THE ARCHAEOLOGY OF HUMAN BONES

The Archaeology of Human Bones provides an up to date account of the analysis of human skeletal remains from archaeological sites, introducing students to the anatomy of bones and teeth and the nature of the burial record.

Drawing from studies around the world, this book illustrates how the scientific study of human remains can shed light upon important archaeological and historical questions. This new edition reflects the latest developments in scientific techniques and their application to burial archaeology. Current scientific methods are explained, alongside a critical consideration of their strengths and weaknesses. The book has also been thoroughly revised to reflect changes in the ways in which scientific studies of human remains have influenced our understanding of the past, and has been updated to reflect developments in ethical debates that surround the treatment of human remains. There is now a separate chapter devoted to archaeological fieldwork on burial grounds, and the chapters on DNA and ethics have been completely rewritten.

This edition of *The Archaeology of Human Bones* provides not only a more up to date but also a more comprehensive overview of this crucial area of archaeology. Written in a clear style with technical jargon kept to a minimum, it continues to be a key work for archaeology students.

Simon Mays is currently Human Skeletal Biologist for Historic England, based in Portsmouth, UK. He is also a Visiting Lecturer at the Department of Archaeology, University of Southampton, and a Honorary Fellow at the School of History, Classics and Archaeology, University of Edinburgh. His research interests span all areas of archaeological human skeletal remains. Previous books include *Advances in Human Palaeopathology* (2008) edited with Ron Pinhasi, and *The Bioarchaeology of Metabolic Bone Disease*, 2nd edition (2020) authored with Megan Brickley and Rachel Ives.

THE ARCHAEOLOGY OF HUMAN BONES

Third edition

Simon Mays

 Routledge
Taylor & Francis Group

LONDON AND NEW YORK

Third edition published 2021
by Routledge
2 Park Square, Milton Park, Abingdon, Oxon OX14 4RN

and by Routledge
52 Vanderbilt Avenue, New York, NY 10017

Routledge is an imprint of the Taylor & Francis Group, an informa business

First edition published by Routledge 1998
Second edition published by Routledge 2010

British Library Cataloguing-in-Publication Data
A catalogue record for this book is available from the British Library

Library of Congress Cataloging-in-Publication Data
Names: Mays, Simon, author.
Title: The archaeology of human bones / Simon Mays.
Description: Third edition. | New York : Routledge, 2021. |
Includes bibliographical references and index.
Identifiers: LCCN 2020029176 (print) | LCCN 2020029177 (ebook) |
ISBN 9781138045606 (hardback) | ISBN 9781138045675 (paperback) |
ISBN 9781315171821 (ebook)
Subjects: LCSH: Anthropometry. | Human remains (Archaeology)–
Methodology. | Paleopathology.
Classification: LCC GN70 .M39 2021 (print) | LCC GN70 (ebook) |
DDC 599.9/4-dc23
LC record available at https://lccn.loc.gov/2020029176
LC ebook record available at https://lccn.loc.gov/2020029177

ISBN: 978-1-138-04560-6 (hbk)
ISBN: 978-1-138-04567-5 (pbk)
ISBN: 978-1-315-17182-1 (ebk)

Typeset in Interstate
by River Editorial Ltd, Devon, UK

To Bonnie, who had an enthusiasm for bones

CONTENTS

FIGURES

TABLES

PLATES

PREFACE

Archaeology is about people and how they lived in the past. The study of the physical remains of those people therefore forms a key part of the discipline. This primarily involves the analysis of skeletal remains (osteoarchaeology), as bones and teeth are the only human remains that survive in most circumstances. The aim of this book is to illustrate the sorts of information that can be obtained from the study of ancient human remains and how this can be harnessed to address questions of general archaeological interest. We shall generally be concerned with the remains of anatomically modern man (*Homo sapiens sapiens*), rather than with tracing the story of human evolution.

Since the publication of the second edition of this book in 2010, nearly all the different areas of osteoarchaeology covered in this book have seen important methodological developments. In some cases, such as the advent of next generation sequencing of DNA, they have supplanted earlier techniques, but in most instances they have supplemented rather than replaced existing methods so that we now have a much broader array of techniques to help us learn about the past from human remains. Debates about what the results of scientific studies of human remains mean for our understanding of key events and processes in the past have also moved on, as have debates on the ethical treatment of excavated human remains. Every chapter in this book has been updated to reflect key developments in these areas. In addition, there is a now a separate chapter devoted to archaeological fieldwork on burial grounds. Several other chapters, including those on ancient DNA and on ethics, have been completely re-written. Others have been expanded to encompass new areas (for example the study of dental calculus in Chapter 9), or to include areas that have matured into significant research foci since the publication of the second edition (for example the study of entheseal changes to investigate activity patterns in Chapter 7). The aim has been to produce not only a more up to date, but also a more comprehensive account.

ACKNOWLEDGEMENTS

The illustrations were reproduced with kind permission. Every effort has been made to trace copyright holders and obtain permissions. Any omissions in this regard that are brought to our attention will be remedied in future editions.

I am grateful to: John Wiley & Sons for permission to reproduce Figures 1.6, 2.5, 4.17, 5.5, Plate 2, 7.14, 7.17, 8.12, 8.17, 8.20a, 8.20b, 9.10b & 10.14; Museum of London Archaeology for Figures 2.3, 3.4 & 9.11a; Martin Carver & Philip Bethell for Figure 2.4; The Wharram Research Project for Figure 2.6; Suffolk County Council Archaeological Service for Figure 3.1; Dorset Natural History and Archaeological Society for Figure 3.2; Warwick Rodwell for Figures 3.6, 3.7 and 14.1a; Elsevier for Plate 1, and Figures 6.5, 8.7, 8.15 and 10.16; Immersion Corporation for Figure 5.4; Paleo-Tech for Figure 6.1; Charles C Thomas for Figure 8.6; The Natural History Museum and the Council for British Archaeology for Figure 8.8; the late Nick Bradford for Figure 8.14; Springer for Figure 8.19; Novium Museum, Chichester District Council for Plate 5; Antiquity for Figure 9.10a; Suffolk Archaeology CIC (Cotswold Archaeology Suffolk) for Figure 9.11b; the late Don Ortner for Figure 10.2; The Natural History Museum for Figure 10.12; Kungliga Vitterhets Historie och Antikvitets Akademien, Stockholm, for Figures 10.18 and 10.19; The British Geological Survey for Plate 8; Nature for Plate 9; Manchester Museum for Plate 11; Joseph Elders for Figure 14.1c; The National Trust for Figure 14.2; The British Museum for Plate 12; and Oxford University Press for Figure 14.3. Other illustrations are Historic England or else public domain.

I am grateful to the following for supplying illustrations, information or publications: Dušan Borić, Megan Brickley, the late Don Brothwell, Carolyn Chenery, Steve Churchill, Margaret Clegg, Yilmaz Erdal, Jane Evans, Karen Hardy, Illinois State Museum, Margaret Judd, Julie Kennard, Scott Maddux, George Milner, Theya Molleson, Stephan Naji, Iñigo Olalde, the late Don Ortner, Stefano Ricci, Duncan Sayer, Dave Swinson and Gordon Turner-Walker. I thank the following for reading and commenting on sections of the text: Gill Campbell, Neil Linford, Alistair Pike and Camilla Speller. Thanks go to Eva Fairnell for her help in dealing with copyright issues and to Stefanie Vincent for taking some of the photographs.

1 The nature of bones and teeth

The human skeleton

There are more than 200 separate bones in the adult human skeleton (Figure 1.1, Table 1.1). They may be divided into three classes according to their basic shape. Long bones are found in the limbs and take the form of hollow tubes closed at both ends. Flat bones take the form of broad bony plates (for example the bones which make up the skull vault), and irregular bones, as their name suggests, fit into neither of the above categories on account of their irregular shape. Examples of irregular bones are the vertebrae and the bones of the skull base.

The composition of bone

Bone is a composite material formed from an organic and an inorganic (mineral) part. By weight, dry bone is about 64% mineral and 26% organics; the remaining 10% is water bound within the bone structure. The great majority of the organic component is collagen, a protein which forms long fibres. The mineral portion is made up of small crystals that are embedded in a matrix of collagen fibres. Bone mineral is chiefly hydroxyapatite, a form of calcium phosphate whose composition approximates to the chemical formula Ca_{10} $(PO4)_6$ $(OH)_2$. The mineral component gives bone its rigidity, and the organic component lends it a slight 'give' or resilience which gives it its strength. The organic part degrades after death, which mainly accounts for the rather brittle nature of most archaeological bone.

The gross structure of bone

In terms of gross structure, there are two different types of bone tissue, cortical and trabecular bone. Cortical bone is the solid, dense part that forms the outer layer of the bones; it is thickest in the diaphyses (shafts) of the long-bones (Figure 1.2). It forms a thin layer around the long-bone ends and around the flat and irregular bones. Trabecular bone is less dense than cortical bone and has a honeycomb structure. Trabecular bone is located within the ends of long-bones (Figure 1.2) and in the interior of the flat and irregular bones.

In living bone, most of the outer surface is surrounded by a thin membrane, the periosteum. The internal walls of the medullary cavities of long-bones are lined with another membrane, the endosteum, which also lines the network of tiny cavities in trabecular bone.

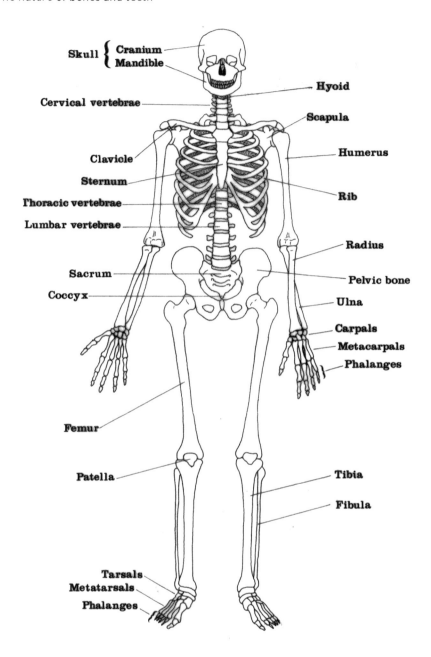

Figure 1.1 The human skeleton

The form and functions of the skeleton

Bones provide a general framework to support the body. They bear ridges for attachment for muscles and tendons, and surfaces which form joints. They also protect vital organs, provide a store of fats and blood-forming marrow, and act as a bank of mineral

Table 1.1 The bones of the adult human skeleton

Skeletal region	Bones	Number
Skull	Various	28 (including mandible and ear ossicles)
–	Hyoid	1
Vertebral column	Presacral Vertebrae	24 (7 cervical, 12 thoracic, 5 lumbar)
	Sacrum	1
	Coccyx	1
Thoracic cage	Ribs	24 (12 pairs)
	Sternum	1
Pectoral girdle	Clavicle	2
	Scapula	2
Pelvic girdle	Pelvic bone	2
Upper limb	Humerus	2
	Radius	2
	Ulna	2
	Carpals	16
	Metacarpals	10
	Phalanges	28
Lower limb	Femur	2
	Patella	2
	Tibia	2
	Fibula	2
	Tarsals	14
	Metatarsals	10
	Phalanges	28
Total		206

Note: In addition to these main elements of the skeleton there are a number of small bones embedded in the tendons of the hands and feet, called sesamoids.

salts. The form of the bones can be understood in terms of these functions. This point is illustrated below with reference to the general structure of long-bones (Figure 1.2).

The tubular form of the long-bones maximises strength and minimises weight; the medullary cavity within the shaft also provides a space for blood-forming cells and fat storage. The flared ends of the shaft (the metaphyses) support the epiphyses which bear the joint surfaces by which the long-bone articulates with its neighbours. Trabecular bone is located beneath the joint surfaces. It is less rigid than cortical bone so is well adapted for the dissipation of mechanical forces at the joints. It also forms a site of red blood cell production in the growing skeleton, and its large surface area facilitates the exchange of minerals to and from bone. The cortical bone which forms the walls of the tube provides strength and rigidity.

On excavation, bones have the appearance of solid, inanimate objects. This is deceptive regarding the nature of living bone. Like most other tissues in the body, bone is living tissue. It is permeated with nerves and blood vessels and, in common with most other tissues, is continually being formed and broken down. The fact that bone tissue is constantly being renewed in this way means that it can repair itself following disease or injury. It also means that, within limits, it can adapt its form according to the strains put on it. This last has been recognised since the nineteenth century, most famously by the German anatomist, Julius Wolff. This bone functional adaptation is still commonly called Wolff's Law. An increase in mechanical forces, due to weight bearing or muscular

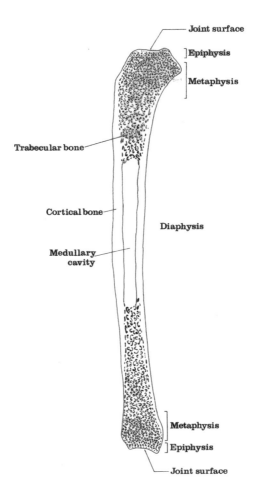

Figure 1.2 The structure of a long-bone

contraction, results in bones that are thicker and stronger, particularly in the orientation in which the loading predominantly occurs (Ruff, 2019). Thus, as well as increasing muscular strength, exercise also increases bone strength. This is illustrated by an X-ray study (Jones et al., 1977) of the arm bones of professional tennis-players, which found that the thickness of the cortical bone of the humerus in the racket arm increased so that it was, on average, about 30% greater than that in the non-playing arm (Figure 1.3). Conversely, bone mineral is lost when the physical strains imposed on the bones are lessened. So, for example, patients who are bed-ridden for some time lose bone mineral (Sievänen, 2010), but regain it when normal activity resumes.

The microscopic structure of bone

Bone is initially laid down as woven or primary bone; woven bone is a temporary tissue which is gradually replaced by mature, or lamellar bone. Woven bone forms the foetal

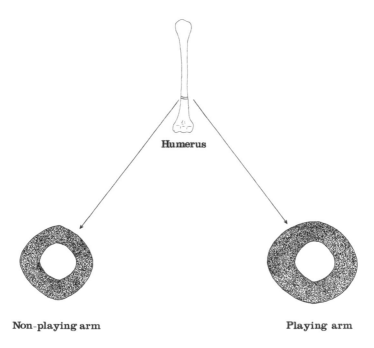

Figure 1.3 Cross-sections of the humeri of a professional tennis player, as inferred from X-ray data. Note the heavily thickened cortical bone in the racket arm
Source: Based on Jones et al. (1977: Figure 4).

skeleton, but by the time an infant is a year old it has almost entirely been replaced by lamellar bone. Woven bone may also be produced in the adult skeleton in response to disease or injury: it may form under the periosteum in response to inflammation, it is produced by some bone tumours, and forms during fracture repair. Woven bone is coarser and more porous than lamellar bone. The two can be distinguished with the naked eye (Figure 1.4).

Lamellar bone is composed of a series of microscopic layers (lamellae) about 4-12 microns thick (1 micron (μm) = one thousandth of a millimetre). It is stronger than woven bone. In the adult, both trabecular and cortical bone have a lamellar structure, but they differ in the way they are organised.

The microstructure of cortical bone is shown in Figures 1.5 and 1.6. Cortical bone is permeated by innumerable, interconnected channels, the Haversian system, upon which it relies for its blood supply. Bony lamellae are arranged concentrically around Haversian canals. There are normally about 4-20 lamellae around each Haversian canal; this unit of bone organisation is called an osteon. Haversian canals run parallel to the long axis of the bone, and interconnect via transverse or oblique channels called Volkmann's canals. There are also some lamellae between the osteons (interstitial lamellae), and some, termed circumferential lamellae, encircle the entire outer and inner surfaces of the bone. Trabecular bone does not have a Haversian system – its fine honeycomb structure allows it to receive sufficient nutrients from blood vessels which meander through it.

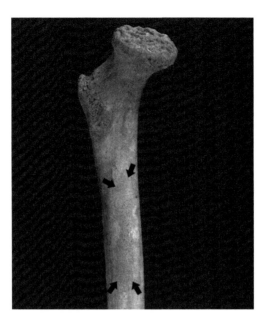

Figure 1.4 A deposit of woven bone on a femur

Bone cells

There are three main types of bone cells. Osteoblasts are responsible for formation of new bone, osteocytes are involved with the maintenance of bone as a living tissue, and osteoclasts are responsible for resorption (removal) of bone.

Osteoblasts are often concentrated on bone surfaces (for example, beneath the periosteum). They are responsible for producing the organic matrix, osteoid, which is then mineralised to form bone.

Osteocytes are situated in spaces (lacunae) within the bone tissue. They receive nutrients via minute channels (the canaliculi) which connect osteocyte lacunae within the same or neighbouring lamellae (Figure 1.5).

Osteoclasts resorb bone both by acidic dissolution of the mineral component and enzymatic degradation of the organic phase. Actively resorbing osteoclasts are located in shallow depressions in bone surfaces called Howship's lacunae.

Bone growth

Formation of the skeleton begins in embryonic life. The clavicle is the first bone to ossify, commencing at about the sixth week following fertilisation. By the time the baby is born, most bones are at least partially ossified but some of the smaller ones (e.g. the carpals and the patellae) only mineralise during infancy and childhood.

Bones form from an embryonic tissue called mesenchyme. Mesenchyme may undergo ossification directly, or it may be replaced by a cartilage model which is then ossified to form bone. The former is intra-membranous ossification; the latter is termed

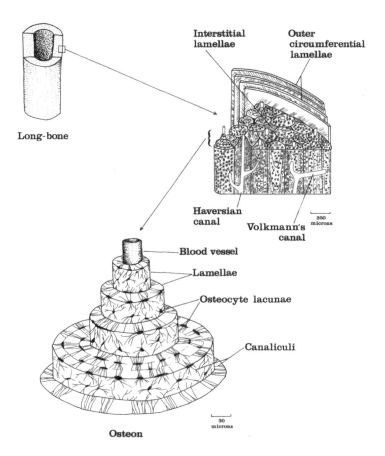

Figure 1.5 The microscopic structure of cortical bone
Source: After White & Folkens (2005: Figure 4.8).

endochondral ossification. Most of the bones in the human skeleton develop via endo-chondral ossification, but some, including the clavicle and most of the bones of the skull, are formed via intra-membranous ossification. The mineralised nature of bone means that it cannot expand; all bone growth is by apposition, the deposition of bone upon some pre-existing surface.

In intra-membranous ossification, osteoblasts lay down bone within a membrane which will eventually form the periosteum. Bone grows in this way from a single ossification centre or from multiple centres which subsequently fuse together.

Endochondral bone growth for a typical long-bone is illustrated in Figure 1.7. Initially the bone is preformed as a cartilaginous model (Figure 1.7a) within a membrane, the perichon-drium. The perichondrium is analogous to the membrane surrounding intra-membranous centres of ossification and likewise later forms the periosteum. The cartilage model grows through the proliferation of cells derived from the perichondrium and the first ossification takes the form of a thin sleeve of bone around the centre of this model (Figure 1.7b), and

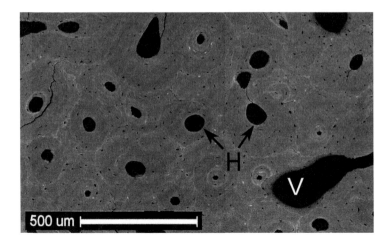

Figure 1.6 Microscopic view of a transverse section of a femur from a Mediaeval archaeological site in Norway, showing well-preserved microstructure. H=Haversian
canals. Note the concentric arrangement of lamellae around each Haversian
canal; the small black dots within the lamellae are osteocyte lacunae. V=Volk-
mann's canal

Source: Reproduced from Turner-Walker (2008: Fig. 1.8a).

subsequently calcium is deposited upon the cartilage within this sleeve (Figure 1.7c).
Blood vessels penetrate the bony sleeve (Figure 1.7d), conveying, among other things,
osteoblasts and osteoclasts, allowing the calcified cartilage within to be converted to
bone. This initial centre of bone formation is termed the primary ossification centre.
Most long-bones have developed a primary ossification centre by the end of
the second month of pre-natal life. As the cartilage cells grow outwards from the primary ossification centre, ossification of the calcified matrix proceeds behind them.
This, together with the elongation of the periosteal sleeve, results in longitudinal
growth of the bone (Figure 1.7e). The interior of the shaft is initially filled with bone,
but as growth continues it is hollowed out by osteoclasts to form the medullary
cavity. During the first few years of post-natal life, secondary centres of ossification,
the epiphyses, appear at long-bone ends (Figures 1.7f, g), united with the shaft via
cartilages – the epiphysial growth plates. When growth is complete, the growth plate
ossifies, fusing the epiphysis with the shaft (Figures 1.7h, i). The age at which the
epiphyses fuse with the shaft ranges from about the mid-teens to the mid-twenties,
depending on the epiphysis.

   The growth in width of a long-bone takes place in a different way. In the diaphysis,
bone is deposited on the outer surface beneath the periosteum, and resorbed from the
internal surface under the endosteum. In a growing bone, the rate of bone resorption
from the endosteal surface is generally exceeded somewhat by the rate of deposition
beneath the periosteum. Thus, as well as an increase in overall width, there is also an
increase in thickness of the walls of the diaphysis during growth.

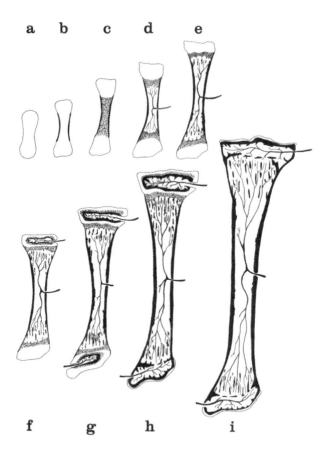

Figure 1.7 Development of a typical long-bone. Cartilage is clear; calcified cartilage is stippled; bone is black

Source: Redrawn from Jee (1988).

Since the metaphyses are flared, their width needs to be reduced during longitudinal growth as metaphysis becomes diaphysis. To achieve this, bone is deposited on the internal surface of the cortex and removed from the periosteal surface.

Teeth

Human teeth are classified into four types according to their shape and function. Incisors are chisel-like teeth for cutting food. The more conical canines are for puncturing and tearing. Premolars and molars have broad, flattened surfaces for crushing and grinding.

Man develops two sets of teeth. The milk or deciduous teeth, which are smaller than their adult counterparts, appear during infancy and early childhood. There are 20 teeth in the deciduous dentition. The upper jaw (maxilla) and lower jaw (mandible) each contain four incisors, two canines and four molars (Figure 1.8). There are no deciduous premolars. During middle childhood, the deciduous teeth are gradually replaced by the

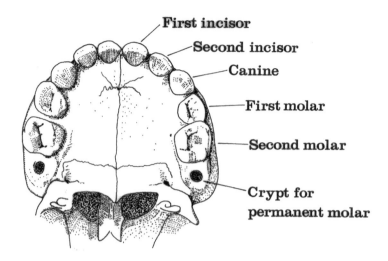

First incisor

Second incisor

Canine

First molar

Second molar

Crypt for
permanent molar

Figure 1.8 The deciduous dentition of the maxilla

permanent teeth (Figure 1.9). All the permanent teeth have erupted by about 18 years, with third molars or wisdom teeth being the last to emerge. The adult mouth normally contains 32 teeth. Each jaw has four incisors, two canines, four pre-molars and six molars (Figure 1.10).

Tooth structure

Each tooth consists of a crown projecting above the gum and one or more tapering roots which occupy sockets (alveoli) in the jaw (Figure 1.11). The junction between the crown and the root is termed the neck or cervix of the tooth.

Teeth consist of three hard tissues: enamel, cementum and dentine, enclosing the dental pulp (soft tissue which includes nerves and blood vessels) in the pulp cavity and the root canal (Figure 1.11). The dental hard tissues lack a blood supply and are not continually turned over as is bone. Thus they cannot reshape themselves once formed, so they do not functionally adapt to mechanical forces like bone does, and they are unable to repair themselves to any great extent in response to injury or disease.

Enamel is almost entirely composed of inorganic matter, whose chemical composition approximates to that of bone mineral (hydroxyapatite), and is arranged in thin rods, or prisms. Enamel lacks a cell structure and, unlike other skeletal hard tissues, is not living tissue.

Dentine consists of about 75% inorganic material (mainly hydroxyapatite); about 20% is a mainly collagen organic component, the remainder being bound water. It lacks cells, except on its inner surface where cells (odontoblasts) line the pulp cavity. Dentine is penetrated by microscopic tubules which run from the pulp cavity to its outer margins.

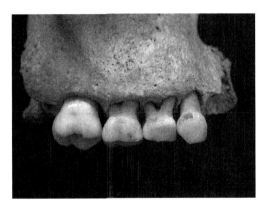

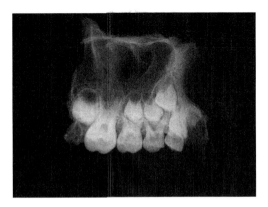

Figure 1.9 The right maxilla of a Mediaeval child, aged about 8 years. (a) The first permanent molar (the tooth furthest to the left in the photograph) is erupted, and anterior to this (to the right in the photograph) are the two deciduous molars and the
deciduous canine. (b) The radiograph (X-ray) of the specimen reveals the developing permanent second molar unerupted within the jaw posterior to the
erupted first molar. The crowns of the developing unerupted premolars and permanent canine are visible within the jaw above the deciduous dentition. Had the
individual lived, the deciduous teeth would in time have been shed and the permanent dentition would have erupted to replace them

Cementum coats the tooth roots. It is about 65% inorganic, 23% organic (mainly collagen), plus bound water. Some of it shows a cell structure.

Tooth formation and development

Formation of the dental hard tissues starts at about the fifteenth week of pre-natal life.
Dentine starts to form first. Odontoblasts secrete an organic matrix, which is then mineralised to form dentine. Dentine, like the other dental hard tissues, is formed in

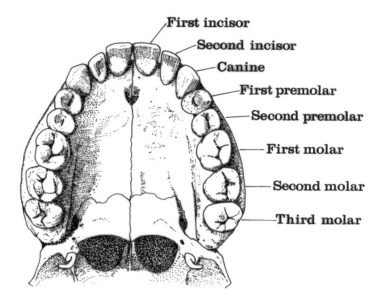

Figure 1.10 The permanent dentition of the maxilla

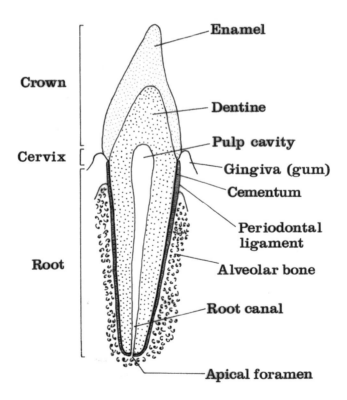

Figure 1.11 The structure of a tooth

microscopic layers. Dentine formation proceeds in a progressive fashion from the crown towards the root tip.

Enamel formation, or amelogenesis, consists of three phases, the formation of an organic matrix, the mineralisation of that matrix, and a maturation phase in which the enamel loses most of its organic content. The enamel-forming cells are called amelo-blasts. Enamel formation begins near the tip of the crown so that the crown grows progressively back towards the cervix until it is complete.

As with the other dental hard tissues, cementum is formed as a result of the laying down of an organic matrix followed by mineralisation of that matrix. It continues to be formed throughout life; the cementum thus increases in thickness with age.

Summary

There are over 200 bones in the adult skeleton. The functions of the skeleton include providing a supporting framework for the body, supplying protection for internal organs and forming a reservoir for essential minerals. Bone tissue has a mineral (mainly hydroxyapatite) and an organic (mainly collagen) component. It is penetrated by many small nerves and blood vessels. Bone tissue is continually renewed, and because of this it is able to repair itself following injury and, to a certain extent, bones are able to adapt their forms according to the mechanical forces imposed upon them. Ossification of the bony skeleton begins in about the sixth week of pre-natal life, and skeletal growth is complete by about 25 years.

Humans develop two sets of teeth. The deciduous dentition emerges during infancy and early childhood and is replaced by the permanent teeth during middle childhood. The permanent dentition is normally fully erupted by about 18 years of age. Teeth are composed of three hard tissues, enamel, dentine and cementum. Unlike bone they lack a blood supply and are not continually renewed.

Further reading

White, T.D. & Folkens, P.A. (2005). *The Human Bone Manual*. Academic Press, London. *A good introduction to skeletal biology and bone and tooth identification, with excellent black and white photographs. Its compact size makes it a good choice for work in the field as well as the laboratory.*

Abrahams, P.H., Spratt, J.D., Loukas, M. & Van Schoor, A-N. (2019). *Abrahams' and McMinn's Clinical Atlas of Human Anatomy* (8th edition). Elsevier, Edinburgh. *Unlike the other books in this list, this is written for medical students rather than archaeologists. The excellent colour photographs are particularly useful for identification of anatomical landmarks on bones, and they clearly show relationships between bones and muscles and other soft tissues.*

Cunningham, C., Scheuer, L., Black S. & Liversidge, H. (2016). *Developmental Juvenile Osteology* (2nd edition). Elsevier, London. *The above two volumes deal mainly with adult bones. This book is the best source for bone identification in, and growth and development of, the juvenile skeleton.*

Hillson, S. (1996). *Dental Anthropology*. Cambridge University Press, Cambridge. *Thorough coverage of dental anatomy, tooth structure and dental development.*

2 The nature of the burial record

When people who are not archaeologists talk to me about my work, it often becomes clear that, if they have thought about it at all, they believe that osteoarchaeology, the archaeological study of human remains, resembles forensic work, the difference being that my 'cases' are just rather older than those the law enforcement agencies deal with. Implicit in this is an assumption that archaeologists tend to concentrate on certain 'interesting' individuals and try to reconstruct their lives and deaths by looking at their skeletons. Although there is a strand of our discipline, termed osteobiography, that does indeed concentrate on building narratives of individual lives (Mays et al., 2018a; Hosek & Robb, 2019), it is not the dominant approach. Today, the main rationale for the study of human remains in archaeology is the biocultural approach, and it is populations rather than individuals that are the focus (Zuckerman & Armelagos, 2011).

In biocultural studies, skeletal data are gathered with the aim of addressing research questions of broad archaeological or historical interest. As the name suggests, it normally means combining the skeletal data with other archaeological and/or historical evidence. These latter sources of evidence might relate to aspects of burial treatment, for example the grave goods with which people are buried. Alternatively, they might comprise general information concerning the type of settlement connected with the cemetery or the specific time period in which the cemetery was used. The data one chooses to obtain from the skeletons are determined by the research questions that the study is aimed at addressing. For example, if we were interested in studying the effects of increasing urbanisation on human health, we might begin by hypothesising that a higher rate of infectious disease might be expected in skeletons from larger, more crowded living environments than in those from smaller settlements. As an initial hypothesis, this seems reasonable, as the former would have been more conducive to the spread of disease. We might then systematically record evidence of infectious disease in skeletons from cemeteries associated with settlements of different sizes to try and test this hypothesis.

In order to address biocultural questions, we usually need to focus on large numbers of skeletons, often from several different cemetery sites. Large numbers of skeletons mean that we stand a better chance of recognising patterns in the data – of finding associations between disease frequency and settlement type in the above example. Statistical analyses are applied to identify and to validate any patterning.

Another type of osteological research is methodological research. This involves testing existing methods for obtaining information from skeletons and developing new ones. This too, normally requires quantitative studies. Osteoarchaeology is therefore largely a statistically based science, and every practitioner needs a working knowledge of statistical methods.

In order avoid errors of interpretation in our research, we need to think carefully about the nature of the relationship between a collection of skeletons (often termed an assemblage) excavated from an archaeological cemetery site and the past community that buried their dead there. Factors that affect the composition of an archaeological assemblage fall into those which relate to the formation of the archaeological record, and those which relate to the archaeological excavation and recovery of the remains. Some of these factors are summarised in Figure 2.1. As we move down Figure 2.1, each successive factor potentially introduces another set of losses and biases into the assemblage, so that each stage in the diagram represents but a sub-sample of the preceding one. On the right in Figure 2.1 are factors which relate to the formation of the burial record, and hence over which archaeologists have no control: the mortality patterns of the ancient human group, the nature of their burial practices, and losses of bones due to destruction in the soil. On the left in

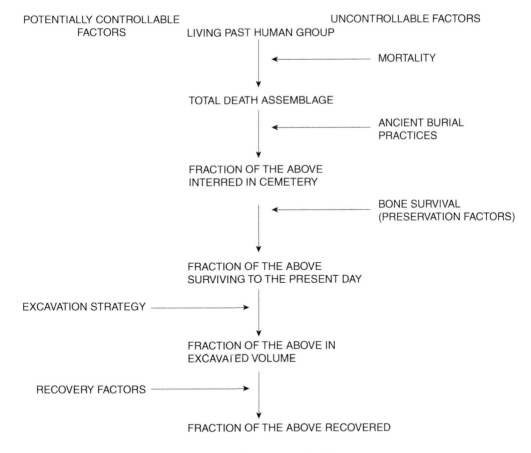

Figure 2.1 Factors affecting an excavated collection of skeletons

Source: Adapted from Meadow (1980).

Figure 2.1 are aspects connected with the strategy and methods of archaeological fieldwork, and hence which are, to a greater or lesser extent, controllable by archaeologists.

This chapter, and the one that follows, are loosely organised around the general outline given in Figure 2.1. In this chapter we concern ourselves with the formation of the burial record. Chapter 3 considers the archaeological excavation and recovery of human remains.

Mortality

A skeletal assemblage is derived from a living population via the intervening variable of mortality: skeletal collections are collections of the dead. This may not seem like a particularly stunning revelation, but it does in fact have some important implications when it comes to trying to understand skeletal data. Because mortality does not affect a human population randomly, the buried population (sometimes called the death assemblage) is not a random sample of the living community. Most obviously, in demographic terms, it means that the age structure of a group of burials bears only an indirect relationship to the age structure of the community that produced it. This is because, in any community, risk of death is different at different ages. For example, in any 21st-century British cemetery, most burials would be of people aged over 60 years. This is obviously not a direct reflection of the age structure of the living population, but is, to a large extent, simply due to the fact that fewer people die at younger ages.

The non-random nature of mortality has ramifications beyond demographic analyses. The relationship between disease frequencies in living and dead populations is complex. For example, in a 21st-century British cemetery, the prevalence of cancers among the burials would be high, and much greater than in the living community. Partly, this reflects that most burials are of people aged over 60 years, the time of life when most cancers start to become more common. But another factor is also at play. If a disease elevates a person's risk of dying then its frequency in the skeletal population will be higher than in the living community (Waldron, 1994: 48–53). The more likely a disease is to cause mortality, the greater the tendency for its over-representation in the death assemblage. Cancer commonly leads to death, elevating its frequency in the death assemblage compared with that in the living community.

The non-random effects of mortality – the mortality bias – as illustrated in the above examples, mean that it is often very difficult to compare data generated from ancient skeletons with data gathered on living populations. However, the mortality bias also operates in more subtle ways even when one does not want to make such a comparison (Wood et al., 1992; Wright & Yoder, 2003). For example, if we are interested in health in children in the past, studying child skeletons may potentially produce biased results, as it would exclude the healthier children who survived to become adults (Milner & Boldsen, 2017). The effects of mortality bias on osteological data continue to be debated (DeWitte & Stojanowski, 2015), and its workings are something to which we shall return in other chapters of this book.

Burial practices

There are many ways to dispose of a dead body. The great variety of funerary practices used by human groups around the world bears witness to this (Ucko, 1969; Parker

Pearson, 1999; Tarlow & Nilsson Stutz, 2013). Many of these, such as disposal in rivers, exposure in trees or on platforms, or abandoning the corpse to be eaten by wild animals, would leave little trace in the archaeological record. Only if ancient funerary rituals culminated in the burial of human remains beneath the soil, or within a tomb, would they usually survive down the centuries to be studied by archaeologists.

In many instances, burials simply involve the straightforward interment of a corpse, so that when it is excavated by archaeologists it is found as a discrete, articulated skeleton. In other cases there may be some pre-treatment accorded to the body before burial. For example, provided there has been no post-depositional disturbance, mingled, disarticulated bones indicate that the soft tissue had been allowed to rot or had been otherwise removed prior to burial of the bones. This type of burial treatment was practised by some earlier human populations. Archaeological finds of burnt human bone show that cremation was another funerary practice used at various periods in antiquity.

Different sectors of a community may receive different treatment in death. As well as biasing our assemblage this may also potentially provide insights into burial practices in antiquity. Differences in burial treatment may take many forms, such as interment with different grave goods, but in the present context we are concerned with those which affect the bones themselves or the overall composition of an assemblage. Into the former category come mutilations or dismemberments characteristic of some ancient funerary rituals, and into the latter fall practices whereby some sector of society was confined to particular parts of cemeteries or was disposed of elsewhere.

In most human groups there are cultural rules governing aspects of burial, such as the orientation of the corpse in the grave, the grave goods, if any, with which it is buried, the location of the grave itself and so on. Just as we would not expect grave goods to be interred with different individuals on a random basis, we should not expect the location of graves in a cemetery to be random, but rather that their placement should be governed by certain principles. Those governing the placing of graves may be difficult or even impossible to determine archaeologically. For example, a combination of several factors may have been taken into account, or the criteria for grave placement may have changed over the period of use of the cemetery.

If a cemetery is only partially excavated, then the burials within the excavated area may be a non-random sample of those on the site as a whole. Whether this affects the conclusions of the osteoarchaeologist depends on the organising principles at the particular site under study. Sometimes grave location within in a burial ground depends on the age or sex of the deceased. In some Mediaeval English and Norwegian churchyards, infant burials are concentrated in specific areas (Boddington, 1996; Sellevold, 1997). In Sweden, in Mediaeval times, ecclesiastical codes specified that women should be buried in the northern part of the churchyard, men in the south, a pattern which has been confirmed archaeologically at some sites (Gejvall, 1960). Of course, when such sites are incompletely excavated a biased impression of the demographic structure of the population is likely.

Cemeteries may show spatial patterning with respect to social rank, status or wealth. Mainfort (1985) studied the bones from the mid-18th-century Native American cemetery at the Fletcher Site, Michigan, USA. The burials there appeared to be laid out in several rows (Figure. 2.2). Historical evidence suggested that these rows probably correspond to the burials of different clans or lineages. The Fletcher Site burials were interred with

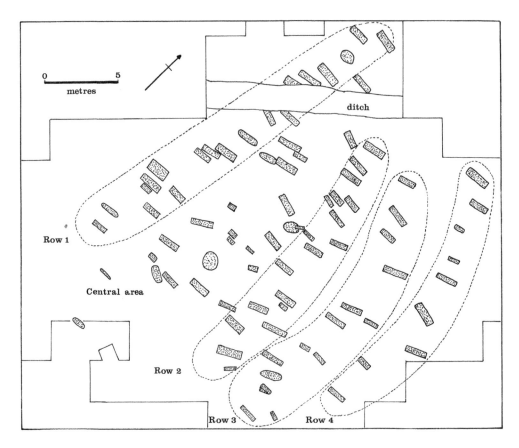

Figure 2.2 The Fletcher Site, Michigan, USA
Source: Adapted from Mainfort (1985).

grave goods, the 18th-century trade value of which, in terms of beaver pelts, could be determined from documentary evidence. Mainfort found that the mean 'value' of the grave goods from burials in the westernmost row (Row One) was approximately 53 beavers. The grave wealth decreased towards the eastern part of the cemetery, the mean for Row Two being 33 beavers, Row Three 18 beavers and Row Four 14 beavers. Mainfort interpreted this patterning as indicating that the rows corresponded to the burials of clans of different wealth or social ranking, the highest-ranking ones being buried towards the western part of the cemetery. In cases like the Fletcher Site, where grave location varies with social status, the potential clearly exists for obtaining a distorted picture if a site is only partially excavated.

   If some part of society was excluded from a cemetery, then even if the entire cemetery was excavated, the data may not be representative of the whole community. In Mediaeval Britain, most burials were made in the local churchyard, but some of the more wealthy members of society elected to be buried in the religious foundations of monks, canons or friars (Mays, 2006a). In cases such as this, a biased view of a past population may be obtained if we are reliant on data from one type of site. Conversely, however, if it is known from other evidence that burial in a particular cemetery was the prerogative of a particular social group then this may enhance the value of the burial data as it allows us to focus on one particular stratum of society.

Ethnographic evidence (Ucko, 1969; Gorecki, 1979) shows that sufferers from disfiguring diseases such as leprosy, smallpox or dropsy may sometimes be excluded from normal burial areas. In Mediaeval Europe, lepers were generally buried in the cemeteries associated with leper hospitals to which they had been confined upon diagnosis of the disease (Magilton, 2008a, b), rather than being returned for burial to the communities where they had previously lived. Clearly this type of practice has important implications for osteoarchaeologists trying to study the prevalence of various diseases in the past using burial evidence.

In many societies, infants may be excluded from cemetery burial. They may be buried outside recognised cemetery areas. For example, in parts of Ireland in post-Mediaeval times, unbaptised infants were excluded from churchyards and instead buried in their own, unconsecrated, burial grounds (Donnelly & Murphy, 2018). In some societies, they may not be given earth burial at all, being disposed of in water or simply left exposed in the countryside (Ucko, 1969). Molleson (1991) attempted to investigate whether infants were excluded from burial in early British cemeteries. She studied the infant (under 2 years old) to juvenile (2–19 years old) ratios for skeletons excavated from various burial grounds dating from AD 100–1300. Using ranges of mortality rates likely to be applicable to rural non-industrialised societies, she estimated the range of ratios of infant: juvenile deaths likely in antiquity. In the sites she studied only one Romano-British (AD 100–400) site fell outside this range, but most of the Anglo-Saxon (AD 400–1066) cemeteries did, showing a deficiency of infants. It seemed unlikely that the systematic difference between Romano-British and Anglo-Saxon periods could be an artifact of preservation or fieldwork biases, so Molleson interpreted it as suggesting that infants were generally excluded from burial on Anglo-Saxon sites. Infant burials are only rarely found on non-cemetery sites from the Anglo-Saxon period in Britain, so it would seem that their bodies were disposed of in such a way as to leave no trace in the archaeological record. Using historical evidence, Molleson suggests that disposal may often have been in water.

Survival and decay of human tissues

Soft tissue

Unless conditions are very cold, unburied bodies are quickly stripped of flesh by insect larvae (maggots). In summer, in temperate regions, a body may be skeletonised in less than a month (Mann et al., 1990). Buried bodies decay much more slowly, due primarily to restriction of access to them by insects, but also to the generally cooler temperatures beneath the soil. Because of the limitation of insect and large carrion activity, breakdown of soft tissue in the buried body is primarily the result of autolysis (the destruction of tissues by enzymes released after death, without intervention of bacteria) and putrefaction (the degradation of the soft tissues by micro-organisms). At death, bacteria which normally inhabit the gut invade the tissues, and in the later stages of decomposition some bacteria may come from the surrounding soil. Initially aerobic species are active, but when these have depleted the tissues of oxygen, they create a favourable environment for the more destructive anaerobic organisms. Putrefaction results in the production of gases, bloating the corpse, and the softening, and eventual liquefaction and disintegration of the soft tissues (Garland & Janaway, 1989; Watson, 1989: 59ff; Clark et al., 1997; Rodriguez, 1997; Janaway et al., 2009).

Different soft tissues show differing resistance to decomposition. Those with ample collagen fibres, such as ligaments and tendons, are slow to decay. Another soft tissue with a relatively high resistance to decomposition is hair. The major constituent of hair is a protein, keratin. The structure of keratin makes it highly resistant to chemical degradation (Wilson et al., 2001; Wilson & Tobin, 2010). Hair is probably the most common soft tissue to survive in archaeological burials, but even so it is present only rarely. When it is preserved in skeletonised remains, it is seen most often in small amounts in relatively recent burials (18th–19th century AD) and is often associated with contact with copper or bronze objects interred with the corpse (Figure 2.3). Copper poisons the micro-organisms

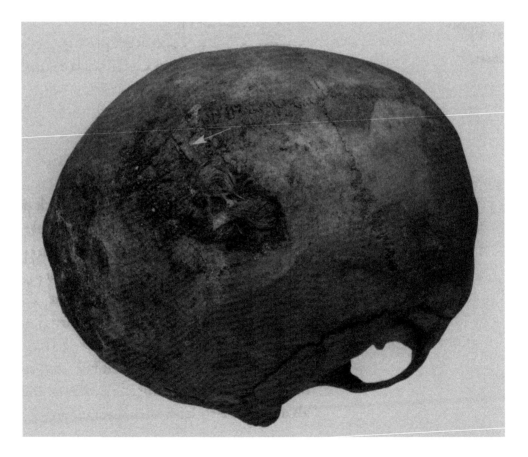

Figure 2.3 A cranium from a 19th century female burial from London. A small amount of hair has survived on the surface of the skull, around a copper alloy hairpin (arrowed)

Source: Walker (2012: Fig. 446).

which would otherwise break down the hair (Janaway, 1987). Occasional instances of more substantial hair survival are known from Roman period interments in coffins packed with gypsum (Green et al., 1981).

The rate of decay of a buried corpse is highly variable. Key factors include temperature, length of time between death and burial, whether the body is fat or thin, adult or child, the availability of water, whether the body is coffined or not and if so the construction of the coffin, whether the body is covered by clothing, the availability of oxygen, the depth of the burial, the nature of the soil and whether decomposition accelerants, such as straw, wood shavings or other vegetable matter are buried with the body (Mant, 1987). Although the above variables appear to be important, information is generally based on qualitative observations; there is a shortage of large-scale, adequately controlled scientific studies to measure their effects (Simmons, 2017). Given the myriad factors potentially influencing decay, it is hardly surprising that the amount of time needed for a buried corpse to be reduced to a skeleton is extremely variable, but in cool-temperate climates about 7–10 years seems a reasonable estimate for an adult body, with a child taking about half that time (Marshall, 1976: 91; Micozzi, 1991: 49).

Hard tissues

Chemical and biological processes in the soil conspire to degrade both the mineral and the organic phases of bone, and in many cases these processes progress to the destruction of the skeleton. Indeed, although bones are popularly viewed as the archetypal archaeological finds, at a very general level their persistence in the burial environment is less usual than their destruction (Collins et al., 2002). Degradation (or diagenesis) of buried bone appears to occur via three principal mechanisms: the chemical dissolution of bone mineral; attack from soil-dwelling micro-organisms (bioerosion), which results in loss of collagen and microstructural alteration of the mineral phase; and the chemical breakdown of collagen. These aspects are considered in turn below.

Chemical dissolution of bone mineral

The most important mechanism responsible for destruction of buried bone is dissolution of the bone mineral by water in the soil. Bone is penetrated by numerous vascular channels and is thus a rather porous material. Most soils are permanently or intermittently damp. Depending upon the soil chemistry (and in particular the soil acidity) bone mineral may be slightly soluble in water. Therefore, in buried bone, dissolution of bone mineral may occur, both from the external surfaces in contact with the soil and from the pore spaces within the bone. Once chemical dissolution has begun, a positive feedback loop is initiated: increased porosity of bone permits greater ingress of water, which in turn promotes greater dissolution of bone mineral further increasing porosity. This may ultimately lead to the destruction of the bone.

Soil acidity is a major influence on bone survival (Smith et al., 2007). Acidity is measured on the pH scale, which ranges from 1 to 14. Values above 7 are alkaline, values below 7 are acid. Most soils and sediments range from about pH 3.5 (very acidic peats) to about pH 8.5 – some soils on chalk geology (Evans, 1978:67). Hydroxyapatite, the chief constituent of the mineral part of bone, is least soluble at about pH 7.8, but increases in solubility in increasingly acidic conditions (Lindsay, 1979: 181–182; Nielsen-Marsh et al., 2000). Alkaline soils are therefore much more conducive to bone survival than acidic soils. A survey of archaeological sites in Europe showed that bone rarely survives when soil pH is less than about 5 (Nielsen-Marsh et al., 2007). In these circumstances a soil stain or 'silhouette' may be all that betrays the presence of burial. For example, at Sutton Hoo, England, the burials were generally only present as soil stains with no survival of bone (Figure 2.4). The soils there were very acidic – pH 3.8–4.9 (Barker et al., 1975). In cases where archaeological bone does survive, its condition may be heavily dependent upon soil acidity. Using sites from Illinois, USA, Gordon and Buikstra (1981) conducted a study on the effect of soil acidity on the preservation of skeletons. They scored preservation into six categories on the basis of visual examination of the bones. Their categories varied from 'strong, complete bones' (termed category 1) through various degrees of superficial erosion of the bones, to total destruction of the skeleton (their category 6). Gordon and Buikstra found that as soil pH decreased (i.e. the soil became more acid) the condition of bone became poorer.

When it does survive, bone from acidic soils often shows dark staining, as does bone from waterlogged, anoxic deposits. This staining is probably from humic acids and transition metal ions which are mobile under such conditions, and hence able to enter the pore structure and interact with the bone substance. Conversely, bones in alkaline soils usually retain their white/cream colour because metal ions in the soil tend to remain locked up in insoluble compounds (Turner-Walker, 2008; Kendall et al., 2018).

Another important factor affecting the degree of dissolution suffered by buried bone is the permeability of the soil to water. In highly permeable soils, water flows repeatedly around and within the bone during weather-dependent wetting/drying cycles, and bone from

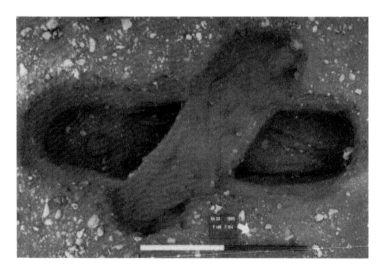

Figure 2.4 Two superimposed burials from Sutton Hoo, England. The bones have been destroyed by the soil acidity at the site; only soil stains indicate their positions
Source: Bethell and Carver (1987: Figure 2.3).

these soils (e.g. sands or gravels) tends to survive poorly. On the other hand, where water movement is restricted due to low permeability (e.g. clay soils) bone survival tends to be better (Nielsen-Marsh et al., 2000). This is because when water movement is negligible, water in contact with the bone becomes saturated in minerals from the bone, markedly slowing the rate of dissolution (Hedges & Millard, 1995; High et al., 2015). Conversely, water movement washes away the dissolved minerals, so dissolution is much more rapid.

Although a combination of low pH and a free-draining soil presents particularly hostile conditions for bone survival, bone survival in highly permeable soils may be negligible even when they are not particularly acidic. At an early Anglo-Saxon (5th–7th century AD) cemetery at Mucking, England, the natural soil had a pH of about 6.6–6.8 (Barker et al., 1975). These values are much more favourable to bone survival than the Sutton Hoo site, but nevertheless skeletal survival at Mucking was very poor, a few scraps of bone were all that remained from most inhumation burials (Mays, 2009). The soils at Mucking were very free-draining sands and gravels lacking a fine particle fraction, and it seemed likely that this was an important cause of the poor bone survival at the site; the passage of water had almost completely leached away the bone mineral.

Microbial degradation (bioerosion)

Soil-dwelling micro-organisms, particularly bacteria, attack bone collagen (Jans et al., 2004; Turner-Walker, 2008). When bacteria attack a collagen fibril they first remove the surrounding hydroxyapatite crystals by dissolving them using extra-cellular organic acids; they then proceed to break down the collagen (Turner-Walker & Syversen, 2002). The results of microbial degradation of buried bone are visible under the microscope. Microscopic study shows that microbial attack on bone tends to be focussed on discrete zones. This results in an increase in bone porosity. Microscopically, porosity due to microbial attack differs from that due to the chemical dissolution discussed above. In microbial degradation, pores tend to be smaller (0.1–8.5µm, compared with more than 8.5µm), and demineralised zones are often surrounded by zones of increased mineral density where the dissolved mineral has been reprecipitated (Turner-Walker & Syversen, 2002; Smith et al., 2007). Bioerosion begins within the bone. Attack on the outer surfaces appears to be inhibited by substances in the soil, so alteration in the outer circumferential lamellae is a late feature (Turner-Walker, 2008).

The degree of microstructural deterioration may be expressed in a semi-quantitative manner using the so-called Oxford Histology Index, or OHI (Hedges et al., 1995; Millard, 2001). This is a six-point scale ranging from zero to five, where five is the best preserved – a histology similar to fresh bone (the Mediaeval bone in Fig. 1.6 would rate an OHI of 5). When degradation is severe, all microstructural features, save the Haversian canals, may be obliterated (an OHI of zero). The bacteria responsible for this type of focal destruction (or 'tunnelling') are evidently aerobic (require oxygen to sustain them), as bones from waterlogged anoxic deposits rarely show this type of attack (Kendall et al., 2018). It may also be absent in bones from contexts where low temperatures inhibit microbial activity (Turner-Walker, 2012). However, bones from most archaeological sites do show bioerosion. When it is present it often tends to be severe (Figure 2.5), and burials within a single site may span the full range of OHI from zero to five (Mays, 2007: Table 10; Dal Sasso et al., 2014; Hollund et al., 2015).

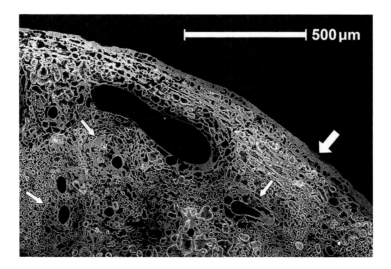

Figure 2.5 Scanning electron micrograph of a transverse section of a Mediaeval long-bone
from Wharram Percy. Throughout the section the microstructure shows considerable bioerosion (compare with Fig 1.6). The mottled appearance is due to
focal dissolution and re-precipitation of bone mineral. Osteons (small arrows)
and circumferential lamellae (large arrow) can still be distinguished
Source: Turner-Walker & Mays (2008: Fig 7.7).

When soil conditions favour chemical dissolution of bone mineral, bioerosion can
increase a bone's vulnerability to that process by increasing its porosity. However, in
more benign soil conditions, even bones showing advanced microstructural alteration
due to microbial attack may be grossly very well preserved, although they may be rather
fragile presumably due mainly to the breakdown of collagen. This is seen in Mediaeval
bones from the churchyard at Wharram Percy in England. Bioerosion is severe (Figure
2.5) but the alkaline soil conditions (pH 7.3–8.3) (Abrahams, 1977; Keeley, n.d.) prevented
chemical dissolution of bone mineral resulting in excellent gross bone survival with negligible erosion of bone surfaces (Figure 2.6).

When skeletons are poorly preserved due to chemical dissolution in the soil, the fragmented bones and eroded surfaces mean that there is severe loss of osteological information – for example it is difficult to diagnose pathologies, to take accurate
measurements and, in extreme cases, even to identify skeletal elements. Although in
most cases, degradation of bone due to microbial attack does not affect gross osteological observations, there is evidence that survival of biomolecules, such as DNA, is less
likely in specimens showing severe bioerosion (Haynes et al., 2002; Hollund et al., 2017;
Kontopoulos et al., 2019). Evaluation of bone microstructure can be a useful tool in
osteoarchaeology, for example for diagnosing disease (Chapter 8); advanced bioerosion
may make it difficult to obtain useful microscopic data of this sort (Turner-Walker &
Mays, 2008; Assis et al., 2015).

Figure 2.6 Well preserved skeletons of a child and an adult from the Mediaeval churchyard at Wharram Percy

Collagen hydrolysis

Collagen in buried bone is broken down by a process of hydrolysis (decomposition by water). At the microscopic level, this causes an increased number of very small pores (less than 0.1μm) without affecting the normal microscopic structure of bone. Normally, loss of collagen from buried bone via this mechanism is very slow, occurring over thousands of years. For example, 12,000 year old bones from Gough's Cave, England, retained organic contents close to modern values (Nielsen-Marsh et al., 2000). Sometimes, however, for reasons that are not yet understood, this process may occur at an accelerated rate, resulting in marked loss of collagen from bones which have been buried for centuries rather than millennia (Smith et al., 2002; Nielsen-Marsh et al., 2007). This results in bones with low collagen contents but, unlike degradation due to microbial attack, microstructural features are preserved (Smith et al., 2002).

Bone survival and the composition of archaeological assemblages

In addition to the factors associated with the burial environment, bone survival also depends on the intrinsic resistance to decay of the bone itself. Because bones differ in their resistance to decay, factors which result in destruction of bones in the soil, as well as causing losses, also have the potential to introduce certain biases into the assemblage.

It has long been asserted (e.g. Weiss, 1973; Johnston & Zimmer, 1989; Guy et al., 1997) that the bones of juveniles, and particularly of infants, survive less well in the soil and hence tend to be under-represented in skeletal assemblages. There is some evidence to support this idea. The density of bones of juveniles is somewhat less than those of adults

(Vinz, 1970), and their bones are rather more porous and the crystals of hydroxyapatite are smaller than in adult bones (Guy et al., 1997). The differences are most marked in infants. Subadult bones are thus more fragile and, if soil conditions are conducive, undergo more rapid dissolution as their porosity facilitates entry of soil water and the small crystal size of the mineral fraction presents a large surface area for demineralisation. Bello et al. (2006) studied bones from three burial grounds in England and France. They found that juvenile skeletons were less complete than those of adults. This could reflect the fact than juvenile bones, particularly infant remains, are small and easily missed on excavation. However, at one of their sites, St Esteve le Pont, France, where soils were acidic, subadult bones also showed more surface erosion than adult bones. This supports the suggestion that here at least, poor survival in the soil contributed to the loss of juvenile remains.

Gordon and Buikstra (1981), in their study of gross bone preservation and soil acidity, found that the preservation of juvenile bones declined more rapidly with increasing soil acidity than did the preservation of adult bones. They also found that the age at death of the immature individuals was correlated with bone preservation, younger individuals tending to have more poorly preserved bones. These observations led them to state that 'at marginal pH ranges all or most of the infants and children may be systematically eliminated from the mortuary sample by preservation bias' (Gordon & Buikstra, 1981: 569).

This under-representation of infants and children may not, however, hold true for sites where soil conditions are less hostile to bone survival. Five hundred and ninety-seven burials were excavated from the Anglican church cemetery in Belleville, Ontario, Canada (Saunders, 1992, 2008). The proportion of subadults in the skeletal assemblage tallied closely with the proportion expected from the burial records, and gross bone preservation was similar to that for adults. At this site, where soil pH was approximately neutral and most bones were well-preserved, there was no evidence for under-representation of infants or children amongst the burials.

Different skeletal tissues differ in their composition and porosity, and show differential resistance both to bioerosion and to chemical dissolution of the mineral phase. Dental enamel contains little organic material, whereas dentine and bone each have significant organic components (see Chapter 1). Consistent with this, enamel does not seem to show bioerosion (Hackett, 1981), and dentine may show it to a lesser degree than bone (Hollund et al., 2015). Dental enamel essentially shows zero porosity. Both dentine and bone are porous materials but, largely because it lacks a Haversian system, dentine has about half the pore volume of bone (Vennat et al., 2009; Figueiredo et al., 2010). Enamel appears to be the most, and bone the least resistant hard tissue to chemical dissolution in the soil, and the differences in porosity are likely to be an important factor in this. When soil conditions are hostile, teeth often survive to a greater extent than bone. At a 7th-9th century AD inhumation cemetery at Whitby, England, skeletal material was in very poor condition. Only about 20% of the weight of bone expected if all skeletons were complete was recovered, but the figure was approximately 45% for teeth (Mays et al., 2012a). When soil conditions are even more aggressive, the enamel crowns may be the only hard tissue present, not only bone but even dentine having been destroyed (e.g. Mays et al., 2006a).

Different bones differ in their vulnerability to decay in the soil. Bone density seems to be a key factor. Willey et al. (1997) studied a large series of adult long-bones from a mass burial of victims of a 14th-century AD massacre at Crow Creek, South Dakota, USA. They compared the numbers of different elements recovered with a reference set of density values from modern specimens (Galloway et al., 1997) and found a general tendency for better survival of denser parts. For example, the femur and tibia are denser than the long-bones of the arm, and were recovered in greater numbers from the Crow Creek site. In the long-bones, there was more frequent preservation of diaphyses than of metaphyseal and epiphyseal areas. The high trabecular bone content of the epiphyses and metaphyses means that they are less dense than the cortical bone of the diaphysis. In addition, the honeycomb structure of trabecular bone presents a large surface area increasing its vulnerability to chemical degradation in the soil (Lambert et al., 1982; Grupe, 1988; López-Costas et al., 2016). Where soil conditions are hostile, the compact bone of the midshaft parts may be all that survives of long-bones.

Bone losses from archaeological contexts may also occur due to the cutting of later features through pre-existing graves, but losses in this way will likely be fairly random. Damage to a cemetery site as a result of natural erosion, or human activities such as ploughing, might selectively remove more of the shallower than the deeper interments. Burials of infants and children are often shallower than those of adults (Manifold, 2012: 60–61), so this may potentially bias the demographic structure of the assemblage.

Summary

Osteoarchaeology is a science based primarily on the statistical analysis of skeletal data. In biocultural studies we use this in order to help us to understand the once-living communities of which the bones are the remaining evidence. In order to make effective inferences about the past we need to consider not only biases in our data that may arise during excavation of the site and recovery of the bones, but also the way in which the burial record is formed. Key factors relating to the formation of the burial record are those of mortality, burial practices and skeletal survival in the soil.

Mortality does not affect a living population in a random way. Hence the skeletal evidence on matters such as demographic composition and disease frequencies is subject to mortality bias and is only an indirect reflection of these parameters in the once-living population.

Different people may be treated differently in death. Not all sectors of a population may be buried in the same way or in the same place. Some parts of a community may not be buried at all, but disposed of in ways that leave no traces archaeologically.

In most archaeological burials, soft tissues have long-since decayed. In many cases, soil conditions mean even the skeleton may be degraded or destroyed completely. The most important mechanism by which this occurs is chemical dissolution of bone mineral. Soils which are acidic and/or free-draining are generally hostile to bone survival; neutral or alkaline soils, and those with low permeabilities to water, are more likely to lead to good bone preservation. Soil-dwelling microorganisms also attack bone. Different parts of the skeleton differ in their resistance to destruction in the soil, and bones of infants and children may often survive less well than those of adults.

These factors means that skeletal remains on an archaeological site form a partial and biased sample of the community that used the cemetery for burial.

Further reading

Some of the difficulties inherent in making inferences about a community from burial evidence were most famously articulated, from the perspective of assessing health in the past, by Wood et al. (1992) The Osteological Paradox: Problems of Inferring Prehistoric Health From Skeletal Samples. *Current Anthropology* 33: 343-370. Milner et al. (2008) Advances in Paleodemography, pp. 561-600 in M.A. Katzenberg & S.R. Saunders (eds) *Biological Anthropology of the Human Skeleton* (2nd Edition). Wiley, Chichester, *consider various topics in palaeodemography, of which the nature of the mortality sample is one.*

Tarlow, S. & Nilsson Stutz, N., eds (2013). *The Oxford Handbook of the Archaeology of Death and Burial*. Oxford University Press, Oxford. *A wide-ranging account of what we can learn from the archaeological study of human burials, and the place of burial archaeology within the discipline as a whole.*

Roberts, C. (2018). *Human Remains in Archaeology: A Handbook* (2nd edition). Practical Handbooks for Archaeology, No. 19. Council for British Archaeology, York. *A useful review of the archaeology of human remains, with a strong British accent. Chapter 3 gives a nice overview of burial practices in Britain in different archaeological periods.*

For a scholarly account of the process of soft-tissue decay see Clark, M.A. et al. (1997) Postmortem Changes in Soft Tissues, pp. 151-164 in W.D. Haglund & M.H. Sorg (eds) *Forensic Taphonomy: The Postmortem Fate of Human Remains*. CRC, London.

Bass, W. & Jefferson, J. (2003). *Death's Acre: Inside the Legendary 'Body Farm'*. Time Warner, London, *is a popular book on the important experimental work done on decay of human corpses by Bill Bass and his colleagues at the so-called 'Body Farm' in Tennessee.*

Kendall et al. (2018). Diagenesis of Archaeological Bone and Tooth. *Palaeogeography, Palaeoclimatology, Palaeoecology* 491: 21-37. *A thorough and up-to-date overview of current knowledge of degradation of hard tissues in the soil.*

3 Archaeological fieldwork on burial grounds

In the previous chapter we saw how mortality bias, ancient burial practices and differential bone survival can affect skeletal assemblages. There is little the archaeologist can do to negate or minimise these effects, the best we can do is to take them into account when planning research projects and interpreting our results. The strategies and methods used in archaeological excavation potentially introduce further biases into an assemblage, but these can, to a greater or lesser extent, be controlled by archaeologists, and our aim should be to try and minimise the effects of these biases.

This chapter describes some of the methods used in archaeological fieldwork projects on burial grounds. It concludes by bringing together some of what we have discussed in this and the last chapter in the form of two case studies. The first of these looks at how we can begin to understand the effects of bone survival and archaeological recovery by looking at the representation of different skeletal elements in a bone assemblage. Building on this, the second illustrates the potential for using element representations to shed light on funerary practices in the past.

Evaluating a burial ground in advance of excavation

Most archaeological excavations are undertaken because a site is threatened with destruction due to modern building work or other development. When fieldwork on an archaeological site is planned, a project team is assembled which, for sites thought likely to yield human remains, should include a Project Osteoarchaeologist (Mays et al., 2018b).

At the outset, it is usual to attempt to obtain an idea of the extent and type of archaeological deposits likely to be encountered. The study of old maps and other documents may reveal, for example, the existence of an early cemetery on the site. Small-scale fieldwork on the site itself is normally undertaken at a preliminary stage to help assess the nature and extent of the archaeological deposits. This work usually comprises trial trenches to evaluate the archaeology directly. In some cases this is preceded by geophysical survey.

Geophysical survey

Geophysical survey comprises a suite of techniques that may permit detection and visualisation of buried archaeological features before a site is excavated. Geophysical methods work by picking up differences in physical properties within the soil, and this potentially allows man-made features, such as pits, ditches, walls etc., to be distinguished. Unfortunately, there is no technique that enables the specific detection of buried human skeletal remains, but if there is sufficient contrast in physical properties between the fill and the surrounding matrix, geophysical methods may enable cut features to be identified. Whether they are graves or not is then a matter of interpretation, based upon their apparent size, shape and orientation.

To conduct a geophysical survey, personnel walk over the site along pre-determined survey lines taking readings at regular intervals with appropriate equipment. Geophysical techniques that have been used to try to detect graves on archaeological sites include ground-penetrating radar (GPR), magnetic survey, soil magnetic susceptibility, electromagnetic conductivity and earth resistance. The choice of technique depends upon the nature of the differences that are anticipated between grave fills and the deposits into which the graves are cut, and this in turn depends upon the nature of the archaeological site and the soil conditions (Hansen et al., 2014). GPR has arguably proved to have been the most consistently useful single technique on burial sites, but each has its strengths and weaknesses, and application of multiple techniques is likely to provide the fullest information (Schmidt et al., 2016: 43; Dick et al., 2017).

The greater the contrast in physical properties between the grave and its surrounding matrix, the better the chances of it being detectable by geophysical survey. Large hollow spaces such as burial vaults are readily visualised (Utsi & Colls, 2017), and cists or stone-lined graves may also tend to show up well (Schmidt et al., 2016: 45). Well-separated, earth-cut graves dug into undisturbed natural soil, as are often found in rural cemeteries, may also be detectable. An American archaeologist, Daniel Bigman, surveyed in and around a 19th-century burial ground in rural Georgia which belonged to the Prior family (Bigman, 2014). The Priors owned slaves before the American Civil War. Slaves were buried outside the family cemetery. Some of the family graves in the cemetery were still visible, but no markers survived to show where the slave burials were. The aims of the geophysical survey were to locate further, unmarked family graves and to try and identify possible locations of slave burials. Electromagnetic conductivity, GPR and magnetic susceptibility were used. Initially these were applied to the known graves in the cemetery in order to create a baseline from which to interpret any anomalies that might be found elsewhere. The survey succeeded in identifying a further 21 anomalies whose regular size, shape and orientation suggested they were graves. Eleven of these lay in a row beyond the cemetery boundary, and this tied in with oral-historical evidence that suggested that slave grave-markers had once been present in that area.

Where archaeological deposits are more complex, geophysical survey may be less useful. In Mediaeval churchyards, burials are usually heavily intercut, and cemetery soils are extensively reworked, meaning that there is little contrast between grave fills and the surrounding matrix. In general, urban environments are less conducive to successful geophysical survey than rural ones – there may be physical impediments to conducting surveys, archaeological deposits are often more complex, graves may be cut into occupation layers instead of natural undisturbed soil, and modern near-surface and above-ground objects may cause interference with results (Schmidt et al., 2016: 44). Nevertheless, on occasion useful results may be obtained. Henry Dick, of Keele University, England, led a survey of Charterhouse Square, an urban park in central London (Dick et al., 2015).

Documentary sources indicated that it was the location of burials of victims of the Mediaeval Black Death plague, and that the edge of that burial ground now forms the modern parish boundary that crosses the square. Eleven graves containing plague burials had been previously excavated to the southwest of the Square. An aim of the geophysical survey was to find out whether more unmarked burials lay beneath the Square. Surveys were carried out using resistivity, electromagnetic conductivity and GPR. Various anomalies were detected that seemed to relate to 15th–20th century structures that historical sources showed had been present on the site. But, in part of the Square, survey identified multiple, evenly spaced anomalies that appeared to be graves. There were at least 200 of them and they showed two different orientations and appeared at three different depths below ground level, suggesting phased use of the site, consistent with the results from the earlier excavations southwest of the Square. These anomalies stopped at the line of the present-day parish boundary, which although it is not now visible on the ground, the geophysics showed was formerly a bank and ditch feature. The finding of individual graves rather than communal burial pits/trenches suggests that, in contrast to some other burial grounds commissioned to cope with the avalanche of mortality in Black Death outbreaks, Charterhouse Square functioned as an emergency cemetery rather than being a location of mass burial.

Evaluation excavation

When a site is threatened by development, the purpose of geophysical survey is not a substitute for a small-scale evaluation excavation but rather to help decide the best places to put the trial trenches. An evaluation excavation is required to 'ground truth' any geophysical survey results. It should be designed so that it provides robust evidence on the ground conditions, including the presence of waterlogging that may lead to survival of organic remains such as wooden coffins, or shrouds and other textiles (e.g. Ives et al., forthcoming). It should also shed light upon the preservation of bone, and the density, depth and spread of burials, so that the overall numbers in the area impacted by the development can be estimated. Proper evaluation of a burial ground in advance of excavation therefore normally requires excavation of trenches down to the base of the archaeological deposits. Before any excavation of burials does take place, either at site evaluation or at the full excavation stage, the Project Director should obtain the appropriate legal permissions.

Excavation strategy

Sometimes, the results of site evaluation mean the developer alters their plans so that disturbance to burials is minimised. If the archaeological impact is too great, or it is thought that excavation would be too expensive, then it is possible that the development may not proceed at all, so no further archaeological excavation occurs. If the development does go ahead, then before the start of the full-scale archaeological excavation of the site, the project team put together a project design, a piece of work detailing the research objectives of the work, how long it is likely to take, and its likely costs, including post-excavation analysis, publication of the findings, and archiving the data and the physical remains. Part of the role of the osteoarchaeologist in the team is to help formulate optimal field recording of burials and recovery strategies for skeletal remains and, at the beginning of the excavation, to familiarise the excavation team with those methods. During excavation, the osteoarchaeologist will normally wish to be present on site to ensure those methods are implemented and, perhaps, to fine-tune them in response to any unexpected finds. The osteoarchaeologist will also carry out whatever post-excavation study of the recovered burials is thought appropriate as part of the archaeological project.

If a burial ground extends beyond the proposed footprint of a development, normally it is only the part that is threatened with destruction that will be excavated. This, together with the fact that not many burial grounds survive down the centuries fully intact, means that only rarely are cemeteries dug in their entirety, and archaeologists normally have little control over which part will be excavated. The proportion of the cemetery lying within the excavated area may not be known with any certainty. Cemeteries often show spatial patterning in terms of status, gender or other social subgroups (see Chapter 2), as well as chronological development. As well as being a subsample, the skeletons in the excavated area may not be fully representative of those in the cemetery as a whole.

On-site recording and recovery of human burials

Most burials on archaeological sites are found as articulated skeletons. In such cases, the on-site procedure is as follows: the grave fill is removed, a record is made of the exposed skeleton, and the remains are lifted. Afterwards the bones are washed, dried, marked and packed into boxes.

Each skeleton should be given a unique context number and dug by hand. When excavating an articulated skeleton, the fill of the grave is carefully removed with a trowel and a hand-brush. As the skeleton is exposed, care is taken not to disturb the positions of any of the bones. Once the bones are revealed, their exposed surfaces should be cleaned of adherent soil using a paint brush and small wooden or plastic implements (those used for modelling clay are quite good); these are less likely to damage bone surfaces than metal tools. The end result should be an undisturbed, cleaned skeleton (Figure 3.1).

Recording

Once the skeleton has been exposed, it is recorded before any bones are lifted. Osteological analyses are best carried out in the laboratory after excavation; the priority in the field is recording information that will be lost once the skeleton is excavated and removed from its context. Records are made of the spatial location of the grave; its relationship to any adjacent graves and other archaeological features; the position of the skeleton within the grave; and its spatial relationship to any grave goods and to any structures or containers such as coffins. Records comprise images, survey points, drawings and written descriptions.

Photographs of burials should be vertical, and should include the whole grave together with a north arrow, scale, context number and site code. Additional close-up shots can be used to record the location of grave goods or any unusual aspects of the burial. The skeleton should also be drawn in plan view, normally at a scale of 1:10. Drawings are useful as back-up if the photographic record becomes corrupted. They may also

Figure 3.1 A Mediaeval skeleton from the Ipswich Blackfriars site, England, after removal of
     the grave fill
Source: Suffolk County Council Archaeological Service.

show features difficult to pick out on images. For example, bone may be difficult to see
on photographs because of poor contrast with the soil (Figure 3.2) and location of grave
goods may not be obvious. It is also usual to fill in a special skeleton recording form. The
form used by Historic England is shown in Figure 3.3. The skeleton recording sheet is

POUNDBURY

L'ATE ROMAN BURIALS, Site C

1414
Co-ord: 641443

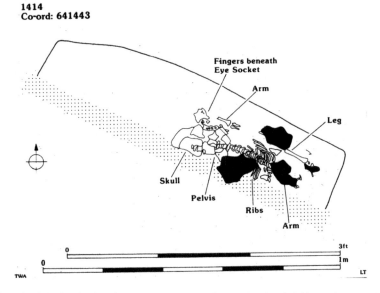

Figure 3.2 A burial of a foetus from Roman Poundbury, England (4th century AD). Although the bones are articulated they are not in the correct anatomical relationships. Their precise disposition is difficult to discern from the site photograph (a), but the annotated drawing (b) makes matters clearer. Post-excavation study showed that the foetus had been dismembered, probably to facilitate its removal from the womb when it became stuck during childbirth. The dismemberment procedure closely followed that recommended in Roman medical texts for safe removal of a foetus to save the mother in cases of obstetric difficulties (Molleson & Cox, 1988)

Source: Molleson (1993: Plate 9, Fig 15).

filled in either in hard copy or digitally. Here, information including the presence of a coffin or cist, basic information on body position and grave orientation, stratigraphic relationships of the grave with other archaeological features is entered. The skeleton sheet also has a standard skeleton diagram so that the excavator can fill in the bones that are present, and there is also a space for noting any unusual aspects of the burial. In the example shown in Figure 3.3, each skeleton is assigned to a burial group where details of finds and soil samples associated with the burial are located.

The location of each grave should be recorded by survey in three dimensions. This is usually accomplished using a total station theodolite, an electronic device that rapidly records three-dimensional coordinates of surveyed points. In an extended burial, points are generally recorded in the grave next to the cranium, pelvis and feet. With more complex skeletal positions, additional survey points may be required. As well as allowing the production of a conventional site plan, in combination with appropriate computer software, this procedure permits virtual 3D reconstruction of all or parts of the burial ground. For example, at the St Pancras burial ground in London, dating from AD1793–1854, burials were laid out in rows and, as is frequently the case in crowded Post-Mediaeval urban cemeteries, several coffins were often found stacked within a single grave shaft. For this site (Emery & Wooldridge, 2011), isometric drawings were rendered from the 3D survey data, with each burial represented as a stylised coffin. These clearly show both the row arrangement of graves and the coffin stacks (Figure 3.4).

In an articulated burial, the position of the corpse when deposited is a key archaeologically discernible aspect of burial treatment. The positions of the bones in the grave upon excavation provides clues to this, but their precise locations depend not only upon the original posture of the body when interred, but also upon any post-depositional movement that may have taken place (Knüsel & Robb, 2016). The ways in which bones may be displaced during decay of the corpse can be understood with reference to a set of principles termed funerary taphonomy[1], or archaeothanatology (Roksandic, 2002; Duday, 2006, 2009). We learnt in Chapter 2 that ligaments tend to be more resistant to decay than other soft tissue, so that they are generally the last things holding the joints together as a body decays. When they do break down, the ligaments at the different joints do so in a predictable sequence (Micozzi, 1991: 49–53; Duday, 2009: 27). In general, the smaller joints, such as those between the cervical vertebrae and in the extremities, become disarticulated before the larger ones such those between the lumbar vertebrae and most of those at the major joints of the limb bones. There are also more detailed patterns: for example, the articulation between the atlas vertebra (the uppermost cervical vertebra) and the occipital bone of the cranium normally persists longer than those between the individual cervical vertebrae (Micozzi, 1991: 51; Duday, 2006). Loss of ligaments and other soft tissues that bind articulations together creates the potential for post-depositional movement of the loose bones within the grave, provided that there is space for them to move into. This movement is more likely to happen if the bones are in an unstable position so that movement may occur due to gravity.

For example, if a corpse was deposited directly in the grave with the upper limbs placed by the sides of the body on the grave floor, then the hand bones would be in a stable position, so there is unlikely to any great post-depositional movement. However, if the corpse was deposited with the hands placed on the chest or abdomen then, as the corpse decays, a void space is created beneath them by the dissolution of the soft

Site name:	Project code:	Year:	Human Remains Record Number:

HUMAN REMAINS RECORD

Every Human Remains record must be accompanied by a Burial Group record

CLASS ATTRIBUTES

Coffin/Cist
(circle as many as apply)   Box   Cist   Coffin   No container identified

Head surveyed? ☐   Pelvis surveyed? ☐   Knees surveyed? ☐   Feet Surveyed? ☐

Survey comments: Survey checked in Intrasis? ☐

Articulated?   *Articulated* ☐   *Disturbed* ☐ | Condition: *Fair* ☐   *Good* ☐   *Poor* ☐

Body Position:
On left hand side: *Crouched* ☐   *Extended* ☐   *Flexed* ☐

On right hand side: *Crouched* ☐   *Extended* ☐   *Flexed* ☐

Prone (extended face down) ☐   *Supine (extended face up)* ☐

Orientation:
(head end recorded first)   *East-West* ☐   *Northeast-Southwest* ☐   *South-North* ☐   *Southwest-Northeast* ☐

North-South ☐   *Northwest-Southeast* ☐   *Southeast-Northwest* ☐   *West-East* ☐

Excavated by/date: Recorded by/date:

RELATIONSHIPS

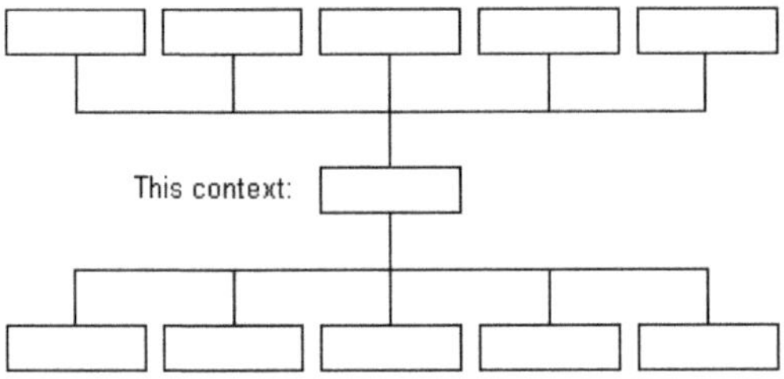

This context:

Burial Group (Structural Group):
Site subdivision:
Fill of:
Cut by:
Sample (head area):
Sample (torso area):
Sample (leg/foot area):

Recording

Photographed? ☐   Photo number(s):

Planned? ☐   Plan number(s):

TEXT - COMMENTS

Figure 3.3 A skeleton recording form for use in the field

HUMAN REMAINS RECORD

page 2

Site name:	Project code:	Year:	Human Remains Record Number:

SKELETON DIAGRAM

Shade in the outline to show the bones present

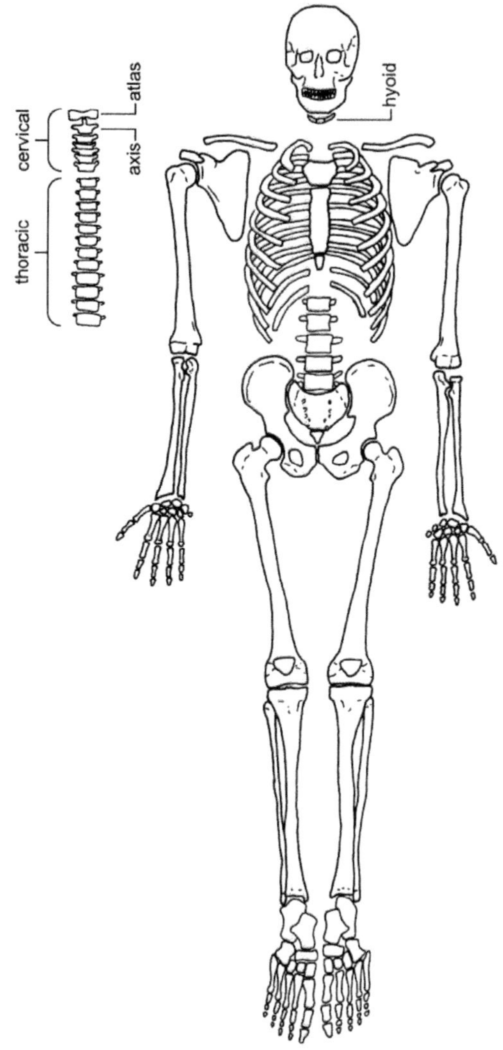

Diagram checked? ☐ Scanned? ☐ Imported into Intrasis? ☐ Relationships entered? ☐

Figure 3.3 Continued

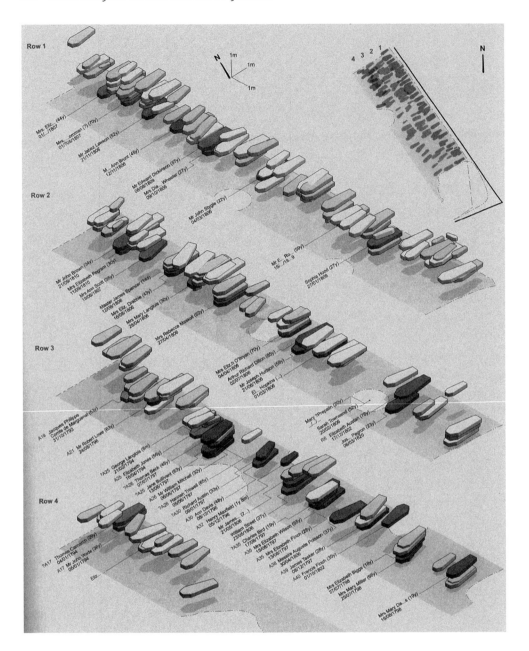

Figure 3.4 (a) Isometric view of four of the burial rows from the St Pancras burial ground. Burials depicted in darker colours are those for which dates of death are known exactly from metal plates attached to the coffins or from identifications in the burial register for the cemetery. (b) Detail of one of the coffin stacks in Row 3. The five individuals in this stack died within a 33-day period in the summer of 1797

Source: Emery & Wooldridge, 2011: Figs 33 & 50.

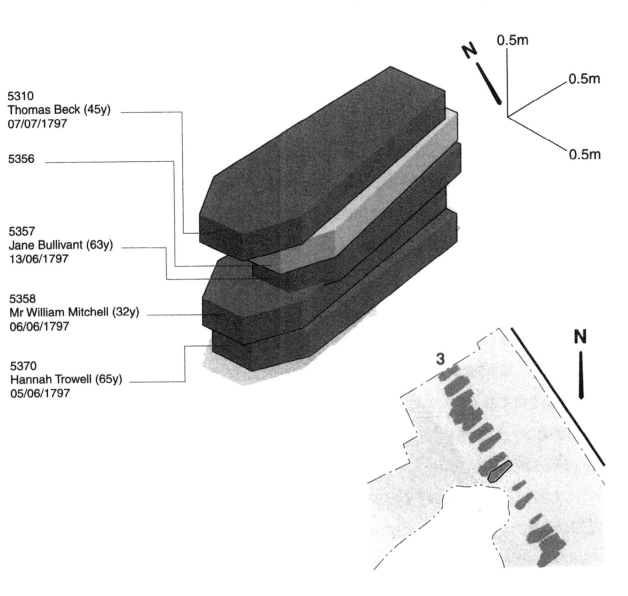

5310
Thomas Beck (45y)
07/07/1797

5356

5357
Jane Bullivant (63y)
13/06/1797

5358
Mr William Mitchell (32y)
06/06/1797

5370
Hannah Trowell (65y)
05/06/1797

0.5m

0.5m

0.5m

N

N

3

gure 3.4 (b)

tissues of the torso. As the ligaments holding the hand bones together rot, the bones may then sink into this void space. This may result in their being found on excavation more or less scattered in the pelvic or torso area (Roksandic, 2002) (Figure 3.5). More general movement of bones may occur if the corpse is interred in a coffin. If the ligaments and other soft tissue holding joints together decay whilst the coffin is still intact, then the void space within the coffin potentially permits movement of the loose bones. Under these circumstances there may sometimes be quite extensive skeletal disarray. The exact processes causing post-depositional movement of bones are incompletely understood, but it might potentially occur as a coffin breaks and collapses under the weight of overburden, or due to movement of liquid within a coffin whilst it is still fairly intact. This extensive movement of bones is sometimes known as 'bone tumble' (Boddington, 1987a) (Figure 3.6).

Bones in a grave may also show 'wall-effects' – that is they may be aligned against some physical limit, such as the sides of a coffin (Duday, 2009: 40). Narrow coffins may result in one type of wall phenomenon, the so-called 'parallel-sided effect' (Boddington, 1987a) where the upper limbs lie tightly against the body with the hands against or on the pelvis and the feet together. A burial from Barton-Upon-Humber, England (Figure 3.7) shows a parallel-sided effect caused by constraint by a narrow coffin, only traces of which survived. There is some scattering of the hand bones (reflecting the fact that the hands

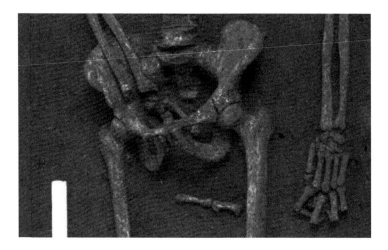

Figure 3.5 Detail from a site-photograph of a 4th-century AD interment from Stanwick, England. The position of the right forearm in this supine extended burial shows that the body was buried with the right hand placed over the lower abdomen. Because of this, as the body decomposed, the right hand bones have become disarticulated and were found somewhat scattered in the pelvic area. The left hand was placed on the floor of the grave so those bones have stayed in articulation. The fingers of the left hand appear clenched. Clenching of the hands may be seen in bodies of individuals who have died in extremes of emotional stress, and this has sometimes been observed archaeologically in burials of executed felons (Waldron & Waldron, 1988). This Stanwick individual had been decapitated (see Fig. 10.13)

Figure 3.6 A 12th-century AD burial from Barton-upon-Humber, England, within a well-
        preserved wooden coffin. There is considerable bone movement ('bone-tumble')
Source: Rodwell & Atkins, 2007: Fig. 181.

were placed upon the pelvic area when the body was deposited), but little evidence of
bone tumble in this case. However, the skull has rolled away from the rest of the body.
This has occurred despite two large stones which had been placed in the coffin either side of
the head. These were used probably in conjunction with a cushion, to prop up the head (Rodwell & Atkins, 2007: 224–5), perhaps when the body was being viewed by mourners. The atlas
vertebra and mandible remain articulated with the cranium in this case even though it has
rolled away from the rest of the vertebral column. This reflects the disarticulation sequence,
referred to above, whereby the atlanto-occipital articulation is more persistent than those
between the cervical vertebrae. There must have been a void space into which the cranium
could roll when ligaments uniting the cervical vertebrae decomposed, indicating that the
coffin was still substantially intact at that point. The fact that there is little movement of other
bones implies that the coffin may have decayed sufficiently to permit soil to infiltrate and surround the body before the dissolution of most of the other ligaments occurred.

Figure 3.7 A 10th–12th-century AD burial from Barton-upon-Humber, showing parallel-sided
effect and post-depositional movement of the skull

Source: Rodwell & Atkins, 2007: Fig. 225.

Phenomena such as bone tumble or parallel-sided effects can be readily visualised in standard vertical photographs of burials, but in many instances more detailed records of bone positions may be useful. This may be accomplished by including detailed photographs of particular areas of the skeleton (e.g. articulations). In addition, recording total station survey points on ends of long-bones and on other major skeletal elements, means that postures of individuals can be rendered virtually as stick figures (Loe et al., 2014) or as schematised bodies or skeletons (Sachau-Carcel et al., 2015). However, an increasingly popular alternative to using multiple survey points to record bone position is photogrammetry (Bedford, 2017; Ulguim, 2017). In essence, this involves taking a series of overlapping photographs of the skeleton from different viewpoints. Photo-targets (markers) are placed around the burial, and surveyed in. The photographs can then be used to create an accurate virtual 3D model of the skeleton, which can be manipulated virtually to study the position of the remains in detail.

A combination of conventional photography and photogrammetry was used to study the posture of two Middle Bronze Age male adult burials (dating to 1495–1285BC) excavated from a site at West Amesbury Farm, near the well-known prehistoric monument of Stonehenge, England (Mays et al., 2018a). The two graves were adjacent to one another, cut into the fill of a boundary ditch (Figure 3.8). Both skeletons were lying on their backs. The more northerly, and stratigraphically later of the two, numbered 8101, had the lower limbs flexed to the right, the more southerly burial (8102) had the lower limbs flexed to the left. Archaeological evidence and radiocarbon dating suggested that these individuals probably died within a very short time of one another.

The two burials were excavated sequentially, but photogrammetry allowed the production of a composite image showing both burials (Figure 3.8) that can be manipulated in three-dimensional space (the 3D image can be viewed in Mays et al., 2018a: Supplementary Figure 1.1). Study of these images confirmed that in each burial, the torso, including shoulder and pelvic girdles, was flat on the grave floor and the lower limb long-bones lay approximately parallel to the grave floor. This position is impossible to attain in a fresh

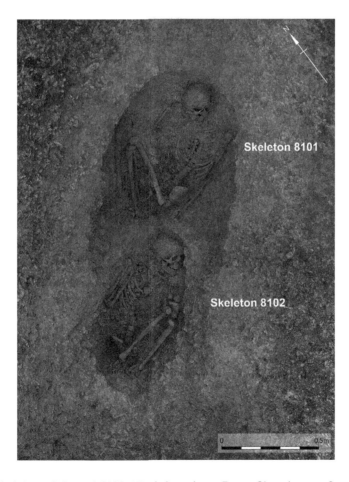

Figure 3.8 Skeletons 8101 and 8102, West Amesbury Farm, Stonehenge. Composite figure derived from photogrammetry

cadaver due to the constraints on the range of motion imposed by the ligaments at the hip joints, so it is unlikely to have been the original posture of the bodies. This appears to be confirmed from the site photographs. In 8102, where the lower limbs are flexed to the left of the torso, there is dislocation of the right sacro-iliac and hip joints (Figures 3.9 and 3.10). In 8101, where the lower limbs lay to the right side, there is dislocation of the left hip and sacro-iliac joints. It seems likely that in each case the lower limbs may originally have been positioned with the knees fully flexed in front of the body so that the heels were in contact with the buttocks. This position was probably maintained by perishable bindings or wrappings. The original placement of the corpse in the grave cannot be determined unambiguously, but the positioning of the torso fully flat on the grave floor may indicate that it is most likely that the body was, in each case, originally positioned on its back. As soil was placed on top of the bodies at burial, the flexed lower limbs may have been pushed to one or other side, creating a poorly filled void space beneath them. As they decayed, the ligaments at the hip and sacroiliac joints would have gradually become less able to resist the weight of the settling overburden, so the lower limbs slumped further to the side.

Given the above discussion, it may be that the posture of the two bodies at deposition was more similar than the skeletal positions as excavated suggest. This was important in the interpretation of these two burials. Mortuary practices are an arena for expressing the social identities of the deceased (Fowler, 2013). Osteological study showed that the two individuals would have differed in appearance, and had different ancestry and geographic origin. These are key components of ethnic identity. Despite this, these two individuals,

Figure 3.9 Burial 8102, West Amesbury Farm, Stonehenge. Detail view from the north, showing dislocation of right sacro-iliac joint. Note that the sacrum is flat on the grave floor

Figure 3.10 Burial 8102, West Amesbury Farm, Stonehenge. Detail view from the south showing dislocation of right hip joint

who died within a short time span, were buried close to one another and in similar ways. This would seem to suggest that aspects of identity that they held in common were considered by those who buried them to be more important than their ethnic differences in determining the manner of deposition of their bodies (Mays et al., 2018a).

Sampling the soil and lifting the remains

Soil samples taken from the abdominal/pelvic area, prior to the lifting of the bones, may reveal gut contents. These may take the form of residues (generally pollen grains or fragments of plant tissue) of food in the gut at time of death or remains of gut parasites. Survival of these remains is variable. If coprolites (remains of faecal material) are preserved in the abdominal area then it is best to sample from them (Rácz et al., 2015), but in skeletonised remains this is seldom the case. In a supine skeleton (one laying on its back), soil samples taken from just above the sacrum and within the sacral foramina seem to offer the best chances of success. Control samples from the grave-fill away from the abdominal area should also be analysed (Berg, 2002; Fugassa et al., 2006).

Once the exposed skeleton has been photographed, planned and recorded, and any pelvic soil samples taken, the bones can be gently lifted by hand, removing any surrounding soil as necessary to loosen them. Although it may be tempting to treat fragile bones with chemical consolidants to try and strengthen them prior to lifting, this in fact does little to facilitate accurate measurement and other osteological study, and it may also cause problems for future chemical or biochemical analyses on the bones. Such treatments are therefore not recommended. Bones from an articulated skeleton should be kept separate from any re-deposited material found in the grave fill which does not belong to it, and if more than one skeleton is interred in a single grave, strenuous efforts must be made to avoid bones from different individuals becoming mixed. Once bones become mixed it is usually very difficult to separate them out once more into discrete individuals. If possible, for each skeleton the different areas of the body should be lifted separately. This is particularly important for the hands and feet as it is difficult to distinguish left and right phalanges once these become mixed.

During hand recovery of human remains it is almost inevitable that some small bones, bone fragments and loose teeth will be missed (Mays et al., 2012a). Sieving of the soil remaining in the grave after the bones have been lifted helps to recover these small elements. The usual procedure is wet-sieving – that is to use water to wash the soil through a series of sieves of different mesh sizes. As well as recovering small bones and bone fragments, this also helps retrieve small grave goods, such as beads. Exact procedures differ between different workers and also depend on the type of soil at the site. I collect the soil left on the grave floor after lifting the skeleton as three subsamples, from the head, the torso and the leg/foot areas. I then wet-sieve each sample through a stack of three sieves, generally with mesh sizes of 8mm, 4mm, and 2mm (Mays et al., 2012a). In practice, most identifiable elements are retained by the 8mm or 4mm meshes. Material that passes through mesh of 4mm or less is mostly unidentifiable, except in the case of foetal or infant remains (Pokines & de la Paz, 2016). Collecting three separate soil samples in the way described above helps to show approximately where in the body any recovered fragments came from. In an experiment at the excavation of a burial ground at Whitby, England, sieving basal grave fills, using the protocol described above, increased retrieval of loose teeth by 54% over the number recovered by hand collection alone (Mays et al., 2012a).

When time pressure on the excavation is severe, some workers routinely recover infant burials by removing the skeleton and remaining grave soil *en bloc* once the burial has been exposed and recorded, and recovering the bone by sieving back in the laboratory. This seems to ensure good recovery of small elements and saves time on site (Brickley et al., 2005: 92–93). Sieving grave soil may also recover tapeworm cysts (Mowlavi et al., 2014), kidney stones (Jaskowiec et al., 2017), bladder stones (Anderson, 2001b), gall stones (Wu & Bellantoni, 2003), remains of calcified soft tissue tumours (Klaus & Ericksen, 2013), calcifications within blood vessels (Binder & Roberts, 2014), ossified cartilage fragments (Ríos et al., 2011) and pleural plaques (Anderson, 1996). These appear as small bone or bone-like fragments and are seldom found in hand-collected material.

Post-excavation processing

The recovered bones need to be cleaned of soil. This is normally accomplished using gentle brushing with a soft tooth-brush using tepid water to loosen adhering soil, although in some dry, sandy soils dry-brushing may be sufficient. Pains should be taken to avoid damage to the remains. Particular care is required not to dislodge deposits of dental calculus (mineralised dental plaque – see Chapter 9) from teeth. Once washed, the remains should then be left to dry slowly, away from direct sunlight and artificial heat sources.

When dry, bones should be marked with the site code and context number in waterproof ink. This is to stop bones accidentally becoming dissociated from the rest of the skeleton, or becoming mixed with those from other burials. The dry, marked remains are put into labelled polythene bags. The different areas of the skeleton are bagged separately, with four separate bags being used to the left and right hands and feet (provided left and right could be recovered separately in the field). The bags should be placed in acid-free cardboard boxes with skulls normally boxed separately from the post-cranial skeleton.

Case study 1: the effects of recovery factors and bone survival on the composition of a skeletal assemblage

At the majority of archaeological cemetery sites, the interments were made as complete corpses. Thus, the numbers of each skeletal element originally present in the assemblage can be taken as known. By studying such assemblages, patterns of loss of the different bones of the skeleton through poor survival in the soil and recovery factors can be investigated. Using a group of 226 Mediaeval (13th–16th century AD) adult burials from the Blackfriars site in Ipswich, England, I calculated the representation of each element of the skeleton by expressing the total number of an element present as a percentage of that expected if all burials were represented by complete skeletons (Mays, 1992). The skeletons from this site were carefully excavated by hand. No sieving for small bones was carried out. The representation of the various skeletal elements in the Ipswich adults is shown in Figure 3.11.

As might be expected, the bones which are in general more poorly represented are the smaller ones and/or those with high trabecular and low cortical bone contents. Many of the bones of the hands and feet are poorly represented, consistent with the likelihood that they may be easily missed if sieving is not carried out. Fewer foot than hand phalanges are present, and fewer carpals than tarsals. This is consistent with the idea that losses of hand and foot bones are primarily deficiencies of recovery: hand and foot phalanges differ little in their relative trabecular and cortical bone contents, and the same is true of carpals and tarsals, but they do differ in size – carpals are smaller than tarsals and foot phalanges are smaller than hand phalanges. The least frequent bones in Figure 3.11 are the foot sesamoids, the smallest of the bones listed and hence the most easily overlooked during excavation.

The limb bones, which have high proportions of dense cortical bone, are well represented. This is particularly so for the tibiae and femora, as expected given the high densities of these weight-bearing bones. The sternum, vertebrae, ribs and hyoid are elements which have high proportions of trabecular bone and these tend to be under-represented. This is as expected given the lesser resistance of trabecular bone to destruction in the soil; the patterning here is probably largely a reflection of differential bone destruction. The hyoid bone is particularly poorly represented; this may be because it is highly fragile, but may also be because it is often omitted from standard skeleton recording forms used in the field, and hence overlooked by excavators unaware of its existence.

Another bone which is rather under-represented is the patella. Patellae are rounded bones appearing as flattened discs several centimetres in diameter. They are quite dense and strong – given their size and ratio of cortical to trabecular bone, we might expect to

Bone

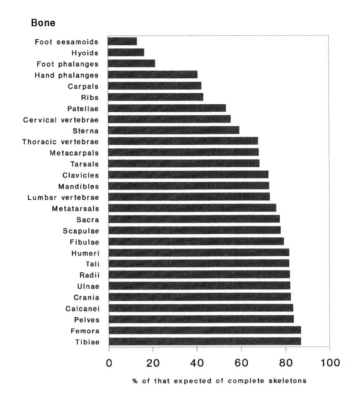

Figure 3.11 Frequency of various skeletal elements in the Mediaeval burials from the Ipswich Blackfriars site

find them in similar numbers to calcanei and tali (the two largest tarsal bones), but as Figure 3.11 shows this is far from being the case. An explanation may be that patellae appear rather undistinctive to excavators and, if dislodged from their anatomical positions during excavation, may not be recognised as bones, particularly if the soil is rather light coloured or stony.

Case study 2: burial practices in the Neolithic of Southern Britain

Provided the effects of archaeological recovery and bone survival are taken into account, the pattern of representation of different parts of the skeleton may sometimes help provide evidence for funerary practices in the past. This is illustrated using a case study of human remains from the Neolithic (c. 4000–2400 BC) of southern Britain.

Human remains are regularly found at several different types of Neolithic site in Britain (Fowler, 2010), including long barrows (Smith & Brickley, 2009). Long barrows take the form of long mounds of earth or chalk rubble, flanked by quarry ditches (Figure 3.12). The bones excavated from beneath these monuments are generally not articulated as discrete skeletons but are, to a greater or lesser extent, disarticulated and mingled.

Study of the human remains from Neolithic sites can shed light on many aspects of burial practices. The specific question we will be considering here is why bones in long

Figure 3.12 An artist's impression of Fussell's Lodge long barrow, viewed from the east, as it may have appeared when first constructed

Source: After Ashbee (1966: Figure 9).

barrows are generally found in a disarticulated state. One possibility is that burials were originally made as fleshed corpses, and the mingling of bones resulted from moving them within the tomb once the soft tissue had decayed, either for 'ritual' reasons or simply to make way for additional interments. A second possibility is that these monuments functioned as ossuaries, repositories for bones from corpses which had previously been buried or stored elsewhere until the flesh had decayed (a practice termed 'excarnation'). We will now look at the evidence from two Neolithic long-barrows, Wayland's Smithy and Fussell's Lodge.

Wayland's Smithy I (Figure 3.13) is a small, unchambered long barrow in Oxfordshire (Atkinson, 1965; Whittle et al., 1991, 2007). Beneath the barrow were found human bones in varying degrees of articulation, from almost complete skeletons, through articulated parts of bodies to completely disarticulated remains. The bones were originally studied by Brothwell and Cullen (1969, report reproduced in Whittle et al., 1991). Following the basic identification of the bones, an important step in the analysis was to estimate the number of individuals buried beneath the monument.

When dealing with a cemetery of discrete, articulated skeletons the number of individuals is clearly equal to the number of skeletons. However, with an assemblage which wholly or partly consists of disarticulated bones, determining the number of individuals present is less straightforward. As was stated above, it is not normally feasible to separate bones into discrete skeletons once they have become mingled. Thus, alternative

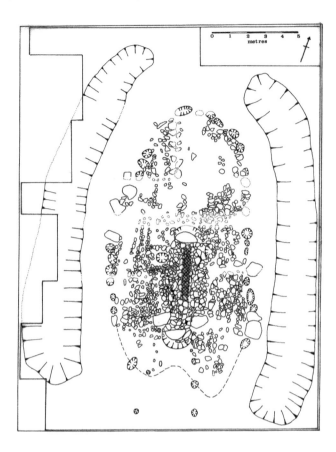

Figure 3.13 Wayland's Smithy, Barrow 1. The human remains were located on the stone
          pavement in the area indicated by the cross-hatching
Source: After Atkinson (1965: Figure 1).

methods of estimating the number of individuals present are needed. One frequently
used measure is the minimum number of individuals (MNI).

MNI is derived from the number of each bone present. There are a variety of methods
for calculating MNI, which differ in detail (Lambacher et al., 2016). In the method presented here, the count of the most abundant element, taking into account its anatomical
frequency, gives the minimum number of individuals which must have contributed to an
assemblage. This means that in order to calculate MNI the elements counted have to
occur in the skeleton with known frequency – in other words we need to count bones not
bone fragments. When dealing with incomplete bones, care needs to be taken to avoid
double counting when compiling totals. The approach is therefore to come to a minimum
number of elements. So, for example, the distal (lower) ends of two left humeri make
a total of two bones but a proximal (upper) and a distal end could come from the same
bone, so make a minimum of one element.

The counts of the major skeletal elements at Wayland's Smithy are given in Table 3.1.
For skulls, the MNI is simply equal to the number of bones, but for paired elements (the

long-bones in the present case) MNI is generally the number of either left or right elements, depending which is the greatest. At Wayland's Smithy, a slight complication occurs with the MNI estimate from the fibulae. When a fibula lacks its proximal and distal ends, as was often the case here, it may be rather difficult to determine whether it is a left or a right, hence the fairly large number of unsided fibulae in Table 3.1. The MNI based on fibulae is not seven, as the number of unsided fibulae needs to be taken into account. The minimum number estimate from this bone will be achieved if we assume that the 12 unsided fibulae are in fact six left and six right; the MNI figure based on fibulae is thus 7 + 6 = 13 individuals.

In order to produce our MNI we assume that all left and right bones may be pairs (whereas an estimate of the maximum number of individuals would involve the assumption that none were pairs), but if we are able to determine, based on observations of bone size etc., whether or not it is possible, in particular cases, that a left and right bone could come from the same individual, then we could refine our MNI estimate. For mixtures of bones from adult skeletons, where differences in bone size etc. are often slight, it is difficult to do this reliably. At Wayland's Smithy, the collection was predominantly of adult bones, so the conservative strategy for calculating MNI is not to attempt to investigate possible matches between left and right elements. Pursuing this strategy, the MNI is 14 individuals. Table 3.1 shows that this figure comes from the total number of skulls present. Of this minimum of 14 individuals, 13 were adults and only one was a child.

Fussell's Lodge (Figure 3.12) is an earthen long barrow in Wiltshire (Ashbee, 1966; Wysocki et al., 2007). Human bones were found in several discrete groups beneath the eastern end of the barrow. Unlike the situation at Wayland's Smithy, nowhere were the bones in articulation. Using information from the report on the bones (Brothwell & Blake, 1966: 49–53), and applying the same method as described for Wayland's Smithy, the collection appears to represent a minimum of 16 adults, together with a similar number of children.

The composition of the adult parts of the bone assemblages from Wayland's Smithy and Fussell's Lodge, in terms of the numbers of skulls, vertebrae, long-bones and hand/foot bones expressed as a percentage of the total numbers of bones recovered from these four regions of the skeleton combined, are given in Figure 3.14.

Table 3.1 Frequencies of some major skeletal elements at different sites, together with MNI derived from them

Bone	Left	Right	Unsided	Total	MNI
Skulls	-	-	-	14	14
Humeri	11	10	0	21	11
Radii	11	9	0	20	11
Ulnae	9	8	0	17	9
Femora	12	13	0	25	13
Tibiae	12	11	1	24	12
Fibulae	7	7	12	26	13

Source: Based on the data of Brothwell and Cullen (in Whittle et al., 1991:72–75).

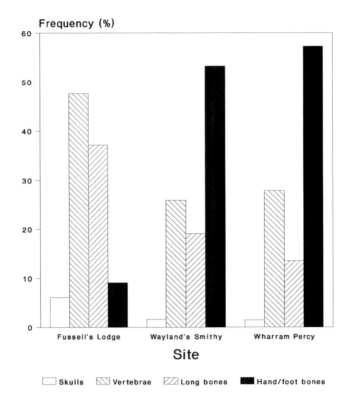

Figure 3.14 Composition of assemblages from Fussell's Lodge, Wayland's Smithy and Wharram Percy in terms of numbers of skulls, vertebrae, long-bones and hand/foot
bones expressed as percentages of the sum of the bones from these four
regions of the skeleton

In order to use the composition of the assemblages from the long barrows to help
assess whether, at each site, the burials were likely to have originally been made as complete, fleshed corpses, it is necessary to have some idea of the composition by skeletal
parts we might expect if this were the case. A way of estimating this is to use an archaeological assemblage where we know that the interments were made as complete
bodies. Because preservation and recovery biases clearly might be expected to vary from
site to site, we need to be careful to select a suitable site to use as a comparison with
our two long barrows. An assemblage from a churchyard, at Wharram Percy, was chosen
for this purpose. The site is located on similar geology to the two barrows (chalk) and
similar recovery techniques were used (hand excavation with no sieving for small bones).
The composition of the Wharram Percy assemblage is also shown in Figure 3.14.

In a complete adult skeleton there is one skull, 24 vertebrae, 12 long-bones from
the upper and lower limbs and 106 hand/foot bones (Table 1.1). At Wharram Percy the
ratio of skulls to vertebrae to long-bones to hand/foot bones is 1:20:10:41. Thus the
ratios of skulls to vertebrae to long-bones are approximately as expected from their

anatomical frequencies. As expected from their greater anatomical frequency, the hand/foot bones are present in the largest numbers of the four classes of bones, but they are in fact under-represented compared with what might be expected from complete skeletons. As we have seen, this is to be expected in hand-collected archaeological assemblages and is probably due mainly to recovery biases. The Wharram Percy data give an idea of the composition expected of an assemblage originally interred as complete corpses once preservation and archaeological recovery factors have taken their toll.

The distributions for Wharram Percy and Wayland's Smithy show a marked resemblance (Figure 3.14). That from Fussell's Lodge, on the other hand, is very different, with a striking deficiency in hand and foot bones – they are six times less frequent in the Fussell's Lodge assemblage than at the other two sites.

If the bones were given temporary earth burial to allow the flesh to rot prior to their exhumation for final deposition in the tomb, then it might be likely that those carrying out the exhumations would tend to overlook small bones or might only bother to retrieve larger ones provided it was not an important part of funerary rituals to collect every scrap of bone. In effect, the assemblage would have been exposed to recovery biases twice over – once in the Neolithic and once when excavated by the archaeologists. If the bodies were exposed above ground to allow the flesh to decay, it is also easy to imagine small bones being lost prior to or during collection of remains for final disposal in the tomb. The lack of any articulated bones at Fussell's Lodge is also consistent with deposition as dry bones rather than fleshed bodies. No evidence for cut-marks or animal scavenging were found on the bones. Weathering on bones in the open air produces splitting and exfoliation of external surfaces. These features were little seen at Fussell's Lodge (Wysocki et al., 2007). It may therefore be that, prior to the placement of their bones in the Fussell's Lodge barrow, the dead were given temporary burial elsewhere until the flesh had rotted (Wysocki et al., 2007).

Clearly, the few fairly complete articulated skeletons from Wayland's Smithy must have been introduced in the fleshed state, but the similarity between Wayland's Smithy and Wharram Percy in terms of overall assemblage composition suggests that this may be true for most or all of the Wayland's Smithy interments. The patterns of bone loss at Wayland's Smithy are those expected from the actions of preservation and recovery factors on an assemblage interred as complete individuals. The remains at Wayland's Smithy which are in a partly or entirely disarticulated state have mostly become so as a result of rearrangement of bones within the tomb when they had been there long enough for the soft tissues partly or completely to decay.

Summary

Most archaeological excavations are undertaken in advance of destruction of the site by modern development. If the site threatened is a cemetery, then an osteoarchaeologist will be a vital member of the archaeological project team. Archaeologists rarely excavate cemeteries in their entirety, only the part that is threatened. Before full-scale fieldwork takes place, it is usual for the archaeological team to prepare by learning as much as possible about the site beforehand. Early maps and other documents might be consulted. Small-scale evaluation excavations may be performed, sometimes preceded by geophysical survey.

To excavate an inhumation burial, the grave fill is first removed to expose the skeleton. A careful record is then made of the aspects of it that will be lost after excavation. This means recording the spatial location of the grave on the site, and of the position of the skeleton in the grave, in three dimensions. Stratigraphic relationships between the grave and other features are noted. A coffin or other container and any structural features of the grave are recorded, as are the locations within the grave of any grave goods. The above aspects are recorded by photography (sometimes including photogrammetry), survey, and by filling in a standard skeleton recording form. The exposed skeleton is also normally drawn in plan view, including the coffin, if there is one, and any grave structural features and locations of grave goods. Soil samples from the pelvic area to retrieve remains of food or gut parasites may also be taken. The bones are then lifted. During excavation, loose teeth, and small bones, such as those of infants or smaller elements of the adult skeleton, are likely to be missed if recovery is by hand collection. Nowadays most excavators combat this problem by sieving the soil remaining on the grave floor to recover these items.

Careful recording on-site, coupled with a knowledge of the principles of funerary taphonomy, helps enable accurate reconstructions of the positioning of the body in the grave, a fundamental aspect of funerary practice in an articulated burial. For remains found in a disarticulated state in undisturbed contexts, patterns of element representation can reveal aspects of mortuary practices, provided the potentially biasing effects of preservation and recovery factors are adequately understood and controlled for.

Note

1 Taphonomy refers to things that happen to remains after death.

Further reading

Parker Pearson, M. (1999). *The Archaeology of Death and Burial*. Sutton, Stroud. *This very readable book contains a succinct guide to excavating human remains, with an emphasis on British practice. For a coverage of this topic using North American examples see*: Ubelaker, M. (1999). *Human Skeletal Remains: Excavation, Analysis, Interpretation* (3rd edition). Taraxacum, Washington.

Roksandic, M. (2002). Position of Remains as a Key to Understanding Mortuary Behavior, pp. 99–117 in W.D. Haglund & M.H. Sorg (eds) *Advances in Forensic Taphonomy*. CRC, Boca Raton. *A clear summary of the ways in which the positions of bones within a grave may alter during decay and burial and how that may affect our understanding of past mortuary practices.*

Bayliss, A. & Whittle, A. eds (2007). Histories of the Dead: Building Chronologies for Five Southern British Long Barrows. *Cambridge Archaeological Journal* 17, Supplement 1. *Papers in this volume present appraisals of Wayland's Smithy, Fussell's Lodge and similar long-barrows based on recent radiocarbon dating together with reviews of evidence from the bones.*

4 The assessment of age and sex

Assessing whether an individual was male or female and estimating age at death are fundamental to the study of skeletal remains. As will become clear in later chapters, they form a necessary background against which other types of osteological data are analysed and interpreted. By combining age and sex data with other burial evidence, such as elaborateness of grave structure or presence of grave goods, we may be able to ascertain whether certain burial practices were associated with particular age groups or with one or other sex. Consideration of age and sex data from large numbers of skeletons may enable us to say something about mortality patterns and demographic compositions of earlier communities.

Assessment of sex

Male and female adult skeletons differ sufficiently for the sex of burials to be assessed. In immature skeletons (those of infants and children), sex differences are much more muted, so sex assessment from skeletal indicators is difficult.

Sex indicators in the adult skeleton

In adults, the degree of skeletal sexual dimorphism (differences in form between males and females) varies between different populations but, in general, it is sufficient for sex to be inferred with reasonable certainty, provided the right areas of the skeleton are present. Although the whole skeleton should be taken into account when determining sex, sexual dimorphism is most consistently expressed in the skull and pelvis. It is the pelvis that is the single most reliable area, and hence should be given most weight in sex determination (Best et al., 2018). The reason for this is that differences here are directly related to functional differences between the sexes. In general, the female pelvis is broader than the male. A narrow pelvis is optimal for locomotion, but in females a broader pelvis is dictated by the fact that it forms the birth canal. Women with very narrow pelvises are more likely to experience potentially life-threatening problems during childbirth, and most researchers agree that the principle reason for the evolution of pelvic sexual dimorphism in man and other primates is natural selection in relation to childbirth in females (Huseynov et al., 2016; Fischer & Mitteroecker, 2017).

The greater width of the female bony pelvis manifests itself in a number of ways. An important area is the sub-pubic angle of the pubic bone. The pubic bone is one of the three elements that make up each pelvic bone (the others are the ilium and ischium), and it lies at the front of the pelvis. The sub-pubic angle is the angle formed between the left and right inferior pubic rami, the lower parts of the pubic bones. It tends to be wider in females than in males (Figure 4.1). In populations of European ancestry, the angle in males is typically less than about 75°; in females it is character-istically greater than about 80° (Small et al., 2012; Karacas et al., 2013; Franklin et al., 2014). Several further features of the pubic bone are also useful in sex determination (Phenice, 1969; Klales et al., 2012). Females generally show development of the ventral arc, a ridge of bone which sweeps down the anterior surface of the pubic bone to merge with the border of the inferior pubic ramus (Figure 4.2). Males characteristically

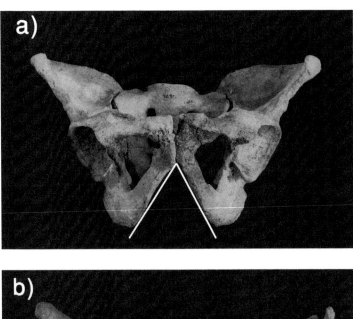

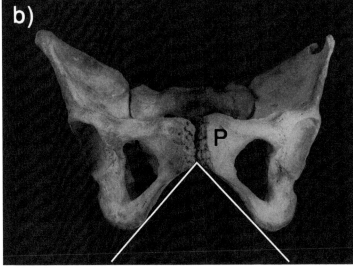

Figure 4.1 Adult male (a) and female (b) pelvic girdles. 'P' denotes the pubic bone. The white lines indicate the sub-pubic angle

Female   **Male**

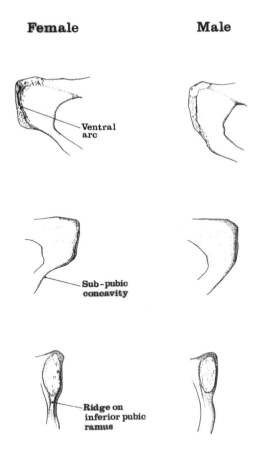

Figure 4.2 Sex differences in the adult pubic bone. The anterior surface of the female
        pubic bone generally shows development of the ventral arc; this is usually lack-
        ing in the male, although slight ridging may occur. Seen from the dorsal aspect,
        the female pubic bone often shows a concavity in the inferior pubic ramus. The
        female pubic bone often shows a ridge on the medial surface of the inferior
        pubic ramus; in the male this area is generally rather flatter

Source: Redrawn from Phenice (1969).

lack the ventral arc. Other aspects of value in sex determination are the sub-pubic
concavity (present in females), and the medial (inner) border of the inferior pubic
ramus, which generally shows a ridge in females but is blunter in males. These aspects
are also depicted in Figure 4.2. These features appear to be associated with differences in muscle attachment sites between males and females, and local differences in
bone growth associated with the broadening of the female pelvis at adolescence
(Budinoff & Tague, 1990; Klales et al., 2012).

   Unfortunately the pubic bone is a rather fragile part of the skeleton, and is often missing or damaged in archaeological material. An important sex indicator situated in the
stronger, posterior part of the pelvis is the greater sciatic notch (Figure 4.3). The greater

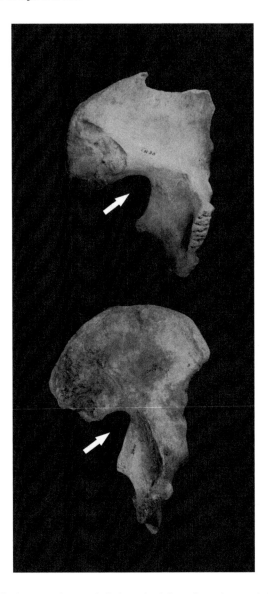

Figure 4.3 Left pelvic bones of an adult female (above) and an adult male (below). The
            greater sciatic notch is indicated on each bone by an arrow

sciatic notch is wider and shallower in females, another manifestation of the broader
female pelvis (Huseynov et al., 2016).

Some aspects of the cranium useful for sex determination include the brow ridge and
forehead shape, the nuchal crest and the mastoid processes (Walker, 2008; Bigoni et al.,
2010); the forehead is more sloping and the other features are more pronounced in the
male (Figure 4.4). The larger brow ridge and sloping forehead in males reflect the
greater growth of the male facial area during adolescence (Rogers, 2005).

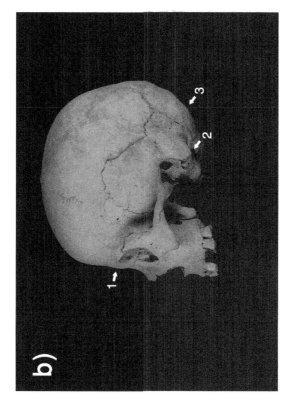

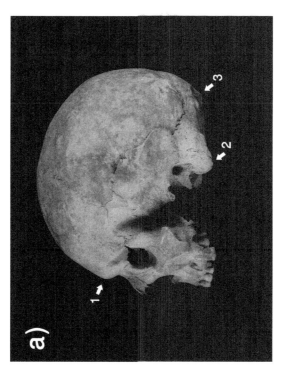

Figure 4.4 Adult male (a) and female (b) crania. The brow ridge (1) is more developed in the male and the forehead is more sloping. In the female the brow ridge is smaller and the forehead more vertical. The mastoid processes (2) and the nuchal crest (3) are more developed in the male

In general, the male skeleton is larger and more robust (i.e. has thicker bones with more developed areas for muscle attachment) than the female. The greater robusticity of the male skeleton is related to the greater muscle mass of the male. The general size and robusticity of the post-cranial skeleton can be used as an auxiliary sex indicator. However, these aspects are more heavily influenced by activity patterns and nutrition, and so are less useful than pelvic and cranial morphology.

The origins of skeletal sexual dimorphism

The origins of sex differences in the skeleton lie in the hormonal differences between males and females. The sex of an individual is established in the chromosomes from the moment of conception, a female having two X chromosomes, a male an X and a Y. The foetus develops ovaries or testes depending upon the chromosomal sex. Studies of the development of human pelvic bones suggest that oestrogens have a marked influence on morphology in females, so that female pelvic morphology diverges strongly from that of males during puberty (Huseynov et al., 2016). In other parts of the skeleton, oestrogens do not appear to be necessary for the development of female skeletal characteristics. Work with animals (Dahinten & Pucciarelli, 1986) suggests that it is testosterone that is responsible for the development of male cranial form. Testosterone also has a profound effect on growth, both of the musculo-skeletal system and other tissues (Tanner, 1989), and so is a prime reason for the greater size and robusticity characteristic of the male skeleton.

Reliability of sex assessment from the skeleton

Methods for sex assessment based on measurements of the pelvic bones, cranium or other elements have been devised but they offer little benefit compared to visual assessment and tend to be highly specific to the population upon which they were devised, working poorly for other groups (Bigoni et al., 2010). Most workers assess sex in adult skeletons from simple visual inspection (Klales, 2013).

For the experienced observer, sex determination from simple visual examination of adult skeletons is quite reliable, providing that the skull and, particularly, the pelvic bones are available for examination. For example, work by Meindl et al. (1985), using modern skeletons of documented sex, found that 97% could be correctly sexed if both pelvis and skull were available. Looking at the skull alone, sex was correctly inferred in 92% of cases; for the pelvis the figure was 96%.

Substantial collections of skeletons from archaeological sites, where sex and other data, such as age at death, are known for individual skeletons from gravestones, inscribed plates attached to coffins, or other means, are few. This limits the opportunities for directly testing methods of ageing and sexing on archaeological material. One important known age and sex archaeological collection was excavated from the crypt of Christ Church, Spitalfields, London. The crypt needed to be cleared due to building work, and this provided the opportunity for study of the skeletons which were interred there. Almost a thousand burials were excavated. About one-third of them had legible coffin plates which gave the name (and hence the sex), age and date of death of the occupant. The burials are of people who died in the 18th and early 19th centuries AD. Although they are quite recent compared with most archaeological material, they do provide a population with living conditions very different to those of today upon which to study the reliability of ageing and sexing methods. Using this collection, Molleson and Cox (1993:206) were able correctly to identify sex in 98% of adult skeletons.

Sex indicators in the immature skeleton

In childhood, not only is skeletal sexual dimorphism less pronounced, but an additional complication when trying to use these slight differences to infer sex is that skeletal morphology changes with age. This latter complication can be overcome by studying teeth, as these are the only skeletal elements which do not change their size and shape once formed.

Sex assessment from teeth

Teeth of males tend to be slightly larger than those of females (Kieser, 1990: 63-70). This appears to reflect the growth-promoting effect of the Y chromosome and of male hormones (Alvesalo, 2009; Ribeiro et al., 2013). Tooth size differences are generally too small to be obvious to the naked eye, so they need to be quantified by measurement. Because teeth cannot change their shape or size once formed, sexual dimorphism in the permanent dentition of children should be similar to that in adults from the same population. Dental measurements offer a way of sex determination in children who have developed at least some of their permanent teeth.

The most sexually dimorphic tooth is generally the lower canine (Mays & Cox, 2000). The degree of dimorphism varies between populations, but occasionally the size difference in lower canines is large enough to allow sexing simply by plotting out crown widths for male and female adult skeletons, and then measuring the permanent canines of children to determine whether they lie in the male or female ranges. This was the strategy used by Molleson (1993) at the Romano-British (3rd-4th century AD) cemetery at Poundbury, Dorset (Figure 4.5). This enabled the sex of children of about 6 years (the age at which the crown of the mandibular permanent canine is formed) and over to be determined.

Poundbury is, however, exceptional – in most skeletal assemblages the degree of sexual dimorphism in the dentition is insufficient to enable sex to be identified from a simple bivariate scatterplot of the dimensions of a single tooth. In such instances, sex of children can often be inferred from a combination of measurements from several teeth using a multivariate statistical technique called discriminant function analysis. This procedure combines a number of measurements in such a way as to maximise the separation between groups (males and females in the present context). The resulting formula can be used to group unknown cases – in the present instance to infer sex of juveniles. The reliability of sexing using a discriminant function analysis of dental measurements can be estimated by determining the percentage of cases in the base population (i.e. the adults of known sex used to generate the discriminant function) correctly classified. This procedure suggests that in many archaeological assemblages the percentage correctly classified may be as high as 80-90%. (This is not quite as impressive as it sounds – remember we could expect to get 50% right by guessing!)

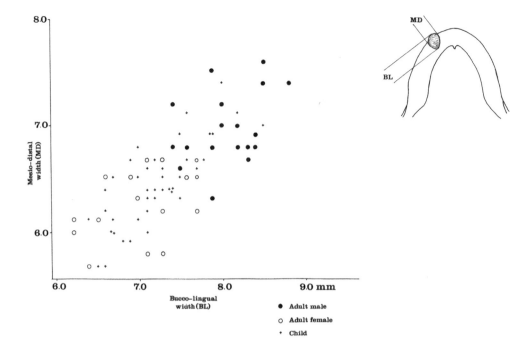

Figure 4.5 Bivariate plot of lower canine dimensions for burials from Poundbury. Since there is little overlap between the adult male and female clusters, the sex of most juveniles with measurable permanent canines can be inferred simply by plotting them onto the graph. The reliability of this method is discussed in the text
Source: After Molleson (1993: Figure 114).

An assumption when sexing children from teeth in this way is that tooth size in children is similar to that in adults of the same sex. There is evidence that sometimes this assumption may be problematic. Experiments with animals (Searle, 1954; Tonge & McCance, 1965; Bunyard, 1972; Luke et al., 1979) suggest that tooth crown size may be reduced by poor nutrition during development, and in man there is evidence (Garn et al., 1979) that maternal health may affect the crown dimensions of teeth developing whilst the baby is in the womb. There is potentially a problem of mortality bias here. Those suffering most from poor nutrition and health problems during growth may tend to die early, hence there is the potential for those who die in childhood to have smaller teeth than those who survived to become adults. It is difficult to know how pervasive this problem might be in archaeological material, but it has the potential to cause too many females to be identified. Some workers (e.g. Gugliardo, 1982; Simpson et al., 1990; Stojanowski et al., 2007) have claimed to have found this phenomenon in archaeological assemblages. Looking at Figure 4.5, the canine dimensions of most children from Poundbury seem to fall into the female range. It is tempting to interpret this as indicating higher childhood mortality in females, perhaps relating to a lower value placed on female children in this community. However, it may be that this bias is simply an artifact of the sexing method if those dying in childhood at this site had smaller teeth than those who survived to adulthood. This illustrates the point that before making archaeological inferences we must first consider the effects of biasing factors on our assemblage and possible shortcomings in our methods.

Sex assessment from the bones

Because some child remains lack the permanent dentition, either because they are too young or because of incomplete survival, studies have been undertaken exploring ways of sexing children from their bones. A natural starting point is to look at aspects of skeletal morphology that are good sex indicators in adults.

The pubic bone appears to show little sexual dimorphism prior to puberty (Klales & Burns, 2017; Estévez Campo et al., 2018), and in any event this element rarely survives intact in non-adult burials on archaeological sites. A number of studies (e.g. Boucher, 1957; Fazekas and Kósa 1978; Schutkowski, 1993; Wilson et al., 2008) have demonstrated sexual dimorphism in the ilium in infant and child skeletons. As in adults, males tend to have narrower, deeper greater sciatic notches than females, but differences are slight. For example Fazekas and Kósa (1978) found that in foetal and infant material the mean greater sciatic notch index (100 x depth/width) was 32 in males, about 4 percentage points greater than the female mean, whereas for adults the mean figures for males and females have been reported as 85 and 63 (Hager, 1996), a difference of fully 22 percentage points. In addition, both notch morphology and the degree of sexual dimorphism vary between populations. Despite these difficulties, some have attempted to devise ways of sexing infant and child skeletons using the greater sciatic notch.

Schutkowski (1993) suggested that the angle of the greater sciatic notch in male juveniles is about 90 degrees but in females it is wider than this (Figure 4.6). He found that this criterion correctly identified the sex of juveniles from Christ Church Spitalfields in about 82% of cases. Sutter (2003) applied this technique to a Chilean archaeological group of known sex with similar success rates. By contrast Vlak et al. (2008) found the technique worked poorly with a Portuguese known sex sample, achieving a success rate of only 54%, little better than chance; Olivares and Aguilera (2016) reported similar results from a Spanish collection. These rather mixed results probably reflect variation in pelvic morphology and the degree of sexual dimorphism between populations – since sex differences are very slight these factors can have a major impact on success rates. In addition, greater sciatic notch morphology varies with age in both sexes (Vlak et al., 2008; Wilson et al., 2015), further complicating the picture.

The problems in identifying sex in juveniles from skeletal morphology mean that, for archaeological assemblages, any results are fraught with uncertainty. For this reason osteologists only routinely attempt to sex adult skeletons. Biomolecular methods of sex assessment offer potential solutions, but are rather expensive and require destructive sampling. Amelogenin proteins, present in small amounts in dental enamel, differ in amino acid sequence in males and females; recent work suggests their potential for sex assessment (Parker et al., 2019). Because DNA can sometimes be extracted and studied

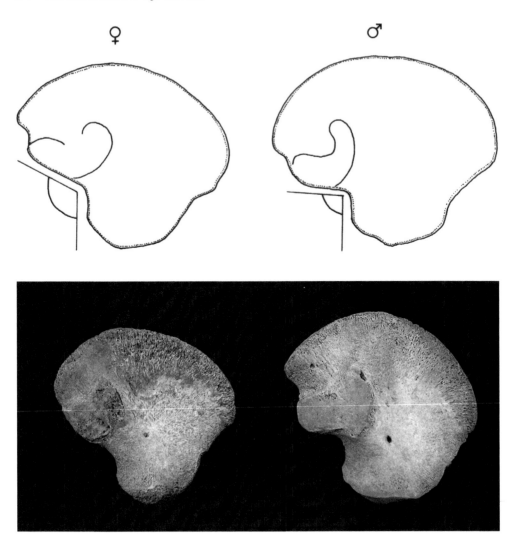

Figure 4.6 Sex difference in the angle of the greater sciatic notch in non-adults reported
         by Schutkowski shown diagrammatically (above) and photographically (below)
Source: diagrams after Schutkowski 1993: Figure 2A.

from ancient skeletal remains, it too offers a method of assessing sex; this is discussed
in Chapter 12.

Age estimation

In immature remains, age at death can be estimated using aspects of skeletal growth and
development. Once skeletal maturity is attained in the adult, age at death can be inferred
from the progress of degenerative conditions and from wear on the teeth. In contrast to
sex assessment, age estimation is more reliable in immature remains than it is for adults.

Age estimation in the immature skeleton

Methods used to estimate age at death in immature remains generally involve the use of growth or developmental standards derived from recent children of known age in order to estimate age in our archaeological skeletons. This sort of approach is known as a reference-target population model, the reference population being the recent children of known age, the target population are the archaeological skeletons whose ages we want to estimate. An assumption here is that growth and development in the ancient skeletons under study follow a similar chronological schedule to that seen in recent children. For some methods this assumption may be broadly valid, for others it is more problematic. The general aim of osteoarchaeologists should be to minimise problems by selecting as age indicators those aspects of growth and development which are least subject to influence by extraneous factors such as disease and nutrition.

Age estimation in the perinatal skeleton

In perinatal skeletons, bone size is closely related to age (Adalian et al., 2002; Sotiriadis et al., 2016). Bone growth in the foetus may be influenced by extrinsic factors such as poor maternal nutrition, but it is much less easily influenced than it is after birth. Maternal malnutrition has to be quite severe to retard growth in the developing foetus (Bagchi & Bose, 1962), as in this situation the foetus is protected at the expense of the mother.

Scheuer et al. (1980) studied the relationship between long-bone length and age using foetal material from medical collections in England. The gestational ages of the foetal skeletons ranged from 27–46 weeks (the average gestational age at birth is 38-41 weeks – Tanner, 1989:43). They measured the length of the limb bones and found that bone length bore a close relationship to age (Figure 4.7). The closeness of the relationship between age at death and long-bone length in foetal remains means that we can use it to estimate age at death to within about two weeks.

Age estimation in the child skeleton: the teeth

After birth, bone growth is heavily affected by extrinsic factors such as nutrition and disease; by comparison growth of the teeth is relatively little affected (Cardoso, 2007; Conceição & Cardoso, 2011; Elamin & Liversidge, 2013). Dental development is therefore the method of choice for age determination in child skeletons.

Tooth formation begins near the tip of the crown and ends at the tip of the root. The crown and the upper portion of the root are formed whilst the tooth is still hidden within the jaw bone; the lower parts of the root are completed after the tooth has emerged through the gum into the mouth (Liversidge & Molleson, 2018). There are thus two components to dental development, the formation of the teeth and their eruption into the mouth. For age determination the former is preferable, as it is less affected by extrinsic factors (Saunders, 2008). The deciduous teeth start to form whilst the baby is still in the womb, and are complete by the time the child is about 3 years old. The permanent dentition starts to form at around time of birth. Growth of most of the permanent teeth is complete by about 15 years of age, although the third molar, or wisdom tooth (which is

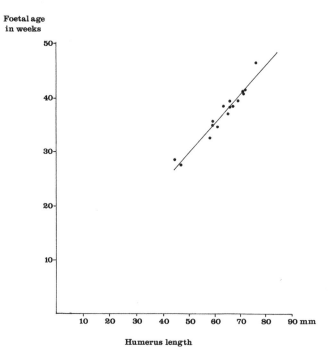

Figure 4.7 Linear regression of gestational age in the foetus against humerus length
Source: Redrawn from Scheuer et al. (1980: Figure 1).

not present in all individuals) may not be completely formed until about 20 years. Dental development therefore provides a potential method of age estimation throughout infancy and childhood.

Our knowledge of the chronology of tooth formation comes principally from radiographic (X-ray) studies of the jaws of living children (Liversidge, 2015). A number of charts relating development to age have been produced (e.g. Schour & Massler, 1941; Ubelaker, 1999; AlQah-tani et al., 2010), but a scheme that is particularly useful for remains of European ancestry is that compiled by two researchers working in Sweden, Gosta Gustafson and Goran Koch. They combined data from different European studies to produce a scheme showing the chronology of the development of the dentition (Gustafson & Koch, 1974). They then tested it by using it to estimate age from dental radiographs in 41 children, aged 3 to 13 years. They found a close correspondence between age as estimated using their scheme and actual age (Figure 4.8). The mean error in age estimation was only two months.

Because it is little affected by extrinsic factors, one might expect modern chronologies of dental development to be broadly applicable to ancient remains. Work on the Spital-fields material seems to bear this out. Sixty-three child skeletons from Spitalfields with ages at death up to 5.4 years were aged using a number of dental development stand-ards (Liversidge, 1994), including that of Gustafson and Koch. All performed well: for example, the mean difference between actual age and the age estimates produced using the chart of Gustafson and Koch (1974) was 0.1 years.

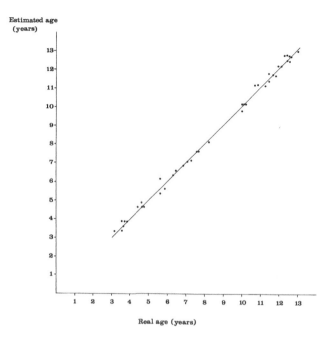

Figure 4.8 Actual age plotted against age estimated from dental radiographs using Gustafson and Koch's dental development scheme. Data for recent Swedish children
Source: Redrawn from Gustafson and Koch (1974: Figure 5).

Chronologies for the development of the deciduous and the permanent teeth are
shown in Figures 4.9 and 4.10. These charts are drawn up from data given by Gustafson
and Koch (1974), except for the third molar, where the data are from Anderson et al.
(1976), Levesque et al. (1981), Garn et al. (1962) and Liversidge (2008). Formation of the
third molar is somewhat more variable in absolute terms (but not in proportion to individual age) than that of the other teeth, but it is still a useful age indicator. For example,
Thorson and Hägg (1991) found that the mean difference between age estimated from
mandibular third molar development and actual age in individuals aged 14.5-20.5 years
old was eight months.

In fragmentary archaeological material, teeth which have erupted into the mouth by time
of death are often loose in their sockets and can easily be removed for examination of their
roots, and if jaws are fragmentary unerupted teeth may be loose for inspection. However,
when the jaw bones are intact with the incompletely formed teeth hidden inside, radiography is necessary in order to determine the state of dental development (Figure 4.11).

Age estimation in the child skeleton: the bones

It may be recalled from Chapter 1 that the extremities of a long-bone are usually formed
from secondary ossification centres (epiphyses), united with the diaphysis (shaft) of the
growing bone by the growth cartilages. Most other bones, save those in the skull and the
ankle and wrist, also possess epiphyses. When bones cease growing the growth cartilage

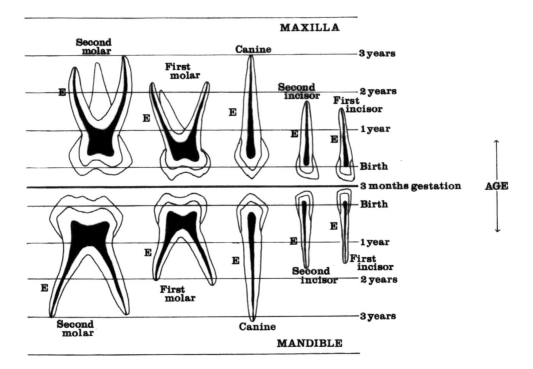

Figure 4.9 Chronology of the development of the deciduous teeth. E denotes approximate
    age at eruption

Note: the style of the diagram is after Stermer Beyer-Olsen and Risnes (1994: Figure 2); data source
Gustafson & Koch (1974).

ossifies, fusing the epiphyses with the diaphysis (Figure 4.12). Epiphysial fusion proceeds in
an orderly manner during adolescence and early adulthood. Although, like other aspects
of bone maturation, it is more affected by extrinsic factors than dental calcification or
eruption (Lewis & Garn, 1960; Conceição & Cardoso, 2011), it is usual to use epiphysial
fusion as a method of estimating age at death in skeletons of adolescents or young
adults where dental development is complete or for which dental remains were not
recovered.

The chronology of epiphysial fusion has been studied both by medical imaging of
living subjects and by examining bones from collections of recent individuals of known
age at death. Some studies document union at a range of epiphyses, others concentrate on particular regions of the skeleton. Studies investigating union at a range of
epiphyses include the dry bone studies of Stevenson (1924) and McKern and Stewart
(1957) on recent US remains, and a series of works by Cardoso and co-workers (Cardoso, 2008a, 2008b; Cardoso & Severino, 2010; Ríos & Cardoso, 2009; Cardonso &
Ríos, 2011; Cardoso et al., 2013; 2014) on recent remains from Portugal, and the radiographic studies of Borovansky and Hnevkovsky (1929) and Flecker (1942) on living individuals of European ancestry. Works concentrating on specific regions of the skeleton
include the dry bone studies of Albert and co-workers on the vertebral body epiphyses

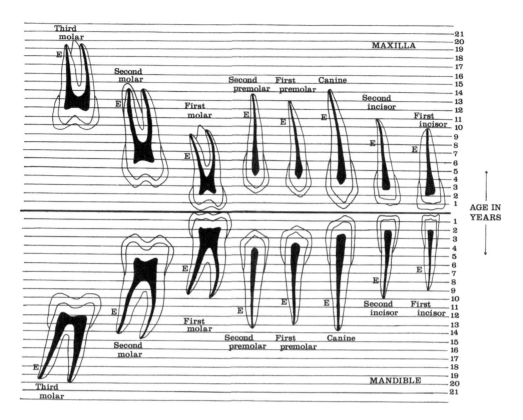

Figure 4.10 Chronology of the development of the permanent teeth. E denotes approximate age at eruption

Note: the style of the diagram is after Stermer Beyer-Olsen and Risnes (1994: Figure 2); for data sources see text.

(Albert & Maples, 1995; Albert et al., 2010), the radiographic study of Schaeffer et al. (2015) on the shoulder and the CT studies of Sullivan et al. (2017) and Kellinghaus et al. (2010) on the pelvic area and clavicle respectively.

There are limitations to both dry-bone and medical imaging studies. Smaller epiphyses and those with complex anatomy may be difficult to visualise adequately using medical imaging techniques. In dry-bone studies, sample sizes are generally small over the age ranges at which epiphyseal union occurs so that the full range of variation may not be adequately captured. Timings of epiphyseal union presented in different studies vary somewhat, but the extent to which this reflects genuine population differences, rather than discrepancies in methodologies or in sample sizes and composition is unclear. No single study is truly comprehensive in including all epiphyses and both sexes, but because of the above factors, combining data from different studies is potentially problematic. Figure 4.13 presents data for the timing of epiphysial fusion, mainly from a study done in Australia by Flecker (1942). This work was conducted using radiography of a large number of hospital patients of European ancestry, ranging in age up to 29 years

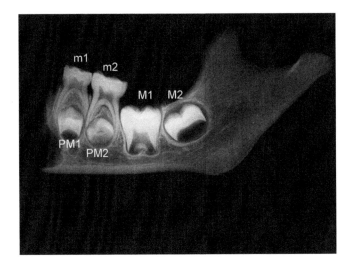

Figure 4.11 Radiograph of part of a mandible from a child from a British archaeological site. Two deciduous molars are fully erupted, and unerupted permanent teeth are clearly visible within the jaw bone. Key: m1=deciduous first molar, m2=deciduous second molar, M1=permanent first molar, M2=permanent second molar, PM1=first premolar, PM2=second premolar. The crowns of the unerupted M2 and PM1 are almost complete. The crown of the PM2 has tilted somewhat within its crypt but it is clear that it is less complete than the PM1. The roots of the M1 have formed to just beyond their bifurcation. Comparison with the schedule for the calcification of the permanent dentition shown in Fig. 4.10 suggests an age at death of about 5–6 years

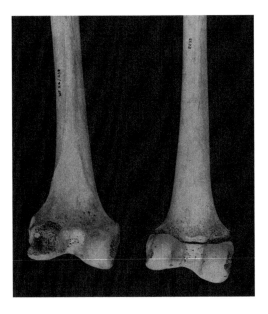

Figure 4.12 The femur on the right is an immature bone with an unfused distal epiphysis. That on the left is a mature bone for comparison

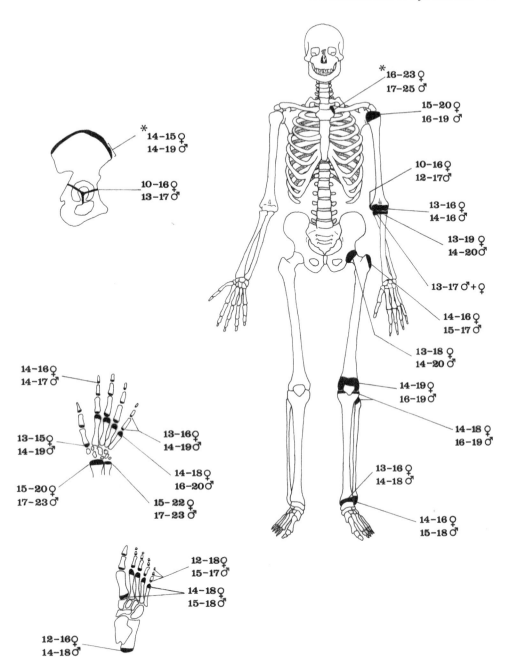

Figure 4.13 Epiphysial fusion. The lower ends of the age ranges are the ages at which fusion of epiphysis to diaphysis was first noted, the upper ends those at which completely unfused epiphyses were last noted

Data are from Flecker (1942), except those marked * which are from Webb and Suchey (1985).

old. These data are supplemented by those for the clavicle and the anterior part of the iliac crest from a dry bone study by Webb and Suchey (1985).

Unfortunately, no adequate collections of adolescent individuals of known age at death exist from archaeological contexts to test the reliability of epiphysial fusion as an ageing method for ancient skeletons. It is also difficult to compare age estimates from epiphysial fusion with those from dental development in archaeological material as assemblages are generally short of adolescent skeletons (in most populations mortality in this age group is low), and in any event the formation of most of the dentition is complete before most of the major epiphyses start to fuse. Nutritional deficits delay epiphysial fusion (Dreizen et al., 1957; Schmeling et al., 2006; Meijerman et al., 2007), extending the growth period. In the 19th century, growth was prolonged, by up to about ten years in the poorer social classes, compared with modern Western populations (see Chapter 6 for further details). This illustrates the potential for significant delay in epiphysial union in earlier human populations. Although this suggests that epiphysial fusion may have the propensity to underage when applied to archaeological material, it is, provided this is borne in mind, still a useful, if rather approximate age indicator.

Age estimation in the adult skeleton

Many methods have been used for estimating age at death in adult skeletons from archaeological sites. All are, in different ways, problematic, and there is currently little consensus over which method is best. Most of the methods rely on assessing aspects of the way in which the skeleton degenerates with age, but this process appears highly variable between individuals, meaning that, at a population level, age indicators are poorly correlated with age. This problem is particularly marked in older adults, as individual skeletal ageing trajectories naturally diverge with age (Nawrocki, 2010). At present, the lack of a satisfactory technique for estimating age at death from adult skeletal remains is one of the thorniest problems in human osteoarchaeology.

The following section briefly describes some of the more important techniques used to estimate age at death in adult skeletons (Figure 4.14). In a book of this nature it is impossible to discuss each method in detail. What follows is a brief summary of each technique. The references given following the name of the method are to review articles (when available) or to major methodological studies, to which the reader is referred for more detail.

1. Cranial suture closure (Masset, 1989; Key et al,. 1994; Galera et al., 1998). Most of the separate bones which make up the cranium interlock at fibrous, non-movable joints called sutures. As an adult individual grows older, the cranial vault sutures tend to progressively fuse and become obliterated. Cranial suture closure is the oldest skeletal ageing technique – that cranial sutures are obliterated with age has been known since the 16th century AD, and practical methods for using this to assess age were first suggested in the 19th century. Over the years, many schemes have been published which purport to show the relationship between suture closure and age. Some of the more important include Acsádi and Nemeskéri (1970), Perizonius (1984) and Meindl and Lovejoy (1985).

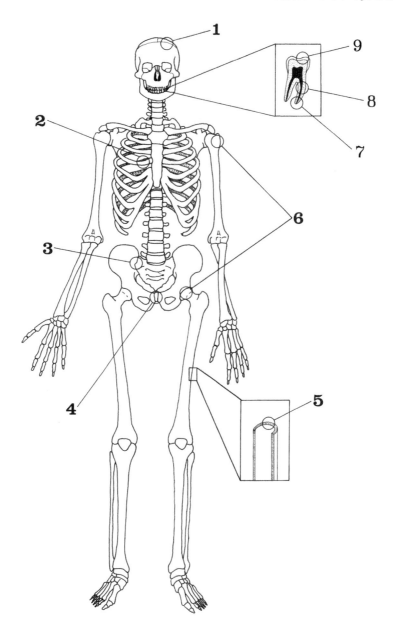

Figure 4.14 Some methods which have been used to estimate age at death in adult skeletons from archaeological sites (for key, see text)

2. Rib-end morphology (Loth, 1995; Hartnett, 2010; İşcan & Steyn, 2013). The ends of
    the ribs are joined to the sternum by lengths of cartilage. Where it joins the cartilage,
    the initially flattish rib-end becomes indented, forming a pit that progressively deep-
    ens. In males, bone is then deposited at the margins of the pit, further deepening it.
    In females bone deposition tends to occur at the base of the pit. İşcan and colleagues

classified these changes into discrete phases and formulated separate ageing schemes for males and females using autopsy material (İşcan et al., 1984, 1985; Loth & İşcan, 1989). The method was originally devised for the fourth rib, but later work (Dudar, 1993; Yoder et al., 2001) showed that changes are quite similar at ribs 2–9. The method suffers from being based on a fragile part of the skeleton that is often missing or damaged in archaeological remains.

3. Auricular surface morphology (Lovejoy et al., 1985; Buckberry & Chamberlain, 2002; Falys et al., 2006). The auricular surface of the ilium is the joint by which this part of the pelvic bone articulates with the sacrum. In young adults, its surface is fine grained and bears transverse striations. These striations are gradually obliterated, and the surface becomes more coarsely textured and porous. Finally the surface becomes more irregular and osteophytes may appear at its margins. Lovejoy et al. (1985) developed this method using a collection of US anatomical skeletons, but several major revisions to their original scheme have since been published (Buckberry & Chamberlain, 2002; Osborne et al., 2004; Igarashi et al., 2005; Falys et al., 2006).

4. Pubic symphysial morphology (Brooks & Suchey, 1990). This is a widely used method and will be discussed in more detail below.

5. Investigation of bone microstructure (Gocha et al., 2019). This involves grinding transverse slices of bone into thin sections, and quantifying frequencies of osteons and various other features under a microscope, a process known as histomorphometry. Histomorphometry was first suggested as an ageing technique in the early 20th century. Despite its antiquity as a method, there remains debate over what microscopic features should be counted, what parts of the skeleton should be sampled (most workers use femur or rib cortical bone), and what proportion of a cut section should be analysed.

6. The 'Complex Method' (Acsádi & Nemeskéri, 1970; Workshop of European Anthropologists, 1980). This involves studying age-related loss of trabecular bone in the femoral and humeral heads, either by radiography or by physically sectioning the bones. Results here are used, in conjunction with pubic symphysis morphology and closure of the cranial sutures, to provide an estimate of age at death. The method was devised by Nemeskéri and co-workers (Nemeskéri et al. 1960) in Hungary, mainly using autopsy specimens. This ageing method has been widely used in Continental Europe (Márquez-Grant & Fibiger, 2011).

7. Tooth root translucency (Megyesi et al., 2006; Tang et al., 2014; Zorba et al., 2018). As an individual grows older, minerals are deposited within the dentinal tubules, which causes the dentine to become translucent. Translucency appears at the root tip in young adults and progresses along the root toward the crown. It is studied in single-rooted teeth; some workers cut longitudinal sections, but most simply place the intact tooth on a light box. The extent of translucency can be used on its own to estimate age (Bang & Ramm, 1970; Singhal et al., 2010) or in conjunction with measurement of the location of the gingival attachment on the tooth (Lamendin et al., 1992; Prince & Ubelaker, 2002), which gradually moves further away from the crown with advancing age. The method was developed using extracted teeth from dental patients and there are difficulties in applying it to archaeological material. The level of the gingival attachment may be difficult to distinguish in ancient remains (Megyesi

et al., 2006) and translucency appears to be affected by diagenesis. For example, 35% of teeth from Spitalfields showed no translucency at all (Megyesi et al., 2006).

8. Cementochronology (Wittwer-Backofen, 2012; Naji et al., 2016). This involves counting incremental layers in cementum that coats tooth roots. This method is discussed in more detail below.

9. Tooth wear (Brothwell, 1989; Miles, 2001). The teeth progressively wear down with age, especially in populations consuming coarse diets. Dental wear ageing is discussed further below.

The methods identified in Figure 4.14 may be divided into two groups. Methods 1-7 use the relationship between the age indicator and age identified in a reference population of known age to estimate age using the state of that indicator in unknown (or target) individuals. As we have seen, a reference-target population approach forms a fairly good basis for age estimation in immature remains, but when the relationship between the age indicator and age is weak and varies between populations, as is the case for adult age markers, then the assumptions and difficulties inherent in this approach may begin to compromise its value. The section which follows discusses some of the problems with the reference-target population approach for adult remains, using as its principal focus pubic symphyseal ageing. This was chosen because it is one of the most widely used ageing methods in osteoarchaeology (Falys & Lewis, 2011). I will then go on to describe the two remaining methods, cementochronology and dental wear. These do not rely on the reference-target population model; the former focuses on the identification of incremental structures that apparently form annually, the latter attempts to identify rate of wear in the particular population under study.

Age estimation in adult remains using the reference-target population model: the case of pubic symphysial ageing

The left and right pubic bones at the front of the pelvis are not fused together in the midline - rather, they are separated by a fibro-cartilaginous disc. This joint is known as the pubic symphysis. The bone surfaces underlying this joint appear to show age-related changes in the adult. Initially the symphysial surface displays ridges and furrows, but these are progressively obliterated and bone builds up around the joint margin. The bony deposits around the margins eventually unite to form a continuous rim. Finally, this rim breaks down and the symphysial surface may become porous and pitted. Figure 4.15 illustrates some of these changes.

Over the years, a number of schemes have been put forward classifying the changes seen at the pubic symphysis and showing the purported relationship of these phases with age at death (Todd, 1920; McKern & Stewart, 1957; Gilbert & McKern, 1973; Brooks & Suchey, 1990). The most important study was carried out by the American forensic anthropologist Judy Myers Suchey and her co-workers (results summarised in Brooks & Suchey, 1990). Her team examined pubic bones dissected during autopsy from 1,225 corpses of known age at death. They classified the age-related changes in morphology into six phases. The earlier studies, referred to above, had shown that male and female pubic bones differ in their morphology, but Suchey and her co-workers were, by concentrating on key features, able to produce a classification of morphological phases applicable to both sexes, although the age-

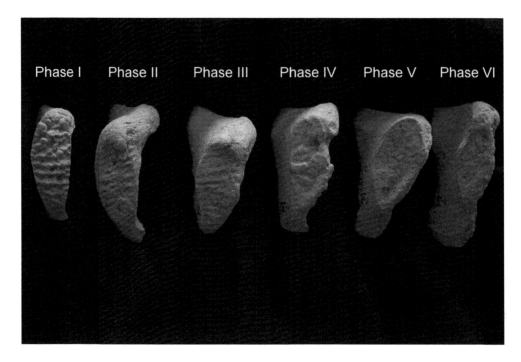

Figure 4.15 Casts of left male pubic bones. These illustrate the appearance of the symphyseal face in the six phases (I=youngest, VI=oldest) of the adult ageing system formulated by Suchey and colleagues. In younger phases, the symphysial face shows a ridge and furrow pattern, but this gradually becomes less visible and is lost entirely by phase V. From phase II onwards, a raised rim begins to develop around the symphysial margin, and this process is complete by phase V. In phase VI the rim begins to break down, and the symphysial face may be pitted or porous, although these latter features are not strongly developed in the specimen illustrating phase VI here. Casts by France Casting, Colorado. For the age spans for each phase found in Suchey and co-workers' autopsy material see Table 4.1

spans corresponding to these phases were different in males and females (Table 4.1). More recent workers (e.g. Hartnett, 2010) have suggested minor modifications to the Suchey-Brooks scheme, but they are rarely used; the original scheme has been the mainstay for age estimation using the pubic symphysis.

The age spans in Table 4.1 are in general very broad. In some instances the age ranges are so large that there is almost complete overlap between those of adjacent phases (e.g. stages IV and V in females). It would seem from the study of Suchey and colleagues that the relationship between pubic morphology and age in all but the youngest of adult age groups is too poor to be of very much use for palaeodemography. Earlier work however, had suggested that it was a much better age indicator; it was the false confidence engendered by such work that lead to the popularity of pubic symphysial ageing for skeletal material. The first study, by T.Wingate Todd (Todd, 1920), had

Table 4.1 Relationship reported between pubic symphysial phases and age in the material studied by Suchey and co-workers

Phase	Age (Years)	
	Females	Males
I	15-24	15-23
II	19-40	19-34
III	21-53	21-46
IV	26-70	23-57
V	25-83	27-66
VI	42-87	34-86

Source: Data from Brooks and Suchey (1990: Table 1).

Note: The age-ranges are those into which 95% of the individuals displaying each particular phase fell.

suggested that individuals could be aged to within five years or less up to the age of 50 and that there was minimal overlap between different phases (Table 4.2).

In a subsequent study, McKern and Stewart (1957) found that for the large collection of male skeletons they worked on, Todd's ageing scheme was unsatisfactory. They found a more elaborate component scores method was required to describe accurately pubic morphology in their sample. Their scheme had broader age-ranges for each stage than Todd's and there was more overlap between age spans (Table 4.3). Todd did not have access to sufficient female skeletons to generate a pubic ageing scheme for females. However Gilbert and McKern (1973) produced standards for females, again using a component scores method (Table 4.4).

It is clear then that since Todd's study a century ago, pubic ageing schemes have undergone heavy revision, with a progressive broadening of age ranges corresponding to particular morphological phases and an increase in age overlap between phases. That such drastic revision should have taken place may seem surprising, and the reasons why are worth considering.

Table 4.2 Relationship found between age at death (in years) and pubic symphysis phases in the Todd Collection. Males only

Phase	I	II	III	IV	V	VI	VII	VIII	IX	X
Age	18-19	20-21	22-24	25-26	27-30	30-35	35-39	39-44	45-50	50+

Source: Data from Todd (1920).

Table 4.3 Relationship found between age at death (in years) and pubic symphysis scores in the material studied by McKern and Stewart. Males only

Score	0	1-2	3	4-5	6-7	8-9	10	11-13	14	15
Age	Under 17	17-20	18-21	18-23	20-24	22-28	23-28	23-39	29+	36+

Source: Data form McKern and Stewart (1957).

Table 4.4 Relationship found between age at death (in years) and pubic symphysis scores in the material examined by Gilbert and McKern. Females only

Score	0	1	2	3	4-5	6	7-8	9	10-11	12	13	14-15
Age	14-18	13-24	16-25	18-25	22-29	25-36	23-39	22-40	30-47	32-52	44-54	52-59

Source: Data from Gilbert and McKern (1973).

Firstly, there were problems associated with the reference collections used by earlier workers. Todd used a collection of skeletons from Cleveland, Ohio, now known as the Hamann-Todd collection. These skeletons came from corpses gathered in the earlier part of the 20th century from local hospitals and medical schools. There are problems with the reliability of the documented ages at death for this material. In some cases age appears to have been estimated by anatomists on the basis of the external appearance of the corpse, rather than known exactly. Furthermore, skeletons in which documented age seemed incompatible with the then accepted skeletal indicators of age were eliminated from Todd's (1920) study. This is a key omission, as it will have the effect of falsely reducing sample variability – if these individuals had been included, then the age spans on Todd's pubic phases would doubtless have been broader.

McKern and Stewart, in their 1957 study, used bones of US Korean War dead. Age at death for these individuals was known accurately, but this sample suffered from other problems. The chief drawback, as McKern and Stewart recognised, was the restricted age range of the material: there were very few individuals over 30 years old. This must have produced a false truncation of the age spans of many phases, and if older individuals had been present in greater numbers they may have shown some phases not seen at all in the material under study.

Age for the female sample studied by Gilbert and McKern (1973) seems to have been reliably documented, and their sample contained a reasonable spread of ages. However, their numbers were rather small (103 individuals, only about one third of the size of McKern and Stewart's male sample, spread over 12 age groups).

Part of the difficulty with the older pubic symphyseal ageing schemata doubtless lies with the problematic nature of the reference samples, but that is unlikely to be the main reason for the wholesale revisions that have been needed over the years. It is probable that there are genuine differences in pubic morphology, and its relationship to chronological age, between populations.

These sorts of problems are not unique to pubic symphyseal ageing. For example, in the decades since it was formulated, the auricular surface ageing method of Lovejoy et al. (1985) has also undergone major revision, the pattern of which carries distinct echoes of that for the pubic symphysis method. The initial scheme, developed by Lovejoy and colleagues using the Hamann-Todd collection, consisted of eight phases each mostly corresponding to an age span of about 5 years and with no overlap (Table 4.5). However subsequent workers (e.g. Buckberry & Chamberlain, 2002; Osborne et al., 2004; Rissech et al., 2012) found that these age bands were too narrow to encompass the variability seen in auricular surface morphology in the skeletal series that they studied. This observation prompted Buckberry and Chamberlain (2002) to introduce a new component scores method which they felt more accurately described auricular surface morphology in their study material (British collections, including the Spitalfields burials). These component scores corresponded to seven phases which were rather broader in age spans than those of Lovejoy et al. and showed considerable overlap (Table 4.5). In 2006, Falys and colleagues looked at auricular surface morphology and age in another large 19th-century London skeletal collection of known age at death, from St Bride's Church, Fleet Street. They attempted to apply the Buckberry & Chamberlain technique but found that the variability seen within age classes was such that only three distinct developmental stages could be defined. The age spans for these three phases were very broad and overlapped to a considerable extent (Falys et al., 2006), leading the authors to question the value of auricular surface morphology as an age indicator.

With the possible exception of cementochronology (see below), the pattern whereby relationships between age indicator and age differ in different populations seems to apply generally for adult age markers. As for pubic symphyseal and auricular surface morphology, empirical evidence shows that other adult skeletal age indicators have different relationships with age in different study samples (e.g. Macaluso & Lucena, 2012; García-Donas et al., 2016; Xanthopoulou et al., 2018; Zorba et al., 2018). This is a severe problem for methods that rely on a reference-target population model.

In addition, in any particular population, the relationship between an age indicator and age is weak. Review of statistical analyses (Mays, 2015) indicated that in general only about 30-40% of the variation in an age indicator reflects variation in age. Quite what accounts for the rest is unclear. The biology of age indicators remains poorly understood, and studies aimed at elucidating the effects of extraneous factors on age markers are only beginning to be undertaken (e.g. Campanacho et al., 2012; Bongiovanni, 2016; Merritt, 2017).

Table 4.5 Relationship between age at death (years) and auricular surface morphological phases in the original formulation of the auricular surface ageing method and in two subsequent revisions

Phase	Age range (years)
Lovejoy et al. (1985)	
1	20-24
2	25-29
3	30-34
4	35-39
5	40-44
6	45-49
7	50-59
8	60+
Buckberry and Chamberlain (2002)	
I	16-19
II	21-38
III	16-65
IV	29-81
V	29-88
VI	39-91
VII	53-92
Falys et al. (2006)	
I	17-69
II	18-90
III	21-91

Some workers (e.g. Hartnett-McCann et al., 2018) have recommended combining several age indicators in a 'multifactorial approach' in order to try and improve results. The use of as many age indicators as possible is intuitively attractive, as consideration of changes in different parts of the skeleton might be thought to give a broader evidential base for estimating age than would concentrating on one indicator alone. On the other hand, simply combining them cannot obviate the problems inherent in each individual technique. It could therefore be argued that there is no reason to expect any improvement in age estimates, and that a better strategy might be to choose the most appropriate or reliable technique(s) for the material in hand. Empirical evidence on this point is equivocal, some studies report improved results when multiple methods are used (e.g. Bedford et al., 1993; Baccino et al., 1999) others (e.g. Schmitt et al., 2002; Martrille et al., 2007) do not.

Testing adult ageing methods on archaeological material

The above discussion might lead one to think that the application of ageing standards derived from recent individuals to archaeological populations, where diet, health and general way of life were very different, might be problematic. Evidence we do have from archaeological collections of skeletons of known age at death seems to confirm this. For example, an overview of a number of studies of pubic symphyseal ageing (sample sizes ranging from 13–68, making a combined total of 171), in 18th–19th-century remains (Saunders et al., 1992; Boyle et al., 2005; Witkin & Boston, 2006; Henderson et al., 2013, 2015) indicates that, in about 20% of cases, actual age fell outside the range indicated by the Brooks & Suchey (1990) standards. This is surprising given the very broad age classes of the Suchey-Brooks scheme, and is much greater than the approximately 5% that might be expected if these populations resembled the Suchey-Brooks reference material.

These results have been reinforced by work on the large skeletal collection of individuals of known age at death from Christ Church Spitalfields, London. Here tooth dentine structure, pubic symphysis morphology, the rib-end technique, cranial suture closure and bone microstructure methods were applied; all performed poorly, showing only very weak associations with individual age (Molleson & Cox, 1993; Aiello and Molleson, 1993; Key et al., 1994; Megyesi et al., 2006; Tang et al., 2014). Molleson and Cox also investigated the utility of the 'Complex Method' of age estimation. The originators of the method claimed that its reliability was such that estimated age should fall within five years of actual age in 80–85% of cases. When tested on the adult skeletons of known age at death from Spitalfields (Molleson & Cox, 1993:167–172) it was found to perform much less well. Less than 30% of individuals were aged correctly to within five years. Molleson and Cox also found a systematic error, younger individuals tended to be over-aged, older ones under-aged. (Figure 4.16). In part, this latter pattern is likely to be a function of the reference sample. The mean age of individuals in Nemeskéri et al.'s (1960) reference sample in most of the oldest phases of their four age indicators were in the 60s; for the earliest phases means were in generally in the late 20s. Errors in age determination in the Spitalfields study were (as is often the case in tests of ageing methods) evaluated as the difference between known age for each individual and the mean age of reference population showing that phase of the age indicator(s). It is thus inevitable that those over 70 and those younger than their late 20s at Spitalfields would

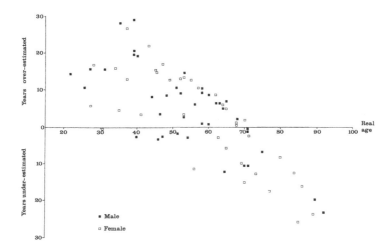

Figure 4.16 Deviation of age estimated using the four criteria of the Complex Method from real age in the Spitalfields adult skeletons

Source: After Molleson and Cox (1993: Figure 12.4).

be classified as under- and over-aged respectively. The pattern by which young adults are over-aged and old adults under-aged is often reported from tests of ageing methods (Martrille et al., 2007; Rivera-Sandoval et al., 2018; Xanthopoulou et al., 2018; Zorba et al., 2018) and may, like at Spitalfields, largely be associated with the nature of the reference samples and the methodologies used in the testing of the ageing methods.

Another more subtle problem with studies of age at death in skeletal populations also relates to the reference samples used to formulate the methods. There appears to be a tendency for age at death distributions generated for archaeological populations using a skeletal age indicator to be biased in the direction of the age structure of the reference sample upon which the method was devised. To understand why this should be so, consider a reference sample that contains many young adults in their 20s and few older ones. The remains of Korean War dead used by McKern and Stewart (1957) for their revision of pubic ageing has this sort of age composition. With this reference material, the possibility remains that an age indicator phase which appeared to correspond to a young adult, could in fact also occur in older age groups and perhaps even be more typical of them. This means that estimated ages for archaeological skeletons would have a general tendency toward being too young so that the age distribution reconstructed for the archaeological group would be biased downwards toward the age structure of the reference population (discussion in Milner et al., 2008). This bias in archaeological age at death distributions toward the age structure of the reference sample has become known as 'age-structure mimicry' (Mensforth, 1990). The effect tends to be most pronounced when the correlation between the age indicator and chronological age is poor (Konigsberg & Frankenberg, 1992), as it is with adult age indicators.

Some have attempted to eliminate age-structure mimicry by statistical manipulation of data using Bayesian analyses, sometimes coupled with statistical analyses aimed at estimating ages at which age indicators transition from one stage to the next (Milner & Boldsen, 2012). A Bayesian analysis begins by assigning probabilities that individuals in the study population belong to a particular age category. These probabilities are known as prior-probabilities. This approach may seem somewhat counter-intuitive and indeed paradoxical, as what we would need to know in order to do this accurately is the age at death distribution of the population, but to know this we would need know ages at death of the individuals! If there is other, independent information on age at death in the population under study (e.g. historical records), we could use that to generate prior-probabilities, but in practice this is rarely the case. One way around this problem is to estimate a likely age distribution using Model Life Tables (schedules that summarize mortality experiences of different types of population around the world) thought to be appropriate for pre-Modern societies (Chamberlain, 2000) and use the resulting data to derive the prior-probabilities. The prior-probabilities (however they are derived) are incorporated into a statistical manipulation of the data which removes the age-structure mimicry bias (see Chamberlain, 2000, for a demonstration of how this may be done). This tends to result in age-at-death distributions for palaeopopulations that appear plausible. However, this may simply be because the use of the prior-probabilities has tended to bias the age distributions toward those of the model populations from which the prior-probabilities were taken. A concern is that because skeletal age indicators are only weakly related to age, the shape of the demographic profile is largely determined by the prior-probabilities selected rather than the skeletal evidence (Jackes, 2000, 2011). The bottom line here is that no statistical manipulation of results can overcome the fact that our skeletal age indicators are simply not very reliable.

The next section discusses two ageing techniques that are not dependent upon chronological standards derived from modern reference populations. This means that many of the problems discussed above are circumvented but, as we shall see, these methods have limitations of their own.

Reference population-free methods: cementochronology

The cementum that coats the tooth roots continues to be laid down in incremental layers throughout life, and unlike bone it does not remodel. There are three main types (Yamamoto et al., 2016), one of which, known as acellular extrinsic fibre cementum (AEFC), shows slow continuous growth by regular increments visible as alternating light and dark bands when a thin section of the tooth is cut and examined under a microscope. Each pair of light and dark bands appears to correspond to cementum deposited in a single year (Grosskopf & McGlynn, 2011). Incremental layers can also be seen in cementum in other mammals, where they are routinely used for age estimation – for example, in wildlife management (Naji et al., 2016; Bertrand et al., 2019a).

Over the years, a variety of sampling sites, sample preparation techniques and microscopy methods have been used in cementochronology of human remains, but recently more consistency in practice has begun to emerge. It is important to sample the AEFC; this is located in the middle and cervical thirds of the root (Yamamoto et al., 2016) and can be identified on the gross specimen (Plate 1). The usual method is to take transverse sections of a single rooted tooth. The tooth root is normally embedded in resin before cutting to stop it crumbling. Sections are cut on a microtome. This is a small, rotating saw that can cut very thin sections – for cementochronology thicknesses of about 70–100µm are generally best (Wittwer-Backofen, 2012). The thin section is examined using a microscope and the regions that show optimal visibility of paired incremental lines are selected for counting, either directly or from a digitally captured image. Normally multiple sections (up to about 8) are counted and an average number of lines calculated. It is unclear exactly when the first incremental line in AEFC forms, but the usual way of calculating age is to add the count of paired lines to the mean age at eruption of the tooth (Figure 4.17).

One way of measuring the reliability of an ageing method is to assess the strength of the relationship between real age and estimated age using the correlation coefficient. Correlation coefficients measure the strength of an association between two variables, and range from zero (no association) to one (perfect correlation). When cementochronology has been trialled on teeth from people of known age, results have been somewhat mixed, with some studies reporting excellent correlations, others finding very poor results (Naji et al., 2016: Table 4.1). To a great extent, this may reflect variations in methodology. For example, some earlier workers appeared to have included cellular cementum in analyses rather than restricting work to AEFC (e.g. Renz & Radlanski, 2006), and obtaining sections of the correct thickness is critical for proper visualisation of lines (Grosskopf & McGlynn, 2011). Recent studies, that have focussed on AEFC and where microscopy techniques are optimised, have reported correlation coefficients with age of more than 0.9 (Wittwer-Backofen et al., 2004; de Broucker et al., 2016; Couoh, 2017; Bertrand et al., 2019b). It appears that the method can work well, provided that the correct methodology is applied.

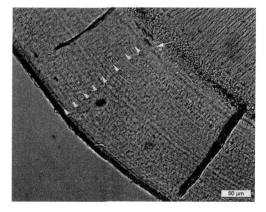

Figure 4.17 Microscopic cross section of the root of a lower canine from a modern individual showing the incremental structure of acellular extrinsic fibre cementum. Long arrow indicates first cementum line, arrowheads indicate groups of 10 paired light and dark lines, the last grouped area is 8 lines. The line count is 78, which added to an age of eruption of about 10 years for this tooth gives an age estimate of 88 years. The true age of this individual was 87.8 years

Source: Wittwer-Backofen et al. (2004: Figure 3).

Even whilst reporting a high overall reliability, some writers have found age estimates to be somewhat less reliable in older individuals (e.g. Bojarun et al., 2004; Meinl et al., 2008; Bertrand et al., 2019b). One reason may be that lines tend to be more densely packed and indistinct in elderly people, making accurate counting more difficult. However, some other workers (e.g. Wittwer-Backofen et al., 2004; de Broucker et al., 2016) have not reported such a pattern. For example, Wittwer-Backofen and co-workers studied teeth from 363 dental patients and found that 97% of estimates were within ± 3 years over the age range 12–96 years (Wittwer-Backofen et al., 2004). The possibility of estimating age in older adults sets cementochronology apart from other methods where it is simply not possible to estimate age in those over about 50 years.

Neither the structural nature of the alternating light and dark bands, nor the physiological basis for their formation are well understood (Colard et al., 2016). Because of this it is hard to know what extraneous factors might impact upon the formation of these incremental structures and hence potentially affect age estimations. One area that has received consideration is the potential influence of dental or oral diseases. Of particular concern is periodontal disease. This is a disease of the supporting tissues of the teeth (Crespo Vázquez et al., 2011). It can be identified in skeletal remains and is common in ancient populations (see Chapter 9). Periodontal disease is associated with alterations to the cementum (Crespo Vázquez et al., 2011). If this affects the periodicity or visibility of incremental structures in AEFC then it is potentially a serious problem for the application of the method. The evidence on this point is mixed. Some workers report that it disrupts the relationship between lines and age (e.g. Dias et al., 2010), but others (Wittwer-Backofen et al., 2004; de Broucker et al., 2016; Couoh, 2017) report no effect. The question requires further attention.

There is a paucity of studies of the effectiveness of cementochronology on archaeological populations of known age at death, but is it clear that alterations to cementum in the burial environment can sometimes prevent accurate line counts. Lanteri et al. (2018) found this to be the case in 17% of burials from a large 16th–18th century burial ground in France; in a study of material from prehispanic sites in Mexico, the figure was 25% (Couoh, 2017).

Cementochronology is time-consuming and expensive, and requires destructive sampling and access to a histology laboratory. Although the method has occasionally been applied to large archaeological collections (e.g. Blondiaux et al., 2016), these considerations still present a major barrier to its routine adoption in osteoarchaeology.

Reference population-free methods: dental wear

The soft, processed diets consumed by modern Western peoples mean that wear on our teeth is slight. However, this was not the case in the past; prior to recent times all human groups consumed a coarse, tough diet which caused considerable dental wear (see Chapter 9). We would thus expect older individuals to show greater tooth wear than younger ones in archaeological groups. Wear is generally most regular on the molar teeth, so it is these which are most often emphasised in ageing studies.

Initially there is wear on the enamel only, but then the underlying dentine is exposed. Eventually the entire enamel crown may be worn away, although secondary dentine formation by the odontoblasts which line the pulp cavity generally prevents exposure of the dental pulp (Figure 4.18). Patterns of dentine exposure have been used as a means of recording dental wear. A number of schemes for recording wear have been proposed; that developed by Brothwell for the molar teeth is shown in Figure 4.19.

An advantage of tooth wear is that it is easily studied in living individuals, as well as in skeletal remains. Some present-day non-Western groups still show heavy dental wear and so are suitable study populations. In high wear populations, the association with age appears greater than for most other skeletal ageing methods – different studies report about 50-90% of variation in molar wear is accounted for by variation in age (Mays, 2015: Supplementary Table 4.1), although for low-wear populations the age correlation appears no better than for bony age indicators (Faillace et al., 2017).

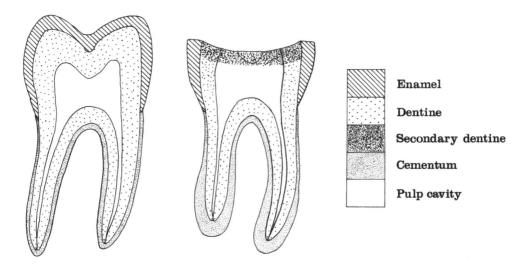

Figure 4.18 Diagrammatic sections through an unworn and a heavily worn molar
Source: After Brothwell (1981: Figure 2.32).

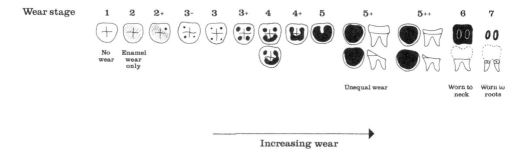

Figure 4.19 A classification of molar wear. White denotes enamel, black exposed dentine
Source: Adapted from Brothwell (1981: Figure 3.9).

As we have seen, the biology of most age indicators is poorly understood. Because of this we are unsure about what extrinsic factors might impact upon their effectiveness, and hence the extent to which they might be applicable to archaeological populations. By contrast, the process of dental wear is fairly well understood. The coarse nature of the diet is largely responsible for the wear customarily seen in archaeological assemblages. The appearance of the phases of wear (Figure 4.19) is a result of the nature of tooth structure and the mechanics of human mastication. We understand, therefore, why dental wear occurs and why the morphological phases into which it can be scored take the form they do. We can therefore also predict what factors are likely to cause differences in wear rates between populations. The chief factor is probably food preparation techniques (see Chapter 9), but differences in types of food consumed are also important. This shows us that it would be futile to try to use modern rates of wear to try to age archaeological populations. Instead, we can estimate the rate of dental wear in the particular archaeological population under study.

Estimation of the rate of molar wear in an archaeological population may be achieved by comparing wear on the different molar teeth. The first molar erupts at about 6 years, the second at about 12 and the third molar at approximately 18 years old (Figure 4.10). This difference between the eruption times of the molars creates a sort of clock against which wear can be calibrated. The most widely used method was devised by A.E.W. Miles (Miles, 1963) and uses dentitions of immature individuals. The amount of wear on the first molar when the second molar erupts gives an indication of the amount of wear expected on a tooth which has been functioning for about six years; when the third molar erupts the first will have 12 years of wear, while the second molar will have about six years. So, if, for example, a second molar in an individual shows a functional age of 12 years, and a third molar a functional age of 6 years, the individual is probably about 24 years old. By looking at the wear on the first molars of such individuals we can gauge the amount of wear which represents about 18 years of tooth function. Those with second molars with functional ages of 18 years will be aged about 30. In this fashion we can estimate age through the entire adult part of an assemblage, starting with the youngest and working our way through to those individuals showing the heaviest wear (Figure 4.20).

There are a number of potential difficulties with dental wear as an ageing method. Firstly, it assumes that individuals in an archaeological group all experienced similar wear rates. Research by Don Brothwell, using child skeletons from British sites from various archaeological periods (see below), suggests that until recently wear rates were stable over extended periods of time. Given this result, it would be surprising if great differences in wear rates often existed in the past between individuals within a single community. Work using tooth crown height measurements provides some support for this supposition. For example, at the Romano-British site at Poundbury, analysis of the relationship between crown height and age in child skeletons aged accurately using dental development showed no evidence for marked inter-individual differences in wear rates (Mays et al., 1995).

One assumption in Miles' calibration is that the different molars wear at similar rates. Miles, looking at a British Anglo-Saxon population, found that there was a slight wear

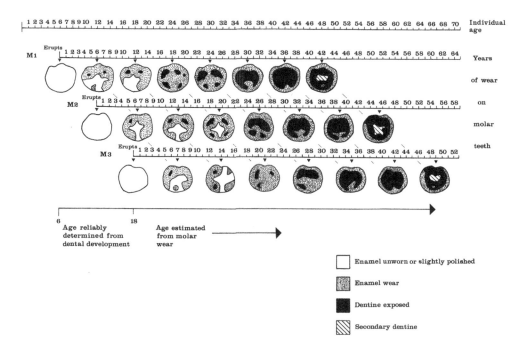

Figure 4.20 Illustration of the Miles method for estimating the rate of dental wear in a skeletal collection, and hence for determining adult age at death

Source: Redrawn from Miles (1963: Figure 10).

gradient, the first molars wearing fastest, the third molars slowest, but the differences made little difference to age estimates (Miles, 2001). Another assumption is that the rate of wear in children is a useful guide to that in adults. In children, fewer teeth are erupted into the mouth than is the case in adulthood. This might be expected to result in an increased rate of wear as the chewing load is shared between fewer teeth. In adults, the jaw muscles are stronger, so this factor would tend to increase wear in adults compared with children. Miles felt that such factors probably tend to cancel one another out, so that his method should work fairly well.

Despite the potential problems, a test of the Miles method conducted by Kieser et al. (1983) on living Lengua Indians from Paraguay has shown that the method appears to work well. The Lengua show heavy dental wear, and the ages of those in Kieser and co-workers' study were known from missionary records. It was found that, at the population level, the Miles method provided a good estimate of true age (Table 4.6).

A reasonable number (perhaps about 20 or more – Nowell, 1978) of child dentitions with erupted permanent molars are needed to calibrate dental wear using the Miles method. Since in most human populations mortality in later childhood and adolescence is low, many archaeological assemblages contain too few individuals of this age. In such cases, a measure of wear rates can potentially be gained by comparing wear on the different molars in adult skeletons, and this information may be used to provide age

Table 4.6 Comparison between mean real ages and mean age estimated from dental wear using the Miles method in Paraguayan Lengua Indians

True age range	No.	Mean true age	Mean estimated age
20-22	18	20.38	20.55
23-24	9	23.50	23.70
25-26	19	25.10	24.89
27-30	11	28.72	29.00
31-36	24	33.60	33.50
37-46	23	40.78	41.56
47-56	23	50.82	53.17

Source: Data from Kieser et al. (1983).

estimates using a method described by Gilmore and Grote (2012). However, the effectiveness of this method has yet to be tested on populations of known age. In any event, for British populations Brothwell (1963) studied children's teeth from various archaeological sites and found that wear rates did not alter greatly from Neolithic (c. 4000 BC) to Mediaeval times (up to the 16th century AD), and later work seems to support this (Field, 2019). By applying methods similar to those of Miles, this allowed him to produce a chart (Figure 4.21) showing the estimated correspondence between actual age and molar wear stages which should be generally applicable to British material from the Neolithic to the Mediaeval period. If insufficient child skeletons are available in an assemblage to determine the rate of molar wear, this chart can be used to estimate age in British material.

Ante-mortem tooth loss: a problem for age estimation using dental wear. Tooth loss during life (ante-mortem tooth loss) is common in most archaeological populations (see Chapter 9). If all molar teeth are missing then we clearly cannot record wear, but even if only some have been lost in life it still presents problems in interpreting the wear on those that remain – for instance when a tooth is lost the wear on its occlusal partner would be expected to cease or at least slow considerably.

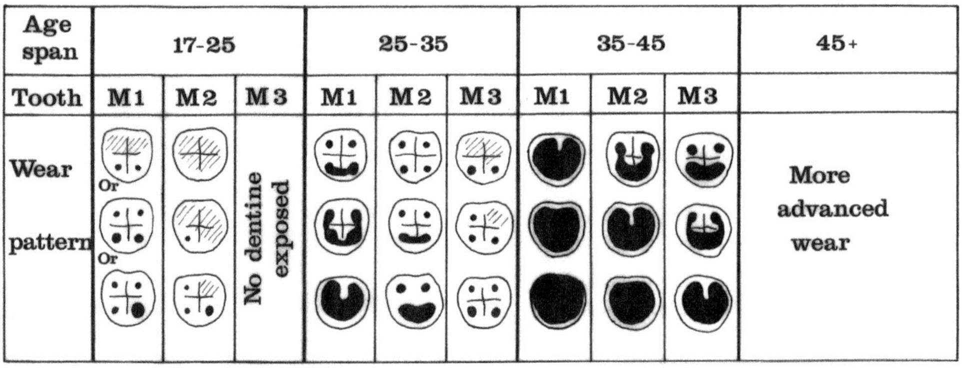

Figure 4.21 Estimated correspondence between adult age at death and molar wear phases for British material from Neolithic to Mediaeval periods

Source: After Brothwell (1981: Figure 3.9).

As we shall see in Chapter 9, loss of teeth can stem from a variety of causes, including dental caries (tooth decay), periodontal disease or, indeed, from heavy dental wear. When wear on a tooth is heavy, it continues to erupt from its socket to maintain occlusion. When wear is advanced, this continued eruption may proceed to the point at which it is only held in its socket by the root tips. This weakening of the support for a tooth may precipitate its loss (Clarke & Hirsch, 1991). This raises the possibility that many molars may be lost before they reach the more extreme wear grades. Consistent with this, in British assemblages it is quite rare to observe the highest grades of molar wear, even though ante-mortem molar loss is common (Mays et al., 1995).

The frequency of conditions such as caries and periodontal disease increases with age. This, together with the observation that advanced wear may precipitate tooth loss, might lead one to suspect that ante-mortem tooth loss would be strongly age correlated, and indeed this has been a finding in both recent and ancient populations (Mays, 2002). Work on populations who did not consume modern Western diets suggests that individuals showing ante-mortem loss of more than about 50% of their teeth are generally more than 50 years of age (e.g. Figure 4.22). On this basis, those showing substantial ante-mortem loss of teeth in archaeological populations are likely predominantly to be past middle age. It is difficult precisely to know what age to assign these individuals, but they cannot simply be omitted from analysis, as to do so would truncate demographic profiles, giving the false impression that few survived past middle age in antiquity. Perhaps the best strategy is simply to assign them to a broad 50+ years age group.

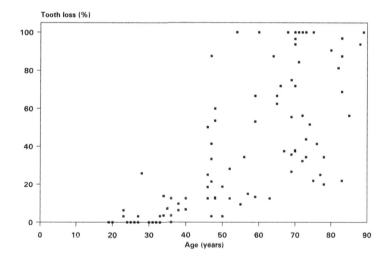

Figure 4.22 Ante-mortem tooth loss (expressed in each individual as the percentage of total observable tooth positions in the mouth showing ante-mortem loss of the tooth) in 19th-century AD burials of documented age at death from Zwolle, the Netherlands. Tooth loss increases markedly once individuals are past middle age

Source: Mays (2002: Figure 11).

Demographic data in archaeological assemblages

What follows are two examples of the use of demographic data to investigate archaeo-logical research questions. The first discusses evidence for the practice of infanticide from perinatal age at death distributions. The second is a study of demographic aspects of adult individuals, particularly age at death, in a British rural Mediaeval community.

Evidence for infanticide

Our ability to estimate age with some precision in perinatal skeletons has provided evidence concerning the practise of infanticide. Infanticide is the killing of unwanted infants. Until recently it was a widely practised and tolerated means of population control in societies around the world (Mays, 2000).

I estimated ages at death in perinatal burials from the Roman period in Britain and from Mediaeval Wharram Percy (Mays, 1993a) from long-bone lengths using the regression equations of Scheuer et al. (1980). I found a difference in age at death distributions. The data from the Roman perinatal infants showed a strong peak at about 38–40 weeks (Figure 4.23a, b), the age corresponding to about a full-term baby. The Mediaeval distribution was much flatter, with no strong peak at full term (Figure 4.23c). I argued that the difference between the Roman and Mediaeval data might reflect differences in the major causes of death. Perinatal burials may be stillbirths, natural deaths in the immediate postnatal period, or victims of infanticide. Age distributions of modern stillbirths and natural deaths soon after birth are shown in Figures 4.23d and e. The Wharram Percy distribution resembles these fairly flat distributions, suggesting that these Mediaeval data represent a 'natural' pattern of perinatal deaths, consisting of some combination of stillbirths and natural deaths in the immediate postnatal period. Since infanticide is generally carried out immediately after birth, the age distribution of victims of this practice would be expected to mimic the gestational age of all live births. Figure 4.23f shows the age distribution for total live births for modern infants. The similarity between this and the age distributions for Romano-British perinatal infants suggest that the Roman assemblages contain substantial numbers of infanticide victims. The fact that the same perinatal age at death pattern holds for Roman cemetery as well as non-cemetery sites (Figure 4.23a, b) indicates that victims of infanticide in Roman times in Britain were not always denied regular burial.

A number of similar studies of perinatal age at death have since been undertaken in Britain and elsewhere. Some other sites (including other Romano-British ones) have produced peaked age distributions; others have produced dispersed distributions more consistent with natural deaths (discussion in Mays, 2014). However, the interpretation of peaked perinatal age at death distributions in terms of infanticide has generated a fair amount of controversy. Gowland & Chamberlain (2002) argued that the peak in the age distribution that I observed in the Romano-British perinatal burials was not indicative of infanticide but simply an artifact of the age-structure mimicry phenomenon (referred to above), and advocated Bayesian statistics to remove this. For theoretical reasons we would expect any bias to be minimal, and re-analysis of the data using regression equations derived from a reference population with a very different age distribution confirmed this (Mays, 2003a). Several studies (Gowland & Chamberlain, 2002; Lewis &

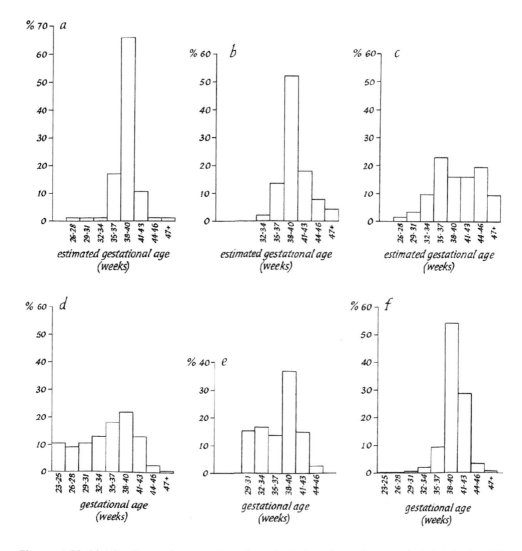

Figure 4.23 Distributions of ages of archaeological and modern perinatal infants: (a) Romano-British settlements (N = 78); (b) Romano-British cemeteries (N = 86); (c) Wharram Percy (N = 61); (d) modern stillbirths (N = 16,702); (e) modern livebirths dying within seven days of birth (N = 196, no data given below 29 weeks); (f) total modern live births (N = 802,532)

Source: After Mays (1993a: Figure 1), where details of the sources for the data may be found.

Gowland, 2007; Mays & Eyers, 2011) show that perinatal age distributions produced by applying the Bayesian method of Gowland & Chamberlain (2002) tend to be more dispersed than those from regression methods, reflecting at least in part a bias inherent in the Bayesian method. In any event, the effect is not very great and the difference in age distributions between Roman and Mediaeval perinatal infants persists even when Bayesian techniques are used (Mays & Eyers, 2011).

More recently, it has been argued that the peak in Romano-British perinatal age distributions may be a product selective burial of full term babies rather than infanticide (Millett & Gowland, 2015). To leave a peak at full term, both premature infants and infants who died during the first weeks of life would have to have been mostly disposed of, not in the cemeteries and settlement sites where we find the full-term babies, but somewhere else where we have yet to locate them. This is clearly not impossible, but by its very nature is an argument that is rather hard to test, and strikes me as a less likely explanation for the Romano-British age distribution than infanticide.

Vigorous debate has always been key to ensuring progress in science. The critique of the infanticide hypothesis led to reanalyses of the data, and has enabled competing explanations to be laid before the scientific community so that other workers may evaluate them and arrive at their own conclusions. Discussion of the evidence for infanticide in Roman Britain has taken place not only in print but also at conferences, and I have also taken part in a recorded debate with one of my critics for the benefit of a student audience. In my experience, students love it when academics openly disagree with one another, so as well as helping to ensure that our interpretations are subject to rigorous examination, properly conducted scientific debate is also important in stimulating interest in our discipline among the next generation of osteoarchaeologists.

Adult age at death in a Mediaeval community

A question one is often asked by members of the public interested in archaeology is 'how long did people live in the past?' Indeed, this sort of basic issue forms a fundamental area of academic enquiry into the demography of past populations. For most of the human past this is a question which can only be investigated by the study of skeletal remains. One way of studying length of life would be to look at the average age of death in the archaeological assemblage of interest. However, that would not be a very informative exercise. For one thing, the figure produced would be heavily influenced by the number of infant burials recovered; a large number of infant burials would, of course, greatly reduce the mean age at death. As we saw in Chapter 2, infants are often underrepresented in archaeological assemblages, as a result of burial practices or other factors, and therefore the degree to which this was so in the assemblage under study will greatly influence the mean age at death figure. What we often mean when thinking about length of life in the past is length of adult life. In order to study this sort of issue for the Mediaeval period I conducted an analysis of the adult skeletons from Wharram Percy. Before describing the analysis, a little more detail about the site is probably in order.

Wharram Percy is a deserted Mediaeval village situated in North Yorkshire, England (Figure 4.24). The only Mediaeval building left standing now is the church, and this is in ruined state, but the remains of earthworks show where peasant houses once stood. A long-running archaeological excavation (Wrathmell, 2012) has taken place there, and as a result nearly 700 skeletons have been recovered from the churchyard (Mays et al., 2007). These burials date from the 10th–19th century AD, but the bulk are Mediaeval (11th–16th century). The burials are mainly of ordinary peasants who lived at Wharram Percy itself and elsewhere in the parish.

To estimate age at death in the Wharram Percy adults I used dental wear. Although there are, as we have seen, problems associated with it, I felt that it was less problematic

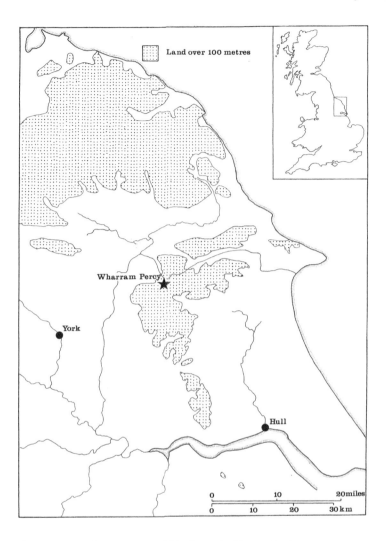

Figure 4.24 The location of the deserted Mediaeval village of Wharram Percy
Source: After Beresford and Hurst (1990: Figure 1).

than reference-target population methods where we are forced to rely completely on standards developed on recent material without knowing whether they are applicable to ancient populations. I also resisted the temptation to use several age indicators, as recommended by some workers. I felt that this would simply risk contaminating data which there is reason to suppose are reasonably reliable (dental wear ages) with those which, as far as archaeological populations are concerned, are of completely unknown reliability. At Wharram Percy there were sufficient child skeletons to calibrate the rate of dental wear using Miles' method. The sex of the adult skeletons was determined using the criteria described earlier in this chapter.

I classified the adults into three broad age categories. It has already been explained that older adults cannot be aged any more precisely than that they are over about 50 years. With some dental wear recording methods it is probably possible to age younger adults into narrower age spans – 10-year age ranges are used by many workers – but for the present purposes the three age groups shown in Table 4.7 were deemed adequate.

About 40% of the adults were aged over 50 years at death (Table 4.7). This appears to suggest that a person on the threshold of adulthood had about a 4 in 10 chance of surviving to at least 50 years of age. However, there are a number of complications to be borne in mind before this interpretation can be accepted.

Firstly, the assemblage represents an aggregate over the period for which the burial ground was used. Longevity may have varied markedly over this period, variations reflecting such factors as climate (and hence success or otherwise of harvests), disease load, etc. Therefore, at different times adult longevity may have been greater or less than that for the whole assemblage.

The impression given of expectation of life from an assemblage of skeletons is also influenced by whether the population of the community was growing or declining. Emigration may be an important point to consider for Wharram Percy. Russell (1948) offers historical evidence that in Mediaeval times populations of urban centres were maintained by immigration from surrounding rural communities. Wharram Percy lies some 20 miles from York, a major urban centre. Documentary data show that many probably migrated this sort of distance to become resident in York (Russell, 1948).

Goldberg (1986) shows that in the later Mediaeval period, many urban centres in northern England had imbalanced adult sex ratios. For example, in Hull, East Yorkshire, it was 0.86, in York 0.91, both in favour of females. Goldberg argued that these skewed sex ratios resulted from female-led migration into towns and cities from surrounding rural areas. Migrant female labour was absorbed into domestic service and into emergent craft industries such as weaving (Goldberg, 1986).

At Wharram Percy, the adult sex ratio is 1.51:1 in favour of males. Not all the churchyard was excavated, but in those parts which were, there is no evidence of anything other than a random intermixing of male and female burials, so it is unlikely that the 'missing' females are lurking in a cluster in some unexcavated area. A better explanation might be that at Wharram Percy we are seeing the other side of the coin concerning Mediaeval migration patterns, with a depletion of adult females due to female-led migration to urban centres like York or Hull.

Table 4.7 Age distribution of Wharram Percy adult burials

Estimated age	Total[*]		Males		Females		Male:female ratio
	Number	%	Number	%	Number	%	
18–29	65	21	35	20	29	23	1.21
30–49	116	39	62	36	52	42	1.19
50+	119	40	75	44	44	35	1.70
Total	300		172		125		1.51[†]

Notes

* Includes a few adults for which, due to the state of the skeleton, sex could not be determined.

† Includes some adults in which age at death could not be determined.

Source: Data from Mays (2007: Table 21).

The effect, if any, of this postulated migration upon the adult age structure of the Wharram Percy burials depends upon the age at which migrants generally left the parish. If most left in adolescence or early adulthood then the effect on the adult age at death distribution should be minimal – those that remained could either die young or live to grow old. If, however, most migrants tended to leave in middle age, this would have the effect of skewing the adult age at death distribution towards the younger ages. Logically, one might expect most migrants to leave in late adolescence or early adulthood. Indeed, the data discussed by Goldberg (1986) for immigrants to York appear to support this, and the observation that the sex ratios in the three adult age groups at Wharram Percy do not differ from one another in any statistically valid manner may also be consistent with this. The effect, therefore, on the Wharram Percy adult age at death distribution may be small.

Whether a community grows or dwindles depends also on the birth and death rates within that population. If birth rate exceeds death rate then, other factors being equal, the population will grow. If the converse is the case, it will decline. If the birth rate exceeds the death rate, the age structure of the excavated skeletons will tend to underestimate the true life expectancy, as at any particular time the younger deaths will be derived from a larger population than that which produced the older deaths (Boddington, 1987b). The opposite is true if death rate exceeds birth rate.

In the Wharram Percy case, use of the burial area covers both a period of growth of population and, from later Mediaeval times onwards, a period of population decline (due to the effects of the Black Death and changing agricultural practices), as well as doubtless many short-term fluctuations and periods of stasis. It may be that the effect of this factor on the overall age structure of the assemblage is fairly minimal.

From the above discussion it may be that the adult age distribution from the skeletons gives a reasonable, though time-averaged impression of adult length of life at Wharram Percy.

In order to help put the Wharram Percy age at death results in context it is helpful to compare them with documentary data on Mediaeval longevity. Reliable documentary data are sparse and do not relate directly to the peasant classes. For example, Russell (1937) studied age at death in the period 1250–1348 using the *Inquisitions Post-Mortem*. These are reports of evidence taken by Royal officials regarding the property and heirs of deceased persons who held land directly from the Crown. The inquests give the age of the heir, not of the deceased, this must be calculated from his age at the death of his predecessor. Data relating to 582 deaths were collected by Russell. They refer solely to males aged 21 years and over (Table 4.8).

Russell's data are not too dissimilar to the Wharram Percy results, but they are in general somewhat older (for example, 50% of individuals seem to have died aged 50 or over, compared with 40% at Wharram Percy). There may be a number of reasons for this.

Russell's ages were calculated from the age of an individual when his predecessor died. Therefore, individuals who pre-deceased their father would not, even if they had died aged over 21, be included in the data. This would tend to make Russell's figures exaggerate age at death somewhat. We would expect particularly deaths in the 21–30 age group to be underrepresented.

Secondly, Russell's figures refer solely to wealthy male landowners. The Wharram Percy peasants represent some of the poorest members of what was a very hierarchical

Table 4.8 Age distribution in Russell's (1937) demographic study

Age range	Number	Percentage
21-29	58	10
30-49	232	40
50+	292	50

society. It can be assumed that their living conditions were much harsher than those of the wealthiest classes so, if anything, we would expect that their longevity would be less. The extent to which the fact that Russell's data relate only to males biases matters is unclear, although in the skeletal data from Wharram Percy there was no suggestion of a sex difference in age at death.

Thirdly, Russell deliberately excluded the great Black Death years of 1348-1350 from his data whilst, of course, the Wharram Percy burials are not purposely selected in this way. This factor too would tend to skew Russell's data towards the older ages.

Another factor is that we are comparing ages estimated from dental wear with ages which were known fairly reliably from documents. Although dental wear circumvents some of the problems associated with other ageing methods, it is, as we have seen, hardly free of potential problems. Nevertheless, the Wharram Percy results are not too dissimilar from those obtained from Mediaeval documents, and the discrepancies which do exist are understandable in the light of differences between the two datasets. The archaeological data would seem to suggest that once adulthood was attained, the inhabitants of Wharram Percy had quite a reasonable chance of surviving to beyond 50 years. However, it is impossible to comment on what proportion of adults survived into their seventies, eighties or even greater old age. Russell's data indicate that, despite a good representation of those in their fifties and sixties, only 8% of those featuring in the *Inquisitions Post-Mortem* survived to 70 years of age or over, although one individual did live to be 100.

Summary

Estimating age at death and assessing the sex of skeletons is of fundamental importance in osteoarchaeology. The best way to assess sex in an adult skeleton is using dimorphic features of the skull and especially the pelvis. If these two indicators are present, then sex can normally be determined correctly in over 95% of cases. Assessing sex in juveniles from their skeletons is much more problematic. This is because skeletal sex differences are very slight until puberty. The difficulties are such that most osteoarchaeologists do not routinely attempt to do this.

In foetal or perinatal infants, age at death can be estimated to within about two weeks using measurement of long-bones. In older infants and children, long-bone length becomes unreliable as an indicator of age; dental development is the best technique to use. This allows age at death to be estimated to within a year or two in most cases. For adults, estimating age at death is much more problematic. Many different ageing techniques have been suggested but none have proved very satisfactory. There is little consensus as to which adult age indicator is the most reliable, although in this chapter I have advocated the use of molar wear in populations where the degree of wear permits this. Given the difficulties, most osteoarchaeologists only attempt to classify individuals as young, middle or older adults, corresponding, approximately, to 18-29, 30-49 and 50+ years respectively. Although further testing is required, in future, application of cementochronology may potentially allow much finer age distinctions to be made.

Further reading

For an overview of methods of estimating age at death see chapter 10 in A.M. Christensen, N.V. Passalacqua & E.J. Bartelink (2014) *Forensic Anthropology: Current Methods and Practice*. Elsevier, London.

For an overview of sex determination in adult and juvenile skeletons see Mays, S & Cox, M. (2000). Sex Determination in Skeletal Remains, pp. 117-130 in M. Cox & S. Mays (eds) *Human Osteology in Archaeology and Forensic Science*. Cambridge University Press, Cambridge.

Mays, S. (2013). A Discussion of Some Recent Methodological Developments in the Osteoarchaeology of Childhood. *Childhood in the Past* 6: 4-21 *contains a more detailed consideration of sex assessment in the immature skeleton.*

To follow up the two case studies presented in this chapter:
Infanticide:

My original Infanticide paper is Mays S. (1993). Infanticide in Roman Britain. *Antiquity* 67: 883-888. *The key contributions to the subsequent debate are:*

Gowland G. & Chamberlain A.T. (2002). A Bayesian Approach to Ageing Perinatal Skeletal Material from Archaeological Sites: Implications for the Evidence of Infanticide in Roman Britain. *Journal of Archaeological Science* 29: 677-685.

Mays S. (2003). Comment on Gowland & Chamberlain's Paper, *Journal of Archaeological Science* 30: 1695-1700;

Mays S. & Eyers J (2011). Perinatal Infant Death at the Roman Villa Site at Hambleden, Buckinghamshire, England. *Journal of Archaeological Science* 28: 555-559;

Millett, M. & Gowland, R. (2015). Infant and Child Burial Rites in Roman Britain: A Study from East Yorkshire. *Britannia* 46:171-189.

Age at death in a Mediaeval community:

For further details of this study, and of the Wharram Percy skeletons in general see my osteological report: Mays S. (2007). The Human Remains, pp. 77-192 & 337-397 in S. Mays, C. Harding & C. Heighway (eds) *Wharram XI: The Churchyard. Wharram: A Study of Settlement in the Yorkshire Wolds, XI.* York University Press, York.

5 Metric variation in the skull

No two skeletons are the same. Firstly, bones and teeth differ in size and shape between individuals. This type of variability, the subject of this chapter and the one that follows, lends itself to recording by measurement, and so is called metric variation. Skeletons also differ in ways which are much more difficult to measure. This type of variability takes the form of minor anatomical variants of the bones and teeth. These sorts of variants are termed non-metric traits, and are usually recorded on a presence-absence basis or according to degree of expression; they are discussed in Chapter 7.

Measurement studies play an important role in the analysis of normal skeletal variation. In the post-cranial skeleton, lengths of limb-bones have been used to assess stature and physique and, because mechanical forces influence the thickness of bone, width measurements have been used to investigate aspects such as activity patterns in past populations. Metric variation in the post-cranial skeleton is covered in the next chapter. Another important focus of metric studies is the quantitative study of variation in the skull (craniometry), particularly for investigating relationships between populations (biodistance) and for discerning evidence for migrations of peoples in the past.

Craniometry is the focus of the present chapter. It starts with a brief discussion of how morphological variation in the skull may be captured and quantified. There then follows a consideration of some of the factors which influence skull form. Later parts of this chapter discuss theoretical and methodological aspects of craniometry, and two archaeological examples are used to illustrate the potential value of craniometric data in the investigation of ancient migrations.

Capturing variation in skull form

Bones are highly irregular in shape. This immediately poses problems for the osteoarchaeologist – given the lack of flat surfaces and right-angles, from what points should one measure? On the skull, this problem has been tackled by defining certain internationally accepted anatomical points, termed 'cranial landmarks'. Cranial landmarks each have their own technical name. Landmark definitions vary slightly between different textbooks. The classic text in this respect is that of Rudolf Martin (Martin, 1928). More recent works (e.g. Howells, 1973; Brothwell, 1981; Buikstra & Ubelaker, 1994) often base their definitions on those of Martin. Because definitions do differ slightly between authors, it is important to state whose landmark and measurement definitions one is following. The ones discussed below are those of Brothwell (1981).

Landmarks may be defined according to a variety of anatomical criteria. Some are defined in terms of maximum projection of the skull in certain directions. For example, the glabella is the most prominent point between the supra-orbital (brow) ridges at the midline (Figure 5.1). Many landmarks, particularly on the cranial vault, are defined according to the points at which certain cranial sutures meet. For example, the bregma is defined as the intersection of the coronal and sagittal sutures (Figure 5.2); the nasion is defined as the midpoint of the suture between the frontal and the two nasal bones (Figure 5.1). Other landmarks are defined on the basis of the locations of anatomical features, such as bony crests for muscle attachment, or with respect to lines projected from them. For example, the nasospinale is the point at the midline lying on a line projected between the lowest parts of the pyriform (nasal) aperture (Figure 5.1).

Traditionally, craniometric variation has been studied using linear measurements between landmarks. Many are taken as straight lines, termed chords, and are generally measured using sliding or spreading callipers (Figure 5.3a, b). These comprise the majority of measurements used by most workers. Less often, dimensions may be taken using a tape measure, measuring along the surface of the bone between two landmarks. These are called arcs. There are also measurements which quantify the relative projection of different parts of the skull. These are called subtenses, and are taken using a co-ordinate calliper (Figure 5.3c).

Whilst linear measurements obviously do contain some information on the relative location of landmarks, much of this information is not captured. For example, measurements between the bregma and the nasion, and between the nasion and the nasospinale would tell us something about the morphology of the frontal bone and facial skeleton,

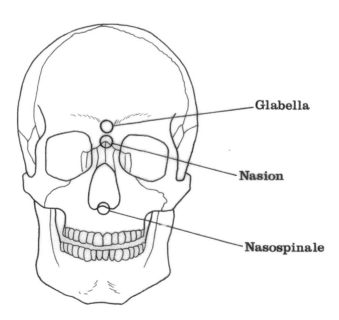

Figure 5.1 Anterior view of skull, showing glabella, nasion and nasospinale

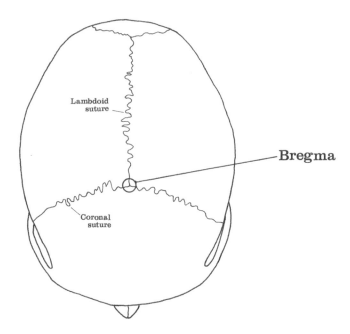

Figure 5.2 Superior view of skull, showing position of bregma

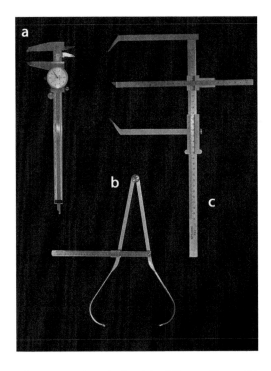

Figure 5.3 Instruments for measuring skulls: (a) sliding calliper; (b) spreading calliper; (c) co-ordinate calliper

but would not enable the geometric relationship between these three landmarks to be reconstructed in three- or two-dimensional space. A solution to this problem is to record not the linear distances between landmarks but the coordinates of the landmarks them-selves. Analysis of two- or three-dimensional landmark coordinates is termed geometric morphometrics. In osteology, this usually involves direct capture of three-dimensional coordinate information from the specimen itself, or two-dimensional coordinate data from radiographs or photographs.

To capture two-dimensional coordinate data, a radiograph or photograph is taken in a standard view (e.g. a lateral view of a cranium). Relevant landmarks are then marked onto the digitised image and their coordinates recorded using computer software. Three-dimensional coordinate information may be captured using a variety of methods. A 3D digitiser is a stylus connected to a base by a flexible arm (Figure 5.4). The digitiser is connected to a computer via a USB port. The coordinates of each landmark in three-dimensional space are recorded when the point of the stylus is brought into contact with it. Increasingly, however, data capture is achieved using surface scanning methods to create a virtual 3D model of the cranium (Friess, 2012). The most common techniques are laser (e.g. Kuzminsky et al., 2018) or structured light scanning (e.g. Stansfield et al., 2017). A visible-light source (laser or white-light) is used to scan the surface of the cranium. Multiple, overlapping views are obtained, either by moving the light source or

Figure 5.4 MicroScribe G2 desktop digitiser for capturing three-dimensional geometric morphometric data

Source: Immersion Corporation, San Jose, USA.

by repositioning the cranium, in order to ensure complete capture of its form. Computer software is used to 'stitch' the views together to create a virtual 3D model. Cranial landmarks can then be placed in their correct anatomical locations, and their positions pinpointed using three-dimensional coordinates.

Some geometric morphometric studies simply use the three-dimensional coordinate data of classic craniometric landmarks (e.g. Kuzminsky et al., 2018). However, analysis of traditional landmark coordinates tells us nothing about the shape of the bone in areas between landmarks. Application of surface-scanning techniques facilitates the placement of so-called semi-landmarks in areas of the cranium between the standard landmarks. Computer software is used to place the same number of semi-landmarks across the surface of each specimen and then to 'slide' them into optimal positions (Gunz & Mitteroecker, 2013) (Figure 5.5). This procedure facilitates the quantification of the topography of curves and surfaces. As well as capturing data for the study of cranial form for biodistance studies, 3D surface scanning is increasingly used in other areas of osteoarchaeology where data on surface form has traditionally been captured using linear measurements or visual assessment. These include the investigation of patterns of sexual dimorphism (Wilson & Humphrey, 2017), growth and development (Stark, 2018) and the study of non-metric variants (Karakostis et al., 2018).

Although traditional calliper measurements continue in use for the quantitative study of cranial morphology, there has recently been a growth in geometric morphometric studies (Mays, 2019a). One might expect that the more complete picture of bone form provided by geometric morphometric methods would lead to improved performance in biodistance studies, but to date, few direct comparisons have been carried out. In those that have, the focus has been on analysing conventional landmark data using the two approaches. In general, the application of geometric morphometrics appears to produce

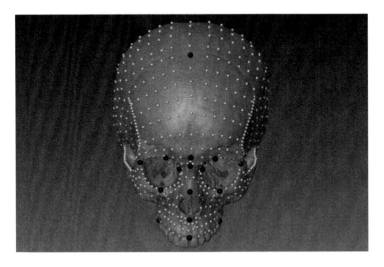

Figure 5.5 Virtual 3D model of a human cranium with traditional landmarks (dark spots) and semilandmarks (light spots) superimposed

Source: Weber (2015: Figure 4).

fairly similar results to the study of linear measurement data (e.g. Stull et al., 2014; Spradley & Jantz, 2016), although there are indications that coordinate-based approaches are somewhat advantageous. For example, McKeown and Jantz (2005) compared geometric morphometric and linear measurement data from a series of Native American crania from the northern Plains of the USA. They found that the results of the two approaches were fairly similar but that the geometric morphometric data provided a clearer picture of the variation with more distinct separation of groups living in different geographical locations. One would expect that the inclusion of semi-landmarks to help characterise surface topography would further increase the advantage of coordinate-based methods over linear measurements in biodistance studies.

As we saw in the last chapter, tooth measurements can be useful in sex determination, particularly for immature skeletons; as will become clear they are also useful for biodistance studies. Most measurements of the teeth are not defined in terms of anatomical landmarks. The two most commonly used dental dimensions are simply the widths of the crown in the bucco-lingual and the mesiodistal directions (see Chapter 4). Biodistance studies using geometric morphometric analyses of dental shape are also beginning to be conducted (e.g. Corny et al., 2017).

Causes of variation in skull form

In order for us to interpret patterning in craniometric data, we clearly need to know something of the causes of variation in cranial morphology. We have already seen in Chapter 4 that age and sex are important determinants of skull form. In the growing child, the skull has yet to assume its final form, hence most population studies of craniometric data confine themselves to adult individuals. The differences between the sexes mean that craniometric data for males and females are either analysed separately or else sex differences are controlled for statistically. As will be shown below, genetic factors play a large part in determining cranial form, but non-genetic factors also have an influence.

Non-genetic influences on skull form

Direct mechanical pressure on the growing skull may influence skull form. Some populations practise deliberate artificial cranial deformation by binding the heads of infants (Tiesler, 2014). Some diseases may affect cranial form. For example, hydrocephalus (water on the brain) results in an enlarged, globular skull (Richards & Anton, 1991). Diseased or artificially deformed skulls can simply be excluded from population studies of cranial morphology. However, there are other, more subtle, influences which need to be borne in mind when interpreting craniometric data. Major non-genetic influences on skull form include nutrition, diet and climate.

Nutrition

Diet may be defined simply as what is eaten; nutrition is the value of that food to the body. Poor nutrition during development can affect the growth and final dimensions of the bones. Larry Angel (Angel, 1982) formulated the hypothesis that the degree of flattening of the base of the cranium in the adult might be an index of growth efficiency, which would in turn be influenced by health and nutrition during childhood. His reasoning was that this part of the skull supports the weight of the brain and head, therefore weakening of the growth of the bone in this area should result in a flattening of the cranial base by compression. He investigated this idea by measuring cranial base height in skulls of recent origin, comparing data from a collection of skeletons of socioeconomically deprived classes in the US, with those from skeletons of middle-class Americans. He found that the poorer social group did indeed show greater cranial base flattening than the middle-class skulls. Consistent with this, Cameron et al. (1990) found that cranial base flattening increased in South African Blacks between 1880 and 1934, and associated this with a decline in their socioeconomic conditions. Using geometric morphometrics, Wescott and Jantz (2005) found a reduction in flattening in the skull base in American populations from AD1850–1975. They associate this with improvements in living conditions during this time, although they felt that the improved conditions permitted greater brain and cranial base growth rather than, as Angel originally suggested, leading to greater resistance to flattening of the cranial base by compression during growth. Kim et al. (2018) report increased cranial vault height (to which lesser cranial base flattening contributes), together with generally larger vault size in Koreans born in the 1970s compared with those born 40 years earlier, and ascribe the changes to improved nutrition.

Some work has also been done on cranial base height in archaeological populations. Looking at ancient Greek archaeological material, Angel and Olney (1981) found that skulls from the Royal tombs at Mycenae showed a greater mean cranial base height (i.e. lesser cranial base flattening) than did those of their counterparts of lower social status. Studying two cemeteries from Mediaeval Poland, Rewekant (2001) found cranial base height was lower in that serving a lower socioeconomic status community. These results suggest that, as one might anticipate in such hierarchical societies, the privileged enjoyed rather better childhood nutrition than those further down the social scale.

The teeth are less vulnerable to environmental insults than the bones. However, as we saw in Chapter 4, poor nutrition during the growth period may influence dental dimensions.

Diet

Bone functional adaptation (Chapter 1) means that bone tissue tends to be built up where it is needed and lost where it is not. This means that mechanical factors may influence the shape as well as the size or thickness of a bone. These observations apply to the skull no less than to any other part of the skeleton.

A major part of the mechanical forces acting on the skull arises from the action of the strong muscles involved in mastication (chewing). The tougher the consistency of the diet, the greater the bite forces required. This leads to greater development of the muscles involved in chewing, and thus to greater development of the bones of the facial skeleton associated with these muscles. Studies on distribution of biomechanical strains in the skulls of non-human primates indicate, not surprisingly, a concentration of forces in the jaw bones and zygomatic arches (cheek-bones) (Lycett & Collard, 2005). Experimental work (e.g. Corruccini & Beecher, 1982) shows that these areas, and the musculature associated with them, become more developed when animals are fed hard diets.

Secular trends in craniometric data have also been understood from a dietary perspective. In general, alterations in food preparation techniques associated with the advent of agriculture resulted in increased cooking efficiency and hence in a softer diet (Larsen, 2015: 279). In addition, animal domestication gave people access to foods such as dairy products that required no or minimal mastication. Looking at more than 500 skulls from around the world, Katz et al. (2017) found that, in farming groups, mandibular and craniofacial size were smaller in relation to vault size than was the case in foraging populations. The lower parts of the face projected less, and were more 'tucked under' the cranial vault. Areas associated with the temporalis and medial pterygoid muscles, key components of the musculature associated with mastication, were reduced indicating smaller muscle sizes. These effects were most pronounced in farming groups primarily reliant upon dairy products rather than cereals.

In Britain, Moore et al. (1968) studied changes in the form of the mandible in populations from Neolithic (c. 4000 BC) to recent times. They found a general reduction in size over time, the greater part of this change occurring after the Mediaeval period. The trend was particularly pronounced for ramus breadth and height, and the mandibular angle (Figure 5.6). These measurements relate to parts of the mandible where powerful chewing muscles attach. Rando et al. (2014) studied Mediaeval and later mandibles from London and report similar findings. Studying the maxilla (upper jaw), Goose (1962) likewise noted a reduction in dimensions between Mediaeval times and the 17th century. The skeletal evidence therefore suggests a transition after the Medieval period to a diet that required much less vigorous mastication. This interpretation is supported by historical data. From the 17th century onward, changes in methods used in the preparation of flour for bread-making in towns meant that an increasing proportion was passed through fine cloth sieves. This would have resulted in the removal not only of the coarser grit particles, but also much of the tough bran material. This would have had the effect of producing a bread that was less resistant to mastication than the coarse, dark rye and bran breads of earlier times. Seventeenth-century diets, at least in urban areas, were softer than previously, and this trend continued in following centuries (Moore & Corbett, 1975; Corbett & Moore, 1976).

Climate

Many of the physical differences between human populations around the world represent adaptations to regional climatic regimes. Skin colour is one obvious example, but some differences in cranial form can also be understood in those terms. In particular, it has long been argued that global variation in aspects of the shape of the human nose is an adaptive response to regional climatic conditions.

An important function of the nose is to warm and moisten inspired air. When air is exhaled, some heat and moisture is lost to the surroundings. Cold air cannot contain as much moisture as warm air so that, for example, hot desert air actually contains more moisture than air in subarctic regions. As well as requiring the most warming, cold air also needs the most humidifying. A high, narrow nose is more efficient at warming and humidifying inhaled air as it maximises air contact with the nasal mucosa; it also restricts loss of heat and moisture on exhalation. Conversely, in hot, humid environments, a low, broad nose better serves to dissipate heat; this may be important as, under these conditions, heat loss through sweating is less efficient (Noback et al., 2011; Maddux et al., 2016, 2017).

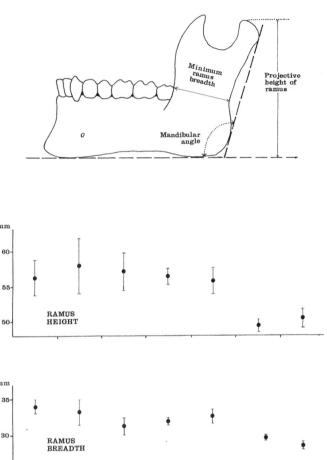

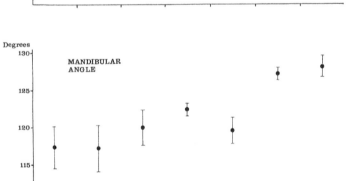

Figure 5.6 Three mandibular measurements, showing trends in British material from the Neolithic to the 19th century AD. The reduction in ramus dimensions is indicative of a reduction in the chewing muscles associated with this part of the jaw. The increase in the mandibular angle is probably partly associated with the reduction in the mandibular ramus, but also reflects a reduction in the development of the angular region itself where the powerful masseter muscle attaches

Source: After Moore et al. (1968: Figures 1, 3 and 4).

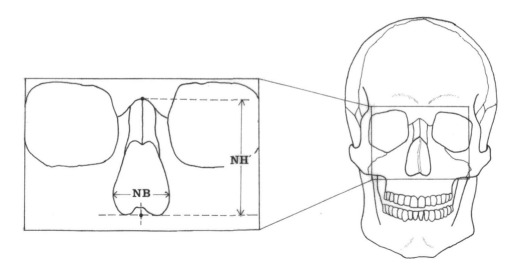

Figure 5.7 Anterior view of skull, showing nasal area and method of taking nasal index. Nasal index is 100 × (NB/NH′)

The relative height and width of the nose may be expressed as the nasal index. In the living person, this is the ratio (expressed as a percentage) of the width across the nostrils, to the length measured between the root of the nose at the nasal bridge and the angle made by the nose and the upper lip. In other words, it is a measure of the width of the nose at the point at which air is inspired relative to its height. When measuring the nasal index in skeletons, the width of the nose is represented by the width of the pyriform aperture and the height by the chord between the nasion and the nasospinale (Figure 5.7). This is closely correlated with living nasal index and there is a mathematical formula for converting one to the other (Davies, 1932). Maddux et al. (2016) assembled nasal index data from more than 15,000 individuals from 148 locations from around the world. Most of the data related to living nasal index, and the few that comprised skeletal nasal index they converted into living values. Their results show clear correlations between nasal index and both temperature and absolute humidity (Plate 2). Populations from cold climates show lower nasal indices than those from warmer more humid environments, as expected if nasal morphology is responsive to climate.

Genetic factors and cranial form

Despite the influences on cranial form of extraneous factors such as climate and diet, the most common use to which craniometric data have been put is to study population history. For this to be a valid strategy there must be a reasonable genetic contribution to population variation in cranial morphology. Evidence for a genetic component in cranial variability comes from family studies and from studies of human populations whose genetic relationships with one another are known or can reasonably be inferred.

Family studies

It is a commonplace observation that members of the same family tend to resemble one another in facial features. It should therefore come as no surprise to learn that the form of the skull bones, the architecture which underlies, and to a large extent determines the features and shape of the face and head, does indeed have a strong inherited component. Family studies of skull form have been done by measuring the heads of volunteers, or by X-raying people's heads and taking measurements from the radiographs. A high degree of inheritance in skull measurements has been a consistent finding (Kohn, 1991; Arya et al., 2002; Jelenkovic et al., 2010; Šešelj et al., 2015).

Population studies

Richard Spielman and Peter Smouse, two American geneticists, studied nine head and three other measurements in living Yanomama Indians from southern Venezuela and northern Brazil (Spielman & Smouse, 1976). The study populations lived in a number of different villages, scattered over an area of about 200 by 300 kilometres. The geneticists classified these settlements into nine clusters (Figure 5.8). These clusters were geographical or were of villages known to have been the product of recent settlement fission. It was

Figure 5.8 Location of Yanomama villages studied by Spielman and co-workers. The dotted lines delineate the settlement clusters defined in Spielman & Smouse's (1976) study

Source: After Spielman et al. (1972: Figure 1).

found that individuals from different village clusters were distinct from one another in terms of measurements. This difference between clusters was great enough that an individual could be assigned to the correct village cluster on the basis of the measurements taken in nearly 60% of cases. Had it been possible to study bone measurements instead of ones which included soft tissue, it is likely that this figure might have been improved upon, as soft tissue thicknesses are likely to show more random idiosyncratic variation between individuals. Salzano et al. (1980), studying groups of indigenous peoples from another part of South America, found a strong correlation between biological relationships between groups revealed by biochemical genetic markers, and those based on anthropological measurement data. Vecchi et al. (1987) conducted a similar study on groups from southern Mexico, and came up with similar results. Perez et al. (2007) studied patterning in geometric morphometric data from crania from archaeological sites from different parts of Argentina, and in genetic markers in modern Native American populations from those regions. They found a good correspondence between the two types of data.

Others have studied data from wider geographic areas. Rightmire (1976) measured crania from six different human groups from southern and eastern Africa. Historical, linguistic and other non-osteological data suggested that these populations were related to one another in the manner shown in Figure 5.9. The measurement data generated the results reproduced in Table 5.1. The numbers in the table are a measure of how similar the crania from the different groups are over the whole suite of measurements, the lower the number the more similar the crania.

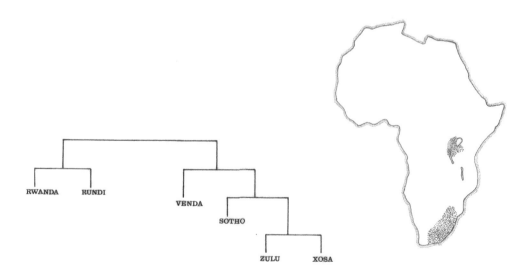

Figure 5.9 Schematic representation of relationships between six African populations as suggested by linguistic, historical and other non-osteological data. Rwanda and Rundi are from the Lake Victoria region of east Africa, the other populations are from southern Africa, as indicated on the map

Source: From Rightmire (1976: Figure 1).

Table 5.1 Distance statistics (Mahalanobis D^2) between six African populations derived from 15 cranial measurements

	Rundi	*Zulu*	*Xosa*	*Sotho*	*Venda*
Rwanda	2.16	8.23	6.10	6.71	3.80
Rundi	–	6.91	8.64	11.35	3.45
Zulu	–	–	1.96	2.16	3.96
Xosa	–	–	–	2.46	3.42
Sotho	–	–	–	–	5.38

Note: Figures from Rightmire (1976: Table 5.2). The Rwanda and the Rundi are from east Africa, the other groups are from southern Africa.

The cranial measurements show a close affinity between the two east African groups (i.e. the value of the distance statistic between Rundi and Rwanda is low), and these two groups are more distant from the Zulu, Xosa and Sotho crania than from the Venda. Among the southern African populations, the closest relationship is between the Xosa and the Zulu. These findings tally closely with the relationships inferred from the linguistic and other non-osteological data depicted in Figure 5.9.

Pucciarelli et al. (2006) measured crania from sites pre-dating European contact from Latin America. The data (Figure 5.10) showed a distinct east-west divide. This was as expected given the barrier presented by the Andes to east-west migration. Previous DNA analyses of living Native American populations had also shown this pattern. In addition, the craniometric data showed a subgroup formed of three groups from Venezuela (numbered 12, 13 and 14 in Figure 5.10); linguistic data had previously suggested a close relationship between these three populations. Pucciarelli and co-workers also included Palaeoamericans (samples dating to 8000–10,000 years old, very much more ancient

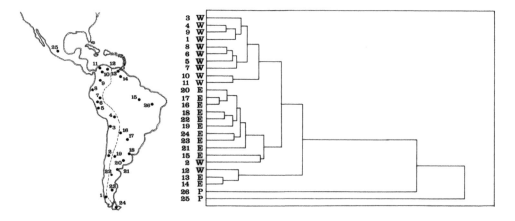

Figure 5.10 Cluster analysis of craniometric data from western (W) and eastern (E) pre-European contact archaeological sites from South America, together with two Palaeoamerican groups (P). The map shows the location of the sites
Source: After Pucciarelli et al. (2006: Figs 3 and 5).

than the other material) from Mexico and Brazil in their analysis. These were sharply separated from the later populations (Figure 5.10), perhaps consistent with previous suggestions that these lineages became extinct soon after the arrival of populations ancestral to recent Native Americans.

On a global scale, cranial morphological data correlate strongly with geographic separation. If one ignores populations known to have migrated recently (e.g. American and Australian populations of European ancestry), in very general terms, cranial morphological similarity between different populations decreases with increasing geographic distance (Relethford, 2004, 2010). Populations with greater geographic separation generally show greater genetic separation – the so-called isolation by distance model. Therefore this suggests that cranial distance reflects genetic distance. This is supported by studies that have directly compared patterning in cranial morphology with that in genetic markers. von Cramon-Taubadel (2009, 2016) studied variation in 442 crania from museum collections relating to 15 recent but preindustrial populations from around the world. She found a strong correlation between interpopulation distances based on cranial morphology and those based on genetic markers – the more closely related the populations, the more similar were their crania.

The results of studies like those discussed above confirm the potential value of cranial measurements for investigating relationships between ancient populations.

Using cranial morphology to investigate ancient migrations

Theoretical aspects

The study of change in prehistory has long been central to archaeology. Archaeologists have employed a variety of theoretical models in order to try and explain important changes in the archaeological record in aspects such as subsistence strategy, material culture or burial practices. Prior to the 1960s, the dominant approach to understanding prehistory was culture historical, in which innovation in the above spheres was ascribed to the influence of more 'advanced' cultures. In northern and central Europe, many innovations were thought to owe their ultimate origin to influences from the civilisations of the Near East or the Mediterranean Basin. Very often, this was thought to have involved migrations of people. For example, discontinuities in the archaeological record in Britain were largely ascribed to a series of influxes of people from Continental Europe bringing with them new objects, ideas or practices (Vander Linden & Roberts, 2011). Large-scale movements of peoples might be expected to leave some trace in the skeletal record, so during this period physical anthropology made a central contribution to archaeology, as skulls were measured in an effort to find evidence for ancient migrations.

The 1960s saw the beginning of a general retreat in migrationism as an explanatory framework in archaeology in many parts of the world (Adams et al., 1978), including Britain. These changes were precipitated both by a revolution in archaeological science – the advent of radiocarbon dating in the 1950s and 60s – and by changes in theoretical approaches in archaeology.

Radiocarbon provided, for the first time, a reliable method of absolute dating for prehistoric remains. This showed that innovations traditionally described to the influence of overseas civilisations, such as the building of megalithic tombs in Britain and some other parts of northern and western Europe, in fact predated their supposed prototypes in the eastern Mediterranean (Renfrew, 1973).

At the same time, archaeologists began to re-think their whole approach to understanding change in prehistory. There was a general realisation that explanations for culture change were likely to be very much more complex than simple migrations and replacements of peoples. In many countries, this was coupled with a rise in processual archaeology. As the term suggests, the processualists advocated a movement away from particularistic approaches to the past, which ascribed changes to unique historical events (such as migrations), toward perspectives which placed an emphasis on attempting to understand process. These processes might be external to the population under study, such as exchange of goods with neighbouring or distant groups, environmental change, or population pressure. On the other hand, they might arise from within ancient societies, for example tensions between the rulers and the ruled. In this theoretical environment, the possibility that migration of peoples might sometimes account for changes observed in the archaeological record was not so much refuted as simply ignored (Adams et al., 1978).

To the processualists, migration studies were viewed as discredited, part of an outdated approach to understanding prehistory. Because of this, archaeological studies of migration languished for several decades, at least in countries such as Britain, where the influence of processualist archaeology was most keenly felt.

Recently in British archaeology there has been a revival of interest in ancient migrations. Just as innovations in archaeological science and alterations in theoretical outlook helped to marginalise the study of migrations, recent developments in these spheres have helped to usher it back toward centre stage. The 1980s and 90s saw the rise in Britain of post-processual models for understanding the past which placed an emphasis on constructing historically specific accounts of earlier societies in which events as well as processes assumed importance (Champion, 1992). Recent years have seen a rise in the archaeology of identity (Knudsen & Stojanowski, 2011), and researchers have begun incorporating theoretical approaches from this field into migration studies (Cabana, 2011), for example exploring how migrants might seek to express and reinterpret their identities in new social situations. Meanwhile, within the processualist camp, there has been an increasing realisation that migrations can be accommodated within a processual framework by treating them as patterned, dynamic human behaviour rather than one-off events (Anthony, 1990, 1997). These developments have helped create theoretical environments more conducive to the study of past population movements. Turning to archaeological science, stable isotopic and ancient DNA studies have provided empirical evidence for migration in prehistory (see Chapters 11 and 12) which has helped force migration issues onto the agenda of those in Britain and elsewhere who study change in prehistoric cultures (e.g. Needham, 2007; Parker Pearson et al., 2016, 2019). The notion that ancient migrations, and population history in general, are important areas of academic enquiry, and should form a core part of archaeology, is once again commanding widespread support. Because genetic factors make a major contribution to skull form, craniometry can be used to study these areas.

Methodological considerations

Choice of landmarks

If one's purpose is to reconstruct biological relationships between ancient human popula-tions using cranial morphology, the question now arises as to how one goes about choos-ing cranial landmarks for generating linear measurements or spatial coordinate data. It may seem reasonable to concentrate mainly on dimensions which have little functional or adaptive significance. If one studies aspects of skull form which do have important functional or adaptive value, then populations would tend to group into those which had similar environments or diets, etc. By contrast, if we concentrate on traits which have little functional or adaptive significance, we might expect that the similarity between the two groups will be proportional to the time elapsed since they shared a common ances-tor – i.e. the similarity on these measurements will be a measure of the genetic relation-ship between the groups (discussion in Brace & Hunt, 1990).

In reality, relationships between cranial landmarks (whether measured as linear dimen-sions using callipers, or captured as spatial coordinates for analysis using geometric mor-phometrics) cannot be neatly divided into those which are of functional or adaptive significance and those which are not. Rather, they grade in a continuum from those which are clearly functionally and adaptively important, to those which have no demon-strable value. However, this does give some basis upon which to make decisions concern-ing choice of variables, and it also needs to be kept in mind when interpreting the results of craniometric studies. To study biological relationships between world populations it would not be desirable to concentrate heavily on data from the mandible or nasal area, since the form of these areas appears to be heavily influenced by diet and climate respectively. For example, von Cramon-Taubadel (2011, 2016) studied mandibular shape in different preindustrial populations and showed that it tracked subsistence strategy (hunter-gatherers vs agriculturalists) not genetics, most probably because of differences in biomechanical loadings due to diet. When the aim is to investigate population history using craniometry, an exploratory approach is generally adopted, in which a number of measurements or landmarks are used in order to gain a general impression of cranial morphology. Spreading measurement or landmark coordinate data over the different areas of the cranium enables one to derive a better overall picture of cranial form. This helps one to understand which cranial areas differ between populations under study and which are morphologically similar.

If one accepts that, for biodistance studies, measurements or landmark coordinate data should be spread over different areas of the cranium, the question remains as to how many measurements or landmarks are needed to gain an adequate impression of cranial form. Of course, the more measurements ones takes, the better, but manually taking large numbers of measurements becomes time-consuming. Because they tend, to a greater or lesser extent, to be correlated with one another, to a degree a 'law of dimin-ishing returns' sets in as one measures more and more dimensions. Using a restricted number of dimensions (between about 10 and 30) tends to give fairly similar results to those obtained from larger sets of measurements (Hanihara, 1993). Most biodistance studies employ a battery of about 10–30 measurements.

Geometric morphometric studies which rely on traditional cranial landmarks tend to use about 10–30 landmarks (e.g. Kuzminsky et al., 2018), but as each is recorded as two or three dimensional coordinates, the information content is greater than if linear measurements were simply taken between them. However, the possibility presented by scanning methods to add large numbers of landmarks and semi-landmarks to the captured image using software applications means that more thorough coverage of bone surfaces can be achieved at little extra time-investment from the operator. This means that geometric morphometric studies often base their analyses on large numbers of data points per specimen. For example, Stansfield et al. (2017) in their analysis of Eurasian Mesolithic and Neolithic crania placed a total of 329 landmarks (89 fixed landmarks plus 240 semilandmarks) on the image of each cranium captured by structured light scanning.

The above are general principals, but the precise number and location of the landmarks one uses for measurement or spatial coordinate data will likely be different for each research project. In the case of spatial coordinate data in geometric morphometrics, decisions will also need to be made concerning whether semi-landmarks are used and, if so, their number and the regions in which they are placed. Detailed decisions regarding these issues will depend both upon the research questions that the study is intended to address and on the condition of the crania.

Statistical techniques

When dealing with a single measurement or index (one measurement divided by another), univariate statistics, such as means and standard deviations, can be used to summarise the data. Early work on cranial form in ancient populations, even when the writers took large numbers of measurements, tended to compare populations on each measurement in turn using univariate statistics. In the early 20th century, multivariate statistical techniques, which can deal with more than one variable at a time, were developed. Calculating multivariate statistics by hand is extremely tedious and time-consuming, so it was only when computers became more widely available in the 1960s and 1970s that multivariate analyses began to make a widespread impact. Nowadays, multivariate statistical techniques are essential for analysing cranial measurement or spatial coordinate data.

A potential problem in statistically analysing craniometric data generated from archaeological remains is that crania are often incomplete whereas multivariate statistical analyses generally require a full set of data for each specimen. If the quantity of missing data is small then missing measurements may be estimated. Estimation methods are normally based on the observation that craniometric measurements, and landmark locations, tend to be correlated with one another. A commonly used method for estimating missing measurements is to use regression equations based on dimensions that show close relationships to the missing measurement (Pietrusewsky, 2019: 558). In geometric morphometrics, algorithms exist for estimating coordinates of missing landmarks based on those that are present (Adams et al., 2013). In order to keep the proportion of data that is estimated to a minimum, biodistance studies generally require fairly complete crania.

Cranial variation contains both shape and size components. It appears that variation in shape better reflects genetic factors than does size (Pinhasi & von Cramon-Taubadel,

2012). In biodistance analysis, it is usual, prior to multivariate analysis, to mathematically remove the size-based element so that analysis deals solely with shape variation. For traditional calliper measurements, size based elements are removed mathematically, for example by dividing each measurement by the geometric mean for all measurements of that specimen (Mosiman, 1970; Gallagher, 2015). In geometric morphometrics, as well as size and shape, the coordinate data will also contain information about the position and orientation of the specimen. As a first step in analysis, size, position and orientation are stripped out by mathematical treatments of the data (normally using a technique known as Generalised Procrustes analysis). This allows visualisation and analysis of shape differences between specimens, and permits the application of standard multivariate statistical procedures (McKeown & Schmidt, 2013; Mitteroecker et al., 2013).

A variety of multivariate techniques are in common use for the analysis of cranial morphological data, among which are principal components, discriminant function and cluster analyses. Principal components analysis uses the correlations between measurements or landmark locations to produce a new set of variables (or axes) which are uncorrelated with one another. These axes are composites of the original variables, and to a certain extent are interpretable in terms of combinations of them. The first new axis accounts for the most original variance, the second the second most, and so on. There are as many new axes as there were original variables, but in many cases the first few axes account for most of the original variance, and hence should provide a simplified, but still valid summary of the data. In this way the visualisation of any groupings or patterning in the data may be facilitated.

Unlike principal components analysis, discriminant function analysis requires that groupings exist within the data, and that which skulls or assemblages belong to which groups be known beforehand. Discriminant function analysis produces a new set of independent variables from the original variables but, unlike principle components, these new variables are constructed from the raw data in such a way as to maximise the separation between the groups.

Cluster analysis is a generic term for an array of techniques which aim to find groupings in a collection of objects. In the type of cluster analysis most often used in the study of cranial morphology, a similarity coefficient, which measures the similarity between skulls or assemblages across the whole battery of variables, is calculated. Alternatively, the inverse of a similarity coefficient, a distance statistic, may be used (see Table 5.1). Similarity data may then be displayed as a dendrogram, a sort of family tree representing the similarities between the skulls or assemblages (see Figure 5.10).

What follows now are two examples of the application of craniometric studies to investigate ancient migrations. These studies, taken from Japanese and British archaeology, are followed by a discussion of the value and limitations of the osteological data in each case.

The Yayoi culture of Japan

During the Jomon period (c. 14,000–900 BC), the Japanese archipelago was populated by human groups with a mainly hunter-gatherer life-style. Although some agriculture does seem to have been practised in Jomon times, it was not until the succeeding Yayoi period (c. 900 BC–AD 300) that the transition to a fully agricultural subsistence strategy was made (Kaner & Yano, 2015). During the Yayoi period, intensive rice agriculture was practised. In addition, there is evidence for a number of important technological innovations, such as metalworking, wheel-made pottery and weaving (Higuchi, 1986). There is also evidence of increased social differentiation at around this time.

Rice is not native to the Japanese islands and so must have been introduced from mainland Asia where it was cultivated long before its appearance in Japan (Aikens, 2012). It has long been believed that the Yayoi cultural package, including intensive rice agriculture, was introduced to Japan by migrants from the Asian mainland (Hanihara, 1991). Craniometric and other studies of skeletal morphology have made a major contribution to our understanding of this question and to Japanese population history in general.

Craniometric studies (e.g. Brace et al., 1989) have shown that, compared with the Yayoi, Jomon skulls tend to have lower, broader faces, narrower noses, and they tend to be generally more robust, with pronounced brow ridges (Figure 5.11). Although some (e.g. Suzuki, 1969) have suggested that cranial morphological changes at the inception of the Yayoi cultural package may have been due to cultural factors (e.g. change in diet) acting on indigenous populations, most have interpreted them as reflecting influx of Yayoi migrants from mainland Asia.

Nakahashi (1993) measured Japanese crania dating from the Jomon period to recent times. The skulls came from an area of south-western Japan comprising northern Kyushu and the western tip of Honshu (Figure 5.12). These areas are important for the present purposes, as they are the parts of Japan which lie closest to the rice growing areas of China and Korea, and hence are the logical places to start looking for evidence of rice-farming immigrants from the mainland. Using the south-western Japanese material, Nakahashi confirmed the differences between Jomon and Yayoi skulls discussed above. He compared his results with data previously published (Suzuki, 1969) for crania from the Kanto region of eastern Honshu (Figure 5.12). The Kanto material did not show the marked change in skull morphology between the Jomon and Yayoi periods which characterised the south-western crania. During the Jomon period cranial form is similar in the two regions, but the marked change in morphology in the south-west means that the Yayoi skulls here are very different from those excavated from the Kanto area. Evidence for rice agriculture, a major feature of

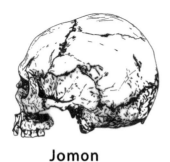

Jomon   **Yayoi**

Figure 5.11 Japanese Jomon and Yayoi crania
Source: After Brace and Nagai (1982: Figures 1 and 2).

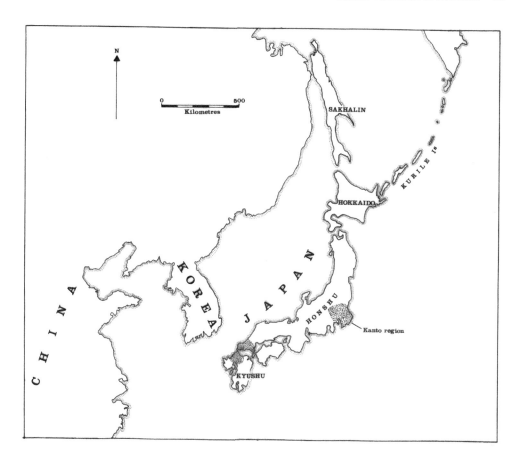

Figure 5.12 Map of Japan. Stippling indicates the area of south-western Japan where the crania studied by Nakahashi (1993) came from, and the Kanto region where the material studied by Suzuki (1969) was found

the Yayoi cultural package, is not confined to Kyushu and western Honshu but seems to have spread quite rapidly though Honshu during the Yayoi era. Nakahashi thus argues that if cultural factors (i.e. diet) were important causes of the changes in skull morphology, similar morphological changes might be expected in the Kanto region. That these were not found suggests that immigration of peoples from mainland Asia to south-western Japan is a better explanation of the osteological data. Nakahashi's study would also seem to suggest that Yayoi culture may have spread to the Kanto region without any great additional movement of people, at least initially. Exploring this question further, using dental measurements, Matsumura (2001) found that most Yayoi burials from various locations in western Honshu resembled those of presumed migrants from the western tip of the island and from northern Kyushu. Although migrants may not have reached as far east as the Kanto region in the Yayoi period, Matsumura's (2001) work suggests that they had colonised much of Honshu west of this region.

Researchers looking at morphological variation on a slightly broader geographical scale have also found evidence consistent with Yayoi migrants. Brace et al. (1989) conducted a craniometric study of various groups in east Asia and the Pacific. Japanese material examined included some from Jomon and Yayoi contexts, as well as more recent Japanese crania. They also studied Ainu crania. The Ainu are a discrete ethnic group, presently concentrated in Hokkaido, as well as in the former Japanese territories of Sakhalin and the Kurile Islands. The Ainu are the aboriginal inhabitants of Hokkaido and perhaps of other parts of the Japanese archipelago. Using cluster analysis of 18 measurements of the skull vault and facial skeleton, Brace et al. (1989) showed that the Yayoi grouped with material from China and Korea, whereas the Jomon and Ainu crania were in a separate cluster (Figure 5.13). Similar results were reported by Ishida et al. (2009) using a somewhat different statistical approach. Ishida and co-workers also found less than the expected variation in Yayoi crania from Kyushu and western Honshu; this was interpreted as consistent with a founder effect stemming from a small population of initial immigrants. These analyses would seem to support the idea that the Yayoi are migrants from the Asian mainland. The Ainu are tranditionally thought to show significant Jomon ancestry, the craniometric evidence is consistent with this, as are ancient and modern DNA data (Adachi et al., 2018).

Brace and Nagai (1982) looked at dental metrics from Japanese and mainland Asian groups. There has generally been a reduction in tooth size in human populations across the

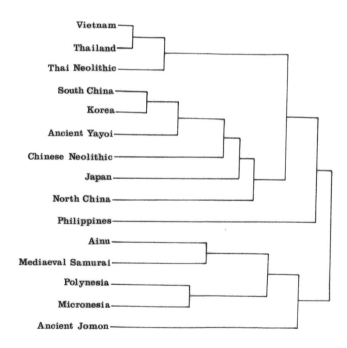

Figure 5.13 Dendrogram from cluster analysis of measurements from Far Eastern and Pacific skulls. All material is of recent origin unless stated

Source: After Brace et al. (1989: Figure 3).

world, particularly in the last 8000 years or so (Brace et al., 1987, 1991). The factors responsible for this are still debated (e.g. Pinhasi & Meiklejohn, 2011). One possibility is that the softer and more cariogenic diet associated with the advent of pottery vessels meant that, if desired, food could be reduced to a drinkable consistency, and this selected for smaller teeth as these present less surface area for carious attack (Calcagno & Gibson, 1988). The Jomon people adopted pottery more than 16,000 years ago, the earliest pottery culture in the world, and also show the greatest dental reduction of any ancient population. Jomon have smaller teeth than those of skeletons from Yayoi contexts (Figure 5.14). Given the general trend for dental reduction discussed above, it is therefore unlikely that the Yayoi are descended from them. Brace and Nagai (1982) found that that Yayoi teeth are similar in size to those from the Chinese Neolithic (Figure 5.14), supporting the idea that the Yayoi might be immigrants from the Asian mainland.

As we shall see in the next chapter, non-metric cranial and dental variants are under a significant degree of genetic control. Studies of non-metric variation support the craniometric data in suggesting immigration to the Japanese islands of people from mainland Asia in the Yayoi period. On the basis of cranial non-metric traits, Yayoi are distinct from the Jomon and Ainu (Dodo & Ishida, 1990; Dodo & Kawakubo, 2002). In the Yayoi period, there is an abrupt change in cranial non-metrical features in south-west Japan,

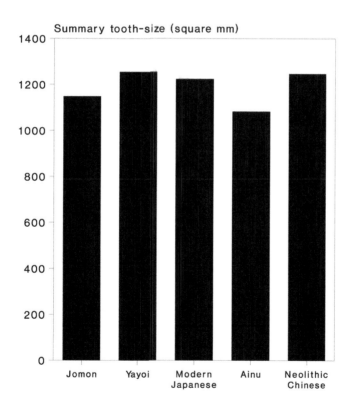

Figure 5.14 Summary tooth size from Japanese and Chinese samples
Source: Based on figures given in Brace and Nagai (1982).

and the Yayoi period skulls here resemble those from the Chinese mainland in terms of their non-metric traits (Kozintsev, 1990); similar patterns have been reported for dental non-metric variants (Hanihara, 1992).

The Neolithic-Bronze Age transition and the problem of the 'Beaker Folk' in Britain

In the southern British Neolithic, the predominant archaeologically visible burial rite involved collective burial in long barrows (see Chapter 3). However, at around 2400BC (Parker Pearson et al., 2016; Jay et al., 2019), during the transition to the Bronze Age, there is a change to individual burial, often beneath round barrows. Unlike most Neolithic burials, those of the Early Bronze Age were generally accompanied by grave goods. A number of other changes are observable in the archaeological record at around this time, including the introduction of metalwork, and the advent of a new pottery style: finely made, elaborately decorated beakers (Figure 5.15).

Beaker pottery shows a patchy distribution in central and western Europe (Figure 5.16). The Beaker cultural package appears first in continental Europe – the earliest Beaker pottery (approximately 2700BC) comes from Iberia (Cardoso, 2014). It seems that the Beaker cultural package was transmitted to Britain from continental Europe, but the question remains as to whether this was predominantly a movement of goods or ideas or else a movement of people. The traditional explanatory framework which dominated British archaeology until the 1960s ascribed it to the arrival of invaders or immigrants. This seemed to be supported by observations made of differences in cranial form between the skulls interred in the Neolithic communal tombs, and those of individuals buried beneath round barrows with Beaker pottery and other grave goods. As long ago as the mid-19th century, the general pattern: 'Long barrows, long skulls; round barrows, round or short skulls' (Thurnam, 1863:158) was noted. Indeed, the difference between Neolithic and Beaker period British skulls is visually striking (Figure 5.17).

The processual approaches of the 1960s and 1970s led to migration or invasion hypotheses for the Beaker phenomenon falling from favour. New explanations were offered, involving movements of goods and ideas rather than people. For example, it was suggested that Beakers represented 'prestige' or valued items, and that they may have been exchanged between elite social groups in Europe (Thorpe & Richards, 1984; Thomas, 1987). It was also argued (Burgess & Shennan, 1976) that the popularity of the Beakers may have been more to do with what they contained than with the vessels themselves. Burgess and Shennan argued that Beakers may have contained some sort of alcoholic beverage, such as beer or mead. They suggested that the Beaker phenomenon might be the material evidence for the spread of a drinking-cult in Early Bronze Age Europe, analogous in some ways to the spread of the Peyote drug cult among North American Indians in the 19th century.

There are difficulties with these theories. Many Beakers would appear ill-suited as drinking vessels, and there is no evidence that they contained alcoholic liquor (Case, 1995; Brodie, 1998). Perhaps not surprisingly, given the difficulties of transporting such fragile items, microscopic analysis shows that Beakers are generally made from local clay sources rather than being traded long distances (Brodie, 1998; Vander Linden,

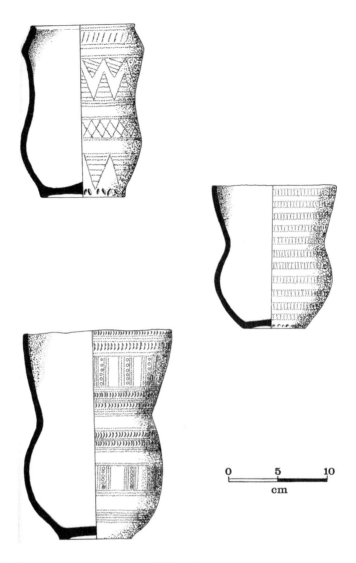

Figure 5.15 Beaker pottery from various British sites
Source: After Critall (1973).

2007). Indeed, it seems likely that those found with burials were specially made for the grave rather than being used in life (Boast, 1995; Shepherd, 2012).

Although some recent commentators continue to deny any great role for influx of new-comers from Continental Europe in the spread of the Beaker phenomenon to Britain (e.g. Parker Pearson et al., 2016; Cummings, 2017), explanations involving movements of people nevertheless appear to be gaining ground. The fragmented distribution of Beakers in Europe (Figure 5.16) suggests, to some, a creeping expansion of Beaker culture by small-scale population movement with interactions between indigenous populations and the new-comers leading to the Beaker package being consolidated in some areas but rejected in others

Figure 5.16 Distribution of the Beaker phenomenon
Source: After Vander Linden, (2007: figure 1).

(Needham, 2007). If Beaker groups were at first widely dispersed then this might give tremendous importance to assertion of identity via distinctive material culture, even through basic equipment such as pottery vessels (Needham, 2005).

Most discussions of the Beaker phenomenon in Britain since the 1960s have tended to focus mainly or entirely on the artifactual data. It is only recently that osteological evidence has begun to be incorporated into this discourse. Commentators who accord a role for human mobility in the Beaker phenomenon (e.g. Needham, 2007; Vander Linden, 2012) have begun to refer to the potential of osteological data to illuminate this question, but it has generally been the potential of isotopic or DNA data that is mentioned, rather than craniometric evidence.

Neolithic

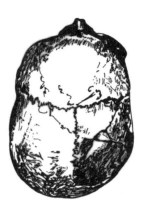

Beaker

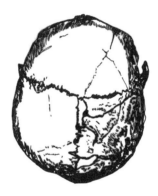

Figure 5.17 Superior view of typical long-headed Neolithic skull and round-headed Beaker
skull. Both specimens are from Britain

Source: After Harrison (1980: Figure 105).

The visual difference in skull shape between the long-headed Neolithic folk and the
rounder-headed Beaker burials, noted since the 19th century, has been confirmed metric-
ally, using the cranial index (the cranial width divided by its length, multiplied by 100)
(Table 5.2).

Table 5.2 The cranial indices of British Neolithic and Bronze Age skulls

		Mean Index	Number of skulls measured
Neolithic	Males	70.4	53
	Females	71.3	28
	Total	70.7	81
Bronze Age	Males	78.1	109
	Females	78.8	48
	Total	78.3	157

Source: Figures calculated from Brodie (1994: Table 8.4).

Multivariate analyses of the crania have been carried out. Brothwell and Krzanowski (1974) studied 11 cranial measurements of Neolithic, Bronze Age and later burials. (In the remainder of this discussion, I treat Beaker burials as belonging to the Early Bronze Age, despite the fact that, initially at least, the metal artifacts from Beaker times are made from unalloyed copper rather than Bronze.) The measurements they used were all of the cranial vault, because in the material available to them few of the more delicate facial bones survived. They used a discriminant function analysis, and were able to achieve a good separation between Neolithic crania on the one hand and Bronze Age, Iron Age and Mediaeval crania on the other.

Twenty years later, Brodie (1994) undertook another study of Neolithic and Early Bronze Age crania. He employed a battery of 20 measurements, and enough crania were available with intact facial bones for Brodie to take measurements here as well as on the cranial vault. I undertook a principle components analysis using Brodie's published data. As already discussed, variation in shape appears to better reflect genetic variation than does variation in size. I therefore first standardised the measurements by normalising each measurement by the geometric mean of all measurements for that individual. This removes the size component, enabling the analysis of cranial shape alone. The results of the principle components analysis on the 20 size-standardised variables is shown in Table 5.3 and Figure 5.18 These data are for males only; there were too few undamaged

Table 5.3 Principle components analysis of 57 Neolithic and Early Bronze Age British crania using size-corrected variables: eigenvalues, percent variance accounted for, and component loadings for the first two components

	PC1	PC2
Eigenvalue	4.18	2.81
% variance accounted for	20.9	14.0
Variable	Component loading	
Maximum cranial length	0.82	-0.22
Maximum breadth	-0.46	0.64
Minimum frontal breadth	-0.36	0.17
Biasterionic breadth	0.17	0.48
Basi-bregmatic height	0.08	-0.37
Frontal arc	0.35	0.48
Parietal arc	0.57	0.32
Occipital arc	0.61	-0.34
Frontal chord	0.50	0.35
Parietal chord	0.71	0.28
Occipital chord	0.61	-0.40
Upper facial height	-0.51	0.02
Basi-nasal length	-0.19	-0.70
Basi-alveolar length	-0.13	-0.70
Orbital height	-0.12	0.20
Orbital breadth	-0.21	0.12
Nasal height	-0.53	0.20
Nasal breadth	-0.47	-0.02
Palatal length	-0.34	-0.19
Palatal breadth	-0.47	-0.16

Sources: The analysis uses data from Brodie (1994), and is identical to that presented in Mays et al. (2018a) except the two Middle Bronze Age crania included in that work are omitted here.

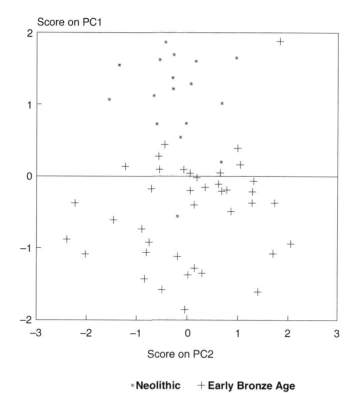

Figure 5.18 Principle components analysis of cranial morphology of Neolithic and Early Bronze Age British crania, using the data of Brodie (1994) with size corrected variables. Scatterplot of first and second principle components

crania in Brodie's data-set to support multivariate analysis of the female data – most Beaker-associated interments are male as, to a lesser extent, are most other Early Bronze Age inhumations and Neolithic burials (Healey, 2012).

In principal components analysis, the sum total of the variance in the data accounted for by a particular component is measured by its eigenvalue. Because there were 20 original variables, the principal components analysis will produce 20 components, but most of them account for very little of the sample variance. It is usual to restrict analysis to components with eigenvalues greater than one – an eigenvalue of less than one would indicate that a component actually accounted for less sample variance than one of the original measurements (Shennan, 1988: 264). In the current analysis, seven components had eigenvalues greater than one but the first two account for 35% of the total variance in the data. The only component upon which Neolithic and Bronze Age crania differ in their scores is component one (PC1). There is little overlap in the point clouds for crania from the two periods in their scores on PC1 (the vertical axis in Fig. 5.18), emphasising their distinct morphology. The loadings of each of the original measurements on PC1 and PC2 are shown in Table 5.3. The loadings are a measure of the correlations between each original variable and the component. As with ordinary correlation coefficients, loadings can vary between −1 and 1. The larger the loading (positive or negative) the more closely that variable is related to the component. A positive loading means as the scores on the component tend to increase the variable increases; a negative loading indicates an inverse relationship.

The Early Bronze Age crania have lower scores on PC1 (Figure 5.18). Vault measurements taken in the sagittal plane (i.e. antero-posteriorly), such as maximum cranial length, have substantial positive loadings on this component, whereas maximum vault breadth has a substantial negative loading, as do most measurements of the facial skeleton (Table 5.3). This means that the Bronze Age crania have shorter, broader cranial vaults (consistent with the cranial index data in Table 5.2), and they have relatively large facial skeletons. Although this analysis only relates to male crania, there is evidence that patterning in female cranial morphology may be similar, at least as far as the cranial vault morphology is concerned. This is evident in Brodie's cranial index data (Table 5.2), and he also conducted a principal components analysis restricted to eight (un-size-standardised) vault measurements and found similar patterns to males with separation of Neolithic and Bronze Age crania.

These studies provide solid evidence for a difference in cranial form between the Neolithic burials in long barrows and elsewhere, and the Beaker associated and other Early Bronze Age burials. It now remains to consider how to interpret this change in cranial morphology.

In general, most British Neolithic bones come from the Early Neolithic (approx. 4000–3500BC); we have very few from Late Neolithic (ca. 3000–2400BC) contexts (Cummings, 2017). No crania dated to the Late Neolithic were sufficiently undamaged that they could be included in the principle components analysis carried out here. There is therefore a large chronological gap between the majority of Neolithic crania and the Beaker burials, which creates uncertainty over the timing of the alterations in cranial morphology. Brodie (1994) was able to take cranial index on 11 Late Neolithic crania. These gave a mean cranial index of 71.5, close to that for the other Neolithic crania. This may suggest that change in cranial vault morphology did indeed occur at or around the transition to the Bronze Age, but with so few Late Neolithic crania it is impossible to be sure.

We have seen that cranial morphology may be modified by alterations in the consistency of the diet, and is sensitive to climatic variables. This raises the question of whether a dietary change or climate change might potentially be responsible for the shorter skulls of the British Beaker period.

If climate was a factor then we might expect to see an alteration in nasal index, the aspect of cranial morphology that has been most consistently associated with climate. This would be expected to show up in the principal components data as markedly different loadings for nasal height and breadth on PC1. In fact, the loadings for both variables are similar (Table 5.3). In any event, although palaeoenvironmental indicators suggest fluctuations in temperature and rainfall throughout the prehistoric period, there is little evidence for systematic differences between the Early Neolithic and the Early Bronze Age (Stevens & Fuller, 2015: Figure 5.4). It seems unlikely that response to climatic change can explain the craniometric results.

As we have seen, a tougher diet tends to be associated with greater relative development of jaws and other areas associated with mastication. Table 5.3 shows that the length and breadth of the palate have substantial negative loadings on PC1. Given that Bronze Age crania have lower scores on this component than Neolithic crania this indicates that the size of the upper jaw in relation to the rest of the cranium tends to be greater in Bronze Age crania. This raises the question of whether a change to a harder diet in the Bronze Age could be responsible for the changes in cranial morphology.

If the diet was harder in the Bronze Age we might expect some alteration to mandibular morphology and/or to patterns of dental wear. Moore et al. (1968) found little difference between the Neolithic and Bronze Age mandibles that they measured (Figure 5.6), and there is no evidence for a systematic difference in the rate of wear on the teeth (Field, 2019). In the cranial data, the observation that morphological changes are not confined to the maxillae but are also observed in the upper face and in the cranial vault (Table 5.3), parts not thought to bear significant masticatory loads (Lycett & Collard, 2005), points away from a dietary interpretation. There is also little archaeological evidence to suggest a significant dietary change at this time. Some have argued, on the basis of evidence from faunal and plant remains, for a greater emphasis on animal products by the middle of the third millennium BC (Bevan et al., 2017), but others (Allen & Maltby, 2012) have urged caution, pointing out the scanty and probably biased nature of the archaeofaunal and archaeobotanical record. A change in the consistency of the diet seems an unlikely explanation for the craniometric data.

Discussion of Japanese Yayoi and British Beaker examples

Both Japan and Britain are islands situated off the Eurasian landmass. In both the Beaker and the Yayoi cases, marked changes were seen both in craniometric data and in other aspects of the archaeological record. In each case, the role, if any, that immigrations from the nearby continental mainland may have played in these discontinuities has been the subject of debate.

Both the Japanese and British craniometric evidence points firmly towards at least limited immigration in the Yayoi and Beaker periods. In the Japanese case, this evidence was strengthened by comparative work which included prehistoric cranial series from the Asian mainland, and the regional pattern of differences in Japanese crania was important in arguing against an environmental or cultural hypothesis for the changes in morphology in Yayoi period crania in south-western Japan. In addition, both dental metrics, and cranial and dental non-metric data support a migration model. The relative profusion of osteological studies aimed at investigating migration stands in contrast to the few that have been carried out on skeletal remains in Britain. This likely reflects the observation that culture history remains a predominant theme in Japanese archaeology, which aims to trace a continuous link between present-day Japan and its remote cultural past (Tsude, 1995). The results of such work are well-integrated into archaeology as a whole, and migration studies were never marginalised as they were for so long in Britain.

In the British case, the specific differences observed between Neolithic and later crania were difficult to explain in terms of extraneous factors known to influence cranial morphology, such as climate or diet. Given the strong association between cranial variation and genetic variation, migration does seem the most parsimonious explanation for the discontinuities observed in cranial form at the Neolithic-Bronze Age transition in Britain. Systematic comparisons with crania from the continental mainland, and studies of dental metrics or cranial and dental non-metrics are lacking but, as we shall see in Chapter 12, the cranial evidence appears to be supported by ancient DNA data which similarly suggest a Neolithic–Beaker period genetic discontinuity (Olalde et al., 2018).

Summary

Cranial form is influenced by both environmental and genetic factors. Among the former are diet, nutrition and climate. The genetic contribution has been assessed by studies of family groups and, on a larger scale, by studies of populations whose relationships can be reconstructed from independent evidence (e.g. DNA or other genetic markers). These studies have consistently demonstrated a high degree of genetic control of cranial morphology. Because of this, the quantitative study of cranial form (craniometry) is a useful tool for investigating relationships between populations (biodistance studies) and for studying population movements in the past.

Cranial morphological data are traditionally recorded using linear measurements between defined anatomical points or landmarks. However, the capture not of measurements but of the coordinates of cranial landmarks in three-dimensional space, and the analysis of this data using geometric morphometrics, is making a growing impact on the field. The advantage with this approach is that, unlike traditional linear measurements, it captures the full geometric relationships between landmarks, and so provides a more comprehensive picture of cranial form. Whichever approach is used, multivariate statistical analysis of the data is essential if we are to successfully identify and understand patterning in cranial morphology in biodistance and migration studies.

Further reading

A useful introduction to geometric morphometrics is given in: McKeown, A.H. and Schmidt, R.W. (2013). Geometric Morphometrics, pp. 325–359 in E.A. Di Gangi and M.K. Moore (eds) *Research Methods in Human Skeletal Biology*. New York, Elsevier.

Brodie, N. (1994). The Neolithic-Bronze Age Transition in Britain. British Archaeological Reports, British Series No. 238. Tempus Reparatum, Oxford. *This provides an overview of the craniometry of Neolithic and Beaker burials.*

For a summary of Japanese population history with a good integration of craniometric and other evidence see Hanihara, K. (1991). Dual Structure Model for the Population History of the Japanese. *Japan Review* 2: 1–33.

6 Metric variation in the post-cranial skeleton

As with cranial metrics, definitions of standard measurements for the post-cranial skeleton are offered in most laboratory manuals of human osteology (e.g. Brothwell, 1981; Bass, 1987; Herrman et al., 1990; Buikstra & Ubelaker, 1994). Although measurement definitions may differ somewhat between authors, most are based on those in Rudolf Martin's classic text (Martin, 1928).

For long-bones, most measurements comprise bone lengths, or else widths of the shaft or articular surfaces. Measurements of length are generally taken with an osteometric board, which consists of a flat surface with a graduated measuring scale and a movable end plate (Figure 6.1). Widths of the shaft or articular surfaces are normally taken with sliding callipers. Less often, shaft circumferences are measured. Circumferences are usually taken with a tape measure or, for more slender bones, with a dampened thread. Widths and circumferences are usually taken at specific landmarks. Very often these landmarks are defined as particular proportions of bone length (e.g. the midshaft). Alternatively, they may be a particular anatomical feature, such as the nutrient foramen in the tibia or the subtrochanteric area of the femur. Articular surface or shaft widths are generally taken in a defined anatomical plane, usually medio-lateral or antero-posterior. Less often, maximum or minimum widths are measured.

Measurements have also been defined for most of the non-long-bone elements of the post-cranial skeleton (Martin, 1928). These are generally maximum or minimum widths measured in different planes, or else distances between defined landmarks.

In addition to being assessed using calliper measurements, the morphology of post-cranial bones can also be captured using surface scanning methods, such as laser or structured light scanning. This data can then be analysed using geometric morphometrics (see Chapter 5) or other methods.

Bone morphology may also be studied using medical imaging techniques. Because radiography and allied techniques allow visualisation of internal features, working with radiological images enables recording not only of surface dimensions but also of dimensions of internal features. At its simplest, this involves taking measurements from radiographs; this used to be done by measuring the hardcopy radiograph with callipers, but it is now more usual to take measurements from digitised images using software applications. CT (computed tomography) scanning goes one better, and allows a bone's

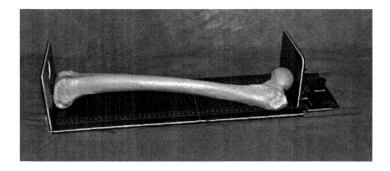

Figure 6.1 An osteometric board for measuring long-bone lengths
Source: Paleo-Tech Concepts Inc.

structure to be visualised as virtual slices or as a three-dimensional image. A major application of quantitative work using medical imaging techniques is study the cross-sectional properties of long-bone shafts.

Metric studies of the post-cranial skeleton have been undertaken for a variety of purposes. For example, measurement of the ribs, sternum, thoracic vertebrae and clavicle in early Andean populations has been used to study thoracic enlargement as an adaptation to high altitude (Weinstein, 2007). Osteometric and geometric morphometric studies on the sacrum and pelvis have assessed adaptation of this area in the female to childbirth (Tague, 1994, 2007; Fischer & Mitteroecker, 2015). The dimensions of the vertebral neural canal, which transmits the spinal cord, have been used as an indicator of malnutrition or other problems during growth (Watts, 2015). However most studies of post-cranial metric variation have concentrated on the appendicular skeleton, principally the major limb long-bones, and it is upon the quantitative study of variation in these elements that this chapter will focus. Firstly, I will discuss the use of long-bone lengths to estimate stature. Secondly, I will consider the use of long-bone shaft cross-sectional properties as a means of investigating activity patterns in past populations.

Stature

Height-for-age in children is strongly dependent upon nutrition and disease experience (Stinson, 2000). The most common causes of retarded growth are inadequate nutrition, infectious disease, or a combination of the two (Humphrey, 2000). Growth-retarded children also tend to be short-statured as adults, but the effect of adverse conditions in childhood upon adult stature tends to be less marked because, when conditions are poor, the growth period is usually prolonged.

Most osteoarchaeological studies of growth in children and stature in adults use them as indicators of the adequacy of childhood nutrition and health. In this section I explain some of the methods for estimating stature from skeletal remains, and I illustrate the value of this sort of data using, as an example, a study of growth in stature from a Mediaeval English site.

Estimating stature from skeletal remains

There are, in essence, three ways of estimating stature from skeletal material. Firstly, one can simply measure the length of the skeleton in the grave. Secondly, one can measure the heights of the different individual bones that contribute to stature, the so-called anatomical method. Lastly, one can measure the lengths of bones (generally long-bones) that bear a known relationship to standing height and use mathematical formulae to estimate stature, the so-called mathematical method. These techniques are discussed in turn below.

Measurement of the skeleton in the grave

This technique involves measuring the length of the articulated skeleton, from the top of the cranium to the feet, before the bones are lifted during excavation (Boldsen, 1984; Petersen, 2005). Clearly this is only a viable strategy where the normative burial practice was interment of the corpse in a fully extended position as, for example, in most Christian burials. The cranium and the foot bones also need to be intact and undisturbed. This may be problematic as crania in archaeological burials are frequently crushed and fragmented by soil pressure. In addition, during the collapse and decay of the body, the bones tend to settle and spread. Where corpses are interred directly in the soil, the surrounding earth may keep this movement to a minimum, but as we have seen in Chapter 3, in coffined burials it may be considerable. To assess the reliability of this method of estimating stature we would need to excavate, and measure *in situ*, skeletal remains of individuals whose height was known in life. This has yet to be done, but comparison of results with those generated from the anatomical method suggest that estimates from skeletal length in the grave are not very reliable (Petersen, 2011). For these reasons it is rarely used in archaeology.

The anatomical technique

This method was developed for estimating stature in adults by Georges Fully, a French physical anthropologist. Following World War II, he was called upon to examine, and if possible identify, skeletonised remains of French citizens killed at Mauthausen concentration camp, Austria (see Stewart (1979) for a brief English language account of Fully's work). Some of these skeletons still bore identification discs. For these identified individuals, the skeletons could be matched with stature taken on entry to the concentration camp or from military records. Working with these remains (102 adult males), for his study of stature Fully selected for measurement those bones that directly contribute to an individual's height (Fully, 1956; Fully & Pineau, 1960). He therefore measured the height of the cranium, the heights of the vertebral bodies, the lengths of the tibia and femur and the articulated height of the talus and calcaneus. He added all these measurements together and termed the sum the skeletal height. By comparing this to the documented stature, he was able to deduce general correction factors (which were different for different skeletal heights) that needed to be added to skeletal height in order to produce an accurate estimate of stature in life. The correction factors were needed to account for the presence of soft tissue (e.g. the intervertebral discs) and other factors that would affect the relationship between skeletal height and actual height, such as the natural spinal curvature.

Fully's anatomical technique was subsequently tested on dissecting hall material where height was measured on cadavers before they were defleshed (King, 2004; Bidmos, 2005; Raxter et al., 2006). (Height measured on a cadaver is not the same as standing height in life. We appear taller after death due to the decomposition and loosening of the soft tissues of the joints. Approximately 2.5cm needs to be deducted from cadaveric height to get height in life (Trotter & Gleser, 1952) Studies that investigate the relationship between stature and osteological measurements using cadaver records take account of this.) The studies of King (2004), Bidmos (2005) and Raxter et al. (2006) found that Fully's correction factors were too small so that his method tended to underestimate height. Raxter et al. (2006) suggested revised equations for estimating height. One of them included an adjustment for age. From a maximum in early adult life, stature tends to progressively decline somewhat, mostly due to shrinkage of soft tissue in the vertebral column (Friedlaender et al., 1977), hence the age adjustment. In archaeological studies, it is primarily maximum stature rather than stature adjusted for age that is of interest, as the former is the more sensitive indicator of nutrition and general living conditions. It has been demonstrated (Raxter et al., 2007; Ruff et al., 2019) that even if it is maximum rather than age-adjusted stature that is of interest, the best way to estimate it is to use Raxter et al.'s (2006) equation with an age term, but to insert an age of 30 years.

The age adjusted equation is:

$$\text{Stature} = 1.009 \times \text{ skeletal height} - 0.0426 \times \text{ age} + 12.1$$

(age in years, other figures in cm)

With an age of 30 years inserted, it becomes:

$$\text{Stature} = 1.009 \times \text{ skeletal height} + 10.82$$

The standard error on the estimate for this equation is 2.22cm. This means that, in Raxter et al.'s reference population, the error on stature estimation was within 2.22cm in about 68% of cases.

Although there are no archaeological collections of known stature upon which to test the method, there seems general agreement that the anatomical method is the most reliable way of estimating stature from skeletal remains (Raxter et al., 2006; Maijanen, 2009). However, the requirement for multiple intact skeletal elements limits the application of this method in osteoarchaeology where fragmentary and incomplete skeletons are the norm. In osteoarchaeology, mathematical techniques, which rely on measuring one or some few bones, are generally used.

Mathematical techniques

Development of mathematical techniques involves measuring a bone or bones in individuals of known stature and deriving a formula by which to estimate height from bone length in remains of individuals of unknown stature. Long-bone lengths bear the most regular relationship to standing height and are thus the most reliable basis for mathematical equations to estimate stature. Among the most commonly used equations for estimating adult stature from long-bone lengths are those formulated by Mildred Trotter and Goldine Gleser (Trotter & Gleser, 1952, 1958, 1977). They used large numbers of skeletonised remains of mid-20th-century repatriated American male war dead whose heights were known from military records, together with 240 female remains from the Robert J. Terry collection, which comprised dissecting hall material from the first half of the 20th century for which stature could be calculated from cadaver measurements taken prior to skeletonisation.

A mathematical technique of stature estimation is a reference–target population technique (see Chapter 4). An inherent assumption is that the body proportions in one's archaeological sample resemble those in the reference sample used to produce the stature formulae (by contrast the anatomical method of stature estimation does not involve this sort of assumption). The sexes differ in their body proportions, hence different equations are required for males and females. There are also differences in body proportions among different world populations. For example, populations from cold climates tend to have shorter distal limb segments (forearms and lower legs) than those from warmer ones. This is thought to represent an adaptation to climate. In a cold climate, shorter distal limb segments help conserve heat, whereas in a warm one longer extremities facilitate heat loss (Trinkaus, 1981). There are therefore different stature equations for different world populations, and one must be careful to choose those which are suitable for the archaeological population in hand. For example, Trotter & Gleser (1952, 1958) produced separate formulae for Whites and Blacks. Others have derived equations for other populations, for example Genoves (1967) for Mesoamericans, and Mahakkanukrauh et al. (2011) for Thais. Trotter and Gleser's equations for Whites and Blacks are reproduced in Table 6.1.

The equations in Table 6.1 are arranged in order of preference according to the standard error of the estimate. So, for example, with a prehistoric male skeleton from England with all long-bones intact for measurement we would choose the White male formula for the femur and tibia. If the maximum femur length was 45.2cm and the length of the tibia omitting the medial malleolus was 34.2cm, then the stature would be estimated as 166.5cm, with a standard error of the estimate of 2.99cm.

Trotter and Gleser's stature formulae were devised for adult skeletons. They work poorly on juvenile remains (Feldesman, 1992; Raxter et al., 2006). This is because body proportions in juveniles differ from those in adults and also vary with age (Maresh, 1959; Ruff, 2007). There are no modern collections with substantial numbers of juvenile skeletons of known stature from which to derive formulae for estimating standing height in the young. Instead, the stature estimation equations we have for juvenile skeletal material are derived from bone measurements taken from radiographs or other medical images of living subjects. One such study is by Marc Feldesman (Feldesman, 1992). He explored the relationship between femur length and stature in children using data from four radiographic studies published in the mid-20th century. These published studies involved X-raying the limbs of White children from the USA and measuring bone lengths from the radiographs, and also recording the children's statures. Feldesman (1992) found that femur length made up a predictable proportion of stature but that this proportion varied with age and sex (Table 6.2).

Feldesman's (1992) method of stature estimation has not been tested on large independent samples of juveniles of documented stature, but a test on a small subsample of

Table 6.1 Mathematical equations for estimating stature from long-bone length (cm) in White and Black adults

White Males		Black Males	
Formula	SEE	Formula	SEE
1.30(Fem+Tib) + 63.29	2.99	1.15(Fem+Tib) + 71.04	3.53
2.38 Fem + 61.41	3.27	2.19 Tib + 86.02	3.78
2.68 Fib + 71.78	3.29	2.11 Fem + 70.35	3.94
2.52 Tib + 78.62	3.37	2.19 Fib + 85.65	4.08
3.08 Hum + 70.45	4.05	3.42 Rad + 81.56	4.30
3.78 Rad + 79.01	4.32	3.26 Ulna + 79.29	4.42
3.70 Ulna + 74.05	4.32	3.26 Hum + 62.10	4.43

White Females		Black Females	
1.39(Fem+Tib) + 53.20	3.55	1.26(Fem+Tib) + 59.72	3.28
2.93 Fib + 59.61	3.57	2.28 Fem + 59.76	3.41
2.90 Tib + 61.53	3.66	2.45 Tib + 72.65	3.70
2.47 Fem + 54.10	3.72	2.49 Fib + 70.90	3.80
4.74 Rad + 54.93	4.24	3.08 Hum + 64.67	4.25
4.27 Ulna + 57.76	4.30	3.67 Rad + 71.79	4.59
3.36 Hum + 57.97	4.45	3.31 Ulna + 75.38	4.83

Data sources: Trotter & Gleser, 1952: Table 13; for females the correction to the radius formula for Blacks detailed in Trotter, 1977 is included. The formulae in this table are also reproduced in Trotter (1970: Table XXVIII), but with the incorrect Black female radius formula. Formulae based on 790 male World War II casualties (710 White, 80 Black) and 240 females (N=63 White, 177 Black) from the Robert J. Terry skeletal collection.

Notes: SEE, standard error of the estimate. All bone lengths should be recorded as maximum lengths, apart from the tibia: tibia lengths should omit the medial maleolus to take account of idiosyncrasies in Trotter's measurement of this bone (Jantz et al., 1994). Note that there is no age correction so that estimates are of maximum (i.e. young adult) stature.

Table 6.2 Femur length: stature ratios by age and sex for children of northern European ancestry

Age (years)	Femur: stature ratio	
	Female	Male
8	0.2626	0.2598
9	0.2663	0.2636
10	0.2691	0.2675
11	0.2717	0.2701
12	0.2735	0.2729
13	0.2730	0.2729
14	0.2721	0.2756
15	0.2711	0.2754
16	0.2706	0.2746
17	0.2697	0.2736
18	0.2695	0.2724

Data source: Feldesman, 1992: Table 5. Note: the 8-year category includes those aged between 8 and 9 years, the 9 year those between 9 and 10 etc. Femur lengths include epiphyses the juvenile data used to generate the ratios (Ruff, 2007) showed that, for all individuals tested (N=20), estimated stature lay within about 6% of true stature.

There are several practical considerations in using the Feldesman (1992) data to estimate stature in archaeological skeletons. Firstly, because the equations were developed using data from American White children, it would seem prudent to restrict their use to archaeological populations of northern European descent.

Secondly, Feldesman's data refer to total bone length, including epiphyses. In archaeological material, epiphyses are present as separate pieces of bone (Figure 4.12). Even when they are recovered undamaged, it is often difficult to refit them accurately to the diaphysis, particularly in younger individuals. Long-bone lengths in archaeological juvenile skeletal remains are usually taken on the diaphysis alone. I measured some juvenile femurs from an archaeological site (Wharram Percy) for which epiphyses were recovered undamaged, and could be refitted accurately to the diaphysis. This showed that the diaphysis makes up about 91% of total femoral length. This figure closely matches those from modern medical imaging studies (Maresh, 1955; Brits et al., 2017). This suggests that femur diaphysial lengths should be divided by 0.91 to estimate total length.

Thirdly, as we saw in Chapter 4, it is not normally possible to determine sex in non-adult skeletons. A way of overcoming this difficulty is to use the mean of male and female ratios to estimate stature in unsexed archaeological material. For individuals, this is somewhat unsatisfactory, but for studies of large numbers of juveniles, where, for example, we are seeking to assess stature increase with age, it seems a reasonable approach. An assumption in doing this is that the juvenile assemblage under study contains similar numbers of males and females in each age group. This assumption is likely to be broadly valid for many cemeteries, and in any case because in most age groups the difference in femur: stature ratio between the sexes is fairly small, this method should be robust to minor sex imbalances.

Child growth in antiquity

The usual way of studying child growth using skeletal remains is to plot a bone dimension (often the length of a long-bone) against age estimated from dental calcification (Humphrey, 2000; Mays, 2018a; Lewis, 2019). Indeed, the study of growth is probably the principal use to which post-cranial metric data in non-adult remains are put. In this way, comparisons of growth patterns can be carried out between different archaeological populations or between subgroups of the same population. Studies have been published assessing the association between growth and type of subsistence economy (Temple et al., 2014), socioeconomic status (Mays et al., 2009), disease in childhood (Pinhasi et al., 2006, 2014), and urban versus rural life (Mays et al., 2008). The few radiographic studies of growth in bone lengths in living children (e.g. Maresh, 1955) also allow limited comparison with some more recent data.

For most growth studies, it is best to compare bone dimensions directly rather than convert them to stature estimates since, as we have seen, estimation of stature introduces its own uncertainties and assumptions. However, in some studies it is useful to work with estimated stature figures rather than bone lengths. For example, in the last two-hundred years, there have been a number of surveys of the heights of living children. If one's aim is to compare growth in an archaeological population with this historical growth data, then stature estimates are needed.

The first large-scale growth studies of living children were undertaken in the early 19th century. These, and subsequent studies, show that there has been a trend toward increased height-for-age in children (and to a lesser extent in final adult stature) in the developed world. Much of this change appears to have occurred in the last 100 years, and in most instances the trend now seems to be slowing or stopping (Tanner, 1989: 156ff; Health Survey for England, 2015). Analysis of archaeological human remains permits the study of trends in growth in height to be extended back into the more remote past.

I studied growth in children from Mediaeval Wharram Percy (Mays, 1999, 2007). Of the nearly 700 burials from this site, over 300 were of children. The large number of juvenile skeletons, together with the excellent gross bone survival at this site, and the fact that the burial ground served a geographically defined community (Wharram Percy village and its surrounding parish) makes this collection ideal for a study of growth. The aims of the work were to shed light on living conditions in this community and also to provide a step towards evaluating whether the trend for increased height-for-age in British children began before the first growth surveys of living children were carried out in the 19th century. The work involved comparing growth at Wharram Percy both with modern and with 19th-century British children.

I estimated standing height in the children from Wharram Percy using Feldesman's (1992) juvenile femur: stature ratios. For example, for a 10-year-old with a femur diaphysial length of 28.5cm, I firstly calculated total femur length as 28.5/0.91 = 31.3cm. Feldesman's (1992) femur stature ratios for 10-year-olds are 0.2691 for females and 0.2675 for males (Table 6.2), giving a midsex mean of 0.2683. The estimated stature of this individual is therefore 31.3/0.2683 = 116.7cm.

The stature estimates for the Wharram Percy children are plotted against age (estimated from dental calcification) in Figure 6.2. Also plotted in this figure are data from recent and 19th-century British children. The recent growth curve is from Freeman et al. (1995) and is for White British children in 1990. The 19th-century data are from a survey done in 1833 in north-west England on children employed in factories (figures reproduced in Tanner, 1981).

Before comparing the archaeological data with those taken from living subjects, a few words of caution are necessary. Firstly, and most obviously, in the archaeological material, both height and age were estimated, whereas in the 19th century and modern studies these were known exactly. Secondly, mortality bias in the archaeological data may prejudice comparisons with living subjects. This is because in archaeological material we are looking at growth in those who died in childhood. It might be suggested that this is not representative of growth in healthier children who survived to become adults. However, a review of this problem (Saunders & Hoppa, 1993) shows that the biasing effect on skeletal growth studies is probably small.

Although these potential difficulties should be kept in mind, some interesting comparisons can be drawn. The most striking thing about Figure 6.2 is the height difference between the modern and the Mediaeval children. For example, the average height for a Wharram Percy 10-year-old is about 117cm, 21cm less than the modern figure (138cm).

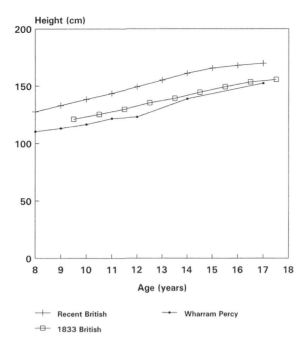

Figure 6.2 Estimated stature plotted against dental age for the Wharram Percy children. Figures for recent and 19th century children are included for comparison

Notes: stature figures are mid-sex means. The 19th-century data have been adjusted to take account of footwear (Tanner, 1981: note 7.5). For data sources see text.

Or, to put it another way, the height of 14-year-olds at Wharram Percy is only about the same as modern 10-year-olds.

The difference between the 19th century and the Wharram Percy children is less pronounced. However, the average height for each age class in the Wharram Percy children is consistently less than for the 1833 subjects; the Mediaeval children lag behind in growth by about 1–2 years at most ages.

Given the relationship between retarded growth and inadequate nutrition and infectious disease burden, the present results suggest that, not surprisingly, the Mediaeval group had poorer nutrition and suffered a greater disease load than modern British children. The observation that the heights of the Wharram Percy children were less than those measured in the 1833 survey may indicate that conditions for the Wharram Percy children were worse even than those for the urban poor in the Industrial Revolution. If the difference between the Mediaeval and the 19th-century children is real, and more broadly valid, then it would imply that the trend for increase in height-for-age in British children may have originated well before the first child height surveys were undertaken in the 19th century. However, such a conclusion would be premature; further studies of large assemblages of British Mediaeval and Post-Mediaeval juvenile skeletons would be needed to substantiate this.

In instances of long-term sub-optimal nutrition, growth is retarded so that children are short for their ages. However, under such circumstances, the growth period is prolonged, so that final adult stature may be unaffected, or at least affected rather less than is height for age in children, although it is reached at a later age. As might be expected from this, concomitant with the recent trend for increased height-for age in childhood, there has also been a trend for final adult stature to be reached earlier.

In modern populations in the developed world, growth in height is virtually complete by 18 years of age (Tanner, 1989: Figure 4). Records show that, in the past, growth was not completed until somewhat later. For example, Morant (1950) studied growth survey data gathered in the 19th century. In the period 1857-1883, final adult stature was not attained until about 29 years of age in the lowest social class. The age of attainment was lower among the more privileged, but still later than it is today – for example it was about 21 years in the 'professional' classes.

Aspects of the Wharram Percy data are consistent with the idea that growth was prolonged in this group compared to modern British subjects. I estimated the heights of female adults from Wharram Percy using Trotter and Gleser's 1952 equation for White females; for the males I used their 1958 White male equation The mean estimated height was 168.8cm for males and 157.8cm for females, giving a midsex mean of 163.4cm. Corresponding figures for modern White British male and female adults are 176.4cm and 163.6cm respectively (Freeman et al., 1995), giving a midsex mean of 170.0cm. Height at 10 years at Wharram Percy was thus about 72% of the mean adult height in that population, whereas height for modern 10-year-olds is about 82% of mean modern adult height. Consistent with this, the difference in height between Mediaeval and modern adults is less than during childhood. The average stature of Wharram Percy adults is about 96% of that in adults today, but the height of a Wharram Percy 10-year-old was only about 85% of that of a modern 10-year-old.

European archaeological evidence (e.g. Bennike, 1985; Šereikienė & Jankauskas, 2002, 2004; Maat, 2005; Cardoso & Gomes, 2009; Niskanen et al., 2018) is consistent with the Wharram Percy results in showing that, in ancient populations, adults were generally somewhat shorter than their modern counterparts. For example, combined data from many British archaeological sites show that stature was in general several centimetres less than today: mean male stature for different periods from the Mesolithic to the 19th century ranges from 165-172cm; the corresponding figures for females are 157-162cm (Roberts & Cox, 2003: Table 8.1). It seems likely that, as with height-for-age in children, the reasons for the greater final adult stature today than in the past reside mainly with lessening of disease and improvements in nutrition (Tanner, 1989: 161).

Bone cross sectional properties and activity patterns

We learnt in Chapter 1 that living bone shows functional adaptation. It is sensitive to mechanical forces placed upon it from weight-bearing or muscular contraction: increased mechanical forces tend to lead to bone being strengthened at skeletal sites subjected to such forces. The density of a bone affects its strength, but most functional adaptation appears to occur not in density but in the amount and distribution of bone tissue (Woo et al., 1981; Warden et al., 2005). A clear illustration of this phenomenon is the increase in thickness in the shafts of bones in the racket arm of regular tennis players (Figure 1.3). Conversely, loss of bone tissue occurs when there is a reduction in mechanical forces, for example in those who are bed-ridden (Sievänen, 2010) or in astronauts subject to weightlessness (Bikle et al., 2003).

Because living bone has this ability to, within limits, alter its morphology in response to mechanical stimuli, osteoarchaeologists have explored the possibility that aspects of bone strength may inform us of activity patterns in past populations. There is little value in attempting to assess the strength of an archaeological bone directly because degradation during burial, particularly of the collagen component, means that its strength will not be a useful guide to that in life. The approach is rather to estimate strength from the amount and distribution of bone tissue. Most workers have concentrated on long-bone shafts, measuring the amount and distribution of cortical bone in cross-section, referred to as the bone's cross-sectional geometry. The first such studies began in the 1970s (e.g. Lovejoy et al., 1976), and since then this is an area that has attracted much interest from researchers.

It will be recalled from Chapter 1 that long-bone shafts have a tubular form in which a wall of cortical bone surrounds the medullary cavity (Figure 1.2). The strength of a tube under compression or tension in the axial plane (i.e. along the long axis of a straight tube) is proportional to the thickness of its walls. However, bones are not straight, they move with body motion, and have irregularly placed muscular insertions upon their surfaces. This means that, in living bone, bending or torsional (twisting) forces are more important modes of loading than pure compression and tension (Larsen, 2015: 219–220). The resistance of a tubular structure to bending or torsion depends not only on the thickness of its walls but also on the diameter of the tube. For a given wall thickness, a wider tube resists bending or torsion better than a narrower one, so, for a bone shaft, both the thickness of the cortical bone, and overall diaphyseal width will affect its strength.

Quantifying cross-sectional properties

The strength of a structure is simply its ability to resist breaking under mechanical loading; its ability to resist deformation is termed rigidity. Both the strength and rigidity of a long-bone diaphysis are associated with its cross-sectional geometry. Mathematical models used by engineers to measure the load-bearing capacity of beams in built structures can be used to assess the strength and rigidity of long-bones. Among the more important measures of rigidity are second moments of area. These are denoted by the letter I and are expressed with respect to a particular axis (for example, antero-posterior or medio-lateral – I_{ap} and I_{ml} respectively) and are a measure of the resistance of bone to bending in that plane. Second moments of area take account both the amount of bone in a cross-section and the square of its distance from the central longitudinal axis (it is the square of the distance because the contribution of a unit of bone in resisting bending is proportional to the square of its distance from the central axis). The polar second moment of area, denoted J, is the sum of two second moments of area in perpendicular planes (e.g. I_{ap} + I_{ml}). It is an index of the overall resistance of a bone to bending and torsional forces, and so is considered a useful indicator of the overall rigidity of the shaft (Ruff, 2019). The strength equivalents of second moments of area are known as section moduli. Section moduli with respect to antero-posterior and medio-lateral axes are denoted Z_{ap} and Z_{ml}, and the polar section modulus is Z_p. Both second moments of area, and section moduli, may be used in studies of bone cross-sectional geometry aimed at investigating ancient activity patterns. Second moments of area and their corresponding section moduli are closely related, and mathematical formulae exist to convert from one to the other (Ruff, 2018).

Cross-sectional properties are generally measured on the major long-bones of the limbs, although some work has also been done on other tubular bones – for example metacarpals (Mays, 2001) and metatarsals (Hagihara & Nara, 2018). They need to be measured at a consistent point on the diaphysis. For most bones, measurements are normally made at the midshaft. An exception is the humerus, where the midshaft is avoided as here there is a large and rather variable crest for muscle attachment (called the deltoid tuberosity). Humerus cross-sectional measurements are normally made at a point 35% of the way from the distal end.

Capturing data on cross-sectional properties of long-bone shafts

The most direct method of measuring cross-sectional properties of a bone is to physically section the bone at the point of interest and digitise the cross-section thus revealed. However, the damage that this causes to skeletal collections is unacceptable in most instances. Most studies therefore use non-invasive methods.

The technique of choice is CT scanning. This is non-destructive and produces an accurate two-dimensional, digitised image of the cross-section of a bone. Various computer programmes have been developed for determining second moments of area and other parameters from digital images of cross-sections (Ruff, 2019).

When cost or other practical constraints preclude CT scanning, an alternative is to use radiography. Two radiographs are taken in perpendicular planes (usually antero-posterior and medio-lateral views). Second moments of area and other parameters can be estimated from radiographic measurements of antero-posterior and medio-lateral total bone widths and medullary widths using geometric formulae, provided one makes assumptions about the shape of a cross-section (for example, for humeral cross-sections at the 35% point along the shaft an elliptical shape is assumed). Comparison of results with those from physically cut sections show that for the humerus (Fresia et al., 1990), femur and tibia (O'Neill & Ruff, 2004) the biplanar radiographic method provides results closely correlated with true values, although there is a slight tendency toward over-estimation of parameters.

The biplanar radiographic method can be refined if the actual contour of the outer surface of the bone is recorded using a latex cast and only the medullary cavity is reconstructed from radiographs. Because bone furthest from the central axis contributes most to shaft rigidity, accurate recording of the subperiosteal contour is more critical than the endosteal contour (O'Neill & Ruff, 2004). Taking this point further, some studies (e.g. Sparacello et al., 2015) estimate cross-sectional geometric properties from the external contour of the bone alone. This can be recorded using the cast method or by surface laser or structured light scanning. This approach has the advantage of obviating the need for radiographic or CT study. Whilst methods that involve the modelling of both periosteal and endosteal contours must be regarded as preferable, correlations between these and data collected just using the external shape are high (Stock & Shaw, 2007; Sparacello & Pearson, 2010), meaning that this latter method is valuable when imaging techniques to reconstruct the endosteal surface are not available. It has been argued (e.g. Pearson, 2000; Wescott, 2006) that useful inferences regarding biomechanical loadings can even be obtained from simple calliper measurements of external bone shaft widths. In addition to the ease and simplicity of recording calliper measurements, because they have long been taken in osteoarchaeology there are large amounts of published data for comparison. However, comparative study (Stock & Shaw, 2007) seems to confirm that external shaft widths are rather crude substitutes for accurate modelling of subperiosteal contours, so they are likely to be less sensitive indicators of loading environment (Ruff, 2002; Larsen, 2015: 247-249).

For comparative purposes, second moments of area and section moduli need to be standardised for body mass and bone length. Body mass contributes to loading directly via the force of gravity, but body mass is also indirectly related to forces imposed on bones from muscular contraction because of the relationship between total body mass and muscle mass. Bending and torsion involve both a force and a moment (or lever) arm, which can be considered proportional to bone length. The best way of standardising for these parameters has been debated for some time (Pearson, 2000; Ruff & Larsen, 2014). Current consensus appears to be that second moments of area should be standardised by body mass multiplied by the square of bone length, and section moduli by body mass multiplied by bone length (Sparacello et al., 2011; Davies & Stock, 2014; Ruff, 2019). Using body mass in standardisation presents some problems because it is difficult to estimate from skeletal remains. Various formulae have been devised, relying on measurement of bi-iliac breadth of the pelvis and stature, femoral head breadth, or cortical bone area at various locations in the femur. Evaluation of these methods on modern subjects of known body mass suggests that they work poorly (Lacoste Jeanson et al., 2017). It has been suggested (Pomeroy et al., 2018) that they might be more accurate for archaeological skeletons as it is likely that, in ancient populations, people generally lacked the large and somewhat variable amounts of adipose tissue that typify people in modern industrialised populations but, as there are no archaeological skeletal series for which body mass was recorded in life, this remains speculative. For second moments of area, an alternative to estimating body mass is to standardise by bone length raised to the power of 5.33, which provides an approximate standardisation for body mass and bone length. Indices, such as I_{ml}/I_{ap}, used to investigate differences between populations in orientation of bone loading, and measures of left-right asymmetry in second moments of area or other parameters, do not need to be standardised for most purposes.

Causes of variation in bone cross-section properties

In addition to mechanical forces, a number of other factors also affect the amount of bone and/or its distribution in cross-section. In adult life, other than *in extremis*, nutrition has little effect on cortical bone thickness (Garn, 1970). However, a consistent link has been found between poor childhood nutrition and reduced cortical thickness (refs in Mays, 2008a). Peak cortical bone thickness in adults in past populations is generally less than in modern subjects, reflecting lesser acquisition of cortical bone during childhood

(Mays, 2008a), likely due to poorer nutrition in the past during the growing years. Most studies indicate the lesser cortical thickness in past populations is due to greater medullary cavity width rather than reduced total bone width (Ruff et al., 2013). Given that bone tissue further from the central axis of a cross-section contributes more to bone strength and rigidity than that nearer the medullary cavity, this means that the effects on these parameters of this deficiency of cortical thickness are minimised.

From middle age onwards, cortical bone becomes thinner due to loss of bone from the endosteal surface bordering the medullary cavity. This is a manifestation of osteoporosis and is particularly marked in women (Mays, 2008a). As above, the pattern of loss means that the effects on diaphyseal strength and rigidity are mitigated, but nevertheless, some authors (e.g. Ogilvie & Hilton, 2011) exclude individuals aged over about 50 years from analysis.

Genetic factors affect bone cross-sectional geometry. A reason for this is that genetic background appears to influence the sensitivity of bone to mechanical forces. This means that different populations vary in the degree to which cross-sectional structural alterations occur in response to loading environment (Wallace et al., 2017). This clearly needs to be considered when interpreting patterned differences between genetically divergent populations. Nevertheless, it is likely that mechanical loading dominates as a cause of variability, particularly in comparisons between groups that are genetically similar.

The evidence connecting increased cross-sectional second moments of area or section moduli with increased loadings on bones is abundant. Body weight has an important effect (Pomeroy et al., 2018), which is why we standardise for it prior to analysis. As regards activity patterns, there is a wide range of human data and animal experimental evidence for an association with bone cross-sectional properties. The human data mostly come from studies of athletes. Comparisons of bone in the playing and non-playing arms of individuals engaged in competitive racket sports (e.g. Jones et al., 1977; Trinkaus et al., 1994; Haapasalo et al., 2000; Bass et al., 2002; Kontulainen et al., 2003) and sports involving repetitive throwing (Warden et al., 2014) are particularly useful as they allow the effects of differences in limb function within individuals to be studied, hence intrinsically controlling for other factors such as age, nutrition etc. However, other studies comparing active versus less active individuals are also of value (e.g. Specker & Binkley, 2003; Iuliano-Barnes et al., 2005). Experimental work with animals has been done by subjecting them to different exercise regimes or artificially imposing loads on bones. For example in one set of experiments (Robling et al., 2002; Warden et al., 2005), rat distal forelimbs were artificially loaded by axial compression (Figure 6.3). This was done (with the rats anaesthetised) in sessions at regular intervals over a period of time. Because the rat ulna is naturally curved, most of the compressive force was translated into a mediolateral bending force (Figure 6.3). Results showed that there was no increase in cortical bone density, but there were changes in the amount and distribution of bone in cross-section. Bone was added mainly in the medio-lateral plane (Figure 6.3), so that second moment of area in this plane increased by 83% compared with an increase of only 14% on the antero-posterior plane. This particular study provides experimental evidence illustrating some key points. Bone responds to load not by changes in material properties, such as density, but by increasing the amount of bone and by alterations in its distribution in cross-section; bone is added principally in the plane where the bending loads are greatest.

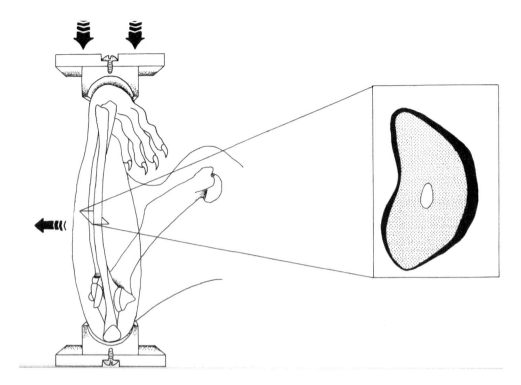

Figure 6.3 Results of experimental loading of the rat ulna by Robling and co-workers (Robling et al., 2002). Because of the natural curvature of the ulna, most of the compressive load applied to the bone by the apparatus was translated to lateral bending strain. Following completion of the experiment, study of the bone cross-section revealed new bone formation (shaded black), mainly on the medial and lateral surfaces, the areas of greatest strain

Source: After Warden et al. (2005: Fig. 1).

As well as indicating that bone responds to mechanical stimuli, overviews of the animal and human studies (Pearson & Lieberman, 2004; Ruff et al., 2006; Wallace et al., 2017) seem to demonstrate the following points. Repetitive, dynamic loading of high intensity has the most effect. Although adults do retain a capacity to increase bone strength in response to exercise, bones are most responsive during the growth period. In addition, during the growth period, exercise tends to increase subperiosteal bone deposition whereas in adulthood its main effect seems to be to reduce endosteal resorption which is less beneficial to strength or rigidity.

The lesser responsiveness in adulthood of bone to mechanical stimuli may mean that cross-sectional properties of an adult long-bone disproportionately reflect adolescent activity patterns. However, it is noteworthy that in many traditional societies, behaviours characteristic of adults are initiated in adolescence, so studies of adult bones should still shed light on 'adult' behaviours even in bone laid down during adolescence (Ruff et al., 2006). However, activity differences between groups or individuals will be more visible if those differences in activities were already established in adolescence than if they were initiated some time during adult life (Knüsel, 1993).

Archaeological work using long-bone cross-sectional properties

By studying second moments of area or section moduli in different planes, workers have attempted to shed light on the orientations of loadings on bones in life. Investigation of polar second moments of area or section moduli have been used to shed light on overall bone rigidity or strength, and hence on the general degree of bending and torsional forces upon a bone. Most work has been comparative, either comparing results from different populations or else sub-groups within a particular population, and most has concentrated on adults.

Work on lower limb cross-sectional geometry helps shed light on aspects of mobility of past populations. For example, Pomeroy (2013) studied femora and tibiae in prehistoric skeletons from San Pedro de Atacama, Chile. Long-distance trade was important economically throughout the periods studied (AD500-1450). Polar second moments of area were lowest in the Middle Horizon (AD500–1000) (Figure 6.4). This suggests lesser mobility, consistent with other evidence that the settlement had a role as a mercantile hub. Values were higher at the subsequent transition to the Late Intermediate Period. This was felt consistent with evidence of a decline in importance of the settlement as a trading centre consequent upon the collapse of the civilisation at Tiwanaku to the north. The disruption of trading networks that this entailed meant that more of the San Pedro de Atacama population would have become actively involved in walking long distances with pack animals for trading purposes. Late Intermediate Period skeletons also showed shape differences in femoral and tibial shaft cross-sections with relatively greater antero-posterior reinforcement. This is also consistent with greater mobility: during locomotion, muscular forces from the quadriceps, hamstrings and calf muscles place increased antero-posterior loads on the femur and tibia.

Cross-sectional geometry of upper limb bones will potentially be an indicator of manual tasks. Other than in groups heavily reliant upon paddled water transport (Weiss, 2003), the human upper limb is free from functional constraints imposed by loadings related to movement around the environment. Studies have focussed on tasks associated with subsistence (Ogilvie & Hilton, 2011), warfare (Rhodes & Knüsel, 2005), craft and other activities (Mays, 2007). The following examples illustrate some of the archaeological questions that can be investigated using upper and lower limb long-bone cross-sectional geometry.

The case of the lop-sided Neanderthals

Neanderthals are premodern humans who lived in Europe and parts of western Asia between about 30,000 and 230,000 years ago, a period corresponding to the Middle Palaeolithic. Neanderthals were succeeded by anatomically modern man in the Upper Palaeolithic (30,000–10,000 years ago) (Churchill, 2014). Study of Neanderthal humeri (Trinkaus et al., 1994) indicates that they show remarkable left-right asymmetries in diaphyseal cross-sectional properties. Neanderthal right humeri are generally markedly more robust than the left, consistent with the idea that Neanderthals were predominantly right-handed like ourselves. The degree of asymmetry is greater than that usually found

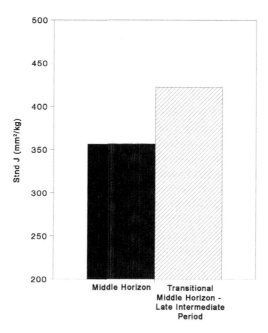

Figure 6.4 Femoral midshaft polar second moment of area for Middle Horizon and Transitional Middle Horizon – Late Intermediate periods at San Pedro de Atacama, Chile. Polar second moments of area are standardised by bone length and estimated body mass

Source: Figures calculated from Pomeroy (2013: Table 1).

in later human groups and approaches that seen in modern tennis players (Table 6.3). This is true of males at least; there was only one Neanderthal female skeleton with both humeri intact available for study and she was less asymmetrical. Assuming that they were not early exponents of racket sports, the question naturally arises as to what Neanderthal men were doing to make their humeri so asymmetric.

Studies of bone and stone points reveal that in the later part of the Middle Palaeolithic through to the earlier Upper Palaeolithic they begin to show features suggestive of a concern with aerodynamics and penetrating ability, implying the advent of projectile hunting weapons (Schmitt et al., 2003). Prior to this, hunters were likely equipped with hand-held close-range weaponry, such as heavy wooden thrusting spears, examples of which have occasionally been found (Churchill, 2014: 61-67). Could forceful use of a heavy thrusting spear result in significant asymmetrical loading of left and right arms, and hence be a possible factor responsible for the humeral asymmetry seen in Neanderthals?

To help find this out, Schmitt et al. (2003) conducted an experiment. They asked volunteers to thrust a large metal rod into a padded target. They placed strain gauges on the rod to collect data on the force applied to it by the trailing and leading hands (Figure 6.5). As one would expect, the volunteers naturally held the rod with their dominant (generally

Table 6.3 Median values for some humeral cross-sectional properties in males in European Palaeolithic material, in four later archaeological groups, and in two modern samples.

	N	Asymmetry in J	N	Right I_{ap}/I_{ml}	N	Left I_{ap}/I_{ml}
Neanderthals	4	53.1	6	1.27	5	1.30
Early Upper Palaolithic	3	21.7	5	1.31	6	1.22
Late Upper Palaeolithic	6	50.9	9	1.16	7	1.12
Aleuts (Alaska, hunter-gatherers)	24	16.4	19	1.04	16	1.02
Jomon (Japan, hunter-gatherers)	10	6.4	10	0.90	10	0.89
Pueblo (USA, agricultural)	14	16.8	16	0.89	19	0.87
Wharram Percy (UK, agricultural)	64	7.4	64	1.16	64	1.19
Modern US Whites	19	7.5	19	1.21	20	1.19
Modern tennis players	34	68.5	-	-	-	-

Notes: Assymmetry in J, asymmetry in polar second moment of area measured as 100 x (max-min)
/min; I_{ap}/I_{ml}, ratio of second moment of area in antero-posterior plane to that in the medio-lateral
plane. All data measured on the humeral shaft 35% of the way from the distal end. Data sources:
Churchill et al., 1996; Mays, 2007 and unpublished data; Ruff et al., 1994.

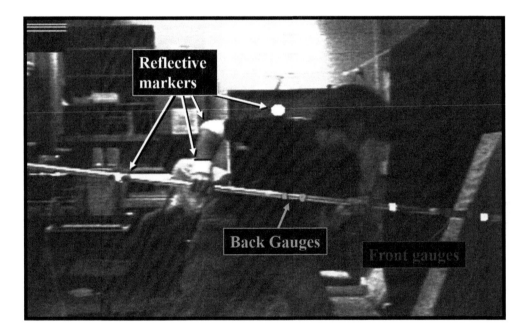

Figure 6.5 Still-frame from a video record of the spear-thrusting experiments of Schmitt
et al. (2003)

Source: reproduced from Schmitt et al. (2003: Fig. 1).

right) arms as the trailing limb. Schmitt et al. found that, on average, the force applied by
the trailing limb was 1.7 times that of the leading limb – the main function of the trailing
limb was to provide the force, that of the leading one was mainly to guide the end of the
implement toward the target. The loads on the 'spear' were considerable, averaging twice

body weight. This suggests that although the use of a thrusting spear is a two-handed activity, it could nevertheless potentially lead to considerable humeral asymmetry. As well as showing high asymmetry, compared with the other groups in Table 6.3, the Neanderthal humeral shafts have a high I_{ap}/I_{ml} ratio, suggesting that they are particularly adapted to resist antero-posterior bending loads. Use of a thrusting spear would be expected to load the upper limbs predominantly in this plane (Churchill et al., 1996). The I_{ap}/I_{ml} data for the Early Upper Palaeolithic males were broadly similar to that for the Neanderthals, although their humeri were less asymmetric. Schmitt and colleagues suggest that both Neanderthal and Early Upper Palaeolithic hunters relied heavily on thrusting spears.

The Late Upper Palaeolithic male humeri are, like those from Neanderthals, highly asymmetrical. However, unlike the Neanderthals or the Early Upper Palaeolithic males, their cross sections have I_{ap}/I_{ml} ratios closer to unity indicating more a more circular shape (Table 6.3). This indicates bones adapted to resisting bending in multiple directions and/or to resisting torsion. Schmitt et al. (2003) note that throwing involves torsional loads on the humerus, and so the high degree of asymmetry, together with the more rounded humeral cross sections in Late Upper Palaeolithic males may indicate that projectile weaponry, such as throwing spears, started to predominate in hunting strategies in this period.

The interpretation that the asymmetry in Neanderthal humeri reflects use of thrusting spears for hunting has been challenged. Shaw et al. (2012) suggest it might reflect not hunting, but another activity that was probably vital to Neanderthals, processing of animal hides. Climate in Eurasia varied a great deal during the 200,000 years when it was home to Neanderthals. This period encompassed both glacial and interglacial phases, but temperatures would generally have been significantly lower than they are today. Palaeoclimatic reconstruction suggests Neanderthals must have tolerated mean winter temperatures down to about −20°C during the colder phases (Churchill, 2014: 113). Although direct archaeological evidence is lacking, they must have used clothing and constructed shelters to help protect themselves from the cold (White, 2006). Recent groups inhabiting Earth's colder regions made good use of animal hides to fashion clothing and build tents to shelter in, and Neanderthals probably did the same. Before hides can be used, the inner surfaces need to be scraped clean of fat and muscle tissue. Stone scrapers (Figure 6.6) are ubiquitous in Middle Palaeolithic finds assemblages (e.g. Rios-Garaizar, 2010; McPherron et al., 2018). Microscopic polishing on their edges and minute residues on their surfaces indicate that in many cases they had been used for hide-scraping (Hardy & Moncel, 2011; Pawlik & Thissen, 2011). In some instances, they show residues of pitch produced by heating birch bark, material known to have been used at this time for hafting (Grünberg, 2002). This suggests that these scrapers were sometimes equipped with handles, presumably of wood (Pawlik & Thissen, 2011).

Shaw et al. (2012) conducted experiments using volunteers that involved both scraping and spear thrusting tasks. They measured the electrical activity in two major muscles of the chest and shoulder using electrodes. Surprisingly, during spear-thrusting, they found that it was the non-dominant (left) side that produced the stronger signals, suggesting that the two muscles were producing greater force on that side. When scraping was conducted as a one-handed task, the results showed, unsurprisingly, that there was greater electrical activity in the muscles of the limb wielding the tool.

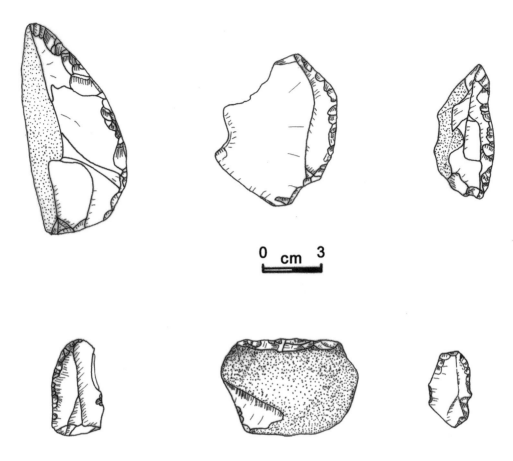

Figure 6.6 Middle Palaeolithic stone scrapers
Source: after Rios-Garaizar (2010) and McPherron et al. (2018).

Shaw et al.'s (2012) finding of greater activity in muscles associated with the upper humerus on the non-dominant side during spear thrusting is puzzling and rather counter-intuitive (Churchill, 2014: 232). It appears to contradict the results of Schmitt et al.'s earlier study although, unlike Schmitt and colleagues, Shaw et al. (2012) did not actually measure the force delivered to the spear by the left and right arms. Their finding of greater muscle use in the dominant limb during one-handed scraping is unremarkable and would presumably characterise any unimanual task, but nevertheless the idea that hide processing was a key activity that might have contributed to the humeral asymmetry deserves consideration. Although it seems reasonable to assume that Neanderthal man spent only a small proportion of his waking hours thrusting spears into animals, hide processing is a lengthy business that would have potentially have consumed a greater proportion of his time. However, it would only work as an explanation if hide processing by Neanderthals was primarily carried out unimanually and that it was an activity of sufficient intensity to elicit significant bone biomechanical adaptation. As regards the first point, if more than one Middle Palaeolithic scraper was mounted in a haft, they could conceivably have formed a tool that could be wielded two-handed, but the size of lithic scrapers means that they must have been used one-handed if unhafted and probably if hafted. As regards the second point, a recent study of Native American skeletons is relevant.

Cameron et al. (2018) compared humeral cross-sectional morphology at two archaeological sites in Virginia. The first dated prior to European contact. Here, hide processing tools are rare and it is likely that deer-skin hides were used to meet the community's domestic needs rather than traded. At the post-contact site, hide scrapers were abundant, and this reflected Native people's engagement in the colonial fur trade, and the consequent high demand for deer-skins. Ethnographic evidence suggested that hide preparation would have been female labour. Given the evidence for increased hide-processing at the later site, if hide-scraping was an activity of sufficient intensity to elicit a bony biomechanical adaptation, we might expect to see differences in cross-sectional geometry, especially in females. However, when humerus cross-sectional properties were compared, differences between pre- and post-contact groups turned out to be minor.

Cameron et al.'s (2018) results might appear to throw doubt on the hide processing explanation for Neanderthal humeral asymmetry. However, because of the likely genetic influence on skeletal responsiveness to mechanical stimuli, care needs to be taken when interpreting bone cross-sectional geometric data from groups like Neanderthals, whose genetic make-up differs significantly from modern humans. If Neanderthal bones were more responsive to biomechanical stimuli than those of anatomically modern man, then a task that might elicit little alteration in cross-sectional geometry in more recent humans might have produced significant effects on a Neanderthal. The Neanderthal genome has been extensively studied, and there are differences between the Neanderthal and the modern human genome in the region harbouring the RUNX2 gene, which is known to affect skeletal physiology (Green et al., 2010; Wallace et al., 2017). If future studies can determine the precise differences in RUNX2 in Neanderthals then it may be possible to shed light on the extent to which genetically mediated differences in bone mechano-responsiveness may have influenced Neanderthal skeletal morphology (Wallace et al., 2017).

The Neanderthal humeral asymmetry data present a number of other difficulties in interpretation besides the potential genetic influence. When dealing with material from the Palaeolithic age, the scarcity of remains means that number of skeletons available for study is low (Table 6.3). This means that it is difficult to verify patterns statistically, and in the Neanderthal case, meant that patterning seen in males could not be adequately compared with that in females which would have helped to place the male results in context and potentially have shed light on differences in gender roles. Another difficulty is that to tie together the osteological data with the other archaeological evidence, we inevitably emphasise in our explanations patterns of specific behaviour that leave archaeological traces. This of course biases our interpretations. In the case of the Neanderthals, hunting with hand-held spears and hide-processing are not mutually exclusive explanations – both may have contributed to the bilateral asymmetry observed in the humerus cross-sectional geometry, but so may myriad other tasks that are now lost to us. For later periods, skeletal material is more plentiful, and there is more opportunity to integrate data from the bones with other sources of evidence to aid interpretations.

Food procurement and processing in different environments: the Stone Age of southern Africa

Combined study of lower and upper limb cross-sectional properties has often been used in an effort to provide a fuller picture of activity patterns. Cameron and Stock (2018) used this integrated approach to study subsistence among Late Stone Age (from approximately 10,000 years ago to the time of European contact) groups from three different regions in southern Africa: the Cape Coast, the southern interior and the Namib Desert (Figure 6.7). These populations were genetically similar to one another, but the ecology of the three areas is very different. The Cape Coast has a Mediterranean climate and is a resource-rich landscape. The interior region is semi-arid, and the Namib Desert is a resource-poor, hyper-arid location.

   Subsistence in all three regions was based around hunting and gathering but with variable amounts of stock herding. Energetic costs of foraging for food resources can be divided into search costs, and handling costs associated with processing and cooking. Cameron & Stock reasoned that search costs are linked closely to mobility of humans in the landscape, and hence potentially to lower limb cross sectional properties. Handling costs are allied to tool technologies and manual tasks, and hence are likely to be linked to upper limb morphology.

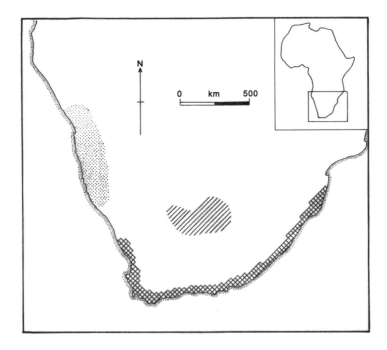

Figure 6.7 Southern Africa, showing coastal (cross-hatched), interior (hatched) and Namib Desert (shaded) regions

Source: after Cameron & Stock (2018: Fig. 1).

Historically documented gender-division of labour in groups from this region involves men hunting game and women gathering and processing plant foods. Southern African rock art also depicts these activities (Vinnicombe, 1976). Hunting involved spears and bows and arrows, whose use would have differentially loaded the left and right upper limbs. Women traditionally used grinding stones to prepare plant foods, and digging sticks to unearth roots and tubers (Figure 6.8). Digging sticks are long sticks, sharpened at one end, and are often weighted with a pierced stone to aid penetration of hard ground. Both grinding stones and digging sticks would have been used two-handed. Against this background, Cameron and Stock (2018) hypothesised that there should be greater humeral asymmetry in males than in females, and that as food resources became sparser with increasing aridity, mobility in the landscape would increase and that this would be reflected in greater lower limb rigidity. To test these hypotheses they studied cross-sectional properties in humeri, femora and tibiae from a total of 155 skeletons from these three regions.

Results showed that, for the humerus, polar second moments of area increase progressively from the Cape Coast, to interior, to Namib Desert regions in females, but there was no trend in males. Asymmetry showed no trend by region but was generally greater in males than in females (overall mean asymmetry for males was 20.8% versus

Figure 6.8 Rock art from South Africa. The woman is about to dig up a tuberous plant using her weighted digging stick. She has a tassled bag slung around her shoulders

Source: After Vinnicombe (1976: Fig. 188).

8.0% for females for the regions combined, and the male mean exceeded the female mean in each region). In the lower limb, polar second moments of area tended to be greater in the Cape Coast, and both femora and tibiae were more strengthened in the antero-posterior relative to the mediolateral plane in this region than in the interior or Namib Desert zones (Figure 6.9).

For the humerus, the asymmetry difference between the sexes accorded with the expectation that male subsistence activities placed more asymmetrical loads on the upper body. The lack of association between environmental zone and humeral rigidity for males suggested that male tasks may have been fairly similar in the different areas. The increased humeral rigidity in females in more arid environments may have reflected the greater difficulty in winning plant resources from hard, dry, stony soils, together with a need to increase processing with grinding stones in order to maximise the nutritional benefit of sparse or poor-quality resources.

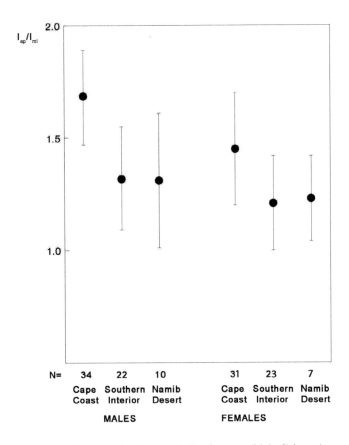

Figure 6.9 Ratio of second moments of area at the femur midshaft in antero-posterior and medio-lateral planes in skeletal material from southern Africa

Notes: N=number of individuals, the spot represents the mean, the lines ±1 standard deviation.
Source: Data from Cameron & Stock (2018).

The patterning in the lower limb cross-sectional properties was not as hypothesised on the basis of foraging theory. The greater rigidity of lower limb bones in Cape Coast populations suggests greater biomechanical demands upon the lower limb, and the greater antero-posterior buttressing in bones from this area is also consistent with this: as we saw earlier in this chapter, during locomotion, muscular forces on the femur and tibia are concentrated in the antero-posterior plane. Cameron and Stock (2018) suggest the lower limb data might be explicable in terms of topography. The Cape Coast region has a more complex and rugged topography than the interior and Namib Desert areas. This may have increased energetic costs of locomotion in search of food despite the greater resource richness of the region. Studies in other areas of the world have reported similar relationships between lower limb bone diaphyseal morphology and terrain (e.g. Holt et al., 2018).

In summary, the theoretical suggestion that, for foraging societies, energetics associated with obtaining and processing foods would leave traces in upper limb bone morphologies appeared largely to be borne out by the data: the patterning was intelligible in terms of gender-related patterns of activity inferred from other sources of evidence. The results from lower limb morphology were not as hypothesised based on resource availability in the different environments, but may have reflected increased energetics involved in resource searching in a more topographically complex environment. This reinforces the importance of considering terrain as well as mobility when making interpretations (Cameron & Stock, 2018).

Summary

Most osteometric work on the post-cranial skeleton has concentrated on the long-bones. In adults, formulae exist by which stature can be estimated from the lengths of the various limb long-bones. In children, post-cranial metric data can be plotted against dental age to study growth. In most cases this is done simply using the raw measurements but, because femur length in children bears a regular relationship to stature, growth in standing height can also be investigated. Growth in children is adversely affected by poor nutrition and a heavy disease burden. Adult stature is also affected by these same factors, but to a lesser extent than height-for-age in childhood. Studies of childhood growth and adult stature have each been used to investigate living conditions for children in past populations.

Studies, both on animals and in man, indicate that, within limits, increased mechanical forces upon a long-bone shaft tend to lead to changes that result in increased strength and rigidity. These alterations primarily consist of thickening of the cortical bone walls, together with widening of the diaphysis as a whole so that more bone is distributed further away from the central axis. The amount and distribution of bone in a shaft cross-section can be assessed using a variety of methods, including CT or radiography. The relationship between cross-sectional properties and mechanical loadings placed upon a bone in life has led to extensive research using these parameters to provide insights into activity patterns in the past. Most work has been comparative, of subgroups within a population or of different populations. In this way researchers have studied ways in which activity patterns relate to gender, social status, subsistence strategy and other variables.

Further reading

For a review of methods of estimating stature from adult skeletons see Willey, P. (2016). Stature Estimation, pp. 308–321 in S. Blau & D. Ubelaker (eds) *Handbook of Forensic Archaeology and Anthropology*, 2nd edition. World Archaeological Congress Handbooks in Archaeology, Routledge, London.

Mays, S. (2018) The Study of Growth in Skeletal Populations, pp. 71–89 in S. Crawford, D.M. Hadley & G. Shepherd (eds) *The Oxford Handbook of the Archaeology of Childhood*. Oxford University Press, Oxford, *considers growth studies in archaeology, and highlights some of the methodological issues in this type of work.*

For overviews of methods and archaeological applications of bone cross-sectional measurements to study activity regimes in past populations see Larsen, C.S. (2015). *Bioarchaeology. Interpreting Behavior from the Human Skeleton*, 2nd edition. Cambridge University Press: Cambridge, pp 308–321 *and* Ruff C. (2019) Biomechanical Analyses of Archaeological Human Skeletons, pp. 189–224 in M.A. Katzenberg & A.L. Grauer (eds) *Biological Anthropology of the Human Skeleton*, 3rd edition, Wiley, Chichester.

7 Non-metric variation

The term 'non-metric variation' is generally taken to encompass any minor variation or anomaly of skeletal anatomy not normally recorded by measurement. Non-metric traits are usually recorded as being either present or absent, or else on an ordinal scale according to their degree of development.

Several hundred non-metric variants have been described for the human bones and teeth (Saunders & Rainey, 2008). For some, there is evidence for a degree of genetic control, and so they have been used to investigate biological relationships between populations or individuals. Others appear to develop primarily in response to non-genetic factors. For example, some seem to be related to biomechanical forces, and have been studied for the light they may throw on activity patterns in the past. For many other traits, however, their causation remains uncertain.

Because they are so heterogeneous, classifying non-metric traits can be problematic. In order to try and illustrate the range of variants which may be encountered in human skeletal material, a six-point classification for bony traits, and a four-fold categorisation of dental variants, are used here.

A classification of non-metric skeletal variants

Bony variants

1. Variations in the numbers of bones. The adult skeleton normally consists of 206 bones. However, fewer or extra elements may be present.

    Extra, or supernumerary, bones may be normal in form (e.g. in the spine an extra vertebra may be present), but more often they are small and irregular in morphology, and are known as ossicles. A particularly common site for supernumerary ossicles is within the cranial sutures, where they may occur singly or in numbers. The lambdoid suture, which separates the occipital bone from the parietal bones at the back of the cranium, is a particularly frequent location (Figure 7.1). Small supernumerary bones are also common in the ankles and wrists (O'Rahilly, 1953). Missing bones are much less common than extra bones.

2. Anomalies of bone fusion. Component parts of a bone may fail to fuse together, or normally discrete skeletal structures may instead be fused. An example of the former is metopism – the retention of the metopic suture in the skull. In the foetus, the frontal bone in the skull is formed via intra-membranous ossification from two halves which make up the left and right sides of the bone. These two parts generally

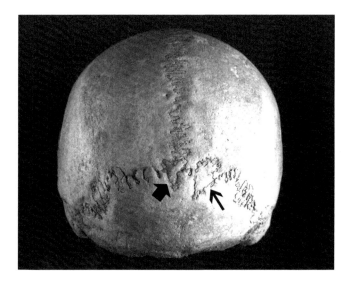

Figure 7.1 Posterior view of a cranium showing an ossicle at the lambda (thick arrow) and
        a lambdoid ossicle (thin arrow)

fuse in the first few years of life to form a single bone. On occasion, however, they
fail to unite, so that the division persists. In such cases, the two parts meet at the
midline in a suture of similar form to those between the other bones of the cranial
vault. This suture is called the metopic suture (Figure 7.2).
3.   Variation in bony foramina. A foramen (pl. foramina) is a small hole in a bone that gener-
     ally transmits a blood vessel and/or nerve. Variants may consist of the presence of

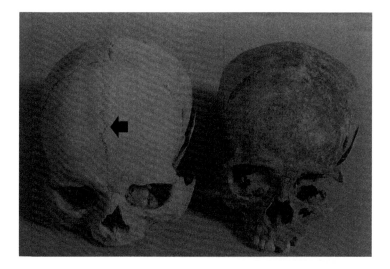

Figure 7.2 The cranium on the left shows retention of the metopic suture. The skull on the
        right is of normal form for comparison

a foramen where none is normally found, or a foramen may be missing where it is usual to find one. The positions of foramina may also vary with respect to features such as cranial sutures etc.

Traits of this type are the skeletal manifestations of variations in the degree and location of branching in nerves or blood vessels. An example of this sort of trait is the presence of parietal foramina. The parietal foramen takes the form of a small hole piercing the parietal bone of the cranial vault, near the midline (Figure 7.3). It transmits a small vein.

4. Articular facet variations. In a human skeleton, the part of the bone at a joint which bore the articular cartilage in life may be recognised, since, as long as it is not diseased, it is of smoother appearance than non-articular bone. Variation in the form of these joint surfaces may occur. Variants may consist of simple extensions or elongations to normal joint surfaces, or else a joint surface may be split into two separate facets. Alternatively, all or part of a joint surface may be in an anomalous position, or small extra articulations may be present. Examples of this type of non-metric trait are the so-called squatting facets which may be present on the distal (lower) end of the tibia. Here, the distal joint surface of the tibia extends onto the anterior surface of the bone (Figure 7.4).

5. Hyperostoses: traits characterised by a localised excess of bone formation. Hyperostoses may take the form of bony spurs or protuberances at sites in the skeleton which do not normally have them. An example is the posterior bridge on the atlas vertebra, the uppermost cervical vertebra, which articulates with the cranial base. On each side of the superior surface of the posterior arch of the atlas is a groove, within which runs an

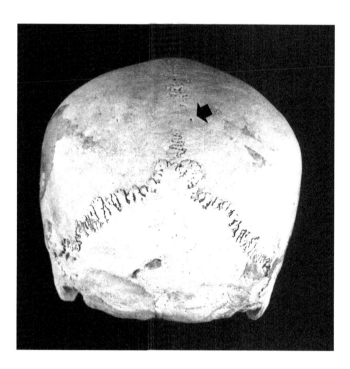

Figure 7.3 A parietal foramen (arrow) is present on the right parietal bone; the trait is absent on the left parietal

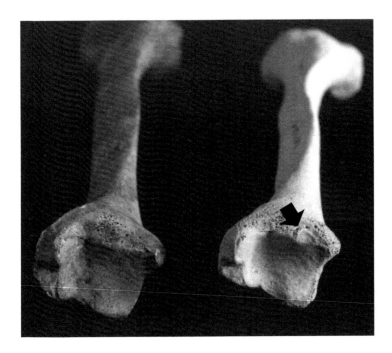

Figure 7.4 The tibia on the right shows a squatting facet (arrow); that on the left is normal
        for comparison

artery and a nerve. Occasionally, a spur of bone running between the articular facet and
the posterior arch transforms this groove into a foramen, through which the nerve and
artery pass (Figure 7.5). This trait is classed here as a hyperostosis rather than
a foraminal variant, as the bony variant is not accompanied by alteration in the anatomy
of the nerve or blood vessel.

Some broader bony overgrowths are called tori (singular, torus). Frequent sites for
tori are the upper and lower jaws. For example, the palatine torus is a low bony ridge
along the midline of the lower surface of the bones which form the hard palate in the
roof of the mouth (Figure 7.6). They may also form in the ear canal, where they are
called auditory tori.

Alterations that predominantly consist of hyperostosis may also occur at places (called
entheses) where ligaments or muscles attach to the skeleton. Sometimes this may be part
of a syndrome of changes caused by certain diseases, but the type of alterations we are
concerned with here occur in the absence of disease. Depending upon the type of enthesis,
new bone formation may take the form either of general roughening and increased prominence, or else marginal bony spurring coupled with new bone deposition on the entheseal
surface. These changes are described in more detail later on in this chapter.

6. Hypo-ostoses: traits characterised by a localised deficiency of bone. Hypo-ostoses
    are perforations or depressions in bones which do not normally bear them. An
    example of a hypo-ostosis is the septal aperture of the humerus, in which the thin
    plate of bone above the distal joint surface is perforated (Figure 7.7).

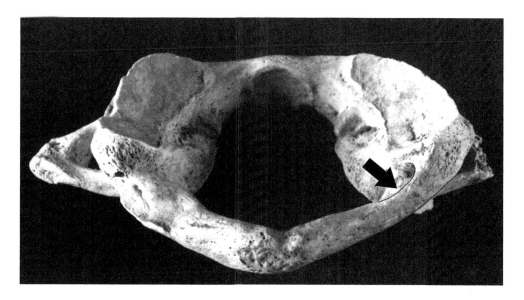

Figure 7.5 An atlas vertebra shows the posterior atlas bridging trait on the right side (arrowed); the trait is absent on the left side

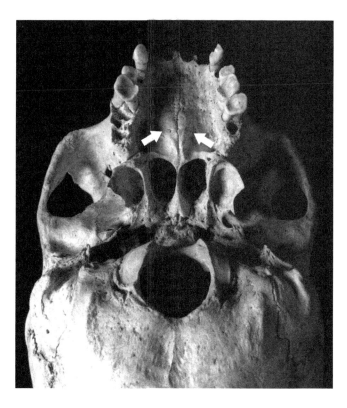

Figure 7.6 The bones forming the hard palate show development of a bony torus along the midline (arrows)

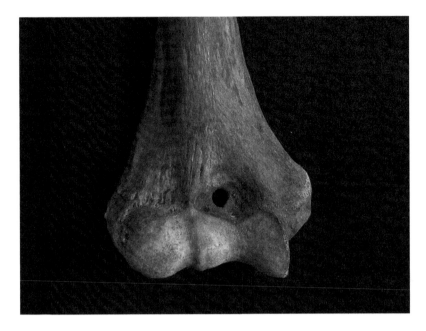

Figure 7.7 The distal part of a right humerus (anterior view). The hole above the distal joint surface is a septal aperture

Dental variants

1. Variation in number of teeth. Unlike the bones, missing elements are more usual than extra teeth. The tooth which most often fails to form is the third molar, or wisdom tooth, but other teeth may also occasionally be absent.
2. Morphological variations affecting the whole tooth. A tooth may be markedly reduced in size and, in such cases, it is often also of abnormal form. Most often affected are third molars and permanent upper lateral incisors; these reduced teeth may be of peg-shaped form (Figure 7.8).
3. Variations in crown morphology. These comprise the majority of dental variants described and used by osteoarchaeologists. These include variations in crown shape, the presence of extra cusps, and more minor variants such as differences in the pattern of pits and fissures on molar or premolar teeth.

    An example of a crown shape variant in the so-called shovel-shaped incisor. This trait (which is generally restricted to the maxillary incisors) takes the form of ridges near the margins of the lingual (inner) surface of the incisor crown, which transform the normally fairly flat lingual surface into a concavity (Figure 7.9).

    One of the more common supernumerary cusps is the Carabelli cusp. This may be found on the antero-medial (mesio-lingual in dental terminology) aspect of a maxillary molar (Figure 7.10).
4. Root variants. The most common of these are variations in root numbers. A tooth may show an extra root. For example, the mandibular canine may sometimes bear two roots

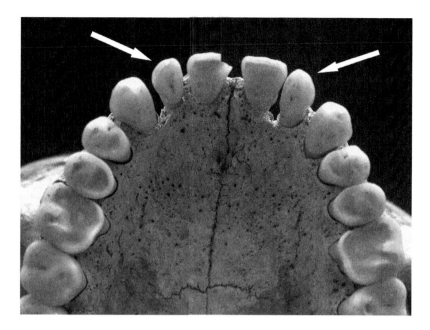

Figure 7.8 An adult dentition showing reduced, peg-shaped maxillary lateral incisors (arrowed)

instead of one (Figure 7.11). Multi-rooted teeth may sometimes show a reduction in root number by union of two or more roots. For example, the mandibular second and third molars are normally twin-rooted but quite often these may instead be fused together into a single root.

The nature of non-metric variation

Most non-metric variants cause no symptoms – you or I may have many of the non-metric traits discussed in this chapter in our own skeletons and be quite unaware of them. They can be considered as part of normal variation. However, the presence of some variants may cause problems. For example, auditory tori, if large, may lead to earache and predispose to ear infections (Moore et al., 2010). A posterior atlas bridge may impinge upon the adjacent nerve and artery and lead to symptoms such as headache or dizziness (Pękala et al., 2017). Certain entheseal changes occur in response to repeated microtraumata of the enthesis and so are considered overuse injuries. The boundary between normal and pathological variation may sometimes be rather blurred.

Causes of non-metric variation

The causes of non-metric variants have been studied for many years and both genetic and non-genetic factors have been investigated.

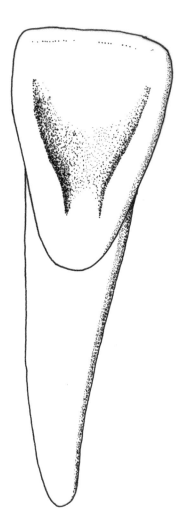

Figure 7.9 A shovel-shaped maxillary permanent central incisor. Normally the lingual surface of the incisor crown is fairly flat, but in this example ridges at its margins
create a shovel shape

Genetic influences

Many of the non-metric variants that have been described in the human skeleton have
analogues in the skeletons of other mammals. Animal studies, most notably on laboratory
mice, have contributed significantly to our understanding of the cause of this type of
morphological variation. In particular, they have addressed the question of the extent to
which traits are under genetic control. This work began, and was carried out most inten-
sively, during the 1950s and 60s (Grüneberg, 1951, 1952, 1963; Berry & Searle, 1963), and
has continued more sporadically ever since (e.g. Self & Leamy, 1978; Cheverud & Buikstra, 1981; Richtsmeier & McGrath, 1986; Nomura et al., 2003; Kangas et al., 2004; Zimmerman et al., 2019).

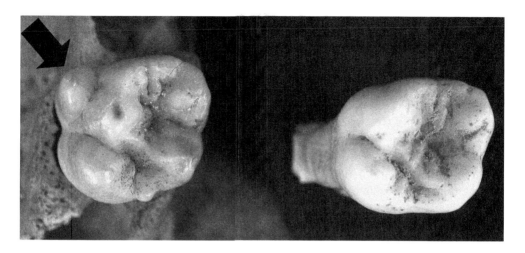

Figure 7.10 A left maxillary permanent molar showing a large Carabelli cusp (arrowed) on its mesio-lingual surface. The other molar is a normal specimen for comparison

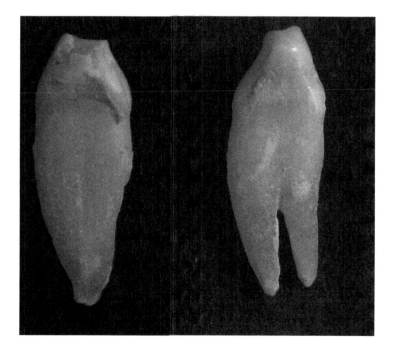

Figure 7.11 A twin-rooted mandibular permanent canine. The canine next to it is of normal morphology for comparison

Taken as a whole, the animal work suggests that many traits have a genetic component in their causation, but that their expression is also affected by non-genetic factors. For example, like humans, mice may sometimes lack their third molars. It has been clear since the early breeding experiments that this trait was under a degree of genetic control (Grüneberg, 1951), and this has been repeatedly confirmed (e.g. Nomura et al., 2003). It appears that whether or not the third molar develops is dependent upon the size of the tooth germ; if it falls below a certain critical size it fails to develop, leading to absence of the third molar. The size of the tooth germ is dependent upon genes determining tooth size and overall body size, but it is also influenced by non-genetic, environmental factors. Thus, the presence or absence of the third molar is not in itself inherited, but the size of the tooth germ to some extent is. This is called a quasi-continuous trait because from a continuum of genetic variation two distinct physical types are produced – those with and without third molars. The occurrence of many other traits also seems to follow this quasi-continuous, threshold model.

In the mouse, the third molar fails to develop if the tooth germ falls below a certain size at about 5-6 days after birth – its development is arrested at this age and it regresses (Grewel, 1962). Environmental factors that may affect whether or not the third molar is missing include poor maternal nutrition while the baby mouse grows in the womb, and deficient nutrition in the growing mouse during the first five days after it is born (Searle, 1954). The expression of other non-metric traits is likewise affected by deficient nutrition, or other deleterious factors such as exposure to toxins, at critical periods in the development of the structures in question (Searle, 1954; Deol & Truslove, 1957; Dahinten & Pucciarelli, 1983; Keller et al., 2007).

In the mouse, the extent of genetic control seems to vary quite markedly between traits, but is often fairly low (Berry & Searle, 1963; Self & Leamy, 1978). Nevertheless, analyses of non-metric traits in wild-living mice and other mammals (Berry, 1979; Ansorge, 2001; Muñoz-Muñoz et al., 2003; Markov et al., 2017) have been successful in distinguishing different populations, showing that useful genetic information can be obtained from these variants.

Studies have been done on inheritance patterns of non-metric traits in human populations. Most work has been done on dental traits. Crown variants can be easily recorded by taking dental casts from the mouths of volunteers. Studies of missing third molars or other teeth are a bit more difficult, as they require radiography to distinguish true cases of absence from those where the tooth is present but unerupted, but dental radiographs are commonplace and hence a plentiful source of data.

Inheritance studies are normally done on families or on twins. Comparison of concordance in trait expression between monozygous ('identical') and dizygous ('non-identical') twins is particularly illuminating. Monozygous twins are genetically identical. Dizygous twins share on average only 50% of their genes in common, no more than ordinary siblings, but like monozygous twins they share similar environments, both within the womb and (usually) whilst growing up. If genes are responsible for expression of a trait, concordance rates should be higher between monozygous than between dizygous twins (Scott et al., 2018: 142).

Twin and familial studies can be used to calculate the heritability of a trait. Heritability is a measure of the extent to which genetics control the variation of a trait within a population (Harris, 2008). It varies from zero to one, higher values indicating greater genetic influence. However, heritability is a property not only of the trait being investigated, but also of the population's genetic composition and the environment in which its members live (Kieser, 1990: 23; Scott et al., 2018: 153). Heritability values are population-specific, and hence can be highly variable. For example, among dental traits, heritabilities of between zero and 0.91 have been reported from different twin studies for Carabelli cusp (Scott et al., 2018: Table 4.1). Because of this, care is needed in their interpretation.

A review (Scott et al., 2018: 129-165) indicates that heritability values for dental crown and root traits generally fall in the range 0.4-0.8. A recent twin study (Trakinienė et al., 2018) reports similar heritability for missing third molars. This evidence supports the idea that, although environmental factors contribute to their causation, genes are a major factor in dental traits.

Turning to bony traits, the tori of the jaws can be observed directly in dental casts so have been studied in living subjects. A recent twin study (Auškalnis et al., 2015) reported a heritability of 0.66. Study of most other bony traits is more difficult as they require medical imaging of the skeletal parts in question in order to visualise them in living people. Because they do not generally cause symptoms there has been little incentive to delve into their genetic background, or ethical justification for exposing people to the ionising radiation that would be required. Because of this, few traits have been investigated, although familial studies by Torgersen (1951a, 1951b, 1954) on metopic suture and sutural ossicles, and by Saunders and Popovich (1978) on posterior atlas bridging, suggest a degree of genetic control for these variants.

For wide-ranging studies of genetic transmission of bony non-metric traits we would need large collections of skeletons of twins or of individuals with other known close family connections. There are none of the former but, although they are very rare, a few of the latter do exist. One such is in Austria.

In many parts of Europe, bones were exhumed from burial grounds when they became full in order to make way for new burials and stored in charnel houses or ossuaries. In the 18th and 19th centuries, in Alpine regions of Austria and Germany, a tradition existed whereby exhumed crania were painted with the name of the deceased and also often decorated with painted designs of leaves and flowers. Unfortunately most collections of these painted crania were re-buried in the early years of the 20th century, but one collection which survives is that from Hallstatt, Austria (the place better known archaeologically for the large Iron Age cemetery found there).

The Hallstatt collection contains about seven hundred decorated crania (Plate 3). This collection has been studied by the Swedish osteoarchaeologist Torstein Sjøvold (Sjøvold, 1984, 1987) and, as part of his work, he investigated patterns of inheritance of some non-metric traits. He used the church records of births, marriages and deaths to reconstruct family trees. Of the 700 crania, 346 fell into 91 families for which at least two members could be identified. Working in the charnel house where the crania were stored, Sjøvold recorded an array of 30 traits for which definitions had been published by Berry and Berry (1967). He selected these variants because they are often routinely recorded in archaeological skeletons. Of these, some had to be excluded from analysis because they were very rare in the Hallstatt material. This left 25 traits whose heritabilities could be studied. Heritabilities ranged from zero to 0.95 but were generally lower than those discussed above for dental traits. Among those he found to be under significant genetic control were metopic suture, various sutural ossicles, and a group of foraminal variants, including parietal foramina.

Another, more recent familial study was carried out on skeletal remains of 34 19th–20th century individuals of known genealogical relationships excavated from tombs used by different branches of a single family in the Czech Republic (Cvrček et al., 2018). Cvrček and his colleagues evaluated more than 200 cranial and post-cranial variants, although many did not occur in sufficient frequencies to be analysed. Sample sizes were too small to permit calculation of heritabilities of individual traits, but there was a tendency for more closely related individuals to share more traits in common. This mainly reflected shared cranial traits, especially those connected with the courses and outlets of nerves and small blood vessels (few sutural ossicles could be scored because many individuals died in old age and so showed advanced suture obliteration). With a few exceptions, such as posterior atlas bridging, most post-cranial variants failed to reflect genetic relationships. To some extent this is an expected pattern as the cranial complex is more highly canalised (i.e. resistant to adverse environmental effects) (Tyrrell, 2000). It also reflects the fact that many of the post-cranial traits recorded by Cvrček et al. (2018) comprised alterations at and around joints and entheses, many of which appear to arise in response to biomechanical forces.

The influence of biomechanical factors

Extremes of motion at a joint may cause bony alteration. For example, it appears that septal aperture of the humerus may form as a result of impingement upon the septum by projections on the ulna during extremes of elbow flexion and/or extension (Mays, 2008b; Ndou, 2018). In keeping with this, there seems to be a tendency for frequencies of septal aperture to be higher in populations with greater frequencies of joint laxity leading to hypermobility (Mays, 2008b).

More sustained extreme motion at a joint appears to promote extension to the joint capsule and articular cartilage, and this is evident in dry bones as extensions to the smooth articular surface, as seen for example in squatting facets on the talus and tibia. In the squatting position there is extreme dorsiflexion of the feet – in other words, the feet are fully bent upwards at the ankles. Prolonged, passive dorsiflexion of the feet puts continuous pressure on the ankle ligaments which tend to elongate, permitting greater dorsiflexion of the joint between the tibia and the talus, leading to anterior extension of the cartilage and joint capsule and hence to the formation of squatting facets (Trinkaus, 1975). Consistent with this, squatting facets have been found to be common in the bones from populations known habitually to rest in the squatting posture. For example they are frequent in south Asians and Australian Aboriginals, but are rare in recent Europeans (Dixit et al., 2012). In an archaeological study (Mays, 2007), they were found to be common at Mediaeval Wharram Percy, a community in which chairs are likely to have been a rarity, but were hardly seen among 18th–19th century middle-class Londoners who would certainly have sat on chairs rather than squatted in repose.

The way in which biomechanical forces influence alterations at entheses is discussed later on in this chapter.

Recording non-metric traits

As with osteological measurements, the precise definitions of non-metric traits vary somewhat between writers, so that it is important to state whose trait definitions one is following. For dental traits, the most widely used scoring system is the one known as the Arizona State University Dental Anthropology System (ASUDAS) that was devised by Christy Turner and his colleagues (Turner et al., 1991). This scheme defines, describes and illustrates some 38 dental traits (Scott & Irish, 2017). Most studies do not use all these traits: for example, some features are difficult to record when tooth wear is significant (Burnett et al., 2013), and some variants are only seen in particular geographic populations. Dental traits are usually scored into grades of expression. For example, ASUDAS recognises eight grades for shovelling of the incisors, ranging from no trace of marginal ridge formation through to extreme development of marginal ridges (Scott & Irish, 2017: 31–36).

For bony traits, Berry and Berry (1967) published a list of 30 cranial variants, and Finnegan (1978) has given definitions of 30 traits of the post-cranial skeleton. These trait lists are widely used. Many more traits are illustrated by Mann et al. (2016). Most bony non-metric traits are scored on a presence-absence basis. Entheseal changes are an exception, and standard scales exist for grading them. An early scheme that was widely used is that of Hawkey and Merbs (1995). More recent methods, that recognise the anatomical differences between different types of enthesis, are now preferred. They include those of Villotte (2006) and Henderson et al. (2016).

For looking at genetic relationships, presence-absence data are normally used. Indeed, most of the research work on the genetic basis of non-metric traits analysed them on this basis. For dental (and other) traits recorded according to degree of expression, scores are usually dichotomised by imposing a cut-off at some point in the scale (Scott & Irish, 2017). For studies of activity patterns using entheseal changes, sometimes grades of expression are used directly in analysis but often they too are condensed into presence-absence scores.

As may already have become apparent, most traits can potentially occur on either side of the body. For example, a parietal foramen may occur on the left and/or right parietal bones (Figure 7.3). For most bony traits, there is marked correlation between left and right sides of the body in their manifestation – most variants tend to occur on both sides of the body if they occur at all (Perizonius, 1979). When they do occur unilaterally (i.e. on one side of the body and not the other) the trait does not usually systematically favour one side over the other (McGrath et al., 1984; Hanihara & Ishida, 2001a). An exception is traits that mainly develop in response to biomechanical forces where, in the upper limb, their occurrence often favours the right side, reflecting the fact that humans are usually right handed (Villotte et al., 2010; Weiss, 2015).

Asymmetry that does not consistently favour one side or the other is called fluctuating asymmetry. Fluctuating asymmetry in the skeleton is generally a reflection of environmental disruption during development, so asymmetry in the occurrence of most non-metric traits is probably best interpreted as an effect of environmental rather than genetic factors. Consistent with this, it has been found (McGrath et al., 1984; Leamy, 1997) that asymmetry in the expression of non-metric variants is not inherited even when the presence or absence of a trait is. Therefore, when traits are recorded with the purpose of elucidating genetic relationships, cases of unilateral trait presence are often combined with cases where it is present on both sides to produce a single 'trait present' category.

There is little asymmetry in most dental traits (Scott & Pilloud, 2019), but there may be significant correlations between the manifestation of a trait between different teeth, especially of the same type. For example, if the central maxillary incisors are shovel-shaped, it is more likely that shovelling will be observed on the lateral maxillary incisors (and perhaps even on the mandibular incisors). Recording shovelling on all incisors would include redundant information. Shovelling expression is best represented by the upper central maxillary incisor, so normally only frequencies based on this tooth would be used in analysis. Similar considerations apply for other crown and root traits that may be evident on multiple teeth. As with shovelling, so-called key-teeth have been defined upon which to base frequency data (Scott & Irish, 2017).

For adults, the frequency of entheseal changes increases with age (Michopoulou et al., 2015), but the age effect on other bony non-metric traits generally seems minor (Berry, 1975). In children, some non-metric traits cannot be recorded. For example, metopic suture cannot be scored in infants and young children, as it is only after the first few years of life that it becomes apparent whether the suture will fuse in the normal way or will be retained. Joint surface variants, such as squatting facets, are also difficult to score in the child skeleton, because joint surfaces are incompletely mineralised. Even for traits which can be reliably scored in immature skeletons, their frequency may vary with age at death.

Most archaeological studies of bony non-metric traits exclude child skeletons from analysis. This is not the case for dental traits. It will be recalled that, unlike bone, dental hard tissues are not continuously turned over, so teeth, once formed, cannot change in morphology. Thus, as long as the relevant part of a permanent tooth has formed, children can be included with adults in analyses. ASUDAS describes variants in the permanent teeth, but many of the traits can also be scored in the deciduous dentition (Paul & Stojanowski, 2015; Paul et al., 2020). Problems in scoring dental traits occur at the other end of the age range in archaeological populations. By middle age, not only may teeth be sufficiently worn to cause problems in scoring some crown variants, but many teeth may also have been lost. Turning to sex differences, most writers have concluded that, both for dental and bony traits, these are trivial (e.g. Hanihara & Ishida, 2001a-d; Scott et al., 2018: 128). Thus, if desired, the sexes can be lumped together for analytical purposes. The exception is for biomechanically-related variants where sex differences in expression are often observed and are potentially informative about gender differences in activities in past populations.

Application of the analysis of non-metric traits to archaeological problems

Investigation of genetic relationships

On a global scale, patterns of relationships between populations obtained from analysis of non-metric traits usually resemble those obtained from study of genetic markers (Hanihara et al., 2003; Hanihara, 2008; Irish et al., 2020). This supports the utility of non-metric variants for this purpose. On a regional scale, we saw in Chapter 5 that studies in non-metric variation in Far Eastern skeletal material provided important support for craniometric data in showing the likely immigration of farming peoples from mainland Asia into the Japanese Islands from about 900 BC onward. Non-metric traits have also been used to investigate population history in other regions of the world (e.g. Hallgrímsson et al., 2004; Nikita et al., 2012; Irish et al., 2014). However, much of the work with skeletal non-metric traits has concentrated on looking at relationships on a smaller scale, either between individuals buried at different cemeteries with a specific local area, or between people in a single cemetery.

Nancy Lovell, of the University of Alberta, Canada, and colleagues studied cranial and dental non-metric variation in skeletons from three cemeteries at the ancient Egyptian site at Naqada (Figure 7.12). The cemeteries date to 3600-3000BC and belong to the Pre-Dynastic period, before the Royal dynasties established a unified Egyptian state and built their well-known monumental architecture, such as the Pyramids of Giza. The excavations at Naqada were carried out in the late 19th century by Sir William Flinders Petrie (Petrie, 1896). There were three cemeteries (Figure 7.12), Cemetery B, Cemetery T and the Great Cemetery, located near a settlement Petrie called South Town. The burials were flexed inhumations; as was usual in this early period, artificial mummification was not practiced. Grave goods consisted of pots and other craft items. The three cemeteries differed in size. Petrie's site plans show 2043 graves in the Great Cemetery, 144 graves from Cemetery B and 69 graves in Cemetery T (Petrie, 1896; Bard, 1989). The field records are problematic, but although it is unlikely that all burials were located, recorded or excavated, it seems probable that cemetery T contained the fewest graves. As well as being smaller, Cemetery T was also richer in grave goods, both in quantity of items and in an increased frequency of items made from exotic materials, such as gold, silver or marble (Bard, 1989). Cemetery T is therefore generally considered to be for an elite segment of Naqada society.

Study of Pre-Dynastic archaeology is crucial to our understanding of the rise of a hierarchical society in Egypt. A major milestone along the road to social complexity is the establishment of elite lineages – i.e. where high social status is ascribed at birth rather than achieved in life. The aim of Lovell and colleagues' work (Johnson & Lovell, 1994; Prowse & Lovell, 1996) was to shed light on whether the high status burials of Cemetery T likely derived from distinct lineages. A total of about 130 skulls survive from the three cemeteries. Lovell and co-workers analysed 9 dental and 47 bony non-metric traits in this material. The results are shown in Table 7.1.

The numbers in Table 7.1 are standardised mean measures of divergence (MMD). These are measures, derived from non-metric trait frequencies, of dissimilarity between

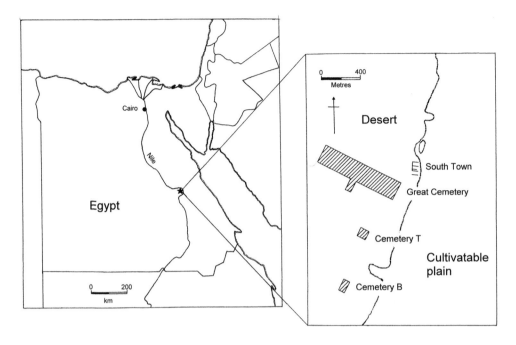

Figure 7.12 Location and site plan of the Naqada excavations of Sir William Flinders Petrie
Source: site plan after Petrie (1896)

Table 7.1 Standardised mean measures of divergence for the three cemeteries at Naqada

	Cemetery T vs Cemetery B	*Cemetery T vs the Great Cemetery*	*Cemetery B vs the Great Cemetery*
Based on cranial traits	2.847	2.033	1.363
Based on dental traits	2.889	1.601	0.219

Source: data from Johnson and Lovell (1994) and Prowse and Lovell (1996)

populations, the higher the number the more divergent the groups. Results from both the dental and the bony non-metric cranial data suggest that burials from Cemetery T are rather distinct from those from the Great Cemetery and Cemetery B which are rather similar to one another. Given the genetic component in the causation of non-metric variants, this would seem to imply that Cemetery T group were genetically distinct from the other two. One explanation that Lovell's team considered is that the burials in Cemetery T were of migrants who originated from outside the Naqada area. However, they felt this was unlikely. The style (if not the richness) of the grave goods in Cemetery T was similar to that in the other cemeteries, suggesting a common culture, and there was no independent archaeological evidence for large-scale population movements at this time. They felt a more likely interpretation was that Cemetery T was used by elite lineages from the local population. The genetic distinctiveness of the high-status Cemetery T individuals, suggested by the non-metric trait analyses, implies that, in Pre-Dynastic Naqada, elite social status was ascribed at birth rather than achieved by deeds in life.

Other studies have looked at patterning of traits within a single site or burial ground. One such was carried out on burials from Cahokia, a large prehistoric archaeological complex in Illinois, USA (Figure 7.13). In the 11th–12th centuries AD, Cahokia was a political, religious and economic centre covering more than 14 km^2 with a population of perhaps 10,000–15,000 (Emerson, 2012). The site contains a large number of monumental earthen mounds. One of these, known as Mound 72, was constructed in about AD1000 and used for about 150 years for the burial of a total of about 270 individuals. One hundred and seventy two of these were in large mass graves (Table 7.2; Figure 7.13).

Individuals in each large mass-grave had, with the likely exception of F229 Upper Layer, died at about the same time, and the idea that they had been deliberately killed seems inescapable. The remains from F105, 205, 214 and 237 were mainly young adult females, showed no signs of violence, and had been buried with care. It was suggested that these were human sacrifices, perhaps of captives taken from other groups during raiding (Fowler et al., 1999). The F229 Lower mass burials (which were separated from the Upper burials by layers of matting) were somewhat different, being more demographically mixed and apparently thrown in rather than deposited carefully. This, together with indications found on the bones of violent death, lead to suggestions that they may have been executed war captives from outside communities (Fowler et al., 1999: 76). A team led by Andrew Thompson, then of the University of Indiana, studied the remains to investigate these possibilities (Thompson et al., 2015). They conducted strontium isotope analysis (for an explanation of this approach see Chapter 11) to try and determine something about where the people buried in Mound 72 came from. Results suggested that most were local or else from some other region of similar geology, but of course that did not exclude the possibility that they came from genetically distinct communities. To look at that, they studied non-metric traits, both among the Cahokia burials, and in burials from neighbouring, approximately contemporary sites.

The soil conditions at Cahokia resulted in poor survival of bone, and even the tooth roots were badly damaged. Thompson et al. (2015) therefore concentrated on the enamel crowns,

Table 7.2 Cahokia, Mound 72 burials

Feature	Number of interments	Deposition
105	53 (28 female, 8 male; mainly young adult/adolescent)	Mass grave, careful placement of bodies
205	22 (14 female, 2 male)	Mass grave, careful placement of bodies
214	24 (16 female: 3 male)	Mass grave, careful placement of bodies
237	19 (12 females, 5 males)	Mass grave, careful placement of bodies
229 Upper Layer	15 (both sexes, adults and children)	Mass grave, evidence for curation of some bodies prior to burial
229 Lower Layer	39 (both sexes, adolescent, adult)	Mass grave, haphazard placement of bodies, some evidence for violent death
Other Mound 72 burials	Approximately 100 (both sexes, adults and children)	Various depositional contexts, high/middle social status

Data sources: Thompson (2013); Emerson et al. (2016). Number of interments: where separate figures are given for males and females, total number of burials exceeds the sum of males plus females because sex could not be determined in some individuals

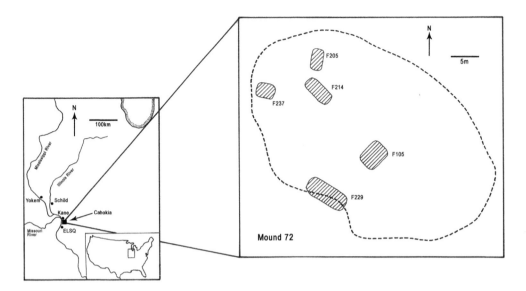

Figure 7.13 Location of Cahokia, showing Mound 72. The locations of the large mass burial
pits within Mound 72 are identified; the locations of other burial features
beneath the mound are not shown. ELSQ, East St Louis Stone Quarry Site
Source: Mound 72 site plan after Fowler et al. (1999: Figure 1.6).

analysing a series of 11 non-metric variants as well as conducting a study of dental crown
measurements. In part, the dental metric study was to determine sex in the remains – something that was needed because the poor survival of bony indicators (Thompson, 2013), but it
was also to support the dental non-metric work – dental crown measurements are also
under a significant degree of genetic control (Dempsey & Townsend, 2001). Mean measures
of divergence between the different groups of burials (the mass graves, the other burials
from Mound 72, plus burials from nearby mounds at the Kane, Yokem, Schild and East St
Louis Stone Quarry sites) were calculated and from the non-metric trait frequencies and the
results displayed using multidimensional scaling (MDS). MDS is a technique that produces,
from measures of similarity (or dissimilarity, such as MMD), a plot summarising the patterning in the divergences between the groups (Everitt & Hothorn, 2011: 105–134). In general, the
larger the MMD between two groups, the greater their separation on the MDS graph.

The results (Figure 7.14) indicate that, in terms of dental non-metric traits, the individuals from most of the large mass graves are similar to one another. They also resemble
burials from other Cahokia contexts, and burials from neighbouring sites. The exception
are the burials from F229 Lower Layer. These are rather separate from the others on
the MDS plot, implying a genetic distinction between them and the rest. Analysis of
dental measurements produced a similar pattern (Thompson et al., 2015).

Perhaps, as originally suggested, the F229 Lower burials were members of a different
community (although not, it would seem, from the Schild, Yokem, Kane or East St Louis
Stone Quarry populations) who were victims of inter-group violence. Alternatively, perhaps
they were a distinct group within Cahokia and were killed as a result of intra-community

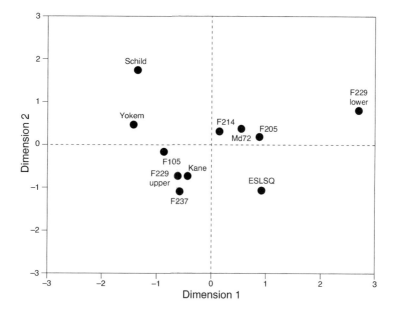

Figure 7.14 Multidimensional scaling plot of mean measures of divergence based on dental non-metric traits among the burials from Mound 72 at Cahokia and from nearby sites

Source: Thompson et al. (2015: Figure 4). Md72, Mound 72 burials not from large mass grave contexts; ESLSQ, East St Louis Stone Quarry site.

violence. By contrast, the dental data suggest that the young, predominantly female individuals in the other mass graves may have been genetically similar to other burials at Cahokia. This would seem to undermine support for the idea that they were provided as tribute by, or were captured from, outlying communities for the purposes of sacrifice, but would be more consistent with them being indigenous to the local community.

Investigation of non-genetic aspects of earlier populations

Auditory tori and the exploitation of aquatic resources

The auditory torus is a hyperostosis which manifests itself as a small, bony protuberance on the inner wall of the ear canal (Figure 7.15). Auditory tori are probably caused by cold water in the ear. The skin in the ear canal is very thin, so the periosteum here is near the surface. Irrigation of the ear canal with cold (below about 19°C) water has been shown to cause prolonged local redness and blood congestion which may traumatise the periosteum, stimulating it to lay down new bone (Kennedy, 1986). In this way auditory tori may be produced. Consistent with this, auditory tori have been elicited experimentally in guinea pigs by irrigating their ears with cold water (Kennedy, 1986). Today, cases of auditory tori in man are generally associated with a history of cold water exposure as a result of participation in water-sports, such as surfing, diving or kayaking, over a prolonged period of time (Sheard & Doherty, 2008; Moore et al., 2010; Alexander et al., 2015).

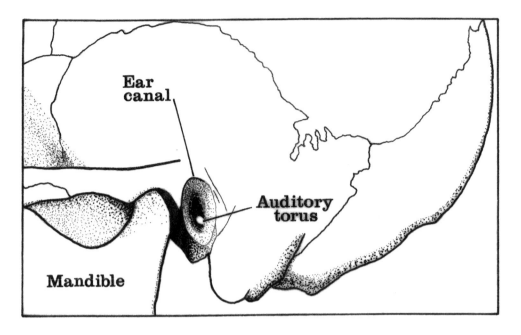

Figure 7.15 Part of the left side of a skull. The posterior wall of the ear canal shows an auditory torus

Auditory tori are potentially a useful indicator of aquatic resource exploitation by diving, or other procurement techniques that require full-body immersion, among groups living at locations where waters are cold enough to produce them (Villotte & Knüsel, 2016). Villotte et al. (2014) studied auditory tori in Mesolithic and Neolithic skeletons from a variety of European locations. Among these were a group of sites located in Serbia, in the Iron Gates region of the Danube. The skeletons spanned the Mesolithic to Middle Neolithic periods (ca. 9500–5500BC). Among the 126 skeletons from the Iron Gates examined by Villotte and his team, 37 (29%) showed auditory tori. The Danube would have been a rich source of aquatic resources and this must have been what attracted settlement to the water's edge (Dinu, 2010). The Iron Gates settlements have produced abundant fish remains (Bonsall & Boroneanţ, 2018). For example, at one habitation site, Vlasac, 60% of the Mesolithic vertebrate fauna were fish (Bökönyi, 1978). Although a few fish spears were found at these settlements, there was no evidence for fish-hooks or other fishing equipment (Dinu, 2010). The waters of the Danube would easily have been cold enough to elicit torus formation, so their high frequency may indicate that the fish were obtained by methods, such as diving or the setting of nets or traps, that involved full-body immersion. These sorts of fishing methods have been associated with elevated frequencies of tori in other populations. For example, auditory tori are common in Aboriginal crania from south-eastern Australia. Ethnographic evidence shows aboriginal inhabitants caught river fish by casting a net into the water, whereupon they would dive in to trap the fish against the river bed (Kennedy, 1986). Among the Aboriginal crania, tori were found mainly in males, which was consistent with ethnographic accounts that it was men who would net the fish in this way. By contrast, in the Iron Gates skeletons, tori were found in similar frequencies in males and females, suggesting that both sexes participated in the task.

Among the burials that could be closely dated, Villotte et al. (2014) found a decline in frequencies of individuals with auditory tori from 50% in the Early – Middle Mesolithic to 7% in Early-Middle Neolithic contexts (Figure 7.16). They suggest that this implies a decline in importance of aquatic foods. Changes in stable isotope evidence from human skeletons at around this time would seem to support their interpretation; they too suggest reliance on riverine resources lessened over time. This evidence is discussed in Chapter 11.

Entheseal changes and activity patterns

Entheses can be classified into two types: fibrocartilagenous and fibrous. Tendon attachments close to joints are of the fibrocartilagenous type: the tendon attaches to bone via a layer of fibrocartilage. The origin of common extensors (a group of muscles that extend the fingers and wrist) on the lateral epicondyle of the humerus is an example of a fibrocartilagenous enthesis. In dry bones the normal appearance of a fibrocartilagenous enthesis is a smooth, well-circumscribed area adjacent to a joint (Figure 7.17a).

Fibrous entheses, on the other hand, lack an intervening layer of fibrocartilage. Whilst the bone is still growing the muscle attaches to the bone via the periosteum, but in many cases the periosteum subsequently disappears so that in the adult the muscle is attached

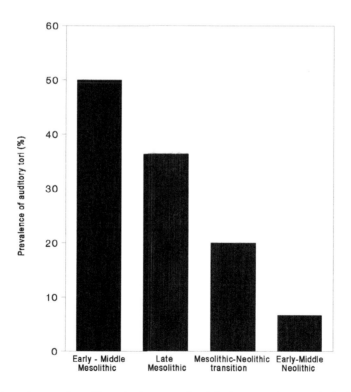

Figure 7.16 Prevalence of auditory tori among burials from various periods from the Iron Gates region of the Danube. Source: based on data in Villotte et al. (2014)

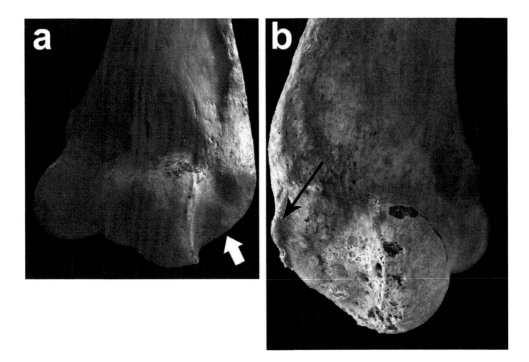

Figure 7.17 (a) Antero-lateral view of the distal end of a left humerus. The smooth area indicated by the arrow is the enthesis at the origin of the common extensor tendon. (b) A lateral view of a right humerus shows that this same area is not smooth, but shows entheseal changes. The surface is roughened and porous and there is an enthesophyte (bony outgrowth) and the entheseal margin (arrowed)

Source: adapted from Palmer & Waters-Rist (2019: Fig 2).

directly to bone. In long-bones, fibrous entheses usually occur on the metaphysis or diaphysis. They are larger in area than fibrocartilagenous entheses with more poorly defined margins; where muscles attach direct to bone entheses normally have a raised somewhat roughened appearance (Benjamin et al., 2002; Shaw & Benjamin, 2007). An example of a fibrous enthesis is the insertion of the deltoid muscle onto the humeral diaphysis (Figure 7.18).

When a muscle contracts, it exerts traction upon its entheses. This may elicit two types of alteration (Foster et al., 2014). The first is an increase in robusticity (roughness and prominence) of the enthesis. This is thought to occur because traction increases local blood flow. This, together with mechanical stimulation of the periosteum, elicits new bone formation increasing entheseal robusticity. Secondly, there is a suite of alterations, termed enthesopathies, that occurs as a consequence of microdamage to the tissues that make up the enthesis. These alterations may be evident on bone as enthesophytes (bony spurring), and porosity and irregularity of the entheseal surface (Figure 7.17b).

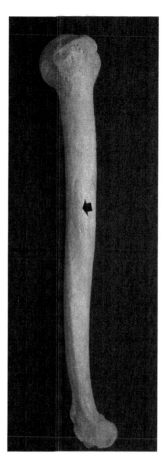

Figure 7.18 Lateral view of a right humerus. The raised, slightly roughened area indicated by the arrow is the enthesis at the insertion of the deltoid muscle

Enthesopathies occur in older individuals as a result of degenerative processes, but overuse can accelerate and intensify these. Today, overuse enthesopathies are seen mainly in sports injuries. It is the fibrocartilagenous entheses that are the more vulnerable to overuse injuries (Shaw & Benjamin, 2007), and enthesopathies at some of them have acquired names linking them with particular sports. For example, tennis elbow is an overuse injury of the common extensor tendon at the elbow – it is linked with repetitive activities involving wrist extension and supination as, for example, in the backhand stroke in racket sports. Conversely, enthesopathy at the common flexor origin, on the medial epicondyle of the humerus, is more associated with throwing sports (Gustas & Lee, 2016). Radiographs of these and other enthesopathies in living patients are often normal, but when bone abnormalities are evident they appear to be similar to those we often see in bones from archaeological sites: enthesophytes and irregularity of the bone surface (Walz et al., 2010; Gustas & Lee, 2016).

The above discussion might seem to suggest that entheseal changes are a good way to study activity patterns in the past. However, there are difficulties. Although it seems indubitable that, especially in the case of enthesopathies at fibrocartilagenous entheses, there is a link with habitual activities, a variety of other factors also affect the prevalence of entheseal changes in a group. Their frequency increases with age (Alves-Cardoso & Henderson, 2010; Michopoulou et al., 2015; Karakostis et al., 2017). Indeed, age seems to be the most important influence on entheseal changes, so it is a variable that always needs to be controlled for. The problems we have in reliably estimating age in adults from their skeletons can make it difficult to do this effectively. There are also other potentially complicating factors. There may be a link between entheseal changes and body size – larger individuals have been reported as showing more advanced changes (Godde et al., 2018). People seem to differ in their inherent tendency toward formation of bone at entheses (Rogers et al., 1997; Mays, 2016). In addition, various factors, including the greater muscle mass and strength and greater body size in males, make direct comparison between the sexes difficult (Weiss et al., 2012; Villotte & Knüsel, 2013; Palmer & Waters-Rist, 2019).

When entheseal changes have been studied in skeletal collections, like Christ Church Spitalfields or from more recent cemeteries or anatomical collections (Henderson & Alves Cardoso, 2018), where activity levels (usually in the form of occupations) are documented for individuals, results have been inconsistent. Some studies have found a greater frequency in those with more strenuous lifestyles or occupations (Villotte et al., 2010; Milella et al., 2015; Karakostis et al., 2017), but others have not (Alves-Cardoso & Henderson, 2010; Michopoulou et al., 2015; Godde et al., 2018). As well as the fact that multiple factors besides activity affect entheses, difficulties in using occupation as a proxy for activity, and inconsistencies in methods (which entheses are studied, how alterations are recorded) may also be at play here.

Some archaeological studies have used entheseal changes to investigate differences in general levels of activity between different social groups or populations (Lieverse et al., 2013; Schrader, 2015; Palmer & Waters-Rist, 2019). For example, Refai (2019) studied entheseal changes at 14 fibrous and fibrocartilagenous entheses among 195 burials dating to 2700-2190BC from around the Great Pyramids at Giza, Egypt. The burials were divided into two classes involved in the building of the pyramids: workers and officials. The former were low socioeconomic status craftsmen and labourers. The latter were high status secular and religious officials who would have organised and overseen the work. Among women, entheseal changes were more frequent in the worker group, consistent with the inference that their work was more strenuous that that of high-status women. A similar pattern was seen in males, and here differences were most consistently expressed in the lower limbs, perhaps because male workers were particularly involved with carrying heavy building materials (Refai, 2019).

Others have attempted to use entheseal changes to investigate more specific activities, such as archery (Molnar, 2006; Thomas, 2014), the throwing of spears or other projectiles, or horse-riding. Villotte and Knüsel (2014) studied entheseal changes at the fibrocartilagenous common extensor and common flexor origins in the humeri of 1261 European skeletons dating from the industrial period (18th-20th centuries AD), pre-industrial historic period (2nd-18th century AD) and prehistoric times (30,000-2700BC). They noted that modern medical studies showed that common extensor enthesopathy ('lateral epicondylosis') is today more frequent than common flexor enthesopathy ('medial epicondylosis') across all activity and occupation groups. The only exception was for baseball pitchers – this should come as no surprise given the association discussed above between this injury and throwing sports. They found that, as with the medical studies, the archaeological skeletons also showed a preference for lateral epicondylosis. The only exception was in right humeri from males from the prehistoric period, where medial epicondylosis predominated. This suggested that prehistoric males were particularly involved in activities that involved hand-thrown projectiles. Hunting was likely important in the prehistoric cultures studied. Ethnographic evidence from around the world showed that use of throwing weapons such as spears, in hunting or other tasks in recent human societies is an overwhelmingly male activity, supporting this interpretation (Villotte & Knüsel, 2014).

Djukic et al. (2018) studied entheseal changes in skeletons from two populations from Serbia. One group dated to the 6th–8th century AD and were from Avar burial grounds. The Avar were traditionally an equestrian people. By the time of these burials, they had transitioned from a nomadic to a settled lifestyle, but horses and horsemanship continued to play a key cultural and socioeconomic role. The other group dated from the 11th–16th centuries AD and were from settlements based on agriculture, trading and craft production; there was no archaeological evidence for horse-riding. The aim of the study was to determine whether there was any evidence in the form of entheseal changes, for the postulated difference in the importance of equestrianism between the two groups.

They began by identifying the muscles of the legs and lower trunk that were important in horse-riding. They recorded a suite of 10 fibrocartilagenous and fibrous entheses in the pelvis and lower limb that related to these in 34 Avar burials and 48 from the later agricultural population. They found a difference at three entheses, and in each case it was the Avars who had the higher frequency of changes. Two of these three relate to adductor muscles – those whose action is to press the knees together. This action is uncommon in everyday activities but is almost continuous during riding. This strengthened the suggestion that the differences between the two groups reflected the importance of riding amongst the Avar. Turning to sex differences, these were significant at only one enthesis in the agricultural population, but at six in the Avar. In each case, the frequency of changes was greater in males. This suggests greater gendered differences in muscle use in the lower limbs among the Avars, and perhaps that riding was a predominantly male activity (Djukic et al., 2018).

Summary

Non-metric skeletal traits are minor variations in the anatomy of bones or teeth which are not normally recorded by measurement, but as present or absent or sometimes by the degree of development.

Work with laboratory animals, as well as studies on man, have shown that some of these traits have a genetic component in their causation. This has led to their use as genetic markers in osteoarchaeology. They have been used, often alongside cranial measurements, to study relationships between populations and to study population history. Another important focus has been the study of genetic relationships at a smaller scale. Some of this has focussed on looking at relationships between groups buried in different cemeteries within the same locale. Other work has investigated patterning within a single burial site.

Many traits do not appear to have any very great genetic component in their causation. Some appear instead to be related to particular environmental factors, such as biomechanical forces exerted on the skeleton. Examples of such variants are alterations at entheses, the attachments of muscle and ligaments to bones. Entheseal changes may arise in response to traction at these sites from repetitive, vigorous muscular contraction. Entheseal changes have been used to investigate differences in activity levels between different social groups or to investigate more specific types of activity, such as horse-riding or the throwing of spears or other projectiles.

Further reading

Scott, G.R. & Pilloud, M.A. (2019). Dental Morphology, pp. 257–292 in M.A. Katzenberg & A.L. Grauer (eds) *Biological Anthropology of the Human Skeleton*, 3rd edition. Wiley, Chichester. This *is a good overview of dental non-metric variants.*

Hauser, G., & De Stafano, G.F. (1989). Epigenetic Variants of the Human Skull. Stuttgart, Schweitzerbart'sche, *covers the developmental bases for many bony non-metric traits of the skull, as well as discussing scoring procedures.* Mann, R.W., Hunt, D.R. & Lozanoff, S. (2016) Photographic Regional Atlas of Non-Metric Traits and Anatomical Variants in the Human Skeleton. Charles C Thomas, Springfield, *illustrates nearly 300 bony variants in the cranial and post-cranial skeleton.*

Stojanowski, C.M. &, Schillaci, M.A. (2006). Phenotypic Approaches for Understanding Patterns of Intracemetery Biological Variation. *Yearbook of Physical Anthropology* 49: 49–88, *offers an overview of the way in which the study of non-metric traits (among other facets of human skeletal biology) can contribute to our understanding of aspects such as kinship and cemetery structure.*

Henderson, C.Y. & Alves Cardoso, F., eds. (2013). Entheseal Changes and Occupation: Technical and Theoretical Advances and Their Applications. *International Journal of Osteoarchaeology* 23, Issue 2. *A special issue of the International Journal of Osteoarchaeology devoted to entheseal changes. There is much useful information; in particular, the article by Villotte & Knüsel is a good review of the anatomical and clinical background.*

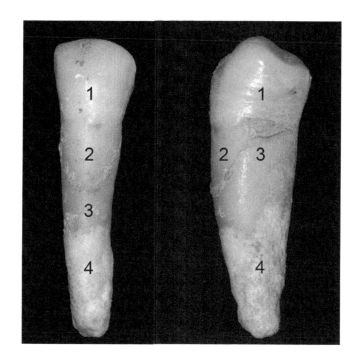

Plate 1 Two views of a mandibular premolar showing identification of acellular extrinsic fibre cementum. 1, Enamel; 2, root dentine not covered by cementum; 3, acellular extrinsic fibre cementum; 4, cellular cementum

Source: Naji et al., (2016: Figure 3).

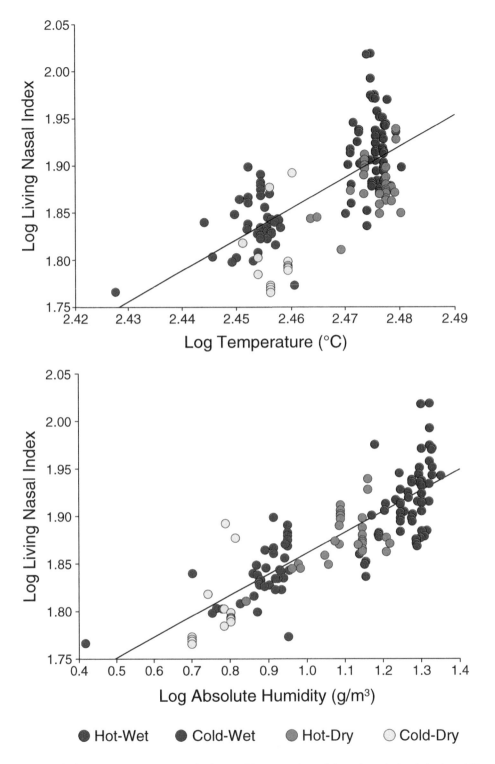

Plate 2 Relationship between nasal index and temperature (above) and absolute humidity (below). For statistical reasons the data are log transformed

Source: Maddux et al. (2016: Fig 3).

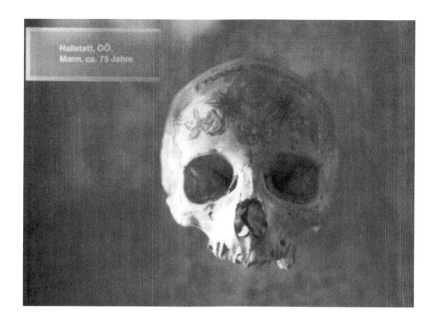

Plate 3 A painted cranium from Hallstatt

a)   b)

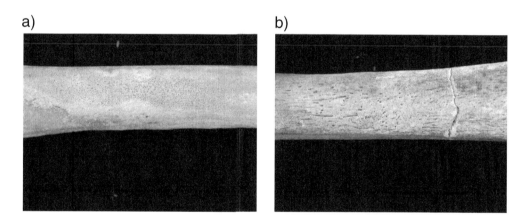

Plate 4 Periostitis. (a) The finely pitted bone on this femur indicates an unremodelled lesion. (b) The smoother, more coarsely pitted / striated appearance of the bone deposit in this tibia is indicative of a remodelled lesion

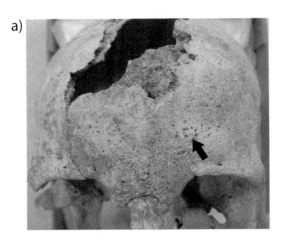

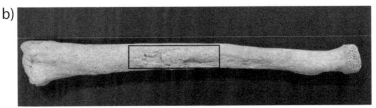

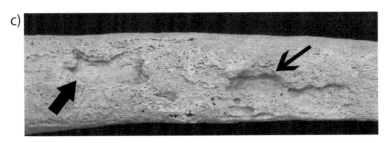

Plate 5 The Apple Down skeleton. (a) Frontal bone. Abnormal pitting is evident above each orbit and toward the midline. The pits vary in size; in places (for example the area indicated by the arrow) they are quite large. The large hole in the cranium visible toward the top of the picture is taphonomic damage. (b) & (c) Left radius. The entire bone shows thickening due to periostitis. The area in the rectangle is shown in more detail in (c). In the area indicated by the thick arrow, the subperiosteal new bone has flaked away post-mortem revealing the former cortical surface. This demonstrates the thickness of new bone that has accumulated. The slender arrow points to a void within the new bone formation. Its edges are smoother suggesting that this hole was present in life. It was perhaps the site of a small gumma

Source: photographs taken and reproduced here with permission of the Novium Museum, Chichester District Council.

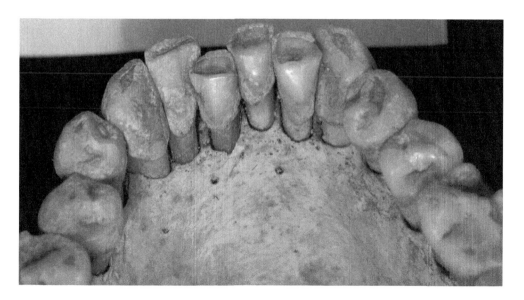

Plate 6 Lingual (posterior) view of the anterior part of a mandible from a Bronze Age burial from near Stonehenge. The lower parts of the crowns of the canines and incisors show deposits of dental calculus

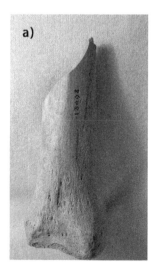
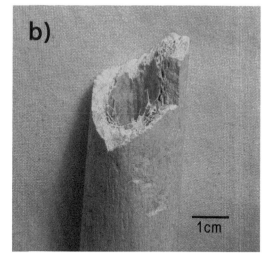

Plate 7 (a). The break at the proximal end of this partial tibia is curvilinear and has a smooth broken surface with sharp edges. These features are characteristic of a perimortal injury. The surface of the break shows a similar level of weathering to the rest of the bone. This too is consistent with a perimortal break. (b). The break in this tibia shows a rough surface, and its profile is jagged with a large step evident in the broken end (on the right side in the photograph). These features are typical of breaks occurring after the bone has lost the slight plasticity / elasticity of fresh bone, suggesting this break occurred long after death. The fresh, white colour of the broken surfaces confirms this, indicating that the damage happened during or after excavation

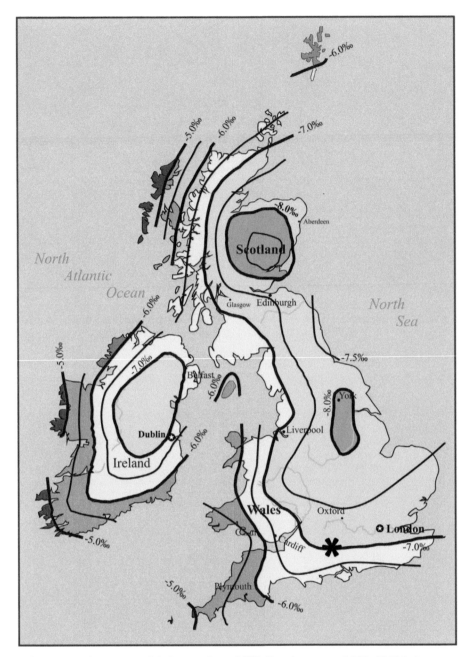

Oxygen Isotope Values for UK Spring and Well Waters

$\delta^{18}O$ -4 to -5	$\delta^{18}O$ -6 to -7	$\delta^{18}O$ -8 to -9
$\delta^{18}O$ -5 to -6	$\delta^{18}O$ -7 to -8	

BGS © NERC, 2004
Isotopic Data from Darling et.al. 2003
Geographical base map adapted from 1996 MAGELLAN GeographixSM Santa Barbara, CA (805)685-3100

Plate 8 $\delta^{18}O$ (‰ versus SMOW) of drinking water across Britain and Ireland. The asterisk marks the location of Stonehenge

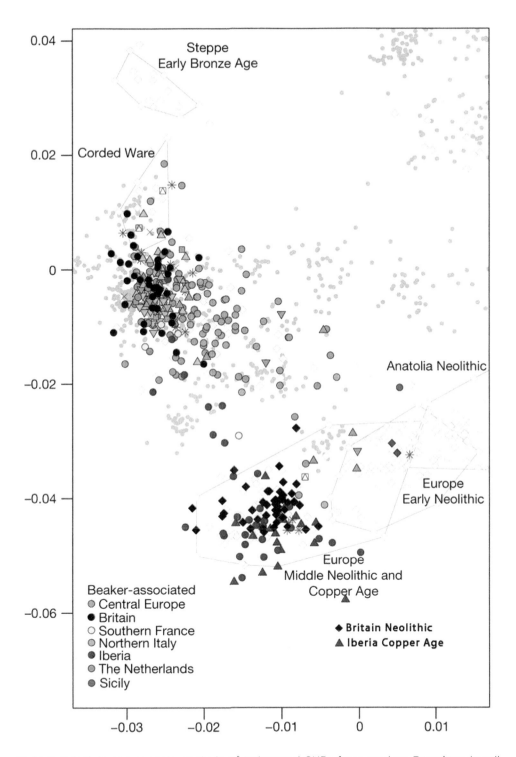

Plate 9 Principle components analysis of autosomal SNPs from modern Eurasians (small grey dots). Ancient data generated by Olalde et al (2018) and previously published ancient data used by those authors (yellow diamonds) are projected onto the plot

Source: adapted from Olalde et al. (2018: Figure 1c).

Plate 10 Visceral (internal) surfaces of two rib fragments from a child from Wharram Percy. The normal smooth bone surface is visible at the end of the lower fragment at the extreme left of the photograph. Elsewhere, the surfaces are covered by deposits of porous bone. This type of lesion is suggestive of a chest infection. Biomolecular analysis (Mays et al., 2002b) showed the presence of *Mycobacterium tuberculosis* complex DNA, indicating that this individual was infected with tuberculosis

Plate 11 Ceremony to mark the handing over of Australian human remains from Manchester Museum, England to Australian Aboriginals

Source: Manchester Museum.

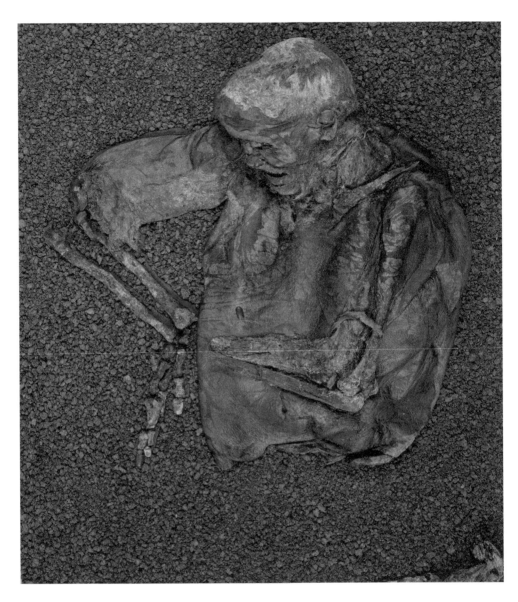

Plate 12 Lindow Man on display at the British Museum
Source: The British Museum.

8 Bone disease

When excavating a burial on an archaeological site, a question one is often asked by visiting members of the public is 'How did he die?' Generally speaking, the answer that one
has to give is that we don't know. Evidence for lethal injury is rarely found in archaeological skeletons, and in any case most deaths in the past were doubtless due to disease
and, unfortunately from the osteoarchaeologist's point of view, most diseases leave no
traces on the skeleton. This is certainly true for the acute infectious diseases which were
the great killers in antiquity. The response of bone tissue to disease is relatively slow, so
that in general only the more long-lasting conditions even have the potential to affect it.
Even for those life-threatening infections which do have the potential to spread to the skeleton, the absence of effective treatment in antiquity would have meant that few individuals
would have survived long enough for them to do so. This would have been particularly so if
the individual's resistance was lowered as a result of having had no previous exposure to the
disease or through poor nutrition. Most skeletons excavated from archaeological sites therefore show no signs of cause of death.

Only a sub-set of the more chronic diseases affect the skeleton, so by studying disease
in archaeological remains we are in fact seeing some of the diseases which individuals must
have endured for some time – often years or even decades. Many of these conditions are
not life-threatening and many are found in a healed state, indicating that the individual
recovered. Most of the diseases we see in archaeological skeletons have little to do with
the cause of death, but may well have affected the individual's lifestyle, at least for some
part of their life. Furthermore, on a population level, the diseases which afflict a human
group are to an extent a reflection of that group's way of life and the general environment
in which they lived. It might be said, then, that studying disease in ancient skeletons generally tells us more about how people lived than about how they died.

The study of disease and injury in ancient skeletons is termed palaeopathology, and it
is to palaeopathology that the next three chapters are devoted. The present chapter
deals with diseases of bone, the following one with dental disease, and Chapter 10 with
traces of injury on the skeleton.

A classification of bone disease

Each disease is unique, but in order to provide a framework for discussion it is useful to
classify in some way those which affect the skeleton. A classification based on the cause
of the disease and the pathological changes in the bones is shown in Figure 8.1.

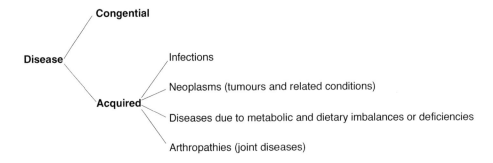

Figure 8.1 A classification of the diseases of bone

Congenital abnormalities *(Barnes, 2012)*

These are present from birth, either as a result of genetic defects or due to problems during pregnancy. They range in severity from those which are incompatible with life and hence would have resulted in the infant being stillborn, through those which would have resulted in disability, to those which would have caused no symptoms and of which the individual would have been unaware. Into the first category come gross malformations such as anencephaly, a condition in which there is almost complete absence of the skull vault and brain. Such a condition has been identified in an Egyptian mummy (Figure 8.2). The infant in question was found buried in catacombs along with sacred ape and ibis, and due to the severity of the deformities there was doubt for a time as to whether it was human. Ironically, the embalmer had attempted to extract the brain in the usual way through the nose, failing to realise the significance of the anomalies in the head and neck (Brothwell & Powers, 1968). Abnormalities which would have resulted in disability rather than death include congenital hip dislocation, club foot and cleft palate, all conditions which have been recognised in ancient skeletons (e.g. Anderson, 1994; Roberts et al., 2004; Mitchell & Redfern, 2011).

Infections *(Ortner, 2008)*

Infections are caused by pathogenic micro-organisms. Infectious lesions in the skeleton may begin due to exposure of the bone to the external environment as, for example, at a open (i.e. compound) fracture, or else may be a direct extension of soft tissue infection to the adjacent bone. For example, infectious lesions of ribs may occur due to contact with adjacent lung infections such as tuberculosis (Roberts et al., 1998), or tibial infections may occur due to overlying skin lesions (Boel & Ortner, 2013). More often, skeletal disease is not due to direct infection of the bone but to secondary spread of disease, via the bloodstream or lymphatic system, from primary seats of infection in soft tissue.

Infection, be it of the soft tissues or of bone, results in inflammation. In the inflammatory process there is increased blood circulation followed by migration of fluid and blood cells into the surrounding tissues. Bone inflammation is often divided into that which affects the outer surface (termed periostitis) and that which affects the compact bone, together with the medullary cavity or trabecular bone within, termed osteomyelitis.

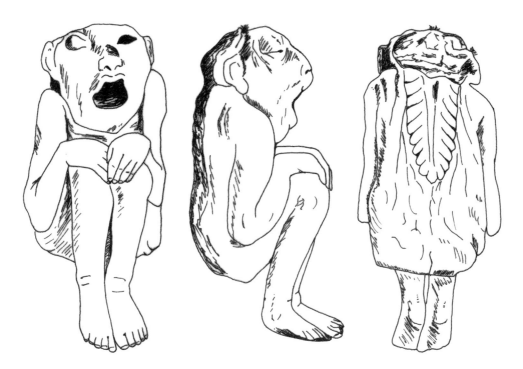

Figure 8.2 Three views of a mummified anencephalic infant from Hermopolis, Egypt
Source: Redrawn from Brothwell and Powers (1968: Figure 3).

Inflammation of the periosteum stimulates it to produce new bone. Periostitis thus results in a deposit of new bone upon the outer surface of the bone. This new bone is initially laid down as woven bone, but is progressively remodelled to lamellar bone (Plate 4).

In osteomyelitis, infection in the marrow cavity leads to pus formation, and the pressure this exerts within this confined space leads to death and subsequent resorption of the nearby cortex due to compression of the blood vessels supplying it. The dead cortex is known as the sequestrum. Exudate from the focus of the infection raises the periosteum, eliciting new bone production beneath it, producing a new shell of bone, the involucrum, enclosing the old cortex. Pressure of pus within the bone leads to the formation of a cloaca, a hole in the cortex through which pus and dead bone fragments are discharged (Roberts, 2019: 297–304). These features are illustrated in Figure 8.3.

For lesions showing new bone deposition it is important to record whether deposits are of woven bone, lamellar bone or both. The presence of woven bone denotes an unremodelled lesion active at time of death, and hence, depending upon its nature, the disease that caused it might be implicated as cause of death. Woven bone alone indicates that the individual died shortly after the disease spread to the skeleton; a mixture of woven and lamellar bone indicates that the individual survived for rather longer. The presence only of remodelled bone indicates a healed (or at least quiescent) lesion.

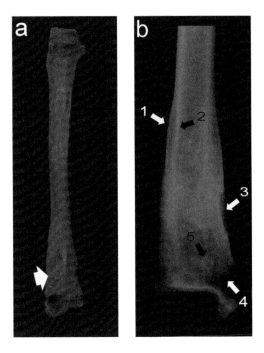

Figure 8.3 Osteomyelitis, (a) There is marked swelling near the distal (lower) end of the tibia. On the medial aspect there is an oval depression (arrowed) which prob- ably represents a healed cloaca, (b) The radiograph (anterior view) shows a shell of new bone (called the involucrum) (1) surrounding the original cortex (the sequestrum) (2) which has been partially resorbed. (3) indicates the site of the healed cloaca. These are typical features of chronic osteomyelitis. The radiolucency (4) is a post-depositional defect. The blotchy radio-opacities at (5) and elsewhere in the metaphysial interior and in the medullary cavity are post-depositional ingress of soil

It is often difficult to determine which micro-organism might have caused the changes seen in an ancient skeleton (i.e. to determine which infectious disease is responsible) because the changes wrought by one infection may be similar to those caused by another. In such cases, the only diagnosis that can be made is non-specific periostitis or osteomyelitis. How- ever, some micro-organisms do elicit lesions which are distinctive in their appearance or dis- tribution in the skeleton. This may enable the identification of specific infections. Infectious diseases which have been identified on ancient skeletons include tuberculosis (Roberts & Buikstra, 2003), syphilis and allied conditions (Cook & Powell, 2012) and leprosy (Roberts 2020). A probable example of skeletal tuberculosis is shown in Figure 8.4.

Neoplasms *(Brothwell, 2008)*

A neoplasm, or tumour, is an uncontrolled growth of cells. Tumours may be benign or malignant. In the former case they tend to be slow-growing and remain localised. In the

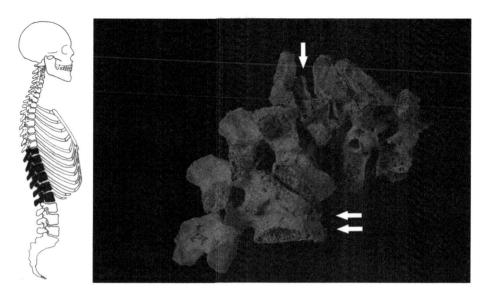

Figure 8.4 The plate shows six contiguous vertebrae (ninth thoracic to second lumbar) showing signs of tuberculosis. The line-drawing shows the location of the diseased bones in the spinal column. The eleventh thoracic vertebra (single arrow) shows complete destruction of its body. There is partial destruction of the bodies of neighbouring vertebrae. The bodies of the first two lumbar vertebrae have collapsed and fused together (twin arrows) as a result of the disease. The whole process has resulted in a kyphosis (forward angulation) of the spine of about 90 degrees

latter they grow more rapidly and spread to other parts of the body, usually via the bloodstream or lymphatic system. About forty different types of tumour may affect bone (Steinbock, 1976:316), but it is often very difficult to distinguish one from another in skeletal material.

The most common benign bony neoplasm in skeletal remains is the osteoma. This is a small, localised overgrowth of dense bone. They are most often found on the external surface of the cranial vault (Figure 8.5), where they are known as button osteomas (Eshed et al., 2002). Benign soft tissue neoplasms may also be evident on the skeleton if they provoke a bony response. Figure 8.6 shows a cranium with massive bony resorption, probably as a result of a large, benign nasal tumour. As their name suggests, benign neoplasms are not of themselves a serious threat to health; they only become so if their size or location compromises nearby tissues (see Sjøvold et al., 1974 for an archaeological case).

Malignant neoplasms ('cancers') are generally life-threatening. Malignant neoplasms in the skeleton may originate in the bone, but more often they are carried to the skeleton from a primary malignant lesion in another tissue; such instances are known as metastatic carcinomas, and occur mainly in older individuals. Malignant neoplasms may be bone forming, bone destroying or a mixture of the two, but bone destruction usually predominates. An example of a malignant neoplasm is shown in Figure 8.7. This is a probable case of

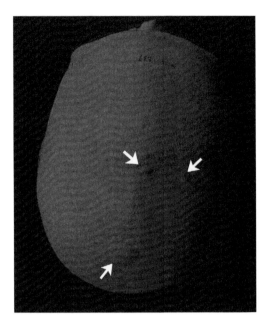

Figure 8.5 A cranium showing several button osteomas

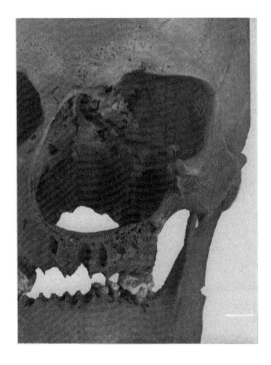

Figure 8.6 The considerable bone resorption seen in the nasal and left orbital region of
this skull is probably due to a large benign nasal tumour

Source: reproduced from Brothwell (1967).

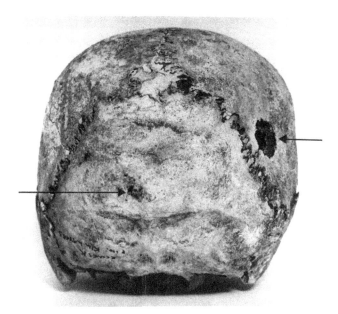

Figure 8.7 Metastatic carcinoma: this skull shows perforations (arrowed) in the bones of
the vault due to the disease
Source: Reproduced from Manchester (1983).

metastatic carcinoma, the cranial perforations (arrowed) have occurred as a result of
detached fragments of a soft tissue cancer spreading to the skeleton (Manchester, 1983).

Metabolic disease *(Brickley et al., 2020)*

Metabolic bone diseases are those where there is disruption of the normal balance
between bone formation and bone resorption due to some metabolic abnormality. They
may be caused by nutritional insufficiency or imbalance, or may arise for other reasons.

Rickets is a metabolic disease that has been recognised in skeletal remains (papers in
Brickley & Mays, 2018). It is a disease of childhood and is a failure of proper mineralisation of growing bone due to inadequate availability of vitamin D. Most vitamin D in man
is not dietary but is synthesised in the body by the action of sunlight on a substance in
the skin. Thus most rickets is caused not by dietary imbalance but by inadequate exposure of the skin to sunlight. The poorly mineralised bones become bent and distorted, particularly those of the legs, and these deformities may persist into adult life (Figure 8.8).

Other metabolic diseases which have been recognised in skeletal remains include
scurvy (papers in Crandall & Klaus, 2014), osteoporosis (Curate, 2014), and Paget's disease of bone (Mays, 2010b).

Arthropathies *(Rogers & Waldron, 1995)*

There are more than one hundred arthropathies (joint diseases) currently defined
(Athanasiou et al., 2017). Most are diseases of old age. They have many different

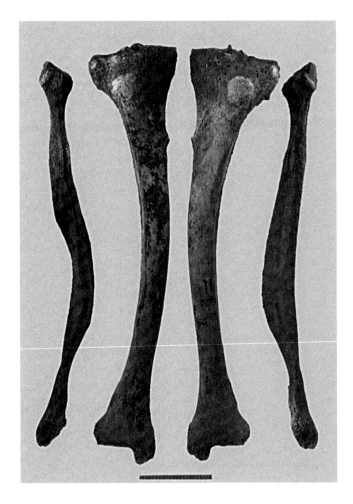

Figure 8.8 The lower leg bones of an adult bowed as a result of childhood rickets
Source: Reproduced from Molleson and Cox (1993: Figure 3.9).

causes. Not all leave diagnostic traces on the bones – only about ten specific arthropathies have been identified with any frequency in skeletons from archaeological sites (Rogers, 2000).

When they leave traces on the skeleton, arthropathies generally result in both bone formation and bone destruction, but they may be classified as proliferative or erosive depending upon which process predominates.

Osteoarthritis and degenerative disc disease are proliferative arthropathies, and are the two most common joint diseases seen on bones from archaeological sites. Degeneration of the intervertebral disc leads to vertebral osteophytosis – formation of osteophytes (bony outgrowths) at the margins of the vertebral body, the weight-bearing part of the vertebra (Figure 8.9). Osteoarthritis is degeneration of the cartilage at a joint. The bony signs are osteophytes at the joint margins coupled with pitting and/or polishing of the joint surface (Figure 8.10). Mechanical loading across a joint due to muscular

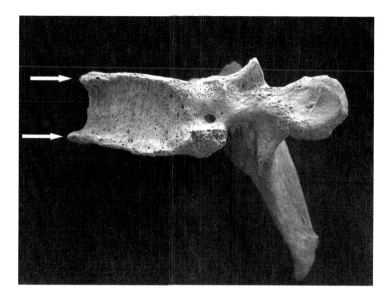

Figure 8.9 Osteophytosis (arrowed) associated with degenerative disc disease in a thoracic vertebra

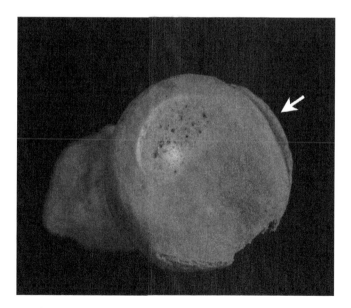

Figure 8.10 The head of a radius showing osteoarthritis. There is pitting and polishing of part of the joint surface, accompanied by some marginal osteophyte formation (arrowed)

contraction or weight-bearing appears to be important in the development of degenerative joint disease, however many other factors also seem to play a part, including age, sex and genetics (Weiss & Jurmain, 2007; Sharma, 2019).

Another proliferative arthropathy which has been identified in ancient bones is diffuse idiopathic skeletal hyperostosis, or DISH for short. This disease is characterised by bone formation in the spinal ligaments and at sites of attachments of tendons onto bone. Ossification of spinal ligaments may progress to unite several vertebral bodies with large flowing osteophytes (Figure 8.11). Its precise cause is uncertain. It is sometimes associated with diabetes and with obesity (Mader et al., 2013), but some individuals appear, for unknown reasons, simply to have an inherent tendency toward this type of bone formation (Rogers et al., 1997; Mays, 2016).

Arthropathies where erosive changes predominate are rarer in palaeopathology. They include gout, rheumatoid arthritis, ankylosing spondylitis, and a group of conditions that may occur in association with urethral or gastrointestinal infection, psoriasis or inflammatory bowel disease. An example of gout is shown in Figure 8.12. In this disease, crystals of urate form in joints. Erosive changes represent bony resorption in response to the growth of tophi, large agglomerations of urate crystals.

The diagnosis of disease in skeletal remains

When confronted with an apparently abnormal bone, the first task is to determine whether the changes occurred during life or simply result from damage to the bone as it

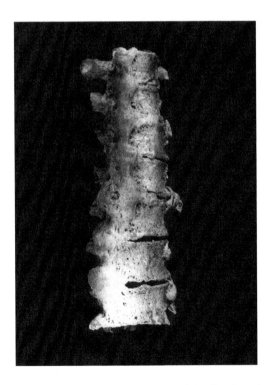

Figure 8.11 Seven thoracic vertebrae, united by a thick, flowing right-sided osteophyte. These changes are characteristic of DISH

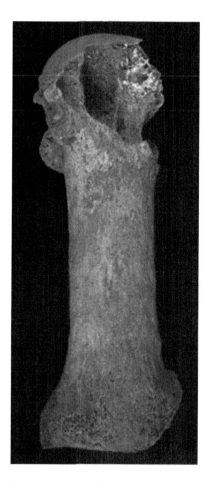

Figure 8.12 Dorsal view of a left first metarsal showing a large erosions typical of gout at its distal end. The white powdery substance visible on exposed trabeculae to the medial side (right in the picture) of the lesions tested positive for uric acid

Source: Swinson et al. (2010: Figure 2)

lay in the soil. Although diseased bones present a myriad variety of appearances, ultimately the only way in which the skeleton can respond to disease is by removal of bone or formation of bone. Clearly, processes occurring in the soil after burial cannot result in new bone formation, but they can destroy bone. The problem, then, is distinguishing erosions or holes in bone which result from disease from those caused by post-depositional damage.

When a cavity in bone is caused by taphonomic (post-depositional) factors, such as soil erosion, it tends to have rather ragged edges. With a cavity due to disease, the trabeculae at its edges are, to a greater or lesser extent, remodelled, a process which is evident as thickening of the bony trabeculae and smoothing of the walls of the lesion (Figure 8.13). This effect is greatest in slow-growing lesions and is least when bone

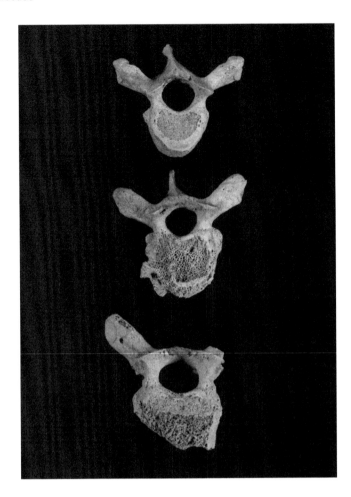

Figure 8.13 An illustration of the distinction between bone destruction caused by a disease process and that due to post-depositional damage. Post-depositional damage is illustrated in the lower vertebra of the three. The trabecular structure of the bone is exposed. The edges of this damaged area are ragged and the trabeculae are fine and unremodelled. The vertebra in the middle of the photograph also shows an area of superficial destruction with exposure of the underlying trabecular bone. However, there is evidence of remodelling of the trabeculae in the form of coarsening and thickening of the honeycomb structure, and the surfaces of the destroyed area are smoother and less ragged. This remodelling indicates that the bone destruction is due to a disease process and not to post-depositional damage. A normal, undamaged vertebra is shown at the top of the photograph for comparison

destruction is rapid (Ortner, 2003: Figure 4.6). In most cases the experienced osteoarchaeologist can distinguish genuine instances of disease from post-depositional damage.

Features due to disease need to be distinguished from normal anatomical variants. A thorough grounding in skeletal anatomy is needed to allow one to do this (Figure 8.14).

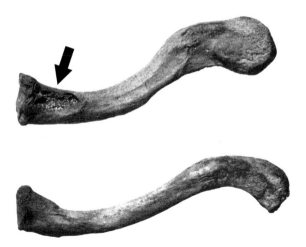

Figure 8.14 Inferior (lower) view of two clavicles. The top one shows a deep cavity towards its sternal end. This is not an abscess cavity but a normal anatomical variant (known as the rhomboid fossa) at the point of attachment of the costo-clavicular ligament. Sometimes this pit is absent, as in the bone in bottom of the picture

As well as being able to talk to the patient, the modern physician has at his or her disposal a wide array of diagnostic techniques, but the great majority of these are not applicable to the study of ancient bones. However, osteoarchaeologists do have one great advantage, they can actually see the bones. Thus careful visual examination and careful recording of the findings, in the form of written descriptions (using proper scientific terminology (Manchester et al., 2017)), augmented as appropriate with photographs and diagrams, are most important in osteoarchaeology.

Osteoarchaeological diagnoses are made from the nature of the lesions themselves and their distribution in the skeleton. The dominant approach is comparative. Lesions in a reference group are used as a basis to help us make a diagnosis in a target skeleton. The target skeleton is the archaeological individual showing lesions. The reference group comprises individuals showing skeletal lesions with independent evidence concerning which disease was present. This reference – target approach is analogous to that used in other areas of osteoarchaeology, for example in age estimation (Chapter 4). However, diagnosis in palaeopathology involves more than simple pattern-matching between reference and target material. The bone lesions produced by a disease may vary due to a variety of factors, such as the length of time the individual had the disease, whether lesions are active or healed at time of death, or the nutritional status of the person (Mays, 2018b). It is in part because of this that it is also important to have a biological understanding of the way in which bone responds to different diseases if we are to understand and (hopefully) correctly interpret lesions seen in the skeleton (Mays, 2018b; Klaus & Lynnerup, 2019).

There are two main sources for the reference material that forms a baseline for interpreting changes in our target archaeological skeletons. The first is bones kept in medical pathology museums or other institutions taken from patients whose disease was diagnosed in life or at autopsy. The second is radiography or other medical imaging of living patients.

Recent dry bone specimens where the disease history is known provide a direct link with disease seen in archaeological bones. However, the number of reliably documented specimens is relatively few. In addition, many were only kept as isolated bones rather than as complete skeletons and this means that it is difficult to determine general patterns of skeletal involvement from these collections. Medical imaging studies of patients, in addition to allowing visualisation of lesion morphology, also provide information on the distribution of alterations in the skeleton.

A potential problem when comparing changes seen in ancient bones with recent cases is that the manifestations of many diseases have been changed in recent times by the development of effective drug and other therapies. This is so, for example, for bacterial infectious diseases, whose courses have been radically altered by the advent of antibiotic treatments in the mid-20th century. By contrast in antiquity, the infection would, in most cases, have proceeded essentially unchecked except by the body's natural defences, until the individual either succumbed or recovered. Documented specimens pre-dating the era of effective antibiotic and other treatments are preferable for establishing baselines for interpreting archaeological cases of disease. For example, to illustrate dry bone lesions in his palaeopathology textbook, Ortner (2003) primarily used specimens from medical and other museums dating to between about AD 1750 and 1930. Material from that period is late enough for the medical diagnosis for the specimens to be reasonably secure, but early enough for the patterns of bone involvement to be unaltered by antibiotics and other modern treatments.

Radiography, the use of X-rays to provide a two-dimensional image, has been applied in a clinical context for over 120 years. Many large-scale radiographic studies of bone lesions in patients, particularly for infectious diseases, were published that predate modern treatment regimes (Mays, 2018b). These tell us not only about lesion morphology, often in advanced cases, but also about typical frequencies with which the skeleton is affected and distributions of lesions amongst the various bones of the skeleton. There are also some early large-scale autopsy studies that provide useful data in these respects (Mays, 2018b). However, some diseases have only recently been recognised as distinct entities. In such instances, we are forced to use bone changes in modern cases as our baseline for interpreting archaeological material. This is so, for example, for many of the arthropathies (Rogers, 2000).

There are a number of laboratory manuals (e.g. Steinbock, 1976; Zimmerman & Kelley, 1982; Aufderheide & Rodriguez-Martin, 1998; Ortner, 2003; Mann & Hunt, 2012; Buikstra, 2019a) which detail the bone changes wrought by various diseases with the aim of providing diagnostic criteria for archaeological cases. Traditionally, these have been orientated toward illustrating the dry bone and radiographic appearance of lesions, but increasingly they are also incorporating images from CT scanning and other techniques. These texts, to varying extents, also discuss the biology of the skeletal response to disease, and this aspect has been increasingly emphasised (Buikstra, 2019a). This means that, as well as providing illustrations of the bone changes in the different diseases, they also attempt to provide a reader with an understanding of why bone changes take the form they do.

A number of techniques are available to the palaeopathologist to assist in examination and diagnosis of diseased bones. These include medical imaging modalities, microscopy and, for infectious disease, analysis of DNA or other biomolecular traces of pathogenic microorganisms.

Radiology

Radiology involves the use of X-rays, to produce an image and in some cases to yield quantitative data on aspects such as bone density. Radiological imaging enables a more complete description of pathological alterations in a specimen to be made. Images made from archaeological specimens can also be directly compared with those from modern patients.

Radiological imaging

In conventional radiography, X-rays produce a two-dimensional image (Fig. 8.3b). Computed tomography (CT) produces two-dimensional virtual slices and, if desired, multiple slices can be integrated or 'stacked' together digitally to form a three-dimensional image (Coqueugniot et al., 2015) which can be manipulated on-screen or 3D-printed to produce a physical model. CT is advantageous because it eliminates the superimposition of overlapping structures characteristic of a radiographic image. This is particularly pertinent in a complex structure such as the cranium. For example, a Mediaeval cranium showed an enlarged middle nasal concha, part of the ethmoid bone that projects into the nasal cavity (Figure 8.15a). For an accurate diagnosis, the internal structure of the concha needed to be visualised, but because of its position in the cranium, in the radiograph, no matter what angle it was taken from, this was obscured by multiple overlapping structures. A CT scan eliminated this problem and clearly revealed an internal void space (Figure 8.15b). This indicated that it was a concha bullosa, an anatomical variant which may cause nasal obstruction (Mays et al., 2011). A related method is micro-CT, a high-resolution (for practical purposes down to tens of μm) CT scan that allows very detailed views of small areas. This is beginning to find application in palaeopathology, for example for 'virtually slicing' lesions to look at their detailed internal structure (Odes et al., 2018).

Although CT provides a fuller picture of the material under study, simple radiography remains the more important tool for the osteoarchaeologist (Mays, 2008c). Partly this is for practical reasons. Radiography is a technique that is fairly readily available to most osteoarchaeologists, and most university departments teaching osteoarchaeology have their own radiographic equipment. By contrast, CT scanners are very expensive and remain the province of medical clinicians or of researchers in engineering or other areas. Osteoarchaeologists usually have to negotiate with hospital radiology or other departments for the use of their CT facilities.

Although radiography is the single most widely used augment to simple visual study of remains, it is fair to say that it plays more of a role in the study of some conditions than in others. It is clearly necessary for the study of lesions which are wholly or partially hidden within the bone (for example, osteomyelitis – Figure 8.3). It is also important for the identification of diseases for which gross bony changes are obvious but their appearance is not specific enough to allow a diagnosis. An example is Paget's disease of bone.

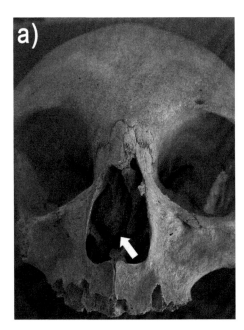 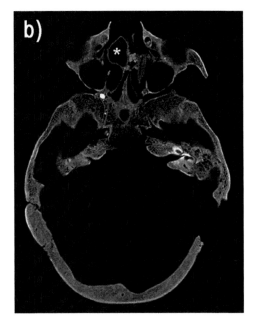

Figure 8.15 (a) Cranium from Mediaeval Huntingdon, England, showing an enlarged right middle nasal concha (arrowed). (b) CT of the same cranium, axial (infero-superior) view. A void space within the concha is clearly visible (asterisk), identifying this as a concha bullosa, an anatomical variant
Source, reproduced from Mays et al. (2011: Figs 2 & 5).

This is a metabolic disease of elderly people in which there is excessive bone remodelling (Tuck et al., 2017). The gross appearance is of thickened, pitted bones, but this appearance is also seen in a variety of other conditions. Although the gross specimen may be difficult to interpret, the chaotic internal structure of the bone in Paget's disease results in a characteristic radiographic appearance (Figure 8.16).

In the case of Paget's disease of bone, clinical radiographic criteria can be directly applied to palaeopathological bones. For other diseases, they may be of limited use for dry bone specimens, so that palaeopathologists need to apply them selectively. For example in rickets, most clinical radiographic diagnostic features relate to bending deformities, bone thickening, concavity of metaphyseal bone ends and 'fraying' of bone beneath the epiphyseal growth plate (Thacher et al., 2000; Pettifor, 2003: 555-557), but these are all readily visible to gross inspection in the dry bone. Radiographic diagnostic criteria for rickets in palaeopathology emphasise aspects such as coarsening/thinning of the trabecular structure and loss of cortico-medullary distinction that are not visible grossly in intact specimens (Mays et al., 2006b). For other diseases, where changes are essentially restricted to bone surfaces, such as osteoarthritis, radiological imaging is less important.

It must be emphasised that radiological imaging of archaeological specimens should be used in addition to careful visual examination of the bones, not as a substitute for it. Post-depositional effects such as soil erosion, breaks in the bone, or ingress of soil

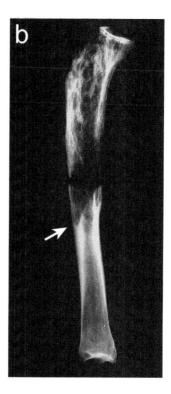

Figure 8.16 (a) The proximal parts of this tibia are thickened, pitted and somewhat bowed. The arrow indicates the boundary between the normal and abnormal bone. (b) The radiograph reveals that the diseased bone has a chaotic internal architecture, giving a mottled appearance on X-ray. The demarcation (arrow) between the normal and abnormal bone is sharp, and the advancing front of diseased tissue is V-shaped. These are typical radiographic features of Paget's disease of bone

particles to the bone interior cause changes in the image (Figure 8.3b) which might be mistaken for those due to disease. Radiographs or CT scans should always be examined in conjunction with the specimen itself.

Quantification of the amount of bone present in a specimen

For studying diseases such as osteoporosis, where changes involve loss of bone mineral without change to the gross anatomical shape of the bone, radiological techniques are available which enable not only production of an image but also quantification of this loss of bone substance. For example, loss of cortical bone can be monitored by measuring the thickness of the cortical bone on a radiograph or on CT. Bone density can be measured using a variety of techniques, the most important of which is dual X-ray absorptiometry, or DXA, in which the attenuation of X-rays as they pass through a specimen is measured and converted into a density figure. An example of an archaeological study using this technique is presented later in this chapter.

Microscopy

In modern medicine, microscopic examination of tissue samples (histology) plays an important role in the diagnosis of some diseases (de Boer & van der Merwe, 2016), but it mostly involves examining tissues that do not normally survive in archaeological burials. However, osteoarchaeologists may sometimes study microscopic alterations in pathological bone to help diagnosis. Microscopy of ancient bones is destructive, but it allows visualisation down to a level that is currently beyond that which can be adequately accessed by non-destructive methods such as micro-CT, and it is a technique that is much more readily available. Small samples, a few millimetres wide, are taken by sawing free a slice of bone (generally a half section so as not to cut completely through the bone) or by removing a plug of bone with a small drill. These samples are then prepared, a process that usually involves embedding them in resin and grinding and polishing the surface to be examined. These sections are studied for abnormalities in their microstructure under a light microscope or scanning electron microscope. Almost no pathological changes seen microscopically are specific to a particular disease. Microscopic analysis should therefore never be used as the sole method of examining a diseased bone. It should only be used to support observations made from visual examination, radiography or other techniques (Turner-Walker & Mays, 2008). Diagenetic change (see Chapter 2) may alter bone microstructure, and if severe may limit the information that can be obtained (Turner-Walker & Mays, 2008; Assis et al., 2015).

Microscopy is particularly useful as a diagnostic aid for bone metabolic disease (Brickley et al., 2020). For example, Paget's disease of bone is one of the few conditions in which the histological picture is firmly diagnostic (Mays, 2008b). Microscopic study is also useful in confirming vitamin D deficiency; the deficient mineralisation of bone is clearly visible at the histological level (Figure 8.17).

Analysis of biomolecules

Diagnosis of infectious disease can sometimes be assisted by analysing residues of biomolecules left by disease-causing microorganisms present in the body at death. For example, identification of lipids specific to the cell-walls of bacteria responsible for tuberculosis and for leprosy has helped diagnose cases of these diseases in skeletal remains (Inskip et al., 2015; Molnár et al., 2015). However, most biomolecular work on infectious disease in ancient skeletal material has concentrated on the study of DNA. This topic will be considered in Chapter 12.

Problems in diagnosing disease in ancient bones

Despite the work which has been directed at enabling palaeopathological diagnosis, identification of disease from bony changes alone remains difficult. The limited ways in which bone can respond to disease means that different diseases may appear alike on the skeleton. Because factors other than the disease which is present can influence bone changes, the same disease may look different in different individuals. A further difficulty in archaeological cases is that skeletons are often incomplete, and the bones which do remain may be damaged by post-depositional processes. Careful study of the lesions and

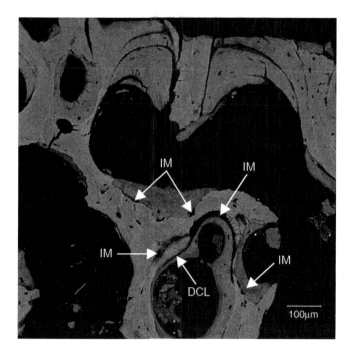

Figure 8.17 Scanning electron micrograph of a rib showing multiple areas of incomplete mineralisation, indicated by the dark areas (arrowed IM), and defectively mineralised bone adjacent to cement lines (boundaries between osteons) (DCL). These features are typical of vitamin D deficiency

Source: reproduced from Brickley et al. (2007).

their distribution in the skeleton may suggest a diagnosis, but in many cases, particularly where the only change is an isolated lump, bump or cavity on a bone, a firm diagnosis may remain elusive.

Quantifying disease frequency in skeletal assemblages

Sometimes, identification of a single case of a disease in a skeleton may be significant – for example it may show the existence of a condition at a time period or location that alters our understanding of the history of the spread of that disease among different human populations. More usually, however, we need to progress beyond the study of the individual skeleton and look at disease occurrence at the population level. This facilitates biocultural studies aimed at tackling meaningful archaeological questions, allowing us to make more general inferences about the past. This means quantifying the frequency of disease in the skeletal assemblage(s) under study.

Disease frequencies in skeletal assemblages are usually measured in terms of prevalence. Prevalence may be expressed with respect to individual skeletons, in which case it is the number of skeletons affected divided by the total number scored for that condition. For conditions that generally affect a particular element of the skeleton we must, when we compute the prevalence in terms of individuals, be careful to include in our calculation only those skeletons preserving the particular element or skeletal part of interest. For example, as we shall see below, anaemia may cause a type of pitting that particularly affects the roofs of the orbits. To record the prevalence of this condition we would divide the total number of individuals showing orbital lesions by the total number of individuals whose crania preserved orbital roofs.

For cases where individual skeletons each possess more than one element which potentially shows the disease of interest, the situation is a little more complex. For example, in a collection of articulated skeletons, the prevalence of osteophytosis of the vertebral bodies (an indication of vertebral disc degeneration – see Figure 8.9) could be scored in terms of individuals affected, i.e. prevalence = number of individuals who have one or more vertebral bodies with osteophytosis, divided by number of individuals. We would clearly want to exclude from study individuals without any vertebrae preserved, but what should we do about skeletons with incomplete spines? If a skeleton with an incomplete vertebral column does show osteophytosis of one or more of the vertebrae, then there is clearly no problem in deciding that vertebral osteophytosis was present in that individual. The situation is less straightforward in individuals with some vertebrae missing who do not show osteophytosis on any of the vertebral bodies that are preserved. In such cases we could not say for certain that osteophytosis was absent in the individual because one or more of the missing vertebrae may have shown a lesion. One way around this difficulty would be only to include in our prevalence rate individuals where the area of the skeleton of interest (the vertebral column in the above example) is complete. In reality this is not usually a viable strategy as, given the incompleteness of most archaeological skeletons, we would be left with very few individuals to work with. The usual thing is to include incomplete skeletons (in the above example, all those with one or more vertebrae available for study) but to bear in mind that because of the uncertainty surrounding negative cases this will result in an underestimation of the prevalence of the condition of interest, and that the degree of underestimation will be greater the fewer elements are available for observation.

An alternative to using the individual as the basis for calculating prevalence is to use the bone or part of the bone (this would be the vertebral body in the above example), so that prevalence is number of bones with a lesion divided by the total number of bones in an assemblage that were examined. This eliminates the problem of reliability of negative evidence (and is the only way of quantification in mingled, disarticulated remains), but a difficulty with the prevalence by element approach is that multiple elements in a given individual (vertebrae in a particular skeleton in the above example) are not independent observations for statistical purposes, meaning that verification of patterning seen in results using standard statistical tests is not possible. In practice, it is often useful to combine both approaches, primarily using the prevalence by individuals, as this is amenable to statistical analyses, but using the prevalence by skeletal element as a back-up to check whether a consistent pattern is obtained comparing assemblages using both methods. In the vertebral osteophytosis example, we would probably calculate an individual prevalence as number of skeletons showing osteophytosis in one or more vertebral bodies divided by number of skeletons preserving at least one vertebral body for study. We would calculate the prevalence by element by dividing total number of vertebral bodies in the assemblage showing osteophytosis by the total number of vertebral bodies scored for the condition.

Another, more sophisticated approach, would be to record the presence or absence of a condition in each skeleton, and include a measure of skeletal completeness in each case as a variable in the analysis. Multivariate statistical techniques, such as logistic regression (Tabachnik & Fidell, 2013: 439–509), can be used to control for the effects of skeletal completeness (and indeed of other variables) on prevalence data when making comparisons within or between skeletal assemblages. In our vertebral osteophytosis example, number of vertebral bodies preserved could be entered for each skeleton as our skeletal completeness variable. Entering a measure of skeletal completeness into a multivariate analysis has been used not only for the study of vertebral pathology (Mays, 2016), but also for other conditions that may potentially affect multiple sites in the skeleton, such as vitamin D deficiency (Mays et al., 2018c).

Because many diseases which may potentially affect the skeleton actually do so only in a minority of cases, care is needed in interpreting prevalence figures in skeletal populations. For example, tuberculosis may affect the skeleton by spread of infection from the soft tissues – often the lungs. From a survey of some of the medical literature pre-dating the advent of antibiotics, Steinbock (1976:175) suggests that untreated, it may do so in only about 5–7% of cases. However, it must be emphasised that this is an average figure. If, for example, tuberculosis spread to a population which had little resistance to it, we would expect few to survive the disease long enough to show bone changes, so less than Steinbock's figure of 5–7% would show skeletal signs. However, in the case of a population which had built up some resistance to tuberculosis, as a result of long association with the bacteria which cause it, we might expect longer survival before succumbing to, or recovering from the disease, and hence a somewhat higher frequency of bone changes. It is worth bearing in mind, then, that differences in frequencies of infectious diseases, such as tuberculosis, in archaeological assemblages may reflect not only differences in the prevalence of a disease in the once-living population from which the assemblages are drawn, but also, to some extent, the resistance of those populations to the disease. This complicating factor in the interpretation of prevalence data from skeletal populations has been recognised for some time, and it has been termed the osteological paradox (Wood et al., 1992). The 'paradox' arises because a skeletal assemblage with few lesions could indicate a population where the disease was rare or alternatively one where the disease was common but individuals had a low resistance to it so few survived long enough to show bone lesions. This point will be returned to in some of the archaeological studies described below.

The prevalences of most specific diseases are usually quite low in skeletal series. The prevalences of infections, such as leprosy or tuberculosis, erosive arthropathies, major congenital defects, and most metabolic diseases and neoplasms, are characteristically less than about 5%, and often under 1%. This means that, unless assemblages are very large, there often too few cases of any particular disease to provide an adequate basis for statistical analysis of results. One way around this problem is to combine diseases together to increase numbers. This can work well when those diseases share risk factors in common (e.g. infectious diseases are often related to overcrowding and poor hygiene), but it is not always appropriate. For example, we would not wish to combine metabolic diseases together to give some overall prevalence figure as they have disparate causes ranging from lack of fresh fruit and vegetables (scurvy), to lack of exposure of the skin to sunlight (rickets) to those where the cause is unknown (Paget's disease of bone). Another stratagem is to concentrate one's population comparisons on conditions that are more common, for example osteoarthritis or non-specific periostitis.

The contribution of palaeopathological study of bone disease to archaeology

What follows are four archaeological examples of the contribution of palaeopathology to the study of the human past. Two comprise cases where study of skeletal remains has enhanced our knowledge of the history of specific diseases. The others consist of studies in which disease data for different populations is used to shed light on broader questions concerning living conditions in past communities.

The history of syphilis in Europe

Syphilis is one of four related infections caused by bacteria of the genus *Treponema* (Centurion-Lara et al., 2006, 2013), the others being bejel (also called endemic syphilis or treponarid), yaws and pinta. Collectively they are termed the treponemal diseases. All except pinta may affect the skeleton. Yaws is a disease of the humid tropics, and is spread by skin contact. Bejel, like yaws, is spread by skin contact or via shared eating and drinking vessels. It is mainly found in warm, dry climates, although in the past it occurred in temperate Europe. Syphilis is the only one of the treponemal diseases which is sexually transmitted, and it may also be passed from an infected mother to the developing foetus so that the child is born with the disease. The distribution of syphilis shows no climatic restrictions (Giacani & Lukehart, 2014).

The bone changes in syphilis

The course of syphilis is generally protracted and may be divided into three stages (Sparling et al., 2008). The primary stage lasts about three weeks and involves the appearance of a sore at the point of infection (usually the genitals). Secondary syphilis marks the spread of the disease through the body via the bloodstream and lymphatic system, and is characterised by fever and a transient skin eruption. Features of the tertiary stage, which commences some 1–20 years after initial infection, include spread of syphilitic damage to different organs, such as the circulatory system, which may result in syphilitic aneurysms, and the central nervous system, which may result in blindness, deafness, paralysis and insanity. Untreated syphilis may cause death, but generally only after the sufferer has had the disease for a long period of time, often several decades.

Diagnostic bone changes are confined to the tertiary stage of the disease (Hackett, 1976; Ortner, 2003: 278–289). Formation of gummata may occur. A gumma is a firm swelling which may form within various tissues, including bone. Skeletal changes in syphilis may be due to the formation of gummata in or adjacent to the bones (gummatous lesions) or simply to chronic inflammation not associated with gumma formation (non-gummatous lesions). Formation of gummata leads to cavities within the bone or on its surface. Chronic inflammation leads to periostitis with marked bone thickening.

In syphilis, the bones most commonly affected include those of the cranial vault (particularly the frontal bone) and the tibia (Figures. 8.18 and 8.19); involvement of the other tubular bones is also frequent (Roberts & Buikstra, 2019: Table 11.7). The lesions in the other treponemal diseases which may affect bone, bejel and yaws, are very similar to those in venereal syphilis (Hackett, 1976; Heathcote et al., 1998; Roberts & Buikstra, 2019: 376), so it is difficult to distinguish one from another on the basis of bone lesions.

Controversy has long existed over the origin and geographical spread of the treponemal diseases, particularly syphilis. Specifically, much discussion has centred on the introduction of syphilis into Europe. One theory, termed the Columbian hypothesis, maintains that it originated in the Americas and was brought to Europe by Columbus and his crew when they returned in 1493 from their first voyage to the New World. Other theories hold that it was already present in Europe prior to this.

Historical evidence for the origin of syphilis

Researchers into the social history of medicine have long recognised that many diseases have origin myths in which their advent is attributed to a specific event involving contact with outsiders. This tends to be especially so when a disease strikes suddenly, seems to be especially threatening, or carries social stigma. Equating such diseases with contact with outsiders is more congenial than the idea that responsibility lies closer to home (Lie, 2007). Although the notion that European syphilis came from the New World seems conform to a classic 'origin myth', there is some evidence to support the theory. Documentary evidence describes a disease, which appears to be syphilis, ravaging Europe in the closing years of the 15th century, an epidemic which appears to have coincided with Columbus's return from the New World. Although there are some pre-Columbian Old World written sources that may refer to syphilis (Kaplan, 2002), there is no unequivocal description and, almost without exception, 16th-century Old-World writers considered it a new disease (Crosby 1969). In Europe, it seems to have followed the classic course of a newly introduced disease of initial virulence followed by a decrease in its severity (Knell, 2004).

Several associates of Columbus felt that that syphilis originated in the New World. For example, the physician, Diaz de Ysla, claimed, in a book published in 1539, that the disease was seen in Columbus's men and that they contracted it on the Caribbean island of Hispaniola. He also described its rapid spread through Barcelona in 1493 after Columbus's return there from the Americas (de Rincon-Ferraz, 1999). Historical sources suggest that syphilis was present in the Americas long before the arrival of Europeans. Bartolome de las Casas, who accompanied Columbus to the New World, learnt from the Native Americans that they had known the disease since time immemorial (Crosby, 1969). Friar Ramon recorded the beliefs of the Arawak natives of Hispaniola in the mid-1490s. He tells of an Arawak folk hero, Guagagiona, who 'had great pleasure' with a woman but soon afterwards had to 'wash himself because he was full of those sores which we call the French disease' [i.e. syphilis] (Crosby, 1969).

Those who have attacked the Columbian theory on the basis of the documentary evidence suggest that syphilis was present in Europe prior to 1493 but that it was not

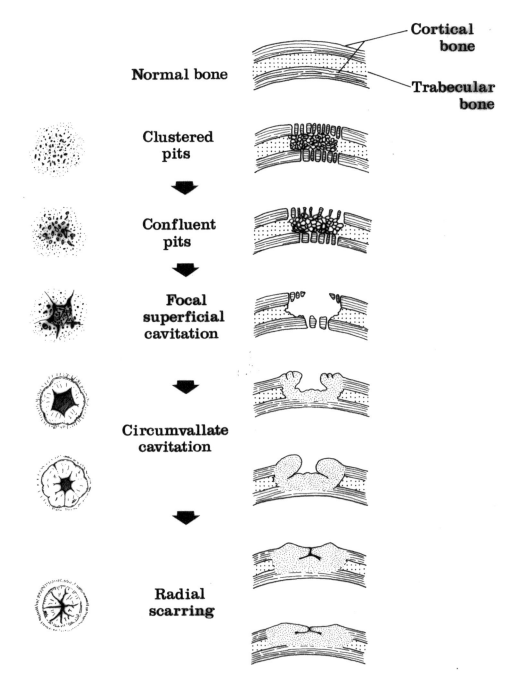

Figure 8.18 Sequence of cranial vault changes in treponemal disease. The series on the left shows the appearance of the lesions on the external cranial surface; that on the right shows them in cross-section

Source: Redrawn from Hackett (1983: Figure 2).

Figure 8.19 Syphilis: four views of a tibia thickened due to non-gummatous periostitis
Source: Reproduced from Hackett (1976: Figure 21).

adequately distinguished from other diseases. For example, Mediaeval documents refer to a condition termed 'venereal' or 'hereditary leprosy'; true leprosy (which Mediaeval authorities certainly could recognise) is not sexually transmitted and does not occur congenitally, so this may refer to syphilis. It is suggested that the 'syphilis epidemic' in late 15th-century Europe may merely have been the widespread recognition of syphilis as a distinct condition rather than it being a truly new disease.

Other criticisms of the Columbian hypothesis have been made on the basis of the historical evidence. A New World origin for syphilis was not mentioned until more than thirty years after Columbus's first voyage, whereas if a relationship existed one might have expected it to be mentioned sooner (Holcomb, 1935). In particular no mention of the disease is made in the documents relating to Columbus's voyages written prior to its apparent outbreak in Europe (Crosby, 1969). Furthermore, even if we accept that there were epidemics of syphilis in the closing years of the 15th century they may not be connected with the Columbus voyage (Holcomb, 1935).

Phylogenetic evidence

Phylogenetic approaches aim to establish the evolutionary development of an organism. Work in this direction has been done using DNA sequences from modern isolates of the bacteria causing the different treponemal diseases. A recent study (Arora et al., 2016) estimated that different modern-day strains of the bacterium causing venereal syphilis split from a common ancestor during 17th–19th century AD. The authors of the study suggest that this could potentially be compatible with a post-Columbian origin for European syphilis (although the estimated timing of the divergence event is obviously much later than the Columbus voyage). However, they also point out that it does not exclude the possibility of the existence of older, pre-Columbian lineages of the bacterium in Europe that have since become extinct.

Neither the documentary nor the phylogenetic evidence has so far resolved the debate on the origins of syphilis. This highlights the importance of the skeletal data.

The contribution of skeletal evidence to the debate

There is abundant skeletal evidence for treponemal disease of pre-Columbian date from the Americas (Powell & Cook, 2005), the oldest of which dates back to at least 3000BC (e.g. Smith, 2006). For a long time, no good cases of treponemal disease which certainly pre-date 1493 were known from Europe. This was taken by many writers (e.g. Crosby, 1969; Baker & Armelagos, 1988) as supporting the Columbian hypothesis.

However, archaeological discoveries have accumulated that have altered this picture. A number of skeletons from pre-1493 archaeological contexts showing signs of treponemal disease have now been reported from Europe (Dawes & Magilton, 1980: 58; Stirland, 1991; 1994; Blondiaux & Alduc-le-Bagousse, 1994; Mays et al., 2003; 2012b) and the Mediterranean Basin (Ortner, 2003: 313–316; Mitchell, 2005, 2009). Kristin Harper and co-workers (Harper et al., 2011) review the cases cited above, together with other Old World cases published as pre-Columbian. They argue that, in all instances, there is a possibility that the dates (which in many cases lie in the centuries immediately preceding the Columbus voyage) could in fact extend into the post-1493 period and/or that (despite the fact that their work did not involve any re-examination of the bones themselves) the diagnoses are uncertain. The position taken by that group of researchers appeared to be that, until there is an Old World skeleton with both an unassailable pre-1493 date and an unequivocal diagnosis, they intend to cling grimly to the Columbian hypothesis. That sort of approach seems unsuited to the equivocal nature of archaeological data, and it may lead to a failure to relinquish a favoured hypothesis long after it becomes clear that the balance of the evidence no longer supports it. I felt that we had arrived at such a situation back in 2013 (see Harper et al., 2013 vs Mays & Vincent, 2013 for a flavour of some of the debate), and subsequent finds seem to show that this is even more clearly the case now.

A skeleton recently described from England suggests that treponemal disease may even have been present in Europe for as long as a millennium before the Columbus voyage. It comes from a cemetery at Apple Down, in southern England, and dates to the 5th–7th century AD. There were both the cranial and post-cranial lesions (Cole & Waldron, 2011; Cole et al., 2015). In the skull, the frontal bone (Plate 5a) showed clusters of pits; some of the larger pits appeared to have been formed by confluence of smaller ones. The postcranial skeleton showed profuse periostitis, with concentric thickening of tubular bones, and some evidence of gummatous changes (Plate 5b, c). The cranial pitting appears to correspond the earlier phases of the treponemal disease sequence (Figure 8.18), and the post-cranial changes are also typical of treponemal disease.

Cole & Waldron (2011) present the Apple Down skeleton as a case of syphilis, but that seems to push the evidence too far. The similarity of bone lesions in yaws, bejel or syphilis means we cannot reliably distinguish them in skeletal remains. Even if we can eliminate yaws as a possibility on the basis that it is a disease of the humid tropics, one could suggest that this (and potentially other pre-1493 cases in Europe) represents bejel rather than syphilis. Historically, bejel was common in many parts of Europe (Willcox, 1972; Anderson et al., 1986; Mehues, 1996). One way of determining specifically whether syphilis was present in pre-1493 Europe and the Mediterannean basin would be if evidence was found of congenital disease. Syphilis may be passed via the placenta to the foetus of an infected mother (Parish, 2000), but there is no firm evidence of congenital transmission of yaws or bejel (Wicher et al., 2000; Peeling & Hook, 2006; Giacani & Lukehart, 2014). In this light a skeleton found in Anatolia is of interest.

Erdal (2006) describes a skeleton of a teenager dated to the 13th century AD from Iznik, near Bursa, in Turkey. It shows the classic gummatous changes of treponemal disease. Congenital cases of syphilis sometimes show malformations of the molar and incisor teeth due to invasion of the developing tooth by the treponemal bacteria (Shafii et al., 2008). Particularly important are the incisor defects (termed Hutchinson incisors), which are specific to syphilis (Hillson et al., 1998; Ioannu et al., 2016). They consist of a notch in the centre of the biting edge of the tooth which is itself narrowed so that the sides of the tooth bulge out below it (Figure 8.20a). An upper central incisor was preserved in the Iznik skeleton and showed this form (Figure 8.20b).

It now seems clear that treponemal disease (in all probability syphilis) was present in pre-1493 Europe. The debate regarding the disease in early Europe has started to move beyond the discussion of individual skeletons, toward looking at disease prevalence. Treponemal disease rarely affects the bones, so it is only in very large cemeteries that we have enough cases to do this. One very large Mediaeval cemetery that has produced evidence for treponemal disease is St Mary Spital in London. Walker et al. (2015) found 25 cases out of 5387 skeletons examined from this site. The cemetery dated from AD1120–1539, but radiocarbon dating showed that seven of the treponemal cases came from phases dating to AD1120–1400, and so were securely pre-Columbian. The remainder came from contexts dating to AD1400–1539, so could be either pre- or post-Columbian or a mixture of the two. The bone lesions were similar in pre- and post-AD1400 cases but the prevalence of the disease was greater in the later phase. It is tempting to equate this rise in prevalence in treponemal disease in the St Mary Spital population to the increase frequency of syphilis described in documentary sources from the closing years of the 15th century, but Walker et al. (2015) are cautious. Firstly, it was not possible to determine if the St Mary Spital cases were syphilis or bejel. There were no dental alterations indicative of congenital disease, but this does not mean the disease was not syphilis – dental changes do not always occur in congenital disease, and in any event most syphilis is acquired in adulthood/adolescence. Mindful of the osteological paradox, Walker et al. (2015) also point out that the greater frequency of skeletal lesions may not be due to an increase in treponemal disease in the population but to a more chronic expression of the disease – perhaps Londoners acquired more resistance to it over time.

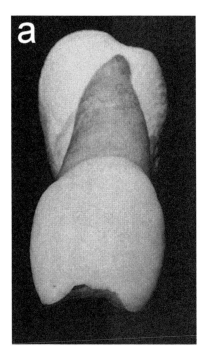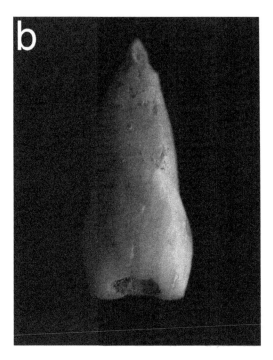

Figure 8.20   (a) An upper incisor from a recent case of congenital syphilis, showing narrowing of the biting edge and a broad notch. (b) An upper incisor from the Mediaeval Iznik case; although the tooth is a little more worn that than in (a), the morphological alterations are clearly similar

Source: (a) reproduced from Hillson et al. (1998); (b) reproduced from Erdal (2006).

Mediaeval osteoporosis

Osteoarchaeology has also made an important contribution to the study of the history of another disease, osteoporosis. This is a metabolic disease involving loss of bone mineral with advancing age. It results in decreased bone strength and increased vulnerability to fracture (Marcus et al., 2013). It particularly affects older women, and it is a major health threat to the elderly today (Kanis et al., 2017). In contrast to syphilis, documentary sources are largely silent on this disease – in order to study the history of osteoporosis we must study bones.

The prime cause of osteoporosis in women is the hormonal changes which accompany the menopause. However, a number of factors associated with modern Western lifestyles also seem to play a part in exacerbating bone loss. It is clearly of interest from the point of view of our present-day understanding of this disease to study its history in earlier European populations with lifestyles very different from our own. One population in which osteoporosis has been studied extensively is Wharram Percy (work summarised in Mays, 2007: 177–181; see also, 2010c).

A variety of techniques have been used to study osteoporosis in past populations (Curate, 2014; Brickley & Mays, 2019). Among those that have been applied at Wharram Percy is dual X-ray absorptiometry (DXA) of the femur neck (Mays et al., 1998). DXA measures bone mineral density (BMD). It is the most important tool for monitoring bone loss in osteoporosis in living patients, and one of the aims of the Wharram Percy work was to compare bone loss in ancient and modern people.

Care is needed when using DXA to study osteoporosis in excavated skeletons. Ingress of soil into the bone interior and chemical changes during burial may potentially affect bone density. To control for the first of these factors, bones were radiographed, and any showing signs of soil ingress were excluded from the analysis (Mays et al., 1998). Micro-scopic analysis (Turner-Walker & Syversen, 2002; Turner-Walker et al., 2002) showed that there was little evidence of minor soil ingress that might have escaped detection on radiographs. Microscopic and chemical analyses, also suggested no great changes in bulk mineral content or composition (Turner-Walker & Syversen, 2002; Mays, 2003b). It seems therefore that at Wharram Percy, once the obviously soil-contaminated specimens were excluded, post-depositional changes in bone density are likely to be minor, permit-ting study of osteoporosis by DXA. Because archaeological specimens lack marrow and soft tissue, absolute DXA BMD values cannot be directly compared with those measured in living people (Lees et al., 1993; Chappard et al., 2004). However, in cases where signifi-cant post-depositional change in BMD can be excluded, valid comparisons of age-related patterns can be made. The results for the Wharram Percy women, together with those for a modern female reference population, are shown in Figure 8.21.

In modern populations, menopause generally begins in the late 40s, and documentary evi-dence suggests that this was also the case in historic times (Pavelka & Fedigan, 1991). Unlike the modern reference data, the Wharram Percy figures seem to show a quite a marked decline in BMD in the 30-49 age group, implying pre-menopausal bone loss (Figure 8.21). This has been seen in other Mediaeval populations (Mays, 2010c), and may be associated with the high parity (i.e. number of births) and late weaning of infants (see Chapter 11) which appear to have been customary in Mediaeval times (Shahar, 1990). In modern populations, minor reduc-tions in BMD may occur during pregnancy and lactation but are quickly recovered (Mays, 2010c). In the past, recovery of bone mass following pregnancy and lactation may often have been prevented or slowed by poor maternal nutrition (Turner-Walker et al., 2001). It may also be that a combination of a rather poor diet and heavy physical work meant that the oestro-gen levels for the Wharram Percy women were generally rather low and their menstrual cycles irregular; this too may have had a negative effect on BMD (Mays, 2010c).

Comparison of BMD values in the 30-49 and 50+ age groups suggests that post-menopausal bone loss is similar in the Wharram Percy and the modern women – in each case the mean value for the 50+ age group is about 89% of that in the 30-49 year group. A problem with this comparison is that, as we learnt in Chapter 4, it is not possible with cur-rent methods of skeletal ageing to break down the 50+ age group in finer age categories. Given the age-progressive nature of osteoporosis, if the age composition of the 50+ group differed between Wharram Percy and the modern reference population then this could ser-iously prejudice results. To tackle this problem, the mean BMD figures from the modern ref-erence data for the decades 50-59, 60-69 and 70-79 were weighted according to the proportions of the 50+ age group dying in these decades in Russell's (1937) documentary study of Mediaeval age at death discussed in Chapter 4. The 50+ age group figure for the modern reference data used in Figure 8.21 was produced by this method. The comparison with the modern BMD data will be accurate if the age composition of the Wharram Percy

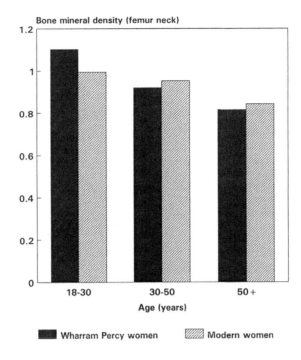

Figure 8.21 Bone mineral density (gcm^{-2}) at the femur neck in women from Wharram Percy (N=54), compared with a modern, living population. Although absolute bone mineral density values in archaeological bone cannot be directly compared with those in living people, valid comparisons of age-related patterns can be made

Sources: Wharram Percy data from Mays et al. (1998); modern reference data from Lunar Corporation (1993).

50+ age group conforms to that of the individuals in Russell's Mediaeval demographic study. If anything, the Wharram Percy people, being of lower socioeconomic status (see Chapter 4), might be expected to have lived less long. This means that post-menopausal bone loss in the Wharram Percy women was likely no less than modern subjects, although it leaves open the possibility that it might have been greater.

Lifestyle factors thought to exacerbate osteoporotic bone loss following the menopause include cigarette smoking, sedentary lifestyle, deficient calcium intake, and perhaps vitamin D deficiency (Ross, 1996; Bonnick et al., 2010). Tobacco was unknown in Mediaeval England. Mediaeval peasants would have had a very physically active lifestyle compared to their modern descendants. This was as true for women as for men (Bennett, 1987). Wharram Percy lies on chalk geology, and many cow bones and fragments of pottery vessels used for dairy products were found there, so diet was unlikely to have been deficient in calcium. The outdoor lifestyle of Mediaeval peasants would seem to make adult vitamin D deficiency unlikely, and no cases of vitamin D deficiency disease were seen in those who survived their early years (Mays, 2007).

The impression is that the lifestyle of Mediaeval women would have been expected to lower their risk of osteoporosis compared with their modern counterparts. That the results indicate that their post-menopausal bone loss was not less than in modern subjects may call into question the importance of lifestyle factors in this respect.

In modern women, osteoporosis leads to increased risk of fracture, particularly at the hip, wrist and the vertebral bodies (Harvey et al., 2013). At Wharram Percy, there were no hip or wrist fractures, but there were compression fractures of the vertebral bodies. Figure 8.22 illustrates two healed vertebral compression fractures in an elderly female from Wharram Percy. The BMD at the femur neck for this individual was only 0.653gcm^{-2}, fully four standard deviations below the young female adult mean at Wharram Percy. Although we can't tell when in the life of this individual these fractures occurred, they are typical of the type seen in osteoporosis.

Anaemia in prehistoric Peru

Anaemia is an impairment of the ability of the red blood cells to transport oxygen to the tissues. Some types of anaemia are congenital. In certain populations, for example some from tropical and Mediterranean regions, congenital anaemias are sufficiently common to be an significant cause of anaemia at the population level. In other areas, anaemia is generally acquired rather than congenital. The most common form of acquired anaemia is iron deficiency anaemia (Brugnara, 2003), but it may also arise due to other causes, such as deficiencies of Vitamin B$_{12}$ or folic acid, which lead to another type, megaloblastic anaemia, in which there is inefficient red blood cell production.

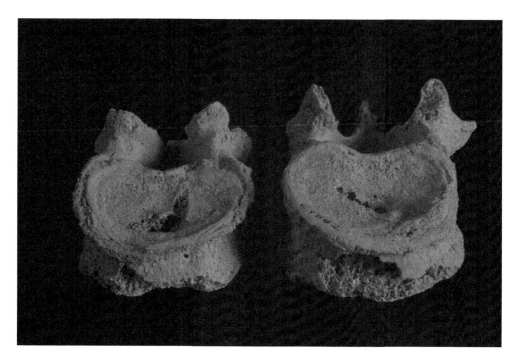

Figure 8.22 Healed compression fractures in the bodies of the twelfth thoracic and first lumbar vertebrae from an elderly female from Wharram Percy

Current consensus is that the most important skeletal manifestation of anaemia is a type of pitting on the orbital roofs and/or cranial vault. This type of pitting is known as porotic hyperostosis, and when it occurs in the orbital roof it is known as cribra orbitalia. Porotic hyperostosis in anaemia is thought to result from thinning of the outer table of the cranium due to overgrowth of the underlying trabecular bone (Figure 8.23). This latter is a location of red blood cell formation, and overgrowth of this layer is thought to represent the body's attempt to combat anaemia by raising red blood cell production (Brickley, 2018). It is not possible to determine, from the bone changes, which form of anaemia was present, but current consensus appears to be that iron deficiency and megaloblastic types are most likely the main types behind porotic hyperostosis (Walker et al., 2009; Oxenham & Cavill, 2010; Mays, 2012: 290–293; McIlvaine, 2015). Of these, iron deficiency anaemia is by far the more common worldwide today (Pasricha et al., 2013), so porotic hyperostosis in skeletal remains

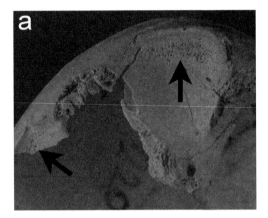

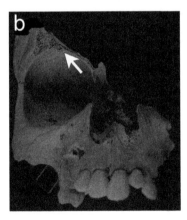

Figure 8.23 (a) Porotic hyperostosis of the orbital roofs (cribra orbitalia). (b) The post-depositional break in the right orbit reveals that the pitting corresponds to an area of overgrowth of the diploe (trabecular bone) and resorption of the thin cortical bone of the orbital roof

may predominantly represent this type. Care is needed in distinguishing porotic hyperostosis of anaemia from pitting due to other causes such as rickets or scurvy (Mays, 2018c; Brickley et al., 2020).

A team led by Deborah Blom, from the University of Vermont, studied the frequency of porotic hyperostosis in prehistoric (6th–15th century AD) populations from Peru (Blom et al., 2005). As part of this work they studied skeletal remains from five sites at different locations in the Moquegua valley (Figure 8.24). They wanted to investigate the effects of site location and subsistence strategies on the prevalence of porotic hyperostosis and hence to shed light on possible factors influencing rates of anaemia in the groups under study. There were 879 individuals from the Moquegua valley with orbital roofs intact so that cribra orbitalia could be scored. The results are summarised in Table 8.1.

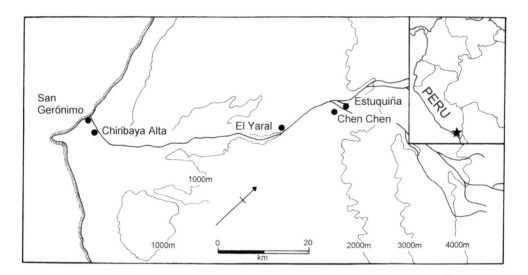

Figure 8.24 Location of burial grounds used in the study of porotic hyperostosis by Blom et al. (2005)

Source: After Blom et al. (2005: Figure 2).

Table 8.1 Frequencies of cribra orbitalia in the prehistoric Moquegua valley

| Site | Subsistence base | Cribra orbitalia | | | |
| | | Children (under 18 years) | | Adults (18+ years) | |
		N	% with lesions	N	% with lesions
San Gerónimo	Fishing	30	56.7	73	45.2
Chiribaya Alta	Fishing, some maize cultivation	91	60.4	160	42.5
El Yaral	Maize cultivation	31	64.5	59	42.4
Chen Chen	Maize cultivation	131	58.8	165	36.4
Estuquiña	Maize cultivation, some marine food	72	44.4	67	4.5

Source: data from Blom et al. (2005: Tables 8 & 9).

At all sites, lesions were more frequent in children than in adults. The pattern whereby porotic hyperostosis is more frequent in children is a general one. At birth, all bone marrow is of the 'red' type which produces red blood cells. When disease leads to increased red-blood cell production, there may be expansion of this red marrow. At most sites in the skeleton, red marrow is gradually replaced during childhood by fatty, yellow marrow that does not produce red blood cells. In adult life, a need to increase red blood cell production to combat anaemia is met by reconversion of yellow back to red marrow rather than by marrow expansion, so there are no bone lesions. In the cranium, the marrow conversion process is complete in the frontal bone (of which the orbital roofs are a part) by about 10 years old (Simonson & Kao, 1992). After this age, cribra orbitalia would be unlikely to occur in response to anaemia; lesions seen in the orbits of older individuals are relics of earlier, childhood disease. The other bones of the cranial vault may retain some capacity to form lesions into adolescence, but for anatomical reasons the propensity to form porotic hyperostotic lesions in response to red marrow over-growth appears less here than in the orbital roof (Brickley, 2018).

Genetic anaemias are not found in pre-contact New World contexts; the anaemia in the prehistoric Moquegua valley is likely to be acquired. One hypothesis Blom and co-workers explored was whether diet could be a significant factor in anaemia in their study samples. For example, a heavy reliance on maize may potentially lead to iron deficiency, as maize contains a substance, phytate, which inhibits absorption of iron from food. It is also low in vitamin B_{12} so overreliance on this crop could lead to megaloblastic anaemia. However, despite the great differences in subsistence base between the various Moquegua groups, there was no evidence for any association between dietary regime and prevalence of cribra orbitalia (Table 8.1).

Other potential causes of anaemia are gut parasites and gut disease. Gut parasites cause anaemia by chronic blood loss and their presence may also interfere with vitamin B_{12} absorption. In diarrhoeal disease, nutrients such as iron and vitamin B_{12} pass through the gut too quickly to be absorbed efficiently, and this can lead to anaemia, especially if diet is low in these items in the first place. Blom et al. (2005) investigated whether gut parasites or disease were likely factors in anaemia in their study populations. They hypothesised that if these factors were important then elevated rates of porotic hyperostosis should be present in communities at lower, more downstream locations, such as San Gerónimo and Chiribaya Alta, as river waters would be contaminated from effluent from settlements further upstream. High rates might also be expected at Chen Chen and El Yaral, as these communities utilised irrigation for agriculture which would enable these sites to support high population densities and would also have provided a ready source of potentially polluted water. Estuquiña would be expected to be the exception to this pattern of high prevalence. This was a fortified site situated on an inaccessible mountain ridge away from the river and the irrigated agrarian sites, so was somewhat removed from these sources of water-borne disease. The results seem consistent with this – the prevalence of cribra orbitalia at Estuquiña is lower that at the other sites, which have similar frequencies to one another. The prevalence of cribra orbitalia among adults from Estuquiña was particularly low. Reasons for this were unclear, however, recalling that lesions seen in adults may generally be relics of childhood disease, Blom et al. (2005) suggest that it may reflect that, although anaemia was apparently less common at Estuquiña than at the other sites, the conditions that caused it at this settlement may more often have been fatal to the children.

Infectious disease in Mediaeval England

Our second example of inter-population comparisons of disease investigates the effects of urban vs rural life on human health using the frequency of periostitis.

Some non-infectious conditions may cause periostitis, including venous stasis ('varicose veins'), scurvy and some types of malignant cancers and congenital disorders. Some of these conditions are recognisable because they also cause other lesions in the skeleton (e.g. scurvy), others are rare (e.g. congenital causes of periostitis), particularly in comparison to infectious disease which was likely common in earlier populations. Current consensus seems to be that infection is likely the most common cause of periostitis in past populations (Roberts, 2019: 292), and it has often been used as a general index of infection (Larsen, 2015: 86–96).

I used the prevalence of periostitis to compare infectious disease at Wharram Percy and in the city of York, which lies about 20 miles away. Anne Grauer (Grauer, 1993) had previously studied the prevalence of periostitis at the York site of St Helen-on-the-Walls. This cemetery dates from the Mediaeval period, and served a poor parish in the city. Comparing Wharram Percy and York St Helen-on-the-Walls enabled conditions of the Mediaeval urban and rural poor to be studied. The results are shown in Table 8.2.

At both Wharram Percy and York St Helens-on-the-Walls, the tibia was the bone most commonly affected by periostitis. At Wharram Percy, 41% of individuals with periostitis showed lesions in the tibia. Or, to look at it using prevalence by bone type, 4.2% of the total tibiae in the Wharram Percy assemblage showed periostitis, one-and-a-half times the prevalence of the next most frequently affected bone which was the fibula at 2.8%. The York data were quantified somewhat differently but also show clear evidence for preferential involvement of the tibia: 62% of bones showing periostitis were tibiae.

The pattern whereby the tibia is the bone most commonly affected by periostitis appears to be a general one in past populations (Larsen, 2015: 88). The reasons for this are obscure, and may be different in different populations. In the current context it is interesting that written records tell us that, in the 18th and 19th centuries, chronic infections of the lower legs were exceedingly common among the poorer classes in England and, in that pre-antibiotic age, were extremely tedious and difficult for doctors to treat. The cause was often minor injuries to the shins which became infected, and which,

Table 8.2 Prevalence of periostitis at Wharram Percy and York St Helen-on-the-Walls

Periostitis	N	% with lesions
Wharram Percy	687	8.4
York St Helen-on-the-Walls	641	22.5

Sources: data from Wharram Percy from Mays (2007: Table 104); data from York from Grauer (1993).

perhaps due to poor diet or generally poor health, failed to heal promptly (Loudon, 1981). The anterior/medial surface of the tibia is only covered by a thin layer of soft tissue, and so would easily have become involved in the infection. There are no adequate medico-historical documents for the Mediaeval period so we cannot confirm that chronic lower leg infections following minor injuries were also common then, but it seems likely, and one wonders whether this might be one reason why the tibia is the bone most commonly affected by periostitis in the York and Wharram Percy groups.

In addition to localised infections, various systemic infectious diseases can also cause periostitis. We have already seen this with treponemal disease (Figure 8.19), but early bone involvement in tuberculosis, before the formation of the characteristic abscess cavities in the spine (Figure 8.4) and elsewhere, may manifest as periostitis (Santos & Roberts, 2001). Pulmonary tuberculosis and other chronic lung infections can cause periostitis on the ribs (Roberts et al., 1998). These conditions can also lead to diffuse periostitis in many areas of the skeleton, a condition known as hypertrophic osteoarthropathy; other chronic lung and abdominal diseases can also do this (Mays & Taylor, 2002; Assis et al., 2011).

Although a multiplicity of different diseases no doubt contributed to the cases of periostitis at both York and Wharram Percy, the higher frequency at York may suggest a higher infectious disease burden in the urban than the rural environment. This result is as expected. A higher population and greater population density, and poorer hygiene chiefly due to contamination of water supplies, of an urban settlement would favour transmission of disease. Crowded, unhygienic conditions typified many Mediaeval cities, and written sources show that York was no exception (Grauer, 1993).

The inference that more bone lesions means greater infectious disease in the urban population is perhaps the intuitive interpretation of the data, but recalling the osteological paradox, the relatively fewer lesions in the Wharram Percy group may also mean that fewer individuals had sufficient resistance to infectious disease to survive for long enough when they did contract it for it to affect the skeleton. Perhaps those at Wharram Percy did not have the long-term exposure from birth to a wide array of pathogens that city-dwellers did, so that when infectious disease did strike, it often killed more quickly, before bone changes had the chance to develop. Study of the bone lesions provides some support for the idea that urban dwellers had a greater resistance to disease. Of the periostitis cases at York, the majority (68%) were remodelled lesions, suggesting that many in that population recovered from infectious disease. By contrast, at Wharram Percy, the majority (64%) were unremodelled, indicating that many failed to survive the diseases responsible for the lesions. In summary, both the higher frequency of lesions at York, and their more often remodelled state, are consistent with the idea of a higher pathogen load in the urban environment.

Summary

In most cases we cannot determine the cause of death from an ancient skeleton, but we can identify some of the diseases that affected people during their lives. Only a small subset of diseases affect the skeleton, so in skeletal remains we see only a very small proportion of disease that afflicted an earlier community.

To diagnose disease in a skeleton, osteoarchaeologists take into account both the nature of the lesions themselves and their distribution in the skeleton. A baseline of reference material showing the changes wrought on the skeleton by different diseases is key to diagnosing disease in archaeological skeletons. In great part, this baseline has been developed from study of bones kept in medical museums from individuals with known diseases, but radiography and CT scans of lesions in living patients helps augment this. Nevertheless, diagnosis of disease in ancient skeletons is frequently difficult because different diseases often overlap in their skeletal manifestations. Diagnoses are therefore characteristically tentative rather than conclusive.

Careful visual examination of the skeleton, together with a written and photographic record of the abnormalities identified, is of paramount importance when studying disease in ancient remains. However other techniques of examination are also useful. The most consistently valuable of these is radiography, but CT scanning, microscopic analysis and, in some cases, analysis for DNA or other biomolecules, may also be helpful.

Congenital abnormalities, infectious diseases, metabolic diseases, benign and malignant tumours and various forms of arthritis are among the types of diseases that have been identified in ancient skeletal remains.

The main applications of the study of skeletal disease to the understanding of the human past are to contribute to our knowledge of the history of particular diseases, and to address archaeological questions. Today, the latter is the principal focus of osteoarchaeological work, and the dominant methodology is to quantify frequency or severity of disease in skeletal populations and relate inter- or intra-population patterning in the data to lifestyles or other cultural factors – the so-called biocultural approach.

Further reading

Roberts, C.A. & Manchester, K. (2005). *The Archaeology of Disease*, 3rd edition. Sutton, Stroud. *A good introduction to many of the diseases that have been identified in ancient skeletons.*

Pinhasi, R. & Mays, S., eds (2008). Advances in Human Palaeopathology. Wiley, Chichester, *gives an account of methodological approaches in palaeopathology and the diagnosis and biocultural interpretation of skeletal disease.* A good compliment to that volume is provided by Grauer, A.L., ed (2012). *A Companion to Paleopathology.* Wiley, Chichester, *which highlights important debates and controversies in different aspects of palaeopathology.*

There are a number of laboratory manuals aimed at assisting palaeopathological diagnosis. A key work in this respect is Buikstra, J.E., ed (2019). Ortner's Identification of Pathological Conditions in Human Skeletal Remains (3rd edition). Academic Press, London. *This book weighs-in at over 800 pages and provides as comprehensive an overview as one could reasonably expect in a single volume. A useful supplement to that book is* Lewis, M.E. (2018). *Paleopathology of Children. Identification of Pathological Conditions in the Human Skeletal Remains of Non-Adults.* Academic Press, London. *As the title suggests this provides greater detail on the expression of disease in infant, child and adolescent skeletons.*

Another laboratory manual is Mann, R.W. & Hunt, D.R. (2012). Photographic Regional Atlas of Bone Disease: A Guide to Pathologic and Normal Variation in the Human Skeleton (3rd edition). Charles C Thomas, Springfield. *Buikstra's and Lewis' books are laid out disease by disease; Mann & Hunt's is organised bone by bone and is particularly useful in helping beginners distinguish bony bumps or cavities due to normal variation from those due to disease.*

9 Dental disease

Most of us have, at some point, suffered the pain of toothache. Dental caries (tooth decay) is not only a common dental problem today, but is also often seen in ancient skeletons. Its occurrence in the past has been extensively studied.

It is well-known that build-up of dental plaque is associated with the formation of caries cavities, but if left undisturbed for long enough, plaque will mineralise to form dental calculus (tartar). Microscopic particles, and biomolecules such as proteins and DNA, appear to preserve quite well in dental calculus on the teeth of ancient skeletons. Microscopic and biomolecular study of calculus is a new, but rapidly growing area of research.

The development of the enamel crowns of the teeth during childhood may be disturbed by environmental insults, specifically episodes of disease or poor nutrition. These growth perturbations may manifest themselves on the tooth crowns as bands of thinned enamel, termed dental enamel hypoplasias. Thus, the teeth may bear scars which give clues concerning the earlier general health of the individual.

This chapter chiefly focuses on dental caries, dental calculus, and dental enamel hypoplasias. In addition, some other commonly seen conditions, such as ante-mortem tooth loss (loss of teeth in life) and periodontal disease, an infection of the gums and other tissues that support the teeth, are also discussed.

Dental caries

The carious process

Dental plaque consists of food debris together with various constituents derived from saliva. Within the dental plaque dwell bacteria. It is acids released by these bacteria when they breakdown sugars present in the mouth as residues of food items, that are the cause of dental caries. Studies on many world populations show a close correspondence between the level of consumption of sweet, sugary foods and rates of dental caries (Moynihan & Kelley, 2014; Sheiham & James, 2015). For example, many European countries showed a dip in caries rates due to restrictions in sugar availability during World War II (e.g. Eriksen et al., 1991).

Starches, another type of dietary carbohydrate, can also be cariogenic if they are broken down into low molecular weight sugars in the mouth. Many plants contain substantial amounts of starches. In plant tissues, starch is held within microscopic granules. If it remains there it cannot be digested, but food-preparation processes, such as grinding or cooking, rupture the granules, liberating the starch (Hillson, 2008). If starchy food residues are retained long enough in the mouth, starch is broken down into low molecular weight sugars by ptyalin, an enzyme present in saliva. Experimental work on laboratory animals (Firestone et al., 1982; Zhu et al., 1997) shows that under these circumstances diets in which starch is the sole carbohydrate are cariogenic, albeit to a lesser extent than diets high in sugars. The potential for starches to be broken down to sugars in the mouth means that, even in the absence of significant intake of sugar, diets rich in carbohydrates have the potential to lead to elevated caries rates. By contrast, fats, oils and meats (including fish) are not cariogenic and may actually inhibit caries (Giacaman, 2018).

Although the type and quantity of carbohydrate in the diet is normally the dominant influence on the rate of dental caries in a population, a number of other factors may also play a part. Certain trace-elements in foods and waters can inhibit caries; the role of fluoride in this respect is well known (Sheiham, 2001). The longer that carbohydrate residues remain in the mouth, the greater their potential to cause caries, so sticky foods which adhere to the teeth are particularly cariogenic (Bibby & Mundorff, 1975). Frequency of eating influences caries rates – more frequent eating means that food and food residues are in contact with the teeth for longer (Cohen & Bowen, 1966; van Loveren, 2019). The texture of the diet also plays a part. Coarse diets, as consumed by most human groups prior to recent times, tend to reduce caries. They help to scour the teeth clean of food debris, reducing excessive build-up of dental plaque, and they wear away the pits and fissures in the crowns of molar and premolar teeth that might otherwise trap food debris (Maat & van der Velde, 1987).

The carious lesion

As has been mentioned in previous chapters, bone is a dynamic tissue; in other words, it is continually being renewed. However, this is not the case for the dental hard tissues, and this has important consequences as far as dental caries and other diseases which may affect the teeth are concerned. Disease in a bone may result in an increase or a decrease in bone substance. Whichever occurs, it is the result of a dynamic response of the bone to the disease process. As was indicated above, dental caries is a passive process of dissolution rather than an active response to disease. Once formed, caries cavities cannot heal.

The initial lesion in dental caries consists of a softened area of enamel. This progresses so that a small cavity forms in the enamel surface. This cavity enlarges as the disease progresses. When it reaches the dentino-enamel junction it tends to spread laterally, due to the increased organic material in this area. This undermines the enamel crown, leaving a fragile shell which may collapse under the strain of mastication (Shafer et al., 1983: 432). In this way, caries may lead to complete destruction of the tooth crown. Inflammation of the pulp may occur, either through direct exposure to the oral environment or via opened, exposed dentinal tubules (Hillson, 1996: 284).

Identifying caries in skeletal remains

There are no dental diseases which an experienced worker is likely to confuse with caries, so the main thing in establishing a diagnosis is to ensure that cavities observed are not confused with post-depositional erosions or anatomical variants.

Unlike erosions produced by post-depositional factors, caries cavities generally have sharp, well-defined edges (Figure 9.1). In addition, the diameter of caries cavities is generally larger within the tooth than on the tooth surface. They also tend to be deeper in relation to their width than do post-depositional erosions, which are often broad and shallow.

Pits and fissures are present on premolar and molar tooth crowns, both as normal features and as anatomical variants. However, the seasoned observer is unlikely to confuse these with caries cavities.

If the carious process leads to infection of the dental pulp, then formation of a dental abscess at the tooth socket may occur by extension of the infection along the root canal. Acute dental abscesses leave no trace on the bone, however infection of the dental pulp may elicit a chronic inflammatory response in the soft tissues at the apex of the root, which may result in the formation of a cavity in the bone at the tip of the root (Dias & Tayles, 1997; Ogden, 2008) (Figure 9.2). In contrast to acute dental abscesses, pain in these cases is characteristically either mild or absent.

Quantifying caries in skeletal remains

We saw in Chapter 8 that when bone disease may potentially affect more than one element in a skeleton, its prevalence in archaeological remains may be expressed by skeleton (i.e. number of affected individuals divided by number of individuals examined) or by bone (number of bones affected divided by the total number of bones

Figure 9.1 A large caries cavity in a molar tooth. The cavity has sharp, well-defined edges and its dimensions are larger within the tooth than where it breaches the tooth surface

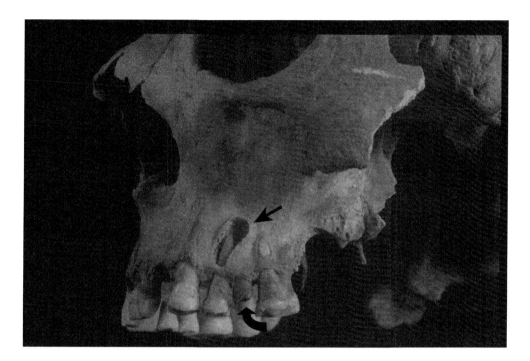

Figure 9.2 There is a periapical void in the maxilla at the tips of the roots of the premolar teeth (straight arrow). The crown of the second premolar has been destroyed by caries (curved arrow), exposing the dental pulp. It is likely that the consequent pulp infection led to a chronic inflammatory response in the bone adjacent to the root tip. Chronic inflammation of this type may result in cyst formation at the root tip. Bone resorption to accommodate the slowly expanding cyst is likely responsible for the void space in the bone seen here

examined). By analogy, the prevalence of caries can be expressed in terms of individuals or by tooth. The strengths and drawbacks of these two methods are similar to the quantification of bone disease by individuals or by bone (Chapter 8). It is often best to quantify both by individuals, so that valid statistical tests can be carried out, and also by teeth, to see whether a consistent picture is obtained comparing assemblages using both methods.

The older an individual, the longer his or her teeth have been exposed to the agents causing caries. This, together with the fact that caries cavities do not heal once formed, means that, in general, assemblages with older ages at death should tend to show higher frequencies of carious teeth than do younger ones (Larsen et al., 1991). Bony pathologies also tend to accumulate with age, and lesions of the jaws are no exception. Indeed, until recently, afflictions such as caries and tooth loss due to disease were primarily conditions of adulthood; child skeletons are rarely affected in archaeological collections. In addition, different tooth types differ in their vulnerability to dental disease. For example, caries and ante-mortem tooth loss are generally more frequent in molars than anterior teeth (Hillson, 1996: 280), and this may bias data for incomplete dentitions. These effects need to be borne in mind when making comparisons between groups.

Caries and tooth loss

In modern Western populations, extraction of carious teeth is the main reason for tooth loss. Therefore, in studies of caries in living subjects in the developed world, numbers of missing teeth are generally combined with those which are carious or filled to produce a DMF (decayed, missing or filled) index. Extraction of painful teeth has a long history. For example, we know it was carried out in Ancient Rome (Jackson, 1988: 119), and such a simple expedient was doubtless practiced long before that. However, in earlier populations, caries may not have been the most important cause of tooth loss. We saw in Chapter 4 that, when dental wear is heavy, super-eruption of teeth may proceed to the point where they are only held in their sockets by their root tips. Periodontal disease, which is very common in past populations (e.g. Kerr, 1998; Wasterlain et al., 2011), shows on the bones as resorption of the bone at the tooth sockets. This results in pitting and concavity of the interdental septa. These are the bony walls between tooth sockets, and in a healthy state they are normally smooth and have convex profiles. The bony resorption also causes enlargement of the diameter of the tooth sockets, loosening the teeth (Hillson, 2008; Ogden, 2008) (Figure 9.3). If a tooth was carious, then the presence of marked super-eruption and/or periodontal disease would have made its extraction easier. However, periodontal disease and marked super-eruption of teeth were also likely to have been major causes of tooth loss in their own rights (Walker & Hewlett, 1990; Clarke & Hirsch, 1991; Kerr & Ringrose, 1998). Other factors may also play a part in tooth loss. If

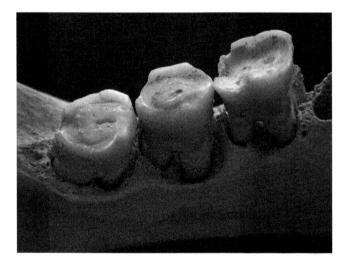

Figure 9.3 Lateral view of the right side of a mandible showing the molar teeth. The tooth sockets have been enlarged by bony resorption, loosening the teeth. The interdental septa are porotic and show resorption. These are indications of periodontal disease

wear is very rapid it may expose the pulp cavity, which may prompt the extraction of the painful, infected tooth. Teeth may sometimes be lost due to violence (Lukacs, 2007) or there may be intentional extraction for ritual or cosmetic purposes (Burnett & Irish, 2017). The multiplicity of possible causes of tooth loss in ancient populations means that it is best treated separately from caries.

Tooth loss occurring during life may be distinguished from instances where teeth have simply dropped out in the soil since, when a tooth is lost in life, the socket becomes obliterated by bony remodelling (Figure 9.4). However, we cannot determine from the appearance of the remodelled socket which of the various causes led to the loss of a tooth. Analogous to dental caries, ante-mortem tooth loss is normally quantified in skeletal populations by giving prevalences both with respect to individuals and with respect to total tooth sockets examined.

Dental caries and ancient diets

Caries frequencies and ancient subsistence strategies

From a survey of literature relating to caries rates around the world, Turner (1979) found that hunter-gatherers showed an average caries frequency of 1.7% of total teeth examined. The figure for those pursuing a mixed strategy involving both hunting/gathering and some plant cultivation was 4.4%, and that for groups solely reliant on agriculture

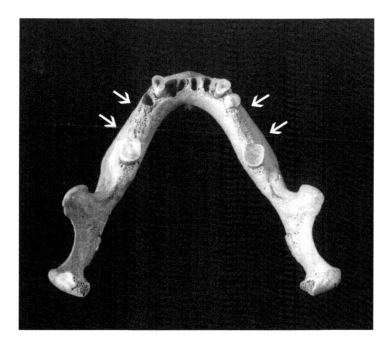

Figure 9.4 The areas delimited by the arrows show where teeth have been lost in life; the sockets have been obliterated by bony remodelling. By contrast, the empty, unremodelled tooth sockets in the anterior part of this mandible show where teeth have fallen out after death

was 8.6%. The increase in dental caries with the advent of plant domestication seems to reflect an increased reliance on carbohydrate-rich plant foods. In addition, innovations in food preparation, such as the use of pottery vessels, grinding stones, etc., which accompany the adoption of agriculture, help to render the food softer and stickier, and hence more cariogenic.

More detailed regional studies have helped us to understand more fully the health implications of differences in diet and subsistence in particular environments or geographical areas. For example, Lumila Menéndez conducted a study of dental caries in prehistoric Argentina (Menéndez, 2016). She studied over 1000 burials from 29 archaeological sites, grouped into eight regions according to their location, ranging from the tropical north to the cold of southern Patagonia (Figure 9.5). The archaeological record shows that prehistoric human groups adopted a range of subsistence strategies to adapt to the opportunities provided by this wide range of environments. The northern zone was favourable to the cultivation of maize and other plant foods. By contrast, hunter-gatherer groups from Patagonia relied more on marine and terrestrial animal resources so their diets contained more proteins and fats and less carbohydrate. At intermediate latitudes a variety of subsistence strategies were practiced. Menéndez hypothesised that there should be a relationship between caries rates and latitude, with northern groups showing the most caries, southern groups the least. This was largely borne out by the data (Figure 9.6). It was also notable that groups living at the northern or southern extremes (the northwest and central highlands, and the central and southern Patagonian groups respectively in Figures 9.5 and 9.6) showed little variation in caries rates. Menéndez (2016) suggests that their diets may have been characterised by specialisation – chiefly maize agriculture in the north and hunter-gatherer-fishers in the south. In contrast, Figure 9.6 shows that caries prevalences in groups from intermediate latitudes varied quite widely, perhaps reflecting the mixture of different subsistence strategies practiced by communities living there.

Looking at a more restricted geographic area, Kelley et al. (1991) studied some dental diseases, including caries and tooth loss, in skeletal assemblages from groups that practiced different types of subsistence in northern Chile (Table 9.1). As with Menéndez's work in Argentina, Kelley et al. (1991) found caries to be rare in those reliant on fishing, but it became progressively more common as agriculture was adopted and intensified. This trend is apparent whether the data are expressed with the tooth or the individual as the unit of analysis.

Kelley and co-workers also argued that causes of tooth loss may have changed over time. At the Morro-1 site, dental attrition was severe and caries rates were low, so they felt that super-eruption or pulp cavity exposure probably accounted for most tooth loss. At the other sites, dental wear is less severe, and the rise in tooth loss over time parallels that in dental caries. Extraction of carious teeth may therefore be an important factor in tooth loss in these assemblages (Kelley et al., 1991).

The impact of refined sugars

Diets with greater proportions of plant foods tend to be more cariogenic, but caries rates rise even more sharply when refined sugars are introduced. For example, in Britain, small amounts of cane sugar began to be imported as early as the 12th century AD, but significant amounts only started to arrive during the 17th century, with the establishment of

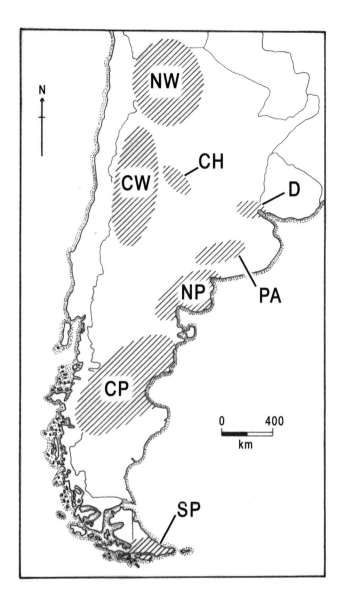

Figure 9.5 Cone of South America, showing location of the skeletal remains from Argentina studied by Menéndez (2016). NW, northwest; CH, central highlands; CW, central-west; D, Paraná delta; PA, Pampa; NP, northern Patagonia; CP, central Patagonia; SP, southern Patagonia

Source: adapted from Menéndez (2016: Figure 1).

sugar-cane plantations in British territories in the Caribbean. From this time, sugar consumption increased in Britain, and in the 19th century, this trend accelerated as import duty on sugar was progressively removed (Corbett & Moore, 1976). Moore and Corbett (1978) studied dental caries in British skeletons dating from various periods up to

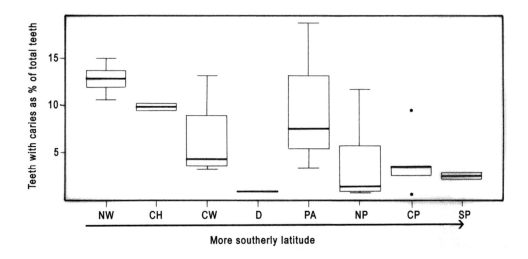

Figure 9.6 Box-plots of caries frequencies in the regions identified in Fig. 9.5. The heavy line is the overall caries frequency for the region. The box represents the inter-quartile range (IQR). The lines from each box extend to the most extreme values that are not outliers. Outliers (more than 1.5 IQR from the overall frequency for each region) are represented by filled circles. Abbreviations as for Figure 9.5.

Source: redrawn from Menéndez (2016: Figure 1).

Table 9.1 Dental caries and tooth loss in four burial sites in northern Chile

	Morro-1 3500-2000BC Fishing	El Laucho 2000-500BC Fishing/some cultivation	Alto Ramirez 1000BC-AD 500 Incipient agriculture	Maitas AD 800-1200 Intensive agriculture
No. of skeletons examined	41	45	41	55
No. of teeth examined	823	476	599	1,160
Individuals with caries as % of total individuals	4.9	15.5	71.7	76.4
Teeth with caries as % of total teeth	0.6	2.5	11.5	14.4
Tooth loss as % of total teeth originally present	4.3	4.6	10.1	16.2

Source: Data from Kelley et al. (1991).

about AD 1900. They showed that there was a marked rise in caries frequency in the 19th century, coinciding with the greatly increased sugar consumption which characterised that period (Figure 9.7).

We learnt in Chapter 5 that, prior to the 17th century AD, diets in Britain were coarse and required vigorous mastication. After this, mainly due to alterations in food preparation techniques, including the way in which flour was processed for bread-making, diets

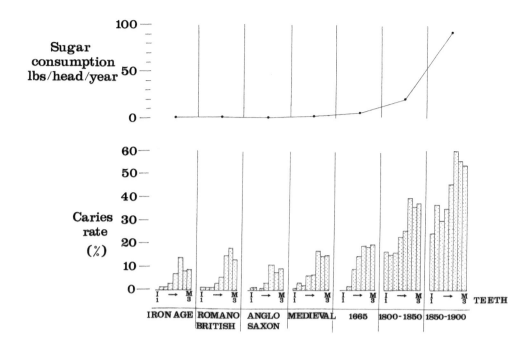

Figure 9.7 Dental caries in relation to sugar consumption in Britain
Source: After Moore and Corbett (1978: Figure 8).

became progressively softer, culminating in the soft, processed foods we consume today. As mentioned above, coarse diets tend to inhibit caries, so the progressive softening of the diet probably played some part in the rise of caries rates over time. The softening of the diet, and the concomitant lessening in dental wear, also led to a change regarding the particular locations on the teeth that most often show cavities.

When dental wear is heavy, caries does not often become established at the occlusal surfaces. However, as the teeth continue to erupt from their sockets to compensate for wear, this exposes the tooth necks to the oral environment and increases the inter-tooth space, permitting increased impaction of food debris between the teeth. When oral hygiene is poor, food residues may remain trapped between the teeth long enough for starchy foods to be broken down by enzymatic action, and the products fermented by plaque bacteria, leading to caries, especially at the cemento-enamel junction (Figure 9.8). Prior to the 17th century this was the prime location for cavities in the posterior dentition (Moore & Corbett, 1978). When, from the 17th century onwards in Britain, diets became progressively softer and less abrasive, this began to change with an increase in the proportion of cavities occurring at other locations on the tooth, particularly the occlusal surfaces (Figure 9.9) (Moore & Corbett, 1978). By the late 19th century (Moore & Corbett, 1978), the distribution broadly resembled the modern pattern (Batchelor & Sheiham, 2004) in which the occlusal surfaces of the posterior teeth are the predominant site of attack. This is because the diet had become insufficiently abrasive to scour these surfaces clean or to wear away the pits and fissures which tend to act as foci for dental caries.

Figure 9.8 A maxilla from a British Mediaeval skeleton. A molar tooth shows a caries cavity at the cemento-enamel junction

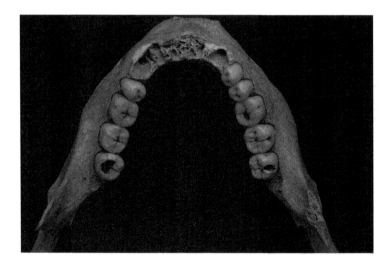

Figure 9.9 A mandible from an 18th century British skeleton. The left third molar and the right first molar show large caries cavities on their occlusal surfaces. The right third molar also shows a large caries cavity, but this probably originated on the side of the crown rather than on the occlusal surface

Dental calculus

If left undisturbed by brushing or other efforts at oral hygiene, the dental plaque will gradually mineralise, due to deposition of calcium salts from the saliva, to form dental calculus. As it mineralises, proteins and other biomolecules, and microscopic particles from foods and other sources, may become entrapped. Calculus may build up on any part of the tooth that is exposed to the oral environment, but occlusal surfaces are generally kept clear by chewing. It is usually the sides of the tooth crowns that are most affected, particularly the lingual (posterior) surfaces of the mandibular anterior teeth. This is because they lie close to salivary gland ducts. In archaeological remains, dental calculus appears as a greenish/brown deposit, most often at the base of the enamel crown approximating to the position of the gum-line in life (Plate 6). The total amount of calculus on the teeth of an archaeological skeleton may vary from zero to about 500mg or more.

Calculus builds up incrementally. The rate of deposition is slow but variable and depends on factors including salivary composition and flow rates, diet, and the mineral content of drinking water (Jin & Yip, 2002). Although, in some archaeological populations, significant deposits may occur in children (e.g. Prowse et al., 2008), they are much more common and extensive in adults. For example, at Wharram Percy, calculus was noted in 22% of child dentitions, but in 89% of adults (Mays, 2007: Table 77). In archaeological collections, calculus often tends to become dislodged during excavation and post-excavation handling, so its true frequency and extent may be underestimated. Standard scales exist for quantifying deposits (e.g. Dobney & Brothwell, 1987).

Microscopic study

This generally involves removing the calculus from one or more teeth, and carefully cleaning it to remove extraneous material. It is then decalcified to release the inclusions, which are then studied under a microscope. Less than 50mg is normally taken, but the larger the sample, the greater the number of particles that are likely to be obtained. Microscopic inclusions may be taken in with food, so have the potential to tell us about diet, or else they may be inhaled, so can reveal aspects of the cultural or natural environment.

The most common inclusions that relate to diet are starch granules. Sometimes they can be identified to species, in which case they can tell us about the plants consumed, but this may be difficult, either because granules are non-diagnostic or because they are damaged (Leonard et al., 2015). It has been suggested that by looking at patterns of damage to the granules we can deduce whether food was cooked. Henry et al. (2011a) identified granules that were increased in size and altered in structure in calculus from Neanderthals. The changes they observed resembled those seen due to heating, so they inferred that Neanderthals were consuming cooked plant foods. Others (Collins & Copeland, 2011) have contended that the changes they saw were a result of diagenesis (alteration occurring in the burial environment) rather than cooking, although the original authors reject this (Henry et al., 2011b). In addition, Hardy et al. (2018) argue that cooked starch granules would be unlikely to be incorporated into calculus because they would have been broken down into sugars in the mouth by ptyalin. We currently lack sufficient knowledge of starch granule survival and diagenesis to settle the debate conclusively. Another consideration is that it is difficult to make quantitative inferences about diet. This is because an individual will likely consume billions of starch granules over a lifetime but only a miniscule proportion of these (usually less than 100) will be recovered from a dental calculus sample.

These factors act to limit our interpretations, but sometimes simply demonstrating the presence of starch granules in archaeological dental calculus can provide important insights. Cristiani et al. (2016) carried out a microscopic analysis of dental calculus from prehistoric burials from Valsač in the Iron Gates region of the Danube (some other aspects of burials from this area are discussed Chapters 7 and 11). A total of seven burials of Late Mesolithic (ca. 6600–6450BC) foragers were studied. In five instances, the calculus samples contained starch granules (numbers of granules varied from 2 to over 100). In three burials, some of the granules could be identified as being from plants from the barley/wheat tribe. These cereals do not have wild progenitors in that region, so this finding showed that the community must have had access to the products of arable agriculture, perhaps via trading contacts with farming groups further south and east, some 400 years before agriculture became established in the area (Cristiani et al., 2016).

Particles less than about 70μm diameter may potentially be inhaled and subsequently incorporated into dental calculus. Some that have been found in ancient calculus, such as fungal spores or pollen grains, likely come from the natural environment (Radini et al., 2017). Other particles may give clues to cultural practices. Microscopic fragments of lapis lazuli, a pigment used for blue colouration in Mediaeval illuminated manuscripts, were found in dental calculus in a 11th–12th century AD burial of woman excavated from the site of a Mediaeval nunnery at Dalheim, Germany. This suggested that the woman was involved in pigment preparation and/or book production, emphasising that Mediaeval women may have been scribes or engaged in the manufacture of artist's materials (Radini et al., 2019).

The lapis lazuli fragments in the woman from Dalheim may have been inhaled as dust or introduced into the mouth whilst licking a paint brush. Other task-related inclusions, cotton fibres, probably introduced into the mouth during production of textiles, were found in dental calculus in four prehistoric (AD900-1100) burials from Ohio (Blatt et al., 2011). Cotton does not grow there, so this suggests links with communities further south and west, where it was cultivated. A wooden fragment recovered from the dental calculus from a Neanderthal seems to derive from an object inserted into the mouth for another purpose – a toothpick. The remains date to 49,000 years ago and come from El Sidrón, Spain. A fragment of pine wood 285μm long was found in calculus from a molar tooth (Radini et al., 2016) (Figure 9.10a). Teeth of Neanderthals, including those from El Sidrón, sometimes show interproximal grooving (Estalrrich et al., 2017) – grooves on the sides of adjacent teeth. These grooves are also often seen in remains of anatomically modern humans (Milner & Larsen, 1991) (Figure 9.10b). A likely explanation for them is that they result from the habitual use of toothpicks to dislodge food caught between the teeth (Estalrrich et al., 2017). The wood fragment discovered in the El Sidrón calculus is consistent with this practice.

DNA analysis

The study of DNA from ancient skeletal remains is discussed in detail in Chapter 12. However, a brief account of some of the DNA work on dental calculus is given here.

(a)

(b)

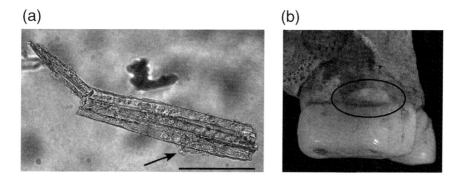

Figure 9.10 (a) A fragment of wood tissue recovered from dental calculus from a molar tooth from a Neanderthal from El Sidrón, Spain. Small flecks of calculus (arrowed) are still attached. Scale bar = 100µm. Source: Radini et al. (2016: Fig. 1). (b) Distal (posterior) view of a first permanent molar from an Upper Palaeolithic burial (approximately 18,000–11,000BC) from Grotta Paglicci, Italy, showing an interproximal groove. Source: Ricci et al. (2016: Figure 2)

A great many bacteria normally live in our bodies. These organisms, termed the microbiome, collectively weigh about 1.5kg, about the same weight as the human brain (Warriner et al., 2015). The bacteria in the microbiome are generally harmless or else play an active role in human health, although in some circumstances they may cause disease, for example when the immune system is compromised (Mackie et al., 2017). A major part of the microbiome is situated in the mouth (Dewhirst et al., 2010). Most of the DNA found in modern calculus, or preserved in ancient calculus, comes from the organisms that make up the oral microbiome (Velsko et al., 2019; Ziesemer et al., 2019). Because of this, most DNA analysis of archaeological dental calculus has focussed on ancient oral microbiomes.

The dominant approach to DNA analysis of dental calculus is metagenomics – the collective study of all the DNA in a sample. This enables inferences to be made regarding the species composition of the oral microbiome. Everyone's oral microbiome is unique, but exploring systematic differences over time and space is of interest because factors such as diet, environment and general way of life influence its composition.

Adler et al. (2013) extracted DNA from calculus samples (less than 0.2g from each skeleton) from 34 European burials ranging from Mesolithic to Mediaeval date. They used a method, amplicon sequencing, focusing on a genetic region that is shared among diverse target species (in this case species of bacteria) to study the oral microbiome. This method allowed the identification of over 800 different species of oral bacteria in a single sample. They found that the oral microbiome composition showed a shift with the introduction of farming in the Neolithic, with a rise in taxa linked to caries and periodontal disease. This may reflect a rise in these conditions with the dietary changes associated with the advent of agriculture (and we have seen that, at least for caries, this is an expected pattern), but there is a need for caution in making direct links between the gene content of the oral microbiome and the presence of disease in individuals. For example, in a study of 18th–19th-century British remains, Velsko et al. (2019) found no difference in microbial profiles of ancient calculus from healthy teeth and from teeth showing caries and/or periodontal disease. Possible reasons for this include the microbiological complexity of the dental plaque and the chance nature of the entrapment of material when it mineralises into calculus.

Some human host DNA is often found in dental calculus (e.g. Ziesemer et al., 2019), but bones or teeth are the more usual substrates for ancient human DNA studies. DNA from items in diet may also be encountered. Weyrich et al. (2017) found DNA from various animal species, including rhinoceros and wild sheep in Neanderthal calculus from Spy in Belgium. Further south, at the El Sidrón site discussed above, no DNA from these species was found, but there was DNA evidence for plant foods such as mushrooms, pine nuts and moss. This result needs to be interpreted with care, but it seems consistent with other evidence in suggesting regional differences in Neanderthal diet.

Proteomics

Proteins are polymers. A polymer is a long molecule made up of repeating subunits; in a protein the subunits are amino acids. It is the sequence of these amino acids that determines the identity and higher-level structure of the protein.

Proteomics is the identification of individual proteins in complex mixtures. Protein fragments are extracted from a small sample (as little as 15mg) of calculus. They are passed through a mass spectrometer. This allows the mass of a fragment to be determined. Comparing these masses with a reference database allows the amino acid sequence to be inferred, and this may permit the protein that it came from to be identified. By this means, hundreds of different proteins may potentially be identified in a single sample (Hendy et al., 2018). We may also be able to identify the organism from which it came – a protein may differ slightly in its amino acid sequence depending upon which species produced it. In addition, particular proteins are often specific to different tissues within an organism – so for example, a protein may be specifically found in milk rather than in other animal products.

As with DNA, most ancient proteins found in dental calculus come from the oral microbiome, but there are contributions from the human host and from food items. In contrast to the DNA studies, much work on the protein content of dental calculus has focussed on ancient diet, but there are difficulties. The study of proteins from meat in the diet is problematic. It is difficult to identify them to species, and hence to distinguish them from those from the human host. Distinguishing plant proteins is more straightforward, but they are often found in low abundance in archaeological dental calculus, despite the fact that plant foods must have been ubiquitous in most ancient diets. Reasons for this are unclear but may include poor survival of proteins from these sources (Hendy et al., 2018). Indeed, proteins of dietary origin often cannot be identified at all. In a study of 100 dental calculus samples from skeletons from British archaeological sites, only 26 yielded evidence for proteins that were clearly dietary in origin (Hendy et al., 2018).

The most consistently identified dietary protein in ancient dental calculus is β-lactoglobulin (e.g. Warriner et al., 2014; Hendy et al., 2018; Jeong et al., 2018; Jersie-Christensen et al., 2018; Mays et al., 2018a; Charlton et al., 2019). This is found in animal milk (humans do not produce it), specifically in the whey fraction. A reason why this protein is the one most often reported in archaeological samples may be because its make-up means that it is especially resistant to decay in the soil (Hendy et al., 2018). Protein fragments from β-lactoglobulin may be identifiable to species. For example, calculus from British Neolithic remains showed evidence for consumption of bovine, sheep and goat milk (Charlton et al., 2019), as did calculus from late Bronze Age burials from Mongolia (Jeong et al., 2018). These groups not only lived in different environments but also practiced very different types of subsistence, the former being settled agriculturalists, the latter steppe herders. The results show that, despite these differences, both exploited multiple species for dairy products.

Warriner et al. (2014) studied dental calculus from burials from two Norse burial grounds in Greenland. One, Tjohildes Church, dates from the earlier years of Norse settlement (AD985-1250), the other, Sandnes (AD1290–1430), from the phase leading up to the abandonment of the region by the Norse in the 15th century. Calculus from two burials from the earlier cemetery produced abundant evidence for β-lactoglobulin, but there was little evidence for it in samples from four burials from the later site. During the earlier years of settlement, the Greenland Norse pursued an agrarian subsistence strategy. When the climate started to deteriorate at the opening of the Little Ice Age cold period, this regime collapsed; there was increased reliance on marine resources until the settlements were abandoned altogether. The dental calculus results could be viewed as consistent with this general scenario (Warriner et al., 2014), but interpretations need to be treated with caution until more skeletons can be analysed.

Other molecules: smoking out our past

The health risks of nicotine are well known, so the study of tobacco use in past populations is of considerable interest. Until recently, the only viable way of identifying smokers from their skeletal remains was from pipe-facets on teeth. Tobacco began to be imported into Europe from North America in the 16th century. Until the introduction of cigarettes in the second half of the 19th century, smokers used pipes. These were normally made of clay and gripped between the teeth. In a long-term habitual smoker, abrasion from the pipe might cause facets to be worn in the teeth (Figure 9.11). These have been identified in Post-Mediaeval skeletal remains from the British Isles (Boston et al., 2015: 67; Geber, 2015: 78-81), the Low Countries (Bouts et al., 1992: 101), Scandinavia (Kvaal & Derry, 1996) and elsewhere (Okumura, 2011). In a study of mid-19th century burials from London (Walker & Henderson, 2010), pipe-notches were found in dentitions of 58 out of 248 individuals, an unusually high prevalence. Only three were female, so pipe-smoking was a predominantly male activity. Interestingly, periosteal new bone deposits on the visceral (inward-facing) surfaces of the ribs were more frequent in individuals showing pipe-facets, perhaps suggesting an association between lung disease and smoking in that population.

Pipe-facets only provide a partial picture of tobacco use as not all smokers will have developed them. Recently, Eerkens et al. (2018) report the identification of nicotine in dental calculus from two Native American burials from pre-contact northern California, one of whom was buried with a pipe. If nicotine proves regularly to survive in ancient

(a)

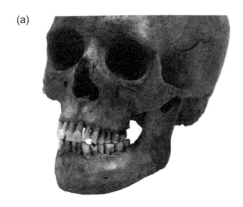

(b)

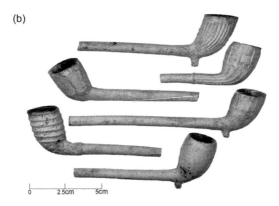

Figure 9.11 (a) A mid-19th-century AD skull from London showing a pipe facet. Source: Walker (2012: Figure 405). (b). Parts of some 19th-century clay pipes, excavated from an archaeological site in Suffolk, England. The stems are broken and so would originally have been rather longer than this. Source: Suffolk Archaeology CIC (Cotswold Archaeology Suffolk)

dental calculus of tobacco-users then it has the potential to provide a more complete picture of tobacco use in the past.

The significance of dental calculus studies

The study of dental calculus is a very young field, but which shows much potential. It offers a useful way of studying the oral microbiome, something that has hitherto been beyond our reach. It also offers direct evidence concerning diet, environment and occupation that is complimentary to other archaeological means of studying these aspects of people's lives. However there are important limitations. Inclusion of biomolecules or microscopic particles in calculus is a chance event, and those preserved will be a tiny sample of those that entered the mouth over an individual's lifetime. This means that inter-individual variation in biomolecular and particulate content of calculus samples is high. This makes interpreting quantitative differences between individuals problematic, and means that study of large numbers of skel-etons will be needed to discern patterned differences between populations or subgroups.

Dental enamel hypoplasias

A dental enamel hypoplasia represents a localised reduction in the normal thickness of enamel. It most often takes the form of a transverse line or band of depressed enamel on the side of a tooth crown (Figure 9.12). Hypoplasias form as a result of disturbance to the growth of the dental enamel or, more specifically, the organic matrix which is subse-quently mineralised to form enamel. This occurs in response to disease or poor nutrition. Dental enamel hypoplasias can only form during that part of childhood when the enamel of the tooth crown is developing. The fact that dental enamel is non-vital tissue means that, once formed, hypoplastic defects are not erased from the tooth unless the enamel is physically removed by dental wear. The tooth crowns therefore provide a 'memory' of biological disruptions which occurred during childhood.

Enamel is laid down in incremental layers. The most prominent microscopic growth layers are the striae of Retzius. These are visible under the microscope in cross-sections of dental enamel. At a point where each stria reaches the surface there is a faint horizontal groove called a perikyma. Perikymata vary in width from about 20–200μm, depending upon the tooth type and the location on the crown (Hillson, 1996: 161), and correspond to about 9 days' worth of enamel formation (Reid & Dean, 2006). At the enamel hypoplasia, the thick-ness of the enamel is less than normal at the location of the affected perikymata. The size of a hypoplastic defect varies from microscopic examples involving just one perikyma, to those involving 20 or more which are clearly visible to the naked eye (Hillson, 2019).

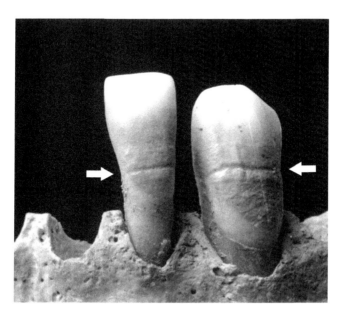

Figure 9.12 Dental enamel hypoplasias (arrowed) on incisor and canine teeth

Enamel layers formed early in crown development are buried beneath subsequent layers (Figure 9.13), so that their striae of Retzius do not form perikymata on the crown surface. Therefore growth disturbances in this part of the tooth enamel do not show as dental enamel hypoplasias on the surface of the crown. The presence of this so-called buried enamel means that teeth do not begin to record surface hypoplasias from the time of enamel crown initiation, but only from some months after this. The proportion of enamel crown formation time represented by this buried enamel varies from 15-20% in anterior teeth to up to 50% in molars (Hillson & Bond, 1997). Thus, for example, although the crown of the maxillary permanent first incisor begins mineralisation when a child is about at about 4 months of age, it is only from about 13-14 months that the tooth potentially records hypoplasias on the crown surface (Reid & Dean, 2006). In the permanent dentition as a whole, hypoplasias visible on the tooth surface record episodes of adverse conditions sufficient to disturb enamel formation occurring between about one and seven years of age (or up to about 13 years if the third molar is included).

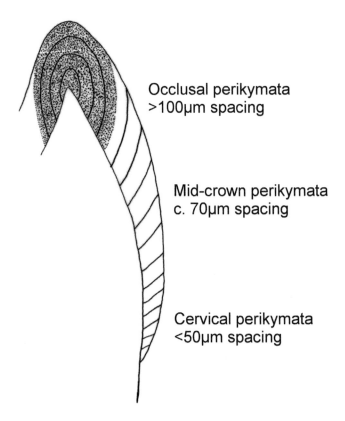

Occlusal perikymata
>100μm spacing

Mid-crown perikymata
c. 70μm spacing

Cervical perikymata
<50μm spacing

Figure 9.13 Schematic representation of a vertical section of a permanent upper central incisor with 168 striae of Retzius, of which 35 are appositional (or buried) striae (shaded). Lines are drawn every 10th stria

Source: After Hillson & Bond (1997: Figure 5).

Causes of dental enamel hypoplasia

Knowledge of the sorts of disease and dietary deficiencies which can cause dental enamel hypoplasias comes both from experimental work on animals and from studies of human populations. This has shown that a wide range of adverse events can lead to enamel defects, including fevers, gut parasites, diarrhoea, rickets, scurvy, measles, allergic reactions, whooping cough, pneumonia, vitamin and other micronutrient deficiencies, and general malnutrition (Pindborg, 1970:138–210; 1982), but the specific cause cannot be discerned from the defect itself. It is often difficult to demonstrate any one-to-one correspondence between an episode of nutritional deficiency or disease and hypoplasia formation. However, much work exists showing a general association between increased nutritional or disease stress, and increased rates of dental enamel defects at the population level. In children from an economically deprived area of Queensland, Australia, there was a strong association between dental enamel hypoplasias and various infectious diseases (Ford et al., 2009). Studies in Guatemalan children showed that those with dental enamel hypoplasias had nearly twice the rate of infectious disease as those without (Sweeney et al., 1969), and there was an inverse correlation between frequency of enamel hypoplasias and nutritional status (Sweeney et al., 1971). Goodman et al. (1991) found that under-nourished children from a Mexican village who had been fed nutritional supplements to increase calorie and protein intakes showed a reduced rate of hypoplasias compared with those on un-supplemented diets. Zhou and Corruccini (1998) found that Chinese subjects who had lived through episodes of famine during childhood had a higher frequency of dental enamel hypoplasias than those who had not.

Recording dental enamel hypoplasia

Dental enamel hypoplasias are quite often visible in ancient skeletons, and the traditional way of recording them is via the careful visual inspection. This is also the way in which studies are carried out in living populations. Visibility of a defect depends not only upon the number of perikymata affected, but also upon the angle with which the striae of Retzius meet the enamel surface and upon the spacing between the perikymata (Hubbard et al., 2009; Hassett, 2012). This means that the visibility of defects differs between different teeth and on different areas of the crown of a given tooth. Hypoplasias are much less visible on deciduous than on permanent teeth, and they tend to be more apparent on the anterior teeth than on molars and premolars. The broadly spaced perikymata in the mid-sections of the crowns of the permanent incisors and canines mean that it is there that hypoplasias are most readily identified, especially upon the fairly flat labial (anterior) surfaces (Figure 9.12).

Tooth crowns grow in a fairly regular manner, so that measuring the location of a defect with respect to some fixed point, such as the cemento-enamel junction, allows estimation of the age of the individual when the hypoplasia occurred. Reid and Dean (2006) present charts for estimating age at formation from a defect's location with respect to the cemento-enamel junction.

Simply identifying dental enamel hypoplasias with the naked eye means that they may be rapidly recorded, facilitating the study of large numbers of individuals. However, there are significant disadvantages. Many hypoplastic lines are quite faint, and this causes problems in scoring them. The enamel on the side of a tooth is never absolutely smooth, so the question arises as to how pronounced a groove has to be before it is classified as a hypoplasia. There is no simple answer to this question. The best that can be done is to ensure that one's results are repeatable – i.e. that identical (or at least similar) results are obtained when the same data are re-scored (It is good practice always to test the repeatability of one's results no matter what skeletal data one might be recording, be they measurements, non-metric traits or scores for pathological lesions.) Repeatability of recording of hypoplastic lines by the same observer is normally reported to be quite good. In a brief test I conducted (Mays, 1995), I found that in 88% of individuals my decision as to whether lines were present or absent was the same on a second inspection done under similar viewing conditions the next day. Others have reported similar results (e.g. Amoroso et al., 2014). However, the difficulties in reliably defining what is to be scored as a defect mean that it is very difficult to compare the results of different writers, as what may be counted as a hypoplasia by one may be disregarded by another.

To gain a fuller picture of enamel hypoplastic defects, microscopic analysis is needed (Hillson, 2014, 2019). Teeth can be physically sectioned and accentuated striae of Retzius recorded under the microscope. Alternatively, sufficient resolution of internal structures may be available from X-ray synchrotron microtomography. This is a non-destructive imaging technique, but the equipment is not widely available. These techniques would be essential to look at growth perturbations in the buried enamel, but more frequently used microscopic techniques concentrate on the surface of the tooth crown. The usual method is to make a mould using silicone dental impression material and then make a resin cast from that. One then has a permanent replica of the tooth surface that can be examined under a microscope.

As well as comprising a furrow of depressed enamel, a hypoplastic line shows perikymata on its occlusal wall that are more widely spaced than normal (Hillson & Bond, 1997). Microscopic methods of recording linear hypoplasias therefore involve either the identification of depressions in the enamel surface, or of variations in the spacing of perikymata where these structures can be seen – in some specimens this may be difficult due to surface wear from diet or deterioration of the enamel surface during burial. Microscopic study may comprise simple visual examination of the image. Alternatively, a measuring microscope can be used to produce a profile of the enamel surface (Cares Henriquez & Oxenham, 2017) or to measure the perikymata spacing (Hassett, 2012). Suitable thresholds can then be defined which furrow dimensions or perikymata spacing have to exceed in order for a defect to be classified as present.

Studying hypoplasias using microscopy is much more time-consuming than using the naked eye, and this places constraints upon numbers of skeletons that it is feasible to analyse in a research study. However it does offer some important advantages (Hillson, 2014, 2019). It provides a more objective way of identifying defects, improves repeatability of scoring, and allows much smaller defects to be identified with confidence. It also permits more accurate estimates of the timing of formation of hypoplasias, and mitigates the biasing effects that differential visibility to the naked eye of defects in different parts of a tooth, and in different teeth, have on interpreting age at insult data. It also facilitates the matching of defects between the crowns of different teeth that were forming at the time of an insult.

Microscopy additionally enables the duration of the event that produced the line to be estimated. The perikymata on the occlusal wall of a defect appear to form during the disease or malnutrition episode itself, whereas those in the rest of the defect seem to relate to the recovery phase (Hillson & Bond, 1997). Counting of perikymata in the occlusal wall under a microscope, and multiplying the total by nine (the approximate number of days' enamel formation represented by a perikyma) produces an estimate of the duration of the insult.

The archaeological study of dental enamel hypoplasia

Because of the increased information obtainable from microscopic analysis, an increasing number of archaeological studies of dental enamel hypoplasias are using microscopy. A team led by Daniel Temple, of George Mason University, examined dental enamel hypoplasias in skeletal remains of prehistoric hunter-gatherers from Japan (ca. 2000–300BC) and Inuit from Alaska (AD1300–1700) (Temple et al., 2013). They found that the frequency of defects in anterior teeth was greater among the prehistoric Japanese. However, estimates provided by perikymata counts from microscopic analysis of a subset of 35 individuals (out of a study group of 113) indicated that median duration of the insults that produced defects was only about 20 days in the Japanese but approximately 40 days among the Inuit. Reasons for these differences in adverse events during childhood in these two populations may be complex, and Temple and co-workers discuss a number of possibilities. Among these was diet. Food types available to the Inuit group were few in number, and diet focused mainly on marine resources. In autumn and winter, when these were essentially the only foods, they may have been deficient in micronutrients such as calcium, deficiencies that are known to cause enamel defects. Such seasonal nutritional problems may explain the long duration of disturbances in enamel seen in this group. The lower-latitude Japanese had a more diverse subsistence base, with a greater range of fall-back foods to mitigate duration of resource scarcity; seasonal and other food insecurities may have been frequent but relatively brief (Temple et al., 2013).

Despite the value of microscopy, most archaeological studies continue to be based solely on recording of defects with the naked eye, and useful results can still be obtained by this method. Mario Šlaus, of the Croatian Academy of Sciences and Arts, investigated various skeletal indicators of health, including dental enamel hypoplasias, in 104 14th-18th century AD burials excavated from a churchyard at Nova Rača (Figure 9.14). Nova Rača was a rural settlement which lay within the Austro-Hungarian Empire in the volatile border area with the Ottoman Turkish Empire.

Šlaus was interested in exploring differences in childhood health in males and females, and in the effects of adverse episodes in childhood on subsequent longevity. Historical evidence suggests that in this region a higher social value was placed on males than on females. Male adults constructed and maintained defences and participated in military actions in the border region. In return they were granted lands and exemption from taxes. This may have led to male offspring being preferred to females. Historic records show that adequate nutrition was frequently a problem in this region. The different social value placed upon male and female offspring may therefore potentially be reflected in differences between male and female diet and health in childhood – when resources were scarce more may have been directed toward male offspring. As part of a study to investigate these aspects, Šlaus (2000) recorded dental enamel hypoplasias in some anterior teeth of burials from the site (Table 9.2).

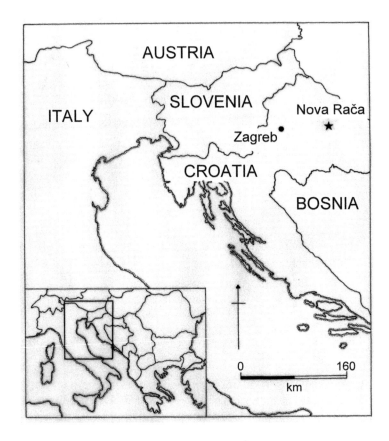

Figure 9.14 Location of the Nova Rača site studied by Šlaus (2000)

Table 9.2 Dental enamel hypoplasia frequencies (%) at Nova Rača

	Children	Adults	
		Males	Females
Maxillary I1	76.9 (13)	16.1 (31)	34.5 (29)
Maxillary C	66.7 (15)	9.7 (31)	48.2 (29)
Mandibular C	64.4 (14)	12.9 (31)	48.2 (29)

Source: figures from Šlaus (2000). Notes: frequencies are expressed as percentage of individuals showing one or more dental enamel hypoplasias; figures in brackets are total number of individuals with teeth present for examination.

Biologically, males show a somewhat greater vulnerability to disturbances of growth (Stinson, 1985; Tanner, 1989). However the effects of this on dental enamel hypoplasia frequencies are probably minor (Guatelli-Steinberg & Lukacs, 1999). Besides, at Nova Rača, it is in fact the females that have the higher frequency of defects (Table 9.2).

Some workers (e.g. Arcini, 1999) have emphasised that dental enamel hypoplasias only occur when individuals recover from adverse events that resulted in arrested tooth crown formation, and suggest that an increased frequency of defects in a population or subgroup may indicate an increased capacity to overcome disease, perhaps implying better living conditions. However this seems an unlikely explanation here. At Nova Rača, as in most archaeological studies, only individuals with complete enamel crowns were analysed. All individuals examined survived the period of crown formation (the anterior dentition records defects occurring between about one and six years of age (Reid & Dean, 2006)); those without defects lived through it without suffering events leading to formation of enamel hypoplasias, those with defects did suffer such events. The sex difference at Nova Rača appears consistent with a cultural bias toward greater investment in male children and perhaps privileged access of male children to food resources during times of shortage.

The data also show a greater frequency of enamel hypoplasias in children than in adults. For females, the inverse relationship between enamel hypoplasias and age at death may have extended into adult life with young female adults (aged approximately 20-30 years at death) appearing to show a higher frequency of defects than older females, although sample size was too small to be certain of this.

An inverse relationship between the prevalence of dental enamel hypoplasias and age at death has also been reported in some other ancient populations (discussion in Armelagos et al., 2009; Temple, 2019). There are a number of possible factors that could contribute to such a pattern (Armelagos et al., 2009). The 'weaker constitution' hypothesis suggests that individuals who fall ill in early childhood continue to do so in later life due to some inherent low resistance to disease. The 'developmental origins of health and disease' or 'biological damage' hypothesis is that adversity during early life may have left people less likely to survive subsequent episodes. A third possibility is that individuals with enamel defects are those who experience life-long social disadvantage resulting both in early childhood dental enamel defects and premature mortality. Regarding the Nova Rača material it is difficult to argue for the first hypothesis to explain the age – hypoplasia association: if the presence of dental enamel defects was simply a marker for individuals with inherently low disease resistance then it would be difficult to explain the association between female sex and hypoplasia frequency, especially since it is naturally females who have a slightly greater resistence to growth disruptions. Perhaps the Nova Rača finding might be explained by some combination of the last two possibilities.

Summary

Dental caries and ante-mortem tooth loss are two of the most frequent dental diseases observed in archaeological human remains. The former may lead to the latter, but periodontal disease, and heavy dental wear with consequent super-eruption of teeth, were also important causes of tooth loss in the past. Dental caries is associated with consumption of carbohydrate foods, particularly sugars. The prevalence of dental caries has been used to shed light on the amount and type of carbohydrate foods in diets in past populations.

Deposits of dental calculus are often found adhering to teeth in ancient skeletons. Proteins and other biomolecules appear to be preserved quite well in dental calculus. In addition, microscopy may allow inclusions from foods or non-food particulates to be identified. Biomolecular and microscopic analysis of dental calculus can potentially tell us not only about diet, but also about task-related activities, and about aspects of the general living environment.

Dental enamel hypoplasias most often consist of a transverse band of depressed enamel on the tooth crown, and they indicate an episode of growth disturbance to the enamel. Hypoplasias are common in ancient skeletons. They range in prominence from defects so small that they are only visible microscopically to gross defects plainly visible to the naked eye. Both microscopic and gross defects share similar causes: episodes of disease and poor nutrition during the period in which the enamel crown was forming. Once formed, hypoplasias remain on the teeth unless physically removed by dental wear. They thus form a permanent record of disease or nutritional stress events suffered during childhood.

Further reading

For a thorough account of dental caries for osteoarchaeologists see Hillson, S. (2008). The Current State of Dental Decay, pp. 111–135 in J.D. Irish & G.C. Nelson (eds) *Technique and Application in Dental Anthropology*. Cambridge, Cambridge University Press.

Ogden, A. (2008). Advances in the Palaeopathology of Teeth and Jaws, pp. 283–307 in R. Pinhasi & S. Mays (eds) *Advances in Human Palaeopathology*. Chichester, Wiley, *gives a useful coverage of the recognition of periodontal disease and the interpretation of periapical voids in skeletal remains.*

Dental calculus: Radini, A. et al. (2017). Beyond Food: The Multiple Pathways of Inclusion of Materials into Ancient Dental Calculus. *Yearbook of Physical Anthropology* 63: 71–83 *provides an overview of microscopic studies.*

Warriner et al. (2015). Ancient Human Microbiomes. *Journal of Human Evolution* 79: 125–136 *is an account of the potential of studying the microbiome in past human populations using calculus and other substrates.*

Hendy et al. (2018). Proteomic Evidence of Dietary Sources in Ancient Dental Calculus. Proceedings of the Royal Society Series B 285: article 20180977 *is a large-scale proteomic study.*

Hillson, S. (2014). *Tooth Development in Human Evolution and Bioarchaeology*. Cambridge, Cambridge University Press. *A useful source on normal development of the teeth, and the record they provide of disruptions to this process. Chapters 7 and 8 provide extended discussion of dental enamel hypoplasias.*

10 Traces of injury on the skeleton

Most injuries, whether accidental or intentional, do not involve the bones at all, only the soft tissues. Of course, with skeletonised remains, most evidence for soft tissue injury will be lost to us. However, in rare cases, these injuries may leave traces on bones. For example, injury to a muscle may occasionally elicit an abnormal cellular response resulting in the formation of a bony mass which may subsequently fuse to the adjacent bone. This type of ossification is termed *myositis ossificans traumatica* (Walczak et al., 2015), and may be manifest as an irregular bony projection (Figure 10.1). Dislocation involves disruption of the normal relationship between the components of a joint. Dislocations of long-standing may produce changes in the bones, including the formation of a secondary joint surface in an abnormal location. For example, shoulder dislocations normally involve anterior displacement of the proximal humerus so that the humeral head lies against the anterior surface of the scapular wing. If the dislocation is not reduced, a novel articular facet for the humeral head may form here (Roberts, 2019: 232) (Figure 10.2).

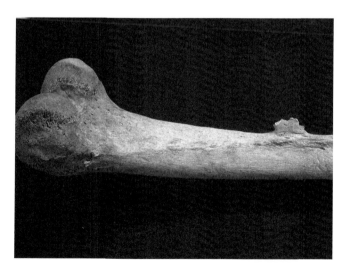

Figure 10.1 The projecting flange of bone on the shaft of this femur is likely due to a muscle injury. The lesion is termed *myositis ossificans traumatica*

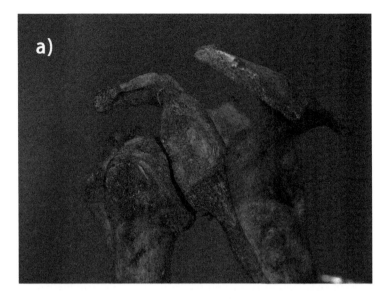

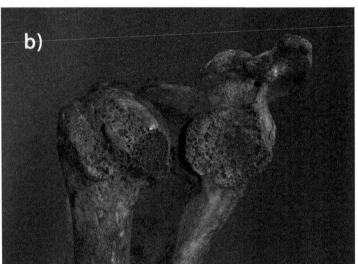

Figure 10.2 An unreduced anterior dislocation of the left shoulder. (a) The head of the humerus lies against the anterior surface of the wing of the scapula, (b) where a secondary joint surface has formed

Source: Supplied by Don Ortner.

Despite occasional evidence for soft tissue injuries, the most frequent indication of injury seen in skeletons is bone fracture. Some diseases, such as osteoporosis, weaken the skeleton. Fractures in bones weakened by disease are known as pathological fractures. Pathological fractures in osteoporosis were discussed in Chapter 8.

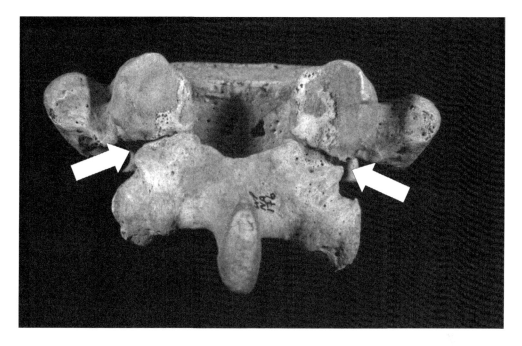

Figure 10.3 Spondylolysis of the 5th lumbar vertebra. There is a fatigue fracture at the *pars interarticularis* on both sides of the neural arch (arrowed). These have failed to unite so that the posterior part of the arch remains as a separate piece of bone

Most fractures occur as a result of excessive force applied to healthy bone tissue. Some result from repetitive stress which causes microscopic damage to a bone to develop at a faster rate than it can be repaired (Datir et al., 2007). These are known as fatigue fractures. An example of a fatigue fracture is spondylolysis of the vertebral neural arch. The break occurs at the *pars interarticularis*, the part of the neural arch between the superior and inferior facet joints. It generally occurs during the growth period, and is normally bilateral (i.e. affects both sides of the neural arch), so that the posterior part of the arch becomes detached from the rest of the bone. These injuries are characteristically found in the lumbar spine, particularly the last lumbar vertebra (Figure 10.3). Spondylolysis has been associated with activities that involve heavy loading of the lumbar spine (Standaert & Herring, 2000). In addition, some individuals seem show an inherent predisposition to it due to the anatomical conformation of their lumbar vertebrae (Ward et al., 2010). However, the majority of fractures are not fatigue failures; they are caused by sudden injury rather than repetitive stress.

Types of fracture

Although fractures are infinitely variable in appearance, most may, for convenience, be classified into a few broad groups based on the type of break (Figure 10.4).

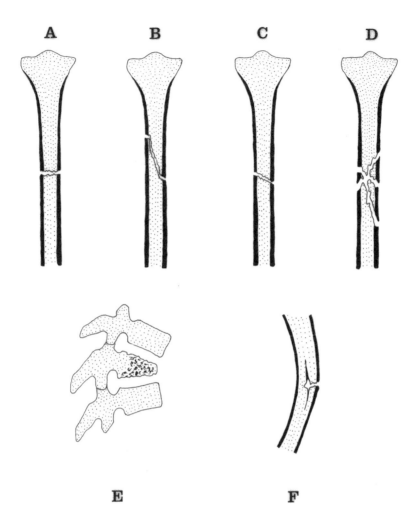

Figure 10.4 Common types of fracture: (a) transverse fracture; (b) spiral fracture; (c) oblique fracture; (d) comminuted fracture; (e) compression fracture; (f) greenstick fracture

Source: Adapted from Hamblen & Simpson (2007: Figure 1.2).

The type of fracture may give a clue as to the nature of the injury that caused it. Bending force or a blow at right angles to the long axis of a bone may cause a transverse fracture (Figure 10.4a); twisting force may cause a spiral fracture (Figure 10.4b). An oblique fracture (Figure 10.4c) may be caused by a combination of bending, twisting and compressive forces. Application of greater force or a crushing injury may lead to bone fragmentation – a comminuted fracture (Figure 10.4d).

The above are all complete fractures – there is a complete break in the bone. In some instances the break may not extend right the way through the bone. Compression and greenstick fractures are examples of incomplete fractures. Compression fractures occur when trabecular bone is crumpled. A frequent site for this type of injury is the vertebral column: forced flexion of the spine may result in wedge-shaped crushing of a vertebral body by compression between its neighbours (Figures 8.22 & 10.4e). Greenstick fractures characteristically occur in children. Children's bones are more springy and resilient than those of adults. A bending force which might result in a transverse break in an adult bone may in a child result in bending and incomplete fracturing, the greenstick fracture (Figure 10.4f).

In archaeological material, an additional type of injury, which is probably best classified as a fracture, is sometimes found: cuts due to slicing of bone by a sharp weapon, such as a sword, or some other implement. These are most often seen on the cranium and are indicative of violent assault. Other evidence for slicing (or sometimes sawing) of bone comes in the form of amputation of limbs or parts thereof. Archaeological examples of amputations may be found in a healed or unhealed state, occasionally with evidence for a prosthesis (Binder et al., 2016a). Sometimes, as with cranial blade injuries, the context suggests that they may reflect violent assault with a sharp weapon (e.g. Mays, 1996). Other cases suggest judicial punishment (e.g. Brothwell & Møller-Christensen, 1963) or surgical treatment of injured or diseased extremities (e.g. Etxeberria, 1999; Fowler & Powers, 2012). Another sort of ancient surgery, for which there is skeletal evidence from most parts of the world, is trepanation (Arnott et al., 2003), the opening of the skull by removing a part of the cranial vault using sharp metal or stone implements. Sometimes this appears to have been carried out to treat cranial fractures (e.g. Mays, 2006b), but in most cases the original therapeutic intent remains obscure.

Fracture repair

The healing of fractures in the diaphyses of tubular bones may be divided into five stages (Figure 10.5).

1. Haematoma formation. Tearing of blood vessels in and around the broken ends results in a collection of blood (haematoma) at the fracture site. As a consequence of damage to minor blood vessels, bone within a few millimetres of the fracture site dies and is subsequently resorbed.
2. Cellular proliferation. Within eight hours of the injury, cells proliferate in the fracture area. This leads to formation of flexible, fibrous tissue which pushes aside the haematoma (which is slowly resorbed) and eventually bridges the break between the bone ends.
3. Callus formation. Osteoblasts lay down bone so that fibrous union between the bone ends is replaced by immature, or woven bone. Osteoclasts remove dead bone from the fracture site. By the end of this stage the fracture is united by a rigid bridge of woven bone.
4. Consolidation. The activities of osteoblasts and osteoclasts gradually convert the woven bone callus the into mature, or lamellar bone. By the end of this stage, the fracture site is bridged by a strong cuff of bone.
5. Remodelling. The bulbous collar of bone surrounding the fracture site is gradually remodelled so that some buttresses of bone are removed and more bone is deposited where stresses are greatest. The medullary cavity reforms.

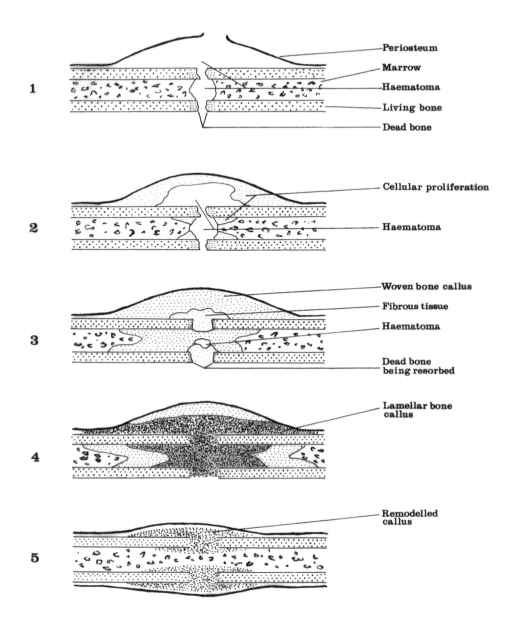

Figure 10.5 Stages in the healing of a fracture in a tubular bone: (1) haematoma formation;
(2) cellular proliferation; (3) callus formation; (4) consolidation; (5) remodelling
Source: After Hamblen & Simpson (2007: Figure 1.5).

Repair of trabecular bone follows a similar pattern to the above. However, as there is no medullary cavity and there is normally a much broader area of contact between the broken fragments than is the case for the diaphysis of a tubular bone, union can occur directly between the bone surfaces – it does not have to take place via internal and external callus. [The above account was taken from Hamblen & Simpson, 2007: 3-19; Nayagam, 2010: 687-692.]

The timing of fracture healing (de Boer et al., 2015) is highly variable. It is faster in children than in adults, and fractures in trabecular bone tend to heal more quickly than those in cortical bone. Factors which hinder fracture repair include inadequate immobilisation of the broken ends, infection at the fracture site and poor local blood supply. In an adult long-bone, the earliest new bone formation may occur as soon as 4-7 days after fracture, but it is not until at least six weeks that the bone ends are firmly united by woven bone callus. The replacement of the woven bone by lamellar bone during the consolidation phase is a gradual process extending over several months. The subsequent remodelling stage is even more protracted – increased remodelling may be observable in long-bone fractures more than a year after injury.

The schedule described above is for optimal cases. At the other end of the scale, if factors hindering healing are severe enough, bony union may never occur. This is generally the case, for example, in spondylolysis (Figure 10.3) where, presumably, it is continued movement of the vertebral column that prevents union. Non-union may also occasionally occur in fractures elsewhere in the skeleton (Figure 10.6). In cases of non-

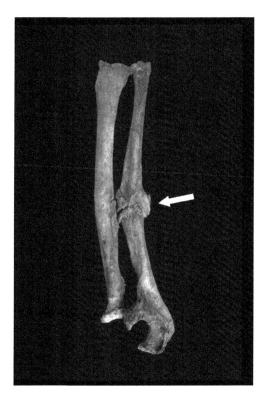

Figure 10.6 A left radius and ulna. There is a midshaft fracture of the ulna which has failed to unite, resulting in the formation of a pseudarthrosis or false joint between the broken ends (arrowed)

union, the bone ends may be united by flexible fibrous tissue, or alternatively a false joint, or pseudarthrosis, may form between them. In the latter case the bone ends are covered by cartilage and enclosed by a capsule containing synovial fluid, in imitation of a normal joint.

After a complete fracture, the broken ends usually become displaced through the force of the injury or through muscular contraction, so if a fracture is left to heal unaided the bones may well unite in a poorly aligned position. Splinting and other forms of reduction and immobilisation to treat fracture have a long history (Roberts, 2019: 246–249). Although such measures may assist healing and reduce displacement, fractures do not normally need treatment in order to heal; fractures usually unite whether they are splinted or not. Even if a fracture in an ancient bone is found united in good alignment, it does not necessarily mean that the individual received treatment in the form of splinting for the injury. Studies on the bones of wild apes (Schultz, 1967) demonstrate that many fractures heal with little deformity even without treatment.

Fractures in ancient bones

Breaks found in bones excavated from archaeological sites may have occurred:

(a) prior to death;
(b) at or around time of death (termed perimortal injuries);
(c) after burial, and may be divided into: (i) ancient breaks occurring whilst the bone is in the soil, and (ii) fresh breaks occurring during excavation or post-excavation processing.

Fractures which occurred some time before death are distinguished from those in categories (b) and (c) by the fact that they show bone production as part of the healing process. If the fracture was in the fairly early stages of healing when death intervened, woven bone callus will be present at the fracture site. Woven bone has a distinctive appearance (see Figure 1.4) so fractures in the early stages of healing should be distinguishable from those which occurred long before death. In the latter, callus appears as a cuff of fairly smooth bone at the fracture site.

An example of a healed fracture in a tibia from an archaeological site is shown in Figure 10.7. Looking first at Figure 10.7a, the bone at the fracture site has a fairly smooth, well-remodelled appearance, suggesting that the fracture occurred long before death. The appearance of the bone also suggests that the broken ends have united in less than perfect alignment – there appears to be some lateral displacement of the distal part. The radiograph (Figure 10.7b) shows that there has been some over-riding of the broken ends resulting in shortening of the bone. The radiograph also shows that it was a spiral fracture. Spiral fractures generally result from twisting forces so it was probably sustained as a result of a severely twisted ankle.

Diagenetic alteration tends to make archaeological bone rather fragile (see Chapter 2 and below). This means that bones are vulnerable to breakage due to careless handling during or after excavation. This damage is relatively easy to identify as it results in 'fresh' breaks; that is, the broken surfaces are white and unweathered. The fragile nature

(a)

(b)

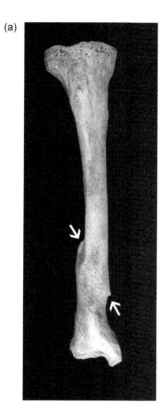
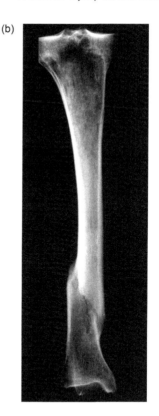

Figure 10.7 (a) Anterior view of the right tibia of an adult showing a healed fracture in its distal third. The fracture site (arrowed) shows smooth, well-remodelled callus. (b) A radiograph of the same bone

of archaeological bone also means that breakage readily occurs as they lie in the soil, due to soil movements associated with changes in moisture content or temperature (Boddington, 1996), or to pressure of overburden (McGowan & Prangnell, 2015). Such breaks may be of considerable antiquity. Hence they show weathering to the broken surfaces. This weathering indicates that they are not of recent origin, but not whether they were perimortal or post-depositional events. Neither fractures in category (b) nor in (c)(i) will show healing, and both types will show weathered edges. However, the differences in mechanical properties between fresh and ancient bone means that they can often be distinguished.

Dry, fresh bone contains about 10% water (Boskey & Robey, 2013), which is loosely bound within the bone's structure. In the weeks and months after death, water content normally decreases (Wieberg & Wescott, 2008; Jordana et al., 2013). This causes alteration to the bone's mechanical properties: it loses its slight 'give' or elasticity, becoming more brittle. This change in properties is accentuated over time as the collagen degrades (Turner-Walker & Parry, 1995). As well increasing its fragility, these alterations also change the way in which it fractures. This is most evident in elements with high cortical bone content: the bones of the cranial vault and the diaphyses of tubular bones. In a long-bone shaft, perimortal fractures tend to be curvilinear, with broken surfaces that are smooth and have sharp edges; post-depositional breaks in long-buried bone tend to be jagged or stepped in outline with rough surfaces (Outram, 2002; Cattaneo & Cappella, 2017). Turning to the cranial vault, perimortal blunt injury tends to cause a 'plastic response' at the site of impact resulting in a depressed fracture in which bone is pushed inwards; on the inner side of the injury, fragments may be 'hinged' inward (Fleming-Farrell et al., 2013). Linear fractures may radiate from the point of impact or else concentric fractures may surround it (Christensen & Passalacqua, 2018: 189–190); the broken surfaces tend to be smooth with straight edges (Fleming-Farrell et al., 2013). By contrast, post-depositional breaks to the skull of a long-buried skeleton tend to be haphazard in orientation, have rough surfaces, do not produce plastic deformation, and may shatter the vault, sometimes into many fragments.

Despite the above differences, it is sometimes difficult to distinguish perimortal from post-depositional breaks. This is due to factors which include overlap in mechanical properties of fresh and ancient bone, and that taphonomic damage may obscure perimortal injuries. For example, in a study of 210 fractures of known origin (27 perimortal, 183 post-depositional) in human remains exhumed 15 years after burial, 76% could be ascribed to their correct origin (perimortal or post-depositional) (Cappella et al., 2014). Most of the errors were for bones with only thin cortical bone (e.g. pelves and long-bone metaphyses). In another experiment, this time focused solely on the cranium and using CT images, Fleming-Farrell et al. (2013) found that fracture surface texture (rough – smooth) and fracture surface outline (straight – irregular) in each case correctly identified whether a break was perimortem or post-depositional in 92% of the 39 cases studied. Applying the criteria of plastic deformation and inward hinging of internal fragments correctly identified only 69% and 56% of cases respectively. However, these latter two features only occurred in perimortal injuries, so their presence would seem a good identifier of perimortal blunt force injury, even if their absence cannot be used to exclude it.

Since post-depositional breaks in ancient buried bone are so common, the best course is to regard all breaks as post-depositional unless application of the above criteria provides compelling evidence that they are perimortal injuries.

A long-bone showing some of the features typical of perimortal breakage is shown in Plate 7a. It is from a collection of disarticulated human remains recovered from a pit in the settlement part of the Mediaeval Wharram Percy site. Bones from the pit showed abundant evidence of burning, knife-marks indicating dismemberment of corpses, and perimortal breakage (Mays et al., 2017). The break at the proximal end of the tibia in Plate 7a is curvilinear in form, the face of the break is smooth and the edges are sharp. The observation that the broken surface shows similar weathering to the rest of the bone supports the idea that this is a perimortal break. By contrast, the break in the bone in Plate 7b shows features typical of a post-depositional break: a jagged, stepped outline and a rough broken surface. The white, unweathered surface indicates that the break occurred after excavation.

A cranial perimortal blunt injury is illustrated in the case of a Mediaeval child excavated from the churchyard at Wharram Percy. The child was about 5–6 years old at death. The lesion is a depression situated on top of the head, just to the right of the midline (Figure 10.8). The cranium is not perforated, but the bone on the external surface shows plastic deformity, being pushed down about 5 mm below the surrounding surface.

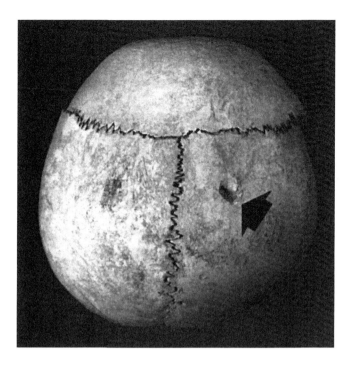

Figure 10.8 Superior view of a skull from Wharram Percy showing an unhealed blunt injury (arrowed)

Looking at the inner side of the injury (Figure 10.9), it can be seen that some of the inner table of the cranium has splintered away exposing the underlying trabecular bone. Some fragments remain attached and are hinged inward. There is no sign of healing, so the injury must have occurred at or around time of death.

In the case of the Wharram Percy child it is impossible to determine whether the cause of the injury was accident (for example a hard object falling on the head) or assault. If the latter, the nature of the wound suggests that the blow was probably delivered using a blunt weapon with a fairly small contact area (to produce the small diameter fracture). The posterior side of the wound slopes more steeply and is deeper than the anterior side (Figure 10.8). This suggests that if it was the result of a blow with a hammer or similar instrument, it was probably delivered from behind the victim. Another type of perimortal injury, where there is normally little doubt that intentional violence was the cause, is the blade injury.

When a sharp metal weapon, such as a sword, strikes bone in a living individual (or, indeed, in a fresh corpse), it tends to slice rather than shatter it. Perimortal blade injuries tend to be linear, without large irregularities to the line of the injury; their edges are generally well defined and clean; the surfaces of the cut edges tend to be fairly flat and smooth and may show polishing (Wenham, 1989; Lewis, 2008).

A blade injury on a Mediaeval skull from Ipswich, England is shown in Figure 10.10. The skull is of an adult male, and the injury takes the form of a linear cut extending from the

Figure 10.9 The inner surface of the Wharram Percy skull at the site of the injury

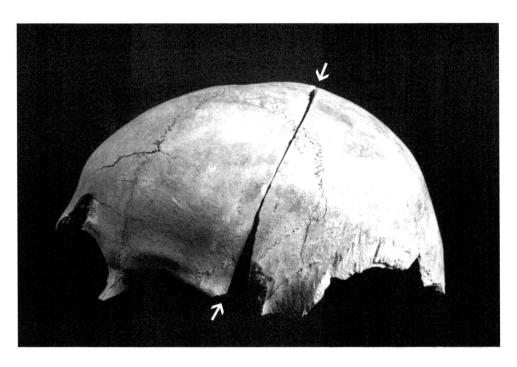

Figure 10.10 A skull from Ipswich showing an unhealed blade injury

area of the left orbit (eye socket) diagonally across the left side of the skull, terminating in the area of the crown of the head. The two sides of the injury do not fit together well due to some distortion of the skull as a result of soil pressure as it lay in the ground. The cut surfaces are fairly flat and parts of them have a polished appearance (Figure 10.11). Had the individual survived the injury for any length of time, new bone would have begun to form at the fracture site and started to obliterate the honeycomb pattern of the trabecular bone on the cut surfaces. Figure 10.11 shows that this has not happened, the honeycomb structure is plainly visible with no signs of new bone formation. Indeed, the brain injury consequent upon the wound must have been so massive that death would have been instantaneous. The lack of fragmentation around the wound edges shows that the weapon used must have been very sharp.

When unhealed blade injuries are examined under a microscope, their cut surfaces often show fine, parallel scratch marks. An experiment was undertaken at Leicester University, England to try and investigate the causes of these (Wenham & Wakely, 1989; Wenham, 1989). Wakely and Wenham purchased fresh pigs' heads from their local

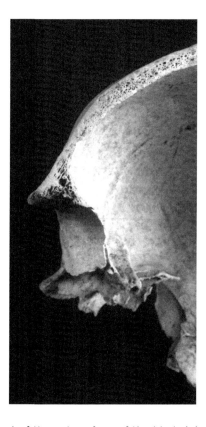

Figure 10.11 The anterior part of the cut surface of the blade injury in the Ipswich skull. The orbit (eye-socket) is on the left in the photograph. The fairly flat cut surface is smooth and has a polished appearance; this is most visible in the anterior part of the lesion, just above the orbit

butcher. They used replicas of Mediaeval swords to strike the pigs' heads with blows whose trajectories were carefully recorded. The cut surfaces on the skulls were then examined microscopically and this showed that the fine, parallel scratches aligned with the passage of the blade through the bone. They appeared to be caused by minute irregularities on the blade's surface. Thus, the orientation of these parallel scratches in archaeological specimens may serve as an indication of the trajectory of the blow which caused the injury.

Examination of the surfaces of the cut on the Ipswich skull under a low-powered microscope revealed fine, parallel scratch marks which were vertically orientated. This suggests that the injury was caused by a downward blow.

A further type of perimortal injury occasionally seen on more recent archaeological material is gunshot wounds. Entrance wounds are often approximately circular; exit wounds are often larger and more irregular in shape. As with blunt injuries, fracture lines may sometimes radiate from the point of impact (Berryman & Haun, 1996; Christensen & Passalacqua, 2018: 191-193). Unlike blunt injuries, holes due to gunshot wounds do not generally show adherent, inwardly directed fragments at their margins: the speed of the bullet means that bone fragments break away rather than bend (Berryman & Haun, 1996). Unless the bullet is retained embedded in the bone, it can be difficult to distinguish gunshot wounds from post-depositional damage on simple visual examination of the remains. This point is illustrated by a 19th century skull from the London Spitalfields site (Cox et al., 1990).

In order not to bias the scientific results, all the data on the Spitalfields skeletons were recorded 'blind' – i.e. without reference to the coffin plates and other sources which provide biographical information about many of the interred individuals. When the biographical data was tied in with the skeletons, it was noted that one of the burials was of William Leschallas, who committed suicide in 1852 by shooting himself in the head with a pistol. The skull in question showed an approximately circular hole in the right temple (Figure 10.12) and a larger more ragged hole in the back of the cranium. These holes looked typical of the sort of taphonomic damage customarily seen on archaeological remains, and indeed were accepted as such by several researchers who had previously examined the skull. When it was realised that the skull belonged to the suicide victim, a radiograph of it was examined and tiny opaque particles were found to be visible. These were lead fragments which had become embedded in the bone. This showed that the two holes were in fact entry and exit wounds from the gunshot. Because gunshot injuries are so difficult to distinguish from post-depositional defects on simple visual examination of the bones, radiography plays an important role in helping to make this distinction in archaeological material where gunshot wounds are suspected.

Strictly speaking, in the perimortal injuries just discussed we cannot determine whether they were delivered to a living person or to a fresh corpse. With the exception of the tibia from Wharram Percy illustrated in Plate 7a, where the specific context of the find suggests it was a mutilation visited upon a corpse (Mays et al., 2017), common sense indicates that they must have been inflicted on living individuals and hence were cause of death. However, with some perimortal injuries, the situation is less clear.

In cemeteries in Britain dating from about the 3rd to the 7th centuries AD it is not uncommon to find a few decapitated burials (Figure 10.13). Decapitated burials can be

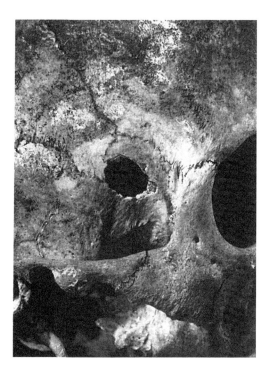

Figure 10.12 The right temple area of the skull of William Leschallas, excavated from the Spitalfields crypt, London. The orbit is visible on the right of the photograph, the ear canal towards the bottom left. The hole in the temple is the entry wound from the bullet which caused his death

Source: Reproduced from Cox et al. (1990: Figure 1).

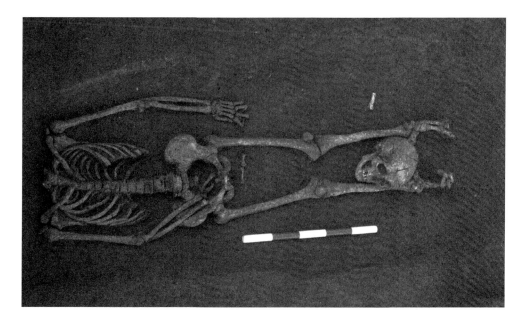

Figure 10.13 A decapitated burial dating to the 4th century AD from a cemetery excavated at Stanwick, England

distinguished from burials in which the skull has been moved by inadvertent disturbance to a long-forgotten grave by the presence of cut or chop marks on the neck vertebrae (Figure. 10.14) and by the observation that the top few vertebrae and the mandible are found still articulated with the cranium (Figure. 10.15). Various explanations for these decapitated burials have been suggested, including executions of criminals or enemies, human sacrifices, mutilations to corpses to prevent ghosts walking and mutilations to dishonour the corpses of enemies (discussion in Philpott, 1991:77–89; Reynolds, 2009: 91–92; Tucker, 2013; 2015). The first two possibilities assume that the decapitation was cause of death, whereas the last two assume that it was inflicted upon a lifeless corpse. In the minority of cases where the head was severed by multiple fine knife cuts, it seems reasonable to suppose the it represented a post-mortem mutilation. But in most cases the method was by chopping with a sword or axe, and here it is impossible to say whether they were executions or occurred after death (although the clenched fingers in the skeleton in Figure 10.13 may suggest a traumatic death – see caption to Figure. 3.5).

Archaeological population studies

Two discussions of injuries in ancient populations are presented below. The first concerns healed fractures and what they tell us about risk of violent or accidental injury. The second focuses on perimortal injuries among casualties of Mediaeval warfare.

Figure 10.14 An axis vertebra from a decapitated skeleton from Towcester, England (4th century AD). A cut from a bladed weapon has removed the odontoid process and part of the left superior articular surface

Source: Reproduced from Anderson (2001a).

Figure 10.15 The skull of another 4th-century AD decapitated burial from Stanwick. Note that the mandible and upper cervical vertebrae are in articulation with the cranium, indicating that the head was removed and placed in its location beneath the knee of this burial whilst still fleshed

Fracture patterns in pre-industrial Denmark

Fractures in a large series of skeletons excavated from Denmark have been studied by a team led by George Milner, of Pennsylvania State University (Milner et al., 2015). The purpose was to compare risk of accidental and violent injury in males and females, and to make comparison with fracture data from a modern hospital.

Milner and colleagues studied healed fractures in the cranial vault and long-bones in 822 adult skeletons (435 males, 387 females) from three archaeological sites. The remains ranged in date from the 12th to the beginning of the 17th century AD. They calculated fracture prevalences as the total number of individuals showing a fracture in a particular skeletal element divided by the total number of individuals preserving that element. The prevalence of fractures calculated in this way in the post cranial skeleton ranged from 6.3% for the radius down to 0.6% for the tibia. A total of 5.7% of crania showed fractures. Among the cranial fractures, all but two were blunt injuries. Further analysis was restricted to fractures in the cranium, clavicle, radius and ulna, as these were the elements showing the largest numbers of injuries.

Except for blade injuries (of which there were only two among the Danish skeletons), it is impossible to be sure in individual cases whether an injury was due to assault or accident. However, some types of fractures are associated with violence more often than others. In violent assault, the head is the natural target (Walker, 1997; Judd, 2004), so skull fractures are more often linked with violence than are post-cranial fractures (Milner et al., 2015). Assault with a blunt instrument is especially associated with injury to the cranial vault (Kremer & Sauvageau, 2009).

Fractures to the ulna shaft may occur when the arm is raised to ward off a blow to the head from a staff or similar weapon. Such fractures are therefore termed parry fractures. Parry fractures are approximately transverse in orientation and generally occur at the midshaft or below (Figure. 10.16); the radius is not normally injured (Judd, 2008). Milner et al. (2015) therefore used cranial vault fractures and parry fractures of the ulna as an index of violent injury.

By contrast, clavicle fractures generally result from accident – typically falls onto the shoulder (Kihlström et al., 2017). Most of the radius fractures in the Danish skeletons occurred near the distal end and are of the type termed Colles' fractures. These are fractures through the distal metaphysis of the bone (Mays, 2006c). Colles' fractures are characteristically the result of a fall onto an outstretched hand (Figure. 10.17). Fractures to the clavicle and distal radius were therefore considered an index of accidental injury.

Of 131 males with the cranial vault and the distal two-thirds of both ulnae present, 16 (12.2%) had fractures at either of these two locations. The figure for females was 4 of 105 (3.8%). This suggests that women were less likely than men to suffer a broken bone as a result of violent assault. The corresponding figures for fractures classified as indicators of accidental injuries were 7/126 = 5.6% for males, and 11/98 = 11.2% for females. It might therefore appear that females were more likely to break bones in accidents, but statistical analysis showed that the difference between the sexes was not significant, which means that there is no valid evidence for any overall difference in clavicle/radius fractures between the sexes. However, some patterning emerged once prevalence of fracture by age at death was considered. Among those over 35 years old, the prevalence of injuries classed as accidental was significantly greater in females. Most of these were

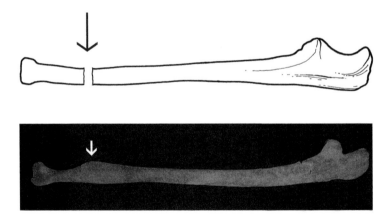

Figure 10.16 Typical location of an ulna parry fracture, together with an archaeological specimen showing a healed example

Source: Reproduced from Judd (2008).

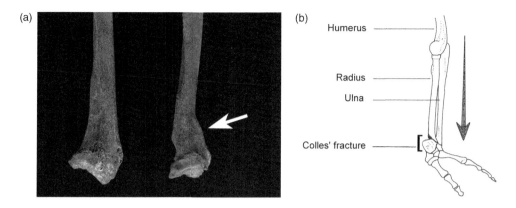

Figure 10.17 (a) A radius showing a healed Colles' fracture (arrowed). The other bone is a normal radius for comparison. (b) The typical cause of Colles' fracture is a fall onto an outstretched hand

Colles' fractures of the radius. These may be attributable to the onset of osteoporosis in females – as we saw in Chapter 8, the 'wrist fracture' (actually Colles' fracture of the radius) is characteristic of osteoporosis.

Using data on patients treated over a period of one year at the Emergency Department at the hospital serving Odense municipality, Milner and colleagues compared risk of cranial fracture in Mediaeval and modern times. The hospital data comprise 128 cases of skull fracture. Making comparisons between data from living patients and from skeletal remains is not straightforward. Although the rate of bone remodelling in early childhood and infancy means that evidence for fractures occurring during early life may in time be obliterated from the skeleton, in adults the fracture site usually remains evident throughout life (Hamblen & Simpson, 2007. 10). Broadly speaking, fractures in a skeleton represent a cumulative record of injuries suffered in adult life. The hospital data, on the other hand, represent injuries that occurred in the incident that prompted attendance at the hospital. This difference means that the total years at risk of acquiring fractures in the archaeological population needs to be accounted for if accurate comparisons are to be made.

To calculate the number of fractures expected in the archaeological population on the basis of the fracture rates observed in the modern data, Milner et al. (2015) first divided the hospital patients into the same 10 year age groups (from 15-25 through to 55+) that they used for the archaeological population. They then calculated the frequency of broken bones in each age group in the modern population by dividing the number of fracture cases in that age group by the number of individuals of that age in the municipality. This was then multiplied by the total years at risk of fracture for that age interval in the archaeological population. Years at risk are calculated from the estimated age at death of the archaeological skeletons. For example, a skeleton of estimated age at death of 25-35 years would have a mid-point age estimate of 30 years, so would contribute 10 years to the 15-25yr interval and 5 years to the 25-35 interval. This exercise indicated that the number of cranial fractures that one might expect in the Mediaeval skeletal assemblage if the risk of fracture was similar to that today was 4.1 for males and 1.3 for females. The actual numbers observed were 14 and 3 respectively. As the authors point out, there are some difficulties in making the comparison – for example fracture diagnosis procedures are obviously different in dry bones and the hospital patients, and age in the skeletons was estimated rather than known accurately. Nevertheless, Milner et al.'s (2015) claim that the comparison should be broadly valid seems reasonable. The risk of cranial fracture would appear to have been considerably greater in Mediaeval times. Given the association between cranial fracture and violence this implies a greater risk of violent injury, especially when one considers that important causes of cranial fracture in modern society, such as motor traffic accidents, would have been absent in the past.

Written sources suggest that violence was part of the fabric of everyday life in late Mediaeval times. They conjure up a vision of a society in which people were quick to take affront and would readily resort to violence to settle disputes, and this at a time when the means of enforcing public order and punishing wrong-doers were generally weak and easily perverted (Bellamy, 1973; Hanawalt, 1976). However, reliable statistics on the actual levels of violence are hard to come by. Perhaps the most usable data relate to legal records of homicides. The extent to which these can be used to estimate homicide rates is controversial (e.g. Sharpe, 1985; Eisner, 2003; Butler, 2018), but analysis of Mediaeval English records (Hanawalt, 1976; Given, 1977), has led to estimates of about 20–50 homicides *per annum* per 100,000 of population in the 13th–14th centuries. Study of late Mediaeval sources from elsewhere in Europe has produced fairly similar figures (Eisner, 2003). The current homicide rate for England and Wales is 1.2 per annum per 100,000 (ONS, 2018), and that for Denmark is similar (Thomsen et al., 2019). Over 80% of homicide victims in the Mediaeval records are male (Hanawalt, 1976; Given, 1977; Eisner, 2003). Making comparisons between ancient and modern rates of violence is difficult, both for osteoarchaeologists and for historians. Both skeletal and written sources have their own biases and shortcomings, but in this instance they both point to the violent nature of Mediaeval society, and that it was men rather than women who were overwhelmingly the victims.

Weapon injuries in Mediaeval warfare

As well as pervading everyday life, violence in Mediaeval times was also expressed through encounters between combatants on the battlefield. Only a few battlefield mass-graves have been excavated. The largest of these is Wisby, which lies on the Swedish island of Gotland in the Baltic Sea.

The Battle of Wisby took place in July 1361. The Danish Army invaded Gotland, and roundly defeated a hastily raised Swedish peasant levy to take the island for Denmark. Three mass-graves (Figure. 10.18) containing skeletons of the fallen were excavated in the earlier part of the 20th century (Thordemann, 1939). Bones representing more than a thousand individuals were recovered. The battle injuries on these bones formed the subject of a classic osteoarchaeological study by the Swedish anatomist, Bo Inglemark (Inglemark, 1939).

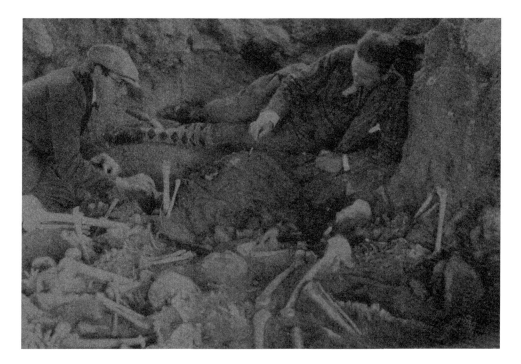

Figure 10.18 One of the mass-graves at Wisby under excavation
Source: Reproduced from Thordeman (1939).

Wounds found on the Wisby skeletons included blade cuts, blunt injuries and arrow wounds. The blade injuries were inflicted with swords, with perhaps some axe wounds. Heavy swords were used at this time, although two-handed swords were rare. The wounds on the Wisby skeletons provide a vivid testament to the brutality of medieval warfare. Many skeletons bear severe multiple injuries (Figure 10.19), showing that the individuals had been felled and mutilated by a series of violent blows. They also illustrate the devastating effectiveness of Mediaeval weaponry. For example, a number of individuals show severed limbs, and in one skeleton both lower legs had been severed by a single sword-slash. Some of the bodies had been cast into the grave pits still wearing their armour. It is clear that in many cases this gave insufficient protection from the Danish heavy weaponry. For example, some skeletons showed fatal cuts which penetrated clean through chain-mail.

Most of the cuts on the skeletons were directed from above, the natural arc of a slashing weapon like the Mediaeval sword. The distribution of blade injuries to the skull and long-bones is shown in Figure 10.20. Many blows landed on the head which, as we have seen, is the natural target in hand-to-hand violence. Inglemark observed an asymmetry in the distribution of the blade injuries on the skull. More blows fell on the left side, the left/right ratio of blade injuries to the skull was 1.6:1. The majority of people are right-handed, so in face-to-face combat an overarm blow with a weapon such as a sword would tend to fall on the upper left side of the victim's head. The lateral asymmetry was most pronounced in those skulls showing a single blade injury (left/right ratio 2.3:1), the distribution being much more

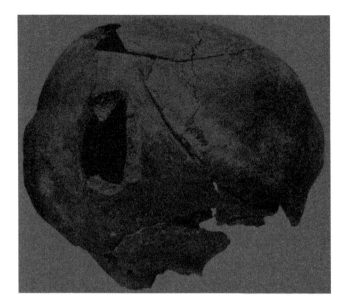

Figure 10.19 A cranium from Wisby showing several cuts in various directions
Source: Reproduced from Inglemark (1939: Figure 175).

even in those showing multiple cuts (left/right ratio 1.2:1). Inglemark felt that this suggested that the single cuts were struck during face-to-face combat, whereas many of the multiple cuts probably came from blows aimed at fallen warriors.

The lower legs are not a naturally favoured target in inter-personal violence (Ström, 1992; Brink et al., 1998), but in the Wisby skeletons a large proportion of cuts were found in this area. Inglemark attributed this to a number of factors. Shields would have provided some protection for the upper body, as would the body armour; however, the lower legs were lightly armoured if at all. Aiming at the lower legs may also have been a deliberate tactic. Blows here would have been difficult to parry and were probably aimed at scything down an opponent prior to administering the coup de grâce. Inglemark also points out that the tibia's superficial location means that it would be injured even by relatively light blows which, had they landed elsewhere on the body, might have stopped in overlying muscle.

Since the Wisby study, several more battlefield mass-graves have been excavated. Bones representing about 60 individuals have been recovered from the site of an early 14th-century battle at Sandbjerget in Denmark (Bennike, 2006; Boucherie et al., 2017). A similar size assemblage has been studied from the so-called Battle of Good Friday in AD1520 at Uppsala, Sweden (Kjellström, 2005). In England, 38 burials come from a mass-grave on the site of the Battle of Towton (AD1461) (Novak, 2000). Detailed comparisons of these assemblages with that from Wisby are problematic, due to factors that include differences in the way in which the remains were excavated and studied, and the condition of the bones. Nevertheless, the data do suggest some differences in the patterns of injury. In particular, the other sites appear to show a greater concentration of injuries

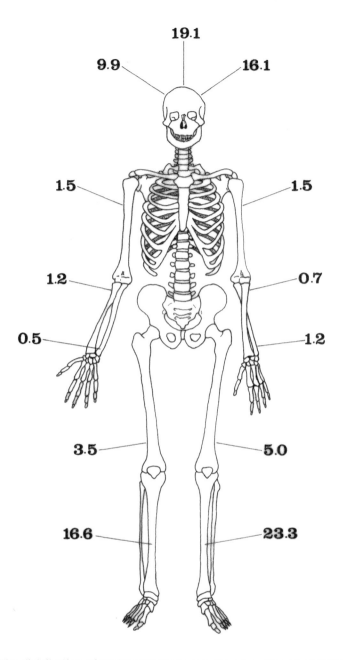

Figure 10.20 The distribution of perimortal blade injuries according to skeletal element and side in the skull and long-bones from Wisby. The large number of skull wounds of indeterminate side is largely because many cuts were identified on skull fragments; in such circumstances it was frequently impossible to determine whether the injury lay mainly on the left or right side

Source: From figures given in Inglemark (1939).

in the skull, with lower left: right side ratios (Figure 10.21a, b). The discrepancies are especially marked at Sandbjerget and Uppsala, where nearly 90% of wounds are to the skull and they lack the left-sided bias observed at Wisby. Perhaps face-to-face combat was not primarily responsible for the casualties from Uppsala and Sandbjerget. For example, if more of the victims here were fleeing than was the case at Wisby, then this might account for the pattern. If this was the case, then we might expect to see more blows directed from behind the victim. The percentage of injuries to the skull that were located upon the occipital bone at Sandbjerget (16%), was similar to that at Wisby (15%). The percentage at Uppsala seems higher (26%), but of course, many blows aimed at a fleeing opponent may have landed parts of the skull other than the occipital, so this is a rather imperfect measure.

As regards the greater concentration of injuries to the skull at Uppsala and Sandbjerget, it may be: that those responsible for the deaths of these individuals used techniques of combat that differed from those employed by the Danish Army at Wisby; that bodies of the victims were more efficiently protected by armour; or that protective head-gear was more easily dislodged during battle (Novak, 2000; Kjellström, 2005; Boucherie et al., 2017). Another possibility is that the blows were delivered by mounted men (Kjellström, 2005;

a)   b)

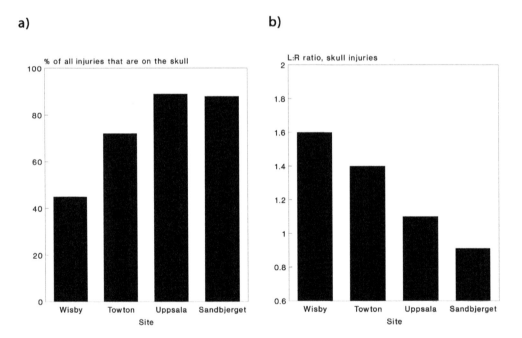

Figure 10.21 Perimortal injuries at Wisby, Towton, Uppsala and Sandbjerget. (a) Percentage of total injuries that are located on the skull. (b) Ratio of left: right sided injuries on the skull

Source: calculated from data from Inglemark (1939), Novak (2000), Kjellström, (2005) and Boucherie et al. (2017). The data relate to blade injuries, except for Towton, where they include some puncture and blunt injuries which would also have mainly resulted from blows from hand-held weapons.

Bennike, 2006; Boucherie et al., 2017). The head of a man on foot would be more readily within reach of a sword swipe than the rest of his body. A scenario whereby a significant number of fatalities were caused by blows inflicted to foot soldiers by horsemen, rather than by fighting between men standing face-to-face, might also account for the relative lack of left side preference in the cranial injuries. At Towton, the proportion of wounds that are located on the skull, and their laterality, differs from Wisby, but not to the same extent as do Sandbjerget and Uppsala (Figure 10.21). Perhaps the element of hand-to-hand fighting between infantry was less than at Wisby but greater than at Sandbjerget or Uppsala.

Summary

Healed fractures are quite readily identified in skeletal remains by the cuff of bony callus present at the fracture site. Bone injuries occurring at or around time of death (termed perimortal injuries) show no signs of bony healing. Ancient bone is a fragile material which readily fragments whilst in the soil and may easily be broken inadvertently during excavation or post-excavation processing. Recent damage is readily identified by the fresh, unweathered state of the broken edges, but breaks occurring in the soil in antiquity will have weathered edges, as will perimortal injuries. Some perimortal injuries, such as wounds from swords and other bladed weapons, are quite characteristic and easily identified. There are also criteria for distinguishing other types of perimortal injuries (fractures in the post-cranial bones, blunt injury to the skull) from breakage occurring in the soil, but these are not fool-proof. Because post-depositional breaks are so ubiquitous in archaeological bone, the best course is to regard breaks that show no sign of healing as post-depositional in origin unless there is compelling evidence to the contrary.

Healed or unhealed cuts from bladed weapons are unequivocal evidence of violence, and the study of their type and distribution in ancient skeletons can tell us much about the nature of warfare and other interpersonal violence in the past. However, unless one is dealing with a battlefield mass grave, most of the fractures seen in an archaeological assemblage are simply healed breaks in bone. In these instances, it is usually unclear whether, in individual cases, the fracture was a result of violence or accident. However, careful study of healed fractures in a skeletal population may allow inferences as to whether violence or accident was the principal cause of the injuries. Evidence for a healed fracture tends to remain on the skeleton throughout life. This means that, in common with many other skeletal pathologies, healed fractures tend to accumulate with age. It is therefore important to control for age when making fracture frequency comparisons.

Further reading

Lovell, N. & Grauer, A.L. (2019). Analysis and Interpretation of Skeletal Trauma in Skeletal Remains, pp 335–383 in Katzenberg M.A. & A.L. Grauer (eds) *Biological Anthropology of the Human Skeleton*. Wiley, Chichester, *is a review of skeletal injury with an emphasis on the types of fracture characteristically found in the different bones of the body.*

The papers in Knüsel, C. & Smith. M. (2013). *The Routledge Handbook of the Bioarchaeology of Human Conflict*. Routledge, London, *provide a wide-ranging survey of the skeletal evidence for violence from prehistory to the present day.*

11 Stable isotope analysis

Isotopes are atoms of an element with different masses. Most elements exist as mixtures of two or more isotopes. Some isotopes are radioactive (for example carbon-14), in which case they steadily decay, transmuting into other elements. Others are stable – that is, they are not radioactive and do not change in abundance over time.

Stable isotope ratios of carbon and nitrogen differ in different classes of foods, and these differences are passed on to the tissues (including skeletal tissues) of the consumer. This makes them useful for elucidation of palaeodiets.

Isotopic ratios of strontium differ according to geology, and oxygen stable isotopes in rainwater vary with climate. This means that they vary in different localities. Strontium and oxygen isotope ratios are passed onto human tissues, including bones and teeth, via foods and drinking water. Skeletal strontium and oxygen isotopic ratios can potentially be used as indicators of the geographical areas in which people lived at different points in their lives.

Palaeodietary analysis using carbon and nitrogen stable isotopes

Carbon occurs in two stable isotopes, of mass 12 and 13 (written as ^{12}C and ^{13}C). The average relative abundances of these is about 98.9% and 1.1% respectively. Nitrogen also has two stable isotopes, ^{14}N and ^{15}N, with relative abundances of approximately and 99.6% and 0.4%.

Most stable isotope palaeodietary studies have concentrated on carbon and nitrogen in collagen, either from bone or dentine. To analyse for stable isotopes, the collagen is extracted and purified. The resulting material is then burnt, and the gases produced analysed using a mass spectrometer. This gives the relative abundance of the different isotopes present.

Because differences in carbon and nitrogen isotopic ratios in different parts of the natural environment, and in different foods, are small, their stable isotope ratios are not normally written as simple ratios of one isotope to another, but as delta units. Delta units measure deviation in isotopic ratio from a particular standard. They are expressed in terms of parts per thousand ('per mil') using the symbol ‰, and calculated according to the formulae below:

$$\delta^{13}C = \left[\frac{(^{13}C/^{12}C)_{Sample}}{(^{13}C/^{12}C)_{Standard}} - 1\right] \times 1000$$

$$\delta^{15}N = \left[\frac{(^{15}N/^{14}N)_{Sample}}{(^{15}N/^{14}N)_{Standard}} - 1 \right] \times 1000$$

The standard for carbon is a mineral called Peedee Belemnite (PDB); for nitrogen it is air. The majority of biological materials have less carbon-13 than the PDB standard, so most $\delta^{13}C$ values are less than zero. Most biological samples have more nitrogen-15 than atmospheric nitrogen, so most $\delta^{15}N$ values are greater than zero.

Carbon stable isotopes in the environment

Carbon stable isotope ratios in plants vary according to the photosynthetic pathway used by the plant to manufacture carbohydrates from atmospheric carbon dioxide. The two major pathways are known as the C3 and C4 mechanisms.

Most temperate zone vegetation uses the C3 pathway, so called because it involves the production of a three-carbon compound as its first step. The mean $\delta^{13}C$ value for C3 plants clusters around -27‰ to -28‰ (O'Leary, 1988).

Some plants from tropical and sub-tropical latitudes, adapted to conditions of high temperature and high light intensity, use a photosynthetic pathway involving the creation of a four-carbon compound as the first step. C4 plants include important cultivated species such as maize, millet, sorghum and sugar-cane. The $\delta^{13}C$ values of C4 plants cluster around a mean of about -12‰ to -13‰ (O'Leary, 1988).

Although the principal determinant of the $\delta^{13}C$ value of a plant is the photosynthetic pathway used, factors affecting the precise figure include water and nutrient availability, light intensity and altitude (O'Leary, 1981; Tieszen, 1991). So, for example, plants growing in dense forest understoreys may produce anomalously negative delta values. This is called the canopy effect and is due to the low light intensity and perhaps uptake of carbon dioxide from rotting vegetation (Bonafini et al., 2013).

The difference in $\delta^{13}C$ values between diet and the flesh of the consumer is small, about 1‰ or less (Tieszen et al., 1983). This means that in a given environment, $\delta^{13}C$ values of animal and plant foods are similar.

Since the Industrial Revolution, the burning of fossil fuels has made the delta value of atmospheric carbon dioxide about 1.5‰ more negative (Friedli et al., 1986). Because carbon in terrestrial food chains ultimately derives from atmospheric carbon dioxide, to estimate $\delta^{13}C$ values for terrestrial foods in antiquity about 1.5‰ needs to be added to modern figures.

Carbon in marine environments derives mainly from dissolved bicarbonate, which is enriched in C-13 compared with atmospheric carbon dioxide (Smith & Epstein, 1971). Marine plants and plankton (which are mainly C3) therefore have less negative $\delta^{13}C$ values than terrestrial C3 plants (Chisholm et al., 1982; Tan, 1989). The flesh of marine mammals and fish has a delta value of about -17‰ to -18‰ (Chisholm et al., 1982).

Nitrogen stable isotopes in the environment

Most plants cannot obtain the nitrogen they need to form proteins and other compounds directly from the atmosphere, they take it up from the soil. Exceptions are legumes, such as peas and beans, which can use atmospheric nitrogen as well as absorbing it from the soil. δ^{15}N values for leguminous plants lie between 0 and +4‰, for other plants they are about +5‰ (DeNiro & Hastorf, 1985). The isotopic ratio for atmospheric nitrogen appears to have remained unchanged for millions of years (DeNiro, 1987), but δ^{15}N in some soils has been reduced somewhat by the use of modern chemical fertilisers (DeNiro & Hastorf, 1985). The precise δ^{15}N of plants varies with climate (Handley et al., 1999; Amundson et al., 2003) and other factors that affect soil chemistry, including the application of natural fertilisers (Bogaard et al., 2007, 2013). In mammals, nitrogen balance may affect δ^{15}N values: insufficient protein intake may result in elevated δ^{15}N (Reitsema, 2013).

Flesh has a somewhat higher δ^{15}N value than diet, so δ^{15}N increases as one ascends a food chain. The magnitude of this trophic level effect is about 3-5‰ (Bocherens & Drucker, 2003). In principle this is sufficient to enable nitrogen stable isotopes to be used to investigate meat: vegetable ratios in human diets, but limitations in our knowledge of other sources of variability in δ^{15}N mean that interpretation of results in these terms is often difficult in practice (Hedges & Reynard, 2007; Makarewicz & Sealy, 2015). However, one area where this trophic level effect has proved of undoubted value is in the study of breastfeeding practices in the past – a suckling infant is living off the product of its mother's tissues and so is one trophic level higher, and this is reflected in its tissue δ^{15}N.

Dissolved nitrates in seawater provide the major nitrogen source for marine food chains. They are enriched in δ^{15}N compared with atmospheric and soil nitrogen so that marine plants have higher δ^{15}N values than do terrestrial ones, and marine animals have higher delta values than do terrestrial species at corresponding positions in food chains (Schoeninger et al., 1983; Schoeninger & DeNiro, 1984). Marine fish have values of about +11‰ to +16‰, and marine mammals +11‰ to +23‰ (Schoeninger & DeNiro, 1984). Marine shellfish δ^{15}N appear somewhat lower than this, at about +7‰ to +10‰ (Sealy et al., 1987; Marchais et al., 2013).

Approximate mean carbon and nitrogen stable isotope values for some major classes of food from temperate terrestrial C3 and C4 environments, and from marine ecosystems are summarised in Figure 11.1. The figures are estimates of likely values obtaining in antiquity; that is, they are adjusted to take into account the effects of atmospheric pollution and the application of chemical fertilisers on modern values. Figure 11.1 is a general guide to the kinds of figures likely for different food classes, but most workers studying ancient diets not only analyse human remains but also faunal remains (and plant remains if available) from nearby archaeological sites in order to provide more precise baseline values for local foods to aid the interpretation of human stable isotope data.

Carbon and nitrogen stable isotope ratios in human bone collagen

Carbon and nitrogen stable isotope ratios in human tissues show a firm relationship with those in diet. The δ^{13}C value of human bone collagen is about 5‰ less negative than diet (Froehle et al., 2010; Fernandes et al., 2012). The δ^{15}N in collagen is about the same as that in flesh (Ambrose, 1993) – about 3-5‰ greater than diet.

C3 environment

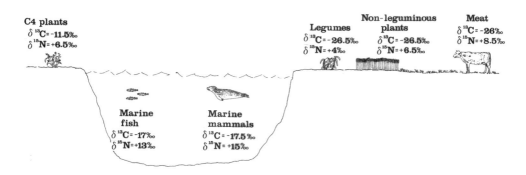

Figure 11.1 Approximate mean stable isotope ratios for some major food classes. Values are
      estimates of those obtaining in antiquity – in other words they are adjusted to
      take into account the effects of fossil fuel burning and the application of chem-
      ical fertilisers on modern values. For sources see text

About three-quarters of the carbon in bone collagen comes from dietary protein
(Fernandes et al., 2012), as does virtually all nitrogen. Carbon stable isotopes primarily,
and nitrogen stable isotopes entirely, reflect those in dietary protein. Bone collagen
turnover in adults is rather slow, about 1.5–4% per year in cortical bone (Hedges et al.,
2007). Collagen stable isotope data from adult skeletons thus yield information on dietary composition averaged over the last few decades of an individual's life. Bone turnover in the growing skeleton is more rapid than in adults, about 10–30% per year in
cortical bone in adolescents (Hedges et al., 2007). It is faster still at younger ages, the
younger the child the more rapid it is. As we know from previous chapters of this book,
the dental hard tissues, unlike bone, are not continually renewed. This means that
stable isotopes in collagen from dentine give an indication of diet at the time the dentine was forming. By analysing dentine in adults we can gain information on what their
diet was like in infancy and childhood.

Intact collagen preserves *in vivo* isotopic ratios. Collagen has a specific atomic carbon:
nitrogen ratio (about 2.9–3.6 (DeNiro, 1985)) and amino acid composition. During diagenesis, a collagen-like amino acid composition (implying the presence of intact collagen)
persists until about 5% of the original protein content remains. Below this figure, an
amino acid composition which differs from that of collagen begins to predominate
(Stafford et al., 1991). A way of detecting intact collagen is to analyse the protein extracted
from a bone to determine whether it retains a collagen-like amino acid signature or
carbon: nitrogen ratio. Alternatively, analysis may be restricted to bone retaining about
5% or more of its original protein (i.e. with an organic residue equal to or greater than
about 1% of the bone weight) (van Klinken, 1999). In practice, most bones from archaeological contexts in temperate zones satisfy these criteria.

Palaeodietary stable isotope work in archaeology

Subsistence change in North America and Europe

Major foci of palaeodietary stable isotope studies have been to investigate the relative contributions of C3 and C4 plants to human diets and to examine the relative use of aquatic as opposed to terrestrial food resources. The approximate $\delta^{13}C$ and $\delta^{15}N$ values expected of human bone collagen from ancient populations on C3 and C4 terrestrial and marine diets is shown in Figure 11.2.

Maize is a C4 plant, so its introduction into temperate regions with natural C3 vegetational cover can be studied using carbon stable isotope ratios. Maize was first domesticated in southern Mexico more than 6000 years ago. It was introduced into temperate North America from the south as a cultigen. In eastern North America, it in time largely replaced existing subsistence strategies based on the cultivation of native plants and the hunting and gathering of wild resources (Blake et al., 2017; Smith, 2017).

Investigation of the introduction of maize agriculture to North America was among the earliest archaeological applications of bone stable isotope work, and many studies have been published (Larsen, 2015: 304–307). The $\delta^{13}C$ data from one such study, of

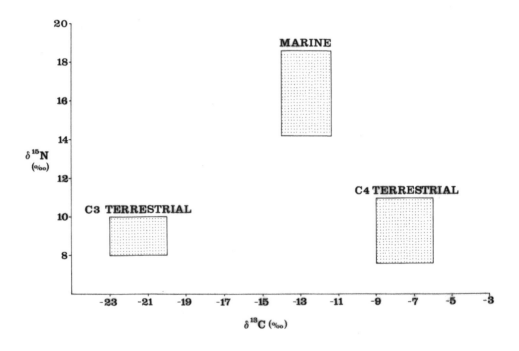

Figure 11.2 Approximate human bone collagen stable isotope ratios expected for archaeological populations consuming pure C3, C4 and marine diets. Pure C3 diets are found in archaeological populations from areas far from the coast with no C4 plants. Exclusively marine and exclusively C4 diets are purely hypothetical

skeletal remains from Arkansas and Missouri (Lynott et al., 1986), are shown in Figure 11.3. Prior to about AD1000, the $\delta^{13}C$ ranges from -19.9‰ to -21.7‰. Reference to Figure 11.2 shows that these values are consistent with a diet of terrestrial C3 foods. After AD1000 there is a sharp rise in carbon isotope ratios. Skeletons after this date give values ranging from -10.4‰ to -15.8‰. This indicates rapid adoption of a major C4 component in diets. Lynott and co-workers interpret this as indicating that intensive maize agriculture began in the region at this time. Radiocarbon dating of fragments of maize from prehistoric settlement sites show that it was present in this region more than 250 years prior to this (Simon, 2017). The pattern whereby the large-scale consumption of maize occurs much later than its initial introduction has also been reported in other regions of eastern North America. For example, comparison of human bone stable isotope data with archaeobotanical evidence indicates that this is so for the Lake Erie basin (Schurr & Redmond, 1991; Hart, 2018) and for southern Ontario (Harrison & Katzenberg, 2003; Blake et al., 2017). The protein content of maize is low – only about 10% (USDA, 2019) – so given that bone collagen $\delta^{13}C$ chiefly reflects protein sources, consumption of small amounts would not show up well in the collagen $\delta^{13}C$ signal. The evidence suggests that, upon its introduction into eastern North America, it was probably eaten only in small quantities, perhaps in ceremonial contexts, and only later adopted as a dietary staple (Smith, 2017; Milner et al., 2018).

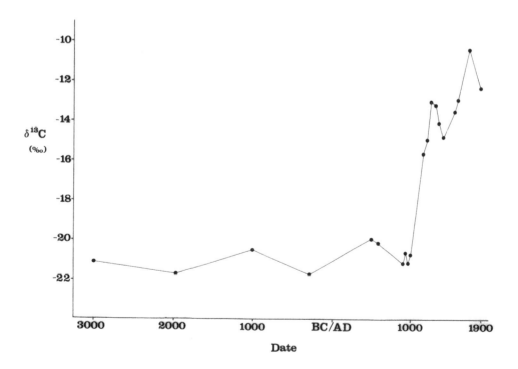

Figure 11.3 Carbon stable isotope ratios for some burials from Missouri and Arkansas, USA
Source: From data in Lynott et al. (1986).

Europe lacks the widespread introduction of a C4 cultigen to parallel the rise of maize in North America. Isotopic study of dietary change at the transition from Mesolithic hunter-gatherer-fisher cultures to the farming communities of the Neolithic focussed on assessing the relative importance of aquatic food resources. A region where this transition has been particularly well-studied is Denmark (Tauber, 1981, 1986; Richards et al., 2003; Fischer et al., 2007; Price et al., 2007). Results show a sharp difference in $\delta^{13}C$ between Mesolithic and Neolithic communities (Figure. 11.4).

The carbon stable isotope values for the Danish Early Mesolithic skeletons (about –17‰ to –22‰) indicate a mainly terrestrial diet. Sea levels in the Early Mesolithic were very much lower than they are today. Most of the sites studied were some distance from the ancient coastline so it is not surprising that those buried there seem to have consumed diets dominated by terrestrial rather than marine foods.

The Middle and Late Mesolithic bones generally came from coastal sites. Their $\delta^{13}C$ values lie in the range from about –11‰ to –17‰, suggesting that protein sources were predominantly made up of marine foods. The importance of seafoods is consistent with finds from coastal settlements of this period. Abundant marine fish remains have been found when the use of sieving techniques allowed the recovery of these small bones (Bødker Enghoff, 1993; Pickard & Bonsall, 2007). Bone fish hooks and, where soil conditions permit their preservation, remains of wooden fish traps and fish spears (Pickard & Bonsall, 2007) have also been found.

With the adoption of agriculture in the transition to the Neolithic, a marked dietary change occurred: $\delta^{13}C$ values from Neolithic and later sites cluster around –20‰ to –21‰ (Figure. 11.4), characteristic of a terrestrial C3 diet. This is true even of Neolithic sites

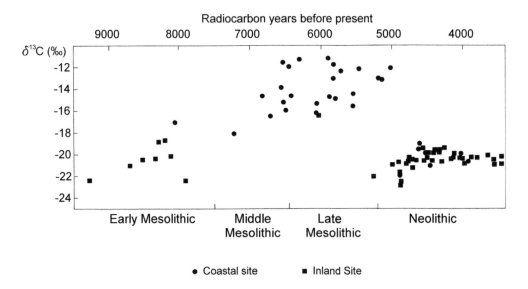

Figure 11.4 Carbon stable isotope results from some human skeletons from Mesolithic and Neolithic Denmark

Source: Data from Fischer et al., 2007: Figure 6.

situated on the coast. The nitrogen stable isotope values were likewise consistent with a change from a primarily marine to a terrestrial diet at this time – Late Mesolithic values range from about 10‰ to 17‰ whereas Neolithic values cluster around 9‰ to 10‰ (Fischer et al., 2007).

Artefactual evidence indicates that the Danish Mesolithic cultures were in contact with farming peoples to the south for more than six hundred years before the first evidence for agriculture in Denmark. Despite this, there is no evidence from the stable isotope data of a gradual adoption of food cultivation. Within the resolution of archaeological dating, the dietary transition seems to have been rapid, and the lack of intermediate delta values between the Mesolithic and Neolithic isotopic groupings (Figure. 11.4) also supports the notion of an abrupt change. It would seem that a fishery resource which had been successfully exploited for centuries was quickly abandoned. An abrupt change in material culture has also been observed at these sites – Andersen (1989, 1991) states that the shift in technological materials from those associated with Mesolithic life-ways to those of Neolithic type occurred within a hundred years or less. It would seem then, that with the dawning of the Neolithic Age in Denmark, the old ways were quickly extinguished by the new.

A similarly sharp dietary transition at the dawn of the Neolithic has also been observed in Britain and at other locations of the Atlantic façade of Europe (Schulting, 2018), but this is not the case everywhere. For example, on the Baltic Island of Öland, burials from two closely adjacent middle Neolithic sites had very different carbon and nitrogen stable isotopic data. One community was heavily reliant on marine resources; the other had a mainly terrestrial diet and had material culture and burial practices that resembled Neolithic groups to the south (Eriksson et al., 2008). These groups coexisted on Öland for more than 1000 years, maintaining their cultural and dietary differences. It is only from the late Neolithic that Öland populations consistently show fully terrestrial stable isotopic values. This suggests that the shift to subsistence farming here was not completed until about 2000 years after the Mesolithic-Neolithic transition.

Stable isotopic data have also been used to study the importance of freshwater fisheries. Although $\delta^{13}C$ in lakes on calcareous geologies may be somewhat elevated (Guiry, 2019), in general, values in freshwater ecosystems overlap with those in terrestrial environments (Dufour et al., 1999). Nitrogen cycles in freshwater ecosystems tend to be rather complex with more trophic levels than terrestrial food webs. Given the trophic level effect in $\delta^{15}N$ referred to earlier, this means that $\delta^{15}N$ from freshwater fish tends to be rather variable but on the whole greater than from terrestrial foods, but without the accompanying elevated $\delta^{13}C$ that characterises marine resources (Müldner & Richards, 2005, 2007; Fleming et al., in prep: Suppl. table 2).

It will be recalled from Chapter 7, that Mesolithic sites in the Iron Gates region of the Danube yield rich freshwater fish bone assemblages, and human remains frequently show auditory tori, suggesting that acquisition of these resources often necessitated human immersion in the river, perhaps to set fish traps. These auditory tori become less common in Neolithic remains. This evidence suggests a heavy reliance on riverine resources in the Mesolithic, which became less in the Neolithic. If this is correct, then we might expect high $\delta^{15}N$ in Mesolithic burials and the decline in the Neolithic, but with a non-marine $\delta^{13}C$ signal for both periods.

Isotopic data from about 200 individuals, dating from the Mesolithic and Neolithic of the Iron Gates region, were collated by Rick Schulting and Dušan Borić (Schulting & Borić, 2017). The plot (Figure. 11.5) shows that for both periods, $\delta^{13}C$ values centre around -20‰ to -19‰, indicating no great input from marine resources. $\delta^{15}N$ for the Mesolithic skeletons cluster around 14‰ to 15‰, rather higher than would be expected from a terrestrial diet (Figure. 11.2). The Neolithic burials are mostly about 2-5‰ lower than this. Burials dating to the Mesolithic-Neolithic transition period are rather variable in their $\delta^{15}N$, with some grouping with the Mesolithic values, others with the Neolithic.

Care is needed when interpreting trends in $\delta^{15}N$ in human remains. However, in this case, the stable isotopic results are consistent with the other skeletal and faunal evidence in suggesting that aquatic resources were key to Mesolithic subsistence but probably declined during the Neolithic. Although lesser consumption of aquatic resources in the Neolithic is likely a prime factor in the decline in $\delta^{15}N$, other variables may also be involved. For example, the trophic level effect means that terrestrial plant foods have low $\delta^{15}N$ compared to most other resources, and these are likely to have been more important to Neolithic farmers than they were to their Mesolithic forebears.

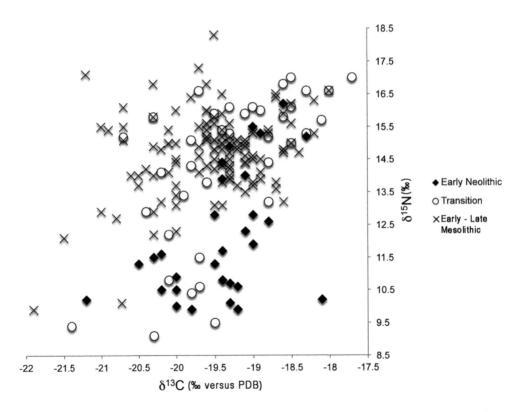

Figure 11.5 Carbon and nitrogen stable isotope data from Mesolithic and Neolithic burials from the Iron Gates region of the Danube

Source adapted from Schulting & Borić (2017: Figure. 7.3).

Working on a broader canvas, Penny Bickle (Bickle, 2018) analysed 66 Mesolithic and 274 Neolithic skeletons from a wide area of inland central Europe. Mean δ^{13}C was about −20‰ in both periods, suggesting no significant marine input. Mean δ^{15}N was 10.1‰ in Mesolithic and 9.4‰ in Neolithic remains. For the Mesolithic in particular, the δ^{15}N figures are lower than for the Iron Gates sites (Figure. 11.5). This probably reflects an unusually large input into Iron Gates region diets from freshwater resources as people took advantage of the rich fisheries offered by the Danube in that region.

The fall in δ^{15}N between Mesolithic and Neolithic in Bickle's (2018) data would seem consistent with a general reduction in importance of freshwater resources over time. In an attempt to reconstruct more closely what her own results might mean in terms of the average composition of early European diets, Bickle used a mathematical mixing model called FRUITS (Fernandes et al., 2014; https://sourceforge.net/projects/fruits/). This works by taking into account both the isotope results for the human remains, and other parameters that include diet to collagen offsets, and the isotope values of potential food sources. Bickle estimated these latter using isotopic analysis of prehistoric faunal remains. Application of this model suggested that mean aquatic food content of Mesolithic diets in central Europe may have been about 19% of total caloric intake; for Neolithic diets it may have been about 6%. Mean inputs from plant foods were estimated as 55% and 84% respectively. As is often the case with mathematical dietary modelling based on isotopic results (e.g. Killian Galván, 2018; Fleming et al., in prep), the uncertainty on these values was very high, with large overlaps between the estimates for the different periods – for example the 95% confidence intervals (between which the true value has a 95% chance of lying) for aquatic contributions to Mesolithic and Neolithic diets were 1%–51% and 0.1%–24% respectively. Despite this uncertainty, her results, together with the other studies discussed above, suggest (as one might perhaps expect), that a decline in aquatic resources as a whole (mainly marine on the coast, freshwater inland), together with a rise in terrestrial plant foods, was a consistent pattern at the Mesolithic–Neolithic transition in Europe.

Breastfeeding in past populations

In most cultures, infants are breastfed from birth, but as time goes on other foods are introduced and breastfeeding declines and eventually ceases, a process known as weaning (Humphrey, 2014). The subject of breastfeeding, and its duration in past societies, has generated much interest among archaeologists and historians. Breastfeeding practices have important demographic consequences. Lactation suppresses ovulation, meaning that duration of breastfeeding is a major determinant of the time interval between successive births (and hence of family size) in societies lacking reliable artificial contraceptives (Vitzthum, 1994; Tsutaya & Yoneda, 2015). Lengthening the birth interval also has implications for women's health as it helps avoid the draining of maternal resources associated with short-spaced, repeated pregnancies. Breastfeeding promotes infant health, both because of the milk's immunological content and because it enables early avoidance of potentially contaminated food and drink (Katzenberg et al., 1996; Mays, 2010c).

A foetus developing in the womb is supplied with nutrients from the mother via the placenta. Therefore, the stable isotope ratios in the foetus resemble those in the mother.

When an infant is breastfeeding, he is consuming the product of his mother's tissues so is one trophic level higher. Given that $\delta^{15}N$ increases with trophic level we would expect the $\delta^{15}N$ of a suckling infant to be higher than that of its mother, but as the child is weaned and breastfeeding ceases, $\delta^{15}N$ should decline again. By plotting $\delta^{15}N$ against age in infants and children we can, therefore, explore duration of breastfeeding in past societies. Some colleagues and I used this approach to study breastfeeding at Mediaeval Wharram Percy (Richards et al., 2002; Mays et al., 2002a).

We conducted nitrogen stable isotope analyses on collagen from rib bone samples from 70 children ranging in age from pre-term foetuses to about 17 years. We also measured $\delta^{15}N$ in 29 adult skeletons. The results are shown in Figure. 11.6.

As expected on theoretical grounds, the $\delta^{15}N$ of foetal skeletons (aged 28–39 weeks *in utero*) resemble adult values. From birth onwards there is a sharp rise in $\delta^{15}N$, presumably reflecting the incorporation of ^{15}N from breastmilk into the bone collagen. The highest infant $\delta^{15}N$ are about 3–4‰ greater than foetal or adult values. This figure resembles that reported in studies of other populations (Reynard & Tuross, 2015), and is toward the low end of the generally accepted trophic level effect, perhaps because milk protein is a little lower in N-15 than other bodily proteins (Tsutaya & Yoneda, 2015). Between one and two years there is a rapid decline in $\delta^{15}N$ so that, by the latter age, values once more lie within the adult range.

The data suggest cessation of breastfeeding between about one and two years of age. It is difficult to be more precise about this because, although the bones of the very young turnover faster than those of adults, rates in infants are not known precisely. However, looking at Figure 11.6, even the youngest post-natal individuals show $\delta^{15}N$ values outside

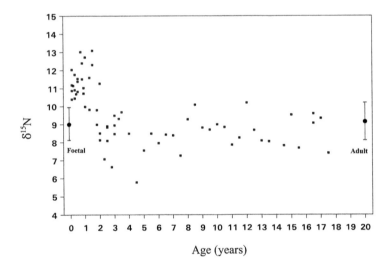

Figure 11.6 Rib bone nitrogen stable isotope data plotted against dental age for infants and children from Mediaeval Wharram Percy, England. Mean values for pre-term foetal remains (aged 28–39 weeks gestation) and for adults are superimposed

Source: Mays et al, 2002a: Figure. 1.

the range of those for foetal material, suggesting that the response of infant bone collagen to a change in isotopic intake is rapid. The strong age-related pattern between one and two years, with little spread of data points, indicates restricted inter-individual variation in timing of weaning. Perhaps breastfeeding was constrained by community-wide cultural factors rather than decisions being made freely according to individual circumstances. The pattern of results is consistent, despite the fact that the analysed burials cover a period of at least 600 years. This suggests that culturally accepted patterns of weaning may have remained essentially unchanged for a prolonged period in this rural community.

For studies like Wharram Percy, which use bone collagen, it could be suggested that a mortality bias is having an effect. This is because they use isotopic data from infants who failed to survive; perhaps weaning practice for them was not typical of that for infants who did survive the weaning period. A way of circumventing this is to study collagen from dentine of older individuals. Because dentine is not remodelled like bone, its collagen preserves the isotopic signal from when it was formed. By analysing dentine from different teeth, and from different parts of teeth, that were forming at different times in infancy and childhood, we can reconstruct weaning patterns for adults and older children who did survive the weaning period.

The most usual approach when analysing dentine for this purpose is to study the first permanent molar. Dentine formation in this tooth begins at around birth and is complete at about 10 years of age (Figure 4.10). Because only very small samples are needed nowadays for stable isotope determinations, multiple subsamples can be taken from the tooth. The most usual method is to take transverse sections about 1mm wide, which, for a first molar, means it normally yields about 10-15 subsamples. Each corresponds to about 9 months of development (Beaumont & Montgomery, 2016; Scharlotta et al., 2018), but only the first few will normally overlap with the breastfeeding period. Because growth layers in dentine are rather oblique in orientation, adjacent transverse sections will overlap somewhat in their chronology, reducing the precision with which the timing of weaning or other dietary changes can be inferred. This effect can be mitigated by microscope-guided sampling (Czermak et al., 2018), but this is a more time-consuming procedure. Although taking multiple subsamples from a tooth means that normally fewer individuals in total are studied, an increasing number of isotopic weaning studies are being done in this way (papers in Chinique de Armas & Roksandic, 2018).

When we analysed dentine in older individuals from Wharram Percy (Fuller et al., 2003), we found no evidence that timing of weaning was very different in those who survived this period. However, studies of other populations have found evidence for a mortality bias. Analysis of ribs from 94 6th–8th century AD children from Kulubnarti, Sudan, suggested that breastfeeding was prolonged, with weaning not generally completed until about 5 years of age (Turner et al., 2007; Sandberg et al., 2014). However, analysis of serial dentine samples from 5 adults suggested cessation of breastfeeding up to three years earlier than this (Sandberg et al., 2014). Although numbers are small, this may be consistent with a mortality bias, with prolonged breastfeeding being more common in children that failed to survive. Sandberg et al. (2014) note that in Africa, extended breastfeeding is often a response to food shortage. Perhaps the rib data include some individuals for which extended breastfeeding represented an unavailing attempt to keep them alive during periods of famine.

Sampling of later forming dentine enables diet later on in childhood to be studied in those who survived to become adults. In a Mediaeval group from Italy, bone $\delta^{15}N$ in children who died aged mainly in the range 4-8 years was lower than it was in second molar crown dentine that forms over a similar time-scale among those that survived into adulthood (Reitsema et al., 2016). It was suggested that children who died relied more heavily on plant rather than animal protein sources, and that such a diet was associated with an elevated risk of early mortality. Fernández-Crespo et al. (2018) report similar findings from a Late Neolithic site in Spain. Such results provide intriguing evidence of the interaction between diet and mortality, but care may needed in interpreting results. Some have argued (Beaumont et al., 2018) that physiological differences in the ways in which nitrogen is incorporated into collagen in dentine and bone means that direct comparisons between the two tissues should be made with caution.

The study of ancient migrations using strontium and oxygen isotopes

Isotopic studies of movement of people have concentrated on oxygen and strontium in hydroxyapatite, which forms the mineral component of bones and teeth. As we saw in Chapter 1, hydroxyapatite is a form of calcium phosphate Strontium has similar chemical properties to calcium, and is incorporated in trace amounts into hydroxyapatite in living organisms. It is these trace amounts of strontium that are analysed in strontium isotopic studies. Phosphate ions contain oxygen atoms, as do carbonate ions which are present in small amounts in biological hydroxyapatite. Oxygen isotope analyses of archaeological human remains more usually target carbonate because analytical procedures are more straightforward and the measurements more precise (Pederzani & Britton, 2019).

For analysis, the strontium and carbonate and/or phosphate components are isolated from the bone or tooth sample in the laboratory, and the isotopic ratios measured using a mass spectrometer.

Strontium isotopes in the environment

Strontium (chemical symbol Sr) naturally occurs in four isotopes of mass 84, 86, 87 and 88, with relative abundancies of 0.6%, 9.9%, 7.0% and 82.6% respectively. Three of these isotopes are stable, but ^{87}Sr is radiogenic in that it is formed from radioactive decay of the rubidium-87. The radioactive decay of rubidium-87 is very slow, occurring over geological time-scales (the half-life is 49 thousand million years), but it is enough to mean that the proportion of ^{87}Sr varies appreciably between different types of rocks, older rocks with high initial ^{87}Rb having accumulated more ^{87}Sr than younger rocks or those with low initial ^{87}Rb levels.

The amount of ^{87}Sr in geological or biological samples is generally expressed as a simple ratio of $^{87}Sr/^{86}Sr$. $^{87}Sr/^{86}Sr$ varies from about 0.703 in volcanic rocks of recent age to about 0.740 in some continental granites (Åberg, 1995). The strontium isotope ratio of seawater has varied between about 0.707 to 0.709 over geological time (McArthur et al., 2001), so marine sedimentary rocks, such as limestones, have values in this range. The variation in strontium isotope ratios between different rocks may seem small, but $^{87}Sr/^{86}Sr$ can be measured very precisely (instrument error is normally 0.00001 or better) and results are routinely reported to five decimal places, so the variation is in fact quite large compared to measurement error (Bentley, 2006).

Although in some areas, airborne dust or sea-spray contributes significantly to strontium in the biosphere, mineral weathering normally predominates so that the underlying geology is the overwhelming determinant of biosphere strontium isotope ratios (Evans et al., 2010). The strontium isotope ratio in soil relates to that in the underlying geology, and a proportion of the soil strontium is labile, that is it is available for uptake by plants. Strontium isotope ratios are not altered by metabolic processes in living organisms, so they remain unchanged in food-webs (Blum et al., 2000). This means that the $^{87}Sr/^{86}Sr$ in bones and teeth reflect the geological area from which the individual obtained his or her food and drink, and by implication lived. Although it is $^{87}Sr/^{86}Sr$ in food and water that generally determines strontium isotope ratios in human bones and teeth, when people ingest substantial amounts of minerals with their food, these can have a significant effect. For example, in the Americas, traditional processing of maize involved soaking it in an alkaline solution, and in some regions (e.g. Mesoamerica) this was made using limestone (Katz et al., 1974). Lime solution (calcium hydroxide) would be rich in strontium and would therefore dominate the $^{87}Sr/^{86}Sr$ signal in human tissues, obscuring the signal from foods or drink from other types of geology (Wright, 2005). In addition, common salt, frequently used as a preservative, is also rich in strontium and could influence human $^{87}Sr/^{86}Sr$ values appreciably, even if consumed in fairly small amounts (Wright, 2005).

Oxygen isotopes in the environment

Oxygen naturally occurs in three stable isotopes, of mass 16, 17 and 18 which have relative abundances of 99.8%, 0.04% and 0.2% respectively. Archaeological oxygen isotope work analyses the ratio of oxygen-18 to oxygen-16. Variation in this ratio in the environment is very small, so oxygen isotope ratios are, like those of carbon and nitrogen, expressed in delta units. The formula for calculating $\delta^{18}O$ is analogous to that for carbon and nitrogen delta values. The standard normally used is standard mean ocean water (SMOW), although for carbonate $\delta^{18}O$ the PDB standard (utilised in carbon stable isotope delta values) is also sometimes used (Coplen, 1996). Skeletal tissues generally have less oxygen-18 than the PDB standard so $\delta^{18}O$ measured against this standard is usually a negative number. Skeletal tissues are enriched in oxygen-18 compared with SMOW, giving $\delta^{18}O$ values greater than zero when measured against the SMOW standard.

Oxygen isotope ratios in air are fairly constant, so in animals it is ingested values that are the main source of within-species variability in $\delta^{18}O$. Unlike the situation for strontium, oxygen isotope ratios are altered by metabolic processes. This means that different foods differ in their $\delta^{18}O$ values. However, this factor has little effect on human tissue $\delta^{18}O$ as, in man, tissue $\delta^{18}O$ is dominated by that in drinking water (Levinson et al., 1987; Daux et al., 2008). The exception to this is suckling infants. During exclusive breastfeeding, an infant receives all his water from his mother's milk, which is enriched in oxygen-18 compared with drinking water. Therefore $\delta^{18}O$ values in tissue forming in infancy may be slightly elevated (Britton et al., 2015). Another complication when interpreting human $\delta^{18}O$ data is that the $\delta^{18}O$ value of water is increased significantly by heating, for example to make beverages or during cooking (Brettell et al., 2012).

Other than on the coast, surface waters and groundwaters are derived exclusively from precipitation (Darling et al., 2003). It has long been known that oxygen isotope ratios in precipitation vary with climate (Dansgaard, 1964) and hence are different in different geographical areas. Lower temperatures mean lower $\delta^{18}O$. For example, in Canada mean annual $\delta^{18}O$ in precipitation in the far north may be as low as -22‰, but this value rises as one moves south so that it is about -12‰ at the border with the USA (Gat, 2010: Figure. 6.2). The relationship with temperature means that seasonal differences in $\delta^{18}O$ of precipitation can be quite marked. For example, in the Swiss Alps, $\delta^{18}O$ is 5–10‰ more negative in winter than in summer (Bentley & Knipper, 2005). This tends to even out in groundwaters and large surface bodies of water. In any event, seasonal variation would not normally be seen in human skeletal tissues as bulk analysis of hydroxyapatite in teeth or bone produces a $\delta^{18}O$ averaged over the years of formation of the tissue. However, microsampling along the teeth of animals whose dentition grows quickly, and which drink from small bodies of surface water, has enabled seasonal variations in temperature in the past to be studied (e.g. Bernard et al., 2009). Precipitation falling at high altitudes generally has lower $\delta^{18}O$. For example, mean annual $\delta^{18}O$ at Bern in Switzerland (elevation approximately 500m) is about -9.7‰, but at Grimsel in the Alps (elevation approximately 2000m) the figure is about -13.3‰ (Bentley & Knipper, 2005). Mean annual $\delta^{18}O$ in precipitation generally decreases as one moves further inland in the direction of the prevailing winds because clouds moving inland progressively lose ^{18}O as the heavier isotope is preferentially rained out (Pederzani & Britton, 2019). For example in Britain, where the prevailing winds are south-westerly, $\delta^{18}O$ is about -5‰ in the southwest and decreases northwards and eastwards to reach about -8‰ in eastern Scotland (Darling et al., 2003).

Strontium and oxygen isotopes in archaeological human remains

As we saw in Chapter 2, bone and dentine are rather porous, so their mineral phases readily undergo chemical exchange with soil water. This means that the isotopic ratios measured in archaeological bone or dentine apatite tend to resemble those of the soils in which they were buried rather than faithfully reflecting those in life. Dental enamel is much less porous, and it is almost entirely inorganic. This means that, unlike bone or dentine, it is not penetrated by soil water and is not subject to attack by soil-dwelling micro-organisms. Enamel is therefore resistant to diagenesis over time-scales of millennia (Montgomery, 2010). Experimental evidence (e.g. Ayliffe et al., 1994; Lee-Thorp & Sponheimer, 2003; Trickett et al., 2003) indicates that the hydroxyapatite of dental enamel generally preserves lifetime isotopic ratios for many thousands of years, even in burial conditions where hydroxyapatite in bone and dentine does not. Because of its resistance to post-depositional change, most workers study strontium and oxygen isotope ratios in dental enamel alone, eschewing the use of bone or dentine.

Because it does not remodel, the isotopic composition of enamel preserves that obtaining during that part of infancy or childhood when the enamel was forming. To investigate whether an individual migrated since childhood, the oxygen or strontium isotope ratios in dental enamel are compared with those in the locality in which the individual was buried (and hence is assumed to have lived immediately before he or she died).

Local $^{87}Sr/^{86}Sr$ baselines can be obtained from geological maps. For some work this may be adequate, but they provide only a general picture of biologically available values because $^{87}Sr/^{86}Sr$ in bedrock is only an approximate guide to that in local water sources (Sillen et al., 1998). For example, rivers may flow through areas of greatly differing geology. Different rocks differ in their strontium contents and in their resistance to weathering, so they differ in their relative contributions to $^{87}Sr/^{86}Sr$ ratios in local waters. Strontium isotope ratios in soils in a particular local area may be highly variable if the geology is diverse. Modern plant and water values may be used to map regional or local variation in bioavailable strontium isotopic ratios (e.g. Evans et al., 2010). Alternatively, or in addition, $^{87}Sr/^{86}Sr$ ratios in faunal remains from archaeological sites from the vicinity of the burials under study may be used (e.g. Bentley et al., 2004).

For oxygen isotope ratios, local baseline values can be established from maps showing modern $\delta^{18}O$ values in local surface waters. These maps are available for most areas of the world (Bowen, 2010). Because oxygen isotope ratios are altered by metabolic reactions in biological systems, ingested $\delta^{18}O$ do not match $\delta^{18}O$ of skeletal tissues, but formulae exist (Longinelli, 1984; Daux et al., 2008) which allow drinking water $\delta^{18}O$ to be estimated from human hydroxyapatite values. Because $\delta^{18}O$ varies with climate, substantial differences are observed in samples from époques, such as ice ages, where the climate was very different from today, but they do not seem to have varied very much during post-glacial times (McDermott, 2004). Therefore, for most archaeological studies, it is probably reasonable to use modern surface water $\delta^{18}O$ to obtain a local baseline.

Archaeological studies of movements of people using stable isotopes

Sometimes useful information can be obtained from analysis of either oxygen or strontium isotopes alone. However, it is more usual combine the two. This will often help to narrow down the number of possible locations where a person may have spent their childhood. In some circumstances, analysis of dietary information from carbon and nitrogen isotope ratios in collagen from dentine may be used, as well as enamel strontium and oxygen isotopes, to help study migration of people.

Sugar plantation slaves in Barbados

Between the 16th and the 19th century AD, Africans were forcibly shipped by western European powers to serve as slave labour in their colonies in the West Indies. Schroeder et al. (2009) studied strontium, oxygen, carbon and nitrogen stable isotopes in skeletal remains from 25 individuals from the slave burial ground at the 17th-19th century AD Newton Sugar Plantation on the West Indian island of Barbados, then a British colony. The aim was to investigate whether individuals were born on Barbados or were first generation migrants from Africa.

In order to investigate childhood diets, $\delta^{13}C$ and $\delta^{15}N$ were studied in collagen from dentine. The $\delta^{13}C$ and $\delta^{15}N$ for most samples fell in the range -12.4‰ to -8.8‰ and 13.1‰ to 17.4‰ respectively (Figure. 11.7). This indicates a diet rich in C4 foods and marine resources. This accords with what is known of slave diet in Barbados. Sorghum, a C4 plant brought from Africa to the New World, was a dietary staple for plantation slaves, as was salted fish (Handler & Lange, 1978: 86-87). The data would therefore suggest that a majority spent

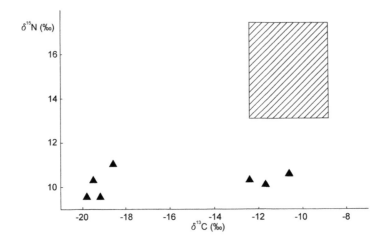

Figure 11.7 Carbon and nitrogen stable isotope ratios in dentine from permanent first molars from skeletons from the slave burial ground at Newton Sugar Plantation, Barbados. The hatched box indicates the range of the bulk of the data. The triangles are the seven outliers tentatively identified as migrants (see text)
Source: Drawn from data presented by Schroeder et al., 2009.

their childhoods on Barbados. Documentary sources are consistent with this, indicating that first generation migrants generally constituted only a small proportion of the slave population (Handler & Lange, 1978: 29).

Results for seven individuals are scattered outside the range of the bulk of the data, indicating childhood diets that differed from that of the rest of the group and also from one another (Figure 11.7). These seven individuals also showed marked differences in δ^{13}C and δ^{15}N between dentine and bone samples, the bone values more closely approximating to those of the rest of the burials. This would seem to suggest that these seven may have been migrants to Barbados from elsewhere, presumably Africa. Strontium and oxygen isotope analyses allowed this possibility to be further evaluated.

West Africa is a complex patchwork of different rocks with many having high ^{87}Sr/^{86}Sr values. By contrast the geology of Barbados is uniformly composed of limestone, with ^{87}Sr/^{86}Sr of about 0.7092. Those who spent their childhoods on the island would be expected to show similar values in their dental enamel. It will be recalled from the discussion above that salt consumption has the potential to shift strontium isotope values. However, the salted fish known to have been part of slave diets would not be expected to complicate the picture in this case as, like local Barbadian terrestrial food and water resources, it also shows a ^{87}Sr/^{86}Sr of about 0.709. Other than the seven individuals already tentatively identified as migrants, the Newton Plantation dental enamel data clustered closely around the ^{87}Sr/^{86}Sr expected for those who spent their childhoods on the island (Figure. 11.8).

Most of the putative Barbadian-born individuals showed dental enamel carbonate δ^{18}O (standardised to PDB) in the range -4.6‰ to -3.9‰, which corresponds to drinking

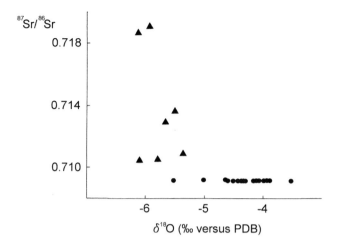

Figure 11.8 Strontium and carbonate oxygen stable isotope ratios in enamel from permanent first molars from skeletons from the slave burial ground at Newton Sugar
Plantation, Barbados. The triangles indicate the same individuals depicted with
triangles in Figure 11.7

Source: Redrawn from Schroeder et al., 2009: Figure 5.

water values of between about -4.7‰ and -3.2‰, consistent with the -5.0‰ to -2.5‰
range found in water sources on the island. Three burials lie outside this range of
$\delta^{18}O$ but nevertheless show $^{87}Sr/^{86}Sr$ consistent with the island geology (Figure. 11.8). It
is possible that these are additional migrants but from areas with similar geology to Barbados (there are some areas in West Africa underlain by sedimentary geology of marine
origin which would be expected to yield similar $^{87}Sr/^{86}Sr$ to Barbados).

The disparate enamel $^{87}Sr/^{86}Sr$ and $\delta^{18}O$ values of the seven probable migrant individuals
(Figure. 11.8) are consistent with the wide spread of their dentine $\delta^{13}C$ and $\delta^{15}N$ in suggesting
diverse origins for this group. For example, $\delta^{13}C$ suggested some came from regions where
C3 crops were the dietary staple, some from C4 regions (Figure. 11.7). West Africa has both
C3 and C4 crop zones, depending upon geographical location. The $\delta^{18}O$ values of these likely
migrants also helped shed light on their origin. These suggested they consumed drinking
water in the range -6.5‰ to -8.1‰. This is inconsistent with coastal West African values,
which are about -2.0‰ to -4.0‰, but is consistent with inland African locations. This
observation is congruent with documentary sources which show that slaves were sometimes
marched hundreds of miles from the interior to embarkation points on the coast.

Some other archaeological studies sample dental tissues forming at different times in
an individual's life (either by sampling different teeth or serial sampling a given tooth) to
build up data on the timing of movement and on patterns of mobility.

Immigration to Imperial Rome

A team led by Tracey Prowse, of McMaster University, Canada, studied oxygen stable isotope ratios in dental enamel carbonate from 61 burials from Portus Romae (Prowse et al.,

2007). Portus Romae lies 23km SW of Rome. In Classical Roman times, it was the main port serving Rome, and the burials date from the 1st–3rd century AD, when the Roman Empire was at its height. As a major port receiving goods from a far-flung empire, it was thought that the origins of Portus Romae's population would likely be diverse. To test this hypothesis, oxygen isotope ratios were measured in the permanent first and third molars. The enamel crowns of these teeth form at about birth–3 years and 9–13 years respectively (Figure. 4.10). Both teeth were analysed to try and shed light on how old people were when they migrated.

Analysis of dental enamel from teeth from modern inhabitants of Rome (Prowse et al., 2007) established that local dental enamel carbonate $\delta^{18}O$ values are about −4‰ to −6‰ (standardised against PDB). This was thought to be in accord with values expected from local precipitation which has a $\delta^{18}O$ of about −5‰ to −6‰ (Figure. 11.9).

The plot of $\delta^{18}O$ in the M1 and M3 from the Portus Romae burials is shown in Figure. 11.10. In about two-thirds of individuals analysed, the M1 produced results in the −4‰ to −6‰

Figure 11.9 Annual mean oxygen stable isotope ratios for precipitation in Italy. The filled circle shows the location of Portus Romae

Source: After Prowse et al., 2007: Figure 2.

range indicated as local by the study on modern teeth. It seems likely that the bulk of these individuals were born locally, although some may have come from areas with similar $\delta^{18}O$ precipitation values, such as elsewhere on the west coast of Italy (Figure. 11.9). Of those with M1 values outside the -4‰ to -6‰ range, most had M3 $\delta^{18}O$ that *were* between -4‰ and -6‰. This combination suggests individuals who migrated to Portus Romae during childhood (i.e. between the time when the first molar enamel was mainly or fully formed but when the third molar enamel had not yet formed). The remainder, whose M3s produced $\delta^{18}O$ outside the local range, likely came to Portus Romae in adolescent or adult life.

The overall range of $\delta^{18}O$ was fairly small, arguing against significant migration from regions with very different climates. Most of the non-local $\delta^{18}O$ signatures were more negative than local precipitation by up to about 2‰. Such values could be consistent with migrants from more northern parts of the Empire, such as Britain, but one does not need to invoke such long-distance migrations to explain them. Areas only a short distance inland from Portus Romae, towards the Apennines, the chain of mountains that runs down the spine of peninsular Italy, have precipitation $\delta^{18}O$ a few per mil lower than coastal values (Figure. 11.9). Most migrants into Portus Romae may therefore have come from less than 100km away. The only individual with a $\delta^{18}O$ signature that provides firm evidence of a migrant from further afield is the lone data point on the far right of Figure 11.10, with a M1 $\delta^{18}O$ of -1.3‰. This elevated value suggests an individual from a warmer climate than the Italian peninsula, perhaps north Africa.

Summing up their findings, Prowse et al. (2007) state that their results show that many migrants came to Portus Romae in childhood. This demonstrates that migration was not limited to young unmarried adults, as might have been expected, but that

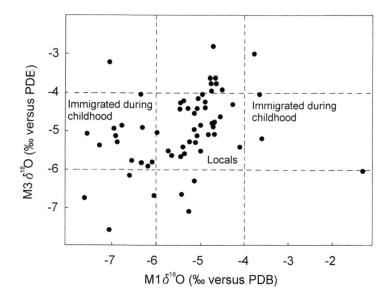

Figure 11.10 Oxygen stable isotope ratios in enamel carbonate from human permanent first and third molars from Portus Romae

Source: after Prowse et al., 2007: Figure 5.

migration of family units also probably occurred. Despite the status of Portus Romae as the main port serving Rome, and hence receiving ships from all over the Roman Empire, the isotopic evidence suggested most of the sampled population were locals, and that those who were not may have come from less than 100km away.

Migration before the time of Stonehenge

Serial subsampling of enamel in $^{87}Sr/^{86}Sr$ and $\delta^{18}O$ studies potentially allows more detailed reconstruction of migration timelines for individual skeletons. This can be undertaken using micro-milling (Dolphin et al., 2016), whereby small samples are cut out at points in the enamel that formed at different ages. For strontium, an alternative is laser ablation, in which a laser is used to remove multiple microsamples (Dolphin et al., 2016; Lugli, 2019).

$\delta^{18}O$ analyses of multiple teeth, coupled with a microsampling approach for strontium, was used with some burials excavated from near the famous Stonehenge prehistoric stone circle in England (Mays et al., 2018a). One of these dated to about 3245–3110BC, the Middle Neolithic, the time immediately before the monument was built. Previous isotopic analysis of other prehistoric burials (Parker Pearson et al., 2016) had established that people were drawn to this area from far afield once construction of the stone monument had started. This individual provided the opportunity to assess whether this was already the case before building had begun. The burial in question was an adult male. Alistair Pike and Beth Linscott, of the University of Southampton, measured $\delta^{18}O$ and $^{87}Sr/^{86}Sr$ in the enamel crowns of the M1, M2 and M3. Taken together, the enamel formation of these teeth covers the period from birth to about 13 years of age (Figure 4.10). $\delta^{18}O$ was analysed in one bulk sample from each tooth; multiple $^{87}Sr/^{86}Sr$ analysis were performed along the tooth section using laser ablation mass spectrometry. The results are summarised in Figure 11.11.

Multiple sampling of a single tooth from the earliest forming enamel to the cervix by laser ablation allows a time-profile of $^{87}Sr/^{86}Sr$ for each tooth crown to be constructed, as shown in Figure 11.11. At Stonehenge, the local geology is chalk. The likely local range for $^{87}Sr/^{86}Sr$ is indicated by the grey box on each profile in Figure 11.11. For the first molar, the $^{87}Sr/^{86}Sr$ profile as a whole is fairly consistent with chalk geology, but the drinking water $\delta^{18}O$ values (Figure 11.11), inferred from the enamel oxygen isotope ratio, are rather less negative than might be expected (water $\delta^{18}O$ is about –7‰ in the Stonehenge region – see Plate 8). One explanation for this might be that, because the formation time of the first molar crown (birth–3 years) partially overlaps the likely breastfeeding period, a breastmilk signal might have elevated the M1 $\delta^{18}O$ value. However, a large-scale study of ancient British teeth (Evans et al., 2012) showed that the first molar enrichment over M2 is generally about 0.2‰ or less. The difference in $\delta^{18}O$ measured in the M1 and M2 enamel in this burial is more than three times this (Mays et al., 2018a: Table 5). A breastfeeding influence is unlikely to be sufficient to account for the elevated M1 values. It is more likely that this person spent his early years somewhere to the west of Stonehenge, where water $\delta^{18}O$ values are higher (Plate 8). Places consistent with both the M1 $\delta^{18}O$ and $^{87}Sr/^{86}Sr$ include Ireland and south Wales. Turning to the M2, the $^{87}Sr/^{86}Sr$ and $\delta^{18}O$ and are both fairly consistent with residence on the local chalklands of southern England, although this does not rule out areas further afield. The $^{87}Sr/^{86}Sr$ profile for the M3 shows a movement off the chalk to an area of different geology (the British Isles are

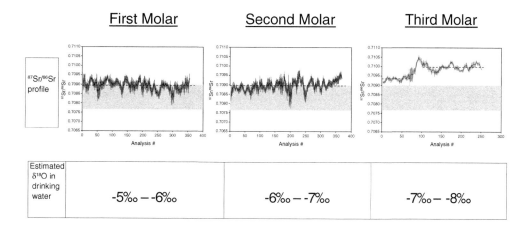

Figure 11.11 Strontium and oxygen isotopic data from the first, second and third molars from the Middle Neolithic burial excavated from near Stonehenge. The strontium data take the form of isotopic profiles along the growth axis of the enamel crown. The left-hand side of each profile corresponds to the start of enamel formation in that tooth, with successive analyses corresponding to older ages as the laser moves along the vertical axis tooth until the profile terminates at the base of the enamel crown. The grey area represents the estimated local strontium isotopic range; the broken line is the mean $^{87}Sr/^{86}Sr$ for the enamel. The $\delta^{18}O$ values are estimates of those in water consumed by this individual at the time that the three enamel crowns were forming during childhood. These were estimated from the measured bulk enamel carbonate $\delta^{18}O$ using the equations of Chenery et al. (2012) and Longinelli (1984)

Source: adapted from Mays et al. (2018a: Figure 12 & Table 5).

geologically complex so this may not have been a very long distance). This seems to have occurred sometime during the earlier part of the formation of the enamel crown, but tying down the timing more precisely is difficult. This is because the residence time of strontium within the body before it becomes incorporated into enamel is uncertain (Montgomery, 2010), and there is a maturation phase after enamel is first laid down during which more mineral (including strontium) is deposited into its structure (Humphrey et al., 2008). The $\delta^{18}O$ for the M3 is broadly compatible with waters local to Stonehenge, but is also consistent with quite large areas of Britain and Ireland (Plate 8).

In summary, the evidence suggests that this person spent their early years to the west of the Stonehenge area. He subsequently moved into an area with drinking water $\delta^{18}O$ resembling that in southern England, but after the age of about 9 years he moved to a different, non-chalk geology, but this latter need not necessarily have been over a long distance. He moved on to (or returned to) the Stonehenge area sometime between about 13 years of age (the completion of enamel formation in the M3) and the end of his life. The dentine $\delta^{13}C$ and $\delta^{15}N$ for this person were also analysed (Mays et al., 2018a). It is known that there are small variations in archaeological human collagen $\delta^{13}C$ and $\delta^{15}N$ between different regions, probably due to environmental factors (such as the canopy effect for $\delta^{13}C$); indeed, isotope ratios from Neolithic burials vary somewhat between different regions of the British Isles (Schulting & Borić, 2017). Intriguingly, the values for our Neolithic person were atypical for England but were consistent with Irish values. It is therefore tempting to suggest that this person lived for part or all of his childhood in Ireland. There is nothing in the isotopic data to contradict that scenario, but placing him specifically in Ireland is no more than a tentative suggestion. In this instance, as is usually the case, although one can suggest plausible scenarios, constructing any more definite narrative of a particular individual's specific locations at different times in his life is usually not possible from isotope data. Nevertheless, the evidence does suggest that he spent his early life some distance from the place where he was buried. If this individual is anything to go by, the landscape that was to become the setting for Stonehenge may have attracted people from far beyond the local area even before construction of the monument began. Analyses of further individuals of similar date would be needed in order to see whether this individual was unusual or whether this was a more general pattern.

Summary

Isotopes are atoms of a chemical element with different masses. Some are radioactive (e.g. carbon-14) and steadily decay, transmuting into other elements. Others are stable, in that they are non-radioactive and do not change in abundance over time. Carbon and nitrogen stable isotopes, generally extracted from human bone collagen, can be used to study ancient diets. Carbon stable isotope ratios differ in plants using different photosynthetic pathways. Most temperate zone vegetation uses the C3 pathway. Some plants from warmer regions, including important cultigens such as maize, use the C4 pathway. Both carbon and nitrogen stable isotope ratios differ in marine and terrestrial foods. Most of the carbon and all of the nitrogen in bone collagen comes from the protein part of the diet. Carbon and nitrogen stable isotope ratios in human bone collagen can therefore tell us about the relative importance, in the protein part of diets, of C3 versus C4 and marine versus terrestrial foods. For nitrogen isotopes, there is a small trophic level effect. Breastfeeding infants are exclusively consuming a product of the mother's body, so they are one trophic level higher. Nitrogen isotope ratios have been used to study duration of breastfeeding in past societies. Another way in which this trophic level effect can be used is to investigate the contribution of freshwater foods to diets – food chains in freshwater ecosystems are often rather longer than in terrestrial ones so that freshwater fish often tend to have elevated nitrogen isotope ratios. When conducting dietary studies, it is useful to analyse local archaeological faunal remains and, if possible, preserved plant remains as this helps the interpretation of the human isotopic data.

Strontium and oxygen isotope ratios in hydroxyapatite, the mineral portion of skeletal tissues, have been used to study geographical movements of people in the past. Strontium isotope ratios vary in different types of rock, but do not vary in different living organisms. There are therefore systematic differences in isotopic ratios in plants and animals in locales with different geology. Oxygen isotopes vary in rainwater in different regions according factors which include climate, altitude and distance from the coast.

Oxygen isotope ratios vary in different living organisms, and hence in different foods, but this does not matter very much for human studies as the isotopic composition of drinking water is the prime determinant of the oxygen isotopic composition of human tissues. Bone and dentine hydroxyapatite is very vulnerable to post-depositional changes in its composition, but dental enamel appears highly resistant to alteration. Therefore, most strontium and oxygen work on human remains uses dental enamel. Because, unlike bone, dental tissues are not continually remodelled, the isotopic composition of dental enamel reflects that in the locale in which the person lived as a child when the enamel was forming. A local baseline for isotopic values in the location in which the individual was buried (and by implication lived immediately prior to death) can be established for oxygen from rainfall maps or from analyses of local surface or well-waters; for strontium from geological maps or from modern plant or water values. If the isotopic composition of dental enamel differs from these baselines then the person likely spent at least part of their childhood elsewhere. Combining oxygen and strontium isotopic data will often help to narrow down the number of possible locations where a person may have spent their childhood. Nevertheless, it is not normally possible to identify unambiguously location(s) where an individual spent part of their childhood. Rather the data will allow some areas to be excluded as candidates on the basis that the person's dental enamel has an isotopic composition incompatible with the rainfall or geology of that locale.

Further reading

A review of carbon and nitrogen isotopic studies is given by Lee-Thorp, J.A. (2008). On Isotopes and Old Bones. *Archaeometry* 50: 925–950.

A special edition of the International Journal of Osteoarchaeology was devoted to isotopic studies of breastfeeding: Chinique de Armas, Y. & Roksandic, M., eds (2018). Breastfeeding and Weaning Practices in Ancient Populations: A Cross-Cultural View. *International Journal of Osteoarchaeology* 28, Issue 5.

For strontium isotope work see: Bentley, R.A. (2006). Strontium Isotopes from the Earth to the Archaeological Skeleton: A Review. *Journal of Archaeological Method and Theory* 13: 135–187; *and* Montgomery, J. (2010). Passports from the Past: Investigating Human Dispersals Using Strontium Isotope Analysis of Tooth Enamel. Annals of Human Biology 37: 325–346.

Pederzani, S. & Britton, K. (2019). Oxygen Isotopes in Bioarchaeology: Principles, Applications, Challenges and Opportunities. *Earth Science Reviews* 188: 77–107, *is a thorough review of oxygen isotope work.*

12 DNA analysis

DNA contains the genetic information which controls the structure, development and metabolism of the body. The complete set of DNA molecules in a living organism is termed the genome. DNA is present in all cells (with a few exceptions such as red blood cells), including the osteocytes, osteoblasts and osteoclasts of bone, and the cells in the dentine and cementum of the teeth. Dental enamel lacks a cell structure, so it contains no DNA.

In the late 1980s it emerged that human DNA survived in, and could be successfully extracted from, ancient skeletal remains (Hagelberg et al., 2014). The genetic information contained in human DNA recovered from ancient skeletons potentially enables us to study kinship between individuals and relationships between populations. It also provides another way of assessing the sex of the individual.

By the mid-1990s it was becoming clear that not only was it possible to extract human DNA from ancient skeletons, but also the DNA of disease-causing micro-organisms which were present in the individual at time of death (Stone & Ozga, 2019). This discovery opened up new avenues for the study of infectious disease in earlier populations, and for studying the way in which pathogens have changed over time.

The nature of DNA (Brown & Brown, 2011: 9-20; Brown, 2012)

DNA (deoxyribonucleic acid) is a linear polymer. As we learnt in Chapter 9, a polymer is a molecule composed of many repeated chemical sub-units. In DNA, these sub-units are called nucleotides, and they each consist of a sugar, a nitrogenous base and a phosphate group. There are four different nucleotides; they differ according to which nitrogenous base they contain, either adenine, guanine, thymine or cytosine. The different nucleotides are referred to as A, G, T and C, according to their nitrogenous base. The structure of DNA is twin-stranded, the strands being joined by hydrogen bonds between pairs of bases on opposite nucleotides, adenine always bonds with thymine, guanine with cytosine. The nucleotide sequence on the two strands is thus complementary, the sequence of one determining that of the other. The two strands are not laid flat, but are wound around one another in the famous double helix pattern (Figure 12.1).

Most of a cell's DNA is located in the chromosomes, thread-like bodies situated in the nucleus. Humans have 23 pairs of chromosomes: 22 pairs of autosomes and one pair of sex chromosomes. Female sex chromosomes consist of a pair of X chromosomes; a male has one X and one Y chromosome. The information within DNA is packaged into discrete units called

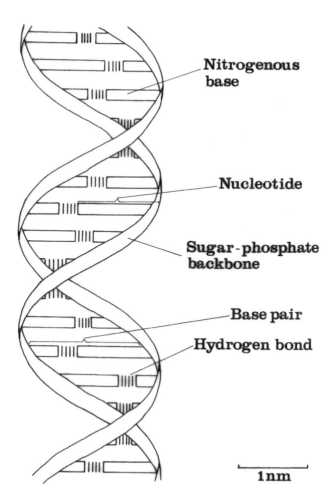

Nitrogenous
base

Nucleotide

Sugar-phosphate
backbone

Base pair

Hydrogen bond

1nm

Figure 12.1 The structure of DNA

genes. Genes are segments of DNA, on average about a thousand base-pairs long, separated from one another by lengths of intergenic DNA (Figure 12.2). Humans have over 20,000 genes. The genetic information in a gene is conveyed by the specific sequence of bases. Given the thousand or so base-pairs typically present in a single gene, the number of possible sequences is practically infinite; so, therefore, is the range of information which can be carried. Twenty-two autosomes, plus one sex chromosome, are inherited from each parent.

Some DNA is also present in mitochondria. Mitochondria lie outside the nucleus and are the cell's energy-generation units. Each cell contains about 800 mitochondria, and each mitochondrion contains about 10 DNA molecules. Each mitochondrial DNA molecule is identical. Mitochondrial DNA is much shorter than chromosomal (nuclear) DNA (16,569 base pairs, as opposed to the many millions of chromosomal DNA), and is of circular rather than strand-like form. Unlike nuclear DNA, mitochondrial DNA is inherited solely from the mother.

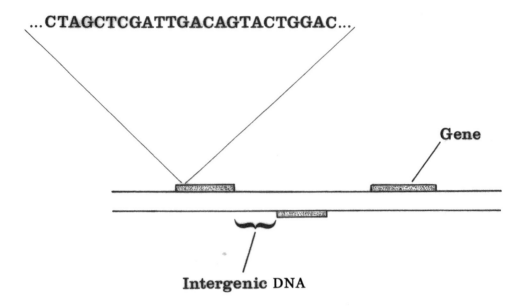

Figure 12.2 DNA molecules bear genes, separated by intergenic DNA

Studying ancient DNA

All components of the human body degrade after death, and DNA is no exception. It decays rapidly, undergoing progressive fragmentation and other chemical damage (Allentoft et al., 2012; Ottoni et al., 2017). In many archaeological specimens, no detectable DNA remains. Even when some does survive, the fragmentation is such that units of more than a few hundred base-pairs are rarely found, and those less than 100 base-pairs long are the norm (Sawyer et al., 2012). In archaeological remains, the overall amounts are small, generally less than about 2% of the levels found in fresh bone (Richards et al., 1995). In addition, endogenous human DNA normally forms only a small proportion of the total DNA found in buried skeletal remains (Marciniak et al., 2015; Key et al., 2017); most of it is exogenous contamination from the soil.

Sampling human remains for DNA

The petrous part of the temporal bone is probably the best part of the skeleton to target in order to recover human DNA (see Figure 13.6c for an illustration of this element). It produces higher yields than other bones or teeth (Pinhasi et al., 2015; Hansen et al., 2017; Furtwängler et al., 2018). Specifically, targeting the otic capsule seems to be the best strategy. This surrounds the sensory apparatus of the inner ear, in the medial part of the temporal bone. It is the densest bone tissue in the body, and it attains full density by the time a child is born (Takahashi et al., 2017). Normally, about 200-300mg of powdered bone is taken, but because the otic capsule is hidden within the temporal bone, this needs to be obtained by sandblasting the surrounding bone away (Pinhasi et al., 2015, 2019) or else drilling in from the cranial base (Sirak et al., 2017). The former appears optimal for DNA recovery but is much more destructive. Recent work (Sirak et al., 2020) suggests that the ear ossicles, if preserved, may be similarly useful sources of DNA and obviate the need for drilling or cutting. If neither the petrous temporal bones nor the auditory ossicles are available, a tooth is probably the next best option.

In contrast to the situation for human DNA, the petrous part of the temporal bone appears to be a poor source of pathogen DNA, perhaps because it has a limited blood supply (Margaryan et al., 2018). When the aim is to study the DNA of infecting bacteria, the best sampling sites are generally skeletal lesions which were active at time of death (if the skeleton shows them), as these are usually where bacterial numbers were greatest. For conditions that spread through the blood-stream, tooth dentine is another good option.

Laboratory procedures

The small amount of DNA which typically survives in archaeological materials means that it has to be amplified so that there is enough to work with. This is done using a technique called polymerase chain reaction (PCR). In the first two decades of research in ancient DNA, the laboratory procedure was essentially to use primers to target a specific region of the DNA molecule that was of interest. Primers are short strands of synthetic DNA. In this single-locus PCR, the primers' nucleotide sequences correspond with sequences at the ends of the region of the DNA molecule that the researcher wishes to study. The primers attach themselves to the site, the region bounded is amplified using PCR, and the nucleotide sequence of the resulting product is then determined. In recent years, this approach has given way to so-called next generation sequencing (NGS) methods (also known as high throughput sequencing), so single-locus PCR will not be described further (but Brown & Brown, 2011: 24–33, provide details).

The first step in the laboratory is to extract the biomolecules from a powdered sample into solution, and then to separate out the DNA. The aim here is to maximise the retrieval of the short fragments that characterise ancient DNA (Matisoo-Smith & Horsburgh, 2012: 66). The next step is to prepare a 'library' of DNA fragments to be sequenced. Much of the damage to the fragments, which is characteristic of ancient DNA, is repaired chemically, and universal adapters, short synthetic single stranded DNA segments, are attached. These permit the amplification and sequencing of all the DNA molecules in the library. There are two main approaches to sequencing (Capellini et al., 2018). The library can be sequenced directly, a procedure known as shotgun sequencing. However, because the proportion of DNA endogenous to the sample is invariably small compared with exogenous DNA from the burial environment, most of the sequences identified by shotgun sequencing will be from unwanted contamination. It is therefore more usual to enrich the library in the DNA of interest prior to sequencing. This is achieved using synthesised 'bait' molecules to capture the sought after DNA, allowing the remainder to be washed away (Linderholm, 2016). The library is sequenced using commercially-available NGS platforms. Bioinformatics techniques (computer-based analyses of the sequencing data) are used 'stitch' together sequences from short DNA strands using overlaps and to align them to a reference genome. This allows the creation of long, continuous sequences covering large parts of the genome. Full mitochondrial genomes and complete nuclear genes have been sequenced (Hofreiter et al., 2014; Brown & Barnes, 2015).

NGS has important advantages over single-locus PCR (Linderholm, 2016; Lan & Lindq-vist, 2018). Because it allows millions of reads in parallel, rather than one at a time, and it dramatically brings down costs of sequencing, whilst allowing much more of the genome to be studied. It also allows sequencing of fragments too short to be accessed via single-locus PCR, a key advantage given the degraded nature of ancient DNA.

The problem of contamination with modern DNA

Modern contamination is one of the most important technical problems that needs to be dealt with when analysing ancient DNA. DNA molecules are ubiquitous in the environment. People shed DNA in their skin cells, sweat and saliva. Stringent protocols are necessary to prevent contamination in the laboratory. All materials and equipment are kept scrupulously clean, protective clothing is worn by laboratory staff and stringent pre-cautions are taken against cross-contamination between different samples under study. It is normal laboratory procedure to process blanks (samples with all reagents but with-out the ancient bone or tooth) alongside the skeletal samples. If DNA is found in these blanks then this clearly indicates a problem in the laboratory. These 'clean lab' proced-ures are essential in any DNA laboratory.

Handling specimens during excavation and study, before they reach the laboratory, will contaminate them with modern DNA. In single-locus PCR work, in theory a single con-taminating molecule could wreck an experiment. In the early days of ancient DNA studies, some writers seriously suggested that excavators routinely wear gloves and face-masks when excavating human remains (and, presumably, that museum curators and researchers studying museum collections should take similar precautions) in case the remains might, at some undefined point in the future, be needed for DNA work. This practice never caught on, probably because it is both impractical and unreasonable to impose these sorts of conditions in perpetuity just in case some future workers might wish to carry out human DNA analyses. It quickly emerged that a better approach would be to develop laboratory techniques for dealing with the problem, especially as these would be necessary for, and are routinely and successfully applied in, studies on existing museum collections.

Procedures that help to remove previous handling contamination from bone surfaces include irradiation with ultra-violet light and sand-blasting. These have long been used, and remain integral to modern laboratory sampling protocols (e.g. Pinhasi et al., 2019). Selection of the correct skeletal sampling site is also important. The high density of the otic capsule makes it a good source not only of highly concentrated, but also of little-contaminated endogenous DNA (Furtwängler et al., 2018).

NGS is optimised for short DNA fragments, so that the likelihood of coamplification of the longer, better preserved fragments of modern contaminating DNA is reduced com-pared with single-locus PCR work (Marciniak et al., 2015). NGS-based methods also facili-tate the quantification of endogenous DNA, and enable the authentication of ancient sequences. The instigation of adequate procedures to deal with contamination, as described below, is essential for any ancient DNA work.

As well as being fragmented, ancient DNA is also damaged in other ways. Identifica-tion of fragments bearing characteristic signs of damage has become the most important means of authenticating endogenous ancient DNA (Capellini et al., 2018; Bos et al., 2019). In single-locus PCR, it is the centre of a fragment that is amplified and sequenced. In NGS it is the whole fragment. This is an important difference because, in ancient DNA, there is a characteristic pattern of damage at the fragment ends, known as cytosine deamination. It is a feature that is regularly present in buried remains over about 100 years old (Sawyer et al., 2012; Velsko et al., 2019). The presence of this type of damage is useful in distinguishing ancient endogenous DNA from recent contamination. The proportion of endogenous DNA in the DNA library can also be increased prior to sequencing by selectively enriching it in damaged DNA molecules (Gansauge & Meyer, 2014). Computational (bioinformatic) analysis can be restricted to damaged (presumed ancient) sequences (Skoglund et al., 2014), or results from the damaged subset can be compared with those from the full population of reads in order to demonstrate that results are not being driven by contamination (Orlando et al., 2015).

Other methods are also available in NGS to help evaluate and quantify contamination (Korneliussen et al., 2014; Renaud et al., 2015; Key et al., 2017). One group of approaches involves determining whether mitochondrial or nuclear DNA comes from more than one source (as would be expected if an ancient sample was contaminated with exogenous human DNA). For example, a set of methods for the nuclear genome relies on study of the X chromosome. Because males have only one X chromosome, reads covering a given location in that chromosome that contain different bases suggest the presence of DNA from a second individual – i.e. contamination (Rasmussen et al., 2011; Moreno-Mayar et al., 2020).

Applications of DNA analyses to archaeological problems

Archaeological studies of ancient DNA from human skeletal remains can be divided into those that study human DNA and those which analyse DNA of infecting micro-organisms present at time of death.

The study of ancient human DNA

The early focus of much ancient DNA work was on mitochondrial DNA, mainly because its presence in multiple copies means that PCR amplification was more likely to be successful. However, the rise of NGS has seen a proliferation of genome-wide or more closely targeted SNP studies of nuclear DNA. SNPs (single nucleotide polymorphisms) are locations in the DNA molecule where different individuals may have different bases. SNPs provide evidence for ancestry, so are useful for conducting kinship or population biodistance studies. They may also give clues as to aspects of phenotype (observable individual characteristics), such as hair or eye colour.

Kinship studies

In personal identification in forensic cases, the dominant DNA approach is to use short tandem repeats (STRs, also known as microsatellites) in nuclear DNA (Iwamura et al., 2016). A typical STR is a sequence of 2–6 base-pairs repeated 5–30 times. Analysis of single STRs is not much use in establishing biological relationships, multiple STRs are needed. Study of 13 is considered to provide a unique profile, and gives good grounds for identification, for example in missing persons cases, when compared with results from close relatives (Baker, 2016). Analysis of STRs has sometimes proven to be of value in kinship studies using ancient DNA (e.g. Haak et al., 2008; Rott et al., 2017), but good DNA survival is needed for it to be useful. The degraded nature of ancient DNA often precludes accurate characterisation of STRs (Brown & Brown, 2011: 173–177; Canturk et al., 2014).

Most kinship studies using ancient DNA are undertaken using mitochondrial and Y-chromosomal DNA, and nuclear SNPs. Because mitochondrial DNA is inherited in the female line, it can tell us about maternal lineages. Individuals sharing a mitochondrial haplotype (mitochondrial DNA sequence) could be closely related, but are not necessarily so – they may share a haplotype by chance, especially if it is one that is common in that population. Y-chromosome DNA can be useful to study paternal lineages, but similar considerations apply, especially as Y-chromosomal DNA is less variable than mitochondrial DNA (Baker, 2016).

Autosomal DNA is inherited from both parents. NGS potentially enables more than a million autosomal SNPs to be typed for each individual. NGS studies of large numbers of SNPs can be used to infer close kin relationships between individuals. However, inferences are still probabilistic rather than definite. The more SNPs two individuals have in common, the closer their likely relationship, but to make reliable inferences we also need to know the expected number of SNPs two unrelated people in the same population might have in common. Using this principle, a team working at the University of Uppsala, led by Jose Monroy Kuhn, developed a mathematical algorithm they called 'READ' (Relationship Estimation from Ancient DNA) that used analysis of SNP data from skeletal remains to infer kinship relationships (Monroy Kuhn et al., 2018).

Each SNP site typed by NGS could be the same or different when two individuals are compared. The proportion of SNPs that are mismatches is 'P0'. The lower P0, the closer the kinship, but to accurately infer kin relationships, the test pair's P0 needs to be normalised by the P0 representative of a pair of unrelated individuals from the same population. The median P0 for all pairs of individuals in the same skeletal population gives a good approximation to the P0 for an unrelated pair. If this cannot be estimated (for example if the group of skeletons under study is small), the value can be based on median P0 in a similar population, or else on the value for two individuals from the study population that other evidence indicates are not close kin.

The READ method enables pairs to be classified as identical (identical twins or two samples belonging to the same individual), first degree relatives (parent – offspring; siblings), second degree relatives (aunt/uncle – nephew/niece; grandparent – grandchild; half-siblings), or unrelated (anything more distant than second degree relatives). READ also estimates the statistical uncertainty behind each assignment. Monroy Kuhn et al. (2018) tested their method on modern DNA data from individuals of known relationships. It worked well. For example, even when the data for over one million SNP sites was reduced to only 2500 in order to simulate the poor genome coverage that might obtain for degraded ancient DNA, the false positive rate (the percentage of unrelated individuals erroneously classified as related) was only about 0.5%.

O'Sullivan et al. (2018) applied the READ technique, along with Y-chromosomal and mitochondrial DNA analysis, to study kinship in a small 7th century AD burial ground at Niederstotzingen, in southwest Germany. There were 13 human burials (10 adults, 3 children). In each case where sex could be determined, the individual was male. The interments were accompanied by rich grave goods, mainly weapons, armour, jewellery and horse fittings. There were also three horse burials in the cemetery. This type of burial ground is thought to be for a household of a powerful family. The main aim of the DNA study was to investigate the extent to which membership of the burial group was determined by close family ties.

Mitochondrial DNA haplotypes could be successfully assigned in all 13 individuals, but only 8 had sufficient nuclear DNA for kinship study. This difference in success rate is not unexpected. At least in part because of its high copy number, mitochondrial DNA sequences can often be recovered even if the coverage of the nuclear genome is too low for reliable SNP calling (Burrell et al., 2015). Applying the READ technique suggested that five of the eight showed first or second degree kinship with one another; the other three were not related to any others (Figure 12.3). Y-chromosomal DNA was successfully analysed in 10 cases; most were haplogroups (major sequence classes) common in this part of Europe today. The exception was burial 3B, which had a haplogroup that is only common in southern Europe, the Caucasus and the Near East. His autosomal SNPs also showed southern European

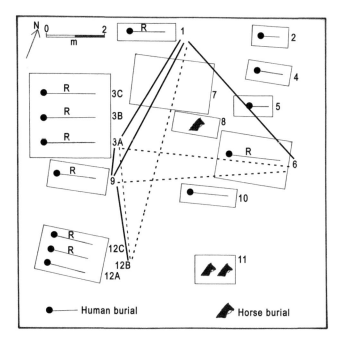

Figure 12.3 The burial ground at Niederstotzingen. R indicates burials included in the 'READ' kinship analysis. Solid lines between burials indicate first degree kinship; dashed lines second degree relationships. Grave 7 contained no burials

Source: after O'Sullivan et al. (2018: Figure 1).

affinities. Previous strontium and oxygen stable isotope work (Wahl et al., 2014) had shown that, in contrast to the local signals shown by most other burials, individual 3B had values consistent with an origin somewhat further south in the Swiss-German Alpine foothills. Putting the autosomal SNP, mitochondrial and Y-chromosome results together enabled the family tree depicted in Figure 12.4 to be tentatively reconstructed.

The results confirmed that close kinship ties were important in determining membership of this burial group (and by implication the noble household). The additional

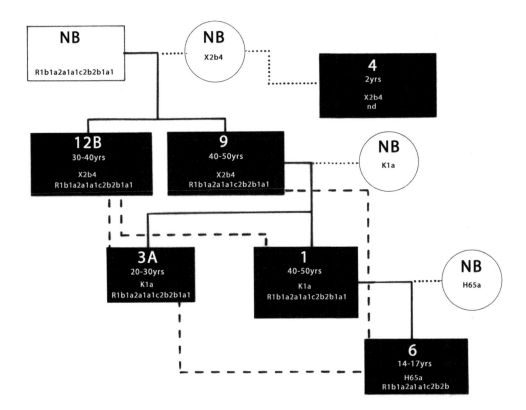

Figure 12.4 Tentative reconstruction of the family tree of some of the burials from Niederstotzingen. Dark rectangles denote male individuals excavated from the burial ground. Information in the dark rectangles is burial number, estimated age at death, and mitochondrial and Y chromosomal DNA haplogroups. Solid lines between burials indicate first degree relationships, dashed lines second degree kinship. The light rectangle indicates a male individual not buried at the burial ground but who contributed Y chromosomal DNA to Niederstotzingen individuals. The light circles indicate female individuals not buried at the burial ground who contributed mitochondrial DNA to Niederstotzingen individuals in the pattern indicated by the dotted lines. Note that Burial 4 could not be included in the READ analysis and is linked solely by mitochondrial DNA

Source: after O'Sullivan et al. (2018: Figure 3).

presence of individuals classified as unrelated suggests other factors, such as social or political ties, sometimes with individuals who originated beyond the local area, were important too. However, it should be recalled that, as READ classifies anything less than a second-degree kinship as unrelated, some of the 'unrelated' individuals may still have been members of a more extended family.

Population History

Biodistance studies aimed at shedding light on population history are undoubtedly the most frequent application of ancient human DNA analyses. Since the widespread adoption of NGS in ancient DNA work about ten years ago, a blizzard of large-scale studies have been published. Analysis of autosomal SNPs, supported by mitochondrial and Y-chromosomal studies, has helped ancient DNA to make important contributions to the study of major research questions in population history. These include the role of migration in the spread of agriculture in Neolithic Europe (e.g. Lipson et al., 2017; Brace et al., 2019); migration patterns in the Eurasian metal ages (e.g. Allentoft et al., 2015; Haak et al., 2015; Jeong et al., 2018); the spread of agriculture on the African continent (e.g. Skoglund et al., 2017; Prendergast et al., 2019); and the dispersal of humans into the Americas (e.g. Skoglund & Reich, 2016; Moreno-Mayer et al., 2018).

As we discussed in Chapter 5, in Britain, the alterations in burial practices and material culture, including the introduction of metalwork and finely decorated pottery Beakers, that occur at the Neolithic-Bronze Age transition, have long been ascribed to the arrival of migrants from Continental Europe. This inference is supported by study of cranial morphology which suggested that people buried with Beaker artifacts differed in ancestry from those excavated from Neolithic contexts. A recent DNA study (Olalde et al., 2018) has helped shed more light on this question.

Olalde et al. (2018) analysed DNA from 400 burials from prehistoric western and central Europe, dating from the Early Neolithic to the Late Bronze Age (approximately 4700–800BC). These were combined with previously published ancient DNA data to form a combined dataset of 683 individuals distributed across Europe and western Asia. Of this total, 120 came from Britain: 51 were Neolithic, 37 had Beaker associations, and 32 were Middle or Late Bronze Age.

Both mitochondrial and nuclear DNA were studied. As part of the analysis of the data on autosomal SNPs, they conducted a principle components analysis on a large modern Eurasian human dataset. Part of the plot of the scores on the first two principle components of these individuals, together with the ancient samples, is shown in Plate 9. In the plot, each point represents one individual. The closer together points are, the more similar their SNP combinations are likely to be, and so the closer their genetic affinity.

The Neolithic burials, including those from Britain, cluster together in the boxes outlined in the lower part of the plot (Plate 9). In contrast, the Beaker affiliated burials are more scattered, suggesting more diversity in their genetic background. Looking in more detail at different regions, in Iberia, the majority of Beaker individuals group with the earlier burials, suggesting considerable genetic continuity across the Neolithic-Bronze Age transition in that region. The pattern is different in Britain. The British Beaker burials form a distinct and separate cluster from the British and other Neolithic data, suggesting that they are genetically distinct. Like Beaker burials from continental northwest Europe, they lie toward the location of the data for the Bronze Age Yamnaya Culture (labelled Steppe Early Bronze Age in Plate 9), a group from the Ukraine and Russia, suggesting that they had a significant proportion of steppe ancestry. Similar patterning was obtained from the analysis of Y-chromosome and mitochondrial DNA haplogroups (Olalde et al., 2018: Figure 3, Supplementary Table 3).

The British burials included in Olalde et al.'s (2018) analysis are a substantially different dataset from that for which craniometric data were described in Chapter 5. For one thing, the latter all are from England, whereas much of Olalde et al.'s (2018) British study material was from Scotland and Wales. Nevertheless, the similarity of the patterns in the British craniometric and DNA data, each showing good separation of Neolithic and Beaker burials, is striking (compare the principle component plots in Plate 9 and Figure 5.18). This similarity should not surprise us. As was discussed in Chapter 5, it has been repeatedly shown that cranial variation aligns closely to genetic variation.

The DNA evidence supports the view, long held on the basis of cranial morphology, that there is a genetic difference between British Neolithic and Beaker burials, and therefore that there was significant migration into the British Isles at around the time of the Neolithic-Bronze Age transition. The DNA study shows that the Neolithic genetic signal in Britain appears to have been extinguished in the Beaker period; the pervasive steppe-related ancestry observed in the Beaker burials persists during the later parts of the Bronze Age (and remains prominent in British populations today) (Olalde et al., 2018). The extinction of the Neolithic DNA signature is also consistent with the craniometric data: Neolithic cranial morphology differs not only from that of Beaker associated burials but is also very different from that of subsequent skeletal populations (Brothwell & Krzanowski, 1974).

Perhaps the most obvious interpretation of these results is that there was a large-scale influx of people into Britain from the Continental Europe at the opening of the Bronze Age, who brought with them the Beaker cultural package. This resulted in the speedy extinction of the native Neolithic British population. In this light, some recent results from a demographic study of prehistoric Britain are interesting. Bevan et al. (2017) conducted a statistical analysis of published radiocarbon dates. They considered not only dates from human remains, but from all archaeological remains. They reasoned that a concentration of dates in a particular time period would suggest greater human activity and, by implication, greater population. This methodology suggested a peak in population in the early Neolithic with a subsequent decline, followed by an increase at around 2500BC, about the time at which Beaker cultural package appears. If this reconstruction of population trends is correct, then Beaker migrants may have arrived into a substantially depopulated landscape, which may have aided their supplanting of Neolithic genetic signals.

Nevertheless, the idea that the craniometric and DNA evidence necessarily indicates a large-scale migration of 'Beaker Folk' into Britain needs to be considered critically. In Chapter 5, it was pointed out that most Neolithic human remains come from the earlier part of that period. Although the few later Neolithic remains that have been analysed group craniometrically, and in terms of DNA, with the earlier Neolithic material rather than with Beaker affiliated individuals, their low numbers make the rapidity and timing of genetic changes, and their precise relationship with changes in burial practice and material culture, difficult to determine with certainty. It is also worth recalling that large-scale genetic turnover need not imply large-scale migration. Quite small evolutionary advantages, conferred by factors such as differential resistance to infectious disease, can lead to significant differences in population growth rates. This means that arrival of even a relatively small population of newcomers can fairly rapidly (in archaeological terms) lead to large-scale genetic turnover (Furholt, 2018).

It has long been appreciated that inhumation, in both the Neolithic and Beaker periods, must have been a rite accorded to only a small minority of the population in Britain (Smith & Brickley, 2009; Cummings, 2017). Burial treatment is an arena for the expression of the social identity of the deceased (Fowler, 2013), of which ancestry is usually an important component (White et al., 2009). So, for example, it may be that inhumation in the Neolithic, beneath long-barrows and elsewhere, might have been restricted to group(s) of specific ancestry. DNA work using the 'READ' approach to reconstruct familial relationships has shown that, in Ireland and Sweden, some Neolithic communal tombs were used for burials of people belonging to particular lineages, rather than representing the larger Neolithic society (Sánchez-Quinto et al., 2019). If this was also the case in Britain, then the genetic background of British Neolithic populations in any one locality was potentially much more diverse than suggested by the burial record. The genetic make-up of the vast majority of the population that were not disposed of by inhumation remains unknown, and for all we know, might have more closely resembled that of the Beaker age and subsequent periods.

When considering questions of population history, we should bear in mind that, over the time-periods studied by archaeologists, processes of population replacement, extinctions and gene flow would be expected for humans and indeed any living organism (Hofreiter et al., 2014). We should not be surprised to see evidence for genetic discontinuities in archaeological data, and we should not be misled into thinking that, by identifying evidence for genetic change, we have somehow 'explained' culture change (Carlin, 2018: 198–200). The genetic data, far from providing the final word, should actually be a starting point toward thinking in more detail about aspects such as the scale, nature and timing of migration, what it may have meant in social terms, and how it might have interacted with other factors to contribute to culture change (Furholt, 2018). Finally, it is always critical to consider the limitations imposed on our understanding of the past by the complex nature of the archaeological record.

Sex determination

Because whether a person is biologically male or female is determined by their chromosomes, DNA analysis offers a way of identifying sex when this is not possible on the basis of skeletal morphology. One method is to study the amelogenin gene (Gibbon et al., 2009). This is a gene which has a role in controlling dental enamel development (it codes for the protein amelogenin, briefly referred to in Chapter 4). Both X and Y chromosomes carry copies which differ slightly in their nucleotide sequence (i.e. they carry different alleles). By targeting suitable areas of the gene, we can infer the sex of the individual. This method has been used since the early days of ancient DNA work (e.g. Faerman et al., 1995), and continues in use today (e.g. Rott et al., 2017; Morales-Arce et al., 2019). Because it uses single-locus PCR, it requires preservation of longer DNA fragments, and is more vulnerable to contamination and other problems than methods that use NGS.

The X chromosome is about three times longer than the Y and, except for small regions at the ends, the bulk of the DNA sequence in each is unique (Brown & Brown, 2011: 157-158). NGS-based methods use the sequence differences to assess the sex of the person. One set of approaches utilises the ratio of reads that map to the Y chromosome, either to those that map to both sex chromosomes (Skoglund et al., 2013) or to those mapping to the autosomes (Fu et al., 2016). Because the bulk of the DNA on the Y chromosome is unique and females lack this chromosome, these ratios in females should be extremely low. Another way is to use a ratio of reads on the X chromosome to those on the autosomes (Mittnik et al., 2016). A sex difference is expected because males, with only one X chromosome, have half the amount of X chromosomal genetic material of females. Each of these methods enables the calculation of a confidence interval that allows the uncertainty of the sex assignment to be quantified. Using shotgun sequencing, Mittnik et al. (2016) measured the ratio of reads on the X chromosome to that on the autosomes on a group of individuals of known sex assignment, and used this to calculate a parameter they called R_x. They showed that if the upper limit of the confidence interval of R_x was less than 0.6, the individual was male; if the lower limit was higher than 0.8 then that indicated female. They tested this method on DNA data from 16 ancient skeletons and found that sex could be confidently assigned, even when only 1000 reads were sampled; that is a very low number and shows that it should work well even with highly degraded DNA.

Sex determination from DNA is not routine, but may be carried out when sex identification in otherwise unsexable individuals addresses some pressing archaeological problem. Under these circumstances, it has been used for immature skeletons (e.g. Hassan et al., 2014; Morales-Arce et al., 2019) or in adult remains where bony sex indicators are ambiguous or poorly preserved.

In 1986, a triple burial was discovered at Dolní Věstonice, Czech Republic (Jelínek, 1987; Klima, 1988; Trinkaus & Svoboda, 2006). It dates to the Upper Palaeolithic, about 26,000 years ago. The bodies had been laid side-by-side in a shallow depression (Figure 12.5). The interment was clearly a single event, the central body (skeleton DV15) being placed first, on its back, and the other two corpses positioned around it. The body on the left side of the grave (DV13) had been laid supine, orientated toward DV15 with the hands extended to touch that individual's pelvic area. The third body (DV14) was placed on the other side of DV15, face down. The heads of all three were covered in red ochre, a natural clay pigment often used in burials of this period, and the central burial also showed this in the pelvic area. They had head ornaments decorated with animal teeth and beads of mammoth ivory.

The three all died in their late teens or early twenties (Hillson et al., 2006). The skeletal morphology of DV13 and DV14 indicated male sex (Brůžek et al., 2006), but the sex indicators of DV15 were somewhat ambiguous, and the sex assignment of this individual has been debated ever since the grave was found (Jelínek, 1987; Klima, 1988; Formicola et al., 2001; Brůžek et al., 2006). Various parts of skeleton DV15 show abnormalities consisting of shortening, bowing and other deformities, which add to the difficulties in determining sex.

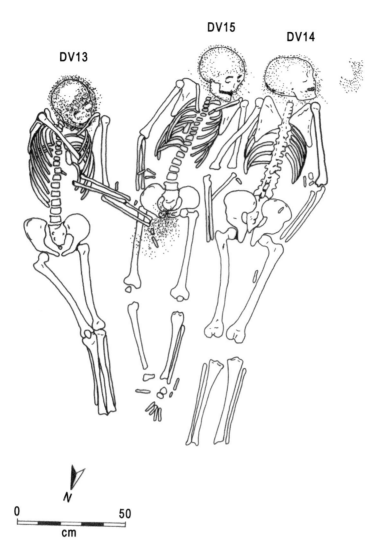

Figure 12.5 The triple burial at Dolní Věstonice. The stippling identifies the principal con-
centrations of red ochre

Source: after Svoboda (2006: Figure 4-4).

The unusual arrangement of the bodies, and the enigmatic signs of disease presented
by DV15, has ensured that this group has featured prominently in discussion of burial
and society (Bahn, 2011; Pettitt, 2011), and palaeopathology (Formicola, 2007) in Upper
Palaeolithic Europe. The question of the sex of DV15 has been key to these debates. An
initial suggestion (Klima, 1988) was that the triple burial could be understood as
a response to the death in childbirth of DV15. Red ochre has been thought to symbolise
life or blood (Bahn, 2011), so the concentration of this substance in the pelvic area might
be symbolic of an obstetric fatality. The layer of ochre around the skull of DV13 formed

a thick crust and was studded with animal teeth and ivory beads. It was thought possible that this represented the death-mask of a shaman, and that the position of DV13's hands indicated this individual had attempted to deliver the child. Klima (1988) suggests that he and the other man might have been thought to have been complicit in the death of DV15, and hence were forced to follow that individual into the afterlife. Turning to the palaeo-pathology of DV15, Formicola et al. (2001) suggest a diagnosis of X-linked dominant chondrodysplasia calcificans punctata for the bony deformities. This is a hereditary condition that is generally lethal in infancy in males, so the survival of this individual into young adulthood would, as Formicola et al. (2001) point out, require that the individual be female.

Mittnik et al. (2016) applied their R_x sexing method to the three burials. The results are shown in Figure 12.6. In each case, R_x was less than 0.6, suggesting male sex. To make sure that modern contamination was not influencing their results, they reanalysed the data excluding any reads from DNA fragments that did not show the cytosine deamination that is the hallmark of ancient DNA. This produced little alteration in R_x values, confirming the reliability of the sex determination. Fu et al. (2016) included the Dolní Věstonice burials in a wider study of DNA from Ice Age Europe. Rather than using shotgun sequencing, their analysis used enrichment to target particular SNPs. Looking at

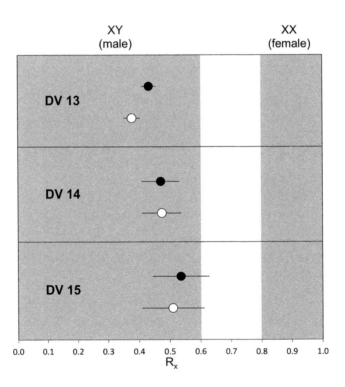

Figure 12.6 R_x values from the three Dolní Věstonice individuals. Black dots are results from unfiltered reads, light dots are results solely from fragments showing cytosine deamination

Source: reproduced from Mittnik et al. (2016: Figure 2).

reads mapping to the Y chromosome normalised with respect to reads mapping to the autosomes, the results consistently suggested male sex for all three burials.

These DNA studies seem to settle the question of the sex of DV15. This helps to eliminate interpretations of the manner of burial that are predicated on DV15 being female (e.g. Klima, 1988; Pettitt, 2011: 209–210). In palaeopathology, the male sex of DV15 makes a diagnosis of X-linked dominant chondrodysplasia calcificans punctata, as suggested by Formicola et al. (2001), unlikely. Although debate concerning the cultural meaning and palaeopathological interpretation of these important remains will continue, the successful resolution of the sex of DV15 will provide a firmer basis for future inferences.

Phenotypic traits

The connection between an individual's genotype (genetic make-up) and phenotype (their observable characteristics) is highly complex and incompletely understood. Nevertheless, probabilistic statements concerning some physical traits, particularly hair, eye and skin pigmentation, can be made on the basis of certain SNPs. This sort of work can be important in personal identification in forensic investigations (Baker, 2016). In archaeology, it can help provide information for facial reconstruction, for example for presenting archaeology to the public, as well as occasionally helping to put a name to a skeleton.

Analysis of functional SNPs undertaken on the skeleton thought to be of the English King Richard III (died AD1485), suggested that there was a 96% probability of blue eye colour, and a 77% probability of blond hair (King et al., 2014). No contemporary portraits of the King exist, but the earliest surviving depiction, painted about 30 years after his death, shows him with blue eyes. The hair in the portrait is brown rather than blond, but DNA predictions relate to childhood colouring, and blond hair can tend to darken with age. These results were consistent with a number of other findings that, taken together, pointed to this skeleton being that of King Richard (King et al., 2014).

On a population level, functional SNPs can help us understand how physical appearance of people varied in different geographic regions or changed over time. In Europe, SNP patterns suggest Mesolithic people showed a variety of intensity of skin pigmentation – for example, the 'Cheddar Man' skeleton from England may have had a dark or black skin (Brace et al., 2019). Later in prehistory, there was an increase in SNPs associated with lighter skin tones – this happened as part of genetic changes observed at about the time of the transition to the Neolithic and again approximately at the transition to the Bronze Age (Mathieson et al., 2015; Olalde et al., 2018).

Another trait that has been extensively studied is lactase persistence. Lactase is an enzyme that enables digestion of lactose, the carbohydrate component in milk. In mammals, this ability is gradually lost after weaning, because lactase is no longer produced. Humans are a partial exception to this. About one third of people worldwide retain a lifelong ability to digest milk, a condition known as lactase persistence (LP). If non-LP people drink milk, not only do they lose some of the caloric benefit but they may also suffer abdominal cramps and nausea. LP frequency is different in different populations, ranging from less than 10% in parts of southern Africa and south-east Asia, to almost 100% in northern Europeans (Itan et al., 2010). LP has a genetic basis, and SNPs associated with it have been identified.

Archaeozoological studies of kill profiles of domestic animals, and analyses of chemical residues in pottery fragments, suggest that dairying was a key component of the subsistence economies of the first farmers in Neolithic Europe (Gerbault et al., 2017). We saw in Chapter 9 that dental calculus from European prehistoric burials has yielded β-lactoglobulin, showing milk consumption. However, the European polymorphism associated with LP is not observed in human remains from that period; it only becomes common in the historic era (Ségurel & Bon, 2017). This suggests LP was not a factor facilitating the adoption and early development of agriculture/pastoralism, but that the trait was selected for once these modes of subsistence had become well-established. Lactose content of fermented dairy products, such as yoghurt, is much less than milk itself, and in contrast to other low-lactose dairy products such as hard cheeses, they retain significant amounts of β-lactoglobulin (Charlton et al., 2019). Perhaps preparing products such as yoghurts helped people without LP in early agricultural populations to enjoy the nutritional benefits of dairy foods.

The study of ancient pathogen DNA

Much work on pathogen DNA amplified from human remains from archaeological sites has concentrated on just two diseases, leprosy and tuberculosis (Marciniak & Poinar, 2018). There are a number of reasons for this. These were important diseases, both epidemiologically and socially, in past populations (Roberts 2020; Roberts & Buikstra, 2003). They are caused by bacteria of the genus *Mycobacteria*, leprosy chiefly by *Mycobacterium leprae*, tuberculosis by several bacilli of the *Mycobacterium tuberculosis* complex, most often *Mycobacterium tuberculosis* or *Mycobacterium bovis*. Mycobacterial DNA seems to survive well in archaeological remains, perhaps in part because of the low permeability of mycobacterial cell walls (Palfí et al., 2015; Daffé, 2015). Lastly, leprosy and tuberculosis leave recognisable lesions on bones, enabling suitable skeletons to be identified and targeted for study.

The earliest use to which analysis of ancient pathogen DNA was put was to help support diagnoses made on osteological grounds (Anastasiou & Mitchell, 2013). DNA can be especially helpful when lesions are ambiguous. For instance, it can help identify when periosteal reactions on the visceral (internal) sides of ribs are associated with tuberculosis rather than with other chest infections (Plate 10) (Mays et al., 2002b; Nicklisch et al., 2012). Another example of this type of application is provided by a skeleton excavated from a 14th-century burial ground at Geridu, Sardinia. It showed no lesions on the bones, but in the pelvic area were found multiple small (under 2cm across) calcified fragments (Kay et al., 2014). Tuberculosis may cause calcifications in the thorax or abdomen (Sood, 2001), and this was the diagnosis that the research team initially suspected, but many other infectious and non-infectious conditions can also potentially do this (Steinbock, 1989; Binder et al., 2016b). Kay et al. (2014) used shotgun sequencing to study DNA extracted from one of the fragments. They mapped their reads against the genomes of several pathogens, including *Mycobacterium tuberculosis*, and *Brucella melitensis*, a causative agent of brucellosis, an infectious disease with a long history in the Mediterranean basin. Reads aligned to *B. melitensis*. This shows that the person was infected with brucellosis, but whether the nodules were a result of this or due to some other co-existing condition is unclear.

For tuberculosis, DNA analyses also potentially enables infection caused by different members of *M. tuberculosis* complex to be distinguished, something that is not possible on the basis of skeletal lesions. *M. tuberculosis* is normally transmitted person-to-person as a droplet infection, whereas *M. bovis* is normally acquired from infected animals or animal products. Different subsistence economies and lifestyles may favour the spread of one or other form of the disease. Therefore making this distinction may be important for understanding relationships between disease and society (Mays et al., 2001; Taylor et al., 2005; Murphy et al., 2009).

Study of residual DNA from pathogens also opens up the possibility of studying diseases that have not left any bony signs of their presence. Diseases that do not enter the bloodstream, for example those like cholera that only affect the intestinal system, are likely to be difficult to study using DNA from skeletal remains; pathogens that are disseminated via the bloodstream offer better prospects (Marciniak & Poinar, 2018). A number of these sorts of diseases have been successfully studied using ancient DNA, including malaria (Marciniak et al., 2016) and enteric (typhoid) fever (Vågene et al., 2018), but it is bubonic plague that has commanded the most attention.

The bubonic plague bacillus, *Yersinia pestis* has been detected in skeletons from mass graves linked by documentary sources to plague outbreaks. Such studies confirm, what had sometimes been doubted, that *Y. pestis* was indeed responsible for the 5th–8th century and the 14th-18th century AD outbreaks in Europe (Seifert et al., 2016; Feldman et al., 2016). Indeed, *Y. pestis* seems to have had a long association with human populations. It has been detected in Neolithic and Bronze Age burials from Europe and Asia (Rasmussen et al., 2015; Valtueña et al., 2017; Spyrou et al., 2019; Rascovan et al., 2019). *Y. pestis* is generally transmitted via a flea carried by rodents. The DNA work shows there seem to have been at least two lineages of the bacillus in the Neolithic–Bronze Age. One genetically resembles more recent strains that are fully adapted to flea transmission; the other may have been less readily transmissible by fleas. There was also a genetic difference between these Neolithic/Bronze Age and more recent isolates that indicated the early strains may have caused plague of the pneumonic form (respiratory disease) or less severe bubonic plague (Valtueña et al., 2017; Spyrou et al., 2019).

Analogous to human ancient DNA studies, in which there is an increasing emphasis on population movements and relationships between different populations, an increasing amount of work on pathogens has concentrated on phylogenetic studies. These investigate relationships between different species and strains, and the ways in which different pathogens have spread into and among human populations.

Today, leprosy is principally a disease of the tropics, but in the past it occurred in Europe. A team led by Verena Scheunemann, of the University of Tübingen, Germany, conducted a phylogenetic study of leprosy in Mediaeval Europe (Scheunemann et al., 2018). They generated SNP data from *M. Leprae* DNA extracted from ten burials with skeletal leprosy from England and Denmark, and combined this with published data from a further seven Mediaeval European leper skeletons. Results showed a high diversity of strains of the bacterium, spanning almost all the major branches of the *M. leprae* phylogenetic tree. One explanation for this would be that leprosy has an origin in western Eurasia. This would seem to be consistent with osteoarchaeological evidence: the earliest convincing cases currently known come from this region. These predominantly date from around the time of the Roman Empire (Inskip et al., 2015), but there is also a recently reported, and fairly convincing case, dating right back to 3780–3650BC (Köhler et al., 2017). An alternative explanation for the high diversity might be that different *M. leprae* strains were introduced into Europe from different parts of the Old World before or during the Mediaeval Age. We currently lack sufficient ancient and modern genomic data on *M. leprae* in different areas of the world in order to distinguish these two possibilities.

In the Americas, modern strains of *M. tuberculosis* are all closely related to those from Europe, so they probably have a European origin. However, skeletal evidence for tuberculosis prior to European contact is abundant (Roberts & Buikstra, 2003). The question of the origins of pre-contact New World tuberculosis is an intriguing one. In order to shed light on this, a team led by Kirsten Bos analysed SNPs in pathogen DNA from three pre-contact (10th–13th century AD) burials from coastal Peru showing clear skeletal signs of tuberculosis. Phylogenetic analysis showed that the genomes clustered, not with strains of *M. tuberculosis* or *M. bovis*, but with another *M. tuberculosis* complex bacterium, *Mycobacterium pinnipedii*. *M. pinnepedii* causes disease in southern hemisphere seals and can be transmitted to other animals, including man (Roe et al., 2019). Bos et al.'s (2014) findings suggest that infection may have been transmitted to Native American humans via their exploitation of marine resources (butchery and consumption of seal meat), and the bacterium subsequently adapted to human hosts. Whether this strain subsequently spread through the New World, and is responsible for prehistoric cases of tuberculosis on a wider scale, is unclear. DNA work on other tuberculous skeletons from the pre-contact New World is needed to shed further light on this.

Summary

DNA contains the genetic information of the organism. In human cells, DNA is present in the chromosomes of the nucleus and also outside the nucleus in the mitochondria. Nuclear DNA is inherited from both parents. Mitochondrial DNA is inherited only from the mother. In skeletal tissues, DNA is present in bone, and in the dentine and cementum of the teeth. It is not present in dental enamel. The genetic information in DNA is conveyed by the sequence of bases in the molecule. In people suffering from infectious diseases, DNA from the pathogenic micro-organisms responsible may remain in the skeleton after death. Both human and pathogen DNA can potentially be extracted from skeletal remains and studied.

Amounts of DNA surviving in ancient skeletons are typically small, and the molecule degrades quickly after death, becoming very fragmented. The site in the skeleton that is sampled needs to be chosen carefully. To recover human DNA, the optimal site appears to be the otic capsule, part of the petrous portion of the temporal bone of the skull. The optimal sampling site for pathogen DNA appears to be skeletal lesions active at time of death or, alternatively, from the dentine at the inner surface of the pulp cavity of a tooth.

Today, so-called next generation sequencing (NGS) techniques dominate laboratory practice. DNA is extracted from a powdered sample, and treated chemically to produce a 'library' of DNA fragments. The fragments are then amplified by polymerase chain reaction to produce multiple copies of each fragment. The library can then be directly sequenced, but because most of the DNA in an ancient sample is normally from the soil rather than being endogenous to the sample, it is more usual to chemically treat the library to enrich it in the DNA of interest (human, pathogen) before sequencing. Sequencing the DNA fragments produces a vast amount of data, and sophisticated bioinformatic techniques (computer algorithms) are needed to organise and analyse it. NGS laboratory techniques are orientated toward working with the highly fragmented DNA molecules that characterise ancient samples. Nevertheless, analysis sometimes fails to produce useful results, either because the DNA was too highly degraded, or for other reasons.

In the analysis of ancient human DNA, both nuclear and mitochondrial DNA are studied but the focus is increasingly on the former. DNA can be used to study kinship between individuals in a cemetery. It can also be used as a way of determining the sex of a person in instances where osteological techniques do not permit this (for example, with infant or child skeletons). Inferences can also sometimes be made about certain physical traits, for example, hair or eye colour. However, the most frequent use to which ancient DNA is put is biodistance studies – investigation of relationships between different human populations and study of migrations in the past.

Analysis of pathogen DNA may be used to confirm presence of an infectious disease (for example, leprosy or tuberculosis) in instances where skeletal lesions are ambiguous. It can also be used to study some diseases that do not leave any marks on the bone at all, for example bubonic plague. Increasingly, ancient pathogen DNA studies are being orientated toward phylogenetic questions – investigations of relationships between species and strains of pathogenic micro-organisms and the ways in which the diseases they cause have spread among human populations in different areas of the world.

Ancient DNA has made some significant contributions to archaeological knowledge. However, it is important not to have unrealistic expectations. Inferences made from DNA are normally probabilistic rather than definite and, just as for any other type of archaeological evidence, our ability to make higher level interpretations about the past from DNA data is constrained by the partial and biased nature of the archaeological record.

Further reading

For an overview of laboratory techniques in DNA analyses see: Marciniak, S. et al. (2015). Ancient Human Genomics: The Methodology Behind Reconstructing Evolutionary Pathways. *Journal of Human Evolution* 79: 21-34.

Such is the pace of advances in ancient DNA that review articles soon become out of date. However, some more recent ones include the following. Capellini, E. et al. (2018). Ancient Biomolecules and Evolutionary Inference. *Annual Reviews in Biochemistry* 87: 1029-60 *reviews DNA and other biomolecues (lipids, proteins) in human and other archaeological remains.* Nieves-Colón, M.A. & Stone, A.C. (2019) Ancient DNA Analysis of Archaeological Remains, pp. 515-544 in M.A. Katzenberg & A.L. Grauer (eds) *Biological Anthropology of the Human Skeleton* (third edition) *focuses more specifically upon human remains.* Stone, A.C. & Ozga, A.T. (2019) Ancient DNA in the Study of Ancient Disease, pp. 183-210 in J.E. Buikstra (ed) *Ortner's Identification of Pathological Conditions in Human Skeletal Remains* (third edition). Elsevier, London. *As the title suggests, this concentrates on pathogens.*

Archaeologists are beginning to make critical appraisals of the strengths and limitations of DNA studies for aiding our understanding of prehistoric populations, culture change and migrations. For example, see Furholt, M. (2018). Massive Migrations? The Impact of Recent aDNA Studies on Our View of Third Millennium Europe. *European Journal of Archaeology* 21: 159-191.

13 Cremated bone

Previous chapters in this book have dealt with inhumation burials. Although these are the most common type of human remains encountered archaeologically, cremation was practiced in many ancient cultures, either alongside inhumation or as the sole archaeologically visible funerary rite. Cremation burials are frequent finds from later prehistory in most parts of Europe (Williams et al., 2017). Cremation was also practiced by early European historic and protohistoric cultures, including many in the Roman Empire (Pearce et al., 2000), and among Anglo-Saxon post-Roman groups in northwest Europe (Lucy, 2000). Cremation burials are also known from prehistoric North America (Goldstein & Myers, 2014; Curtin, 2015), and from various parts of Asia (Crubézy et al., 2006; Kutterer et al., 2012; Ward & Tayles, 2015), South America (Ulguim, 2015; Strauss, 2016), and Oceania (Bowler et al., 2003; Scott et al., 2010). Most osteoarchaeologists therefore deal with archaeological cremation burials on a regular or occasional basis. This chapter discusses the nature of cremated human remains and the information which can be gained from their study.

The process of cremation

Our understanding of the process of cremation has been aided by studies conducted in modern crematoria (Evans, 1963; Wahl, 1982; McKinley, 1994; Schultz et al., 2015). When a corpse is exposed to fire, initially there is scorching and burning of the skin and hair. About 60% of body-weight is water. This is driven off by the heat early on in the cremation process, and as a result muscles and tendons may contract, giving rise to visible movements of the extremities (although tales of muscle contractions causing corpses suddenly to sit up in the furnace are apocryphal!). There may be swelling of the abdomen due to gaseous expansion within, before the skin and muscles split. As cremation progresses, destruction of overlying soft tissues causes parts of the skeleton to be revealed. Eventually all soft parts are destroyed (the ligaments and brain tissue are often the last to go) leaving only the bones. Temperatures in modern crematoria routinely reach about 800–900°C, and may climb beyond 1000°C. As we shall see, similar temperatures were often attained on ancient cremation pyres.

Bones and teeth are not destroyed on heating but they fragment. Following cremation, bone fragments are generally a maximum of only a few centimetres long. In modern cremations, the fragment size of the 'ashes' (actually bone fragments) is much smaller, as they are ground to a gritty or gravel-like consistency in a special machine following cremation (McKinley, 1994; Schultz et al., 2015). The teeth also fragment. In particular, the enamel crowns of erupted teeth separate from the dentine and disintegrate into tiny fragments (Beach et al., 2015). However, enamel crowns of unerupted teeth may survive the cremation process intact (Wahl, 2015).

Alterations to bone composition also occur during heating. Over the range of temperatures likely to be attained by cremated bone, three major changes occur (Munro et al., 2007, 2008; Figueiredo et al., 2010; Snoeck et al., 2014a; Greiner et al., 2019). Firstly, water content is driven off. This process is complete once the remains reach about 250°C. Secondly, combustion of the organic component (chiefly collagen) occurs. This begins at approximately 275°C and is mainly complete by about 500°C. The third phase is loss of structural carbonate from the mineral fraction; this is driven off as carbon dioxide between about 400°C and 750°C.

Colour changes take place as bone is heated, and they appear to be associated with the destruction of the organic component. A great many studies have investigated the way in which bone changes colour under heating (e.g. Binford, 1963; Wahl, 1982; Shipman et al., 1984; Nicholson, 1993; Mays, 1998: 217; Munro et al., 2007; Walker et al., 2008; Galeano & García-Lorenzo, 2014; Greiner et al., 2019; Krap et al., 2019; Ellingham & Sandholzer, 2020). The results differ in detail, but in essence, bone initially darkens, and orange or reddish-brown colours are seen. By about 200°C, it may be dark brown. At about 300–400°C, the bone is black, and above this temperature it progressively lightens in colour, through tones of tan and grey, until by about 650–800°C it becomes predominantly white. The black colouration at about 300°C appears to correspond to the initial charring of the organic component and the lightening thereafter to its progressive loss via combustion. Burnt bone which is whitish in colour due to loss of the organic component is often termed 'calcined' (Stiner et al., 1995; Symes et al., 2015; Ellingham & Sandholzer, 2020).

As well as fragmenting the bones, the cremation process also results in shrinkage of the fragments (Shipman et al., 1984; Thompson, 2005; Ellingham & Sandholzer, 2020). The degree of shrinkage varies between different skeletal elements, and in different parts of the same bone so that fragments often distort. In general, shrinkage tends to be minor (less than about 5%) at temperatures below about 700°C. The amount of shrinkage is markedly greater above about 700°C, and rises sharply with increasing temperature. In bone heated to 900°C, some dimensions may be reduced by more than 30%. Most shrinkage appears to occur upon cooling of the fragments.

Shrinkage appears to be predominantly associated with microstructural changes which occur to the bone mineral (hydroxyapatite). Key amongst these is alteration in crystallinity. High crystallinity denotes large crystal size and absence of structural defects in a mineral, qualities which tend to be found together. In living bone, the crystals of bone mineral are very small, but on heating an increase in crystallinity is observed. These changes have been studied by heating modern bone samples in a furnace, and subjecting them to analysis using various scientific techniques (reviewed in Ellingham et al., 2015; Mamede et al., 2018). Among the more important of these are X-ray diffraction (XRD) and Fourier transform infra-red spectroscopy (FTIR).

When X-rays are passed through a crystalline structure, they are diffracted, the diffraction pattern being determined by the nature of the crystal structure. FTIR works in a different way. Chemical bonds between atoms vibrate. The absorption of infra-red light by a chemical bond depends upon its specific vibrational properties. Vibrational properties of particular bonds alter with changes in crystallinity. Therefore, both XRD and FTIR can be used to measure crystallinity. Results can either be assessed simply from the visual output – the diffractogram or spectrum – or the results are used to provide a quantitative measure in the form of a 'crystallinity index'.

XRD studies on experimentally heated bone samples (e.g. Kalsbeek & Richter, 2006; Munro et al., 2008; Greiner et al., 2019) have produced very consistent results (Figure 13.1). There is a minor increase in crystallinity up to about 600°C. This is indicated by the narrowing and sharpening of the peaks in the diffraction pattern (Figure 13.1). However between about 600°C and 700°C the peaks abruptly become much narrower, indicating a fairly rapid transition to a much more highly crystalline structure. There is little further change above about 700°C.

Because of the fundamental differences between XRD and FTIR techniques, measures of crystallinity produced by the two methods cannot be directly compared (Thompson, 2015). Nevertheless, the alteration in crystallinity at about 600–700°C, seen so clearly on the XRD trace, is also evident on FTIR. However, pattern reported at higher temperatures varies between different FTIR studies. Some, as with XRD, report little further change in crystallinity over about 700°C (e.g. Figueiredo et al., 2010). Others report an increase (e.g. Piga et al., 2016), others a decrease (e.g. Ellingham et al., 2016). Because XRD directly reflects the microstructural organisation of a crystalline substance, it is generally regarded as the 'gold standard' for assessing crystallinity (Farlay et al., 2010; Mamede et al., 2018). The variability in the FTIR results may reflect differences in methodology between studies, and the observation that, at higher temperatures, partial conversion of hydroxyapatite to other minerals may occur and this may interfere with the accurate calculation of a crystallinity index using FTIR (Piga et al., 2016, 2018).

An advantage with FTIR is that, as well as estimating crystallinity, it can also be used to study aspects of compositional change. For example, the absorption due to the carbonyl group (present in organic compounds) and the carbonate group can each be measured (Thompson et al., 2009, 2013). When normalised against phosphate absorption they can, respectively, be used to quantity loss of the organic component, and of the carbonate component of bone mineral (Ellingham et al., 2016). In practice, crystallinity index (CI) and carbonate: phosphate ratio (C/P) are the most commonly reported parameters in FTIR work on burnt bone. A plot of CI and C/P measured using FTIR in bone heated to different temperatures is shown in Figure 13.2.

Although temperature is the principle factor predicting the compositional and other changes in bone, other variables also play a part. Sufficient duration of heat is necessary to elicit these changes (Snoeck et al., 2014a; Greiner et al., 2019). For efficient combustion of the organic component, sufficient oxygen supply is also necessary (Walker et al., 2008). The state of the bone is therefore only an approximate guide to firing temperature.

Survival of cremated bone in the soil

It has long been noted (e.g. De Jong, 1926) that cremated bone tends to survive better in the soil than unburnt bone, and recent studies have demonstrated this systematically. Study of burnt and unburnt archaeofaunal remains from rockshelters in Australia and

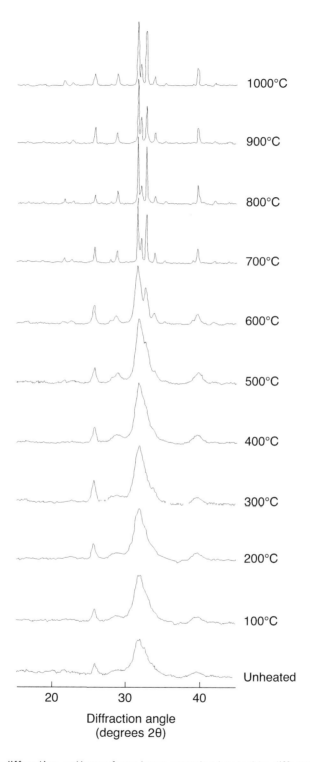

Figure 13.1 X-ray diffraction patterns from bone samples heated to different temperatures. A gradual sharpening of peaks is observed at temperatures up to 600°C. Between 600°C and 700°C there is a shift to a pattern with much narrower peaks. This shows a transition to a structure of increased crystallinity

Source: after Kalsbeek & Richter, 2006: Fig. 2.

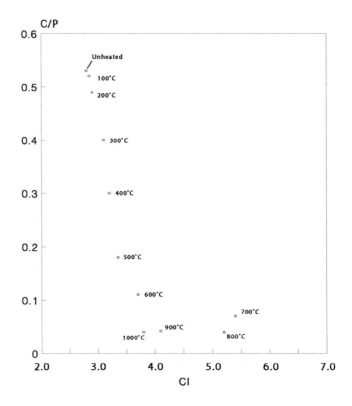

Figure 13.2 Crystallinity index (CI) plotted against carbonate: phosphate ratio (C/P) for bone samples heated to different temperatures. Both CI and C/P were measured using Fourier transform infra-red spectroscopy using attenuated total reflectance mode

Source: drawn from Ellingham et al. (2016: Figure 2).

New Guinea (Aplin et al., 2016) showed that burnt bone less often showed superficial erosion. That study also showed that, in acidic soil conditions (which, as we saw in Chapter 2, are generally destructive toward bone) the ratio of burnt: unburnt bone was consistently greater than at sites on alkaline geology. This suggests that burnt bone had a greater resistance to destruction in acidic conditions. In some regions, soil conditions are simply inimicable to the survival of unburnt bone. For example, in Finland, prehistoric inhumations are normally devoid of bone, but cremated bone does survive (Saipio, 2017). Reasons why cremated bone is more resistant to dissolution in the soil are unclear, but it is presumably connected with the microstructural alterations that occur in response to heating. The small size of the hydroxyapatite crystals mean that unburnt bone presents a large surface area for interaction with soil water. This is reduced when crystallinity is increased in burnt bone. It will be recalled from Chapter 2 that microbial degradation also plays a part in deterioration of buried bone. Because calcined bone lacks an organic component it is not attractive to microorganisms. This may also potentially play a part in aiding its survival.

Archaeological funerary contexts yielding cremated bone

Burnt human remains may be found in a variety of archaeological funerary contexts. Sometimes, finds are made of so-called *'bustum'* burials in which the burning and the burial take place in the same spot. This may be recognised archaeologically by evidence of *in situ* burning (reddening of the soil), much charcoal, and burial of a single individual. Examples have been excavated in which a mound was simply heaped over the remains of the pyre (Ulguim, 2015); the pyre was built over a pit into which the remains fell (Martín-Seijo & César Vila, 2019); or, more rarely, where a fire was lit in the grave next to the body (Weitzel & McKenzie, 2015).

More usually, however, burning and burial take place at separate locations. Pyre sites have sometimes been identified archaeologically, and they yield variable quantities of human remains, representing the residual material, not collected for burial, of single or multiple cremation events. Archaeological pyre sites assume a variety of appearances. They may simply be spreads of burnt material (charcoal, burnt stones, burnt human remains) and heat-affected soil. Others may have shallow X, T or Y-shaped ditches (Figure 13.3), which appear to represent flues dug to aid air flow (Fitzpatrick, 1997). Pyre sites range in

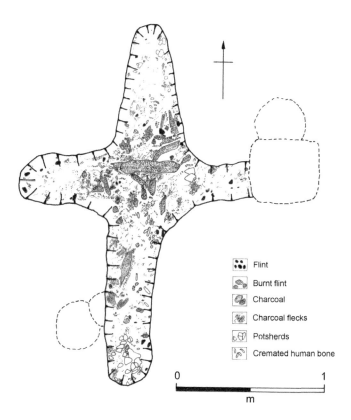

	Flint
	Burnt flint
	Charcoal
	Charcoal flecks
	Potsherds
	Cremated human bone

0   1
m

Figure 13.3 A pyre site at the late Iron Age (approx. 90–50BC) cemetery at Westhampnett, England. The crossed ditches represent flues for the pyre

Source: After Fitzpatrick, 1997: Figure 18.

size from ovoid areas a few metres in length, which may be the residuum of a single cremation event (e.g. Metzler et al., 1991), to more amorphous spreads of material tens of
metres in diameter, which represent the result of multiple cremation events in the same
general location (e.g. Polfer, 2000).

The most common feature yielding cremated bone on archaeological sites is the cremation burial – i.e. the deposition of burnt bone and other material (mainly charcoal) that
has been collected from a pyre. These burials are generally made in small pits. On excavation, the bones may often be found in an urn or other container (Fig. 13.4a). However
they may also be found directly in the soil, indicating either that they were not placed in
a container prior to burial or that they were interred in a container of perishable material
(Figure 13.4b).

Recovery of cremated remains in the field

Material from fills of cremation urns or pits generally consists of fragments of bone and
charcoal. Because of the small fragment size, recovery of the cremated remains by hand
is likely to result in significant loss of material. Instead, the entire pit fill or the whole urn
is recovered on site. For large urns or pits, the contents may be removed in several spits
in order to help study the vertical distribution of bone and charcoal. Very large features
(e.g. pyre sites) may be divided into blocks so the horizontal distribution of bone and
other remains can also be investigated.

Once the soil from a cremation-related feature has been recovered, the bone and
charcoal need to be separated out. The usual procedure is to place the soil in water. The
residue (soil, stones and bone) sinks; the charcoal floats off. Larger pieces of charcoal
can often be identified to specific types of wood, so it is a valuable source of information

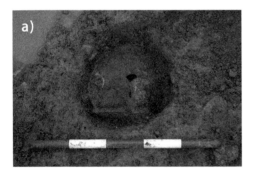 

Figure 13.4 Two 2nd–3rd century AD cremation burials from the Roman site at Birdoswald,
    on Hadrians Wall, England. (a) An urn, containing cremated bone. Despite being
    placed on its side in the pit, the contents have not spilled out, so perhaps a lid
    of perishable material was originally in place. (b) In this cremation burial, the
    presence of iron nails showed that the stones lining the pit had been positioned
    around a wooden box (now decayed). Cremated bone found in the pit had ori-
    ginally been placed within this box. The urn incorporated into one of the side-
    walls of the pit contained charcoal but no bone

about the fuel used for the pyre. For example, at a Bronze Age site in Ireland, taxonomic diversity in charcoal from cremation deposits was less than from domestic hearths, showing a narrower range of wood types was selected for use as fuel in pyres (O'Donnell, 2016). At a Roman-period site in Spain, *bustum* burials showed a narrower range of wood taxa than cremation burials that were burnt in a separate pyre area. This would be consistent with repeated use of pyre sites with consequent mixing of charcoal from different types of wood used in the cremation of different individuals (Martín-Seijo & César Vila, 2019).

The residue from the cremation-related feature is washed through sieves to recover the bone. Exact procedures vary between different field units. I generally wet-sieve residues through sieves of 4mm and 2mm mesh sizes, the 4mm sieve being stacked on top of the 2mm one. Care is taken during this process not to fragment the remains further. The bone fragments are hand-sorted (i.e. picked out by hand) from the material caught by the 4mm mesh. It would be very tedious and time-consuming to do this for material that passes through the 4mm sieve to be retained by the 2mm mesh. In fact, few bone fragments small enough to pass through a 4mm mesh are identifiable. In my two-sieve system, the material from the 2mm mesh is not sorted but is retained for study so that it can be scanned for any diagnostic fragments. Material recovered from a cremation urn using this method is shown in Figure 13.5. When the bone has been sieved, sorted and left to dry, it is ready for study.

5cm

Figure 13.5 Bone from a cremation burial after sieving. a) Bone sorted from the material retained by the 4mm mesh. b) The residue from the 2mm mesh: it has not been sorted

The osteoarchaeological study of cremated bone

Identification of bone fragments

Even in material from the 4mm sieve, bone fragment size is generally fairly small, often on average about 1–2cm, although occasional fragments up to about 10cm long may be present. The small size and distorted nature of most of the fragments means that even their identification presents a major challenge. To a great extent, the proportion of material which can be identified is dependent upon fragment size. However, other factors also play a part. Pieces from some parts of the skeleton are easier to identify than others. Very small bones such as terminal phalanges, sesamoids and carpals often survive cremation without fragmenting. They are thus easier to identify than the larger bones which shatter into many pieces. There are also differences between the larger bones in terms of 'identifiability'. For example, even when very small, cranial vault fragments are quite distinctive. By contrast, it may be impossible to determine from which particular skeletal element even quite large long-bone fragments come. A factor which assists in identification of cremated bone fragments is that, when subject to heat, bones do not shatter in a completely random way. Fracture patterns are influenced by bone anatomy. The seasoned observer gets used to seeing similar fragments in cremation after cremation, and tends to be on the look-out for them. Commonly occurring fragments include the odontoid process of the axis vertebra, the mandibular condyles and the petrous part of the temporal bone at the base of the skull (Figure 13.6).

Although many osteoarchaeologists divide their identified fragments into broad categories such as skull, axial skeleton and upper and lower limbs, more precise identification of as many fragments as is practicable is important. We cannot assume that a cremation deposit contains the remains of only one person. Any duplication of skeletal elements indicates the presence of more than one individual.

In most cremation deposits, a substantial portion of the bone cannot be identified to skeletal element, or even, in many cases, to broader categories such as axial skeleton etc. This severely limits the data which can be obtained from them.

Careful examination of the remains may reveal that not all are human. Burnt animal bones may be found in cremation burials. These may represent food offerings, sacrifices, or parts of hides or furs in which the corpse may have been wrapped before burning (Bond & Worley, 2004, 2006; Kirkinen, 2017).

Even small fragments that cannot be identified to specific skeletal element may bear clues as to whether they are human or non-human. For example, the cortical bone of large animals, like cattle or horses, is markedly thicker than that of human long-bones. Animal bones may have trabecular structures that are coarser or finer than that characteristic of human bones. Non-human mammal bone often has a smoother cortical surface than does human bone.

For unburnt bone, fragments that cannot be positively identified as human or non-human on morphological grounds can usually be identified using proteomics (analysis of proteins). This is possible because the amino acid sequence in collagen differs between species. The most common laboratory method is known as 'zooarchaeology by mass spectrometry', or ZooMS for short (Buckley et al., 2009; Charlton et al., 2016; Welker, 2018). However, because

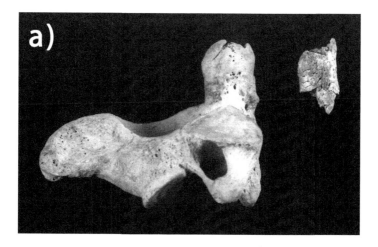

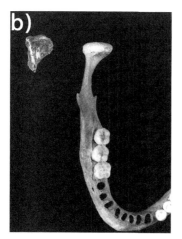
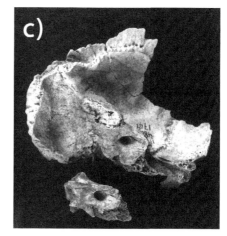

Figure 13.6 Commonly occurring fragments in cremation burials: (a) the odontoid process of an axis vertebra; (b) a mandibular condyle; (c) the petrous part of a temporal bone. Unburnt bones are shown next to each cremated specimen to illustrate where the cremated fragments come from

the organic fraction is destroyed during cremation, this is not viable for burnt bone. There are some differences in microstructure between human and animal bones, so examination of microscopic features may be useful in identification. Human bone tends to differ from bone of domestic animal species in terms of the diameter of the Haversian canals and osteons. Bone microstructure generally survives burning (Imaizumi et al., 2014), but these features may alter in size during cremation (Ellingham et al., 2015) which complicates matters. There are also differences in the frequency of Volkmann's canals, and in qualitative aspects such as the arrangement of osteons (Hillier & Bell, 2007; Brits et al., 2014; Mulhern, 2016) which, whilst not absolute, may, in many cases, allow a distinction to be made.

Given that in most cremation burials there is a huge number of tiny fragments which are unidentifiable, it is clearly impractical to apply microscopic analysis to attempt to confirm each one as human or non-human. However, in some circumstances, judicious application of microscopic analysis may be warranted. If one could identify some burnt bone fragments in a collection of burnt material from an archaeological feature as human or non-human, this might have major implications for its archaeological interpretation. For example, animal bone alone might suggest a hearth, human bone a pyre or the remains of a cremation burial.

Estimation of age at death

Because teeth which were unerupted at time of death may survive intact in cremated material, in some child burials dental development can be used as an age indicator. In cremated bone of immature skeletons, fragments of unfused epiphyses may be noted. However, because different epiphyses fuse at different times, difficulties in identification to specific skeletal element hamper the use of this technique. In instances where dental development cannot be used for ageing immature remains, one is often reduced to using the fragments to gain an impression of the general size of the bones, and using this to give a very approximate guide to age at death.

It was argued in Chapter 4 that dental wear and, potentially, cementochronology, may be the best ways of estimating age at death in adult remains. The destruction of tooth crowns means that dental wear is not a viable method for most cremation burials. Tooth roots often survive burning wholly or partially intact (Schmidt, 2015). Thermal alteration to the cementum makes counting of the incremental lines problematic (Gocha & Schutkowski, 2013). It may still be possible to apply cementochronology, but results are likely to be less reliable than for unburnt remains (Oliveira-Santos et al., 2017). Because bone microstructure generally survives cremation, bone histological ageing methods can potentially be applied. However, in addition to the difficulties with these methods outlined in Chapter 4, in burnt bone there are problems caused by thermal alterations in osteon size. Many of the other parts of the skeleton which have been used as indicators of age at death (Figure 4.14) tend to survive poorly the cremation process. For example, for the large assemblage of cremated bone from Spong Hill, England, dating from the 5th–early 6th century AD (Hills & Lucy, 2013), in only 4% of cases did the pubic symphysis survive (McKinley, 1994: 16).

The relative ease with which cranial vault fragments can be picked out facilitates the use of cranial suture closure over other methods of ageing adult cremated remains. The uncertain reliability of this method has already been referred to in Chapter 4, and in cremations its use is further complicated as, with a bone fragment, it is often difficult to identify which part of a suture one is dealing with. This is important, as published ageing schemes rely on scoring closure at different sites in the various cranial vault sutures (Perizonius, 1984; Meindl & Lovejoy, 1985). Nevertheless, some idea of the general state of suture closure can often be gained. On occasions, signs of joint degeneration may be visible, in the form of pitting or porosis of the joint surfaces or osteophyte formation at the joint margins. In modern populations such changes are not common before middle age. If we can assume that the same was true in antiquity then they may be used, to some extent at least, as auxiliary age indicators. However, the safest course is often to classify fully mature material (i.e. when fragments seem to come from adult-sized bones and there is no evidence of unfused epiphyses) simply as adult and not to attempt any finer age distinctions.

Assessment of sex

The highly fragmented and distorted nature of cremated bone makes it very difficult to gain an impression of bone shape. This makes the use of the sexing criteria outlined in Chapter 4 problematic. Sometimes though, by happy chance, diagnostic areas survive, often parts of the skull such as the nuchal crest or brow ridge areas. If such fragments are not available, sex may have to be determined from the general size and robusticity of the skeleton, as inferred from the bone fragments. However, it must be borne in mind that in a population which was generally of heavy build an excess of males may be identified; the converse is likely in groups of slender build. An additional complication in sex determination is the shrinkage suffered by bone during cremation. It is important to take at least a subjective account of this when attempting to gain an impression of the general size and robusticity of the skeleton from cremated remains.

Unsurprisingly, in view of the problems discussed above, sex can usually only be determined in a fairly modest proportion of burials. For example, Kirsty Squires examined over 800 cremation burials from Elsham and Cleatham, two 5th–7th century AD sites in eastern England (Squires, 2012). In only 50% of the adults could any identification of sex (however tentative) be made, and in only 19% could sex be assigned with confidence.

The study of normal and pathological skeletal variation

The nature of the material means that metric studies, of the type described in Chapters 5 and 6, play little part in the analysis of cremated bone. Although non-metric variants and disease-related changes may sporadically be noted, little useful data on the frequencies of these features can be obtained.

Biomolecular analyses

In cremations where combustion of the organic component is incomplete, sufficient collagen may remain for carbon and nitrogen stable isotope ratios to be determined. However, heating leads to alterations in $\delta^{13}C$ and $\delta^{15}N$ in collagen (DeNiro et al., 1985; Schurr et al., 2015), so in burnt bone they are not useful indicators of palaeodiets.

Strontium isotopic ratios, and carbon and oxygen stable isotope ratios, can be measured in the mineral fraction of bone. In unburnt bone this is normally avoided because its propensity for chemical exchange with the burial environment means that values are unlikely to be indicative of those obtaining during life. However, the more ordered and compact microstructure of thoroughly burnt bone seems to make it resistant to post-depositional alteration (Snoeck et al., 2015, 2016). Strontium isotopic ratios appear unaltered by heating (Snoeck et al., 2015), meaning that they may still be useful for mobility studies. Cremation does cause alterations in bone mineral $\delta^{13}C$ and $\delta^{18}O$ (Munro et al., 2007, 2008; Snoeck et al., 2014b, 2016). In pyre-burnt remains, a prime cause appears to be intake of carbon dioxide from the combustion of fuel in the pyre (Snoeck et al., 2015, 2016). This means that, unlike for unburnt bone, they cannot be used for dietary and mobility studies; nevertheless, as the following study illustrates, results may still be useful.

Snoeck et al. (2018) carried out isotopic analyses on cranial bones from the cremated remains of 25 individuals excavated from Stonehenge. The burials date from the period 3180–2380BC, around the time of the monument's initial construction. Fifteen individuals returned strontium isotopic ratios consistent with the chalk geology that is local to Stonehenge. The others had signals consistent with older geologies. This might be con-sistent with those individuals having an origin in west Wales, the place where the famous bluestones, that form an early construction phase of the monument, are thought to come from. These 'non-locals' tended to have lower $\delta^{13}C$ values in their bone mineral. $\delta^{13}C$ in pyre-cremated bone largely reflects that in the wood used as fuel; the depressed $\delta^{13}C$ may relate to the so-called 'canopy effect' (see Chapter 11). This suggests that the wood used as fuel for these cremations may have come from a more heavily forested environment than the rather open prehistoric landscape around Stonehenge. This again would be consistent with west Wales. At least some of these non-locals may have been cremated elsewhere, and their burnt remains brought to the Stonehenge area for burial, possibly in conjunction with the transport and raising of the bluestones (Snoeck et al., 2018).

Experimental evidence (Imaizumi et al., 2014) indicates that DNA cannot be amplified from bone exposed to more than about 250°C. Consistent with this, attempts to obtain DNA from petrous temporal bones from prehistoric cremations have failed (Hansen et al., 2017).

Cremated bone and ancient funerary practices

In part due to the limitations on what can be learnt in the fields of demography, normal skeletal variation and palaeopathology, much work on cremated bone has concentrated on the study of ancient funerary practices. The following sections discuss firstly how we can estimate the temperature of firing, and secondly what can be learnt about burial practices from studying the weights of bone present in ancient cremations.

Temperature of firing

The temperature reached in funerary pyres has long been thought a key aspect of early cremation practices. It is an indication of the thoroughness with which the corpse was burnt, and it is dependent upon aspects of 'pyre technology' – the ways in which the pyre was constructed and tended. It is also dependent upon notions in ancient societies of what was considered an appropriate level of incineration of a corpse – modern crema-toria thoroughly cremate a body, leaving only calcined remains, but this need not have been viewed as either necessary or desirable in earlier cultures.

In addition to study of the bone, sometimes remains of artifacts burnt on the pyre with the body can give clues as to the temperatures reached. I examined bone from some early Anglo-Saxon (5th–7th century AD) cremation burials from Mucking, England (Mays, 2009). The X-ray diffraction pattern showed narrow, sharp peaks (Figure 13.7). Comparison with Figure 13.1 shows that this is consistent with exposure to temperatures of more than about 600°C. The colour of the bone fragments was predominantly white,

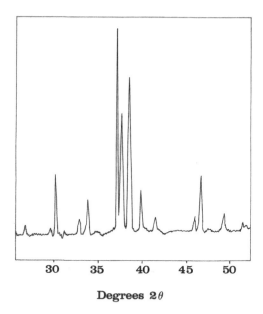

Degrees 2θ

Figure 13.7 X-ray diffraction pattern from a cranial fragment from a Mucking cremation. The fragment was white in colour, suggesting exposure to a temperature in excess of about 600°C. The sharp peaks on the X-ray diffraction spectrum are consistent with this (compare with Figure 13.1)

Note: The peaks in this spectrum occur at slightly different diffraction angles (2θ) than those in Figure 13.1; this is because radiation of a different wavelength was used to produce this spectrum – the overall pattern is unaffected.

which would also be consistent with this. The lack of any significant further changes in X ray diffraction pattern or colour in bone heated to temperatures beyond about 600°C means that we cannot say anything more precise about firing temperature at Mucking on the basis of this evidence. However, some bone fragments had blobs of melted glass (Figure 13.8) or splashes or molten bronze adhering to them. These must come from artifacts cremated with the body. Chemical analysis of the glass (Finney, 1996), showed a composition typical of Anglo-Saxon soda-glass used in the manufacture of beads. Earlier work (Wells, 1993) showed that this becomes fully molten at about 940°C. Copper melts at 1085°C, but the melting point of bronze, a copper-tin alloy, usually with a tin content of less than 20%, would be somewhat lower, probably about 800–1000°C (Turner-Walker, 2009: Figure 1.2). Taken together, the state of the bone and the remnants of artifacts are consistent with a pyre temperature in excess of about 950°C. At Mucking, there was a predominance of oak in the charcoal assemblages from the cremations (Hather, 2009). This is consistent with the evidence for high firing temperatures: oak has a high calorific value and gives a long-lasting burn (Martín-Seijo & César Vila, 2019).

The temperatures attained in the Mucking pyres need not surprise us. In a series of experimental wood camp-fires made using oak and other Mediterranean hardwoods, Stiner et al. (1995) recorded temperatures of 900–1000°C using a thermocouple. Wahl (1982),

Figure 13.8 A section through a cranial vault fragment from one of the Mucking cremations showing a fused mass of glass on its outer surface

working in Mainz, Germany, noted the general similarity in appearance between ancient cremations and bone fragments recovered from a furnace at a modern crematorium. He comments on the high efficiency of firing that this shows could be achieved in ancient times.

A team led by Tim Thompson, of Teesside University, studied cremation practices at Roman period (late 1st-early 5th century AD) military sites in Britain (Thompson et al., 2016). To investigate intensity of firing using bone from the burials, they studied a number of variables, including bone colour, but the main technique was FTIR. The main burial sites they focussed on were Carlisle and Beckfoot, which lay in the vicinity of Hadrian's Wall, a fortification that marked the effective northern limit of the Roman Empire, and two legionary fortresses further south, at Lincoln and Malton.

They applied FTIR (using a specific method known as attenuated total reflectance spectroscopy) to long-bone fragments from a total of 49 individuals. A number of parameters were calculated, but they concentrated particularly on the crystallinity index (CI) and the carbonate: phosphate ratio (C/P). The results, together with some data from the 5th-6th century AD Anglo-Saxon burials from Elsham, in Lincolnshire, are shown in Figure 13.9.

The CI and C/P values are fairly similar across the four Roman sites (Figure 13.9). This indicates little difference in cremation intensity between them. Thompson et al. (2016) argue that this suggests a shared cultural model of what constituted appropriate funerary practice. The data concentrate around a CI of approximately 3.5-4.0 and a C/P of about 0.1-0.2. Comparison with figure 13.2 indicates that this is suggestive of a moderate degree of firing with sustained maximum temperatures of about 500-600°C. An even temperature

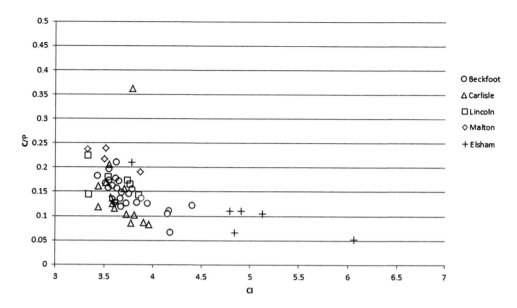

Figure 13.9 Crystallinity index (CI) plotted against carbonate: phosphate ratio (C/P) for bone samples from four sites from Roman Britain, and from Anglo-Saxon Elsham, in eastern England. Both CI and C/P were measured using Fourier transform infra-red spectroscopy using attenuated total reflectance mode

Source: adapted from Thompson et al. (2016: Fig. 8).

throughout an ancient cremation pyre is unlikely, so some variation around this value would be expected, meaning that, in a given burial, some elements may have been exposed to these temperatures only briefly or may have only reached lesser temperatures. As discussed above, destruction of bone's organic part tends to occur at about 275–500°C, so in some instances heat-exposure may not have been sufficient for its complete combustion. The colour of the fragments was consistent with this. At each site, remains exhibited a range of colours. Some were white, showing calcination; others showed darker colours (e.g. brown, black) characteristic of incomplete destruction of organics. At the largest site, Beckfoot, charcoal remains showed that the predominant fuel was alder and hazel (Thompson et al., 2016). These burn quickly, so perhaps pyres were short lived so that some parts did not have the chance to attain high temperatures, or did so only briefly.

At Elsham, the CI was higher, and the C/P generally lower than at the Roman sites. Comparison with Figure 13.2 indicates that this is consistent with more intense firing of remains at Elsham. It is tempting to see this as evidence of a cultural difference in the approach to cremation in the Roman and Anglo-Saxon periods, but in view of the small sample size (they only had results from 6 individuals from Elsham), Thompson et al. (2016) refrain from making any generalisations.

As we have seen, methods such as FTIR and XRD can give numeric outputs that are related to intensity of firing of bone. Recent studies (e.g. Krap et al., 2019) are beginning to do the same with colour, using a technique called colourimetry in which colours are expressed in terms of numerical coordinates (e.g. combinations of red/blue/green values). These are significant steps forward in our study of cremated bone. Not only can burning intensity be studied graphically (as in the above example), but this also provides data on burning intensity that can readily be analysed statistically, meaning that patterned differences between groups can potentially be tested and validated.

Burial practices

A number of workers have measured the ash-weight of the human skeleton (e.g. Malinowski & Porawski, 1969; Trotter & Hixon, 1974; McKinley, 1993; Warren & Maples, 1997; Bass & Jantz, 2004; van Deest et al., 2011; Gonçalves et al., 2013). The ash-weight is the weight of the mineral portion of the skeleton that remains after combustion. Weights reported vary widely. In the studies cited above, for adults of European ancestry, mean skeletal ash-weights for males range from 2004g to 3380g; for females from 1539 to 2350g. In general, for adults, female weights are about 65–70% of those of males. Skeletal ash-weight declines somewhat with adult age, particularly in females.

Skeletal weight is correlated both with stature and with body weight (Warren & Maples, 1997; May, 2011). In general, the higher mean skeletal ash-weights tend to come from recent studies of US populations (Warren & Maples, 1997; Murad, 1998; Bass & Jantz, 2004; van Deest et al., 2011). The well-known secular trends toward increased stature and, especially, higher body weight, characteristic of recent Western populations, are likely to be factors behind this. It would seem probable that results from older studies more closely resemble skeletal ash-weights likely for individuals from ancient populations. Data from the work by Trotter and Hixon (1974), which used cadavers from individuals dying in the first half of the 20th century, are shown in Table 13.1. However, even these are likely to over-estimate values for ancient humans because there has been a secular trend for an increase in the thickness of long-bone cortices. Cortical thickness for archaeological groups has been consistently reported as somewhat lower than that in mid-20th-century populations. This reflects less acquisition of cortical bone during the growth period, probably due to poorer nutrition in antiquity (Mays, 2008a).

In archaeological burials, it is rare to find cremations containing the full amount of bone expected from a cremated corpse (McKinley, 2013) even where there is no evidence for loss of bone through post-depositional disturbance of the burial. The phenomenon of 'missing' bone from cremation burials was apparent at a Romano-British (2nd century AD) burial site at Rectory Farm, Godmanchester, England (Mays, 2019b). Some of the burials had suffered

Table 13.1 The ash weight of the human skeleton

Age group	Mean weight (grams)
0–6 months	54
6 months–3 years	185
3–13 years	661
13–25 years	2,191
Adult	1,919 (males 2,288 [range 1,534–3,605], females 1,550 [range 952–2,278])

Source: Figures calculated from Trotter and Hixon (1974).

damage due to deep ploughing of the site in recent times, but many remained undamaged. Twenty-eight undamaged urns contained the remains of only one adult individual each. The bone, which generally had a white, well-fired appearance, was recovered from the earth fills of the pots by sieving through a stack of sieves of 4mm, 2mm, and 0.5mm mesh. Only the residue retained by the 4mm sieve was sorted. The mean weight of bone from these burials was 777g (Figure 13.10). This is less than half of the bone that might be expected if each burial contained the complete remains from a cremated body.

One possibility in explaining the relative lack of bone initially appeared to be that the shortfall might be made up by the bone in the unsorted (and hence unweighed) fractions retained by the mesh sizes 2mm and under. However, scanning these residues showed that in fact they contained little bone. Even if these fractions had been sorted and the bone fragments weighed, they would have added little to the overall bone weights. It might also be suggested that some trabecular bone may have crumbled to dust and hence been lost, but against this, many trabecular bone fragments were in fact present, and in any case trabecular bone makes a fairly modest contribution to the overall weight of the skeleton compared with the much denser cortical bone. These two factors certainly cannot account for the 'missing' bone.

It might be argued that destruction of much cremated bone had taken place whilst the burials lay in the soil. As already discussed, cremated bone is markedly more resistant to destruction in the soil than is unburnt bone. In addition to the cremations, there were

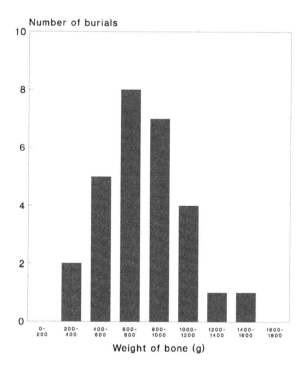

Figure 13.10 The distribution of bone weights from the adult cremation burials from Godmanchester

also a few Romano-British inhumations at Godmanchester (Mays, 1993b, 2019b). Undis-turbed adult inhumations were skeletally fairly complete, but many bones showed super-ficial soil erosion. By contrast, there was no surface erosion visible on the cremated bone. It seems unlikely that there were substantial losses of cremated bone when the less resistant unburnt bone survived well and the fragments of cremated bone which were present showed no evidence of eroded surfaces.

It is also possible that weight of bone may alter whilst it is in the soil. Few studies of this phenomenon have been conducted, but the indications are that alterations to the weight of calcined cortical bone (which forms the bulk of the remains at Godmanchester) are minor (Amarante et al., 2019).

There was no evidence for burning of the soil in the area that the cremation urns were buried; the pyres must have been outside the excavated area. A likely source for most of the bone loss is during collection of remains from the pyre in antiquity prior to burial.

Some cremations contained fragments of charcoal, but amounts were generally small. This suggests that bone was picked out from the pyre for burial fairly carefully. If bone and other materials were simply picked up haphazardly and put in an urn we would expect a lot more charcoal. If we are right in our inference that bone was carefully col-lected, why are the burials so short on bone? One possibility seemed to be that the limit-ing factor was the capacity of the pot. However, in most cases the pots do not seem to have been filled: the amount of bone found in them was very much less than they could have held, even allowing for some post-depositional settling and fragmentation. It is pos-sible that some uncombusted pieces of wood and soft tissue survived the pyre and were placed in the urns but have since decayed. Although this possibility cannot be completely discounted, the presence of such material would seem at odds with the thorough firing of most of the bone fragments and the apparent care with which they were collected.

Even if it is accepted that the pots were unlikely ever to have been completely filled with bone, it could be argued that the size of pot might still have been an influence on the amount of bone collected, the tendency being to collect a larger amount of bone for a larger pot. To test this hypothesis, I investigated whether there was a relationship between quantity of bone and vessel volume (the sizes of the pots varied quite a lot). No evidence of any such relationship was found (Figure 13.11): vessel volume did not seem to have influenced the amount of bone collected.

The amount of bone in the pots shows that it must have been an important part of funerary practices to collect a substantial quantity of bone from the pyre for burial, a token amount was clearly not acceptable. Equally, however, it cannot have been important to try and collect all the bone. It is possible that many smaller fragments of bone may have been inadvertently overlooked when the bone was picked out of the pyre for burial in antiquity. However, practical experiments (Piontek, 1976) show that bone fragments are quite easy to spot and retrieve from pyre remains, even by the inexperienced, and in the Godmanchester urns quite small fragments were indeed present. It may be, rather, that a certain quantity (perhaps about 600-1000g) appeared to those involved in the funerary rituals at Godmanchester to be a sufficient or appropriate amount to collect and bury. The fairly marked central tendency in the distribution of bone weights (Figure 13.10) would appear to support this – if there was no set notion of what constituted a seemly amount for burial we might expect a more random spread of weights.

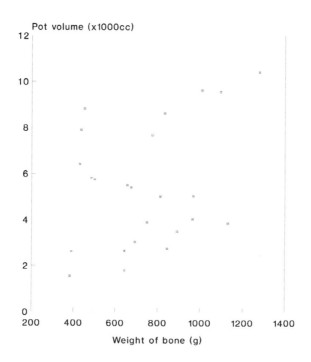

Figure 13.11 Pot volume versus the weight of bone recovered from adult Godmanchester cremations

Although the above scenario provides a plausible way of accounting for the distribution of bone weights at Godmanchester, it is an interpretation which must remain tentative, not least because of the relatively small number of burials upon which it is based. Nevertheless, it does, together with the earlier discussion, serve to illustrate the sort of information concerning ancient funerary practices potentially available from the study of cremated bone from archaeological sites.

Summary

Although inhumations are the most frequently encountered archaeological human remains, cremation was practiced in many ancient cultures, either exclusively or alongside inhumation. Depending upon the area of the world in which they work, most osteoarchaeologists deal with cremated human remains, either on a frequent or occasional basis. Archaeologically, most burnt human remains come from deliberate burials of cremated bone, although some come from the remains of pyre sites.

Temperatures in ancient cremations frequently reached 800–1000°C, similar to those in modern crematoria. Burning of bone to these temperatures results in loss of water, combustion of the organic component and alterations to the structure and composition of the inorganic fraction. During cremation there is fragmentation of bones and teeth. Tooth crowns usually disintegrate into tiny fragments. Bone fragments more than a few centimetres long are rare in most archaeological cremations. The fragments also suffer shrinkage and distortion. Cremated bone tends to survive better in hostile soil conditions than does unburnt bone.

Because of the nature of burnt bone, it is often not possible to identify sex in cremated human remains nor to determine age at death more precisely than adult versus child. Studies of metric and non-metric variation, and analyses of pathological conditions play little part in the study of cremated bone. The application of DNA analyses is problematic, but some information can be obtained from isotopic studies. Most work on archaeological cremations concentrates on elucidating ancient funerary practices. Valuable insights may be gained concerning pyre temperatures. Traditionally, colour of bone fragments has been used to shed light on this, but X-ray diffraction (XRD) and Fourier transform infra-red spectroscopy (FTIR) are increasingly being used for this purpose as well. The use of multiple techniques is likely to provide the fullest picture of firing intensity. Analysis of other variables, such as quantity of remains present, can shed light on other aspects of funerary practices.

Further reading

Various edited volumes on the study of archaeological cremation burials have appeared in recent years. Cerezo-Román, J., Wessman, A. & Williams, H., eds (2017). *Cremation and the Archaeology of Death.* Oxford University Press, Oxford *concentrates on cremation in prehistoric and protohistoric Europe. Another collection of archaeological studies, from Europe and North America, is* Kuijt, I., Quinn, C.P. & Cooney, G., eds (2014) *Transformation by Fire: The Archaeology of Cremation in Cultural Context.* University of Arizona Press, Tucson. *The emphasis in these two volumes is mainly on the socio-cultural interpretation of cremation burials.*

Thompson, T., ed. (2015) *The Archaeology of Cremation: Burned Human Remains in Funerary Studies.* Oxbow, Oxford, *and* Schmidt, C.W. & Symes, S.A., eds (2015), *The Analysis of Burned Human Remains* (second edition). Academic Press, London *are collections of papers on archaeological (and, particularly in the case of the latter, also forensic) burnt human remains. Compared to the Cerezo-Román et al. and Kuijt et al books described above, both these volumes have more of an emphasis on scientific methods for analysing remains.*

If you are looking for a snappy guide to ways of estimating firing temperature from burnt bones, read Ellingham, S.T.D., Thompson, T.J.U., Islam, M. & Taylor, G. (2015). Estimating Temperature Exposure of Burnt Bone – A Methodological Review. *Science & Justice* 55: 181–188. *For those hungry for more detail on diffractometric and spectroscopic methods for examining burnt bone, a user-friendly introduction is*: Mamede, A.P., Gonçalves, D., Marques, M.P.M. & Batista de Carvalho, L.A.E. (2018). Burned Bones Tell Their Own Stories: A Review of Methodological Approaches to Heat-Induced Diagenesis. *Applied Spectroscopy Reviews* 53: 603–635.

14 Ethics and human remains

Because human remains are the remnants of once living people, they have a special significance in all human societies. In many countries, the distinct status of human remains in archaeology is recognised under law (Márquez-Grant & Fibiger, 2011). For example, in England, special legal permission is needed to excavate an archaeological site that includes human burials (Mays, 2017: Figure 1).

The special nature of human remains means that dealing with them raises moral issues that do not arise with other sorts of archaeological finds. Scientists have a duty to consider the moral implications of what they do, especially as most scientific work is undertaken with public funds. There is a tacit social contract that science should act in the interests of society and will conduct itself in accordance with high ethical standards (Jones, 2007). Ethics is a coherent system of values concerned with moral aspects of human conduct. Ethical principles are therefore useful in providing a basis for moral decisions concerning the treatment of human remains.

What constitutes respectful treatment of the dead varies widely between different cultures. The treatment of human remains may be a source of disagreement and may arouse strong feelings. Osteoarchaeologists must familiarise themselves with the legal framework and behavioural norms pertaining to human remains of the country in which they are working

Most archaeological excavations of human remains are not initiated by archaeologists but are necessary because a burial ground is to be built over or otherwise destroyed by development. As we shall see, in some countries (for example, Israel) disturbance of human remains is itself controversial. In general though, there is an acceptance, albeit tacit, that sometimes the dead must make way for the living. This is especially so in densely populated areas, where pressure on land is intense and ancient burial grounds are often threatened by development. In countries with a developed archaeological sector, archaeological excavation of ancient remains is undertaken in advance of construction work.

An important area regarding ethics and archaeological human remains concerns what should happen to them once they have been excavated. The nub of the matter is generally whether remains should be kept in museums and other institutions, primarily for the purposes of research, or whether they should be reburied. This is probably the oldest ethical debate relating to archaeological human remains, and it continues to be of prime importance today, so it is to this topic that most of this chapter will be devoted. However, it is also worth noting that, in the last ten years or so, ethical debates have begun to broaden out to encompass other issues. In part, this has been driven by recent advances in scientific techniques and in digital applications.

Analytical innovations in proteomics, DNA analyses and stable isotopic studies, as described in previous chapters of this book, have meant that museum curators are being faced with increasing requests for destructive analyses of human remains in collections under their care. The tension between the potential for generation of new knowledge using these methods, and the need to keep collections intact for future researchers, is at the heart of many of the ethical dilemmas that this raises (Mays et al., 2013; Fox & Hawks, 2019). The rise of social media platforms has fuelled online trading in human remains. This commodification of human remains for financial gain is ethically objectionable, so professional osteological organisations feel that it is important to try to stamp it out (e.g. https://babao.org.uk/publications/ethics-and-standards/); Huffer and Charlton (2019) set out some of the ethical issues involved. The ethical implications of making images of human remains (Harries et al., 2018) and disseminating them online (Errickson & Thompson, 2019) are now beginning to be explored. Increasing consideration is also being given as to how we can communicate our research to the public, for example via popular media, in a way that is engaging and attracts interest, whilst avoiding rendering what are often quite complex stories simplistic, and minimising the risks that our results will be distorted or sensationalised (Buikstra, 2019b).

Retention versus reburial of human remains

Activism for return ('repatriation') of human remains, normally for reburial, has been a feature in some countries formerly colonised by Europeans, particularly in North America and Australasia. In a movement that gathered pace in the 1980s, indigenous groups have, with a large degree of success, claimed for reburial collections of aboriginal human remains. These remains were dug up, or otherwise obtained, mainly in the late 19th and 20th centuries, by non-indigenous archaeologists or other scientists, and held in museums and other research institutions, both in their home countries and around the world (Plate 11). In some other countries, religious groups are pressing for reburial of human remains. In the sections below, I explain some of the arguments both in favour of reburial, and in favour of retention of remains for study. I follow this with a brief review of the situation regarding retention versus reburial of human remains in some different areas of the world.

Why rebury human remains?

Groups who make claims for return of human remains present diverse cases, but perusal of the literature (e.g. Mihesuah, 2000; Quigley, 2001; Fforde et al., 2002; Weiss, 2008; Nilsson Stutz, 2013; Colomer, 2014; Rathouse, 2016; Jenkins, 2016a; Colwell, 2017; Svestad, 2019) identifies a number of common themes. Claimants see the retention of remains in museums as offensive to their spiritual/religious beliefs. The aim, from the claimants' point of view, is to take control of remains, which they perceive as theirs, normally so that they can be reburied or otherwise 'laid to rest' according to the cultural traditions of the claimant group. For indigenous minorities, return of remains is often seen as a step toward restitution for injustices suffered by their ancestors during a period of colonial domination. Claimants may also assert that continued retention of remains in a museum perpetuates grief in their community, which can only be assuaged by their return and reburial. There is usually also a political dimension. Return of remains helps claimant communities assert their cultural identity, and may be part of other political processes aimed at bolstering the rights of indigenous groups in former colonies of European powers. It may also be seen as a step toward recognising past wrongs and aiding reconciliation.

The argument that the knowledge to be gained from the scientific study of human remains is important sometimes cuts little ice with indigenous groups. It may be felt that archaeological or other scientific knowledge is a Western construct and of little value to people who already 'know' their own past through oral traditions and religious beliefs. Knowledge gained from scientific study may be viewed not only as superfluous but also as potentially subversive as it may conflict with established beliefs and may lead to the questioning of authority of traditional religious leaders (Lambert & Walker, 2019).

Why keep human remains in museums?

If, as I fondly imagine, you are reading this book from cover to cover, earlier chapters should have shown you that study of human remains can reveal important insights into past lives. Most would consider the acquisition of knowledge a significant benefit for humanity (Scarre, 2003). Hence osteoarchaeology is a worthy pursuit. Retention of human remains for study is fundamental to the survival of osteoarchaeology as a science. Some might suggest that skeletal material can be reburied following osteological recording of data for use by future workers. However, recording of data from a collection cannot substitute for the availability of the collection itself. For one thing, it is impossible to predict what future researchers, working on research projects as yet unformulated, might require in the way of data. This is illustrated by the data-recording protocols implemented in the USA as a response to the reburial of collections. Data from this massive recording exercise has been available to scholars since the mid-1990s. However little use has been made of it. Analysis of 691 primary research articles on human remains published in the period 2001–2007 showed that only five made use of data from existing skeletal databases; 686 required study of skeletal collections curated in museums or elsewhere (Mays, 2010a).

It is fundamental to the scientific method that the data and conclusions of earlier workers can be reassessed, and re-examination of remains is essential for this. Innovations in techniques also enable new data to be obtained from old collections. This may help new light to be shed on questions that have long been of interest. For example, in Britain, many Neolithic tombs were excavated many years ago. Then, as now, a focus of examination of skeletal remains was to reconstruct population affinities. Traditionally, this was done using cranial morphology. Whilst this approach remains valid today, measurements applied to assess the morphology of these crania have been updated over the years (see Chapter 5), and morphological studies have recently been complimented by analysis of these remains for DNA (Chapter 12). In addition, changes in theoretical orientation of academic disciplines mean that we continue to ask new questions of existing skeletal collections. Sticking with our example of remains from Neolithic tombs, recent work on them has yielded new insights into mortuary ritual (see Chapter 3), diet (see Chapter 11) and other aspects of the lives of these early farmers (Smith & Brickley, 2009). The above considerations mean that important collections are returned to time and again by researchers (Roberts & Mays, 2011). Loss of human remains for reburial is therefore a loss of information about our past.

Repatriation and reburial of human remains around the world

In the USA, the Native American Graves Protection and Repatriation Act (NAGPRA) was passed into law in 1990. This required publicly funded museums to inventory their Native American skeletal remains and offer them for return to affiliated indigenous claimant groups.

Affiliation is established on the basis of preponderance of evidence based on geography, kinship, biology, archaeology, linguistics, folk-lore, oral traditions, historical evidence and other information. Establishing this was intended to ensure that any claimant had a reasonable connection with the remains (Ousley et al., 2005). However, about three-quarters of human remains in American Museums could not be affiliated to tribe in this way. In 2010, NAGPRA was amended so that provision was made to transfer unaffiliated remains to Native American groups with present-day or historical connections to the land upon which the remains were found (NAGPRA, 2013).

Since the passage of NAGPRA in 1990, many thousands of human remains have been repatriated to Native American groups. Occasionally, solutions have been reached whereby remains are placed under Native American control but there is continued access for scientific study (Lambert & Walker, 2019), but the overwhelming majority have been reburied. Reburial places them beyond the reach of science, and this is likely to be permanent, due to loss of contextual integrity and because fragile remains deteriorate rapidly once reinterred (e.g. During, 1997; Weiss, 2008: 90). By 2006, remains representing about 30,000 individuals had been affiliated to tribe and repatriated (Weiss, 2008: 71-72). Since then, affiliated remains have continued to be repatriated as, since 2010, have unaffiliated remains. In the nine years since the 2010 amendment, nearly 16,000 sets of unaffiliated remains have been claimed, which is about 12% of total museum holdings of such remains (NAGPRA, 2019).

Reburial of Native American remains under NAGPRA had an immediate impact on osteoarchaeology. In the 15 years following its passage, the proportion of research papers on Native American remains published in the American Journal of Physical Anthropology, the major US journal in the discipline, fell by half compared with the previous 15 years (Weiss, 2008: 69-71).

In Australia, any remains predating AD1770 are legally aboriginal and are therefore under the control of aboriginal authorities. This has led to removal of remains from museums in Australia for reburial by aboriginal groups. They, with the support of the Australian government, have also been active in making claims for return of Australian aboriginal remains held in museums in other countries. Various museums in the Europe and North America have repatriated remains (Weiss-Krejci, 2016). Major collections have been reburied. Australian research on indigenous skeletal remains has effectively ceased; osteoarchaeologists in Australia now focus their work on remains from other countries (Pardoe, 2013).

The New Zealand government established a repatriation programme for Native New Zealand (Maori) remains in 2003. Remains have been repatriated from Museums around the world, and museums in New Zealand have also handed over remains to Maori tribal representatives. Maori tribal groups have the authority to determine the disposal of Maori remains, and they may sometimes allow scientific research. For example, osteologists, working collaboratively with Maori communities, conducted a project on a site at Wairau Bar.

Burials there were some of the oldest in New Zealand. A variety of analytical studies were carried out and produced important information concerning the earliest settlement of the islands (Buckley & Petchey, 2018; Gilmore et al., 2019). The remains were reburied afterwards, but the project may stimulate future collaborative research.

In Canada, a Royal Commission on Aboriginal peoples was established in 1991 to encourage museums to return voluntarily indigenous remains to appropriate First Nations groups (First Nations is the Canadian term for indigenous peoples). This has resulted in large-scale reburial of material (Weiss, 2008: 52–54).

Although Central and South American countries have a colonial past, there has not been a concerted movement by indigenous groups toward reburial of human remains. Museums in Latin America hold large collections, and it is commonplace to see both skeletonised and mummified remains on display in public galleries. Latin America is a large and culturally diverse region, and reasons for differences in attitudes to human remains here compared with indigenous groups further north are equally complex and diverse, but a few factors can be highlighted. The customs and beliefs of many Andean and Central American indigenous cultures emphasise interacting with rather than shunning the dead. Display of ancient human remains by indigenous communities in museums and cultural centres may be an important assertion of cultural identity, showing how their ancestors cared for their dead (Overholtzer & Argueta, 2017). In many parts of the region, people often have a mixed background, with both indigenous and non-indigenous ancestry, so that categorising them into opposing 'indigenous' and 'non-indigenous' communities may be inappropriate (Retamal et al., 2018). In addition, in many cases, indigenous contributions to the past have been integrated into a national identity that is important to all citizens (Ubelaker & Grant, 1989).

In northern Europe, there are certain parallels, in terms of debates over cultural heritage, between the indigenous Sámi people and indigenous groups in North America and Australasia. The Sámi are indigenous to northern mainland Scandinavia. In their ancestral region, cemetery sites were excavated by non-Sámi, and remains removed to museums further south. Sámi heritage has been marginalised in the narratives of the national pasts of the Scandinavian countries rather than being incorporated into mainstream national identity (Nilsson Stutz, 2016). In recent years, Sámi have had considerable success in obtaining the return of human remains from Finnish, Swedish and Norwegian Museums. Mostly these have been reburied, but some have been deposited in museums in Sámi communities (Svestad, 2019).

Agitation for reburial, primarily on religious grounds, has occurred in some other countries. In Israel, ultra-orthodox religious groups object to the handling and disturbance of human remains. This arises from their interpretation of the part of the Halakha, the Jewish religious laws, that relates to burials. This maintains that Jewish burials should remain eternally undisturbed. However, the arguments of the Halakha do not resonate equally for all Jews. What they should mean in practice depends heavily upon rabbinical interpretation, and upon the branch of Judaism that is applied (Colomer, 2014). Ultra-orthodox religious groups take a fundamentalist approach to the Halakha, refusing to make accommodations for secular society. They wield considerable political power in Israel. Violent protests have been orchestrated at archaeological excavations at burial grounds. In 1992, excavations of ossuaries in Jerusalem led to three days of rioting. In

1994, the government's chief legal advisor ruled that human remains found on archaeo-logical sites should not be considered as archaeological material but should be trans-ferred to the Ministry of Religious Affairs for immediate reburial. In Israel, it is illegal to move excavated human remains to a laboratory for study; brief osteological recording on-site is all that is permissible (Hallote & Joffe, 2002; Nagar, 2002, 2011).

In most of Europe, unless remains are associated with some minority faith groups, for example Jews (Sayer, 2010: 79–82; Colomer, 2014), excavation and study of burials does not normally attract significant controversy. Nevertheless, current, normative cultural practices concerning disposal of the recently dead differ in different countries, and this seems to colour attitudes toward archaeological burials when it comes to the question of reburial of remains. In southern Europe, it is usual for grave plots in cemeteries to be rented for a certain period of time (e.g. 5 years), during which the body decays to a skeleton. The bones are then exhumed, so that the grave can be reused, and placed in an ossuary of some sort or else otherwise disposed of. For example, in Portugal, if the relatives agree to pay a fee, the exhumed bones are put in a stone block compartment, otherwise they are buried in a communal grave or incinerated. In several Portuguese cities, universities or museums have obtained legal permission to collect unclaimed skel-etons, and through this they have built up some internationally renowned research collec-tions where age at death and other biographical information can be linked to individual remains (Alves-Cardoso, 2019). Research collections in other southern European countries have been assembled in similar ways (e.g. Eliopoulos et al., 2007; Alemán et al., 2012), as have some in South American countries whose religious and burial traditions derive from those in southern Europe (e.g. García-Mancuso et al., 2019). In northern Europe, where this translation of skeletal remains is not now practiced, the grave has come to be viewed as the final resting place for human remains. The influence of this on attitudes toward arch-aeological burials is seen in the Church of England's stance on reburial of archaeological human remains from Christian burial grounds.

In England, both secular and ecclesiastical laws may apply to archaeological burials. The secular laws do not generally mandate reburial. When reburial does occur, it is often due to cost and logistical considerations when large burial grounds are impacted by development (some 19th century British burial grounds contain thousands of burials (Mays et al., 2015)). Reburial as a result of these factors is becoming a significant prob-lem in British archaeology, and has been a prime reason why some large and important skeletal collections have been lost.

In England, for human remains excavated from land under Church of England jurisdic-tion, Ecclesiastical Law applies in instead of secular law. This means that permission to excavate them is required from the Church of England. In practice this applies to church-yards. Most churchyards in Britain have been in use for many centuries, and may contain burials more than 1000 years old.

In Christian theology, although the mortal remains have no import for the resurrected life of the individual, they should be treated with respect. In keeping with the idea of the grave as final resting place, the Church of England interpret this as meaning that burials should not be disturbed without good reason, and if they must be disturbed they should, following their exhumation, be returned to a consecrated place, unless there is compel-ling reason not to do so (Mays, 2017).

Although the Church of England is not averse to scientific research on human remains, permissions for excavation of human remains under Ecclesiastical Law normally carry the proviso that they be reburied at some specific point in the future. For collections of high research value, Church authorities are normally open to arguments for extending this period. For example, this has been done with the collection of 18th–19th century burials from Christ Church, Spitalfields in London, referred to earlier in this book (see Chapter 4, for example): the Church has periodically renewed permission for them to be kept in the Natural History Museum in London. Nevertheless, the feeling of the Church is that, even for highly important collections, remains should ultimately be reinterred in consecrated ground (Mays, 2017). As a general solution, in 2005 the Church of England and English Heritage (then the chief advisor to the UK Government on archaeology in England) agreed a policy whereby such collections could be retained in redundant or par-tially redundant churches. This fulfils the Church's desire that remains be returned to consecrated ground (redundant churches remain consecrated, theologically speaking) whilst ensuring that remains continue to be available for study. For example, the excava-tions in the churchyard of St Peters Church, Barton-upon-Humber, yielded more than 2700 skeletons dating from the 10th–19th century AD. St Peter's Church is now redun-dant, and this internationally important collection is now stored there (Figure. 14.1) where it continues to be available for scientific research (Mays, 2013).

(a)

Figure 14.1 (a) St Peter's Church, Barton-upon-Humber, is now no longer used for worship. It is under the care of English Heritage and is open to the public. (b) The interior houses an exhibition on the history of the church and on what has been learnt from the scientific study of the remains excavated from the churchyard, and features some of the skeletons excavated from the site. (c) The skeletons from the site not used in the exhibition are stored in a separate area behind the blind arcading. This is not accessible to the public. The human remains are available for study by researchers by arrangement. A committee composed of members of Historic England, English Heritage, the local community and an external advisor, oversees research access to the remains

Source: (a) Warwick Rodwell; (c) Joseph Elders.

(b)

(c)

Figure 14.1 (Continued)

In Britain, there is no widespread public pressure for the wholesale reburial of existing collections of remains of British origin housed in museums and elsewhere. However, some practitioners of modern Pagan religions (such as Druidism) have pressed for reburial of prehistoric remains which, for them, hold spiritual significance. Although this is not a widespread movement, it does raise some interesting issues, and demands for reburial have been made for some important collections. This is further discussed later on in this chapter.

Decisions concerning treatment of human remains

Decisions concerning the treatment of human remains potentially need to take into account the moral interests of both the living and the dead. However, the degree to which the dead can be said to have moral interests is controversial (e.g. Scarre, 2003; Ott, 2012; Boonin, 2019). To some extent, current guidelines devised for ethical treatment of human remains appear to assume that they do. For example, in Britain, cremation followed by interment of the remains was sometimes suggested as a way of disposing of archaeological human remains after study when reburial is mandated. In a document giving ethical and other guidance for the treatment of excavated burials from Christian sites in England (Mays, 2017), it was felt that this method was normally inappropriate. This was not because this course of action was felt likely to offend the living. Cremation is the most frequent way of disposing of the dead in Britain today. However, it was not practiced in Britain prior to about 1880 and would have been anathema to Christians before this. It was this consideration in relation to the moral interests of the dead which led the working group which produced that document to regard cremation as normally inappropriate for Christian remains from archaeological sites. However, in instances where remains potentially pose a health risk (for example in some cases with extensive soft tissue survival), health and safety considerations were pre-eminent over the (presumed) wishes of the dead, and under those circumstances it was felt that cremation of remains was permissible.

Although the dead may have moral interests, it may be that they hold them only in attenuated form and that they may often be subservient to those of the living. In addition, in archaeological cases, they are on an individual basis normally unknowable. Most legal frameworks and non-statutory guidelines for treatment of human remains, particularly those dealing with the question of retention or reburial, mainly concern themselves with the moral interests of the living.

A framework for evaluating claims for reburial of human remains in Britain

In some countries, statutory frameworks, for example in the USA provided by NAGPRA and other legislation, govern the way in which claims for repatriation of human remains are dealt with. More often, procedures for handling claims are not enshrined in law. In such cases, museums and other institutions have a need for professional guidelines for decision-making. In Britain, the government Department of Culture, Media and Sport (DCMS) assembled an expert committee to produce a national set of guidelines covering the care of human remains in museums. The resulting document (Swain, 2005) included guidance for handling requests for return of remains.

A museum or other institution holding human remains may be considered to have stewardship of the material. That is, they hold it in trust for the benefit of the wider community and for the benefit of future generations. An important part of this benefit is in the form of knowledge which may be derived from study of the material. There is thus a moral imperative toward preservation of collections. On the other hand, sometimes this benefit may be outweighed by harm caused by retention of remains to particular groups or communities who have special links with the remains. When a claim for remains is received, these considerations need to be weighed in the balance. Ethical principles are helpful in guiding thinking in such instances. The DCMS guideline adopted the following principles:

1. Non-maleficence. This means doing no harm, whether to a community or to the general public, wherever possible.
2. Respect for diversity of belief. For example, this requires a museum to recognise that a community may place a particular cultural value on remains even if this is not shared by others.
3. Respect for the value of science. Individuals and communities now and in the future benefit from the fruits of scientific knowledge.
4. Solidarity. This means furthering humanity via cooperation and consensus in relation to human remains. This means that efforts should be made toward finding a consensus among competing interests that all parties can accept.
5. Beneficence. Ensuring that your actions have good outcomes wherever possible. This might include preserving knowledge for the benefit of humanity or respecting the wishes of an individual or community by returning remains for reburial.

Of course, in reality these principles may frequently come into conflict with one another. This is particularly so when dealing with claims for reburial. Because of this, more detailed practical guidance is also needed. The DCMS document therefore outlines a set of criteria that can be used to evaluate a claim. As with frameworks like NAGPRA, a key consideration is establishing the nature of the links between the claimants and the remains. Both genetic and cultural links are considered, but given that most archaeological remains are not of known personal identity, it is cultural links that are normally crucial. Under the DCMS guidelines, for a valid claim, the claimants should normally be able to demonstrate continuity of beliefs, customs or language, or else be able to demonstrate why this was not the case (e.g. due to disruption of indigenous culture during the colonial period (Swain, 2005: 26-27)). The DCMS guidance notes that demonstrating cultural continuity far back into the past is usually difficult, so that claims for remains over about 300 years old are unlikely to be successful and are unlikely to be considered for remains over 500 years old. In addition, even when a claimant has established a valid link with the remains being claimed, this does not mean their claim will automatically succeed. The guideline states that museums need to be willing to consider the views of all those with interests in the remains, with no one view having automatic pre-eminence (Swain, 2005: 13).

When a valid link has been established, other criteria which have a bearing on the strength of a claim include how the remains were initially acquired (if remains were acquired without dispute that weakens the claim; if they were acquired against the will of local communities that strengthens it), the spiritual and religious significance of the remains to the claimant community, the value of the remains for contributing to scientific and historical knowledge, and the fate of the remains if returned. In keeping with the ethical principal of solidarity (see above) the guideline urges that when dealing with valid claims, efforts should be made to proceed through compromise and consensus. The DCMS guideline was crafted in order to provide a common framework for dealing both with claims for repatriation of material from overseas indigenous groups, and with any claims for reburial of remains excavated from British archaeological sites.

Claims for repatriation by indigenous groups of remains of overseas origin

The DCMS guidelines have been widely adopted by museums in Britain as a basis for assessing claims for repatriation of human remains from indigenous overseas communities. This has resulted in rejection of some claims, either because they fail to satisfy the DCMS criteria or because the scientific benefits of retaining the remains were thought to outweigh the arguments for repatriation, but some important remains have been repatriated (Wellcome Institute, 2013; McKinney, 2014; Pitt Rivers Museum, 2017; Clegg, 2020). Among these latter are remains of 138 individuals from the Torres Strait area of northern Australia, whose release was agreed by the Natural History Museum in London (Clegg & Long, 2015). The Natural History Museum has long had engagement in repatriation issues, and has used this as an opportunity to build relationships with the living descendants of some of the peoples whose human remains they hold. This would seem to be in keeping with the ethos of the DCMS guideline, and in practical terms those ties mean that indigenous communities can learn more about the work of the museum, and what scientific study of remains actually involves, and museum staff can understand more about indigenous cultures (Clegg, 2020: 117). Forging these sorts of links may help build trust and establish common ground for the future between museums and indigenous peoples.

Modern pagans and reburial of British prehistoric remains

Modern Pagans are a somewhat diverse group, but they share spiritual beliefs which are broadly 'nature orientated', and prehistoric monuments, such as stone circles and burial mounds, hold spiritual significance (Rountree, 2015; Doyle White, 2016). Particular Pagan traditions include Wicca and Druidism. Whilst many Pagans take their cues from what they perceive to have characterised pre-Christian spirituality, the modern Pagan movement essentially dates from the second half of the 20th century (for example Wicca was invented in the 1950s by a retired British Civil Servant), although its ethos can arguably be traced to the Romantic movement of the 18th and 19th centuries (McIntosh, 2004). Paganism has only a small number of adherents; in the most recent British National Census, about 0.2% of the population professed a Pagan religion.

As might be expected, given the diversity of Pagan belief systems, there is also a diversity of views among Pagans concerning what constitutes respectful treatment of human remains and whether reburial is desirable (White, 2019). Nevertheless, in 2006 a Druidic organisation, calling themselves The Council of British Druid Orders (CoBDO) submitted a request for reburial of some human remains (and associated grave goods) from a major prehistoric monument in southern England.

Avebury is a large prehistoric stone circle in Wiltshire (Figure 14.2). CoBDO's claim for reburial concerned some prehistoric human remains excavated in the vicinity of the monument and which were kept in the museum at Avebury. The claim was submitted to English Heritage (EH) and the National Trust (NT), who jointly administered the site. All three parties agreed that the claim should be assessed using the DCMS guideline (Swain, 2005).

Figure 14.2 Part of Avebury stone circle
Source: The National Trust.

English Heritage were my employers at the time, and I was involved in their assessment of this claim.

In their submission, CoBDO argued that holding of the remains in the museum severed the connection between the ancestors and the land, and this was a cause of pain to the Druid community. Reburial was needed to correct this injustice. They made no claim to cultural continuity with the remains, but argued that, as indigenous British, they do have a genetic link (CoBDO, 2008).

In considering this claim, EH and the NT took a view that, because there is no reason to believe that modern Pagans are any more closely related to Neolithic people than anyone else in Britain, any genetic link between them and the remains is not a specific and close genealogical link in the sense meant in the DCMS guideline. EH and the NT recognised the spiritual importance of the Avebury monument and landscape to members of modern Druid orders but pointed out that these are important to many other people as well – there is widespread interest in archaeology in Britain. The scientific importance of the remains was assessed. The Avebury monument complex is of international significance and the human skeletal material buried there is of similar high importance, and is a major source of evidence regarding our understanding of Avebury and surrounding monuments. In addition, one of the skeletons subject to the claim for reburial was on display in the Avebury Museum. This display had an important educational role and provided the public with an enhanced understanding of the prehistory of Avebury, and a survey showed it was popular with visitors (English Herritage & The National Trust, 2008).

It was felt that, as well as evaluating the claim itself, it was important to take into account wider opinion on the matter. For this purpose, a public consultation was set up. CoBDO's claim and a draft report on the case prepared by EH and the NT, together with other supporting documentation were placed on the EH and the NT websites. Invitations to comment were sent out to a list of 78 individuals and organisations drawn up by CoBDO, EH and the NT. The existence of the consultation was also widely publicised and it was open to anyone at all to respond. Responses were received from a total of 73 organisations and 567 individuals. As regards the eventual fate of the remains, consult- ees were asked to choose which of three options they thought best: reburial, reburial in such a way as to permit continuing public and research access to remains, and retention in the museum with access (where reasonable) for CoBDO and other groups. Ignoring a small number of 'don't knows' responses in favour of these three were 5%, 5% and 90% respectively (Thackray & Payne, 2009).

Responses to a consultation may not be a good guide to the views of the general public. This is because in this case those who responded were selected by the claimants or by those who ran the site, or else were people who had heard about the consultation and felt motivated to respond. Because of this, EH approached a professional opinion-polling com- pany to conduct a survey into public attitudes. This took the opportunity to focus not simply on the Avebury question but on broader public attitudes to the question of keeping archaeological human remains in museums. The reason for this was to provide a general background against which the Avebury decision could be taken, and to provide information that might inform broader policy regarding human remains from archaeological sites. In surveys of public opinion, the way in which questions are framed can affect the answers one receives, especially for topics such as this, to which most people have probably not previously devoted much thought. Taking advice from a professional polling organisation helped ensure that questions were framed as neutrally as possible. Results of the poll showed, that of 864 respondents, 91% felt that museums should be allowed to keep human bones from archaeological digs for research purposes (Mills & Tranter, 2010).

Considering the evidence, EH and the NT felt that CoBDO's claim failed on the DCMS criteria. This, coupled with the results of the consultation and the public opinion poll, led EH and the NT to decide to refuse the request for reburial and to continue to keep the remains in Avebury Museum (Thackray & Payne, 2010).

Following this process, there was some criticism of EH and the NT from people who thought we had spent disproportionate resources on assessing what they felt was a claim from a fringe group. This point also emerged in the consultation (Thackray & Payne, 2009, 2010), and has in the past been made to me at archaeological meetings, sometimes rather forcefully! However, simply because a group is small does not mean that their case does not deserve a fair hearing. In the years leading up to the claim, some academics and museum staff were quite vocal in supporting this and other Pagan reburial claims for prehistoric remains. However, their responses following the Avebury decision have been rather muted (e.g. Wallis & Blaine, 2011; Wallis, 2015). I think that the systematic and open way in which the case was evaluated has played a part in this. In general, applying proper procedure helps ensure transparency of decision-making, and helps to show that cases have been dealt with equitably. In addition, it was intended that the Avebury case would act as a reference point, helping to simplify matters for those considering similar claims in the future. In the years leading up to the Avebury claim, Pagan groups, although small, were becoming increasingly vocal regarding prehistoric human remains, and some museums clearly felt under pressure from them. In a commentary on British human remains and Pagan groups, Liz White (White, 2019) believes that, since the Avebury case, requests for reburial of prehistoric remains have abated. It is difficult to be certain, but, save for a few exceptions, this is also my impres- sion. The Avebury example may have acted as a useful precedent. I also think that the public opinion poll, commissioned as part of that exercise, has helped more broadly, placing deci-sion-making regarding human remains on a more confident footing.

Display of human remains in museums

Most countries in Europe hold in their museums large collections of human remains that have been excavated over the years from archaeological sites. It is also usual to see human remains among the displays in public galleries (Nilsson Stutz, 2016) – so the Ave-bury Museum is quite usual in that respect.

In general terms, the purpose of displaying human remains in museum galleries is to help public understanding and engagement with archaeology (Nilsson Stutz, 2016; Williams, 2016) and, on occasion, with other subjects, such as early medicine (Bekvalac, 2015). The DCMS guideline supports public display of remains when it is justified in these terms (Swain, 2005: 20). Being able to relate a narrative of a person's life, con-structed through osteoarchaeology, to the real, physical remains of that particular individual, provides a uniquely powerful and personal connection to the past for a museum visitor. In archaeological galleries, displays of skeletal remains help to humanise and populate a past which, if presented solely using displays of artifacts, can sometimes appear rather remote and impersonal. Human remains, properly integrated into dis-plays of other types of archaeological evidence, may act as a focus to help to bring to life for visitors something of what it may have been like to be a person living in an ancient community.

Evidence confirms the appeal that museum displays of human remains hold for the visiting public. Special exhibitions featuring archaeological burials draw large numbers of visitors (Swain, 2006; Redfern & Bekvalac, 2013). There have been a number of surveys in Britain of the attitudes of visitors to museums toward human remains. Results (Table 14.1) have consistently shown strong support for their display in public galleries. Of course, these are only the views of people who have chosen to visit museums. However, the wider public also seems supportive. A question in the public opinion survey commis-sioned by English Heritage, referred to above, was whether people thought museums should be allowed to display human bones from archaeological digs – 91% said that they should (Mills & Tranter, 2010).

Although displays of archaeological human remains are regularly seen in British museums, they are not wholly without controversy, but the nature of this may not

Table 14.1 Surveys of visitors to museums in England to gauge support for display of archaeological human remains in museum galleries.

Museum	Year	Number of respondents	Percentage in favour of display	Reference
Avebury Museum	1999	465	91%	Cleal (2000)
Petrie Museum	2002	100	81%	Kilmister (2003)
Museum of London	2004	99	88%	Museum of London (2005)
Museum of London	2005	162	99%	Swain (2006)
Wellcome Institute	2008	803	99%	Aldous & Payne (2009)
Museum of London	2008	100	92%	Gopinath (2008)
Manchester Museum	2009	412	91%	Manchester Museum (2009)

always be as anticipated by museum professionals. In 1984, the remains of a body were dug up from a peat bog at Lindow Moss, Cheshire, in north-west England. The remains had been rather damaged by the peat cutting machinery, but the conditions in the bog had resulted in substantial preservation of soft tissue, including skin and hair (Plate 12). The remains come from 1st century AD. This bog body, known as 'Lindow Man', is of national importance, and is kept on display at the British Museum in London (Joy, 2009, 2014).

In 2008, Lindow Man's remains were loaned for temporary exhibition to Manchester Museum (which is quite close to where the remains were found). This exhibition was quite controversial. It tried to provide views of Lindow Man from different perspectives, including from an archaeologist, someone from the local community and (presumably because Iron Age Lindow Man comes from pre-Christian times) from a Pagan (Exell, 2016). This, together with the fact that there was relatively little information given about the Iron Age, left many visitors to the exhibition baffled, the story of Lindow Man's life being rather submerged beneath a welter of different modern-day personal opinions and reflections (Jenkins, 2016b). Manchester Museum also assumed that the public was becoming increasingly 'sensitive' to the display of human remains. Having raised with focus-groups the question of whether Lindow Man's remains should now be reburied, they attempted to use the body as an opportunity to promote wider debate over the question of display of human remains in museums. Perhaps not surprisingly in view of the results of visitor opinion surveys that had been conducted up to that time (Table 14.1), the issue failed to gain much traction with the general public.

The reality is that there was public controversy over the display of Lindow Man's remains. However, this has centred not on *whether*, but on *where* his remains should be displayed. When the remains were first taken to the British Museum in the 1980s there was a campaign for their 'repatriation' for display at a museum in northwest England, close to where they were found. Because of his national importance, Lindow Man's permanent home is at the British Museum, but, as a compromise, the remains have been regularly loaned out, not only to Manchester but also to other regional museums to make them more accessible around the country (Joy, 2014).

In general, museums are centres for community engagement with the past. The public fascination with human remains means that archaeological burials are often the centre-pieces of displays of local archaeology (e.g. Tatham, 2016). They may also be foci for special projects that involve active community participation (e.g. www.heritageeastbourne. co.uk/ancestors.aspx). As archaeological excavations, including those of burial grounds, increasingly see it as important to offer opportunities for community engagement (Figure. 14.3), showing results of new excavations, including where relevant, displays of human remains, in local museums may become increasingly expected by the public (e.g. Sayer & Sayer, 2016).

Osteoarchaeology in the wider world

In the last thirty years, the success of repatriation claims from indigenous groups has led to large-scale losses of museum collections of human remains, particularly those originating from North America and Australasia. Loss of a significant part of its evidence-base

Figure 14.3 Visitors to the excavations of the 6th century AD (Early Anglo-Saxon) cemetery at the village of Oakington, England. People were encouraged to visit the site and to talk to the archaeologists

Source: Sayer & Sayer (2016: Figure. 7.3).

cannot be good for any science, and there is little doubt that this has had a serious impact on osteoarchaeology as practiced in those parts of the world. Nevertheless, most osteoarchaeologists, whilst mourning the loss of information, feel that it is probably right to cede authority for control over remains to modern communities who have strong and demonstrable links to them.

In North America and Australasia, many museum curators actively supported the indigenous repatriation movement. To them (Colwell, 2017), the panorama of empty shelves in museum stores that once held human remains might instil a feeling of satisfaction in a job well done, and a sense that indigenous groups have to a great extent won out over the scientists in the 'bone wars'. Another view (Lambert, 2012; Pardoe, 2013) is that the years spanning the late 20th and early 21st centuries, with the mass reburial of human remains that took place, may be looked upon in future as the time at which large chunks of the indigenous past were forever erased by taking actions that had irreversible consequences. In many instances, this occurred in response to a fractious political climate that existed at that time. Some museum curators were guilty of helping to create such a climate by polarising debates, making compromise solutions more difficult to broker.

One feature that many repatriation claims have in common is that there is a 'clash of cultures' between the values of the claimants on the one hand, based on religious or other spiritual beliefs, and the scientific rationalism of those who would study the remains. Wider engagement between osteoarchaeologists and indigenous groups may increase mutual understanding, meaning that the 'clash of cultures' becomes less intense and there is more common ground. On the one hand, osteoarchaeologists who deal with indigenous remains are learning more about traditional indigenous cultures and perspectives. On the other hand, communities currently hostile to science may begin to see it less as a threat but rather as complimentary to other ways of looking at indigenous pasts. In some regions, more indigenous people are becoming archaeologists with an interest in preserving remains in such a way that they are potentially accessible to research in future (Clegg, 2020). Finding common ground, building trust and formulating collaborative projects will, one hopes, enable a future to be built for indigenous osteoarchaeology.

In most other parts of the world, attitudes regarding human remains are very different, but being mindful of wider opinion regarding burial archaeology is no less important. In Britain, public interest in archaeology, and in burial archaeology in particular, is high. The public is supportive of retention of human remains in museums for research purposes, and expects to see museum displays of archaeological human remains that showcase the results of that research. Archaeology and human remains are often important to community identity and people may expect remains from the local area to be displayed in local museums rather than being sent elsewhere. Building community engagement into fieldwork and laboratory-based archaeological research projects is increasingly routine. The ethical importance of this is recognised by research councils and increases the chances of projects being funded. As well as carrying out good science, osteoarchaeologists need to play a part in ensuring that community involvement with burial archaeology is undertaken in an engaging and appropriate way.

Summary

Human remains, as the remnants of once-living people, have a special significance in all human societies. Their study in archaeology raises profound moral issues over and above those involved in dealing with other classes of archaeological finds. Although archaeological burials are important for the information that they can provide about the past, they may also be important to other communities for a variety of reasons. There may sometimes be disagreement over their treatment, and these disputes may arouse strong feelings.

Ethics is a system of values concerned with moral aspects of human conduct. Ethical principles are useful for providing guidance in moral decisions concerning the treatment of archaeological human remains. In a few countries, even removing human remains to make way for roads, buildings or other construction work is controversial, but the most pressing ethical issues more often revolve around what to do with remains once they have been excavated: whether to keep them in a museum or to rebury them. On the one hand, keeping them will enable current and future generations to learn from them. In many countries, the public is strongly supportive of this. In some countries, however, groups with close biological or cultural affinities to the remains may feel that retaining remains in a museum offends their religious beliefs and that social justice demands that authority be ceded to them to rebury or otherwise treat remains as they see fit.

Moral arguments can be found to support both retention and reburial of human remains. When there are opposing views, compromise solutions should be sought when appropriate, but in reality, reconciling conflicting opinions may be difficult or impossible. Frameworks for dealing with claims from descendant groups demanding return of remains for reburial have been provided in some countries by the legal system (for example, the USA), and in others (for example, Britain) by non-statutory guidelines.

Activism toward reburial of museum collections of remains has been most prominent among indigenous groups in former colonies of the European powers in Australasia and North America. Many human remains excavated from archaeological sites have been reburied in response to indigenous and other activists. Whilst mourning the loss of data, many osteoarchaeologists concede that when links between claimants and the material claimed are strong, then the case for ceding control over remains to their modern descendants carries moral force. Rebuilding an indigenous osteoarchaeology in these countries is likely to depend upon osteoarchaeologists and indigenous groups finding common ground and developing collaborative projects. In many other countries, such as Britain, the public is supportive of the retention, study, and display of human remains in museums, but being mindful of public opinion concerning what constitutes appropriate treatment of human remains is no less important. Building community engagement into archaeological projects is increasingly routine. The high public interest in skeletal remains means that, provided it is done appropriately, projects involving osteoarchaeology provide a good opportunity for increasing public appreciation and understanding of our past.

Further reading

Nilsson Stutz, L. (2013). Claims to the Past: A Critical View of the Arguments Driving Repatriation of Cultural Heritage and Their Role in Contemporary Identity Politics. *Journal of Intervention and Statebuilding* 7(2): 170–195 *provides a general overview of some of the issues behind repatriation of indigenous human remains.*

For a personal account of what it was like being an osteologist at the sharp end of the repatriation debate in Australia read Pardoe, C. (2013). Repatriation, Reburial, and Bioarchaeological Research in Australia, pp. 733–762 in L. Nilsson Stutz & S. Tarlow (eds) *The Oxford Handbook of the Archaeology of Death and Burial.* Oxford University Press, Oxford.

Williams, H. & Giles, M., eds (2016). *Archaeologists and the Dead: Mortuary Archaeology in Contemporary Society,* Oxford University Press, Oxford *has a mainly European focus and concentrates particularly on public engagement, especially issues connected with museum display of human remains.*

Squires, K., Errickson, D. & Márquez-Grant, N., eds (2019). *Ethical Approaches to Human Remains. A Global Challenge in Bioarchaeology and Forensic Anthropology.* Springer, Cham *broadens the canvas still further by considering a wide spectrum of ethical debates that arise in connection with human remains.*

Bibliography

Åberg, G. (1995). The Use of Natural Strontium Isotope Ratios as Tracers in Environmental Studies. *Water, Air and Soil Pollution* 79: 309-322.

Abrahams, P. (1977). *Soil Report from Wharram Percy, North Yorkshire.* Ancient Monuments Laboratory Report 2360. Historic England, Portsmouth.

Acádi, G. & Nemeskéri, J. (1970). *History of Human Lifespan and Mortality.* Akademiai Kiado, Budapest.

Adachi, N., Kakuda, T., Takahashi, R., Kanzawa-Kiriyama, H., & Shinoda, K. (2018). Ethnic Derivation of the Ainu Inferred from Ancient Mitochondrial DNA Data. *American Journal of Physical Anthropology* 165: 139-148.

Adalian, P., Piercecci-Marti, M.-D., Bourlière-Najean, B., Panuel, M., Leonetti, G., & Dutour, O. (2002). Nouvelle Formule De Détermination De L'âge D'un Fetus. *Comptes Rendus Biologies* 325: 261-269.

Adams, D.C., Rohlf, F.J., & Slice, D.E. (2013). A Field Comes of Age: Geometric Morphometrics in the 21st Century. *Hystrix, the Italian Journal of Mammalogy* 24: 7-14.

Adams, W.Y., van Gerven, D.P., & Levy, R.S. (1978). The Retreat from Migrationism. *Annual Review of Anthropology* 7: 483-532.

Adler, C.J., Dobney, K., Weyrich, L.S., Kaidonis, J., Walker, A.W., Haak, W. et al. (2013). Sequencing Ancient Calcified Dental Plaque Shows Changes in Oral Microbiota with Dietary Shifts of the Neolithic and Industrial Revolutions. *Nature Genetics* 45: 450-455.

Aiello, L. & Molleson, T. (1993). Are Microscopic Ageing Techniques More Accurate than Macroscopic Ageing Techniques? *Journal of Archaeological Science* 20: 689-704.

Aikens, C.M. (2012). Origins of the Japanese People, pp. 55-65 in K.F. Friday (ed) *Japan Emerging: Premodern History to 1850.* Routledge, London.

Albert, A.M. & Maples, W.R. (1995). Stages of Epiphyseal Union for Thoracic and Lumbar Vertebral Centra as a Method of Age Determination for Teenage and Young Adult Skeletons. *Journal of Forensic Sciences* 40: 623-633.

Albert, M., Mulhern, D., Torpey, M.A., & Boone, E. (2010). Age Estimation Using Thoracic and First Two Lumbar Vertebral Ring Epiphyseal Union. *Journal of Forensic Sciences* 55: 287-294.

Alcmán, I., Irurita, J., Valencia, A.R., Martínez, A., López-Lázaro, S., Viciano, J. et al. (2012). The Granada Osteological Collection of Identified Infants and Young Children. *American Journal of Physical Anthropology* 149: 606-610.

Alexander, V., Lau, A., Beaumont, E., & Hope, A. (2015). The Effects of Surfing Behaviour on the Development of External Auditory Canal Exostoses. *European Archives of Otorhinolaryngology* 272: 1643-1649.

Allen, M.J. & Maltby, M. (2012). Chalcolithic Land-Use, Animals and Economy – A Chronological Changing Point? pp. 281-297 in M.J. Allen, J. Gardiner, & A. Sheridan (eds) *Is There a British Chalcolithic? People, Place and Polity in the Late 3rd Millennium.* Prehistoric Society Research Paper 4. Oxbow, Oxford.

Allentoft, M.E., Collins, M., Harker, D., Haile, J., Oskam, C., Hale, M.L. et al. (2012). The Half-Life of DNA in Bone: Measuring Decay Kinetics in 158 Dated Fossils. *Proceedings of the Royal Society of London B* 279: 4724-4733.

Allentoft, M.E., Sikora, M., Sjögren, K-G., Rasmussen, S., Rasmussen, M., Stenderup, J. et al. (2015). Population Genomics of Bronze Age Eurasia. *Nature* 522: 167-172.

AlQahtani, S.J., Hector, M.P., & Liversidge, H.M. (2010). The London Atlas of Human Tooth Development and Eruption. *American Journal of Physical Anthropology* 142: 481-490.

Alvesalo, L. (2009). Human Sex Chromosomes in Oral and Craniofacial Growth. *Archives of Oral Biology* 54S: S18-S24.

Alves-Cardoso, F. (2019). "Not of One's Body": The Creation of Identified Skeletal Collections with Portuguese Human Remains, pp. 503-518 in K. Squires, D. Errickson, & N. Márquez-Grant (eds) *Ethical Approaches to Human Remains: A Global Challenge in Bioarchaeology and Forensic Anthropology.* Springer, Cham.

Alves-Cardoso, F. & Henderson, C.Y. (2010). Enthesopathy Formation in the Humerus: Data from Known Age at Death and Known Occupation Skeletal Collections. *American Journal of Physical Anthropology* 141: 550-560.

Amarante, A., Ferreira, M.T., Makhoul, C., Vassalo, A.R., Cunha, E., & Gonçalves, D. (2019). Preliminary Results of an Investigation on Postmortem Variations in Human Skeletal Mass of Buried Bones. *Science & Justice* 59: 52-57.

Ambrose, S.H. (1993). Isotopic Analysis of Palaeodiets: Methodological and Interpretative Considerations, pp. 59-130 in M.K. Sandford (ed.) *Investigations of Ancient Human Tissue.* Gordon & Breach, Reading.

Amoroso, A., Garcia, S.J., & Cardoso, H.F.V. (2014). Age at Death and Linear Enamel Hypoplasias: Testing the Effects of Childhood Stress and Adult Socioecomonic Circumstances on Premature Mortality. *American Journal of Human Biology* 26: 461-468.

Amundson, R., Austin, A.T., Schuur, E.A.G., Yoo, K., Matzek, V., Kendall, C. et al. (2003). Global Patterns of Isotopic Composition of Soil and Plant Nitrogen. Global *Biogeochemical Cycles* 17(1) article 1031.

Anastasiou, E. & Mitchell, P.D. (2013). Palaeopathology and Genes: Investigating the Genetics of Infectious Diseases in Excavated Human Skeletal Remains and Mummies from Past Populations. *Gene* 528: 33-40.

Andersen, S.H. (1989). Norsminde. A 'Køkkenmødding' with Late Mesolithic and Early Neolithic Occupation. *Journal of Danish Archaeology* 8: 13-40.

Andersen, S.H. (1991). Bjørnsholm. A Stratified Køkkenmødding on the Central Limfjord, North Jutland. *Journal of Danish Archaeology* 10: 59-96.

Anderson, D.L., Thompson, G.W., & Popovich, F. (1976). Age of Attainment of Mineralisation Stages of the Permanent Dentition. *Journal of Forensic Sciences* 21: 191-200.

Anderson, T. (1994). Medieval Example of Cleft Lip and Palate from St Gregory's Prior, Canterbury. *Cleft Palate – Craniofacial Journal* 31: 466-472.

Anderson, T. (1996). Recovery and Identification of Rarely Encountered Bone Elements and Abnormal Calcifications. *Journal of Palaeopathology* 8: 111-118.

Anderson, T. (2001a). Two Decapitations from Roman Towcester. *International Journal of Osteoarchaeology* 11: 400-405.

Anderson, T. (2001b). A Recently Discovered Medieval Bladder Stone from Norwich, with A Review of British Archaeological Bladder Stones and Documentary Evidence for Their Treatment. *British Journal of Urology International* 88: 351-354.

Anderson, T., Arcini, C., Anda, S., Tangerud, A., & Robertsen, T. (1986). Suspected Endemic Syphilis (Treponarid) in Sixteenth Century Norway. *Medical History* 30: 341-350.

Angel, J.L. (1982). A New Measure of Growth Efficiency: Skull Base Height. *American Journal of Physical Anthropology* 59: 297-305.

Angel, J.L. & Olney, L.M. (1981). Skull Base Height and Pelvic Inlet Depth from Prehistoric to Modern Times. *American Journal of Physical Anthropology* 54: 197.

Ansorge, H. (2001). Assessing Non-metric Skeletal Characters as a Morphological Tool. *Zoology* 104: 268-277.

Anthony, D. (1997). Prehistoric Migration as Social Process, pp. 21-32 in J. Chapman & H. Hamerow (eds) *Migrations and Invasions in Archaeological Explanation*. British Archaeological Reports, International Series No. 664. Archaeopress, Oxford.

Anthony, D.W. (1990). Migration in Archaeology: The Baby and the Bathwater. *American Anthropologist* 92: 895-914.

Aplin, K., Manne, T., & Attenbrow, V. (2016). Using a 3-Stage Burning Categorization to Assess Post-Depositional Degradation of Archaeofaunal Assemblages: Some Observations Based on Multiple Prehistoric Sites in Australasia. *Journal of Archaeological Science Reports* 7: 700-714.

Arcini, C. (1999). *Health and Disease in Early Lund*. Investigationes de Antiqvitatibus Urbis Lundae VIII. Department of Community Health Sciences, Medical Faculty, Lund University, Lund.

Armelagos, G.J., Goodman, A.H., Harper, K.N., & Blakey, M.L. (2009). Enamel Hypoplasia and Early Mortality: Bioarchaeological Support for the Barker Hypothesis. *Evolutionary Anthropology* 18: 261-271.

Arnott, R., Finger, S., & Smith, C.U.M. (eds) 2003. *Trepanation: History, Discovery, Theory*. Swets & Zeitlinger, Abingdon.

Arora, N., Scheuenemann, V.J., Jäger, G., Peltzer, A., Seitz, A., Herbig, A. et al. (2016). Origin of Modern Syphilis and Emergence of a Pandemic *Treponema Pallidum* Cluster. *Nature Microbiology* 2: article 16245.

Arya, R., Duggirala, R., Comuzzie, A.G., Puppala, S., Modem, S., Busi, B.R., & Crawford, M.H. (2002). Heritability of Anthropometric Phenotypes in Caste Populations of Visakhapatnam, India. *Human Biology* 74: 325-344.

Ashbee, P. (1966). The Fussell's Lodge Long Barrow Excavations 1957. *Archaeologia* 100: 1-80.

Assis, S., Santos, A.L., & Roberts, C.A. (2011). Evidence for Hypertrophic Osteoarthropathy in Individuals from the Coimbra Skeletal Identified Collection (Portugal). *International Journal of Palaeopathology* 1: 155-163.

Assis, S., Keenleyside, A., Santos, A.L., & Cardoso, F.A. (2015). Bone Diagenesis and Its Implication for Disease Diagnosis: The Relevance of Bone Microstructure Analysis for the Study of Past Human Remains. *Microscopy and Microanalysis* 21: 805-825.

Athanasiou, K.A., Darling, E.M., Hu, J.C., DuRaine, G.D., & Reddi, A.H. (2017). *Articular Cartilage*, second edition. CRC Press, Boca Raton.

Atkinson, R.J.C. (1965). Wayland's Smithy. *Antiquity* 39: 126-133.

Aufderheide, A.C. & Rodriguez-Martin, C. (1998). *The Cambridge Encyclopaedia of Human Palaeopathology*. Cambridge University Press, Cambridge.

Auškalnis, A., Bernhardt, O., Putnienė, E., Šidlauskas, A., Andriuškevičiūtė, I., & Basevičienė, N. (2015). Oral Bony Outgrowths: Prevalence and Genetic Factor Influence. Study of Twins. *Medicina* 51: 228-232.

Axelsson, G. & Hedegard, B. (1981). Torus Mandibularis Among Icelanders. *American Journal of Physical Anthropology* 54: 383-389.

Ayliffe, L.K., Chivas, A.R., & Leakey, M.G. (1994). The Retention of Primary Oxygen Isotope Compositions of Fossil Elephant Skeletal Phosphate. *Geochimica et Cosmochimica Acta* 58: 5291-5298.

Baccino, E., Ubelaker, D.H., Hayek, L.C., & Zerelli, A. (1999). Evaluation of Seven Methods of Estimating Age at Death from Mature Human Skeletal Remains. *Journal of Forensic Sciences* 44: 931-936.

Bagchi, K. & Bose, A.K. (1962). Effect of Low Nutrient Intake during Pregnancy on Obstetrical Performance and Offspring. *American Journal of Clinical Nutrition* 11: 586-592.

Bahn, P.G. (2011). Religion and Ritual in the Upper Palaeolithic, pp. 344-357 in T. Insoll (ed) *The Oxford Handbook of the Archaeology of Ritual and Religion*. Oxford University Press, Oxford.

Baker, B.J. & Armelagos, G.J. (1988). The Origin and Antiquity of Syphilis. *Current Anthropology* 29: 703-737.

Baker, B.J., Dupras, T.L., & Tocheri, M.W. (2005). *The Osteology of Infants and Children.* Texas A&M University, College Station.

Baker, L. (2016). Biomolecular Applications, pp. 416-429 in S. Blau, S. & D.H. Ubelaker (eds) *Handbook of Forensic Anthropology and Archaeology* (2nd edition). World Archaeological Congress Research Handbooks in Archaeology. Routledge, London.

Bang, G. & Ramm, E. (1970). Determination of Age in Humans from Root Dentin Transparency. *Acta Odontologica Scandinavica* 28: 3-35.

Bard, K.A. (1989). The Evolution of Social Complexity in Predynastic Egypt: An Analysis of the Naqada Cemeteries. *Journal of Mediterranean Archaeology* 2: 223-248.

Barker, H., Hughes, M.J., Oddy, W.A., & Werner, A.E. (1975). Report on Phosphate Analysis Carried Out in Connection with the Cenotaph Problem, pp. 550-572 in R.L.S. Bruce-Mitford (ed.) *The Sutton Hoo Ship Burial* (Volume 1). British Museum, London.

Barnes, E. (2012). *Atlas of Developmental Field Anomalies of the Human Skeleton.* Wiley-Blackwell, Hoboken.

Bass, S., Saxon, L., Daly, R.M., Turner, C.H., Robling, A.G., Seeman, E., & Stuckey, S. (2002). The Effect of Mechanical Loading on the Size and Shape of Bone in Pre-, Peri- and Post-Pubertal Girls: A Study in Tennis Players. *Journal of Bone and Mineral Research* 17: 2274-2280.

Bass, W.M. (1987). *Human Osteology: A Laboratory and Field Manual* (3rd edition). Missouri Archaeological Society: Columbia.

Bass, W.M. & Jantz, R.L. (2004). Cremation Weights in East Tennessee. *Journal of Forensic Sciences* 49: 901-904.

Batchelor, P.A. & Sheiham, A. (2004). Grouping of Tooth Surfaces by Susceptibility to Caries: A Study in 5-16 Year-Old Children. *BMC Oral Health* 4: article 2.

Beach, J.J., Passalacqua, N.V., & Chapman, E.N. (2015). Heat-Related Changes in Tooth Colour, pp. 139-147 in C.W. Schmidt & S.A. Symes (eds) *The Analysis of Burned Human Remains* (2nd edition). Academic Press, London.

Beaumont, J. & Montgomery, J. (2016). The Great Irish Famine: Identifying Starvation in the Tissues of Victims Using Stable Isotope Analysis of Bone and Incremental Dentine Collagen. *PloS One* 11(8): e0160065.

Beaumont, J., Craig-Atkins, E., Buckberry, J., Haydock, H., Horne, P., Howcroft, R., Mackenzie, K. & Montgomery, J. (2018). Comparing Apples and Oranges: Why Infant Bone Collagen May Not Reflect Dietary Intake in the Same Way as Dentine Collagen. *American Journal of Physical Anthropology* 167: 524-540.

Bedford, J. (2017). *Photogrammetric Applications for Cultural Heritage.* Historic England, Swindon.

Bedford, M.E., Russell, K.F., Lovejoy, C.O., Meindl, R.S., Simpson, S.W., & Stuart-Macadam, P.L. (1993). Test of the Multifactorial Ageing Method Using Skeletons with Known Ages-at-Death from the Grant Collection. *American Journal of Physical Anthropology* 91: 287-297.

Bekvalac, J. (2015). The Display of Archaeological Human Skeletal Remains in Museum Exhibitions, pp. 114-121 in R. Redmond-Cooper (ed) *Heritage, Ancestry and the Law. Principles, Policies and Practices in Dealing with Historical Human Remains.* Institute of Art and Law, Builth Wells.

Bellamy, J. (1973). *Crime and Public Order in England in the Late Middle Ages.* Routledge, London.

Bello, S.M., Thomann, A., Signoli, M., Dutour, O., & Andrews, P. (2006). Age and Sex Bias in the Reconstruction of Past Population Structures. *American Journal of Physical Anthropology* 129: 24-38.

Benjamin, M., Kumai, T., Milz, S., Boszczyk, B.M., Boszczyk, A.A., & Ralphs, J.R. (2002). The Skeletal Attachment of Tendons – Tendon 'Entheses'. *Comparative Biochemistry and Physiology Part A* 133: 931-945.

Bennett, J.M. (1987). *Women in the Mediaeval English Countryside*. Oxford University Press, Oxford.

Bennike, P. (1985). *Palaeopathology of Danish Skeletons*. Akademisk Forlag, Copenhagen.

Bennike, P. (2006). Rebellion, Combat and Massacre: A Mediaeval Mass Grave at Sandbjerg Near Naestved in Denmark, pp. 305-318 in T. Otto, H. Thrane, & H. Vandkilde (eds) *Warfare and Society. Archaeological and Social Anthropological Perspectives*. Aarhus University Press, Aarhus.

Bentley, R.A. (2006). Strontium Isotopes from the Earth to the Archaeological Skeleton: A Review. *Journal of Anthropological Archaeology* 13: 135-187.

Bentley, R.A. & Knipper, C. (2005). Geographical Patterns in Biologically Available Strontium, Carbon and Oxygen Isotope Signatures in Prehistoric SW Germany. *Archaeometry* 47: 629-644.

Bentley, R.A., Price, T.D., & Stephan, E. (2004). Determing the 'Local' 87Sr/86Sr Range for Archaeological Skeletons: A Case Study from Neolithic Europe. *Journal of Archaeological Science* 31: 365-375.

Beresford, M. & Hurst, J. (1990). *Wharram Percy Deserted Medieval Village*. English Heritage/ Batsford, London.

Berg, G.E. (2002). Last Meals: Recovering Abdominal Contents from Skeletonised Remains. *Journal of Archaeological Science* 29: 1349-1365.

Bernard, A., Daux, V., Lécuyer, C., Brugal, J.-P., Genty, D., Wainer, K., Gardien, V., Fourel, F. & Jaubert, J. (2009). Pleistocene Seasonal Temperature Variations Recorded in the $\delta^{18}O$ of *Bison Priscus* Teeth. *Earth and Planetary Science Letters* 283: 133-143.

Berry, A.C. (1975). Factors Affecting the Incidence of NonMetrical Skeletal Variants. *Journal of Anatomy* 120: 519-535.

Berry, A.C. & Berry, R.J. (1967). Epigenetic Variation in the Human Cranium. *Journal of Anatomy* 101: 361-379.

Berry, R.J. (1979). Genes and Skeletons Ancient and Modern. *Journal of Human Evolution* 8: 669-677.

Berry, R.J. & Searle, A.G. (1963). Epigenetic Polymorphism in the Rodent Skeleton. *Proceedings of the Zoological Society of London* 140: 577-615.

Berryman, H.E. & Haun, S.J. (1996). Applying Forensic Techniques to Interpret Cranial Fracture Patterns in an Archaeological Specimen. *International Journal of Osteoarchaeology* 6: 2-9.

Bertrand, B., Oliveira-Santos, I., & Cunha, E. (2019a). Cementochronology: A Validated but Disregarded Method for Age at Death Estimation, pp. 169-186 in J. Adserias-Garriga (ed) *Age Estimation. A Multidisciplinary Approach*. Academic Press, London.

Bertrand, B., Cunha, E., Bécart, A., Gosset, D., & Hédouin, V. (2019b). Age at Death Estimation by Cementochronology: Too Precise to Be True or Too Precise to Be Accurate? *American Journal of Physical Anthropology* 169: 464-481.

Best, K.C., Garvin, H.M., & Cabo, L.L. (2018). An Investigation into the Relationship Between Human Cranial and Pelvic Dimorphism. *Journal of Forensic Sciences* 63: 990-1000.

Bethell, P.H. & Carver, M.O.H. (1987). Detection and Enhancement of Decayed Inhumations at Sutton Hoo, pp. 10-21 in A. Boddington, A.N. Garland, & R.C. Janaway (eds) *Death, Decay and Reconstruction*. Manchester University Press, Manchester.

Bevan, A., Colledge, S., Fuller, D., Shennan, S., & Stevens, C. (2017). Holocene Fluctuations in Human Population Demonstrate Repeated Links to Food Production and Climate. *Proceedings of the National Academy of Sciences of the USA* 115: e10524-e10531.

Bibby, B.G. & Mundorff, S.A. (1975). Enamel Demineralisation by Snack Foods. *Journal of Dental Research* 54: 461-470.

Bickle, P. (2018). Stable Isotopes and Dynamic Diets: The Mesolithic-Neolithic Dietary Transition in Terrestrial Central Europe. *Journal of Archaeological Science Reports* 22: 444-451.

Bidmos, M.A. (2005). On the Non-equivalence of Documented Cadaver Lengths to Living Stature Estimates Based on Fully's Method on Bones in the Raymond A. Dart Collection. *Journal of Forensic Sciences* 50: 501-506.

Bigman, D.P. (2014). Mapping Social Relationships: Geophysical Survey of a Nineteenth-century American Slave Cemetery. *Archaeological and Anthropological Sciences* 6: 17-30.

Bigoni, L., Velemínska, J., & Brůžek, J. (2010). Three-dimensional Geometric Morphometric Analysis of Cranio-Facial Sexual Dimorphism in a Central European Sample of Known Sex. *HOMO – Journal of Comparative Human Biology* 61: 16-32.

Bikle, D.D., Sakata, T., & Halloran, B.P. (2003). The Impact of Skeletal Unloading on Bone Formation. *Gravitational and Space Biology Bulletin* 16(2): 45-54.

Binder, M. & Roberts, C.A. (2014). Calcified Structures Associated with Human Skeletal Remains: Possible Atherosclerosis Affecting the Population Buried at Amara West, Sudan (1300-800BC). *International Journal of Paleopathology* 6: 20-29.

Binder, M., Eitler, J., Deutschman, J., Landstätter, S., Glaser, F., & Fiedler, D. (2016). Prosthetics in Antiquity – An Early Mediaeval Wearer of a Foot Prosthesis (6th Century AD) from Hemmaberg/Austria. *International Journal of Paleopathology* 12: 29-40.

Binford, L. (1963). An Analysis of Cremations from Three Michigan Sites. *Wisconsin Archaeologist* 44: 98-110.

Blake, M., Benz, B., Moreiras, D., Masur, L., Jakobsen, N., & Wallace, R. (2017). *Ancient Maize Map, Version 2.1: An Online Database and Mapping Program for Studying the Archaeology of Maize in the Americas*. http://en.ancientmaize.com/. Laboratory of Archaeology, University of B.C., Vancouver.

Blom, D.E., Buikstra, J.E., Keng, L., Tomczak, P.D., Shoreman, E., & Stevens-Tuttle, D. (2005). Anemia and Childhood Mortality: Latitudinal Patterning along the Coast of Pre-Columbian Peru. *American Journal of Physical Anthropology* 127: 152-169.

Blondiaux, J. & Alduc-le-Bagousse, A. (1994). Une Treponematose Du Bas-Empire Romain En Normande?, pp. 99-100 in O. Dutour, G. Palfi, J. Berato, & J.-P. Brun (eds) *L'Origine De La Syphilis En Europe, Avant Ou Apres 1493?* Editions Errance, Centre Archeologiques du Var.

Blondiaux, J., Naji, S., Audureau, E., & Colard, T. (2016). Cementochronology and Sex: A Reappraisal of Sex-Associated Differences in Survival in Past French Societies. *International Journal of Palaeopathology* 15: 152-163.

Blum, J.D., Taliaferro, E.H., Weisse, M.T., & Holmes, R.T. (2000). Changes in Sr/Ca, Ba/Ca and 87Sr/86Sr Ratios between Trophic Levels in Two Forest Ecosystems in the Northeastern USA. *Biogeochemistry* 49: 87-101.

Boast, R. (1995). Fine Pots, Pure Pots, Beaker Pots, pp. 69-80 in I. Kinnes & G. Varndell (eds) *'Unbaked Urns of Rudely Shape'. Essays on British and Irish Pottery for Ian Longworth*. Oxbow Monograph 55. Oxbow, Oxford.

Bocherens, H. & Drucker, D. (2003). Trophic Level Isotopic Enrichment of Carbon and Nitrogen in Bone Collagen: Case Studies from Recent and Ancient Ecosystems. *International Journal of Osteoarchaeology* 13: 46-53.

Boddington, A. (1987a). Chaos, Disturbance and Decay in an Anglo-Saxon Cemetery, pp. 27-42 in A. Boddington, A.N. Garland, & R.C. Janaway (eds) *Death, Decay and Reconstruction*. Manchester University Press, Manchester.

Boddington, A. (1987b). From Bones to Population: The Problem of Numbers, pp. 180-197 in A. Boddington, A.N. Garland, & R.C. Janaway (eds) *Death, Decay and Reconstruction*. Manchester University Press, Manchester.

Boddington, A. (1996). *Raunds Furnells: The Anglo-Saxon Church and Churchyard*. English Heritage Archaeological Report 7. English Heritage, London.

Bødker Enghoff, I. (1989). Fishing from the Stone Age Settlement Norsminde. *Journal of Danish Archaeology* 8: 41-50.

Bødker Enghoff, I. (1991). Mesolithic Eel Fishing at Bjørnsholm, Denmark, Spiced with Exotic Species. *Journal of Danish Archaeology* 10: 105-118.

Bødker Enghoff, I. (1993). Coastal Fishing, p. 69 in S. Hvass & B. Storgaard (eds) *Digging into the Past. 25 Years of Archaeology in Denmark*. Aarhus University Press, Aarhus.

Boel, L.W.T. & Ortner, D.J. (2013). Skeletal Manifestations of Skin Ulcer in the Lower Leg. *International Journal of Osteoarchaeology* 23: 303-309.

Bogaard, A., Heaton, T.H.E., Poulton, P., & Merbach, I. (2007). The Impact of Manuring on Nitrogen Isotope Ratios in Cereals: Archaeological Implications for Reconstruction of Diet and Crop Management Practices. *Journal of Archaeological Science* 34: 335-343.

Bogaard, A, Fraser, R., Heaton, T.H.E., Wallace, M., Vaiglova, P., Charles, M. et al. (2013). Crop Manuring and Intensive Land Management by Europe's First Farmers. *Proceedings of the National Academy of Sciences of the USA* 110(31): 12589-12594.

Bojarun, R., Jankauskas, R., & Garmus, A. (2004). Altersbestimmung Mithilfe Von Wachstumslinien Des Zahnzements. *Rechtsmedizin* 14: 405-408.

Bökönyi, S. (1978). The Vertebrate Fauna of Vlasac, pp. 35-65 in D. Srejovic & Z. Letica (eds) *Vlasac: A Mesolithic Settlement in the Iron Gates*. Serbian Academy of Sciences, Belgrade.

Boldsen, J. (1984). A Statistical Evaluation of the Basis for Predicting Stature from Lengths of Long Bones in European Populations. *American Journal of Physical Anthropology* 65: 305-311.

Bonafini, M., Pellegrini, M., Ditchfield, P., & Pollard, A.M. (2013). Investigation of the 'Canopy Effect' in the Isotope Ecology of Temperate Woodlands. *Journal of Archaeological Science* 40: 3926-3935.

Bond, J.M. & Worley, F.L. (2004). The Animal Bone, PP. 311-331 in H.E.M. Cool (ed) *The Roman Cremation Cemetery at Brougham, Cumbria. Excavations 1966-67*. Britannia Monograph Series No. 21. Society for the Promotion of Roman Studies, London.

Bond, J.M. & Worley, F.L. (2006). Companions in Death: The Role of Animals in Anglo-Saxon and Viking Cremation Rituals in Britain, pp. 89-98 in R. Gowland & C. Knüsel (eds) *Social Archaeology of Funerary Remains*. Oxbow, Oxford.

Bongiovanni, R. (2016). Effects of Parturition on Pelvic Age Indicators. *Journal of Forensic Sciences* 61: 1034-1040.

Bonnick, S.L., Harris, S.T., Kendler, D.L., McClung, M.R., & Silverman, S.L. (2010). Management of Postmenopausal Osteoporosis in Women: 2010 Position Statement of the North American Menopause Society. *Menopause* 17, 25-54.

Bonsall, C. & Boroneanţ, A. (2018). The Iron Gates Mesolithic – A Brief Review of Recent Developments. *L'Anthropologie* 122: 264-280.

Boonin, D. (2019). *Dead Wrong: The Ethics of Posthumous Harm*. Oxford University Press, Oxford.

Borovansky, L. & Hnevkovsky, O. (1929). Growth of the Body and Process of Ossification in Prague Boys from 4 to 19 Years. *Anthropologie (Prague)* 7: 169-208.

Bos, K.I., Harkins, K.M., Herbig, A., Coscolla, M., Weber, N., Comas, I. et al. (2014). Pre-Columbian Mycobacterial Genomes Reveal Seals as a Source of New World Human Tuberculosis. *Nature* 514: 494-497.

Bos, K., Kühnert, D., Herbig, A., Esquivel-Gomez, L.R., Valtueña, A.A., Barquera, R. et al. (2019). Palaeomicrobiology. Diagnosis and Evolution of Ancient Pathogens. *Annual Review of Microbiology* 73: 639-666.

Boskey, A.L. & Robey, P.G. (2013). The Composition of Bone, pp. 49-58 in C.J. Rosen (ed) *Primer on the Metabolic Bone Diseases and Disorders of Mineral Metabolism* (8th edition). Wiley, Chichester.

Boston, C., Witkin, A., Boyle, A., & Wilkinson, D.P. (2015). *'Safe Moor'd in Greenwich Tier'. A Study of the Skeletons of the Royal Navy Sailors and Marines Excavated at the Royal Hospital Greenwich*. Oxford Archaeology, Oxford.

Boucher, B.J. (1957). Sex Differences in the Foetal Pelvis. *American Journal of Physical Anthropology* 15: 581-600.

Boucherie, A., Jørkov, M.L.S., & Smith, M. (2017). Wounded to the Bone: Digital Microscopic Analysis of Traumas in a Mediaeval Mass Grave Assemblage (Sandbjerget, Denmark, AD 1300-1350). *International Journal of Paleopathology* 19: 66–79.

Bouts, W.H.M., Constandse-Westermann, T., Pot, T., & Verhoeven, H. (1992). De Gebisresten Uit De Broerenkerk, Zwolle, Circa 1800AD, pp. 99–141 in H. Clevis & T. Constandse-Westermann, eds *De Doden Vertellen: Opgraving in Der Broerenkerk Te Zwolle 1987-88*. Stichting Archeologie Ijssel/ Vechtstreek, Kampen.

Bowen, G.J. (2010). Statistical and Geostatistical Mapping of Precipitation Water Isotope Ratios, Pp. 139-160 in G.J. Bowen, T.E. Dawson, & K.P. Tu (eds) *Isoscapes: Understanding Movement, Pattern and Process on Earth Through Isotope Mapping*. Springer, New York.

Bowler, J.M., Johnston, H., Olley, J.M., Prescott, J.R., Roberts, R.G., Shawcross, W. & Spooner, N.A. (2003). New Ages for Human Occupation and Climatic Change at Lake Mungo, Australia. *Nature* 421: 837–840

Boyle, A., Boston, C., & Witkin, A. (2005). *The Archaeological Experience at St Luke's Church, Old Street, Islington*. Oxford Archaeology, Oxford.

Brace, C.L. & Hunt, K.D. (1990). A Nonracial Cranial Perspective on Human Variation: A(ustralia) to Z(uni). *American Journal of Physical Anthropology* 82: 341–360.

Brace, C.L. & Nagai, M. (1982). Japanese Tooth Size: Past and Present. *American Journal of Physical Anthropology* 59: 399–411.

Brace, C.L., Rosenberg, K.R., & Hunt, K.D. (1987). Gradual Change in Human Tooth Size in the Late Pleistocene and Post Pleistocene. *Evolution* 41: 705–720.

Brace, C.L., Brace, M.L., & Leonard, W.R. (1989). Reflections on the Face of Japan: A Multivariate Craniofacial and Odonto Metric Perspective. *American Journal of Physical Anthropology* 78: 93–113.

Brace, C.L., Smith, S.L., & Hunt, K.D. (1991). What Big Teeth You Had Grandma! Human Tooth Size Past and Present, pp. 33–57 in M.A. Kelley & C.S. Larsen (eds) *Advances in Dental Anthropology*. Wiley-Liss, Chichester.

Brace, S., Diekmann, Y., Booth, T.J., van Dorp, L., Faltyskova, Z., Rohland, N. et al. (2019). Ancient Genomes Indicate Population Replacement in Early Neolithic Britain. *Nature Ecology and Evolution* 3: 765–771.

Brettell, R., Montgomery, J., & Evans, J. (2012). Brewing and Stewing: The Effect of Culturally Mediated Behaviour on the Oxygen Isotope Composition of Ingested Fluids and the Implications of Human Provenance Studies. *Journal of Analytical and Atomic Spectrometry* 27: 778–785.

Brickley, M., Berry, H., & Western, G. (2005). The People: Physical Anthropology, pp. 90–151 in M. Brickley, S. Butuex, J. Adams, & R. Cherrington *St Martins Uncovered: Investigations in the Churchyard of St Martin's-in-the-Bull Ring, Birmingham, 2001*. Oxbow: Oxford.

Brickley, M., Mays, S., & Ives, R. (2007). An Investigation of Vitamin D Deficiency in Adults: Effective Markers for Interpreting Past Living Conditions and Pollution Levels in 18th and 19th Century Birmingham, England. *American Journal of Physical Anthropology* 132: 67–79.

Brickley, M., Ives, R., & Mays, S. (2020). *The Bioarchaeology of Metabolic Bone Disease* (2nd edition). Academic Press, London.

Brickley, M.B. (2018). Cribra Orbitalia and Porotic Hyperostosis: A Biological Approach to Diagnosis. *American Journal of Physical Anthropology* 167: 896–902.

Brickley, M.B. & Mays, S. (2019). Metabolic Disease, pp. 531–566 in J.E. Buikstra, (ed). *Ortner's Identification of Pathological Conditions in Human Skeletal Remains* (3rd edition). Academic Press, London.

Brink, O., Vesterby, A., & Jensen, J. (1998). Pattern of Injuries Due to Interpersonal Violence. *Injury* 29: 705-709.

Brits, D., Steyn, M., & L'Abbé, E.L. (2014). A Histomorphological Analysis of Human and Non-Human Femora. *International Journal of Legal Medicine* 128: 369-377.

Brits, D.M., Bidmos, M.A., & Manger, P.R. (2017). Stature Estimation from the Femur and Tibia in Black South African Sub-Adults. *Forensic Science International* 270: 277e1-277e10.

Britton, K., Fuller, B.T., Tütken, T., Mays, S., & Richards, M.P. (2015). Oxygen Isotope Analysis of Human Bone Phosphate Evidences Weaning Age in Archaeological Populations. *American Journal of Physical Anthropology* 157: 226-241.

Brodie, N. (1994). *The Neolithic–Bronze Age Transition in Britain*. British Archaeological Reports, British Series, No. 238. Tempus Reparatum, Oxford.

Brodie, N. (1998). British Bell Beakers: Twenty-Five Years of Theory and Practice, pp. 43-56 in M. Benz & S. van Willigen (eds) *Some New Approaches to the Bell Beaker 'Phenomenon'. Lost Paradise ... ? Proceedings of the Second Meeting of the "Association Archéologie Et Gobelets", Feldberg (Germany) 18th-20th April 1997*. British Archaeological Reports, International Series No. 690. Archaeopress, Oxford.

Brooks, S. & Suchey, J.M. (1990). Skeletal Age Determination Based on the Os Pubis: A Comparison of the Acsádi-Nemeskéri and Suchey–Brooks Methods. *Human Evolution* 5: 227-238.

Brothwell, D.R. (1963). *Digging Up Bones* (1st edition). Oxford University Press/British Museum (Natural History), Oxford.

Brothwell, D.R. (1967). The Evidence for Neoplasms, pp. 320-345 in D. Brothwell & A.T. Sandison (eds) *Diseases in Antiquity*. Charles C Thomas, Springfield.

Brothwell, D.R. (1981). *Digging Up Bones* (3rd edition). Oxford University Press/British Museum (Natural History), Oxford.

Brothwell, D.R. (1989). The Relationship of Tooth Wear to Ageing, pp. 303-316, in M.Y. İşcan (ed) *Age Markers in the Human Skeleton*. Charles C Thomas, Springfield.

Brothwell, D.R. (2008). Tumours and Tumour-like Processes, pp. 253-281 in R. Pinhasi & S. Mays (eds) *Advances in Human Palaeopathology*. Wiley, Chichester

Brothwell, D.R. & Blake, M.L. (1966). The Human Remains from Fussell's Lodge Long Barrow: Their Morphology, Discontinuous Traits and Pathology. *Archaeologia* 100: 48-63.

Brothwell, D.R. & Cullen, R. ([1969] 1991). Wayland's Smithy, Oxfordshire: The Human Bone. *Proceedings of the Prehistoric Society* 57: 72-80.

Brothwell, D.R. & Krzanowski, W., (1974). Evidence of Biological Differences between Early British Populations from Neolithic to Mediaeval Times, as Revealed by Eleven Commonly Available Cranial Vault Measurements. *Journal of Archaeological Science* 1: 249-260.

Brothwell, D.R. & Møller-Christensen, V. (1963). Medico-Historical Aspects of a Very Early Case of Mutilation. *Danish Medical Bulletin* 10: 21-25.

Brothwell, D.R. & Powers, R. (1968). Congenital Malformations of the Skeleton in Earlier Man, pp. 173-203 in D.R. Brothwell (ed.) *The Skeletal Biology of Earlier Human Populations*. Pergamon, Oxford.

Brown, T. & Brown, K. (2011). *Biomolecular Archaeology: An Introduction*. Wiley-Blackwell, Chichester.

Brown, T.A. (2012). *Introduction to Genetics: A Molecular Approach*. Garland Science, London.

Brown, T.A. & Barnes, I.M. (2015). The Current and Future Applications of Ancient DNA in Quarternary Science. *Journal of Quarternary Science* 30: 144-153.

Brůžek, J., Franciscus, R.G., Novotný, V., & Trinkaus, E. (2006). The Assessment of Sex, pp. 46-62 in E. Trinkaus & J.A. Svoboda (eds) *Early Modern Human Evolution in Central Europe. The People of Dolní Věstonice and Pavlov*. Oxford University Press, Oxford.

Bryant, J.D. & Froehlich, P.N. (1996). Oxygen Isotope Composition of Human Tooth Enamel from Mediaeval Greenland: Linking Climate and Society: Comment and Reply. *Geology* 24: 477-479.

Bryant, J.D., Koch, P.L., Froehlich, P.N., Showers, W.J., & Genna, B.J. (1996). Oxygen Isotope Partitioning between Phosphate and Carbonate in Mammalian Apatite. *Geochimica et Cosmochimica Acta* 60: 5145-5148.

Buckberry, J.L. & Chamberlain, A.T. (2002). Age Estimation from the Auricular Surface of the Ilium: A Revised Method. *American Journal of Physical Anthropology* 119: 231-239.

Buckley, H.R. & Petchey, P. (2018). Human Skeletal Remains and Bioarchaeology in New Zealand, pp. 93-110 in B. O'Donnabhain & M.C. Lozada (eds) *Archaeological Human Remains: Legacies of Imperialism, Communism and Colonialism*. Springer, Cham.

Buckley, M., Collins, M., Thomas-Oates, J., & Wilson, J.C. (2009). Species Identification by Analysis of Bone Collagen Using Matrix-assisted Laser Desorption/Ionisation Time-of-Flight Mass Spectroscopy. *Rapid Communications in Mass Spectrometry* 23: 3843-3854.

Budinoff, L.C. & Tague, R.G. (1990). Anatomical and Developmental Bases for the Ventral Arc of the Human Pubis. *American Journal of Physical Anthropology* 82: 73-79.

Buikstra, J.E., (ed) (2019a). *Ortner's Identification of Pathological Conditions in Human Skeletal Remains* (3rd edition). Academic Press, London.

Buikstra, J.E., (ed) (2019b). *Bioarchaeologists Speak Out. Deep Time Perspectives on Contemporary Issues*. Springer, Cham.

Buikstra, J.E. & Ubelaker, D.H. (1994). *Standards for Data Collection from Human Skeletal Remains*. Arkansas Archaeological Society Research Series No. 44. Arkansas Archaeological Society, Fayetteville.

Bunyard, M.W. (1972). Effects of High Sucrose Cariogenic Diets with Varied Protein-Calorie Levels on the Bones and Teeth of the Rat. *Calcified Tissue Research* 8: 217-227.

Burgess, C. & Shennan, S. (1976). The Beaker Phenomenon: Some Suggestions, pp. 309-331 in C. Burgess & R. Miket (eds) *Settlement and Economy in the 3rd and 2nd Millenia BC*. British Archaeological Reports, British Series, No. 33. Tempus Reparatum, Oxford.

Burnett, S.E. & Irish, J.D., (eds) (2017). *A World View of Bioculturally Modified Teeth*. University Press of Florida, Gainesville.

Burnett, S.E., Irish, J.D., & Fong, M.R. (2013). Wear's the Problem? Examining the Effect of Dental Wear on Studies of Crown Morphology, pp. 535-554 in G.R. Scott & J.D. Irish (eds) *Anthropological Perspectives on Tooth Morphology: Genetics, Evolution, Variation*. Cambridge University Press, Cambridge.

Burrell, A.S., Disotell, T.R., & Bergey, C.M. (2015). The Use of Museum Specimens with High-Throughput DNA Sequencers. *Journal of Human Evolution* 79: 35-44.

Butler, S.M. (2018). Getting Medieval on Stephen Pinker. Violence and Medieval England. *Historical Reflections* 44(1): 29-40.

Cabana, G.S. (2011). The Problematic Relationship between Migration and Culture Change, pp. 16-28 in G.S. Cabana & J.J. Clark (eds) *Rethinking Anthropological Perspectives on Migration*. University Press of Florida, Boca Raton.

Cameron, M.E. & Stock, J.T. (2018). Ecological Variation in Later Stone Age Southern African Biomechanical Properties. *Journal of Archaeological Science Reports* 17: 125-136.

Cameron, M.E., Lapham, H., & Shaw, C. (2018). Examining the Influence of Hide Processing on Native American Upper Limb Morphology. *International Journal of Osteoarchaeology* 28: 332-342.

Cameron, N., Tobias, P.V., Fraser, W.J., & Nagdee, M. (1990). Search for Secular Trends in Calvarial Diameters, Cranial Base Height, Indices, and Capacity in South African Negro Crania. *American Journal of Human Biology* 2: 53-61.

Campanacho, V. & Santos, A.L. (2013). Comparison of Entheseal Changes of the *Os Coxae* of Portuguese Males (19th-20th Centuries) with Known Occupation. *International Journal of Osteoarchaeology* 23: 229-236.

Campanacho, V., Santos, A.L., & Cardoso, H.F.V. (2012). Assessing the Influence of Occupational and Physical Activity on the Rate of Degenerative Change of the Pubic Symphysis in Portuguese Males from the 19th to 20th Century. *American Journal of Physical Anthropology* 148: 371-388.

Canturk, K.M., Emre, R., Kinoglu, K., Başpinar, B., Sahin, F., & Ozen, M. (2014). Current Status of the Use of Single-Nucleotide Polymorphisms in Forensic Practices. *Genetic Testing and Molecular Biomarkers* 18(7): 455-460.

Capellini, E., Prohaska, A., Racimo, F., Welker, F., Pedersen, M.W., Allentoft, M.E. et al. (2018). Ancient Biomolecules and Evolutionary Inference. *Annual Reviews in Biochemistry* 87: 1029-1060

Cappella, A., Amadasi, A., Castoldi, E., Mazzarelli, D., Gaudio, D., & Cattaneo, C. (2014). The Difficult Task of Assessing Perimortem and Postmortem Fractures on the Skeleton: A Blind Test on 210 Fractures of Known Origin. *Journal of Forensic Sciences* 59: 1598-1601.

Cardoso, H.F.V. (2007). Environmental Effects on Skeletal versus Dental Development: Using a Documented Subadult Skeletal Sample to Test a Basic Assumption in Human Osteological Research. *American Journal of Physical Anthropology* 132: 223-233.

Cardoso, H.F.V. (2008a). Epiphyseal Union at the Innominate and Lower Limb in a Modern Portuguese Skeletal Sample, and Age Estimation in Adolescent and Young Adult Male and Female Skeletons. *American Journal of Physical Anthropology* 135: 161-170.

Cardoso, H.F.V. (2008b). Age Estimation of Adolescent and Young Adult Male and Female Skeletons II: Epiphyseal Union in the Upper Limb and Scapular Girdle in a Modern Portuguese Skeletal Sample. *American Journal of Physical Anthropology* 137: 97-105.

Cardoso, H.F.V. & Gomes, J.E.A. (2009). Trends in Adult Stature of Peoples Who Inhabited the Modern Portuguese Territory from the Mesolithic to the Late 20th Century. *International Journal of Osteoarchaeology* 19: 711-725.

Cardoso, H.F.V. & Ríos, L. (2011). Age Estimation from Stages of Epiphyseal Union in the Presacral Vertebrae. *American Journal of Physical Anthropology* 14: 238-247.

Cardoso, H.F.V. & Severino, R.S.S. (2010). The Chronology of Epiphyseal Union in the Hand and Foot from Dry Bone Observations. *International Journal of Osteoarchaeology* 20: 737-746.

Cardoso, H.F.V., Campanacho, V., Gomes, J., & Marinho, L. (2013). Timing of Fusion of the Ischiopubic Ramus from Dry Bone Observations. *Homo - Journal of Comparative Human Biology* 64: 454-462.

Cardoso, H.F.V., Pereira, V., & Ríos, L. (2014). Chronology of Fusion of the Primary and Secondary Ossification Centers in the Human Sacrum and Age Estimation in Child and Adolescent Skeletons. *American Journal of Physical Anthropology* 153: 214-225.

Cardoso, J.L. (2014). Absolute Chronology of the Beaker Phenomenon North of the Tagus Estuary: Demographic and Social Implications. *Trabajos De Prehistoria* 71: 56-75.

Cares Henriquez, A. & Oxenham, M.F. (2017). An Alternative Objective Microscopic Method for the Identification of Linear Enamel Hypoplasia (LEH) in the Absence of Visible Perikymata. *Journal of Archaeological Science Reports* 14: 76-84.

Carlin, N. (2018). *The Beaker Phenomenon? Understanding the Character and Context of Social Practices in Ireland 2500-2000 BC*. Sidestone Press, Leiden.

Case, H. (1995). Beakers: Loosening a Stereotype, pp. 55-67 in I. Kinnes & G. Varndell (eds) *'Unbaked Urns of Rudely Shape'. Essays on British and Irish Pottery for Ian Longworth*. Oxbow Monograph 55. Oxbow, Oxford.

Cattaneo, C. & Cappella, A. (2017). Distinguishing Between Peri- and Post-Mortem Trauma on Bone, pp. 352-368 in E.M.J. Schotsmans, N. Márquez-Grant, & S.L. Forbes (eds) *Taphonomy of Human Remains: Forensic Analysis of the Dead and Depositional Environment*. Wiley, Chichester.

Centurion-Lara, A., Molini, B.J., Gordones, C., Sun, E., Hevner, K., van Voorhis, W.C., & Lukehart, S.A. (2006). Molecular Differentiation of *Treponema Pallidum* Subspecies. *Journal of Clinical Microbiology* 44: 3377-3380.

Centurion-Lara, A., Giacani, L., Godornes, C., Molini, B., Brinck Reid, T., & Lukehart, S.A. (2013). Fine Analysis of Genetic Diversity of the Tpr Gene Family among Treponemal Species, Subspecies and Strains. *PloS Neglected Tropical Diseases* 7(5): e2222.

Chamberlain, A. (2000). Problems and Prospects in Palaeodemography, pp. 101-115 in M. Cox & S. Mays (eds) *Human Osteology in Archaeology and Forensic Science*. Cambridge University Press, Cambridge.

Champion, T. (1992). Migration Revived. *Journal of Danish Archaeology* 9: 214-218.

Chappard, D., Moquereau, M., Mercier, P., Gallois, Y., Legrand, E., Baslé, M.F. & Audran, M. (2004). Ex Vivo Bone Mineral Density of the Wrist: Influence of Medullar Fat. *Bone* 34: 1023-1028.

Charlton, S., Alexander, M., Collins, M., Milner, N., Mellars, P., O'Connell, T.C., Stevens, R.E. & Craig, O.E. (2016). Finding Britain's Last Hunter-Gatherers: A New Biomolecular Approach to 'Unidentifiable' Bone Fragments Utilising Bone Collagen. *Journal of Archaeological Science* 73: 55-61.

Charlton, S., Ramsøe, A., Collins, M., Craig, O.E., Fischer, R., Alexander, M. & Speller, C. (2019). New Insights into Neolithic Milk Consumption through Proteomic Analysis of Dental Calculus. *Archaeological and Anthropological Sciences* 11: 6183-6196.

Chenery, C.A., Pashley, V., Lamb, A.L., Sloane, H.J., & Evans, J.A. (2012). The Oxygen Isotope Relationship between the Phosphate and Structural Carbonate Fractions of Human Bioapatite. *Rapid Communications in Mass Spectrometry* 26: 309-319.

Cheverud, J.M. & Buikstra, J.E. (1981). Quantitative Genetics of Skeletal Nonmetric Traits in the Rhesus Macaques on Cayo Santiago. I Single Trait Heritabilities. *American Journal of Physical Anthropology* 54: 43-49.

Chinique de Armas, Y. & Roksandic, M., (eds) (2018). Breastfeeding and Weaning Practices in Ancient Populations: A Cross-Cultural View. *International Journal of Osteoarchaeology* 28(5).

Chisholm, B.S. (1989). Variation in Diet Reconstructions Based on Stable Carbon Isotopic Evidence, pp. 10-37 in T.D. Price (ed.) *The Chemistry of Prehistoric Human Bone*. Cambridge University Press, Cambridge.

Chisholm, B.S., Nelson, D.E., & Schwarcz, H.P. (1982). Stable Carbon Isotope Ratios as a Measure of Marine versus Terrestrial Protein in Ancient Diets. *Science* 216: 1131-1132.

Christensen, A.M. & Passalacqua, N.V. (2018). *A Laboratory Manual for Forensic Anthropology*. Elsevier, London.

Churchill, S.E. (2014). *Thin on the Ground: Neandertal Biology, Archaeology and Ecology*. Wiley, Chichester.

Churchill, S.E., Weaver, A.H., & Niewoehner, W.A. (1996). Late Pleistocene Human Technological and Subsistence Behaviour: Functional Interpretations of Upper Limb Morphology. *Quaternaria Nova* 6: 413-447.

Clark, M.A., Worrell, B.B., & Pless, J.E. (1997). Postmortem Changes in Soft Tissues, pp. 151-164 in W.D. Haglund & M.H. Sorg (eds) *Forensic Taphonomy: The Postmortem Fate of Human Remains*. CRC, London.

Clarke, N.G. & Hirsch, R.S. (1991). Physiological, Pulpal and Periodontal Factors Influencing Alveolar Bone, pp. 241-266 in M.A. Kelley & C.S. Larsen (eds) *Advances in Dental Anthropology*. Wiley-Liss, Chichester.

Cleal, R., (2000). Questionnaire on the Display of Human Remains from Windmill Hill – Autumn 1999. English Heritage, Avebury. Reprinted as Appendix 4, 18-32 in D. Thackray & S. Payne (eds) *Draft Report on the Request for the Reburial of Human Remains from the Alexander Keiller Museum at Avebury*.

Clegg, M. (2020). *Human Remains: Curation, Reburial and Repatriation*. Cambridge University Press, Cambridge.

Clegg, M. & Long, S. (2015). The Natural History Museum and Human Remains, pp. 104-113 in R. Redmond-Cooper (ed) *Heritage, Ancestry and the Law. Principles, Policies and Practices in Dealing with Historical Human Remains*. Institute of Art and Law, Builth Wells.

CoBDO (2008). *Request for Reburial of Human Remains and Grave Goods, Avebury, from the Council of British Druid Orders*. CoBDO, Bath.

Cohen, B. & Bowen, W.H. (1966). Dental Caries in Experimental Monkeys. *British Dental Journal* 121: 269-276.

Colard, T., Falgayrac, G., Bertrand, B., Naji, S., Devos, O., Balsack, C. Delannoy, Y. & Penel, G. (2016). New Insights on the Composition and the Structure of the Acellular Extrinsic Fiber Cementum by Raman Analysis. *PloS One* 11(12): e0167316.

Cole, G. & Waldron, T. (2011). Apple Down 152: A Putative Case of Syphilis from Sixth Century AD Anglo-Saxon England. *American Journal of Physical Anthropology* 144: 72-79.

Cole, G., Waldron, T., & Edwards, C.J. (2015). Apple Down 152 Putative Syphilis: Pre-Columbian Date Confirmed. *American Journal of Physical Anthropology* 156: 489.

Collet, P., Uebelhart, D., Vico, L., Hartmann, D., Roth, M., & Alexandre, C. (1997). Effects of 1- and 6-Month Spaceflight on Bone Mass and Biochemistry in Two Humans. *Bone* 20: 547-551.

Collins, M.J. & Copeland, L. (2011). Ancient Stach: Cooked or Just Old? *Proceedings of the National Academy of Sciences of the USA* 108: E145.

Collins, M.J., Nielsen-Marsh, C.M., Hiller, J., Smith, C.I., & Roberts, J.P. (2002). The Survival of Organic Matter in Bone: A Review. *Archaeometry* 44: 383-394.

Colomer, L. (2014). The Politics of Human Remains in Managing Archaeological Medieval Jewish Burial Grounds in Europe. *Nordisk Kulturpolitisk Tidsskrift* 17: 168-186.

Colwell, C. (2017). *Plundered Skulls and Stolen Spirits: Inside the Fight to Reclaim Native America's Culture*. University of Chicago Press, Chicago.

Conceição, E.L.N. & Cardoso, H.F.V. (2011). Environmental Effects on Skeletal versus Dental Development II: Further Testing of a Basic Assumption in Human Osteological Research. *American Journal of Physical Anthropology* 144: 463-470.

Cook, D.C. (1981). Mortality, Age Structure and Status in the Interpretation of Stress Indicators in Prehistoric Skeletons: A Dental Example from the Lower Illinois Valley, pp. 133-144 in R. Chapman, I. Kinnes, & K. Randsborg (eds) *The Archaeology of Death*. Cambridge University Press, Cambridge.

Cook, D.C. & Powell, M.L. (2012). Treponematosis: Past Present and Future, pp. 472-491 in A.L. Grauer (ed) *A Companion to Paleopathology*. Wiley-Blackwell, Chichester.

Coplen, T.B. (1996). New Guidelines for Reporting Stable Hydrogen, Carbon, and Oxygen Isotope-Ratio Data. *Geochimica et Cosmochimica Acta* 60: 3359-3360.

Coqueugniot, H. & Weaver, T.D. (2007). Infracranial Maturation in the Skeletal Collection from Coimbra, Portugal: New Aging Standards for Epiphyseal Union. *American Journal of Physical Anthropology* 134: 424-437.

Coqueugniot, H., Dutailly, B., Desbarats, P., Boulestin, B., Pap, I., Baker, O., Montaudon,M., Panuel, M., Karlinger, K., Balázs Kovács; K., Alida, L., Pálfi, G., Dutour, O. (2015). Three-dimensional Imaging of Past Skeletal TB: From Lesion to Process. *Tuberculosis* 95: S73-S79.

Corbett, M.E. & Moore, W.J. (1976). Distribution of Dental Caries in Ancient British Populations: IV the 19th Century. *Caries Research* 10: 401-414.

Corny, J., Galland, M., Arzarello, M., Bacon, A-M., Demeter, F., Grimaud-Hervé, D. et al. (2017). Dental Phenotypic Shape Variation Supports a Multiple Dispersal Model for Anatomically Modern Humans in Southeast Asia. *Journal of Human Evolution* 112: 41-56.

Corruccini, R.S. & Beecher, R.M. (1982). Occlusal Variation Related to Soft Diet in a Non-Human Primate. *Science* 218: 74-75.

Couoh, L.R. (2017). Differences between Biological and Chronological Age-at-Death in Human Skeletal Remains: A Change of Perspective. *American Journal of Physical Anthropology* 163: 671-695.

Cox, M. (1989). *The Human Bones from Ancaster*. AML Report 93/89. English Heritage, London.

Cox, M., Molleson, T., & Waldron, T. (1990). Preconception and Perception: The Lessons of a 19th Century Suicide. *Journal of Archaeological Science* 17: 573-581.

Crandall, J. & Klaus, H., (eds) (2014). Advances in the Paleopathology of Scurvy: Papers in Honor of Donald J. Ortner. *International Journal of Paleopathology* 5: 1-106.

Crespo Vázquez, E., Crespo Abelleira, A., Suárez Quintanilla, J.M., & Rodriguez Cobos, M.A. (2011). Correlation between Occlusal Contact and Root Resorption in Teeth with Periodontal Disease. *Journal of Periodontal Research* 46: 82-88.

Cristiani, E., Radini, A., Edinborough, M., & Borič, D. (2016). Dental Calculus Reveals Mesolithic Foragers in the Balkans Consumed Domesticated Plant Foods. *Proceedings of the National Academy of Sciences of the USA*. 113: 10298-10303.

Critall, E. (1973). A History of Wiltshire, Volume 1, Part 2. Victoria County History, University of London Institute for Historical Research, London.

Crosby, A.W. (1969). The Early History of Syphilis: A Reappraisal. *American Anthropologist* 71: 218-227.

Crubézy, E., Ricaut, F.X., Martin, H., Erdenebataar, S., Coqueugnot, H., Maureille, B., & Giscard, P.H. (2006). Inhumation and Cremation in Mediaeval Mongolia: Analysis and Analogy. *Antiquity* 80: 894-905.

Cummings, V. (2017). *The Neolithic of Britain and Ireland*. Routledge, London.

Curate, F. 2014. Osteoporosis and Palaeopathology: A Review. *Journal of Anthropological Science* 92: 119-146.

Curtin, A.J. (2015). Putting Together the Pieces, pp. 219-226 in C.W. Schmidt & S.A. Symes (eds) *The Analysis of Burned Human Remains* (2nd edition) Academic Press, London.

Cvrček, J., Veleminský, P., Dupej, J., Vostrý, L., & Brůžek, J. (2018). Kinship and Morphological Similarity in the Skeletal Remains of Individuals with Known Genealogical Data (Bohemia, 19th-20th Centuries): A New Methodological Approach. *American Journal of Physical Anthropology* 167: 541-556.

Czermak, A., Schermelleh, L., & Lee-Thorp, J. (2018). Imaging-Assisted Time-Resolved Dentine Sampling to Track Weaning Histories. *International Journal of Osteoarchaeology* 28: 535-541.

Daffé, M. (2015). The Cell Envelope of Tubercle Bacilli. *Tuberculosis* 95: S155-S158.

Dahinten, S.L. & Pucciarelli, H.M. (1983). Effects of Protein-Calorie Malnutrition During Suckling and Post-Weaning Periods on Discontinuous Cranial Traits in Rats. *American Journal of Physical Anthropology* 60: 425-430.

Dahinten, S.L. & Pucciarelli, H.M. (1986). Variations in Sexual Dimorphism in the Skulls of Rats Subjected to Malnutrition, Castration and Treatment with Gonadal Hormones. *American Journal of Physical Anthropology* 71: 63-67.

Dal Sasso, G., Maritan, L., Usai, D., Angelini, I., & Artioli, G. (2014). Bone Diagenesis at the Micro-scale: Bone Alteration Patterns During Multiple Phases at Al Khiday (Khartoum, Sudan) Between the Early Holocene and the II Century AD. *Palaeogeography, Palaeoclimatology, Palaeoecology* 416: 30-42.

Dansgaard, W. (1964). Stable Isotopes in Precipitation. *Tellus* 16: 436-468.

Darling, W.G., Bath, A.H., & Talbot, J.C. (2003). The O and H Stable Isotopic Composition of Fresh Waters of the British Isles. 2. Surface Waters and Groundwaters. *Hydrology and Earth System Sciences* 7: 183-195.

Datir, A.P., Saini, A., Connell, A., & Saifuddin, A. (2007). Stress-Related Bone Injuries with Emphasis on MRI. *Clinical Radiology* 62: 828-836.

Daux, V., Lécuyer, C., Héran, M-A., Amiot, R., Simon, L., Fourel, F., Martineau, F., Lynnerup, N., Reychler, H. & Escarguel, G. (2008). Oxygen Isotope Fractionation Between Human Phosphate and Water Revisited. *Journal of Human Evolution* 55: 1138-1147.

Davies, A. (1932). A Re-Survey of the Morphology of the Nose in Relation to Climate. *Journal of the Royal Anthropological Institute* 62: 337-359.

Davies, M.R.R. (1982). *The Law of Burial, Cremation and Exhumation* (5th edition). Shaw, London.

Davies, T.G. & Stock, J.T. (2014). Human Variation in Periosteal Geometry of the Lower Limb: Signatures of Behaviour Among Human Holocene Populations, pp. 67-90 in K.J. Carlson & D. Marchi (eds) *Reconstructing Mobility: Environmental, Behavioral and Morphological Determinants*. Springer, New York.

Dawes, J.D. & Magilton, J.R. (1980). *The Cemetery of St Helen-on-the-Walls, Aldwark*. The Archaeology of York 12/1. Council for British Archaeology, York.

de Boer, H.H. & van der Merwe, A.E. (2016). Diagnostic Dry Bone Histology in Human Palaeopathology. *Clinical Anatomy* 29: 831-843.

de Boer, H.H., van der Merwe, A.E., Hammer, S., Steyn, M., & Maat, G.J.R. (2015). Assessing Post-Traumatic Time Interval in Human Dry Bone. *International Journal of Osteoarchaeology* 25: 98-109.

de Broucker, A., Colard, T., Penel, G., Blondiaux, J., & Naji, S. (2016). The Impact of Periodontal Disease on Cementochronology Age Estimation. *International Journal of Paleopathology* 15: 128-133.

De Jong, W.F. (1926). La Substance Mineral Dans Les Os. *Receuil Des Traveaux Chimiques De Pays-Bas* 45(6).

de Rincon-Ferraz, A.A.B. (1999). Early Work on Syphilis: Diaz De Ysla's Treatise on the Serpentine Disease of Hispaniola Island. *International Journal of Dermatology* 38: 222-227.

Dempsey, P.J. & Townsend, G.C. (2001). Genetic and Environmental Contributions to Variation in Human Tooth Size. *Heredity* 86: 685-693.

DeNiro, M.J. (1985). Postmortem Preservation and Alteration of *in Vivo* Bone Collagen Isotope Ratios in Relation to Palaeodietary Reconstruction. *Nature* 317: 806-809.

DeNiro, M.J. (1987). Stable Isotopy and Archaeology. *American Scientist* 75: 182-191.

DeNiro, M.J. & Hastorf, C.A. (1985). Alteration of 15N/14N and 13C/12C Ratios of Plant Matter during the Initial Stages of Diagenesis: Studies Utilizing Archaeological Specimens from Peru. *Geochimica et Cosmochimica Acta* 49: 97-115.

DeNiro, M.J., Schoeninger, M.J., & Hastorf, C.A. (1985). Effect of Heating on Stable Carbon and Nitrogen Isotope Ratios of Bone Collagen. *Journal of Archaeological Science* 12: 1-7.

Deol, M.S. & Truslove, G.M. (1957). Genetical Studies on the Skeleton of the Mouse. XX. Maternal Physiology and Variation in the Skeleton of C57BL Mice. *Journal of Genetics* 55: 288-312.

Dewhirst, F.E., Chen, T., Izard, J., Paster, B.J., Tanner, A.C.R., Yu, W-H. et al. (2010). The Human Oral Microbiome. *Journal of Bacteriology* 192: 5002-5017.

DeWitte, S. & Stojanowski, C.M. (2015). The Osteological Paradox 20 Years Later: Past Perspectives, Future Directions. *Journal of Archaeological Research* 23: 397-450.

Dias, G. & Tayles, N. (1997). 'Abscess Cavity' – A Misnomer. *International Journal of Osteoarchaeology* 7: 548-554.

Dias, P.E.M., Beaini, T.L., & Melani, R.F.H. (2010). Age Estimation from Dental Cementum Incremental Lines and Periodontal Disease. *Journal of Forensic Odontostomatology* 28 (1): 13-21.

Dick, H.C., Pringle, J.K., Sloane, B., Carver, J., Wisniewski, K.D., Haffenden, A., Porter, S., Roberts, D. & Cassidy, N.J (2015). Detection and Characterisation of Black Death Burials by Multi proxy Geophysical Methods. *Journal of Archaeological Science* 59: 132-141.

Dick, H.C., Pringle, J.K., Wisniewski, K.D., Goodwin, J., van der Putten, R., Evans, G.T., Francis, J.D., Cassella, J.P. & Hansen, J.D. (2017). Determining Geophysical Responses from Burials in Graveyards and Cemeteries. *Geophysics* 82: B245-B255.

Dinu, A. (2010). Mesolithic Fish and Fishermen of the Lower Danube (Iron Gates). *Documenta Preahistorica* 37: 299-310.

Dixit, S.G., Kaur, J., & Kakar, S. (2012). Racial Variation on Articular Surface of Talus (Astragalus) in North Indian Population. *Journal of Forensic and Legal Medicine* 19: 152-157.

Djukic, K., Miladinovic-Radmilovic, N., Draskovic, M., & Djuric, M. (2017). Morphological Appearance of Muscle Attachment Sites on Lower Limbs: Horse Riders versus Agricultural Population. *International Journal of Osteoarchaeology* 28: 656-668.

Dobney, K. & Brothwell, D. (1987). A Method for Evaluating the Amount of Dental Calculus on Teeth from Archaeological Sites. *Journal of Archaeological Science* 14: 343-351.

Dodo, Y. & Ishida, H. (1990). Population History of Japan as Viewed from Cranial Non-Metric Variation. *Journal of the Anthropological Society of Nippon* 98: 269-287.

Dodo, Y. & Kawakubo, Y. (2002). Cranial Affinities of the Epi-Jomon Inhabitants in Hokkaido, Japan. *Anthropological Science* 110: 1-32.

Dokladal, M. (1970). Ergebnisse Experimenteller Verbrennungen Zur Feststellung Von Form- Und Grössenveränderung Von Menschenknochen Unter Dem Einfluss Von Hohen Temperaturen. *Anthropologie (Brno)* 8(2): 3-17.

Dolphin, A.E., Teeter, M.A., White, C.D., & Longstaffe, F.J. (2016). Limiting the Impact of Destructive Analytical Techniques through Sequential Microspatial Sampling of the Enamel from Single Teeth. *Journal of Archaeological Science Reports* 5: 537-541.

Donnelly, C.J. & Murphy, E.M. (2018). Children's Burial Grounds (Cillíní) in Ireland: New Insights into an Early Modern Religious Tradition, pp. 608-628 in S. Crawford, D.M. Hadley, & G. Shepherd (eds) *The Oxford Handbook of the Archaeology of Childhood*. Oxford University Press, Oxford.

Doyle White, E. (2016). Old Stones, New Rites: Contemporary Pagan Interactions with the Medway Megaliths. *Material Religion* 12(3): 346-372.

Dreizen, S., Snodgrasse, R.M., Webb-Peploe, H., & Spies, T.D. (1957). The Effect of Prolonged Nutritive Failure on Epiphysial Fusion in the Human Hand Skeleton. *American Journal of Roentgenology* 78: 461-470.

Dudar, J.C. (1993). Identification of Rib Number and Assessment of Intercostal Variation at the Sternal Rib End. *Journal of Forensic Sciences* 38: 788-797.

Duday, H. (2006). Archaeothanatology, or the Archaeology of Death (Translated from the French by Christopher J Knüsel.), pp. 30-56 in R. Gowland & C. Knüsel (eds) *Social Archaeology of Funerary Remains*. Oxbow, Oxford.

Duday, H. (2009). *The Archaeology of the Dead. Lectures in Archaeothanatology (Translated from the French by M. Cipriani and J. Pearce)*. Oxbow, Oxford.

Dufour, E., Bocherens, H., & Mariotti, A. (1999). Palaeodietary Implications of Isotopic Variability in Eurasian Lacustrine Fish. *Journal of Archaeological Science* 26: 617-627.

During, E.M. (1997). The Skeletal Remains from the Swedish Man-of-War *Vasa* - A Survey. *HOMO - Journal of Comparative Human Biology* 48: 135-160.

Eerkens, J.W., Tushingham, S., Brownstein K.J., Garibay, R., Perez, K., Murga, E. et al. (2018). Dental Calculus as a Source of Ancient Alkaloids: Detection of Nicotine by LC-MS in Calculus Samples from the Americas. *Journal of Archaeological Science Reports* 18: 509-515.

Eisner, M. (2003). Long-Term Historical Trends in Violent Crime. *Crime and Justice* 30: 83-142.

Elamin, F. & Liversidge, H.M. (2013). Malnutrition Has No Effect on the Timing of Human Tooth Formation. *PloS ONE* 8(8): e72274.

Eliopoulos, C., Lagia, A., & Manolis, S. (2007). A Modern, Documented Human Skeletal Collection from Greece. *Homo: Journal of Comparative Human Biology* 58: 221-228.

Ellingham, S. & Sandholzer, M.A. (2020). Determining Volumetric Shrinkage Trends of Burnt Bone Using Micro-CT. *Journal of Forensic Sciences* 65(1): 196-199.

Ellingham, S.T.D., Thompson, T.J.U., Islam, M., & Taylor, G. (2015). Estimating Temperature Exposure of Burnt Bone - A Methodological Review. *Science & Justice* 55: 181-188.

Ellingham, S.T.D., Thompson, T.J.U., & Islam, M. (2016). The Effect of Soft Tissue on Temperature Estimation from Burnt Bone Using Fourier Transform Infrared Spectroscopy. *Journal of Forensic Sciences* 61(1): 153-159.

Emerson, T.E. (2012). Cahokia Interaction and Ethnogenesis in the Northern Midcontinent, pp. 398-409 in T.R. Pauketat (ed) *Oxford Handbook of North American Archaeology*. Oxford University Press, Oxford.

Emerson, T.E., Hedman, K.M., Hargrave, E.A., Cobb, D.E., & Thompson, A.R. (2016). Paradigms Lost: Reconfiguring Cahokia's Mound 72 Beaded Burial. *American Antiquity* 81: 405-425.

Emery, P.A. & Wooldridge, K. (2011). *St Pancras Burial Ground. Excavations for St Pancras International, the London Terminus of High Speed 1, 2002-3*. Gifford/High Speed 1, London.

English Heritage & The National Trust (2008). *Draft Report on the Request for the Reburial of Human Remains from the Alexander Keiller Museum at Avebury*.

Erdal, Y.S. (2006). A Pre-Columbian Case of Congenital Syphilis from Anatolia (Nicaea, 13th Century AD). *International Journal of Osteoarchaeology* 16: 16–33.

Eriksen, H.M., Grytten, J., & Holst, D. (1991). Is There a Long-Term Caries-Preventative Effect of Sugar Restrictions During World War II? *Acta Odontologica Scadinavica* 49: 163–167.

Eriksson, G., Linderholm, A., Fornander, E., Kanstrup, M., Schoultz, P., Olofsson, H., & Lidén, K. (2008). Same Island, Different Diet: Cultural Evolution of Food Practice on Öland, Sweden, from the Mesolithic to the Roman Period. *Journal of Anthropological Archaeology* 27: 520–543.

Errickson, D. & Thompson, T.J.U. (2019). Sharing Is Not Always Caring: Social Media and the Dead, pp. 299-313 in K. Squires, D. Errickson, & N. Márquez-Grant (eds) *Ethical Approaches to Human Remains: A Global Challenge in Bioarchaeology and Forensic Anthropology*. Springer, Cham

Eshed, V., Latimer, B., Greenwald, C.M., Jellema, L.M., Rothschild, B.M., Wish-Baratz, S. & Hershkovitz, I. (2002). Button Osteoma: Its Etiology and Pathophysiology. *American Journal of Physical Anthropology* 118: 217–230.

Estalrrich, A., Alarcón, J.A., & Rosas, A. (2017). Evidence of Toothpick Groove Formation in Neandertal Anterior and Posterior Teeth. *American Journal of Physical Anthropology* 162: 747–756.

Estévez Campo, E.J., López-Lázero, S., Rodríguez, C.L.-M., Aguilera, I.A., & López, M.C.B. (2018). Specific-age Group Sex Estimation of Infants through Geometric Morphometrics Analysis of Pubis and Ischium. *Forensic Science International* 286: 185-192.

Etxeberria, F. (1999). Surgery in the Spanish War of Independence (1807-1813), Between Desault and Lister. *Journal of Paleopathology* 11(3): 25-40.

Evans, J.A., Chenery, C.A., & Montgomery, J. (2012). A Summary of Strontium and Oxygen Isotope Variation in Archaeological Human Tooth Enamel Excavated from Britain. *Journal of Analytical Atomic Spectrometry* 27: 754-764.

Evans, J.A., Montgomery, J., Wildman, G., & Boulton, N. (2010). Spatial Variations in Biosphere 87Sr/86Sr in Britain. *Journal of the Geological Society London* 167: 1-4.

Evans, J.G. (1978). *An Introduction to Environmental Archaeology*. Elek, London.

Everitt, B. & Hothorn, T. (2011). *An Introduction to Applied Multivariate Analysis with R*. Springer, New York.

Excll, K. (2016). Covering the Mummies at Manchester Museum: A Discussion of Authority, Authorship, and Agendas in the Human Remains Debate, pp. 233-250 in H. Williams & M. Giles (eds) *Archaeologists and the Dead. Mortuary Archaeology in Contemporary Society*. Oxford University Press, Oxford.

Faerman, M., Filon, D., Kahila, G., Greenblatt, C.L., Smith, P., & Oppenheim, A. (1995). Sex Identification of Archaeological Human Remains Based on Amplification of X and Y Amelogenin Alleles. *Gene* 167: 327–332.

Faillace, K.E., Bethard, J.D., & Marks, M.K. (2017). The Applicability of Dental Wear in Age Estimation for a Modern American Population. *American Journal of Physical Anthropology* 164: 776–787.

Falys, C.G. & Lewis, M.E. (2011). Proposing A Way Forward: A Review of Standardisation in the Use of Age Categories and Ageing Techniques in Osteological Analysis (2004-2009). *International Journal of Osteoarchaeology* 21: 704-716.

Falys, C.G., Schutkowski, H., & Weston, D.A. (2006). Auricular Surface Ageing: Worse Than Expected? A Test of the Revised Method on A Documented Historic Skeletal Assemblage. *American Journal of Physical Anthropology* 130: 508-513.

Farlay, D., Panczer, G., Rey, C., Delmas, P.D., & Boivin, G. (2010). Mineral Maturity and Crystallinity Index are Distinct Characteristics of Bone Mineral. *Journal of Bone and Mineral Metabolism* 28: 433-445.

Fazekas, I.G. & Kósa, F. (1978). *Forensic Foetal Osteology.* Akademiai Kiado, Budapest.

Feldesman, M.R. (1992). Femur/Stature Ratio and Estimates of Stature in Children. *American Journal of Physical Anthropology* 87: 447–459.

Feldesman, M.R., Kleckner, J.G., & Lundy, J.K. (1990). Femur/Stature Ratio and Estimates of Stature in Mid- and Late-Pleistocene Fossil Hominids. *American Journal of Physical Anthropology* 83: 359–372.

Feldman, M., Harbeck, M., Keller, M., Spyrou, M.A., Rott, A., Trautmann, B. et al. (2016). A High-Coverage *Yersinia Pestis* Genome from A Sixth-Century Justinianic Plague Victim. *Molecular Biology and Evolution* 33(11): 2911–2923.

Fernandes, R., Nadeau, M.J., & Grootes, P.M. (2012). Macronutrient-Based Model for Dietary Carbon Routing in Bone Collagen and Bioapatite. *Archaeological and Anthropological Sciences* 4: 291–301.

Fernandes, R., Millard, A.R., Brabec, M., Nadeau, M.J., & Grootes, P. (2014). Food Reconstruction Using Isotopic Transferred Signals (FRUITS): A Bayesian Model for Diet Reconstruction. *PloS One* 9(2): e87436.

Fernández-Crespo, T., Czermak, A., Lee-Thorp, J., & Schulting, R.J. (2018). Infant and Childhood Diet in the Passage Tomb of Alto De La Huesera (North-central Iberia) from Bone Collagen and Sequential Dentine Isotope Composition. *International Journal of Osteoarchaeology* 28: 542–551.

Fforde, C., Hubert, J., & Turnbull, P. (eds) (2002). *The Dead and Their Possessions. Repatriation in Principal, Policy and Practice.* Routledge, London.

Field, S. (2019) *Re-evaluating the Use of Dental Wear as a Tool for Estimating Age at Death in British Archaeological Skeletal Remains.* PhD Thesis, University of Southampton.

Figueiredo, M., Fernando, A., Martins, G., Freitas, J., Judas, F., & Figueiredo, H. (2010). Effect of the Calcination Temperature on the Composition and Microstructure of Hydroxyapatite Derived from Human and Animal Bone. *Ceramics International* 36: 2383–2393.

Finnegan, M. (1978). Non-Metric Variation of the Infracranial Skeleton. *Journal of Anatomy* 125: 23–37.

Finney, T. (1996). *Investigation of a Skull Fragment from Cremation 704, Mucking, Essex.* AML Report 1/96. English Heritage, London.

Firestone, A.R., Schmid, R., & Mühlemann, H.R. (1982). Cariogenic Effects of Cooked Wheat Starch Alone or with Frequency-Controlled Feeding in Rats. *Archives of Oral Biology* 27: 759–763.

Fischer, A., Olsen, J., Richards, M., Heinemeier, J., Sveinbjörnsdóttir, A.E., & Bennike, P. (2007). Coast-Inland Mobility and Diet in the Danish Mesolithic and Neolithic: Evidence from Stable Isotope Values of Humans and Dogs. *Journal of Archaeological Science* 34: 2125–2150.

Fischer, B. & Mitteroecker, P. (2015). Covariation between Human Pelvis Shape, Stature and Head Size Alleviates the Obsetric Dilemma. *Proceedings of the National Academy of Sciences of the USA* 112(18): 5655–5660.

Fischer, B. & Mitteroecker, P. (2017). Allometry and Sexual Dimorphism in the Human Pelvis. *Anatomical Record* 300: 698–705.

Fitzpatrick, A.P. (1997). *Archaeological Excavations on the Route of the A27 Westhampnett Bypass, West Sussex, 1992.* Wessex Archaeology Report No. 12. Trust for Wessex Archaeology, Salisbury.

Flecker, H. (1942). Time of Appearance and Fusion of Ossification Centres as Observed by Roentgenographic Methods. *American Journal of Roentgenology* 47: 97–159.

Fleming, R., Crosby, V., Cool, H., Wardle, A., Bayliss, A., Bronk Ramsey, C., Dunbar, E., & Mays, S. (in prep). Late-Roman Stanwick, Northamptonshire. *Journal of Archaeological Science Reports*

Fleming-Farrell, D., Michailidis, K., Karantanas, A., Roberts, N., & Kranioti, E.F. (2013). Virtual Assessment of Perimortem and Postmortem Blunt Force Cranial Trauma. *Forensic Science International* 229: 162.e1–162.e6.

Ford, D., Seow, W.K., Kazoullis, S., Holcombe, T., & Newman, B. (2009). A Controlled Study of Risk Factors for Enamel Hypoplasia in the Permanent Dentition. *Pediatric Dentistry* 31: 382–388.

Formicola, V. (2007). From the Sunghir Children to the Romito Dwarf. Aspects of the Upper Palaeolithic Funerary Landscape. *Current Anthropology* 48: 446–453.

Formicola, V., Pontradolfi, A., & Svoboda, J. (2001). The Upper Palaeolithic Triple Burial of Dolní Věstonice: Pathology and Funerary Behavior. *American Journal of Physical Anthropology* 115: 372–379.

Foster, A., Buckley, H., & Tayles, N. (2014). Using Enthesis Robusticity to Infer Activity in the Past: A Review. *Journal of Archaeological Method and Theory* 21: 511–533.

Fowler, C. (2010). Pattern and Diversity in the Early Neolithic Mortary Practices of Britain and Ireland: Contextualising the Treatment of the Dead. *Documenta Praehistorica* 37: 1–22.

Fowler, C. (2013). Identities in Transformation: Identities, Funerary Rites, and the Mortuary Process, pp. 511–526 in L. Nilsson Stutz & S. Tarlow (eds) *The Oxford Handbook of the Archaeology of Death and Burial*. Oxford University Press, Oxford.

Fowler, L. & Powers, N. (2012). *Doctors, Dissection and Resurrection Men. Excavations in the 19th-Century Burial Ground of the London Hospital, 2006*. MOLA Monograph 62. Museum of London Archaeology, London.

Fowler, M., Rose, J., Vander Leest, B., & Ahler, S.R. (1999). *The Mound 72 Area: Dedicated and Sacred Space in Early Cahokia*. Illinois State Museum Reports of Investigations No. 54. Illinois State Museum, Springfield.

Fox, K. & Hawks, J. (2019). Use Human Remains More Wisely. *Nature* 572: 581–583.

Franklin, D., Cardini, A., Flavel, A., & Marks, M.K. (2014). Morphometric Analysis of Pelvic Sexual Dimorphism in a Contemporary Western Australian Population. *International Journal of Legal Medicine* 128: 861–872.

Freeman, J.V., Cole, T.J., Chinn, S., Jones, P.R.M., White, E.M., & Preece, M.A. (1995). Cross-Sectional Stature and Weight Reference Curves for the UK, 1990. *Archives of Disease in Childhood* 73: 17–24.

Fresia, A.E., Ruff, C.B., & Larsen, C.S. (1990). Temporal Decline in Bilateral Asymmetry of the Upper Limb on the Georgia Coast, pp. 121–132 in C.S. Larsen (ed) *The Archaeology of the Mission Santa Catalina De Guale: 2. Biocultural Interpretation of a Population in Transition*. Anthropological Papers of the American Museum of Natural History No. 68. American Museum of Natural History, New York.

Friedlaender, J.S., Costa, P.T., Bosse, R., Ellis, E., Rhoads, J.G., & Stoudt, H.W. (1977). Longitudinal Physique Changes among Healthy White Veterans at Boston. *Human Biology* 49: 541–558.

Friedli, H., Lotscher, H., Oescheger, H., Siegenthaler, U., & Stauffer, B. (1986). Ice Core Record of the 13C/12C Ratio of Atmospheric CO in the Past Two Centuries. *Nature* 324: 237–238.

Friess, M. (2012). Scratching the Surface? The Use of Surface Scanning in Physical and Paleoanthropology. *Journal of Anthropological Sciences* 90: 7–31.

Froehle, A.W., Kellner, C.M., & Schoeninger, M.J. (2010). Effect of Diet and Protein Source on Carbon Stable Isotope Ratios in Collagen: Follow up to Warriner and Tuross (2009). *Journal of Archaeological Science* 37: 2662–2670.

Fu, Q.,Posth, C., Hajdinjak, M., Petr, M., Mallick, S., Fernandes, D. et al. (2016). The Genetic History of Ice Age Europe. *Nature* 534: 200–205.

Fugassa, M.H., Araújo, A., & Guichón, R.A. (2006). Quantitative Paleoparasitology Applied to Archaeological Sediments. *Memorias Do Instituto Oswaldo Cruz* 101(Supplement 2): 29–33.

Fuller, B.T., Richards, M.P., & Mays, S.A. (2003). Stable Carbon and Nitrogen Isotope Variations in Tooth Dentine Serial Sections from Wharram Percy. *Journal of Archaeological Science* 30: 1673–1684.

Fully, G. (1956). Une Nouvelle Méthode De Détermination De La Taille. *Annales De Médicine Légale* 36: 266-273.

Fully, G. & Pineau, H. (1960). Détermination De La Stature Au Moyen Du Squelette. *Annales De Médicine Légale* 40: 145-154.

Furholt, M. (2018). Massive Migrations? The Impact of Recent aDNA Studies on Our View of Third Millennium Europe. *European Journal of Archaeology* 21: 159-191.

Furtwängler, A., Reiter, E., Neumann, G.U., Siebke, I., Steuri, N., Hafner, A. et al. (2018). Ratio of Mitochondrial to Nuclear DNA Affects Contamination Estimates in Ancient DNA Analysis. *Scientific Reports* 8: 14075.

Galeano, S. & García-Lorenzo, M.L. (2014). Bone Mineral Change During Experimental Calcination: An X-Ray Diffraction Study. *Journal of Forensic Sciences* 59(6): 1602-1606.

Galera, V., Ubelaker, D.H., & Hayek, L.C. (1998). Comparison of Macroscopic Cranial Methods of Age Estimation Applied to Skeletons in the Terry Collection. *Journal of Forensic Sciences* 43: 933-939.

Gallagher, A. (2015). Determination of a Novel Size Proxy in Comparative Morphometrics. *South African Journal of Science* 111: Article 2014-2221.

Galloway, A., Willey, P., & Snyder, L. (1997). Human Bone Mineral Densities and Survival of Bone Elements: A Contemporary Sample, pp. 295-317 in W.D. Haglund & M.H. Sorg (eds) *Forensic Taphonomy: The Postmortem Fate of Human Remains*. CRC, London.

Ganiaris, H., 2001. London Bodies: An Exhibition at the Museum of London, pp. 267-274 in E. Williams (ed) *Human Remains: Conservation, Retrieval and Analysis, Proceedings of a Conference Held in Williamsburg*, Virginia, *November 7th-11th 1999*. British Archaeological Reports British Series 934, Archaeopress, Oxford.

Gansauge, M.T. & Meyer, M. (2014). Selective Enrichment of Damaged DNA Molecules for Ancient Genome Sequencing. *Genome Research* 24: 1543-1549.

García-Donas, J.G., Dyke, J., Paine, R.R., Nathena, D., & Kranioti, E.F. (2016). Accuracy and Sampling Error of Two Age Estimation Techniques Using Rib Histomorphometry on a Modern Sample. *Journal of Forensic and Legal Medicine* 38: 28-35.

García-Mancuso, R., Plischuk, M., Desántolo, B., Garizoain, G., & Sardi, M.L. (2019). Ethical Considerations in Human Remains Based Research in Argentina, pp. 447-463 in K. Squires, D. Errickson, & N. Márquez-Grant (eds) *Ethical Approaches to Human Remains: A Global Challenge in Bioarchaeology and Forensic Anthropology*. Springer, Cham

Garland, A.N. & Janaway, R.C. (1989). The Taphonomy of Inhumation Burials, pp. 15-37 in C. Roberts, F. Lee, & J. Bintliff (eds) *Burial Archaeology Current Research, Methods and Developments*. British Archaeological Reports, British Series, No. 211. British Archaeological Reports, Oxford.

Garn, S.M. (1970). *The Earlier Gain and Later Loss of Cortical Bone*. Charles C Thomas, Springfield.

Garn, S.M., Lewis, A.B., & Bonne, B. (1962). Third Molar Formation and Its Developmental Course. *The Angle Orthodontist* 32: 270-279.

Garn, S.M., Osborne, R.H., & McCabe, K.D. (1979). The Effect of Prenatal Factors on Crown Dimensions. *American Journal of Physical Anthropology* 51: 665-678.

Gat, J.R. (2010). *Isotope Hydrology: A Study of the Water Cycle*. Imperial College Press, London.

Geber, J. (2015). *Victims of Ireland's Great Famine. The Bioarchaeology of Mass Burials at Kilkenny Union Workhouse*. University Press of Florida, Gainesville.

Gejvall, N.G. (1960). *Westerhus: Mediaeval Population and Church in the Light of Skeletal Remains*. Hakak Ohlsson, Lund.

Genoves, S. (1967). Proportionality of the Long Bones and Their Relation to Stature among Mesoamericans. *American Journal of Physical Anthropology* 26: 67-78.

Gerbault, P., Walker, C., Brown, K., Yonova-Doing, E., & Thomas, M.G. (2017). The Evolution of Lactase Tolerance in Dairying Populations, in J. Lee-Thorp & M.A. Katzenberg (eds) *The Oxford Handbook of the Archaeology of Diet*. Oxford University Press, Oxford.

Giacaman, R.A. (2018). Sugars and Beyond. The Role of Sugars and Other Nutrients and Their Potential Impact on Caries. *Oral Diseases* 24: 1185-1197.

Giacani, L. & Lukehart, S.A. (2014). The Endemic Treponematoses. *Clinical Microbiology Reviews* 27: 89-115.

Gibbon, V., Paximadis, M., Štrkalj, G., Ruff, P., & Penny, C. (2009). Novel Methods of Molecular Sex Identification from Skeletal Tissue Using the Amelogenin Gene. *Forensic Science International: Genetics* 3: 74-79.

Gilbert, B.M. & McKern, T.W. (1973). A Method for Ageing the Female Os Pubis. *American Journal of Physical Anthropology* 38: 31-38.

Gilmore, C.C. & Grote, M.N. (2012). Estimation of Age from Adult Occlusal Wear: A Modification of the Miles Method. *American Journal of Physical Anthropology* 149: 181-192.

Gilmore, H., Aranui, A., & Halcrow, S.E. (2019). Ethical Issues of Bioarchaeology in New Zealand-Aotearoa: Relationships, Research, and Repatriation, pp. 431-444 in K. Squires, D. Errickson, & N. Márquez-Grant (eds) *Ethical Approaches to Human Remains: A Global Challenge in Bioarchaeology and Forensic Anthropology*. Springer, Cham.

Given, J.B. (1977). *Society and Homicide in Thirteenth Century England*. Stanford University Press, Stanford.

Gocha, T.P. & Schutkowski, H. (2013). Tooth Cementum Annulation for Estimation of Age-at-Death in Thermally Altered Remains. *Journal of Forensic Sciences* 58(S1): S151-S155.

Gocha, T.P., Robling, A.G., & Stout, S.D. (2019). Histomorphometry of Human Cortical Bone: Applications to Age Estimation, pp. 145-187 in M.A. Katzenberg & A.L. Grauer, eds *Biological Anthropology of the Human Skeleton* (3rd edition). Wiley-Blackwell, Chichester.

Godde, K., Wilson Taylor, R.J., & Gutierrez, C. (2018). Entheseal Changes and Demographic/Health Indicators in the Upper Extremity of Modern Americans: Associations with Age and Physical Activity. *International Journal of Osteoarchaeology* 28: 285-293.

Goldberg, P.J.P. (1986). Female Labour, Service and Marriage in the Late Mediaeval Urban North. *Northern History* 22: 18-38.

Goldstein, L. & Myers, K. (2014). Transformation and Metaphors. Thoughts on Cremation Practices in the Precontact Midwestern United States, pp. 207-232 in I. Kuijt, C.P. Quinn, & G. Cooney, (eds) *Transformation by Fire: The Archaeology of Cremation in Cultural Context*. University of Arizona Press, Tucson.

Gonçalves, D., Cunha, E., & Thompson, T.J.U. (2013). Weight References for Burned Human Skeletal Remains from Portuguese Samples. *Journal of Forensic Sciences* 58(5): 1134-1140.

Goodman, A.H., Martinez, C., & Chavez, A. (1991). Nutritional Supplementation and the Development of Linear Enamel Hypoplasias in Children from Tezontepan, Mexico. *American Journal of Clinical Nutrition* 53: 773-781.

Goose, D.H. (1962). Reduction of Palate Size in Modern Populations. *Archives of Oral Biology* 7: 343-350.

Gopinath, S. (2008). *Evaluation of Human Bone Survey in London before London Gallery at the Museum of London*. Museum of London, London

Gordon, C.G. & Buikstra, J.E. (1981). Soil pH, Bone Preservation and Sampling Bias at Mortuary Sites. *American Antiquity* 46: 566-571.

Gorecki, P.P. (1979). Disposal of Human Remains in the New Guinea Highlands. *Archaeology & Physical Anthropology in Oceania* 14: 107-117.

Gowland G. & Chamberlain A.T. (2002). A Bayesian Approach to Ageing Perinatal Skeletal Material from Archaeological Sites: Implications for the Evidence of Infanticide in Roman Britain. *Journal of Archaeological Science* 29: 677-685.

Grauer, A.L. (1993). Patterns of Anaemia and Infection from Mediaeval York, England. *American Journal of Physical Anthropology* 91: 203-213.

Grayson, D.K. (1979). On the Quantification of Vertebrate Archaeofaunas. *Advances in Archaeological Method and Theory* 2: 199-237.

Green, C.J.S., Paterson, M., & Biek, L. (1981). A Roman Coffin Burial from Crown Buildings, Dorchester with Particular Reference to the Head of Well-Preserved Hair. *Proceedings of the Dorset Natural History and Archaeological Society* 103: 67–100.

Green, R.E., Krause, J., Briggs, A.W., Maricic, T., Stenzel, U., Kircher, M. et al. (2010). A Draft Sequence of the Neandertal Genome. *Science* 328 (5979): 710–722.

Greiner, M., Rodríguez-Navarro, A., Heinig, M.F., Mayer, K., Kocsis, B., Göhring, A., Toncala, A., Grupe, G., & Schmahl, W.W. (2019). Bone Incineration: An Experimental Study on Mineral Structure, Colour and Crystalline State. *Journal of Archaeological Science Reports* 25: 507–518.

Grewel, M.S. (1962). The Development of an Inherited Tooth Defect in the Mouse. *Journal of Embryology & Experimental Morphology* 10: 202–211.

Grosskopf, B. & McGlynn, G. (2011). Age Diagnosis Based on Incremental Lines in Dental Cementum: A Critical Reflection. *Anthropologischer Anzeiger* 66: 275–289.

Grünberg, J.M. (2002). Middle Palaeolithic Birch-Bark Pitch. *Antiquity* 76: 15–16.

Grüneberg, H. (1951). The Genetics of a Tooth Defect in the Mouse. *Proceedings of the Royal Society of London, Series B* 138: 437–451.

Grüneberg, H. (1952). Genetical Studies on the Skeleton of the Mouse IV. Quasi-Continuous Variations. *Journal of Genetics* 51: 95–114.

Grüneberg, H. (1963). *The Pathology of Development*. Blackwell, Oxford.

Grupe, G. (1988). Impact of the Choice of Bone Samples on Trace Element Data in Excavated Human Skeletons. *Journal of Archaeological Science* 15: 123–129.

Guatelli-Steinberg, D. (2016). Dental Stress Indicators from Micro- to Macroscopic, pp. 450–464 in J.D. Irish & G.R. Scott (eds) *A Companion to Dental Anthropology*. Wiley, Chichester.

Guatelli-Steinberg, D. & Lukacs, J.R. (1999). Interpreting Sex Differences in Enamel Hypoplasia in Human and Non-Human Primates: Developmental, Environmental and Cultural Considerations. *Yearbook of Physical Anthropology* 42: 73–126.

Gugliardo, M.F. (1982). Tooth Crown Size Differences Between Age Groups: A Possible New Indicator of Stress in Skeletal Samples. *American Journal of Physical Anthropology* 58: 383–389.

Guiry, E. (2019). Complexities of Stable Carbon and Nitrogen Isotope Biogeochemistry in Ancient Freshwater Ecosystems: Implications for the Study of Past Subsistence and Environmental Change. *Frontiers in Ecology and Evolution* 7: article 313.

Gunz, P. & Mitteroecker, P. (2013). Semilandmarks: A Method for Quantifying Curves and Surfaces. *Hystrix, the Italian Journal of Mammalogy* 24: 103–109.

Gustafson, G. & Koch, G. (1974). Age Estimation up to 16 Years of Age Based on Dental Development. *Odontologisk Revy* 25: 297–306.

Gustas, C.N. & Lee, K.S. (2016). Multimodality Imaging of the Painful Elbow. Current Imaging Concepts and Image-Guided Treatments for the Injured Thrower's Elbow. *Radiologic Clinics of North America* 54: 817–839.

Guy, H., Masset, C., & Baud, C. (1997). Infant Taphonomy. *International Journal of Osteoarchaeology* 7: 221–229.

Haak, W., Lazaridis, I., Patterson, N., Rohland, N., Mallick, S., Llamas, B. et al. (2015). Massive Migration from the Steppe Was a Source for Indo-European Languages in Europe. *Nature* 522: 207–211.

Haapasalo, H., Kontulainen, S., Sievänen, H., Kannus, P., Järvinen, M., & Vuori, I. (2000). Exercise Induced Bone Gain Is Due to Enlargement in Bone Size without A Change in Volumetric Bone Density: A Peripheral Quantitative Computed Tomography Study of the Upper Arms of Male Tennis Players. *Bone* 27: 351–357.

Hackett, C.J. (1976). *Diagnostic Criteria of Syphilis, Yaws and Treponarid (Treponematoses) and of Some Other Disease in Dry Bones*. Springer, Berlin.

Hackett, C.J. (1981). Microscopic Focal Destruction (Tunnels) in Exhumed Bone. *Medicine, Science and the Law* 21: 243–265.

Hackett, C.J. (1983). Problems in the Palaeopathology of the Human Treponematoses, pp. 106–128 in G.D. Hart (ed) *Disease in Ancient Man*. Clarke-Irwin, Toronto.

Hagelberg, E., Hofreiter, M., & Keyser, C. (2014). Ancient DNA: The First Three Decades. *Philosophical Transactions of the Royal Society B* 370: 20130371.

Hager, L. (1996). Sex Differences in the Sciatic Notch of Great Apes and Modern Humans. *American Journal of Physical Anthropology* 99: 287–300.

Hagihara, Y. & Nara, T. (2018). Diaphyseal Cross-Sectional Geometry of the Metatarsal Bones in the Jomon Population. *American Journal of Physical Anthropology* 166: 745–752.

Hallgrímsson, B., Ó Donnabháin, B., Walters, G.B., Cooper, D.M.L., Gudbjartsson, D., & Stefánsson, K. (2004). Composition of the Founding Population of Iceland: Biological Distance and Morphological Variation in Early Historic Atlantic Europe. *American Journal of Physical Anthropology* 124: 257–274.

Hallote, R.S. & Joffe, A.H. (2002). The Politics of Israeli Archaeology: Between 'Nationalism' and 'Science' in the Age of the Second Republic. *Israel Studies* 7: 84–116.

Hamblen, D.L. & Simpson, A.H.R.W. (2007). *Adam's Outline of Fractures Including Joint Injuries* (12th edition). Churchill-Livingstone, London.

Hanawalt, B. (1976). Violent Death in Fourteenth and Early Fifteenth Century England. *Comparative Studies in Society and History* 18: 297–320.

Handler, J.S. & Lange, F.W. (1978). *Plantation Slavery in Barbados: An Archaeological and Historical Investigation*. Harvard University Press, Cambridge.

Handley, L.L., Austin, A.T., Robinson, D., Scrimgeour, C.M., Raven, J.A., Heaton, T.H.E., Schmidt, S. & Stewart, G.R (1999). The ^{15}N Natural δ^{15}N Abundance of Ecosystem Samples Reflects Measures of Water Availability. *Australian Journal of Plant Physiology* 26: 185–199.

Hanihara, K. (1991). Dual Structure Model for the Population History of the Japanese. *Japan Review* 2: 1–33.

Hanihara, T. (1992). Negritos, Australian Aborigines, and the 'Proto-Sundadont' Dental Pattern: The Basic Populations in East Asia, V. *American Journal of Physical Anthropology* 88: 183–196.

Hanihara, T. (1993). Population Prehistory of East Asia and the Pacific as Viewed from Craniofacial Morphology: The Basic Populations in East Asia, VII. *American Journal of Physical Anthropology* 91: 173–187.

Hanihara, T. (2008). Morphological Variation of the Major Human Populations Based on Dental Nonmetric Traits. *American Journal of Physical Anthropology* 136: 169–182.

Hanihara, T. & Ishida, H. (2001a). Frequency Variation of Discrete Cranial Traits in Major Human Populations. I. Supernumerary Ossicle Variations. *Journal of Anatomy* 198: 689–706.

Hanihara, T. & Ishida, H. (2001b). Frequency Variation of Discrete Cranial Traits in Major Human Populations. II. Hypostotic Variations. *Journal of Anatomy* 198: 707–725.

Hanihara, T. & Ishida, H. (2001c). Frequency Variation of Discrete Cranial Traits in Major Human Populations. III. Hyperstotic Variations. *Journal of Anatomy* 199: 251–272.

Hanihara, T. & Ishida, H. (2001d). Frequency Variation of Discrete Cranial Traits in Major Human Populations. IV. Vessel and Nerve Related Variations. *Journal of Anatomy* 199: 273–287.

Hansen, H.B., Damgaard, P.B., Margaryan, A., Stenderup, J., Lynnerup, N., Willerslev, E. & Allentoft, M.E. (2017). Comparing Ancient DNA Preservation in Petrous Bone and Tooth Cementum. *PloS One* 12(1): e0170940.

Hansen, J.D., Pringle, J.K., & Goodwin, J. (2014). GPR and Bulk Ground Resistivity Surveys in Graveyards: Locating Unmarked Burials in Contrasting Soil Types. *Forensic Science International* 237: e14–e29.

Hardy, B.L. & Moncel, M. H. (2011). Neanderthal Use of Fish, Mammals, Birds, Starchy Plants and Wood 125-250,000 Years Ago. *PloS ONE* 6(8): e23768.

Hardy, K., Buckley, S., & Copeland, L. (2018). Pleistocene Dental Calculus: Recovering Information on Palaeolithic Food Items, Medicines, Palaeoenvironmental and Microbes. *Evolutionary Anthropology* 27: 234–246.

Harper, K.N., Zuckermam, M.K., Harper, M.L., Kingston, J.D., & Armelagos, G.J. (2011). The Origin and Antiquity of Syphilis Revisited: An Appraisal of the Old World Pre-Columbian Evidence for Treponemal Infection. *Yearbook of Physical Anthropology* 54: 99–133.

Harper, K.N., Zuckerman, M.K., & Armelagos, G.J. (2013). A Possible (But Not Probable) Case of Treponemal Disease. *International Journal of Osteoarchaeology* 626–627.

Harries, J., Fibiger, L., Smith, J., Adler, T., & Szöke, A. (2018). Exposure: The Ethics of Making, Sharing and Displaying Photographs of Human Remains. *Human Remains and Violence* 4(1): 3–24.

Harris, E.F. (2008). Interpreting Heritability Estimates in the Orthodontic Literature. *Seminars in Orthodontics* 14(2): 125–134.

Harrison, R.G. & Katzenberg, M.A. (2003). Paleodiet Studies Using Carbon Stable Isotopes from Bone Apatite and Collagen: Examples from Southern Ontario and San Nicholas Island, California. *Journal of Anthropological Archaeology* 22: 227–244.

Harrison, R.J. (1980). *The Beaker Folk*. Thames & Hudson, London.

Hart, J.P. (2018). New Trends in Prehistoric North-eastern North American Agriculture Evidence: A View from Central New York, in J. Lee-Thorp & M.A. Katzenberg (eds) *The Oxford Handbook of the Archaeology of Diet*. Oxford University Press, Oxford.

Hartnett, K.M. (2010). Analysis of Age-at-Death Estimation Using Data from a New, Modern Autopsy Sample. – Part I Pubic Bone. *Journal of Forensic Sciences* 55: 145–1151.

Hartnett-McCann, K., Fulginiti, L.C., & Seidel, A. (2018). Adult Age-at-death Estimation in Unknown Decedents: New Perspectives on an Old Problem, pp. 65–85 in K. Latham, E. Bartelink, & M. Finnegan (eds) *New Perspectives in Forensic Human Skeletal Identification*. Elsevier, London.

Harvey, N., Dennison, E., & Cooper, C. (2013). The Epidemiology of Osteoporotic Fractures, pp. 348–356 in C.J. Rosen (ed) *Primer on the Metabolic Bone Diseases and Disorders of Mineral Metabolism* (8th edition). Wiley-Blackwell, Chichester.

Hassett, B.R. (2012). Evaluating Sources of Variation in the Identification of Linear Hypoplastic Defects of Enamel: A New Quantified Method. *Journal of Archaeological Science* 39: 560–565.

Hather, J. (2009). The Charcoal from the Cremation Burials and Its Environmental Implications, pp. 426–428 in S. Hirst & D. Clark (eds) *Excavations at Mucking Volume 3: The Anglo-Saxon Cemeteries*. Museum of London Archaeology, London.

Hawkey, D.E. & Merbs, C.F. (1995). Activity-Induced Musculoskeletal Stress-Markers (MSM) and Subsistence Strategy Changes Among Ancient Hudson Bay Eskimos. *International Journal of Osteoarchaeology* 5: 324–338.

Haynes, S., Searle, J.B., Bretman, A., & Dobney, K.M. (2002). Bone Preservation and Ancient DNA: The Apllication of Screening Methods for Predicting DNA Survival. *Journal of Archaeological Science* 29: 585–592.

Healey, F. (2012). Chronology, Corpses, Ceramics, Copper, and Lithics, pp. 144–163 in M.J. Allen, J. Gardiner, & A. Sheridan (eds) *Is There a British Chalcolithic? People, Place and Polity in the Late 3rd Millennium*. Prehistoric Society Research Paper 4. Oxbow, Oxford.

Health Survey for England (2015). *Trend Tables – Child Tables*. https://digital.nhs.uk/data-and-information/publications/statistical/health-survey-for-england/health-survey-for-england-2015-trend-tables

Heathcote, G.M., Stodder, A.L.W., Buckley, H.R., Hanson, D.B., Douglas, M.T., Underwood, J. H., Taisipic, T.F. & Diego, V.P (1998). On Treponemal Disease in the Western Pacific: Corrections and Critique. *Current Anthropology* 39: 359–368.

Hedges, R.E.M. & Millard, A.R. (1995). Bones and Groundwater: Towards the Modelling of Diagenetic Processes. *Journal of Archaeological Science* 22: 155–164.

Hedges, R.E.M. & Reynard, L.M. (2007). Nitrogen Isotopes and the Trophic Level of Humans in Archaeology. *Journal of Archaeological Science* 34: 1240-1251.

Hedges, R.E.M., Millard, A.R., & Pike, A.W.G. (1995). Measurements and Relationships of Diagenetic Alteration of Bone from Three Archaeological Sites. *Journal of Archaeological Science* 22: 201-209.

Hedges, R.E.M., Clement, J.G., Thomas, D.L., & O'Connell, T.C. (2007). Collagen Turnover in the Adults Femoral Midshaft: Modelled from Anthropgenic Radiocarbon Tracer Measurements. *American Journal of Physical Anthropology* 133: 808-816.

Henderson, C.Y. & Alves Cardoso, F., (eds) (2018). *Identified Skeletal Collections: The Testing Ground of Anthropology?* Archaeopress, Oxford.

Henderson, C.Y., Mariotti, V., Pany-Kucera, D., Villotte, S., & Wilczak, C. (2016). The New 'Coimbra Method': A Biologically Appropriate Method for Recording Specific Features of Fibrocartilagenous Entheseal Changes. *International Journal of Osteoarchaeology* 26: 925-932.

Henderson, M., Miles, A., & Walker, D. (2015). *St Marylebone's Paddington North Burial Ground. Excavations at Paddington Street, London W1, 2012-13*. Museum of London Archaeology, Archaeology Studies Series 34. Museum of London Archaeology, London.

Henderson, M., Miles, A., Walker, D., Connell, B., & Wroe-Brown, R. (2013). *'He Being Dead yet Speaketh'. Excavations at Three Post-Mediaeval Burial Grounds in Tower Hamlets, East London, 2004-10*. Museum of London Archaeology Monograph 64. Museum of London Archaeology, London.

Hendy, J., Warriner, C., Bouwman, A., Collins, M.J., Fiddyment, S., Fischer, R. et al. (2018). Proteomic Evidence of Dietary Sources in Ancient Dental Calculus. *Proceedings of the Royal Society Series B* 285: article 20180977.

Henry, A.G., Brooks, A.S., & Piperno, D.R. (2011a). Microfossils in Calculus Demonstrate Consumption of Plants and Cooked Foods in Neanderthal Diets (Shanidar III, Iraq; Spy I and II, Belgium). *Proceedings of the National Academy of Sciences of the USA* 108: 486-491.

Henry, A.G., Brooks, A.S., & Piperno, D.R. (2011b). Reply to Collins and Copeland: Spontaneous Gelatinization Not Supported by Evidence. *Proceedings of the National Academy of Sciences of the USA* 108: E146.

Herrman, D., Grupe, G., Hummel, S., & Piepenbrink, H. (1990). *Prähistorische Anthropologie. Leitfaden Der Feld- Und Labormethoden*. Springer, Berlin.

High, K., Milner, N., Panter, I., & Penkman, K.E.H. (2015). Apatite for Destruction: Investigating Bone Degradation Due to High Acidity at Star Carr. *Journal of Archaeological Science* 59: 159-168.

Higuchi, T. (1986). Relationships between Japan and Asia in Ancient Times: Introductory Comments, pp. 121-125 in R.J. Pearson, G.L. Barnes, & K.L. Hutterer (eds) *Windows on the Japanese Past: Studies in Archaeology and Prehistory*. Center for Japanese Studies, Ann Arbor.

Hiller, J.C., Thompson, T.J.U., Evison, M.P., Chamberlain, A.T., & Wess, T.J. (2003). Bone Mineral Change during Experimental Heating: An X-ray Scattering Investigation. *Biomaterials* 24: 5091-5097.

Hillier, M.L. & Bell, L.S. (2007). Differentiating Human Bone from Animal Bone: A Review of Histological Methods. *Journal of Forensic Sciences* 52: 249-263.

Hills, C. & Lucy, S. (2013). *Spong Hill. Part IX: Chronology and Synthesis*. McDonald Institute Monograph, McDonald Institute for Archaeological Research, Cambridge.

Hillson, S. (1996). *Dental Anthropology*. Cambridge University Press, Cambridge.

Hillson, S. (2005). *Teeth* (2nd edition). Cambridge University Press, Cambridge.

Hillson, S. (2014). *Tooth Development in Human Evolution and Bioarchaeology*. Cambridge University Press, Cambridge.

Hillson, S. (2019). Dental Pathology, pp. 295-333 in M.A. Katzenberg & A.L. Grauer, (eds) *Biological Anthropology of the Human Skeleton* (3rd edition). Wiley-Blackwell, Chichester.

Hillson, S. & Bond, S. (1997). Relationship of Enamel Hypoplasia to the Pattern of Tooth Crown Growth: A Discussion. *American Journal of Physical Anthropology* 104: 89–103

Hillson, S., Grigson, C., & Bond, S. (1998). Dental Defects of Congenital Syphilis. *American Journal of Physical Anthropology* 107: 25–40.

Hillson, S.W., Franciscus, R.G., Holliday, T.W., & Trinkaus, E. (2006). The Ages at Death, pp. 31–45 in E. Trinkaus & J.A. Svoboda (eds) *Early Modern Human Evolution in Europe. The People of Dolní Věstonice and Pavlov.* Oxford University Press, Oxford.

Hofreiter, M., Paijmans, J.L.A., Goodchild, H., Speller, C.F., Barlow, A., Fortes, G.G. et al. (2014). The Future of Ancient DNA: Technical Advances and Conceptual Shifts. *Bioessays* 37: 284–293.

Holcomb, R.C. (1935). The Antiquity of Syphilis. *Medical Life* 42: 275–325.

Hollund, H.I., Arts, N., Jans, M.M.E., & Kars, H. (2015). Are Teeth Better? Histological Characterisation of Diagenesis in Bone-Tooth Pairs and a Discussion of the Consequences for Archaeometric Sample Selection and Analysis. *International Journal of Osteoarchaeology* 25: 901–911.

Hollund, H.I., Teasdale, M.D., Mattiangeli, V., Sverrisdóttir, O.O., Bradley, D.G., & O'Connor, T. (2017). Pick the Right Pocket. Sub-sampling of Bone Sections to Investigate Diagenesis and DNA Preservation. *International Journal of Osteoarchaeology* 27: 365–374.

Holt, B., Whittey, E., Niskanen, M., Sládek, V., Berner, M., & Ruff, C.B. (2018). Temporal and Geographic Variation in Robusticity, pp. 91–132 in C.B. Ruff (ed) *Skeletal Variation and Adaptation in Europeans. Upper Palaeolithic to the Twentieth Century.* Wiley-Blackwell, Chichester.

Hosek, L. & Robb, J. (2019). Osteobiography: A Platform for Archaeological Research. *Bioarchaeology International* 3: 1–15.

Howells, W.W. (1973). *Cranial Variation in Man. A Study by Multivariate Analysis of Patterns of Difference among Recent Human Populations.* Papers of the Peabody Museum, No. 67, Harvard University Press, Cambridge.

Hubbard, A., Guatelli-Steinberg, D., & Sciulli, P.W. (2009). Under Restrictive Conditions, Can the Widths of Linear Enamel Hypoplsias Be Used as Relative Indicators of Stress Episode Duration? *American Journal of Physical Anthropology* 138: 177–189.

Huffer, D. & Charlton, N. (2019). Serious Enquiries Only, Please: Ethical Issues Raised by the Online Human Remains Trade, pp. 95–129 in K. Squires, D. Errickson, & N. Márquez-Grant (eds) *Ethical Approaches to Human Remains: A Global Challenge in Bioarchaeology and Forensic Anthropology.* Springer, Cham.

Humphrey, L. (2000). Growth Studies of Past Populations: An Overview and an Example, pp. 23–38 in M. Cox & S. Mays (eds) *Human Osteology in Archaeology & Forensic Science.* Cambridge University Press, Cambridge.

Humphrey, L.T. (2014). Isotopic and Trace Element Evidence of Dietary Transitions in Early Life. *Annals of Human Biology* 41: 348–357.

Humphrey, L.T., Dean, M.C., Jeffries, T.E., & Penn, M. (2008). Unlocking Evidence for Early Diet from Tooth Enamel. *Proceedings of the National Academy of Sciences of the USA* 105(19): 6834–6839.

Huseynov, A., Zollikofer, C.P.E., Coudyzer, W., Gascho, D., Kellenberger, C., Hinzpeter, R., & Ponce de Leon, M.S. (2016). Developmental Evidence for Obstetric Adaptation of the Human Female Pelvis. *Proceedings of the National Academy of Sciences of the USA* 113 (19): 5227–5232.

Igarashi, Y., Uesu, K., Wakebe, T., & Kanazawa, E. (2005). New Method for Estimation of Adult Skeletal Age at Death from the Morphology of the Auricular Surface of the Ilium. *American Journal of Physical Anthropology* 128: 324–339.

Imaizumi, K., Taniguchi, K., & Ogawa, Y. (2014). DNA Survival and Physical and Histological Properties of Heat-Induced Alterations in Burnt Bones. *International Journal of Legal Medicine* 128: 439–446.

Inglemark, B. (1939). The Skeletons, pp. 149–205 in B. Thordemann (ed) *Armour from the Battle of Wisby, 1361.* Vitterhets Historie och Antikvitets Akademien, Stockholm.

Inskip, S.A., Taylor, G.M., Zakrzewski, S.R., Mays, S.A., Pike, A.W.G., Llewellyn, G., Williams, C. M., Lee, O.Y.-C., Wu, H.H.T., Minniken, D.E., Besra, G.S. & Stewart, G.R. (2015). Osteological, Biomolecular and Geochemical Examination of an Early Anglo-Saxon Case of Lepromatous Leprosy. *PloS One* 10(5): e0124282.

Ioannu, S., Sassani, S., Henneberg, M., & Henneberg, R.J. (2016). Diagnosing Congenital Syphilis Using Hutchinson's Method: Differentiating between Syphilitic, Mercurial and Syphilitic-Mercurial Dental Defects. *American Journal of Physical Anthropology* 159: 617–629.

Irish, J.D., Black, W., Sealy, J., & Ackermann, R.R. (2014). Questions of Khoesan Continuity: Dental Affinities among Indigenous Holocene Peoples of South Africa. *American Journal of Physical Anthropology* 155: 33–44.

Irish, J.D., Morez, A., Flink, L.G., Phillips, E.L.W., & Scott, G.R. (2020). Do Dental Nonmetric Traits Actually Work as Proxies for Neutral Genomic Data? Some Answers from Continental- and Global-Level Analyses. *American Journal of Physical Anthropology* 172: 347–375.

İşcan, M.Y. & Steyn, M. (2013). *Human Skeleton in Forensic Medicine*. Charles C Thomas, Springfield.

İşcan, M.Y., Loth, S.R., & Wright, R.K. (1984). Metamorphosis at the Sternal Rib End: A New Method to Estimate Age at Death in White Males. *American Journal of Physical Anthropology* 65: 147–156.

İşcan, M.Y., Loth, S.R., & Wright, R.K. (1985). Age Estimation from the Rib by Phase Analysis: White Females. *Journal of Forensic Sciences* 30: 853–863.

Ishida, H., Hanihara, T., Kondo, O., & Fukumine, T. (2009). Craniometric Divergence History of the Japanese Population. *Anthropological Science* 117: 147–156.

Itan, Y., Jones, B.L., Ingram, C.J.E., Swallow, D.M., & Thomas, M.G. (2010). A Worldwide Correlation of Lactase Persistence Phenotype and Genotype. *BMC Evolutionary Biology* 10: article 36.

Iuliano-Barnes, S., Stone, J., Hopper, J.L., & Seeman, E. (2005). Diet and Exercise During Growth Have Site-Specific Skeletal Effects: A Co-Twin Control Study. *Osteoporosis International* 16: 1225–1232.

Ives, R., MacQuarrie, H., & Hogg, I. (forthcoming). *An East-End Opportunity – Insights into Post-Medieval Life, Death and Burial from Excavations at Kilday's Burial Ground, Bethnal Green.* AOC Archaeology, London.

Iwamura, E.S.M., Guimarães, M.A., & Evison, M.P. (2016). DNA Methods to Identify Missing Persons, pp. 337–352 in S.J. Morewitz & C. Sturdy Culls (eds) *Handbook of Missing Persons*. Springer, Cham.

Jackes, M. (2000). Building the Bases for Paleodemographic Analysis: Adult Age Determination, pp. 417–466 in M.A. Katzenberg & S.R. Saunders (eds) *Biological Anthropology of the Human Skeleton* (1st edition), Wiley, Chichester.

Jackes, M. (2011). Representativeness and Bias in Archaeological Skeletal Samples, pp. 107–146 in S.C. Agarwal & B.A. Glencross (eds) *Social Bioarchaeology*. Wiley-Blackwell, Chichester.

Jackson, R. (1988). *Doctors and Diseases in the Roman Empire*. British Museum Press, London.

Janaway, R.C. (1987). The Preservation of Organic Materials in Association with Metal Artifacts Deposited in Inhumation Graves, pp. 127–148 in A. Boddington, A.N. Garland, & R.C. Janaway (eds) *Death, Decay and Reconstruction*. Manchester University Press, Manchester.

Janaway, R.C., Percival, S.L., & Wilson, A.S. (2009). Decomposition of Human Remains, pp. 313–333 in S.L. Percival, (ed) *Microbiology and Aging*. Springer, Berlin.

Jans, M.M.E., Nielsen-Marsh, C.M., Smith, C.I., Collins, M.J., & Kars, H. (2004). Characterisation of Microbial Attack on Archaeological Bone. *Journal of Archaeological Science* 31: 87–95.

Jantz, R.L., Hunt, D.R., & Meadows, L. (1994). Maximum Length of the Tibia: How Did Trotter Measure It? *American Journal of Physical Anthropology* 93: 525–528.

Jaskowiec, T.C., Grauer, A.L., Lee, M., & Rajnic, S. (2017). No Stone Unturned: The Presence of Kidney Stones in a Skeleton from 19th Century Peoria, Illinois. *International Journal of Paleopathology* 19:18-23.

Jay, M., Richards, M.P., & Marshall, P. (2019). Radiocarbon Dates and Their Bayesian Modelling, pp. 43-80 in M. Parker Pearson, A. Sheridan, M. Jay, A. Chamberlain, M.P. Richards, & J. Evans (eds) *The Beaker People. Isotopes, Mobility and Diet in Prehistoric Britain*. Prehistoric Society Research Paper 7. Oxbow, Oxford.

Jee, W. (1988). Bone, in L. Weiss (ed) *Cell and Tissue Biology* (6th edition). Urban & Schwartzenberg, Baltimore.

Jelenkovic, A., Poveda, A., Susanne, C., & Rebato, E. (2010). Common Genetic and Environmental Factors among Craniofacial Traits in Belgian Nuclear Families: Comparing Skeletal and Soft Tissue Related Phenotypes. *HOMO: Journal of Comparative Human Biology* 61: 191-203.

Jelínek, J. (1987). A New Palaeolithic Triple Burial Find. *Anthropologie (Brno)* 25: 189-190.

Jenkins, T. (2016a). *Keeping Their Marbles: How the Treasures of the Past Ended up in Museums … and Why They Should Stay There*. Oxford Universty Press, Oxford.

Jenkins, T. (2016b). Making an Exhibition of Ourselves: Using the Dead to Fight the Battles of the Living, pp. 251-267 in H. Williams & M. Giles (eds) *Archaeologists and the Dead. Mortuary Archaeology in Contemporary Society*. Oxford University Press, Oxford.

Jeong, C., Wilkin, S., Amgalantugs, T., Bouwman, A., Taylor, W.T.T., Hagan, R.W. et al. (2018). Bronze Age Population Dynamics and the Rise of Dairy Pastoralism on the Eastern Eurasian Steppe. *Proceedings of the National Academy of Sciences of the USA* 115: E11248-E11255.

Jersie-Christensen, R.R., Lanigan, L.T., Lyon, D., Mackie, M., Belstrøm, D., Kelstrup, K.D. et al. (2018). Quantitative Metaproteomics of Medieval Dental Calculus Reveals Individual Oral Health Status. *Nature Communications* 9: article 4744.

Jin, Y. & Yip, H. K. (2002). Supra-Gingival Calculus: Formation and Control. *Critical Reviews in Oral and Biological Medicine* 15: 426-441.

Johnson, A.L. & Lovell, N.C. (1994). Biological Differentiation at Predynastic Naqada, Egypt: An Analysis of Dental Morphological Traits. *American Journal of Physical Anthropology* 93: 427-433.

Johnston, F.E. & Zimmer, L.O. (1989). Assessment of Growth and Age in the Immature Skeleton, pp. 11-21 in M.Y. İşcan & K.A.R. Kennedy (eds) *Reconstruction of Life from the Skeleton*. Liss, New York.

Jones, H.H., Priest, J.D., Hayes, W.C., Tichenor, C.C., & Nagel, D.A. (1977). Humeral Hypertrophy in Response to Exercise. *Journal of Bone and Joint Surgery* 59A: 204-208.

Jones, N.L. (2007). A Code of Ethics for the Life Sciences. *Science and Engineering Ethics* 13: 25-43.

Jordana, F., Colat-Parros, J., & Bénézech, M. (2013). Diagnosis of Skull Fractures According to Postmortem Interval: An Experimental Approach in a Porcine Model. *Journal of Forensic Sciences* 58: S156-S162.

Joy, J. (2009). *Lindow Man*. British Museum, London.

Joy, J. (2014). Looking Death in the Face: Different Attitudes Towards Bog Bodies and Their Display with a Focus on Lindow Man, pp. 10-19 in A. Fletcher, D. Antoine, & J.D. Hill (eds) *Regarding the Dead: Human Remains in the British Museum*. British Museum Research Publication 197. British Museum Press, London.

Judd, M. (2004). Trauma in the City of Kerma: Ancient versus Modern Injury Patterns. *International Journal of Osteoarchaeology* 14: 34-51.

Judd, M. (2008). The Parry Problem. *Journal of Archaeological Science* 35: 1658-1666.

Kalsbeek, N. & Richter, J. (2006). Preservation of Burned Bones: An Investigation of the Effects of Temperature and pH on Hardness. *Studies in Conservation* 51: 123-138.

Kanaseki, H. (1986). The Evidence for Social Change Between the Early and Middle Yayoi, pp. 317–333 in R.J. Pearson, G.L. Barnes, & K.L. Hutterer (eds) *Windows on the Japanese Past: Studies in Archaeology and Prehistory*. Center for Japanese Studies, Ann Arbor.

Kaner, S. & Yano, K. (2015). Early Agriculture in Japan, pp. 353–386 in G. Barker & C. Goucher (eds) *Cambridge World History*. Cambridge University Press, Cambridge.

Kangas, A.T., Evans, A.R., Thesleff, I., & Jernvall, J. (2004). Nonindependence of Mammalian Dental Characters. *Nature* 432: 211–214.

Kanis, J.A., Cooper, C., Rizzoli, R., Abrahamsen, B., Al-Daghri, N.M., Brandi, M.L. et al. (2017). Identification and Management of Patients at Increased Risk of Osteoporotic Fracture: Outcomes of an ESCEO Expert Consensus Meeting. *Osteoporosis International* 28: 2023–2034.

Kaplan, G.B. (2002). The (Columbian) Myth of Syphilis: A Textual Perspective. *Hispanófila* 134: 21–35.

Karacas, H.M., Harma, A., & Alicioglu, B. (2013). The Subpubic Angle in Sex Determination: Anthropometric Measurements and Analyses on Anatolian Caucasians Using Multidetector Computed Tomography Datasets. *Journal of Forensic and Legal Medicine* 20: 1004–1009.

Karakostis, F.A., Hotz, G., Scherf, H., Wahl, J., & Harvati, K. (2017). Occupational Manual Activity Is Reflected on the Patterns Among Hand Entheses. *American Journal of Physical Anthropology* 164: 30–40.

Karakostis, F.A., Hotz, G., Scherf, H., Wahl, J., & Harvati, K. (2018). A Repeatable Geometric Morphometric Approach to the Analysis of Hand Enthesial Three-dimensional Form. *American Journal of Physical Anthropology* 166: 246–260.

Katz, S.H., Hediger, M.L., & Valleroy, L.A. (1974). Traditional Maize Processing Techniques in the New World. *Science* 184: 765–773.

Katz, D.C., Grote, M.N., & Weaver, T.D. (2017). Changes in Human Skull Morphology across the Agricultural Transition are Consistent with Softer Diets in Preindustrial Farming Groups. *Proceedings of the National Academy of Sciences of the USA* 114(34): 9049–9055.

Katzenberg, M.A., Herring, D.A., & Saunders, S.R. (1996). Weaning and Infant Mortality: Evaluating the Skeletal Evidence. *Yearbook of Physical Anthropology* 39: 177–199.

Kay, G.L., Sergeant, M.J., Guiffra, V., Bandiera, P., Milanese, M., Bramanti, M. et al. (2014). Recovery of a Mediaeval *Brucella Melitensis* Genome Using Shotgun Metagenomics. *MBio* 5 (4):article e01337-14.

Keeley, H. (n.d.). *Wharram Percy, Yorkshire, Soil Report*. Manuscript on file at Historic England.

Keller, J.M., Huet-Hudson, Y.M., & Leamy, L.J. (2007). Qualitative Effects of Dioxin on Molars Vary Among Inbred Mouse Strains. *Archives of Oral Biology* 52: 450–454.

Kelley, M.A., Levesque, D.R., & Weidl, E. (1991). Contrasting Patterns of Dental Disease in Five Early Northern Chilean Groups, pp. 203–213 in M.A. Kelley & C.S. Larsen (eds) *Advances in Dental Anthropology*. Wiley-Liss, Chichester.

Kellinghaus, M., Schulz, R., Vieth, V., Schmidt, S., & Schmeling, A. (2010). Forensic Age Estimation in Living Subjects Based on the Ossification Status of the Medial Clavicular Epiphysis as Revealed by Thin-Slice Multidetector Computed Tomography. *International Journal of Legal Medicine* 124: 149–154.

Kendall, C., Høier Eriksen, A.-M., Kontopoulos, I., Collins, M.J., & Turner-Walker, G. (2018). Diagenesis of Archaeological Bone and Tooth. *Palaeogeography, Palaeoclimatology, Palaeoecology* 491: 21–37.

Kennedy, G.E. (1986). The Relationship Between Auditory Exostoses and Cold Water: A Latitudinal Analysis. *American Journal of Physical Anthropology* 71: 401–415.

Kerr, N.W. (1998). The Prevalence and Natural History of Periodontal Disease in Britain from Prehistoric to Modern Times. *British Dental Journal* 185: 527–535.

Kerr, N.W. & Ringrose, T.J. (1998). Factors Affecting the Lifespan on the Human Dentition in Britain Prior to the Seventeenth Century. *British Dental Journal* 184: 242-246.

Key, C.A., Aiello, L.C., & Molleson, T. (1994). Cranial Suture Closure and Its Implications for Age Estimation. *International Journal of Osteoarhaeology* 4: 193-207.

Key, F.M., Posth, C., Krause, J., Herbig, A., & Bos, K. (2017). Mining Metagenomic Data Sets for Ancient DNA: Recommended Protocols for Authentication. *Trends in Genetics* 33: 508-520.

Kieser, J.A. (1990). *Human Adult Odontometrics*. Cambridge University Press, Cambridge.

Kieser, J.A., Preston, C.B., & Evans, W.G. (1983). Skeletal Age at Death: An Evaluation of the Miles Method of Ageing. *Journal of Archaeological Science* 10: 9-12.

Kihlström, C., Möller, M., Lönn, K., & Wolf, O. (2017). Clavicle Fractures: Epidemiology, Classification and Treatment of 2442 Fractures in the Swedish Fracture Register; an Observational Study. *BMC Musculoskeletal Disorders* 18: article 82.

Killian Galván, V.A.K. (2018). Models for Paleodietary Research: Three Case Studies from Arid and Semi-Arid Environments in Northwest Argentina. *Journal of Archaeological Science Reports* 18: 606-616.

Kilmister, H., (2003). Visitor Perceptions of Ancient Egyptian Human Remains in Three United Kingdom Museums. *Papers from the Institute of Archaeology* 14: 57-69

Kim, Y.S., Park, I.S., Kim, H.J., Kim, D., Lee, N.J., & Rhyu, I.J. (2018). Changes in Intracranial Volume and Cranial Shape in Modern Koreans over Four Decades. *American Journal of Physical Anthropology* 166: 753-759.

King, K.A. (2004). A Test of the Fully Anatomical Method of Stature Estimation. *American Journal of Physical Anthropology Supplement* 38: 125.

King, T.E., Fortes, G.G., Balaresque, P., Thomas, M.G., Balding, D., Delser, P.M. et al. (2014). Identification of the Remains of King Richard III. *Nature Communications* 5: article 5631.

Kirkinen, T. (2017). "Burning Pelts" - Brown Bear Skins in the Iron Age and Early Mediaeval (1-1300AD) Burials in South-Eastern Fennoscandia. *Estonian Journal of Archaeology* 21(1): 3-29.

Kjellström, A. (2005). A Sixteenth-Century Warrior Grave from Uppsala, Sweden: The Battle of Good Friday. *International Journal of Osteoarchaeology* 15: 23-50.

Klales, A.R. (2013). Current Practices in Physical Anthropology for Sex Estimation in Unidentified, Adult Individuals. *American Journal of Physical Anthopology* Suppl. 56: 168 (abstact).

Klales, A.R. & Burns, T.L. (2017). Adapting and Applying the Phenice (1969) Adult Morphological Sex Estimation Technique to Subadults. *Journal of Forensic Sciences* 62: 747-752.

Klales, A.R., Ousley, S.D., & Vollner, J.M. (2012). A Revised Method of Sexing the Human Inominate Using Phenice's Nonmetric Traits and Statistical Methods. *American Journal of Physical Anthropology* 149: 104-114.

Klaus, H.D. & Ericksen, C.M. (2013). Paleopathology of an Ovarian Teratoma: Description and Diagnosis of an Exotic Abdominal Bone and Tooth Mass in a Historic Peruvian Burial. *International Journal of Paleopathology* 3: 294-301.

Klaus, H.D. & Lynnerup, N. (2019). Abnormal Bone: Considerations for Documentation, Disease Process Identification, and Differential Diagnosis, in J.E. Buikstra, ed. *Ortner's Identification of Pathological Conditions in Human Skeletal Remains* (3rd edition). Academic Press, London.

Klima, B. (1988). A Triple Burial from the Upper Palaeolithic of Dolní Věstonice, Czecheslovakia. *Journal of Human Evolution* 16: 831-835.

Knell, R.J. (2004). Syphilis in Renaissance Europe: Rapid Evolution of an Introduced Sexually Transmitted Disease? *Proceedings of the Royal Society of London B* (Supplement) 271: S174-S176.

Knudsen, K.J. & Stojanowski, C.M. (eds) 2011. *The Bioarchaeology of Identity in the Americas*. University Press of Florida, Boca Raton.

Knüsel, C. (1993). On the Biomechanical and Osteoarthritic Differences between Hunter-Gatherers and Agriculturalists. *American Journal of Physical Anthropology* 91: 523–527.

Knüsel, C. & Robb, J. (2016). Funerary Taphonomy: An Overview of Goals and Methods. *Journal of Archaeological Science Reports* 10: 655–673.

Köhler, K., Marcsik, A., Zádori, P., Szeniczey, T., Fábián, S. et al. (2017). Possible Cases of Leprosy from the Late Copper Age (3780-3650 cal BC) in Hungary. *Plos One* 12(10): e0185866.

Kohn, L.A.P. (1991). The Role of Genetics in Craniofacial Morphology and Growth. *Annual Review of Anthropology* 20: 261–278.

Konigsberg, L.W. & Frankenberg, S.R. (1992). Estimation of Age Structure in Anthropological Demography. *American Journal of Physical Anthroplogy* 89: 235–256.

Kontopoulos, I., Penkman, K., McAllister, G.D., Lynnerup, N., Damgaard, P.B., Hansen, H.B., Allentoft, M., & Collins, M.J. (2019). Petrous Bone Diagenesis: A Multi-Analytical Approach. *Palaeogeography, Palaeoclimatology, Palaeoecology* 518: 143–154.

Kontulainen, S., Sievänen, H., Kannus, P., & Vuori, I. (2003). Effects of Long-Term Impact Loading on Mass, Size, and Estimated Strength of Humerus and Radius of Female Racquet Sports Players: A Perpipheral Quantitative Computed Tomography Study between Young and Old Starters and Controls. *Journal of Bone and Mineral Research* 18: 352–359.

Korneliussen, T., Albrechtsen, S.A., & Nielsen, R. (2014). ANGSD: Analysis of Next Generation Sequencing Data. *BMC Bioinformatics* 15: article 356.

Kozintsev, A. (1990). Ainu, Japanese, Their Ancestors and Neighbours. *Journal of the Anthropological Society of Nippon* 98: 247–267.

Krap, T., Ruijter, J.M., Nota, K., Karel, J., Burgers, A.L., Aalders, M.C.G., Oostra, R-J. & Duijst, W. (2019). Colourimetric Analysis of Thermally Altered Human Bone Samples. *Scientific Reports* 9: article 8923.

Kremer, C. & Sauvageau, A. (2009). Discrimination of Falls and Blows in Blunt Head Trauma: Assessment of Predictability through Combined Criteria. *Journal of Forensic Sciences* 54: 923–926.

Kutterer, A.U., Doppler, S., Uerpman, M., & Uerpman, H.P. (2012). Neolithic Cremation in South-East Arabia: Archaeological and Anthropological Observations at FAY-NE10 in the Emirate of Sharjah (UAE). *Arabian Archaeology & Epigraphy* 23: 125–144.

Kuzmirsky, S.C., Ráez, O.R., Arriaza, B., Méndez, C., Standen, V.G., San Román, M., Muñoz, I., Herrera, Á., & Hubbe, M. (2018). Investigating Cranial Morphological Variation of Early Human Skeletal Remains from Chile: A 3D Geometric Morphometric Approach. *American Journal of Physical Anthropology* 165: 223–237.

Kvaal, S.I. & Derry, T.K. (1996). Tell-Tale Teeth: Abrasion from the Traditional Clay Pipe. *Endeavour* 20: 28–30.

Lacoste Jeanson, A., Santos, F., Villa, C., Dupej, J., & Lynnerup, N. (2017). Body Mass Estimation from the Skeleton: An Evaluation of 11 Methods. *Forensic Science International* 281: 183e1–183e8.

Lambacher, N., Gerdau-Radonic, K., Bonthorne, E., & Montero, F.J.V.D. (2016). Evaluating Three Methods to Estimate the Number of Individuals from a Commingled Context. *Journal of Archaeological Science Reports* 10: 674–683.

Lambert, J.B., Vlasak, S.M., Thometz, A.C., & Buikstra, J.E. (1982). A Comparative Study of the Chemical Analysis of Ribs and Femurs in Woodland Populations. *American Journal of Physical Anthropology* 59: 289–294.

Lambert, P.M. (2012). Ethics and Issues in the Use of Human Skeletal Remains in Paleopathology, pp. 17–33 in A.L. Grauer (ed) *A Companion to Paleopathology*. Wiley-Blackwell, Chichester.

Lambert, P.M. & Walker, P.L. (2019). Bioarchaeological Ethics: Perspectives on the Use and Value of Human Remains in Scientific Research, pp. 1–42 in M.A. Katzenberg & A.L. Grauer, (eds) *Biological Anthropology of the Human Skeleton* (3rd edition). Wiley-Blackwell, Chichester.

Lamendin, H., Baccino, E., Humbert, J.F., Tavernier, J.C., Nossintchouk, R.M., & Zerelli, A. (1992). A Simple Technique for Age Estimation in Adult Corpses: The Two Criteria Dental Method. *Journal of Forensic Sciences* 37: 1373-1379.

Lan, T. & Lindqvist, C. (2018). Technical Advances and Challenges in Genome-Scale Analysis of Ancient DNA, pp. 3-29 in C. Lindqvist & O.P. Rajora (eds) *Palaeogenomics. Genome-Scale Analysis of Ancient DNA*. Springer, Berlin

Lanteri, L., Bizot, B., Saliba-Serre, B., Gaudart, J., Signoli, M., & Schmitt, A. (2018). Cemento-chronology: A Solution to Assess Mortality Profiles from Individual Age-at-Death Estimates. *Journal of Archaeological Science Reports* 20: 576-587.

Larsen, C.S. (2015). *Bioarchaeology: Interpreting Behavior from the Human Skeleton* (second edition). Cambridge University Press, Cambridge.

Larsen, C.S., Shavit, R., & Griffen, M.C. (1991). Dental Caries Evidence for Dietary Change: An Archaeological Context, pp. 179-202 in M.A. Kelley & C.S. Larsen (eds) *Advances in Dental Anthropology*. Wiley-Liss, Chichester.

Leamy, L. (1997). Genetic Analysis of Fluctuating Asymmetry for Skeletal Characters in Mice. *Journal of Heredity* 88: 85-92.

Lees, B., Molleson, T., Arnett, T.R., & Stevenson, J.C. (1993). Differences in Proximal Femur Bone Density over Two Centuries. *Lancet* 341: 673-675.

Lee-Thorp, J. & Sponheimer, M. (2003). Three Case Studies Used to Reassess the Reliability of Fossil Bone and Enamel Isotope Signals for Palaeodietary Studies. *Journal of Anthropological Archaeology* 22: 208-216.

Leonard, C., Vashro, L., O'Connell, J.F., & Henry, A.G. (2015). Plant Microremains in Dental Calculus as A Record of Plant Consumption: A Test with Twe Forager-Horticulturalists. *Journal of Archaeological Science Reports* 2: 449-457.

Levesque, G.Y., Demirjian, A., & Tanguay, R. (1981). Sexual Dimorphism in the Development, Emergence and Agenesis of the Mandibular Third Molar. *Journal of Dental Research* 60: 1735-1741.

Levinson, A.A., Luz, B., & Kolodny, Y. (1987). Variations in Oxygen Isotopic Compositions of Human Teeth and Urinary Stones. *Applied Geochemistry* 2: 367-371.

Lewis, A.B. & Garn, S.M. (1960). The Relationship between Tooth Formation and Other Maturational Factors. *The Angle Orthodontist* 30: 70-77.

Lewis, J.E. (2008). Identifying Sword Marks on Bone: Criteria for Distinguishing between Cut Marks Made by Different Classes of Bladed Weapons. *Journal of Archaeological Science* 35: 2001-2008.

Lewis, M.E. (2019). Children in Bioarchaeology: Methods and Interpretations, pp. 119-144 in M.A. Katzenberg & A.L. Grauer (eds) *Biological Anthropology of the Human Skeleton*. Wiley-Blackwell, Chichester.

Lewis, M.E. & Gowland, R. (2007). Brief and Precarious Lives: Infant Mortality in Contrasting Sites from Mediaeval and Post-Mediaeval England (AD850-1859). *American Journal of Physical Anthropology* 134: 117-129.

Lie, A.K. (2007). Origin Stories and the Norwegian Radesyge. *Social History of Medicine* 20: 563-579.

Lieverse, A.R., Bazaliiskii, V.I., Goriunova, O.I., & Weber, A.W. (2013). Lower Limb Activity in the Cis-Baikal: Entheseal Changes Among Middle Holocene Siberian Foragers. *American Journal of Physical Anthropology* 150: 421-432.

Linderholm, A. (2015). Ancient DNA: The Next Generation – Chapter and Verse. *Biological Journal of the Linnean Society* 117: 150-160.

Lindsay, W.L. (1979). *Chemical Equilibria in Soils*. Wiley, New York.

Lipson, M., Szécsényi, A., Mallick, S., Pósa, A., Stégmár, B., Keerl, V. et al. (2017). Parallel Palaeogenomic Transects Reveal Complex Genetic History of Early European Farmers. *Nature* 551: 368-372.

Liversidge, H.M. (1994). Accuracy of Age Estimation from Developing Teeth of a Population of Known Age (0 to 5.4 Years). *International Journal of Osteoarchaeology* 4: 37-45.

Liversidge, H.M. (2008). Timing of Human Mandibular Third Molar Formation. *Annals of Human Biology* 35: 294-321.

Liversidge, H.M. (2015). Controversies in Age Estimation from Developing Teeth. *Annals of Human Biology* 42: 397-406.

Liversidge, H.M. & Molleson, T.I. (2018). Human Tooth Development, Tooth Length and Eruption; a Study of British Archaeological Dentitions. *Historical Biology* 30: 166-173.

Loe, L., Barker, C., Brady, K., Cox, M., & Webb, H. (2014). *'Remember Me to All'. The Archaeological Recovery and Identifications of Soldiers Who Fought and Died at the Battle of Fromelles, 1916*. Oxford Archaeology Monograph No. 23. Oxford Archaeology, Oxford.

López-Costas, O., Lantez-Suárez, Ó., & Martínez-Cortzas, A. (2016). Chemical Compositional Changes in Archaeological Human Bones Due to Diagenesis: Type of Bone Vs Soil Environment. *Journal of Archaeological Science* 67: 43-51.

Loth, S.R. & İşcan, M.Y. (1989). Morphological Assessment of Age in the Adult: The Thoracic Region, pp. 105-135 in M.Y. İşcan (ed) *Age Markers in the Human Skeleton*. Charles C Thomas, Springfield.

Loudon, I.S.L. (1981). Leg Ulcers in the 18th and Early 19th Centuries. *Journal of the Royal College of General Practitioners* 31: 263-273.

Lovejoy, C.O., Burstein, A.H., & Heiple, K.G. (1976). The Biomechanical Analysis of Bone Strength: A Method and Its Application to Platycnemia. *American Journal of Physical Anthropology* 44: 489-506.

Lovejoy, C.O., Meindl, R.S., Pryzbeck, T.R., & Mensforth, R.P. (1985). Chronological Metamorphosis of the Auricular Surface of the Ilium: A New Method of Determining Adult Age at Death. *American Journal of Physical Anthropology* 68: 15-28.

Lugli, F. (2019). Accurate Sr Isotope Determination of Human Bone and Tooth Samples by LA-MC-ICP-MS: A Comment on "Meijer Et Al. (2019)". *International Journal of Osteoarchaeology* 29: 1109-1111.

Lukacs, J.R. (2007). Dental Trauma and Antemortem Tooth Loss in Prehistoric Canary Islanders: Prevalence and Contributing Factors. *International Journal of Osteoarchaeology* 17: 157-173.

Luke, D.A., Tonge, C.H., & Reid, D. (1979). Metrical Analysis of Growth Changes in the Jaws and Teeth or Normal, Protein Deficient and Calories Deficient Pigs. *Journal of Anatomy* 129: 449-457.

Lunar Corporation. (1993). *Lunar DPX Technical and Operator's Manuals, Version 3.6*. Lunar Corporation, Madison.

Lycett, S.J. & Collard, M. (2005). Do Homiologies Impede Phylogenetic Analyses of the Fossil Hominids? An Assessment Based on Extant Papionin Craniodental Morphology. *Journal of Human Evolution* 49: 618-642.

Lynott, M.J., Boutton, T.W., Price, J.E., & Nelson, D.E. (1986). Stable Carbon Isotope Evidence for Maize Agriculture in Southeast Missouri and Northeast Arkansas. *American Antiquity* 51: 51-65.

Maat, G.J.R. (2005). Two Millennia of Male Stature Development and Population Health and Wealth in the Low Countries. *International Journal of Osteoarchaeology* 15: 276-290.

Maat, G.J.R. & van der Velde, E.M. (1987). The Caries-Attrition Competition. *International Journal of Anthropology* 2: 281-292.

Macaluso, P.J. & Lucena, J. (2012). Test of a New Components Method for Age-at-Death Estimation from the Medial End of the Fourth Rib Using a Modern Spanish Sample. *International Journal of Legal Medicine* 126: 773-779.

Mackie, M., Hendy, J., Lowe, A.D., Sperduti, A., Holst, M., Collins, M.J. & Speller, C.F. (2017). Preservation of the Metaproteome: Variability of Protein Preservation in Ancient Dental Calculus. *Science and Technology of Archaeological Research* 3: 58-70.

Maddux, S.D., Yokley, T.R., Svoma, B.M., & Franciscus, R.G. (2016). Absolute Humidity and the Human Nose: A Reanalysis of Climate Zones and Their Influence on Nasal Form and Function. *American Journal of Physical Anthropology* 161: 309-320.

Maddux, S.D., Butaric, L.N., Yokley, T.R., & Franciscus, R.G. (2017). Ecogeographic Variation Across Morphofunctional Units of the Human Nose. *American Journal of Physical Anthropology* 162: 103–119.

Mader, R., Verlan, J.-J., & Buskila, D. (2013). Diffuse Idiopathic Skeletal Hyperostosis: Clinical Features and Pathogenic Mechanisms. *Nature Reviews Rheumatology* 9: 741–750.

Magilton, J. (2008a). Leprosy, Lepers and Their Hospitals, pp. 9–26 in J. Magilton, F. Lee, & A. Boylston (eds) *Lepers outside the Gate. Excavations at the Cemetery at the Hospital of St James and St Mary Magdelene, Chichester 1986-87 and 1993*. Chichester Excavations 10. CBA Research Report 158. Council for British Archaeology, York.

Magilton, J. (2008b). Mediaeval and Early Modern Cemeteries in England: An Introduction, pp. 27–47 in J. Magilton, F. Lee, & A. Boylston (eds) *Lepers outside the Gate. Excavations at the Cemetery at the Hospital of St James and St Mary Magdelene, Chichester 1986-87 and 1993*. Chichester Excavations 10. CBA Research Report 158. Council for British Archaeology, York.

Mahakkanukrauh, P., Khanpech, P., Prasitwattanseree, S., Vichairat, K., & Case, T.D. (2011). Stature Estimation from Long Bone Lengths in a Thai Population. *Forensic Science International* 210: 279e1–279e7.

Mainfort, R.C. (1985). Wealth, Space and Status in a Historic Indian Cemetery. *American Antiquity* 50: 555–579.

Makarewicz, C.A. & Sealy, J. (2015). Dietary Reconstruction, Mobility, and the Analysis of Ancient Skeletal Tissues: Expanding the Prospects of Stable Isotope Research in Archaeology. *Journal of Archaeological Science* 56: 146–158.

Malinowski, A. & Porawski, R. (1969). Identificationsmöglichkeiten Menschlicher Brandknochen Mit Besonderer Berucksichtigung Ihres Gewichters. *Zacchia* 5: 392–410.

Mamede, A.P., Gonçalves, D., Marques, M.P.M., & Batista de Carvalho, A.E. (2018). Burned Bones Tell Their Own Stories: A Review of Methodological Approaches to Assess Heat-Induced Diagenesis. *Applied Spectroscopy Reviews* 53: 8: 603–635.

Manchester, K. (1983). Secondary Cancer in an Anglo-Saxon Female. *Journal of Archaeological Science* 10: 475–482.

Manchester, K., Ogden, A., & Storm, R. (2017). *Nomenclature in Palaeopathology*. Palaeopathology Association. https://paleopathology-association.wildapricot.org/resources/Documents/Nomenclature%20in%20Palaeopathology%20Web%20Document.pdf. Accessed July 2019.

Manchester Museum (2009). *Criticism, Lindow Man Exhibition* [online], available from: http://lindowmanchester.wordpress.com/category/criticism/[18thMarch2020]

Manifold, B.M. (2012). Intrinsic and Extrinsic Factors Involved in the Preservation of Non-Adult Skeletal Remains in Archaeology and Forensic Science. *Bulletin of the International Association of Paleodontology* 6(2): 51–69.

Mann, R.W. & Hunt, D.R. (2012). *Photographic Regional Atlas of Bone Disease: A Guide to Pathologic and Normal Variation in the Human Skeleton* (3rd edition). Charles C Thomas, Springfield.

Mann, R.W., Bass, W.M., & Meadows, L. (1990). Time Since Death and Decomposition of the Human Body: Variables and Observations in Case and Experimental Field Studies. *Journal of Forensic Sciences* 35: 103–111.

Mann, R.W., Hunt, D.R., & Lozanoff, S. (2016) *Photographic Regional Atlas of Non-Metric Traits and Anatomical Variants in the Human Skeleton*. Charles C Thomas, Springfield.

Mant, A.K. (1987). Knowledge Acquired from Post-War Exhumations, pp. 65–78 in A. Boddington, A.N. Garland, & R.C. Janaway (eds) *Death, Decay and Reconstruction*. Manchester University Press, Manchester.

Marchais, V., Schaal, G., Grall, J., Lorrain, A., Nerot, C., Richard, P. & Chauvaud, L. ((2013). Spatial Variability of Stable Isotope Ratios in Oysters (*Crassostrea Gigas*) and Primary Producers along an Estuarine Gradient (Bay of Brest, France). *Estuaries and Coasts* 36: 808–819.

Marciniak, S. & Poinar, H.N. (2018). Ancient Pathogens Through Human History: A Palaeo-genomic Perspective, pp. 115-138 in C. Lindqvist & O.P. Rajora (eds) *Palaeogenomics. Genome-Scale Analysis of Ancient DNA*. Springer, Berlin.

Marciniak, S., Klunk, J., Devault, A., Enk, J., & Poinar, H. (2015). Ancient Human Genomics: The Methodology Behind Reconstructing Evolutionary Pathways. *Journal of Human Evolution* 79: 21-34.

Marciniak, S., Prowse, T.L., Herring, D.A., Klunk, J., Kuch, M., Duggan, A.T. et al. (2016). *Plasmodium Falciparum* Malaria in 1st-2nd Century CE Southern Italy. *Current Biology* 26: R1205-R1225.

Marcus, R., Dempster, D.W., & Bouxsein, M.L. (2013). The Nature of Osteoporosis, pp. 21-30 in R. Marcus, D.W. Dempster, J.A. Cauley, & D. Feldman, eds *Osteoporosis* (4th edition). Academic Press, London.

Maresh, M.M. (1955). Linear Growth of the Long Bones of the Extremities from Infancy through Adolescence. *American Journal of Diseases of Children* 89: 725-742.

Maresh, M.M. (1959). Linear Body Proportions. A Roentgenographic Study. *American Journal of Diseases of Children* 98: 27-49.

Margaryan, A., Hansen, H.B., Rasmussen, S., Sikora, M., Moiseyev, V., Khklov, A. et al. (2018). Ancient Pathogen DNA in Human Teeth and Petrous Bones. *Ecology & Evolution* 8: 3534-3542.

Markov, G., Colak, E., Yigit, N., & Dimitrov, H. (2017). Epigenetic Variation and Population Uniqueness of the Forest Dormouse (*Dryomys Nitedula*) as Revealed by Craniological Nonmetric Traits. *Comptes Rendus De l'Academie Bulgare Des Sciences* 70: 381-386.

Márquez-Grant, N. & Fibiger, L., eds. (2011). *The Routledge Handbook of Archaeological Human Remains and Legislation. An International Guide to Laws and Practice in the Excavation and Treatment of Archaeological Human Remains*. Routledge, London.

Marshall, T.K. (1976). Changes After Death, pp. 78-100 in F.E. Camps (ed.) *Gradwohl's Legal Medicine* (3rd edition). John Wright, Bristol.

Martin, R. (1928). *Lehrbuch Der Anthropologie in Systematischer Darstellung*. Fischer, Jena.

Martín-Seijo, M. & César Vila, M. (2019). Oak, Ash and Pine: The Role of Firewood in Funerary Rituals at the Roman Site of Reza Vella (Ourense, Spain). *Archaeological and Anthropological Sciences* 11: 1911-1926.

Martrille, L., Ubelaker, D.H., Catteneo, C., Seguret, F., Tremblay, M., & Baccino, E. (2007). Comparison of Four Skeletal Methods for the Estimation of Age at Death on White and Black Adults. *Journal of Forensic Sciences* 52: 302-307.

Masset, C. (1989). Age Estimation on the Basis of Cranial Sutures, pp. 71-103 in M.Y. İşcan (ed) *Age Markers in the Human Skeleton*. Charles C.Thomas, Springfield.

Mathieson, I., Lazaridis, I., Rohland, N., Mallick, S., Patterson, N., Alpasian Roodenberg, S. et al. (2015). Genome-Wide Patterns of Selection in 230 Ancient Eurasians. *Nature* 528: 499-503.

Matisoo-Smith, E. & Horsburgh, K.A. (2012). *DNA For Archaeologists*. Left Coast Press, Walnut Creek.

Matsumura, H. (2001). Differentials of Yayoi Immigration to Japan as Derived from Dental Metrics. *Homo-Journal of Comparative Human Biology* 52: 135-156.

May, S. (2011). The Effects of Body Mass on Cremation Weight. *Journal of Forensic Sciences* 56(1): 3-9.

Mays, S. (1989). *The Anglo-Saxon Human Bone from School Street, Ipswich, Suffolk*. AML Report 115/89. Historic England, Portsmouth.

Mays, S. (1991). *The Mediaeval Burials from the Blackfriars Friary, School Street, Ipswich, Suffolk*. AML Report 16/91. Historic England, Portsmouth.

Mays, S. (1992). Taphonomic Factors in a Human Skeletal Assemblage. *Circaea* 9: 54-58.

Mays, S. (1993a). Infanticide in Roman Britain. *Antiquity* 67: 883-888.

Mays, S. (1993b). *The Human Bone from Godmanchester, Cambridgeshire (1988–92 Excavations)*. AML Report 39/93. Historic England, Portsmouth.

Mays, S. (1995). The Relationship between Harris Lines and Other Aspects of Skeletal Development in Adults and Juveniles. *Journal of Archaeological Science* 22: 511–520.

Mays, S. (1996). Healed Limb Amputations in Osteoarchaeology and Their Causes: A Case Study from Ipswich, UK. *International Journal of Osteoarchaeology* 6: 101–113.

Mays, S. (1998). *The Archaeology of Human Bones* (1ˢᵗ edition). Routledge, London.

Mays, S. (1999). Linear and Appositional Long Bone Growth in Earlier Human Populations: a Case Study from Mediaeval England, pp. 290–3312 in R.D. Hoppa & C.M. Fitzgerald (eds.) *Human Growth in the Past: Studies from Bones and Teeth*. Cambridge University Press, Cambridge.

Mays, S. (2000). The Archaeology and History of Infanticide, pp. 180–190 in J. Sofaer-Derevenski (ed) *Children and Material Culture*. Routledge, London.

Mays, S. (2001). Effects of Age and Occupation of Cortical Bone in a Group of 18ᵗʰ-19ᵗʰ Century British Men. *American Journal of Physical Anthropology* 116: 34–44.

Mays, S. (2002). The Relationship between Molar Wear and Age in an Early 19ᵗʰ Century AD Archaeological Human Skeletal Series of Documented Age at Death. *Journal of Archaeological Science* 29: 861–871.

Mays, S. (2003a). Comment on 'A Bayesian Approach to Ageing Perinatal Skeletal Material from Archaeological Sites: Implications for the Evidence for Infanticide in Roman Britain' by R.L. Gowland and A.T. Chamberlain. *Journal of Archaeological Science* 30: 1695–1700.

Mays, S. (2003b). Bone Strontium : Calcium Ratios and Duration of Breastfeeding in a Mediaeval Skeletal Population. *Journal of Archaeological Science* 30: 731–741.

Mays, S. (2006a). The Osteology of Monasticism in Mediaeval England, pp. 179–189 in R. Gowland & C. Knüsel (eds) *Social Archaeology of Funerary Remains*. Oxbow, Oxford.

Mays, S. (2006b). A Possible Case of Surgical Treatment of Cranial Blunt Force Injury from Mediaeval England. *International Journal of Osteoarchaeology* 16: 95–103.

Mays, S. (2006c). A Palaeopathological Study of Colles' Fracture. *International Journal of Osteoarchaeology* 16: 415–428.

Mays, S. (2007). The Human Remains, pp. 77–192 & 337–397, in S. Mays, C. Harding & C. Heighway (eds) *Wharram XI: The Churchyard*. Wharram: A Study of Settlement in the Yorkshire Wolds, XI. York University Press, York.

Mays, S. (2008a). Metabolic Bone Disease, pp. 215–251 in R. Pinhasi & S. Mays (eds.) *Advances in Human Palaeopathology*. Wiley, Chichester.

Mays, S. (2008b). Septal Aperture of the Humerus in a Mediaeval Human Skeletal Population. *American Journal of Physical Anthropology* 136: 432–440.

Mays, S. (2008c). Radiography and Allied Techniques in the Palaeopathology of Skeletal Remains, pp. 77–100 in R. Pinhasi & S. Mays (eds) *Advances in Human Palaeopathology*. Wiley, Chichester.

Mays, S. (2009). The Human Remains, pp. 436–440 in S. Hirst & D. Clark (eds) *Excavations at Mucking Volume 3: The Anglo-Saxon Cemeteries*. Museum of London Archaeology, London.

Mays, S. (2010a). Human Osteoarchaeology in the UK 2001-2007: a Bibliometric Perspective. *International Journal of Osteoarchaeology* 20: 192–204.

Mays, S. (2010b). Archaeological Skeletons Support a North-West European Origin for Paget's Disease of Bone. *Journal of Bone & Mineral Research* 25: 1839–1841.

Mays, S. (2010c). The Effects of Infant Feeding Practices on Infant and Maternal Health in a Mediaeval Community. *Childhood in the Past* 3: 63–78.

Mays, S. (2012). The Relationship between Palaeopathology and the Clinical Sciences, pp. 285–309 in A.L. Grauer (ed) *A Companion to Paleopathology*. Wiley-Blackwell, Chichester.

Mays, S. (2013). Curation of Human Remains at St Peter's Church, Barton-upon-Humber, England, pp. 109–121 in M. Giesen (editor) *Curating Human Remains: Caring for the Dead in the United Kingdom*. Boydell, Woodbridge.

Mays, S. (2014). The Bioarchaeology of the Homicide of Infants and Children, pp. 99–122, in J.L. Thompson, M.P. Alfonso-Durutty. & J.L. Crandall (eds) *Tracing Childhood. Bioarchaeological Investigations of Early Lives in Antiquity*. University Press of Florida, Gainesville.

Mays, S. (2015). The Effect of Factors Other Than Age Upon Skeletal Age Indicators in the Adult. *Annals of Human Biology* 42: 330–339.

Mays, S. (2016). Bone-Formers and Bone-Losers in an Archaeological Population. *American Journal of Physical Anthropology* 159: 577–584.

Mays, S., ed. (2017). *Guidance for Best Practice for the Treatment of Human Remains Excavated from Christian Burial Grounds in England*, 2nd edition. Advisory Panel on the Archaeology of Burials in England, London.

Mays, S. (2018a). The Study of Growth in Skeletal Populations, pp. 71–89 in S.C. Crawford, D.M. Hadley & G. Shepherd (eds) *The Oxford Handbook of the Archaeology of Childhood*. Oxford University Press, Oxford.

Mays, S. (2018b). How Should we Diagnose Disease in Palaeopathology? Some Epistemological Considerations. *International Journal of Palaeopathology* 20: 12–19.

Mays, S. (2018c). Micronutrient Deficiency Diseases, in W. Trevathan (ed) *The International Encyclopaedia of Biological Anthropology*. Wiley, Chichester.

Mays (2019a). *Palaeopathology in South America and Beyond: a Bibliometric Perspective*. Paper presented at the 2019 Palaeopathology Association Meeting in South America (PAMinSA), Sao Paulo, Brazil.

Mays, S. (2019b). Human Skeletal Remains, pp. 362–367 in A. Lyons (ed), *Rectory Farm, Godmanchester, Cambridgeshire. Excavations 1988–1995. Neolithic Monument to Roman Villa Farm*. East Anglian Archaeology Report 170. Oxford Archaeology East, Cambridge.

Mays, S. & Cox, M. (2000). Sex Determination in Skeletal Remains, pp. 117-130 in M. Cox & S. Mays (eds) *Human Osteology in Archaeology and Forensic Science*, Cambridge University Press, Cambridge.

Mays, S. & Eyers, J. (2011). Perinatal Infant Death at the Roman Villa Site at Hambleden, Buckinghamshire, England. *Journal of Archaeological Science* 38: 1931-1938.

Mays, S. & Taylor, G.M. (2002). Osteological and Biomolecular Study of Two Possible Cases of Hypertrophic Osteoarthropathy from Mediaeval England. *Journal of Archaeological Science* 29: 1267-1276.

Mays, S. & Vincent, S. (2013). Probable and Possible Cases of Treponematosis: A Response to the Comment 'A Possible (But not Probable) Case of Treponemal Disease' by Harper, Zuckerman & Armelagos. *International Journal of Osteoarchaeology* 23: 628-629.

Mays, S., de la Rua, C. & Molleson, T. (1995). Molar Crown Height as a Means of Evaluating Existing Wear Scales for Estimating Age at Death in Human Skeletal Remains. Journal of Archaeological Science 22: 659-670.

Mays, S., Lees, B. & Stevenson, J.C. (1998). Age-Dependent Bone Loss in the Femur in a Mediaeval Population. *International Journal of Osteoarchaeology* 8: 97-106.

Mays, S., Taylor, G.M., Legge, A.J., Young, D.B. & Turner-Walker, G. (2001). Palaeopathological and Biomolecular Study of Tuberculosis in a Mediaeval Skeletal Collection. *American Journal of Physical Anthropology* 114: 298-311.

Mays, S., Richards, M.P. & Fuller, B.T. (2002a). Bone Stable Isotope Evidence for Infant Feeding in Mediaeval England. *Antiquity* 76: 654-656.

Mays, S., Fysh, E. & Taylor, G.M. (2002b). Investigation of the Link Between Visceral Surface Rib Lesions and Tuberculosis in a Mediaeval Skeletal Series from England Using Ancient DNA. *American Journal of Physical Anthropology* 119: 27-36.

Mays, S., Krane-Cramer, G. & Bayliss, A. (2003). Two Probable Cases of Treponemal Disease of Mediaeval Date from England. *American Journal of Physical Anthropology* 120: 133-143.

Mays, S., Turner-Walker, G. & Brown, K. (2006a). Human Bone, pp. 20-23 C. Johns (ed) An Iron Age Sword and Mirror Cist Burial from Bryher, Isles of Scilly. *Cornish Archaeology* 41-42: 20-23.

Mays, S., Brickley, M.B., & Ives, R. (2006b). Skeletal Manifestations of Rickets in Infants and Young Children in an Historic Population from England. *American Journal of Physical Anthropology* 129: 362–374.

Mays, S., Harding, C. & Heighway, C. (2007). *Wharram XI: The Churchyard*. Wharram: A Study of Settlement in the Yorkshire Wolds, XI. York University Press, York.

Mays, S., Brickley, M. & Ives, R. (2008). Growth in an English Population from the Industrial Revolution. *American Journal of Physical Anthropology* 136: 85–92.

Mays, S., Ives, R. & Brickley, M. (2009). The Effects of Socioeconomic Status on Endochondral and Appositional Bone Growth in Children from 19th Century Birmingham, England. *American Journal of Physical Anthropology* 140: 410–416.

Mays, S., Vincent, S., Snow, M. & Robson-Brown, K. (2011). Concha Bullosa: A Neglected Condition in Palaeopathology. *International Journal of Palaeopathology* 1: 184–187.

Mays, S., Vincent, S. & Campbell, G. (2012a). The Value of Sieving of Grave Soil in the Recovery of Human Remains: An Experimental Study of Poorly Preserved Archaeological Inhumations. *Journal of Archaeological Science* 39: 3248–3254.

Mays, S., Vincent, S. & Meadows, J. (2012b). A Possible Case of Treponemal Disease from England Dating to the 11th-12th Century AD. *International Journal of Osteoarchaeology* 22: 366–372.

Mays, S., Elders, J., Humphrey, L., White, W. & Marshall, P. (2013). *Science and the Dead. A Guideline for the Destructive Sampling of Archaeological Human Remains for Scientific Analysis*. Advisory Panel for the Archaeology of Burials in England, London.

Mays, S., Sidell, J., Sloane, B., White, W. & Elders, J. (2015). *Large Burial Grounds. Guidance on Sampling in Archaeological Fieldwork Projects*. Advisory Panel on the Archaeology of Burials in England, London.

Mays, S., Fryer, R., Pike, A.W.G., Cooper, M.J. & Marshall, P. (2017). A Multidisciplinary Study of a Burnt and Mutilated Assemblage of Human Remains from a Deserted Mediaeval Village in England. *Journal of Archaeological Science Reports* 16: 441–455.

Mays, S., Roberts, D., Marshall, P., Pike, A.W.G., van Heekeren, V., Bronk Ramsey, C., Dunbar, E., Reimer P., Linscott, B., Radini, A., Lowe, A., Dowle, A., Speller, C., Vallender, J. & Bedford, J. (2018a). Lives Before and After Stonehenge: An Osteobiographical Study of Four Prehistoric Burials Recently Excavated From Stonehenge World Heritage Site. *Journal of Archaeological Science Reports* 20: 692–710.

Mays, S., Brickley, M., Dodwell, N. & Sidell, J. (2018b). *The Role of the Human Osteologist in an Archaeological Fieldwork Project*. Historic England / BABAO, Swindon.

Mays, S., Prowse, T., George, M. & Brickley, M.B. (2018c). Latitude, Urbanization, Age, and Sex as Risk Factors for Vitamin D Deficiency Disease in the Roman Empire. *American Journal of Physical Anthropology* 167: 484–496.

McArthur, J.M., Howarth, R.J., & Bailey, T.R. (2001). Strontium Isotope Stratigraphy: LOWESS Version 3: Best Fit to the Marine Sr-Isotope Curve for 0-509 Ma and Accompanying Look-up Table for Deriving Numerical Age. *Journal of Geology* 109: 155–170.

McDermott, F. (2004). Palaeo-Climate Reconstruction from Stable Isotope Variations in Speleothems: A Review. *Quarternary Science Reviews* 23: 901–908.

McGowan, G. & Prangnell, J. (2015). A Method for Calculating Soil Pressure Overlying Human Burials. *Journal of Archaeological Science* 53: 12–18.

McGrath, J.W., Cheverud, J.M., & Buikstra, J.E. (1984). Genetic Correlations between Sides and Heritability of Asymmetry for Non-Metric Traits in Rhesus Macaques on Cayo Santiago. *American Journal of Physical Anthropology* 64: 401–411.

McIlvaine, B.K. (2015). Implications of Reappraising the Iron Deficiency Anaemia Hypothesis. *International Journal of Osteoarchaeology* 25: 997–1000.

McIntosh, C. (2004). The Pagan Revival and Its Prospects. *Futures* 36: 1025–1048.

McKeown, A.H. & Jantz, R.L. (2005). Comparison of Coordinate and Craniometric Data for Biological Distance Studies, pp. 215–230 in D.E. Slice (ed) *Modern Morphometrics in Physical Anthropology*. Kluwer Academic/Plenum Publishers, New York.

McKeown, A.H. & Schmidt, R.W. (2013). Geometric Morphometrics, pp. 325–359 in E.A. Di Gangi & M.K. Moore (eds) *Research Methods in Human Skeletal Biology*. Elsevier, New York.

McKern, T.W. & Stewart, T.D. (1957). *Skeletal Age Changes in Young American Males*. Quartermaster Research and Development Command, Natick.

McKinley, J.I. (1993). Bone Fragment Size and Weights of Bone from Modern British Cremations and the Implications for the Interpretation of Archaeological Cremations. *International Journal of Osteoarchaeology* 3: 283–287.

McKinley, J.I. (1994). *Spong Hill. Part VIII, The Cremations*. East Anglian Archaeology Report No. 69.

McKinley, J.I. (2013). Cremation, pp. 147–172 in L. Nilsson Stutz & S. Tarlow (eds), *The Oxford Handbook of the Archaeology of Death and Burial*. Oxford University Press, Oxford.

McKinney, N. (2014). Ancestral Remains from Oceania: Histories and Relationships in the Collection of the British Museum, pp. 34–42 in A. Fletcher, D. Antoine, & J.D. Hill (eds) *Regarding the Dead: Human Remains in the British Museum*. British Museum Research Publication 197. British Museum Press, London.

McPherron, S.J.P., Dibble, H.L., Sandgathe, D.M., Goldberg, P., Lin, S.L., & Turq, A. (2018). The Lithic Assemblages, pp. 117–219 in H.L. Dibble, S.J.P. McFerron, P. Goldberg, & D.M. Sandgathe (eds) *The Middle Palaeolithic Site of Pech De l'Azé IV*. Springer, Berlin.

Meadow, R.H. (1980). Animal Bones: Problems for the Archaeologist Together with Some Possible Solutions. *Paleorient* 6: 65–77.

Megyesi, M.S., Ubelaker, D.H., & Sauer, N.J. (2006). Test of the Lamendin Aging Method on Two Historic Skeletal Samples. *American Journal of Physical Anthropology* 131: 363–367.

Mehues, A. (1996). The Non-Venereal Treponematoses. *Medicine (Baltimore)* 24: 69–71.

Meijerman, L., Maat, G.J.R., Schulz, R., & Schmeling, A. (2007). Variables Affecting the Probability of Complete Fusion of the Medial Clavicular Epiphysis. *International Journal of Legal Medicine* 121: 463–468.

Meindl, R.S. & Lovejoy, C.O. (1985). Ectocranial Suture Closure: A Revised Method for Determining Skeletal Age at Death Based on the Lateral Anterior Sutures. *American Journal of Physical Anthropology* 68: 57–66.

Meindl, R.S., Lovejoy, C.O., Mensforth, R.P., & Carlos, L.D. (1985). Accuracy and Direction of Error in the Sexing of the Skeleton. *American Journal of Physical Anthropology* 68: 79–85.

Meinl, A., Huber, C.D., Tangl, S., Gruber, G.M., Teschler-Nicola, M., & Watzek, G. (2008). Comparison of the Validity of Three Dental Methods for the Estimation of Age at Death. *Forensic Science International* 178: 96–105.

Menéndez, L.P. (2016). Spatial Variation of Dental Caries in Late Holocene Samples of Southern South America: A Geostatistical Study. *American Journal of Human Biology* 28: 825–836.

Mensforth, R.P. (1990). Paleodemography of the Carlston-Annis (Bt-5) Late Archaic Skeletal Population. *American Journal of Physical Anthropology* 82: 81–99.

Merritt, C.E. (2017). Innaccuracy and Bias in Adult Age Estimation: Assessing the Reliability of Eight Methods on Individuals of Varying Body Sizes. *Forensic Science International* 275: 315.e1–315.e11.

Metzler, J., Waringo, R., & Metzler-Zens, N. (1991). *Clemency et Les Tombes De l'Aristocratie en Gaule Belgique*. Dossiers D'Archeologie du Musee Nationale d'Histoire et d'Art I, Luxembourg.

Michopoulou, E., Nikita, E., & Valakos, E.D. (2015). Evaluating the Efficiency of Different Recording Protocols for Entheseal Changes in Regards to Expressing Activity Patterns Using Archival Data and Cross-Sectional Geometric Properties. *American Journal of Physical Anthropology* 158: 557–568.

Micozzi, M.S. (1991). *Postmortem Change in Human and Animal Remains*. Charles C Thomas, Springfield.

Mihesuah, D.A. (ed) (2000). *Repatriation Reader. Who Owns American Indian Remains?* University of Nebraska Press, Lincoln.

Milella, M., Alves Cardoso, F., Assis, S., Lopreno, G.P., & Speith, N. (2015). Exploring the Relationship between Entheseal Changes and Physical Activity: A Multivariate Study. *American Journal of Physical Anthropology* 156: 215–223.

Miles, A.E.W. (1963). The Dentition in the Assessment of Individual Age in Skeletal Material, pp. 191–209 in D.R. Brothwell (ed) *Dental Anthropology*. Pergamon, Oxford.

Miles, A.E.W. (2001). The Miles Method of Assessing Age from Tooth Wear Revisited. *Journal of Archaeological Science* 28: 973–982.

Millard, A. (2001). The Deterioration of Bone pp. 637–647 in D.R. Brothwell & A.M. Pollard, (eds) *Handbook of Archaeological Sciences*. Wiley, Chichester.

Millett, M. & Gowland, R. (2015). Infant and Child Burial Rites in Roman Britain: A Study from East Yorkshire. *Britannia* 46: 171–189.

Mills, S. & Tranter, V. (2010). *Research Into Issues Surrounding Human Bones in Museums*. Business Development Research Consultants, London. https://historicengland.org.uk/advice/technical-advice/archaeological-science/human-remains-advice/avebury-reburial-results/

Milner, G.R. & Boldsen, J.L. (2012). Transition Analysis: A Validation Study with Known-Age Modern American Skeletons. *American Journal of Physical Anthropology* 148: 98–110.

Milner, G.R. & Boldsen, J.L. (2017). Life Not Death: Epidemiology from Skeletons. *International Journal of Paleopathology* 17: 26–39.

Milner, G.R. & Larsen, C.S. (1991). Teeth as Artifacts of Human Behaviour: Intentional Mutilation and Accidental Modification, pp. 357–378 in M.A. Kelley & C.S. Larsen (eds) *Advances in Dental Anthropology*. Wiley-Liss, Chichester.

Milner, G.R., Wood, J.W., & Boldsen, J.L. (2008). Advances in Paleodemography, pp. 561–600 in M.A. Katzenberg & S.R. Saunders (eds) *Biological Anthropology of the Human Skeleton* (2nd Edition). Wiley, Chichester.

Milner, G.R., Boldsen, J.L., Weise, S., Lauritsen, J.M., & Freund, U.H. (2015). Sex-Related Risks of Trauma in Medieval to Early Modern Denmark, and Its Relationship to Change in Interpersonal Violence over Time. *International Journal of Paleopathology* 9: 59–68.

Milner, G.R., Buikstra, J.E., & Novotny, A.C. (2018). A Stepwise Transition to Agriculture in the American Midcontinent. in J. Lee-Thorp & M.A. Katzenberg (eds) *The Oxford Handbook of the Archaeology of Diet*. Oxford University Press, Oxford.

Mitchell, P.D. (2005). Pre-Columbian Treponemal Disease from 14th Century AD Safed, Israel, and the Implications for the Medieval Eastern Mediterranean. *American Journal of Physical Anthropology* 121: 117–124.

Mitchell, P.D. (2009). Revised Radiocarbon Date for a Case of Treponemal Disease from Safed, Israel, from the 15th Century AD. *American Journal of Physical Anthropology* 139: 274.

Mitchell, P.D. & Redfern, R.C. (2011). Developmental Dysplasia of the Hip in Mediaeval London. *American Journal of Physical Anthropology* 144: 479–484.

Mitteroecker, P., Gunz, P., Windhager, S., & Schaefer, K. (2013). A Brief Review of Shape, Form, and Allometry in Geometric Morphometrics, with Applications to Human Facial Morphology. *Hystrix, the Italian Journal of Mammalogy* 24: 59–66.

Mittnik, A., Wang, C.-C., Svoboda, J., & Krause, J. (2016). A Molecular Approach to the Sexing of the Triple Burial at the Upper Palaeolithic Site of Dolní Věstonice. *PloS One* 11(10): e0163019.

Molleson, T. (1991). Demographic Implications of the Age Structure of Early English Cemetery Samples. *Actes Des Journées Anthropologiques* 5: 113–121.

Molleson, T. (1993). The Human Remains, pp. 142–214 in D.E. Farwell & T.I. Molleson, *Excavations at Poundbury 1966-80*. Volume II: The Cemeteries. Dorset Natural History &

Archaeology Society Monograph Series Number 11. Dorset Natural History and Archaeology Society, Dorchester.

Molleson, T. (1995). Rates of Ageing in the Eighteenth Century, pp. 199–222 in S. Saunders & A. Herring (eds) *Grave Reflections*. Canadian Scholars' Press, Toronto.

Molleson, T. & Cox, M. (1993). *The Spitalfields Project*. Volume 2: The Anthropology. CBA Research Report 86. Council for British Archaeology, York.

Molleson, T.I. & Cox, M. (1988). A Neonate With Cut Bones from Poundbury Camp. *Bulletin De La Société Royale Belge d'Anthropologie Et De Préhistoire* 99: 53–59.

Molnár, E., Donoghue, H.D., Lee, O.Y-C., Wu, H.H.T., Besra, G.S., Minniken, D.E., Bull, I.D., Llewellyn, G., Williams, C.M., Spekker, O. & Pálfi, G. (2015). Morphological and Biomolecular Evidence for Tuberculosis in 8th Century AD Skeletons from Bélmegyer-Csömöki Domb, Hungary. *Tuberculosis* 95: S35–S41.

Molnar, P. (2006). Tracing Prehistoric Activities: Musculoskeletal Stress Marker Analysis of a Stone-Age Population on the Island of Gotland in the Baltic Sea. *American Journal of Physical Anthropology* 129: 12–23.

Monroy Kuhn, J., Jakobsson, M., & Günther, T. (2018). Estimating Genetic Kin Relationships in Prehistoric Populations. *PloS One* 13(4): e0195491.

Montgomery, J. (2010). Passports from the Past: Investigation of Human Dispersals Using Strontium Isotope Analysis of Tooth Enamel. *Annals of Human Biology* 37: 325–346.

Moore, R.D., Schuman, T.A., Scott, T.A., Mann, S.E., Davidson, M.A., & Labadie, R.F. (2010). Exostoses of the External Auditory Canal in White-Water Kayakers. *Laryngoscope* 120: 582–590.

Moore, W.J. & Corbett, M.E. (1975). Distribution of Dental Caries in Ancient British Populations: III. The 17th Century. *Caries Research* 9: 163–175.

Moore, W.J. & Corbett, M.E. (1978). Dental Caries Experience in Man, pp. 3–19 in N.H. Rowe (ed) *Diet, Nutrition and Dental Caries*. University of Michigan School of Dentistry & the Dental Research Institute, Chicago.

Moore, W.J., Lavelle, C.L.B., & Spence, T.F. (1968). Changes in the Size and Shape of the Human Mandible in Britain. *British Dental Journal* 125: 163–169.

Morales-Arce, A.Y., McCafferty, G., Hand, J., Schmill, N., McGrath, K., & Speller, C. (2019). Ancient Mitochondrial DNA and Population Dynamics in Postclassic Central Mexico: Tlatelolco (AD1325-1520) and Cholula (AD900-1350). *Archaeological and Anthropological Sciences* 11: 3459–3475.

Morant, G.M. (1950). Secular Changes in the Heights of British People. *Proceedings of the Royal Society of London* 137B: 443–452.

Moreno-Mayer, J.V., Vinner, L., Damgaard, P. de B., de la Fuente, C., Chan, J., Spence, J.P., et al (2018). Early Human Dispersals within the Americas. *Science* 362: eaav2621.

Moreno-Mayar, J.V., Korneliussen, T.S., Dalal, J., Renaud, G., Albrechtsen, A., Nielsen, R. & Malaspinas, A-S (2020). A Likelihood Method for Estimating Present-Day Human Contamination in Ancient Male Samples Using Low-Depth X-Chromosome Data. *Bioinformatics* 36: 828–841.

Mosiman, J.E. (1970). Size Allometry: Size and Shape Variables with Characterizations of the Lognormal and Generalized Gamma Distributions. *Journal of the American Statistical Association* 65: 930–945.

Mowlavi, G., Kacki, S., Dupouy-Camet, J., Mobedi, I., Makki, M., Harandi, M.F., & Naddaf, S.R. (2014). Probable Hepatic Capillariosis and Hydatidosis in an Adolescent from the Late Roman Period Buried in Amiens, France. *Parasite* 21: 9.

Moynihan, P.J. & Kelley, S.A.M. (2014). Effect on Caries of Restricting Sugars Intake: Systematic Review to Inform WHO Guidelines. *Journal of Dental Research* 93: 8–18.

Müldner, G., Richards, M.P. (2005). Fast or Feast: Reconstructing Diet in Later Mediaeval England by Stable Isotope Analysis. *Journal of Archaeological Science* 32: 39–48.

Müldner, G., Richards, M.P. (2007). Stable Isotope Evidence for 1500 Years of Human Diet in the City of York, UK. *American Journal of Physical Anthropology* 133: 682–697.

Mulhern, D.M. (2016). Differentiating Human from Nonhuman Skeletal Remains, pp. 197–212 in S. Blau & D.H. Ubelaker (eds) *Handbook of Forensic Anthropology and Archaeology* (2nd edition). World Archaeological Congress Research Handbooks in Archaeology. Routledge, London.

Muñoz-Muñoz, F., Sans-Fuentes, M.A., López-Fuster, M.J., & Ventura, J. (2003). Non-Metric Morphological Divergence in the Western House Mouse, *Mus Musculus Domesticus*, from the Barcelona Chromosomal Hybrid Zone. *Biological Journal of the Linnean Society* 80: 313-322.

Munro, L.E., Longstaffe, F.J., & White, C.D. (2007). Burning and Boiling of Modern Deer Bone: Effects on Crystallinity and Oxygen Isotope Composition of Bioapatite Phosphate. *Palaeogeography, Palaeoclimatology, Palaeoecology* 249: 90-102.

Munro, L.E., Longstaffe, F.J., & White, C.D. (2008). Effects of Heating on Carbon and Oxygen-Isotope Compositions of Structural Carbonate in Bioapatite from Modern Deer Bone. *Palaeogeography, Palaeoclimatology, Palaeoecology* 266: 142-150.

Murphy, E.M., Chistov, Y.K., Hopkins, R., Rutland, P., & Taylor, G.M. (2009). Tuberculosis among Iron Age Individuals from Tuva, South Siberia: Palaeopathological and Biomolecular Findings. *Journal of Archaeological Science* 36: 2029-2038.

Museum of London. (2005). *Opinion Survey of Visitors to the Centre for Bioarchaeology, Museum of London, July 2004*. Museum of London, London

Nagar, Y. (2002). Bone Reburial in Israel: Legal Restrictions and Methodological Implications, pp. 87–90 in C. Fforde, J. Hubert, & P. Turnbull (eds) *The Dead and Their Possessions. Repatriation in Principal, Policy and Practice*. Routledge, London.

Nagar, Y. (2011). Israel, pp. 613–620 in N. Márquez-Grant & L. Fibiger (eds) *The Routledge Handbook of Archaeological Human Remains and Legislation. An International Guide to Laws and Practice in the Excavation and Treatment of Archaeological Human Remains*. Routledge, London.

NAGPRA. (2013). *43 CR § 10.11- Disposition of Culturally Unidentifiable Human Remains*. www.law.cornell.edu/cfr/text/43/10.11

NAGPRA. (2019). *National NAGPRA Online Databases*. https://home1.nps.gov/nagpra/ONLINEDB/index.htm

Naji, S., Colard, T., Blondiaux, J., Bertrand, B., d'Incau, E., & Bocquet-Appel, J.-P. (2016). Cementochronology, to Cut or Not to Cut? *International Journal of Paleopathology* 15: 113-119.

Nakahashi, T. (1993). Temporal Craniometric Changes from the Jomon to the Modern Period in Western Japan. *American Journal of Physical Anthropology* 90: 409-425.

Nawrocki, S.P. (2010). The Nature and Sources of Error in the Estimation of Age at Death from the Skeleton, pp. 79–101 in K.E. Latham & M. Finnegan (eds) *Age Estimation of the Human Skeleton*. Charles C Thomas, Springfield.

Nayagam, S. (2010). Principles of Fractures, pp. 687–732 in L. Solomon, D. Warwick, & S. Nayagam (eds) *Apley's System of Orthopedics and Fractures* (9th edition). Hodder & Arnold, London.

Ndou, R., Pillay, S., & Schepartz, L.A. (2018). Characterization of the Tissue Crossing the Supratrochlear Aperture of the Humerus Using Histochemical Techniques. *Surgical and Radiological Anatomy* 40: 1371-1377.

Needham, S. (2005). Transforming Beaker Culture in Northwest Europe; Processes of Fusion and Fission. *Proceedings of the Prehistoric Society* 71: 171-217.

Needham, S. (2007). Isotopic Aliens: Beaker Movement and Cultural Transmissions, pp. 41-46 in M. Larsson & M. Parker Pearson (eds) *From Stonehenge to the Baltic. Living with Cultural Diversity in the 3rd Millennium BC*. British Archaeological Reports International Series No. 1692. Archaeopress, Oxford.

Nemeskéri, J., Harsányi, L., & Acsádi, G. (1960). Methoden Zur Diagnose Der Lebensalters Von Skelettfunden. *Anthropologischer Anzeiger* 24: 70-95.

Nicholson, R. (1993). A Morphological Investigation of Burnt Animal Bone and an Evaluation of Its Utility in Archaeology. *Journal of Archaeological Science* 20: 411–428.

Nicklisch, N., Maixner, F., Ganslmeier, R., Friederich, S.Dresely, V., Meller, M. et al. (2012). Rib Lesions in Skeletons from Early Neolithic Sites in Central Germany: On the Trail of Tuberculosis at the Onset of Agriculture. *American Journal of Physical Anthropology* 149: 391–404.

Nielsen-Marsh, C., Gernaey, A., Turner-Walker, G., Hedges, R., Pike, A., & Collins, M. (2000). The Chemical Degradation of Bone, pp. 439–454 in M. Cox & S. Mays (eds) *Human Osteology in Archaeology and Forensic Science*. Cambridge University Press, Cambridge.

Nielsen-Marsh, C.M., Smith, C.I., Jans, M.M.E., Nord, A., Kars, H., & Collins, M.J. (2007). Bone Diagenesis in the European Holocene II: Taphonomic and Environmental Considerations. *Journal of Archaeological Science* 34: 1523–1531.

Nikita, E., Mattingly, D., & Lahr, M.M. (2012). Sahara: Barrier or Corridor? Nonmetric Cranial Traits and Biological Affinities of North African Late Holocene Populations. *American Journal of Physical Anthropology* 147: 280–292.

Nilsson Stutz, L. (2013). Claims to the Past. A Critical View of the Arguments Driving Repatriation of Cultural Heritage and Their Role in Contemporary Identity Politics. *Journal of Intervention and Statebuilding* 7: 170–195.

Nilsson Stutz, L. (2016). To Gaze upon the Dead: The Exhibition of Human Remains as Cultural Practice and Political Process in Scandinavia and the USA, pp. 268–292 in H. Williams & M. Giles (eds) *Archaeologists and the Dead. Mortuary Archaeology in Contemporary Society*. Oxford University Press, Oxford.

Nilsson Stutz, L. & Tarlow, S., (eds) (2013). *The Oxford Handbook of the Archaeology of Death and Burial*. Oxford University Press, Oxford.

Niskanen, M., Ruff, C.B., Holt, B., Sládek, V., & Berner, M. (2018). Temporal and Geographic Variation in Body Size and Shape of Europeans from the Late Pleistocene to Recent Times, pp. 49–89 in C.B. Ruff (ed) *Skeletal Variation and Adaptation in Europeans. Upper Palaeolithic to the Twentieth Century*. Wiley-Blackwell, Chichester.

Noback, M.J., Harvati, K., & Spoor, F. (2011). Climate-Related Variation of the Human Nasal Cavity. *American Journal of Physical Anthropology* 145: 599–614.

Nomura, R., Shimizu, T., Asada, Y., Hirukawa, S., & Maeda, T. (2003). Genetic Mapping of the Absence of Third Molars in EL Mice to Chromosome 3. *Journal of Dental Research* 82: 786–790.

Novak, S. (2000). Battle-Related Trauma, pp. 90–102 in V. Fiorato, A. Boylston, & C. Knüsel (eds) *Blood Red Roses. The Archaeology of a Mass Grave from the Battle of Towton, 1461*. Oxbow, Oxford.

Nowell, G.W. (1978). An Evaluation of the Miles Method of Ageing Using the Tepe Hissar Dental Sample. *American Journal of Physical Anthropology* 49: 271–276.

O'Donnell, L. (2016). The Power of the Pyre – A Holistic Study of Cremation Focusing on Charcoal Remains. *Journal of Archaeological Science* 65: 161–171.

O'Leary, M.H. (1981). Carbon Isotope Fractionation in Plants. *Phytochemistry* 20: 553–567.

O'Leary, M.H. (1988). Carbon Isotopes in Photosynthesis. *BioScience* 38: 328–336.

O'Neill, M.C. & Ruff, C.B. (2004). Estimating Human Long Bone Cross-Sectional Geometric Properties: A Comparison of Non-Invasive Methods. *Journal of Archaeological Science* 47: 221–235.

O'Rahilly, R. (1953). A Survey of Carpal and Tarsal Anomalies. *Journal of Bone & Joint Surgery* 35A: 626–642.

O'Sullivan, N., Posth, C., Coia, V., Schuenemann, V.J., Price, T.D., Wahl, J. et al. (2018). Ancient Genome-Wide Analyses Infer Kinship Structure in an Early Medieval Alemannic Graveyard. *Science Advances* 4: eaao1262.

Odes, E.J., Delezene, L.K., Randolph-Quinney, P.S., Smilg, J.S., Augustine, T.N., Jakata, K., & Berger, L.R. (2018). A Case of Benign Osteogenic Tumour in *Homo Naledi*: Evidence for

Peripheral Osteoma in the U.W. 101-1142 Mandible. *International Journal of Palaeopathology* 21: 47-55.

Ogden, A. (2008). Advances in the Palaeopathology of the Teeth and Jaws, pp. 283-307 in R. Pinhasi & S. Mays (eds) *Advances in Human Palaeopathology*. Wiley, Chichester.

Ogilvie, M.D. & Hilton, C.E. (2011). Cross-Sectional Geometry in the Humeri of Foragers and Farmers from the Prehispanic American Southwest: Exploring Patterns in the Sexual Division of Labour. *American Journal of Physical Anthropology* 144: 11-21.

Okumura, M. (2011). The End of Slavery: Disease Patterns and Cultural Behaviours of African Americans in Suriname. *International Journal of Osteoarchaeology* 21: 631-642.

Olalde, I., Brace, S., Allentoft, M.E., Armit, I., Kristiansen, K., Booth, T. et al. (2018). The Beaker Phenomenon and the Genomic Transformation of Northwest Europe. *Nature* 555: 190-196.

Olivares, J.I. & Aguilera, I.A. (2016). Validation of the Sex Estimation Method Elaborated by Schutkowski in the Granada Osteological Collection of Identified Infant and Young Children: Analysis of the Controversy Between the Different Ways of Analysing and Interpreting the Results. *International Journal of Legal Medicine* 130: 1623-1632.

Oliveira-Santos, I., Gouveia, M., Cunha, E., & Gonçalves, D. (2017). The Circle of Life: Age at Death Estimation in Burnt Teeth through Tooth Cementum Annulations. *International Journal of Legal Medicine* 131: 527-536.

ONS. (2018). *Office of National Statistics: Homicide in England and Wales: Year Ending March 2018*. www.ons.gov.uk/peoplepopulationandcommunity/crimeandjustice/articles/homicideinenglandandwales/yearendingmarch2018. Accessed October 2019.

Orlando, L., Gilbert, M.T.P., & Willerslev, E. (2015). Reconstructing Ancient Genomes and Epigenomes. *Nature Reviews Genetics* 16: 395-408.

Ortner, D.J. (2003). *Identification of Pathological Conditions in Human Skeletal Remains*, (2nd edition). Academic Press, London.

Ortner, D.J. (2008). Differential Diagnosis of Skeletal Lesions in Infectious Disease, pp. 191-214 in R. Pinhasi & S. Mays (eds) *Advances in Human Palaeopathology*. Wiley, Chichester.

Osborne, D.L., Simmons, T.L., & Nawrocki, S.P. (2004). Reconsidering the Auricular Surface as an Indicator of Age at Death. *Journal of Forensic Sciences* 49: 905-911.

Ott, W. (2012). Are There Duties to the Dead? *Philosophy Now* 89: 14-16.

Ottoni, C., Bekaert, B., & Decorte, R. (2017). DNA Degradation: Curent Knowledge and Progress in DNA Analysis, pp. 65-80 in E.M.J. Schotsmans, N. Márquez-Grant, & S.L. Forbes (eds) *Taphonomy of Human Remains: Forensic Analysis of the Dead and the Depositional Environment*. Wiley, Chichester.

Ousley, S.D., Billeck, W.T., & Hollinger, R.E. (2005). Federal Repatriation Legislation and the Role of Physical Anthropology in Repatriation. *Yearbook of Physical Anthropology* 48: 2-32.

Outram, A.K. (2002). Bone Fracture and Within-Bone Nutrients: An Experimentally Based Method for Investigating Levels of Marrow Extraction, pp. 51-63 in P. Miracle & N. Milner (eds) *Consuming Passions and Patterns of Consumption*. McDonald Institute, Cambridge.

Overholtzer, L. & Argueta, J.R. (2017). Letting Skeletons Out of the Closet: The Ethics of Displaying Ancient Mexican Human Remains. *International Journal of Heritage Studies* 24: 508-530.

Oxenham, M.F. & Cavill, I. (2010). Porotic Hyperostosis and Cribra Orbitalia: The Erythropoietic Response to Iron Deficiency Anaemia. *Anthropological Science* 118: 199-200.

Palfí, G., Dutour, O., Perrin, P., Sola, C., & Zink, A. (2015). Tuberculosis in Evolution. *Tuberculosis* 95: S1-S3.

Palmer, J.L.A. & Waters-Rist, A.L. (2019). Acts of Life: Assessing Entheseal Change as an Indicator of Social Differentiation in Postmediaeval Aalst (Belgium). *International Journal of Osteoarchaeology* 29: 303-313.

Pardoe, C. (2013). Repatriation, Reburial, and Biological Research in Australia, pp. 733-762 in L. Nilsson Stutz & S. Tarlow (eds) *The Oxford Handbook of the Archaeology of Death and Burial*. Oxford University Press, Oxford.

Parker, G.J., Yip, J.M., Eerkens, J.W., Salemi, M., Durbin-Johnson, B., Kiesow, C. et al. (2019). Sex Estimation Using Sexually Dimorphic Amelogenin Protein Fragments in Human Enamel. *Journal of Archaeological Science* 101: 169–180.

Parker Pearson, M. (1999). *The Archaeology of Death and Burial*. Sutton, Stroud.

Parker Pearson, M.,Chamberlain, A., Jay, M., Richards, M., Sheridan, A., Curtis, N., Evans, J., Gibson, A., Hutchison, M., Mahoney, P., Marshall, P., Montgomery, J., Needham, S., O'Mahoney, S., Pellegrini, M., Wilkin, N. (2016). Beaker People in Britain: Migration, Mobility and Diet. *Antiquity* 90, 620–637.

Parker Pearson, M., Sheridan, A., Jay, M., Chamberlain, A., Richards, M.P., & Evans, J. (eds) (2019). *The Beaker People. Isotopes, Mobility and Diet in Prehistoric Britain*. Prehistoric Society Research Paper 7. Oxbow, Oxford.

Pasricha, S.R., Drakesmith, H., Black, J., Hipgrave, D., & Biggs, B.A. (2013). Control of Iron Deficiency Anemia in Low- and Middle-Income Countries. *Blood* 121:2607–2617.

Paul, K.S. & Stojanowski, C.M. (2015). Performance Analysis of Deciduous Morphology for Detecting Biological Siblings. *American Journal of Physical Anthropology* 157: 615–629.

Paul, K.S., Stojanowski, C.M., Hughes, T.E., Brook, A.H., & Townsend, G.C. (in press). Patterns of Heritability across the Human Diphyodont Dental Complex: Crown Morphology of Australian Twins and Families. *American Journal of Physical Anthropology*

Pavelka, M.S.M. & Fedigan, L.M. (1991). Menopause: A Comparative Life History Perspective. *Yearbook of Physical Anthropology* 34: 13–38.

Pawlik, A.F. & Thissen, J.P. (2011). Hafted Armatures and Multi-Component Tool Design at the Micoquian Site of Inden-Altdorf, Germany. *Journal of Archaeological Science* 38: 1699–1708.

Payne, S. (1972). Partial Recovery and Sample Bias: The Results of Some Sieving Experiments, pp. 49–64 in E.S. Higgs (ed) *Papers in Economic Prehistory*. Cambridge University Press, Cambridge.

Pearce, J., Millett, M., & Struck, M. (eds) (2000). *Burial, Society and Context in the Roman World*. Oxbow, Oxford.

Pearson, O.M. (2000). Activity, Climate, and Postcranial Robusticity. *Current Anthropology* 569–607.

Pearson, O.M. & Lieberman, D.E. (2004). The Aging of Wolff's "Law": Ontogeny and Responses to Mechanical Loading in Cortical Bone. *Yearbook of Physical Anthropology* 47: 63–99.

Pederzani, S. & Britton, K. (2019). Oxygen Isotopes in Bioarchaeology. Principles and Applications, Challenges and Opportunities. *Earth-Science Reviews* 188: 77–107.

Peeling, R.W. & Hook, E.W. (2006). The Pathogenesis of Syphilis: The Great Mimicker Revisited. *Journal of Pathology* 208: 224–232.

Pękala, P.A., Henry, B.M., Pękala, J.R., Saganiak, K., Taterra, D., Walocha, J.A., Tubbs, R.S., & Tomaszewski, K.A. (2017). Lateral and Posterolateral Foraminal Variants of the Atlas: A Meta-Analysis. *Journal of Clinical Neuroscience* 40: 74–82.

Perez, S.I., Bernal, V., & Gonzalez, P.N. (2007). Evolutionary Relationships among Prehistoric Human Populations: An Evaluation of Relatedness Patterns Based on Facial Morphometric Data Using Molecular Data. *Human Biology* 79: 25–50.

Perizonius, W.R.K. (1979). Non-Metric Cranial Traits: Symmetry and Side Difference. *Proceedings of the Koninklijke Nederlandse Akademie Van Wettenschappen, Series C* 82: 91–112.

Perizonius, W.R.K. (1984). Closing and Non-Closing Sutures in 256 Crania of Known Age and Sex from Amsterdam (AD1883-1909). *Journal of Human Evolution* 13: 201–216.

Petersen, H.C. (2005). On the Accuracy of Estimating Living Stature from Skeletal Length in the Grave and by Linear Regression. *International Journal of Osteoarchaeology* 15: 106–114.

Petersen, H.C. (2011). A Re-Evaluation of Stature Estimation from Skeletal Length in the Grave. *American Journal of Physical Anthropology* 144: 327–330.

Petrie, W.M.F. (1896). *Naqada and Ballas*. Bernard Quaritch, London.

Pettifor, J.M. 2003. Nutritional Rickets, pp. 541–565 in F. Glorieux, J. Pettifor, & H. Jüppner (eds) *Pediatric Bone: Biology and Diseases*. Academic Press, New York.

Pettitt, P. (2011). *The Palaeolithic Origin of Human Burial*. Taylor Francis, London.

Phenice, T.W. (1969). A Newly Developed Visual Method of Sexing the Os Pubis. *American Journal of Physical Anthropology* 30: 297–302.

Philpott, R. (1991). *Burial Practices in Roman Britain*. British Archaeological Reports, British Series, No. 219. Tempus Reparatum, Oxford.

Pickard, C. & Bonsall, C. (2007). Late Mesolithic Coastal Fishing Practices, pp. 176–183 in B. Hårdh, K. Jennbert, & D. Olausson (eds) *On the Road: Studies in Honour of Lars Larssen*. Acta Archaeologica Lundensia, Series 4, Volume 26. Almqvist & Wiksell International, Lund.

Pickering, M. (2006). Repatriation at the National Museum of Australia. *Paper Delivered at the Australian High Commission*, London, May 2006.

Pietrusewsky, M. (2019). Traditional Morphometrics and Biological Distance: Methods and an Example, pp. 547–591 in M.A. Katzenberg & A.L. Grauer (eds) *Biological Anthropology of the Human Skeleton* (3rd edition). Wiley, Chichester.

Piga, G., Gonçalves, D., Thompson, T.J.U., Brunetti, A., Malgosa, A., & Enzo, S. (2016). Understanding the Crystallinity Indices Behavior of Burned Bones and Teeth by ATR-IR and XRD in the Presence of Bioapatite Mixed with Other Phosphate and Carbonate Phases. *International Journal of Spectroscopy* 2016: article 4810149.

Piga, G., Amarante, A., Makhoul, C., Cunha, E., Malgosa, A., Enzo, S., & Gonçalves, D. (2018). β-Tricalcium Phosphate Interferes with the Assessment of Crystallinity in Burned Skeletal Remains. *International Journal of Spectroscopy* 2018: article 5954146.

Pindborg, J.J. (1970). *Pathology of the Dental Hard Tissues*. Munksgaard, Copenhagen.

Pindborg, J.J. (1982). Aetiology of Developmental Enamel Defects Not Related to Fluorosis. *International Dental Journal* 32: 123–134.

Pinhasi, R. & von Cramon-Taubadel, N. (2012). A Craniometric Perspective on the Transition to Agriculture in Europe. *Human Biology* 84: 45–66.

Pinhasi, R. & Meiklejohn, C. (2011). Dental Reduction and the Transition to Agriculture in Europe, pp. 451–474 in R. Pinhasi & J.T. Stock (eds) *Human Bioarchaeology of the Transition to Agriculture*. Wiley, Chichester.

Pinhasi, R., Shaw, P., White, B. & Ogden, A.R. (2006). Morbidity, Rickets and Long-Bone Growth in Post-Mediaeval Britain – A Cross-Population Analysis. *Annals of Human Biology* 33: 372–389.

Pinhasi, R., Timpson, A., Thomas, M. and Šlaus, M. (2014). Bone Growth, Limb Proportions and Non-Specific Stress in Archaeological Populations from Croatia. *Annals of Human Biology* 41: 127–137.

Pinhasi, R., Fernandes, D., Sirak, K., Novak, M., Connell, S., Alpasian-Roodenberg, S. et al. (2015). Optimal Ancient DNA Yields from the Inner Ear Part of the Human Petrous Bone. *PloS One* 10(6): e0129102.

Pinhasi, R., Fernandes, D.M., Sirak, K. & Cheronet, O. (2019). Isolating the Human Cochlea to Generate Bone Powder for Ancient DNA Analysis. *Nature Protocols* 14: 1194–1205.

Piontek, J. (1976). The Process of Cremation and Its Influence on the Morphology of Bones in the Light of Results from Experimental Research. *Archaeologica Polski* 21: 254–280.

Pitt-Rivers Muiseum. (2017). *Press Release from The Karanga Repatriation Programme of Te Papa Tongarewa (The National Museum of New Zealand) and the Pitt Rivers Museum, University of Oxford, 25 May 2017*. www.prm.ox.ac.uk›media›repatriation.maori_.pressrelease.pdf

Pokines, J.T. & de la Paz, J.S. (2016). Recovery Rates of Human Fetal Skeletal Remains Using Varying Mesh Sizes. *Journal of Forensic Sciences* 61: S184–S189.

Polfer, M. (2000). Reconstructing Funerary Rituals: The Evidence of *Ustrina* and Related Archaeological Structures, pp. 30–37 in J. Pearce, M. Millett, & M. Struck (eds) *Burial, Society and Context in the Roman World*. Oxbow, Oxford.

Pomeroy, E. (2013). Biomechanical Insights into Activity and Long Distance Trade in the South Central Andes. *Journal of Archaeological Science* 40: 3129–3140.

Pomeroy, E., Macintosh, A., Wells, J.C.K., Cole, T.J., & Stock, J.T. (2018). Relationship Between Body Mass, Lean Mass, Fat Mass, and Limb Bone Cross-Sectional Geometry: Implications for Estimating Body Mass and Physique from the Skeleton. *American Journal of Physical Anthropology* 166: 56–69.

Powell, M.L. & Cook, D.C. (eds) (2005). *The Myth of Syphilis: The Natural History of Treponematosis in North America*. University of Florida Press, Gainesville.

Prendergast, M.E., Lipson, M., Sawchuk, E.A., Olalde, I., Ogola, C.A., Rohland, A. et al. (2019). Ancient DNA Reveals a Multistep Spread of the First Herders into Sub-Saharan Africa. *Science* 365: eaaw6275.

Price, T.D., Ambrose, S.H., Bennike, P., Heinemeier, J., Noe-Nygaard, N., Brinch-Petersen, E., Vang-Petersen, P. & Richards, M. (2007). New Information on the Stone Age Graves at Dragsholm, Denmark. *Acta Archaeologica* 78(2): 193–219.

Prince, D.A. & Ubelaker, D.H. (2002). Application of Lamendin's Adult Dental Aging Technique to a Diverse Skeletal Sample. *Journal of Forensic Sciences* 47: 107–116.

Prowse, T.L. & Lovell, N.C. (1996). Concordance of Cranial and Dental Morphological Traits and Evidence for Endogamy in Ancient Egypt. *American Journal of Physical Anthropology* 101: 237–246.

Prowse, T.L., Schwarcz, H.P., Garnsey, P., Knyf, M., Macchiarelli, R., & Bondioli, L. (2007). Isotopic Evidence for Age-Related Immigration to Imperial Rome. *American Journal of Physical Anthropology* 132: 510–519.

Prowse, T.L., Saunders, S.R., Schwarcz, H.P., Garnsey, P., Macchiarelli, R., & Bondioli, L. (2008). Isotopic and Dental Evidence for Infant and Young Child Feeding Practices in an Imperial Roman Skeletal Sample. *American Journal of Physical Anthropology* 137: 294–308.

Pucciarelli, H.M., Neves, W.A., González-José, R., Sardi, M.L., Rozzi, F.R., Struck, A. & Bonilla, M.Y. (2006). East-West Cranial Differentiation in Pre-Columbian Human Populations from South America. *Homo- Journal of Comparative Human Biology* 57: 133–150.

Quigley, C. (2001). *Skulls and Skeletons. Human Bone Collections and Accumulations*. McFarland, Jefferson.

Rácz, S.E., Pucu De Araújo, E., Jensen, E., Mostek, C., Morrow, J.J., Van Hove, M.L., Bianucci, R., Heller, F., Araújo, A. & Reinhard, K.J. (2015). Parasitology in an Archaeological Context: Analysis of Medieval Burials in Nivelles, Belgium. *Journal of Archaeological Science* 53: 304–315.

Radini, A., Buckley, S., Rosas, A., Estalrrich, A., de la Raisilla, M., & Hardy, K. (2016). Neanderthals, Trees and Dental Calculus: New Evidence from El Sidrón. *Antiquity* 90: 290–301.

Radini, A., Nikita, E., Buckley, S., Copeland, L., & Hardy, K. (2017). Beyond Food: The Multiple Pathways for Inclusion of Materials into Ancient Dental Calculus. *Yearbook of Physical Anthropology* 63:71–83.

Radini, A.,Tromp, M., Beach, A., Tong, E., Speller, C., McCormick, M., Dudgeon, J.V., Mollins, M.J., Rühli, F., Kröger, R. & Warriner, C. (2019). Medieval Women's Early Involvement in Manuscript Production Suggested by Lapis Lazuli Identification in Dental Calculus. *Science Advances* 5: eaau7126.

Rando, C., Hillson, S., & Antoine, D., (2014). Changes in Mandibular Dimensions During the Mediaeval to Post-Mediaeval Transition in London: A Possible Response to Decreased Masticatory Load. *Archives of Oral Biology* 59: 73–81.

Rascovan, N., Sjögren, K.-G., Kristiansen, K., Nielsen, R., Willerslev, E., Desnues, C., & Rasmussen, S. (2019). Emergence and Spread of Basal Lineages of *Yersinia Pestis* During the Neolithic Decline. *Cell* 176: 295–305.

Rasmussen, M., Guo, X., Wang, Y., Lohmueller, K.E., Rasmussen, S., Albrechtsen, A. et al. (2011). An Aboriginal Australian Genome Reveals Separate Human Dispersals Into Asia. *Science* 334: 94–98.

Rasmussen, S., Allentoft, M.A., Nielsen, K.,Orlando, M., Sikora, K. Sjögren, K-G. et al. (2015). Early Divergent Strains of *Yersinia Pestis* in Eurasia 5,000 Years Ago. *Cell* 163: 571–582.

Rathouse, W. (2016). Contemporary Pagans and the Study of the Ancestors, pp. 333–344 in H. Williams & M. Giles (eds) *Archaeologists and the Dead. Mortuary Archaeology in Contemporary Society*. Oxford University Press, Oxford.

Raxter, M.H., Auerbach, B.M., & Ruff, C.B. (2006). Revision of the Fully Technique for Estimating Stature. *American Journal of Physical Anthropology* 130: 374–384.

Raxter, M.H., Auerbach, B.M., & Ruff, C.B. (2007). Technical Note: Revised Fully Stature Estimation Technique. *American Journal of Physical Anthropology* 138: 817–818.

Redfern, R. & Bekvalac, J. (2013). The Museum of London: An Overview of Policies and Practice, pp. 87–98 in M. Giesen (ed) *Curating Human Remains: Caring for the Dead in the United Kingdom*. Boydell, Woodbridge.

Redfern, R. & Roberts, C. (2019). Trauma, pp. 211–284 in J.E. Buikstra, (ed). *Ortner's Identification of Pathological Conditions in Human Skeletal Remains* (3rd edition). Academic Press, London.

Refai, O. (2019). Entheseal Changes in Ancient Egyptians from the Pyramid Builders of Giza - Old Kingdom. *International Journal of Osteoarchaeology* 29: 513–524.

Reid, D.J. & Dean, M.C. (2006). Variation in Modern Human Enamel Formation Times. *Journal of Human Evolution* 50: 329–346.

Reitsema, L.J. (2013). Beyond Diet Reconstruction: Stable Isotope Applications to Human Physiology, Health and Nutrition. *American Journal of Human Biology* 25: 445–456.

Reitsema, L.J., Vercelotti, G., & Boano, R. (2016). Subadult Dietary Variation at Trino Vercellese, Italy, and Its Relationship to Adult Diet and Mortality. *American Journal of Physical Anthropology* 160: 653–664.

Relethford, J.H. (2004). Global Patterns of Isolation by Distance Based on Genetic and Morphological Data. *Human Biology* 76: 499–513.

Relethford, J.H. (2010). Population-Specific Deviations of Global Human Craniometric Variation from a Neutral Model. *American Journal of Physical Anthropology* 142: 105–111.

Renaud, G., Sion, V., Duggan, A.T., & Kelso, J. (2015). Schmutzi: Estimation of Contamination and Endogenous Mitochondrial Consensus Calling for Ancient DNA. *Genome Biology* 16: article 224

Renfrew, C. (1973). *Before Civilisation*. Penguin, Harmondsworth.

Renz, H. & Radlanski, R.J. (2006). Incremental Lines in Root Cementum of Human Teeth - A Reliable Age Marker? *Homo - Journal of Comparative Human Biology* 57: 29–50.

Retamal, R., Pacheco, A., & Uribe, M. (2018). Bioarchaeology in Chile: What It Is, Where We are and Where We Want to Go, pp. 7–24 in B. O'Donnabhain & M.C. Lozada (eds) *Archaeological Human Remains: Legacies of Imperialism, Communism and Colonialism*. Springer, Cham.

Reynard, L.M. & Tuross, N. (2015). The Known, the Unknown and the Unknowable: Weaning Times from Archaeological Bones Using Nitrogen Isotope Ratios. *Journal of Archaeological Science* 53: 618–625.

Reynolds, A. (2009). *Anglo-Saxon Deviant Burial Customs*. Oxford University Press, Oxford.

Reynolds, E.L. (1947). The Bony Pelvis in Prepubertal Childhood. *American Journal of Physical Anthropology* 5: 165–200.

Rhodes, J.A. & Knüsel, C.J. (2005). Activity-Related Skeletal Change in Medieval Humeri: Cross-Sectional and Architectural Alterations. *American Journal of Physical Anthropology* 128: 536–546.

Ribeiro, D.C., Brook, A.H., Hughes, T.E., Sampson, W.J., & Townsend, G.C. (2013). Intrauterine Hormone Effects on Tooth Dimensions. *Journal of Dental Research* 92: 425–431.

Ricci, S., Capecchi, G., Boschin, F., Arrighi, S., Ronchitelli, A., & Condemi, S. (2016). Toothpick Use among Epigravettian Humans from Grotta Paglicci (Italy). *International Journal of Osteoarchaeology* 26: 281-289.

Richards, G.D. & Anton, S.C. (1991). Craniofacial Configuration and Post-cranial Development of a Hydrocephalic Child (Ca. 2500B.C. - 500A.D.): With a Review of Cases and a Comment on Diagnostic Criteria. *American Journal of Physical Anthropology* 85: 185-200.

Richards, M.B., Sykes, B.C., & Hedges, R.E.M. (1995). Authenticating DNA Extracted from Ancient Skeletal Remains. *Journal of Archaeological Science* 22: 291-299.

Richards, M.P., Mays, S., & Fuller, B.T. (2002). Stable Carbon and Nitrogen Isotope Values of Bone and Teeth Reflect Weaning Age at the Mediaeval Wharram Percy Site, Yorkshire, UK. *American Journal of Physical Anthropology* 119: 205-210.

Richards, M.P., Price, T.D., & Koch, E. (2003). Mesolithic and Neolithic Subsistence in Denmark: New Stable Isotope Data. *Current Anthropology* 44: 288-295.

Richtsmeier, J.T. & McGrath, J.W. (1986). Quantitative Genetics of Cranial Nonmetric Traits in Randombred Mice: Heritability and Etiology. *American Journal of Physical Anthropology* 69: 51-58.

Rightmire, G.P. (1976). Metric versus Discrete Traits in African Skulls, pp. 383-407 in E. Giles & J.S. Friedlaender (eds) *The Measures of Man: Methodologies in Biological Anthropology*. Peabody Press, New York.

Ríos, L. & Cardoso, H.F.V. (2009). Age Estimation from Stages of Union from the Vertebral Epiphyses of the Ribs. *American Journal of Physical Anthropology* 140: 265-274.

Ríos, L., García-Rubio, A., Martínez, B., Coch, C., & Llidó, S. (2011). Field Recovery and Potential Information Value of Small Elements of the Skeleton. *HOMO - Journal of Comparative Human Biology* 62: 270-279.

Rios-Garaizar, J. (2010). Organización Económica De Las Sociedades Neandertales: El Case Del Nivel VII De Amalda (Zestoa, Gipuzkoa). *Zephyrus* 65: 15-37.

Rissech, C., Wilson, J., Winburn, A.P., Turbón, D., & Steadman, D. 2012. A Comparison of Three Established Age Estimation Methods on an Adult Spanish Sample. *International Journal of Legal Medicine* 126: 145-155.

Rivera-Sandoval, J., Monsalve, T., & Catteneo, C. (2018). A Test of Four Innominate Bone Age Assessment Methods in A Modern Skeletal Collection from Medellin, Colombia. *Forensic Science International* 282: 232.e1-232.e8.

Roberts, C. & Buikstra, J. (2003). *The Bioarchaeology of Tuberculosis*. University of Florida Press, Gainesville.

Roberts, C. & Cox, M. (2003). *Health and Disease in Britain from Prehistory to the Present Day*. Sutton, Stroud.

Roberts, C. & Mays, S. (2011). Study and Restudy of Curated Skeletal Collections in Bioarchaeology: A Perspective on the UK and Its Implications for Future Curation of Human Remains. *International Journal of Osteoarchaeology* 21: 626-630.

Roberts, C.A. (2019). Infectious Disease: Introduction, Periostosis, Periostitis, Osteomyelitis and Septic Arthritis, pp. 285-319 in J.F. Buikstra, (ed) *Ortner's Identification of Pathological Conditions in Human Skeletal Remains* (3rd edition). Academic Press, London.

Roberts, C.A. (2020). *Leprosy Past and Present*. University of Florida Press, Gainesville.

Roberts, C.A. & Buikstra, J.E. (2019). Bacterial Infections, pp. 321-439, in J.E. Buikstra, (ed). *Ortner's Identification of Pathological Conditions in Human Skeletal Remains* (3rd edition). Academic Press, London.

Roberts, C.A., Boylston, A., Buckley, L., Chamberlain, A.C., & Murphy, E.M. (1998). Rib Lesions and Tuberculosis: The Palaeopathological Evidence. *Tubercle and Lung Disease* 79: 55-60.

Roberts, C.A., Knüsel, C.J., & Race, L. (2004). A Foot Deformity from A Romano-British Cemetery at Gloucester, England, and the Current Evidence for Talipes in Palaeopathology. *International Journal of Osteoarchaeology* 14: 389-403.

Robling, A.G., Hinant, F.M., Burr, D.B., & Turner, C.H. (2002). Improved Bone Structure and Strength after Long-Term Mechanical Loading Is Greatest if Loading Is Separated into Short Bouts. *Journal of Bone and Mineral Research* 17: 1545-1554.

Rodriguez, W.C. (1997). Decomposition of Buried and Submerged Bodies, pp. 459-467 in W. D. Haglund & M.H. Sorg (eds) *Forensic Taphonomy: The Postmortem Fate of Human Remains*. CRC, London.

Rodwell, W. & Atkins, C. (2007). *St Peter's Barton-upon-Humber, Lincolnshire. A Parish Church and Its Community. Volume 1. History, Archaeology and Architecture*. Oxbow, Oxford.

Roe, W.D., Lenting, B., Kokosinska, A., Hunter, S., Duigan, P.J., Gartrell, B. et al. (2019). Pathology and Molecular Epidemiology of *Mycobacterium Pinnipedii* Tuberculosis in Native New Zealand Marine Mammals. *PloS One* 14(2): e0212363.

Rogers, J. (2000). The Palaeopathology of Joint Disease, pp. 163-182 in M. Cox & S. Mays (eds) *Human Osteology in Archaeology and Forensic Science*. Cambridge University Press, Cambridge.

Rogers, J. & Waldron, T. (1995). *A Field Guide to Joint Disease*. Wiley, Chichester.

Rogers, J., Shepstone, L., & Dieppe, P. (1997). Bone Formers: Osteophyte and Enthesophyte Formation are Positively Associated. *Annals of the Rheumatic Diseases* 56: 85-90.

Rogers, T. (2005). Determining the Sex of Human Remains through Cranial Morphology. *Journal of Forensic Sciences* 50: 493-500.

Roksandic, M. (2002). Position of Remains as a Key to Understanding Mortuary Behavior, pp. 99-117 in W.D. Haglund & M.H. Sorg, (eds). *Advances in Forensic Taphonomy*. CRC, Boca Raton.

Ross, P.D. (1996). Prediction of Fracture Risk II: Other Risk Factors. *American Journal of Medical Science* 312: 260-269.

Rott, A., Turner, N., Scholz, U., von Heyking, K., Immler, F., Peters, J., et al. (2017). Early Medieval Stone-Lined Graves in Southern Germany: Analysis of an Emerging Noble Class. *American Journal of Physical Anthropology* 162: 794-809.

Rountree, K. (2015). Holy Sites, Archaeological Monuments and the Perennial Contest over Material Heritage. *Journal for the Academic Study of Religion* 28(2): 104-128.

Ruff, C.B. (2000). Body Mass Prediction from Skeletal Frame Size in Elite Athletes. *American Journal of Physical Anthropology* 113: 507-517.

Ruff, C.B. (2002). Long Bone Articular and Diaphyseal Structure in Old World Monkeys and Apes. I: Locomotor Effects. *American Journal of Physical Anthropology* 119: 305-342.

Ruff, C.B. (2007). Body Size Prediction from Juvenile Skeletal Remains. *American Journal of Physical Anthropology* 133: 698-716.

Ruff, C.B. (2018). Quantifying Skeletal Robusticity, pp. 39-47 in C.B. Ruff (ed) *Skeletal Variation and Adaptation in Europeans. Upper Palaeolithic to the Twentieth Century*. Wiley-Blackwell, Chichester.

Ruff, C.B. (2019). Biomechanical Analyses of Archaeological Human Skeletons, pp. 189-224 in M.A. Katzenberg & A.L. Grauer (eds) *Biological Anthropology of the Human Skeleton* (3rd edn). Wiley, Chichester.

Ruff, C.B. & Larsen, C.S. (2014). Long Bone Structural Analyses and the Reconstruction of Past Mobility: A Historical Review, pp. 13-29 in K.J. Carlson & D. Marchi (eds) *Reconstructing Mobility: Environmental, Behavioral and Morphological Determinants*. New York, Springer.

Ruff, C.B., Scott, W.W., & Liu, A.Y.-C. (1991). Articular and Diaphysial Remodelling of the Proximal Femur with Changes in Body Mass in Adults. *American Journal of Physical Anthropology* 86: 397-413.

Ruff, C.B., Walker, A., & Trinkaus, E. (1994). Postcranial Robusticity in *Homo*. III: Ontogeny. *American Journal of Physical Anthropology* 93: 35–54.

Ruff, C.B., Holt, B., & Trinkaus, E. (2006). Who's Afraid of the Big Bad Wolff?: "Wolff's Law" and Bone Functional Adaptation. *American Journal of Physical Anthropology* 129: 484–498.

Ruff, C.B., Garofalo, E., & Holmes, M.A. (2013). Interpreting Skeletal Growth in the Past from a Functional and Physiological Perspective. *American Journal of Physical Anthropology* 150: 29–37.

Ruff, C.B., Niskanen, M., Maijanen, H., & Mays, S. (2019). Effects of Age and Body Proportions on Stature Estimation. *American Journal of Physical Anthropology* 168: 370–377.

Russell, J.C. (1937). Length of Life in England 1250–1348. *Human Biology* 9: 528–541.

Russell, J.C. (1948). *British Medieval Population*. University of New Mexico Press, Albuquerque.

Sachau-Carcel, G., Castex, D., & Vergnieux, R. (2015). Archaeoanthropology: How to Construct a Picture of the Past, pp. 29–41 in K. Gerdau-Radonić & K. McSweeney (eds) *Trends in Biological Anthropology, Volume 1*. Oxbow, Oxford.

Saipio, J. (2017). The Emergence of Cremations in Eastern Fennoscandia, pp. 201–230 in J. Cerezo-Román, A. Wessman, & H. Williams, (eds), *Cremation and the Archaeology of Death*. Oxford University Press, Oxford.

Salzano, F.M., Callegari, J., Franco, M.H.L.P., Hutz, M.H., Weimer, R.S.S., & da Rocha, F.J. (1980). The Caingang Revisited: Blood Genetics and Anthropometry. *American Journal of Physical Anthropology* 53: 513–524.

Sánchez-Quinto, F., Malmström, H., Fraser, M., Girdland-Flink, L., Svensson, E.M., Simões, L.G. et al. (2019). Megalithic Tombs in Western and Northern Neolithic Europe Were Linked to a Kindred Society. *Proceedings of the National Academy of Sciences of the USA* 116 (19): 9469–9474.

Sandberg, P.A., Sponheimer, M., Lee-Thorp, J., & van Gerven, D. (2014). Intra-Tooth Stable Isotope Analysis of Dentine: A Step toward Addressing Selective Mortality in the Reconstruction of Life History in the Archaeological Record. *American Journal of Physical Anthropology* 155: 281–293.

Santos, A.L. & Roberts, C.A. (2001). A Picture of Tuberculosis in Young Portuguese People in the Early 20th Century: A Multidisciplinary Study of the Skeletal and the Historical Evidence. *American Journal of Physical Anthropology* 115: 38–49.

Saunders, S.R. (1992). Subadult Skeletons and Growth Related Studies, pp. 1–20 in S.R. Saunders & M.A. Katzenberg (eds) *Skeletal Biology of Past Peoples: Research Methods*. Wiley-Liss, Chichester.

Saunders, S.R. (2008). Juvenile Skeletons and Growth-Related Studies, pp. 117–147 in M.A. Katzenberg & S.R. Saunders (eds) *Biological Anthropology of the Human Skeleton* (2nd edition). Wiley, Chichester.

Saunders, S.R. & Hoppa, R.D. (1993). Growth Deficit in Survivors and Non-Survivors: Biological Mortality Bias in Subadult Skeletal Samples. *Yearbook of Physical Anthropology* 36: 127–151.

Saunders, S.R. & Popovich, F. (1978). A Familial Study of Two Skeletal Variants: Atlas Bridging and Clinoid Bridging. *American Journal of Physical Anthropology* 49: 193–204.

Saunders, S.R. & Rainey, D.L. (2008). Nonmetric Trait Variation in the Skeleton: Abnormalities, Anomalies and Atavisms, pp. 533–559 in M.A. Katzenberg & S.R. Saunders (eds) *Biological Anthropology of the Human Skeleton* (2nd edition). Wiley-Liss, Chichester.

Saunders, S.R., Fitzgerald, C., Rogers, T., Dudar, C., & McKillop, H. (1992). A Test of Several Methods of Skeletal Age Estimation Using A Documented Archaeological Sample. *Canadian Society of Forensic Science Journal* 25: 97–117.

Sawyer, S., Krause, J., Guschanski, K., Savolainen, V., & Pääbo, S. (2012). Temporal Pattern of Nucleotide Misincorporations and DNA Fragmentation in Ancient DNA. *PloS One* 7(3): e34131.

Sayer, D. (2010). *Ethics and Burial Archaeology*. Duckworth, London.

Sayer, F. & Sayer, D. (2016). Bones without Barriers: The Social Impact of Digging the Dead, pp. 139–165 in H. Williams & M. Giles (eds) *Archaeologists and the Dead. Mortuary Archaeology in Contemporary Society*. Oxford University Press, Oxford.

Scarre, G. (2003). Archaeology and Respect for the Dead. *Journal of Applied Philosophy* 20: 237–249.

Schaeffer, M., Aben, G., & Vogelsberg, C. (2015). A Demonstration of Appearance and Union Times of Three Shoulder Ossification Centers in Adolescent and Post-Adolescent Children. *Journal of Forensic Radiology and Imaging* 3: 49–56.

Scharlotta, I., Goude, G., Herrscher, E., Bazaliiskii, V.I., & Weber, A.W. (2018). Shifting Weaning Practices in Early Neolithic Cis-Baikal, Siberia: New Insights from Stable Isotope Analysis of Molar Microsamples. *International Journal of Osteoarchaeology* 28: 579–598.

Scheuenemann, V.J., Avansi, C., Krause-Kyora, B., Seitz, A., Herbig, A., Inskip, S. et al. (2018). Ancient Genomes Reveal a High Diversity of Mycobacterium Leprae in Medieval Europe. *PloS Pathogens* 14(5): e1006997.

Scheuer, J.L., Musgrave, J.H., & Evans, S.P. (1980). Estimation of Late Foetal and Perinatal Age from Limb Bone Lengths by Linear and Logarithmic Regression. *Annals of Human Biology* 7: 257–265.

Schmeling, A., Schultz, R., Danner, B., & Rösing, F.W. (2006). The Impact of Economic Progress and Modernization in Medicine on the Ossification of Hand and Wrist. *International Journal of Legal Medicine* 120: 121–126.

Schmidt, A., Linford, P., Linford, N., David, A., Gaffney, C., Sarris, A., & Fassbinder, J. (2016). *EAC Guidelines for the Use of Geophysics in Archaeology. Questions to Ask and Points to Consider*. EAC Guidelines 2. Europae Archaeologiae Consilium, Namur.

Schmidt, C.W. (2015). Burned Human Teeth, pp. 61–81 in C.W. Schmidt & S.A. Symes (eds) *The Analysis of Burned Human Remains* (2nd edition). Academic Press, London.

Schmitt, A., Murail, P., Cunha, E., & Rougé, D. (2002). Variability in the Pattern of Aging on the Human Skeleton: Evidence from Bone Indicators and Implications on Age at Death Estimation. *Journal of Forensic Sciences* 47: 1203–1209.

Schmitt, D., Churchill, S.E., & Hylander, W.L. (2003). Experimental Evidence Concerning Spear Use in Neanderthals and Early Modern Humans. *Journal of Archaeological Science* 30: 103–114.

Schoeninger, M.J. & DeNiro, M.J. (1984). Nitrogen and Carbon Isotopic Composition of Bone Collagen from Marine and Terrestrial Animals. *Geochimica et Cosmochimica Acta* 48: 625–639.

Schoeninger, M.J., DeNiro, M.J., & Tauber, H. (1983). Stable Nitrogen Isotope Ratios of Bone Collagen Reflect Marine and Terrestrial Components of Prehistoric Diet. *Science* 220: 1381–1383.

Schour, L. & Massler, M. (1941). The Development of the Human Dentition. *Journal of the American Dental Association* 28: 1153–1160.

Schrader, S.A. (2015). Elucidating Inequality in Nubia: An Examination of Entheseal Changes at Kerma (Sudan). *American Journal of Physical Anthropology* 156: 102–202.

Schroeder, H., O'Connell, T.C., Evans, J.A., Shuler, K.A., & Hedges, R.E.M. (2009). Trans-Atlantic Slavery: Isotopic Evidence of Forced Migration to Barbados. *American Journal of Physical Anthropology* 139: 547–557.

Schulting, R. (2018). Dietary Shifts and the Mesolithic-Neolithic Transition in Europe: An Overview of the Stable Isotope Data, in J. Lee-Thorp & M.A. Katzenberg (eds) *The Oxford Handbook of the Archaeology of Diet*. Oxford University Press, Oxford.

Schulting, R. & Borić, D. 2017. A Tale of Two Processes of Neolithisation: Southeast Europe and Britain/ Ireland, pp. 82–104 in P. Bickle, V. Cummings, D. Hofmann, & J. Pollard (eds) *The Neolithic of Europe: Papers in Honour of Alasdair Whittle*. Oxbow, Oxford.

Schultz, A.H. (1967). Notes on Diseases and Healed Fractures of Wild Apes, pp. 47–55 in D. R. Brothwell & A.T. Sandison (eds) *Diseases in Antiquity*. Charles C. Thomas, Springfield.

Schultz, J.J., Warren, M.W., & Krigbaum, J.S. (2015). Analysis of Human Cremains, pp. 83–103 in C.W. Schmidt & S.A. Symes (eds) *The Analysis of Burned Human Remains* (2nd edition). Academic Press, London.

Schurr, M.R. & Redmond, B.G. (1991). Stable Isotope Analysis of Incipient Maize Horticulturalists from the Gard 2 Site. *Mid-Continental Journal of Archaeology* 16: 69–84.

Schurr, M.R., Hayes, R.G., & Cook, D.C. (2015). Thermally Induced Changes, pp. 105–118 in C.W. Schmidt & S.A. Symes (eds) *The Analysis of Burned Human Remains* (2nd edition). Academic Press, London.

Schutkowski, H. (1993). Sex Determination of Infant and Juvenile Skeletons: I Morphognostic Features. *American Journal of Physical Anthropology* 90: 199–205.

Scott, G.R. & Irish, J.D. (2017). *Tooth Crown and Root Morphology: The Arizona State University Dental Anthropology System*. Cambridge University Press, Cambridge.

Scott, G.R. & Pilloud, M.A. (2019). Dental Morphology, pp. 257–292 in M.A. Katzenberg & A.L. Grauer (eds) *Biological Anthropology of the Human Skeleton* (3rd edition). Wiley: Chichester.

Scott, G.R., Turner, C.G., Turner, G.C., & Martinón-Torres, M. (2018). *The Anthropology of Modern Human Teeth* (2nd edition). Cambridge University Press, Cambridge.

Scott, R.M., Buckley, H.R., Spriggs, M., Valentin, F., & Bedford, S. (2010). Identification of the First Reported Lapita Cremation in the Pacific Islands Using Archaeological, Forensic and Contemporary Burning Evidence. *Journal of Archaeological Science* 37: 901–909.

Sealy, J.C., van der Merwe, N.J., Lee-Thorp, J.A., & Lanham, J.L. (1987). Nitrogen Isotopic Ecology in Southern Africa: Implications for Environmental and Dietary Tracing. *Geochimica et Cosmochimica Acta* 51: 2707–2717.

Searle, A.G. (1954). Genetical Studies on the Skeleton of the Mouse XI. The Influence of Diet on Variation within Pure Lines. *Journal of Genetics* 52: 413–424.

Ségurel, L. & Bon, C. (2017). On the Evolution of Lactase Persistence in Humans. *Annual Reviews in Human Genetics* 18: 297–319.

Seifert, L., Wiechmann, I., Harbeck, M., Thomas, A., Grupe, G., Projahn, M. et al. (2016). Genotypic *Yersinia Pestis* in Historical Plague: Evidence for Long-Term Persistence of *Y. Pestis* in Europe from the 14th-17th Century. *PloS One* 11(1): e0145194.

Self, S.G. & Leamy, L. (1978). Heritability of Quasi-Continuous Skeletal Traits in a Randombred Population of House Mice. *Genetics* 88: 109–120.

Sellevold, B.J. (1997). Children's Skeletons and Graves in Scandinavian Archaeology, pp. 15–25 in G. De Boe & F. Verhaeghe, (eds) *Death and Burial in Medieval Europe. Papers of the 'Medieval Europe Brugge 1997' Conference, Volume 2*. Instituut voor het Archeologisch Patrimonium Rapporten 2. Instituut voor het Archeologisch Patrimonium, Doornveld.

Šešelj, M., Duren, D.L., & Sherwood, R.J. (2015). Heritability of the Human Craniofacial Complex. *Anatomical Record* 298: 1535–1547.

Shafer, W.G., Hine, M.K., & Levy, B.M. (1983). *A Textbook of Oral Pathology* (4th edition). W.B.Saunders, London.

Shafii, T., Radolf, J.T., Sánchez, P.J., Schulz, K.F., & Murphy, F.K. (2008). Congenital Syphilis, pp. 1577–1612 in K.K. Holmes, P.F. Sparling, W.E. Piot, J.N. Wasserheit, L. Corey, M.S. Cohen, & D.H. Watts (eds) *Sexually Transmitted Diseases* (4th edition). McGraw-Hill, London.

Shahar, S. (1990). *Childhood in the Middle Ages*. Routledge, London.

Sharma, L. (2019). Local and Systemic Risk Factors for Incidence and Progression of Osteoarthritis, pp. 1513–1521 in M.C. Hochberg, E.M. Gravellese, A.J. Silman, J.S. Smolen, M.E. Weinblatt, & M.H. Weisman (eds) *Rheumatology* (7th edition). Elsevier, Philadelphia.

Sharpe, J.A. (1985). The History of Violence in England: Some Observations. *Past and Present* 108: 206–215.

Shaw, C.N., Hofmann, C.L., Petraglia, M.D., Stock, J.T., & Gottschall, J.S. (2012). Neandertal Humeri May Reflect Adaptation to Scraping Tasks, but Not Spear Thrusting. *PloS ONE* 7 (7): e40349.

Shaw, H.M. & Benjamin, M. (2007). Structure-Function Relationships of Entheses in Relation to Mechanical Load and Exercise. *Scandinavian Journal of Medicine and Science in Sports* 17: 303-315.

Sheard, P.W. & Doherty, M. (2008). Prevalence and Severity of External Auditory Exostoses in Breath-Hold Divers. *Journal of Laryngology and Otology* 122: 1162-1167.

Sheiham, A. (2001). Dietary Effects on Dental Diseases. *Public Health Nutrition* 4(2B): 569-591.

Sheiham, A. & James, W.P.T. (2015). Diet and Dental Caries: The Pivotal Role of Free Sugars Reemphasized. *Critical Reviews in Oral Biology and Medicine* 94: 1341-1347.

Shennan, S. (1988). *Quantifying Archaeology*. Edinburgh University Press, Edinburgh.

Shepherd, A. (2012). Stepping Out Together: Men, Women and Their Beakers in Time and Space, pp. 257-280 in M.J. Allen, J. Gardiner, & A. Sheridan (eds) *Is There a British Chalcolithic? People, Place and Polity in the Late 3rd Millennium*. Prehistoric Society Research Paper 4. Oxbow, Oxford.

Shipman, P., Foster, G., & Schoeninger, M. (1984). Burnt Bones and Teeth: An Experimental Study of Colour, Morphology, Crystal Structure and Shrinkage. *Journal of Archaeological Science* 11: 307-325.

Sievänen, H. 2010. Immobilisation and Bone Structure in Humans. *Archives of Biochemistry and Biophysics* 503: 146-152.

Sillen, A. (1989). Diagenesis of the Inorganic Phase of Cortical Bone, pp. 211-229 in T.D. Price (ed) *The Chemistry of Prehistoric Human Bone*. Cambridge University Press, Cambridge.

Sillen, A., Hall, G., Richardson, S., & Armstrong, R. (1998). 87Sr/86Sr Ratios in Modern and Fossil Food-webs of the Sterkfontein Valley: Implications for Early Hominid Habitat Preference. *Geochimica et Cosmochimica Acta* 62: 2463-2473.

Simmons, T. (2017). Post-Mortem Interval Estimation: An Overview of Techniques, pp. 134-142 in E.M.J. Schotsmans, N. Márquez-Grant, & S.L. Forbes (eds) *Taphonomy of Human Remains: Forensic Analysis of the Dead and the Depositional Environment*. Wiley, Chichester.

Simon, M. (2017). Reevaluating the Evidence for Middle Woodland Maize from the Holding Site. *American Antiquity* 82: 140-150.

Simonson, T.M. & Kao, S.C.S. (1992). Normal Childhood Developmental Patterns in Skull Bone Marrow by MR Imaging. *Pediatric Radiology* 22: 556-559.

Simpson, S.W., Hutchinson, D.L., & Larsen, C.S. (1990). Coping with Stress: Tooth Size, Dental Defects and Age at Death, pp. 66-77 in C.S. Larsen (ed) *The Archaeology of the Mission Santa Catalina De Guale: 2. Biocultural Interpretations of a Population in Transition*. Anthropological Papers of the American Museum of Natural History No. 68. American Museum of Natural History, New York.

Singhal, A., Ramesh, V., & Balamurali, P.D. (2010). A Comparative Analysis of Root Dentin Transparency with Known Age. *Journal of Forensic Dental Sciences* 2(1): 18-21.

Sirak, K., Fernandes, D., Cheronet, O., Harney, E., Mah, M., Mallick, S. et al. (in press). *Human Auditory Ossicles as an Alternative Optimal Source of Ancient DNA*. Genome Research

Sjøvold, T. (1984). A Report on the Heritability of Some Cranial Measurements and Non-Metric Traits, pp. 223-246 in G.N. van Vark (ed) *Multivariate Statistical Methods in Physical Anthropology*. Reidel, Groningen.

Sjøvold, T. (1987). Decorated Skulls from Hallstatt, Austria: The Development of a Research Project, pp. 5-21 in G. Burenhult, A. Carlsson, A. Hyenstrand, & T. Sjøvold (eds) *Theoretical Approaches to Artifacts, Settlement and Society*. British Archaeological Reports, International Series, No. 366. British Archaeological Reports, Oxford.

Sjøvold, T., Swedborg, I., & Diener, L. (1974). A Pregnant Woman from the Middle Ages with Exostosis Multiplex. *Ossa* 1: 3-23.

Skoglund, P. & Reich, D. (2016). A Genomic View of the Peopling of the Americas. *Current Opinion in Genetics and Development* 41: 27-35.

Skoglund, P., Storå, J., Götherström, A., & Jakobsson, M. (2013). Accurate Sex Identification of Ancient Human Remains Using DNA Shotgun Sequencing. *Journal of Archaeological Science* 40: 4477-4482.

Skoglund, P., Northoff, B.H., Shunkov, M.V., Derevianko, A.P., Pääbo, S., Krause, J., & Jakobsson, M. (2014). Separating Endogenous Ancient DNA from Modern Contamination in a Siberian Neanderthal. *Proceedings of the National Academy of Sciences of the USA* 111(6): 2229-2234.

Skoglund, P., Thompson, J.C., Predegast, M.E., Mittnik, A., Sirak, K., Hajdinjak, M. et al. (2017). Reconstructing Prehistoric African Population Structure. *Cell* 171: 59-71.

Šlaus, M. (2000). Biocultural Analysis of Sex Differences in Mortality Profiles and Stress Levels in the Late Mediaeval Population from Nova Rača, Croatia. *American Journal of Physical Anthropology* 111: 193-209.

Small, C., Brits, D.M., & Hemingway, J. (2012). Quantification of the Subpubic Angle in South Africans. *Forensic Science International* 222: 395.e1-395.e6.

Smith, B.D. (2017). Tracing the Initial Diffusion of Maize in North America, pp. 332-348 in N. Boivin, R. Crassard, & M. Petraglia (eds) *Human Dispersal and Species Movement: From Prehistory to the Present*. Cambridge University Press, Cambridge.

Smith, B.H. (1991). Standards of Human Tooth Formation and Dental Age Assessment, pp. 143-168 in M.A. Kelley & C.S. Larsen (eds) *Advances in Dental Anthropology*. Wiley-Liss, Chichester.

Smith, B.N. & Epstein, S. (1971). Two Categories of 13C/12C Ratios for Higher Plants. *Plant Physiology* 47: 380-384.

Smith, C.I., Nielsen-Marsh, C.M., Jans, M.M.E., Arthur, P., Nord, A.G., & Collins, M.J. (2002). The Strange Case of Apigliano: Early "Fossilisation" of Medieval Bone in Southern Italy. *Archaeometry* 44: 405-415.

Smith, C.I., Nielsen-Marsh, C.M., Jans, M.M.E., & Collins, M.J. (2007). Bone Diagenesis in the European Holocene I: Patterns and Mechanisms. *Journal of Archaeological Science* 34: 1485-1493.

Smith, L. (2004). The Repatriation of Human Remains – Problem or Opportunity. *Antiquity* 78: 404-413.

Smith, M. & Brickley, M. (2009). *People of the Long Barrows. Life, Death and Burial in the Earlier Neolithic*. History Press, Stroud.

Smith, M.O. (2006). Treponemal Disease in the Middle Archaic to Early Woodland Periods of the Western Tennessee River Valley. *American Journal of Physical Anthropology* 205-217.

Snoeck, C., Lee-Thorpe, J.A., & Schulting, R.J. (2014a). From Bone to Ash: Compositional and Structural Changes in Burned Modern and Archaeological Bone. *Palaeogeography, Palaeoclimatology, Palaeoecology* 416: 55-68.

Snoeck, C., Brock, F., & Schulting, R.J. (2014b). Carbon Exchanges between Bone Apatite and Fuels during Cremation: Impact on Radiocarbon Dates. *Radiocarbon* 56: 591-602.

Snoeck, C., Lee-Thorp, J., Schulting, R., de Jong, J., Debouge, W., & Matielli, N. (2015). Calcined Bone Provides a Reliable Substrate for Strontium Isotope Ratios as Shown by an Enrichment Experiment. *Rapid Communications in Mass Spectrometry* 29: 107-114.

Snoeck, C., Schulting, R.J., Lee-Thorp, J., Lebon, M., & Zazzo, A. (2016). Impact of Heating Conditions on the Carbon and Oxtgen Isotope Composition of Calcined Bone. *Journal of Archaeological Science* 65: 32-43.

Snoeck, C., Pouncett, J., Claeys, P., Goderis, S., Matielli, N., Parker Pearson, M., Willis, C., Zazzo, A., Lee-Thorp, J.A. & Schulting, R.J. (2018). Strontium Isotope Analysis on Cremated Human Remains from Stonehenge Support Links with West Wales. *Scientific Reports* 8: article 10790.

Sood, R. (2001). Diagnosis of Abdominal Tuberculosis: Role of Imaging. *Journal, Indian Academy of Clinical Medicine* 2: 169-177.

Sotiriadis, A., Eleftheriades, M., Chatzinikolaou, F., Hassiakos, D., Chrousos, G.P., & Pervani-dou, P. (2016). National Curves of Foetal Growth in Singleton Foetuses of Greek Origin. *European Journal of Clinical Investigation* 46: 425–433.

Sparacello, V.S. & Pearson, O.M. (2010). The Importance of Accounting for the Area of the Medullary Cavity in Cross-Sectional Geometry: A Test Based on the Femoral Midshaft. *American Journal of Physical Anthropology* 143: 612–614.

Sparacello, V.S., Pearson, O.M., Coppa, A., & Marchi, D. (2011). Changes in Skeletal Robusti-city in an Iron Age Agropastoral Group: The Samnites from the Alfedena Necropolis (Abruzzo, Central Italy). *American Journal of Physical Anthropology* 144: 119–130.

Sparacello, V.S., d'Ercole, V., & Coppa, A. (2015). A Bioarchaeological Approach to the Reconstruction of Changes in Military Organization among Iron Age Samnites (Vestini) from Abruzzo, Central Italy. *American Journal of Physical Anthropology* 156: 305–316.

Sparling, P.F., Swartz, M.N., Musher, D.M., & Healy, B.P. (2008). Clinical Manifestations of Syphilis, pp. 661–684 in K.K. Holmes, P.F. Sparling, W.E. Piot, J.N. Wasserheit, L. Corey, M. S. Cohen, & D.H. Watts (eds) *Sexually Transmitted Diseases* (4th edition). McGraw-Hill, London.

Specker, B. & Binkley, T. (2003). Randomized Trial of Physical Activity and Calcium Supple-mentation on Bone Mineral Content in 3- to 5-Year Old Children. *Journal of Bone and Mineral Research* 18: 885–892.

Spielman, R.S. & Smouse, P.E. (1976). Multivariate Classification of Human Populations I. Allocation of Yanomama Indians to Villages. *American Journal of Human Genetics* 28: 317–331.

Spielman, R.S., de Rocha, F.J., Weitkamp, L.R., Ward, R.H., Neel, J.V., & Chagnon, N.A. (1972). The Genetic Structure of a Tribal Population, the Yanomama VII. Anthropometric Differ-ences among Yanomama Villages. *American Journal of Physical Anthropology* 37: 345–356.

Spigelman, M. & Donoghue, H.D. (2003). Palaeobacteriology with Special Reference to Pathogenic Mycobacteria, pp. 175–188 in C. Greenblatt & M. Spigelman (eds) *Emerging Pathogens. Archaeology, Ecology and Evolution of Infectious Disease*. Oxford University Press, Oxford.

Spradley, M.K. & Jantz, R.L. (2016). Ancestry Estimation in Forensic Anthropology: Geomet-ric Morphometric versus Standard and Nonstandard Interlandmark Distances. *Journal of Forensic Sciences* 61(4): 892–897.

Spyrou, M.A., Tukhbatova, R.I., Wang, C.C., Valentuña, A.A., Lankapalli, A.K., Kondrashin, V. V. et al (2019). Analysis of 3800-Year-Old *Yersinia Pestis* Genomes Suggests Bronze Age Origin for Bubonic Plague. *Nature Communications* 9: article 2234.

Squires, K.E. (2012). Populating the Pots: The Demography of the Early Anglo-Saxon Ceme-teries at Elsham and Cleatham, North Lincolnshire. *Archaeological Journal* 169: 312–342.

Stafford, T.W., Hare, P.E., Currie, L., Jull, A.J.T., & Donahue, D.J. (1991). Accelerator Radio-carbon Dating at the Molecular Level. *Journal of Archaeological Science* 18: 35–72.

Standaert, C.J. & Herring, S.J. (2000). Spondylolysis: A Critical Review. *British Journal of Sports Medicine* 34: 415–422.

Stansfield, E., Rasskasova, A., Berezina, N., & Soficaru, A.D. (2017). Resolving Relationships between Several Neolithic and Mesolithic Populations in Northern Eurasia Using Geomet-ric Morphometrics. *American Journal of Physical Anthropology* 164: 163–183.

Stark, S.Y. (2018). *The Shape of Childhood: A Morphometric Growth Study of the Anglo-Saxon to Post-Medieval Period*. PhD Thesis, University of Southampton.

Steinbock, R.T. (1976). *Paleopathological Diagnosis and Interpretation*. Charles C.Thomas, Springfield.

Steinbock, R.T. (1989). Studies in Ancient Calcified Soft Tissues and Organic Concretions. I: A Review of Structures, Diseases and Conditions. *Journal of Paleopathology* 3: 35–38.

Stermer Beyer-Olsen, E.M. & Risnes, S. (1994). Radiographic Analysis of Dental Develop-ment Used in Age Determination of Infant and Juvenile Skulls from a Mediaeval Archaeo-logical Site in Norway. *International Journal of Osteoarchaeology* 4 299–303.

Stevens, C.J. & Fuller, D.Q. (2015). Alternative Strategies to Agriculture: The Evidence for Climatic Shocks and Cereal Declines during the British Neolithic and Bronze Age (A Reply to Bishop). *World Archaeology* 47: 856-875.

Stevenson, P.H. (1924). Age Order of Epiphyseal Union in Man. *American Journal of Physical Anthropology* 7: 53-93.

Stewart, T.D. (1979). A Tribute to the French Forensic Anthropologist Georges Fully (1926-1973). *Journal of Forensic Sciences* 24: 916-924.

Stiner, M.C., Kuhn, S.L., Weiner, S., & Bar-Yosuf, O. (1995). Differential Burning, Recrystallisation and Fragmentation of Archaeological Bone. *Journal of Archaeological Science* 22: 223-237.

Stinson, S. (1985). Sex Differences in Environmental Sensitivity During Growth and Development. *Yearbook of Physical Anthropology* 28: 123-147.

Stinson, S. (2000). Growth Variation: Biological and Cultural Factors, pp. 423-463 in S. Stinson, B. Bogin, R. Huss-Ashmore, & D. O'Rourke (eds.) *Human Biology: An Evolutionary and Biocultural Perspective*. Wiley-Liss, Chichester.

Stirland, A. (1991). Pre-Columbian Treponematosis in Mediaeval Britain. *International Journal of Osteoarchaeology* 1: 39-47.

Stirland, A. (1994). Evidence for Precolumbian Treponematosis in Mediaeval Europe, pp. 109-115 in O. Dutour, G. Palfi, J. Berato, & J.P. Brun (eds) *L'Origine De La Syphilis En Europe, Avant Ou Apres 1493?* Editions Errance, Centre Archeologiques du Var.

Stock, J.T. & Shaw, C.N. (2007). Which Measures of Diaphyseal Robusticity are Robust? A Comparison of External Methods of Quantifying the Strength of Long Bone Diaphyses to Cross-Sectional Geometric Properties. *American Journal of Physical Anthropology* 134: 412-423.

Stojanowski, C.M., Larsen, C.S., Tung, T.A., & McEwan, B.G. (2007). Biological Structure and Health Implications from Tooth Size at Mission San Luis De Apalachee. *American Journal of Physical Anthropology* 132: 207-222.

Stone, A.C. & Ozga, A.T. (2019). Ancient DNA in the Study of Ancient Disease, pp. 183-210 in J.E. Buikstra (ed) *Ortner's Identification of Pathological Conditions in Human Skeletal Remains* (3rd edition). Elsevier, London.

Strauss, A. (2016). Os Padrões De Sepultamento Do Sítio Arqueológico Lapa Do Santo (Holoceno Inicial, Brasil). *Boletim Do Museu Paranese Emílio Goeldi. Ciênces Humanas* 11 (1): 243-276.

Ström, C. (1992). Injuries Due to Violent Crimes. *Medicine, Science and the Law* 32: 123-132.

Stull, K.E., Kenyhercz, M.W., & L'Abbé, E.N. (2014). Ancestry Estimation in South Africa Using Craniometrics and Geometric Morphometrics. *Forensic Science International* 245: 206e1-206e7.

Sullivan, S., Flavel, A., & Franklin, D. (2017). Age Estimation in a Sub-Adult Western Australian Population Based on the Analysis of the Pelvic Girdle and Proximal Femur. *Forensic Science International* 281: 185.e1-185.e10.

Sutter, R.C. (2003). Nonmetric Subadult Skeletal Sexing Traits: I. A Blind Test of the Accuracy of Eight Previously Proposed Methods Using Prehistoric Known-Sex Mummies from Northern Chile. *Journal of Forensic Sciences* 48: 927-935.

Suzuki, H. (1969). Microevolutional Changes in the Japanese Population from the Prehistoric Age to the Present Day. *Journal of the Faculty of Science, University of Tokyo, Section 5 (Anthropology)* 3: 279-309.

Svestad, A. (2019). Caring for the Dead? An Alternative Perspective on Sámi Reburial. *Acta Borealia* 36: 23-52.

Svoboda, J.A. (2006). The Archaeological Contexts of the Human Remains, pp. 15-26 in E. Trinkaus & J.A. Svoboda (eds) *Early Modern Human Evolution in Central Europe. The People of Dolní Věstonice and Pavlov*. Oxford University Press, Oxford.

Swain, H. (ed) (2005). *Guidance for the Care of Human Remains in Museums*. DCMS. www.culture.gov.uk/NR/rdonlyres/0017476B-3B86-46F3-BAB3-11E5A5F7F0A1/0/GuidanceHumanRemains11Oct.pdf

Swain, H. (2006). Public Reaction to the Displaying of Human Remains at the Museum of London, pp. 97-101 in J. Lohman & K. Goodnow (eds) *Human Remains in Museum Practice*. UNESCO/Museum of London, London.

Sweeney, E.A., Cabera, J., Urrutia, J., & Mata, L. (1969). Factors Associated with Linear Hypoplasia of Human Deciduous Incisors. *Journal of Dental Research* 48: 1275-1279.

Sweeney, E.A., Saffir, A.J., & de Leon, R. (1971). Linear Hypoplasia of Deciduous Incisor Teeth in Malnourished Children. *American Journal of Clinical Nutrition* 24: 29-31.

Swinson, D., Snaith, J., Buckberry, J., & Brickley, M. (2010). High Performance Liquid Chromatography (HPLC) in the Investigation of Gout in Palaeopathology. *International Journal of Osteoarchaeology* 20: 135-143.

Symes, S.A., Rainwater, C.W., Chapman, E.N., Gipson, D.R., & Piper, A.L. (2015). Patterned Thermal Destruction in a Forensic Setting, pp. 17-59 in C.W. Schmidt & S.A. Symes (eds) *The Analysis of Burned Human Remains* (2nd edition) Academic Press, London.

Tabachnik, B.G. & Fidell, L.S. (2013). *Using Multivariate Statistics* (6th edition). Pearson, London.

Tague, R.G. (1994). Maternal Mortality of Prolonged Growth: Age at Death and Pelvic Size in Three Prehistoric Amerindian Populations. *American Journal of Physical Anthropology* 95: 27-40.

Tague, R.G. (2007). Costal Process of the First Sacral Vertebra: Sexual Dimorphism and Obstetrical Adaptation. *American Journal of Physical Anthropology* 132: 395-405.

Takahashi, K., Morita, Y., Ohshima, S., Izumi, S., Kubota, Y., & Horii, A. (2017). Bone Density Development of the Temporal Bone Assessed by Computed Tomography. *Otology and Neurology* 38: 1445-1449.

Tan, F.C. (1989). Stable Carbon Isotopes in Dissolved Inorganic Carbon in Marine and Estuarine Environments, pp. 171-217 in P. Fritz & J.C. Fontes (eds) *Handbook of Environmental Isotope Geochemistry. Volume 3: The Marine Environment*. Elsevier, Oxford.

Tang, N., Antoine, D., & Hillson, S. (2014). Application of the Bang & Ramm Age at Death Estimation Method to Two Known Age Archaeological Assemblages. *American Journal of Physical Anthropology* 155: 332-351.

Tanner, J.M. (1981). *A History of the Study of Human Growth*. Cambridge University Press, Cambridge.

Tanner, J.M. (1989). *Foetus into Man* (2nd edition). Castlemead, Ware.

Tatham, S. (2016). Displaying the Dead: The English Heritage Experience, pp. 184-203 in H. Williams & M. Giles (eds) *Archaeologists and the Dead. Mortuary Archaeology in Contemporary Society*. Oxford University Press, Oxford.

Tauber, H. (1981). 13C Evidence for Dietary Habits of Prehistoric Man in Denmark. *Nature* 292: 332-333.

Tauber, H. (1986). Analysis of Stable Isotopes in Prehistoric Populations, pp. 31-38 in B. Herrmann (ed) *Innovative Trends in Prehistoric Anthropology*. Mitteilungen der Beliner Gesellschaft Für Anthropologie, Ethnologie und Urgeschichte, Band 7.

Taylor, G.M., Young, D.B., & Mays, S.A. (2005). Genotypic Analysis of the Earliest Known Prehistoric Case of Tuberculosis in Britain. *Journal of Clinical Microbiology* 43: 2236-2240.

Temple, D.H. (2019). Bioarchaeological Evidence for Adaptive Plasticity and Constraint: Exploring Life-History Trade-Offs in the Human Past. *Evolutionary Anthropology* 28: 34-46.

Temple, D.H., McGroarty, J.N., Guatelli-Steinberg, D., Nakatsukasa, M., & Matsumura, H. (2013). A Comparative Study of Stress Episode Prevalence and Duration among Jomon Period Foragers From Hokkaido. *American Journal of Physical Anthropology* 152: 230-238.

Temple, D.H., Basaliiski, V., Goriunova, O., & Weber, A. (2014). Skeletal Growth in Early and Late Neolithic Foragers from the Cis-Baikal Region of Eastern Siberia. *American Journal of Physical Anthropology* 153: 377-386.

Thacher, T.D., Fischer, P.R., Pettifor, J.M., Lawson, J.O., Manaster, B.J., & Reading, J.C. (2000). Radiographic Scoring Method for the Assessment of the Severity of Nutritional Rickets. *Journal of Tropical Pediatrics* 46: 132-139.

Thackray, D. & Payne, S. (2009). *Report on Consultation on the Request for Reburial of Prehistoric Human Remains from The Alexander Keiller Museum at Avebury*. English Heritage and The National Trust, Swindon. https://historicengland.org.uk/advice/technical-advice/archaeological-science/human-remains-advice/avebury-reburial-results/

Thackray, D. & Payne, S. (2010). *Avebury Reburial Request: Summary Report*. English Heritage and The National Trust, Swindon. https://historicengland.org.uk/advice/technical-advice/archaeological-science/human-remains-advice/avebury-reburial-results/

Thomas, A. (2014). Bioarchaeology of the Middle Neolithic: Evidence for Archery among Early European Farmers. *American Journal of Physical Anthropology* 154: 279-290.

Thomas, J. (1987). Relations of Production and Social Change in the Neolithic of Northwest Europe. *Man* 22: 405-430.

Thompson, A.R. (2013). Odontometric Determination of Sex at Mound 72, Cahokia. *American Journal of Physical Anthropology* 151: 408-419.

Thompson, A.R., Hedman, K.M., & Slater, P.A. (2015). New Dental and Isotopic Evidence of Biological Distance and Place of Origin for Mass Burial Groups at Cahokia's Mound 72. *American Journal of Physical Anthropology* 158: 341-357.

Thompson, T.J.U. (2005). Heat-Induced Dimensional Changes in Bone and Their Consequences for Forensic Anthropology. *Journal of Forensic Sciences* 50: 1008-1015.

Thompson, T.J.U. (2015). The Analysis of Heat-Induced Crystallinity Change in Bone, pp. 323-337, in C.W. Schmidt & S.A. Symes (eds) *The Analysis of Burned Human Remains* (2nd edition) Academic Press, London.

Thompson, T.J.U., Gauthier, M., & Islam, M. (2009). The Application of a New Method of Fourier Transform Infrared Spectroscopy to the Analysis of Burned Bone. *Journal of Archaeological Science* 36: 910-914.

Thompson, T.J.U., Islam, M., & Bonniere, M. (2013). A New Statistical Approach for Determining the Crystallinity of Heat-Altered Bone Mineral from FTIR Spectra. *Journal of Archaeological Science* 40: 416-422.

Thompson, T.J.U., Szigeti, J., Gowland, G.L., & Witcher, R.E. (2016). Death on the Frontier: Military Cremation Practices in the North of Roman Britain. *Journal of Archaeological Science Reports* 10: 828-836.

Thordemann, B. (1939) *Armour from the Battle of Wisby, 1361*. Vitterhets Historie och Antikvitets Akademien, Stockholm.

Thorpe, I.J. & Richards, C. (1984). The Decline of Ritual Authority and the Introduction of Beakers into Britain, pp. 67-84 in R. Bradley & J. Gardiner (eds) *Neolithic Studies: A Review of Some Current Research*. British Archaeological Reports, British Series, No. 133. British Archaeological Reports, Oxford.

Thorson, J. & Hägg, U. (1991). The Accuracy and Precision of the Third Mandibular Molar as an Indicator of Chronological Age. *Swedish Dental Journal* 15: 15-22.

Thurnam, J.T. (1863). On the Principal Forms of Ancient British and Gaulish Skulls. *Memoirs of the Anthropological Society of London* 1: 120-168.

Tiesler, V. (2014). *The Bioarchaeology of Artificial Cranial Modifications. New Approaches to Head-Shaping and Its Meaning in Pre-Columbia Mesoamerica and Beyond*. Springer, New York.

Tieszen, L.L. (1991). Natural Variation in the Carbon Isotope Values of Plants: Implications for Archaeology, Ecology and Palaeoecology. *Journal of Archaeological Science* 18: 227-248.

Tieszen, L.L., Boutton, T.W., Tesdahl, K.G., & Slade, N.A. (1983). Fractionation and Turnover of Stable Carbon Isotopes in Animal Tissues: Implications for Delta 13C Analysis of Diet. *Oecologia* 57: 32-37.

Todd, T.W. (1920). Age Changes in the Pubic Bone. I. The Male White Pubis. *American Journal of Physical Anthropology* 3: 285-339.

Tonge, C.H. & McCance, R.A. (1965). Severe Undernutrition in Growing and Adult Animals. 15. The Mouth, Jaws and Teeth of Pigs. *British Journal of Nutrition* 19: 361-372.

Torgersen, J.H. (1951a). The Developmental Genetics and Evolutionary Meaning of the Metopic Suture. *American Journal of Physical Anthropology* 9: 193-205.

Torgersen, J.H. (1951b). Hereditary Factors in the Sutural Patterns of the Skull. *Acta Radiologica* 36: 374-382.

Torgersen, J.H. (1954). The Occiput, the Posterior Cranial Fossa and the Cerebellum, pp. 396-418 in J. Jansen & A. Brodal (eds) *Aspects of Cerebellar Anatomy*. Gundersen, Oslo.

Trakinienė, G., Šidlauskas, A., Andriuškevičiūtė, I., Šalomskienė, L., Švalkauskienė, V., Smailienė, D., & Trakinis, T. (2018). Impact of Genetics on Third Molar Agenesis. *Scientific Reports* 8: article 8307.

Trickett, M.A., Budd, P., Montgomery, J., & Evans, J. (2003). An Assessment of Solubility Profiling as a Decontamination Procedure for the 87Sr/86Sr Analysis of Archaeological Human Skeletal Tissue. *Applied Geochemistry* 18: 653-658.

Trinkaus, E. (1975). Squatting among the Neanderthals: A Problem in the Behavioral Interpretation of Skeletal Morphology. *Journal of Archaeological Science* 2: 327-351.

Trinkaus, E. (1981). Neanderthal Limb Proportions and Cold Adaptation, pp 187-224 in C.B. Stringer (ed) *Aspects of Human Evolution*. Taylor-Francis, London.

Trinkaus, E. & Svoboda, J., (eds). (2006). *Early Modern Human Evolution in Central Europe. The People of Dolní Věstonice and Pavlov*. Oxford University Press, Oxford.

Trinkaus, E., Churchill, S.E., & Ruff, C.B. (1994). Post-Cranial Robusticity in *Homo* II: Humeral Bilateral Asymmetry and Bone Plasticity. *American Journal of Physical Anthropology* 93: 1-34.

Trotter, M. (1970). Estimation of Stature from Intact Limb Long Lones, pp. 71-83 in T.D. Stewart (ed) *Personal Identification in Mass Disasters*. Smithsonian Institution, Washington.

Trotter, M. & Gleser, G.C. (1951). The Effect of Ageing on Stature. *American Journal of Physical Anthropology* 9: 311-324.

Trotter, M. & Gleser, G.C. (1952). Estimation of Stature From Long-Bones of American Whites and Negroes. *American Journal of Physical Anthropology* 10: 463-514.

Trotter, M. & Gleser, G.C. (1958). A Re-Evaluation of Estimation of Stature Based on Measurements of Stature Taken During Life and of Long-Bones after Death. *American Journal of Physical Anthropology* 16: 79-123.

Trotter, M. & Gleser, G.C. (1977). Corrigenda to "Estimation of Stature From Long-Bones of American Whites and Negroes", American Journal of Physical Anthropology (1952). *American Journal of Physical Anthropology* 47: 355-356.

Trotter, M. & Hixon, B.B. (1974). Sequential Changes in Weight, Density and Percentage Ash Weight of Human Skeletons From an Early Foetal Period Through to Old Age. *Anatomical Record* 179: 1-18.

Tsude, H. (1995). Archaeological Theory in Japan, pp. 298-311 in P.J. Ucko (ed) *Theory in Archaeology, A World Perspective*. Routledge, London.

Tsutaya, T. & Yoneda, M. (2015). Reconstruction of Breastfeeding and Weaning Practices Using Stable Isotope and Trace Element Analyses: A Review. *Yearbook of Physical Anthropology* 59: 2-21.

Tuck, S.P., Layfield, R., Walker, J., Mekkayil, B., & Francis, R. (2017). Adult Paget's Disease of Bone: A Review. *Rheumatology* 56: 2050-2059.

Tucker, K. (2013). The Osteology of Decapitation Burials from Roman Britain, pp. 213-236 in C. Knüsel & M. Smith (eds) *The Routledge Handbook of the Bioarchaeology of Human Conflict*. Routledge, London.

Tucker, K. (2015). *An Archaeological Study of Decapitation Burials*. Pen & Sword, Barnsley.

Turner, B.L., Edwards, J.L., Quinn, E.A., Kingston, J.D., & van Gerven, D.P. (2007). Age-Related Variation in Isotopic Indicators of Diet at Mediaeval Kulubnarti, Sudanese Nubia. *International Journal of Osteoarchaeology* 17: 1-25.

Turner, C.G. (1979). Dental Anthropological Indications of Agriculture among the Jomon People of Central Japan. *American Journal of Physical Anthropology* 51: 619-636.

Turner, C.G., Nichol, C.R., & Scott, G.R. (1991). Scoring Procedures for Key Morphological Traits of the Permanent Dentition, pp. 13-31 in M.A. Kelley & C.S. Larsen (eds) *Advances in Dental Anthropology*. Wiley-Liss, Chichester.

Turner-Walker, G. (2008). The Chemical and Microbial Degradation of Bones and Teeth, pp. 3-29 in R. Pinhasi & S. Mays (eds) *Advances in Human Palaeopathology*. Chichester, Wiley.

Turner-Walker, G. (2009). *A Practical Guide to the Conservation of Metals*. Headquarters Administration of Cultural Heritage Council for Cultural Affairs, Taipei.

Turner-Walker, G. (2012). Early Bioerosion in Skeletal Tissues: Persistence through Deep Time. *Neuers Jahrbuch Für Geologie Und Paläontologie* 265: 165-183.

Turner-Walker, G. & Mays, S. (2008). Histological Studies on Ancient Bone, pp. 121-146 in R. Pinhasi & S. Mays (eds) *Advances in Human Palaeopathology*. Chichester, Wiley.

Turner-Walker, G. & Parry, T.V. (1995). The Tensile Strength of Archaeological Bone. *Journal of Archaeological Science* 22: 185-191.

Turner-Walker, G. & Syversen, U. (2002). Quantifying Histological Changes in Archaeological Bones Using BSE-SEM Image Analysis. *Archaeometry* 44: 461-468.

Turner-Walker, G., Syversen, U., & Mays, S. (2001). The Archaeology of Osteoporosis. *Journal of European Archaeology* 4: 263-268.

Turner-Walker, G., Nielsen-Marsh, C.M., Syversen, U., Kars, H., & Collins, M.J. (2002). Sub-Micron Spongiform Porosity Is the Major Ultra-Structural Alteration Occurring in Archaeological Bone. *International Journal of Osteoarchaeology* 12: 407-414.

Tyrrell, A. (2000). Skeletal Non-Metric Traits and the Assessment of Inter- and Intra-Population Diversity: Past Problems and Future Potential, pp. 289-306 in M. Cox & S. Mays (eds) *Human Osteology in Archaeology and Forensic Science*. Cambridge University Press, Cambridge.

Ubelaker, D.H. (1999). *Human Skeletal Remains: Excavation, Analysis, Interpretation* (3rd edition). Taraxacum, Washington.

Ubelaker, D.H. & Grant, L.G. (1989). Human Skeletal Remains: Preservation or Reburial? *Yearbook of Physical Anthropology* 32: 249-287.

Ucko, P.J. (1969). Ethnography and Archaeological Interpretation of Funerary Remains. *World Archaeology* 1: 262-280.

Ulguim, P.F. (2015). Analysis Cremated Human Remains from the Southern Brazilian Highlands: Interpreting Archaeological Evidence of Funerary Practice at Mound and Enclosure Complexes in the Pelotas River Valley, pp. 173-212 in T. Thompson (ed) *The Archaeology of Cremation. Burned Human Remains in Funerary Studies*. Oxbow, Oxford.

Ulguim, P.F. (2017). Recording *in Situ* Human Remains in Three Dimensions: Applying Digital Image-based Modelling, pp. 71-92 in D. Erricksen & T. Thompson, (eds). *Human Remains: Another Dimension. The Application of Imaging to the Study of Human Remains*. Academic Press, London.

USDA. (2019). United States Department of Agriculture, Food Data Central. Corn Grain, Yellow (*Zea Mays*) https://fdc.nal.usda.gov/fdc-app.html#/food-details/170288/nutrients. Consulted 13/5/2020.

Utsi, E.C. & Colls, K.S. (2017). The GPR Investigation of the Shakespeare Family Graves. *Archaeological Prospection* 24: 335-352.

Vågene, Å.J., Herbig, A., Campana, M.G., Garcia, N.M.R., Warriner, C., Sabin, S. et al. (2018). *Salmonella Enterica* Genomes from Victims of a Major Sixteenth-Century Epidemic in Mexico. *Nature Ecology and Evolution* 2: 520-528.

Valtueña, A.A., Mittnik, A., Key, F.M., Haak, W., Allmäe, R., Belinskij, A. et al. (2017). The Stone Age Plague and Its Persistence in Eurasia. *Current Biology* 27: 3683-3691.

van Deest, T.L., Murad, T.A., & Bartelink, E.J. (2011). A Re-examination of Cremains Weight: Sex and Age Variation in A Northern California Sample. *Journal of Forensic Sciences* 56 (2): 344-349.

van Klinken, G.J. (1999). Bone Collagen Quality Indicators for Palaeodietary and Radiocarbon Measurements. *Journal of Archaeological Science* 26: 687-695.

van Loveren, C. (2019). Sugar Restriction for Caries Prevention: Amount and Frequency. Which Is More Important? *Caries Research* 53: 168-175.

Vander Linden, M. (2007). What Linked the Bell Beakers in Third Millennium BC Europe? *Antiquity* 81: 343-352.

Vander Linden, M. (2012). The Importance of Being Insular: Britain and Ireland in Their North-western European Context during the Third Millennium BC, pp. 71-84 in M.J. Allen, J. Gardiner, & A. Sheridan (eds) *Is There a British Chalcolithic? People, Place and Polity in the Late 3rd Millennium*. Prehistoric Society Research Paper 4. Oxbow, Oxford.

Vander Linden, M. & Roberts, B.W. (2012). A Tale of Two Countries: Contrasting Archaeological Culture History in British and French Archaeology, pp. 23-40 in B.W. Roberts & M. Vander Linden (eds) *Investigating Archaeological Cultures: Material Culture, Variability and Transmission*. Springer, London.

Vecchi, F., Coppa, A., & Priori, R. (1987). Morphological Distance between Four Ethnic Groups in Southern Mexico. *Rivista Di Antropologia (Roma)* 65: 223-234.

Velsko, I.M., Yates, J.A.F., Aron, F., Hagan, R.W., Frantz, L.A.F., Loe, L. et al. (2019). Microbial Differences between Dental Plaque and Historic Dental Calculus are Related to Oral Biofilm Maturation Stage. *BMC Microbiome* 7: article 102.

Vennat, E., Bogicevic, C., Fleureau, J.-M., & Degrange, M. (2009). Demineralized Dentin 3D Porosity and Pore Size Distribution Using Mercury Porosimetry. *Dental Materials* 25: 729-735.

Villotte, S. (2006). Connaissances Médicales Actuelles, Cotation De Enthésopathies: Nouvelle Méthode. *Bulletins Et Mémoires De La Société d'Anthropologie De Paris* 18(1-2): 65-85.

Villotte, S. & Knüsel, C. (2013). Understanding Entheseal Changes: Definition and Life Course Changes. *International Journal of Osteoarchaeology* 23: 127-136.

Villotte, S. & Knüsel, C. (2014). "I Sing of Arms and of a Man ...": Medial Epicondylosis and the Sexual Division of Labour in Prehistoric Europe. *Journal of Archaeological Science* 43: 168-174.

Villotte, S. & Knüsel, C. (2016). External Auditory Exostoses and Prehistoric Aquatic Resource Procurement. *Journal of Archaeological Science Reports* 6: 633-636.

Villotte, S., Castex, D., Couallier, V., Dutour, O., Knüsel, C., & Henry-Gambier, D. (2010). Enthesopathies as Occupational Stress Markers: Evidence from the Upper Limb. *American Journal of Physical Anthropology* 142: 224-234.

Villotte, S., Stefanović, S., & Knüsel, C. (2014). External Auditory Exostoses and Aquatic Activities during the Mesolithic and the Neolithic in Europe: Results from a Large Prehistoric Sample. *Anthropologie (Brno)* 52: 73-89.

Vinnicombe, P. (1976). *People of the Eland. Rock Paintings of the Drakensberg Bushmen as a Reflection of Their Life and Thought*. University of Natal Press, Pietermaritzburg.

Vinz, H. (1970). Untersuchingen Über Die Dichte, Den Wasser- Und Den Mineralgehalt Des Kompacten Menschlichen Knochengewebes in Abhängigkeit Vom Alter. *Gegenbauers Morphologisches Jarhbuch* 115(3): 273-283.

Vitzthum, V.J. (1994). Comparative Study of Breastfeeding Structure and Its Relation to Human Reproductive Ecology. *Yearbook of Physical Anthropology* 37: 307-349.

Vlak, D., Roksandic, M., & Schillaci, M.A. (2008). Greater Sciatic Notch as a Sex Indicator in Juveniles. *American Journal of Physical Anthropology* 137: 309-315.

Volkman, S.K., Galecki, A.T., Burke, D.T., Paczas, M.R., Moalli, M.R., Miller, R.A., & Goldstein, S.A. (2003). Quantitative Trait Loci for Femoral Size and Shape in a Genetically Heterogeneous Mouse Population. *Journal of Bone and Mineral Research* 18: 1497-1505.

von Cramon-Taubadel, N. (2009). Revisiting the Homiology Hypothesis: The Impact of Phenotypic Plasticity on the Reconstruction of Human Population History from Craniometric Data. *Journal of Human Evolution* 57: 179-190.

von Cramon-Taubadel, N. (2011). Global Human Mandibular Variation Reflects Differences in Agricultural and Hunter-Gatherer Subsistence Strategies. *Proceedings of the National Academy of Sciences of the USA* 108(49): 19546-19551.

von Cramon-Taubadel, N. (2016). Population Biodistance in Global Perspective: Assessing the Influence of Population History and Environmental Effects on Patterns of Craniomandibular Variation, pp. 425-445 in M.A. Pilloud & J.T. Hefner (eds) *Biological Distance Analysis: Forensic and Bioarchaeological Perspectives*. Elsevier, London.

Wahl, J. (1982). Leichenbranduntersuchungen: Ein Uberblick Über Die Bearbeitungs- Und Aussagemoglichkeiten Von Brandgräbern. *Praehistorische Zeitschrift* 57: 1-125.

Wahl, J. (2015). Investigations on Pre-Roman and Roman Cremation Remains, pp. 163-179 in C.W. Schmidt & S.A. Symes (eds) *The Analysis of Burned Human Remains* (2nd edition). Academic Press, London.

Wahl, J.,Cipollini, G., Coia, V., Francken, M., Harvati-Papatheodorou, K., Kim, M-R. et al. (2014). Neue Erkentmisse Zur Frümittelalterlichen Separatgrablege Von Niederstotzingen, Kreis Heidenheim. *Fundberichte Aus Baden-Wurttemberg* 34(2): 341-390.

Walczak, B.E., Johnson, C.N., & Howe, B.M. (2015). Myositis Ossificans. *Journal of the American Academy of Orthopedic Surgeons* 23: 612-622.

Waldron, T. (1994). *Counting the Dead. The Epidemiology of Skeletal Populations*. Wiley, Chichester.

Waldron, T. & Waldron, G. (1988). Two Felons from Surrey. *London Archaeologist* 5: 443-445.

Walker, D. (2012). *Disease in London, 1st-19th Centuries. An Illustrated Guide to Diagnosis*. Museum of London Archaeology Monograph 56. Museum of London Archaeology, London.

Walker, D. & Henderson, M. (2010). Smoking and Health in London's East End in the First Half of the 19th Century. *Post-Medieval Archaeology* 44: 209-222.

Walker, D., Powers, N., Connell, B., & Redfern, R. (2015). Evidence of Skeletal Treponematosis from the Mediaeval Burial Ground of St Mary Spital, London, and Implications for the Origins of the Disease in Europe. *American Journal of Physical Anthropology* 156: 90-101.

Walker, P.L. (1997). Wife Beating, Boxing and Broken Noses: Skeletal Evidence for the Cultural Patterning of Violence, pp. 145-179 in D.L. Martin & D.W. Frayer (eds) *Troubled Times: Violence and Warfare in the Past*. Gordon & Breach, Amsterdam.

Walker, P.L. (2008). Sexing Skulls Using Discriminant Function Analysis of Visually Assessed Traits. *American Journal of Physical Anthropology* 136: 39-50.

Walker, P.L. & Cook, D.C. (1998). Gender and Sex: Viva La Difference. *American Journal of Physical Anthropology* 106: 255-259.

Walker, P.L. & Hewlett, B.S. (1990). Dental Health, Diet and Social Status among Central African Foragers and Farmers. *American Anthropologist* 92: 383-398.

Walker, P.L., Miller, K.W.P., & Richman, R. (2008). Time, Temperature and Oxygen Availability: An Experimental Study of the Effects of Environmental Conditions on the Colour and Organic Content of Cremated Bone, pp. 129-135 in C.W. Schmidt & S.A. Symes (eds) *The Analysis of Burned Human Remains* (1st edition). Academic Press, London.

Walker, P.L., Bathurst, R.R., Richman, R., Gjerdrum, T., & Andrushko, V.A. (2009). The Causes of Porotic Hyperostosis and Cribra Orbitalia: A Reappriasal of the Iron-Deficiency-Anemia Hypothesis. *American Journal of Physical Anthropology* 139: 109-125.

Wallace, I.J., Demes, B., & Judex, J. (2017). Ontogenic and Genetic Influences on Bone's Responsiveness to Mechanical Signals, pp. 233-253 in C.J. Percival & J.T. Richtsmeier (eds) *Building Bones. Bone Formation and Development in Anthropology*. Cambridge University Press, Cambridge.

Wallis, R.J. (2015). Paganism, Archaeology and Folklore in Twenty-First Century Britain: A Case Study of 'The Stonehenge Ancestors'. *Journal for the Academic Study of Religion* 28(2): 129-157.

Wallis, R.J. & Blaine, J. (2011). From Respect to Reburial: Negotiating Pagan Interest in Prehistoric Human Remains in Britain, through the Avebury Consultation. *Public Archaeology* 10: 23-45.

Walz, D.M., Newman, J.S., Konin, G.P., & Ross, G. (2010). Epicondylitis: Pathogenesis, Imaging, and Treatment. *RadioGraphics* 30: 167-184.

Ward, C.V., Mays, S.A., Child, S., & Latimer, B. (2010). Lumbar Vertebral Morphology and Isthmic Spondylolysis in a British Mediaeval Population. *American Journal of Physical Anthropology* 141: 273-280.

Ward, S.M. & Tayles, N. (2015). The Use of Ethnographic Information in Cremation Studies: A Southeast Asian Example, pp. 381-402 in C.W. Schmidt & S.A. Symes (eds) *The Analysis of Burned Human Remains* (2nd edition) Academic Press, London.

Warden, S.J., Hurst, J.A., Sanders, M.S., Turner, C.H., Burr, D.B., & La, J. (2005). Bone Adaptation to a Mechanical Loading Program Significantly Increases Skeletal Fatigue Resistance. *Journal of Bone and Mineral Research* 20: 809-816.

Warden, S.J., Mantila Roosa, S.M., Kersh, M.E., Hurd, A.L., Fleisig, G.S., Pandy, M.G., & Fuchs, R.K. (2014). Physical Activity When Young Provides Lifelong Benefits to Cortical Bone Size and Strength in Men. *Proceedings of the National Academy of Sciences of the USA* 111(14): 5337-5342.

Warren, M.W. & Maples, W.R. (1997). The Anthropometry of Contemporary Commercial Cremation. *Journal of Forensic Sciences* 42: 417-423.

Warriner, C., Hendy, J., Cappellini, E., Fischer, R., Trachsel, C., Arneborg, J. et al. (2014). Direct Evidence of Milk Consumption from Ancient Human Dental Calculus. *Scientific Reports* 4: article 7104.

Warriner, C., Speller, C., Collins, M.J., & Lewis, C.M. (2015). Ancient Human Microbiomes. *Journal of Human Evolution* 79: 125-136.

Wasterlain, S.N., Cunha, E., & Hillson, S. (2011). Periodontal Disease in a Portuguese Identified Skeletal Sample from the Late Nineteenth and Early Twentieth Centuries. *American Journal of Physical Anthropology* 145: 30-42.

Watson, A.A. (1989). *Forensic Medicine. A Handbook for Professionals*. Gower, Aldershot.

Watts, R. (2015). The Long-Term Impact of Developmental Stress. Evidence from Later Medieval and Post-Medieval London (AD1117-1853). *American Journal of Physical Anthropology* 158-569-580.

Weaver, D.S. (1980). Sex Differences in the Ilia of a Known Sex and Age Sample of Fetal and Infant Skeletons. *American Journal of Physical Anthropology* 52: 191-195.

Webb, P.A.O. & Suchey, J.M. (1985). Epiphyseal Union of the Anterior Iliac Crest and Medial Clavicle in a Modern Multiracial Sample of American Males and Females. *American Journal of Physical Anthropology* 68: 457-466.

Weber, A.W. (1995). The Neolithic and Early Bronze Age of the Lake Baikal Region, Siberia: A Review of Recent Research. *Journal of World Prehistory* 9: 99-165.

Weber, A.W., Link, D.W., & Katzenberg, M.A. (2002). Hunter-Gatherer Culture Change and Continuity in the Middle Holocene of the Cis-Baikal, Siberia. *Journal of Anthropological Archaeology* 21: 230-299.

Weber, G.W. (2015). Virtual Anthropology. *Yearbook of Physical Anthropology* 156: 22-42.

Weinstein, K.J. (2007). Thoracic Skeletal Morphology and High-Altitude Hypoxia in Andean Prehistory. *American Journal of Physical Anthropology* 134: 36-49.

Weiss, E. (2003). Effects of Rowing on Humeral Strength. *American Journal of Physical Anthropology* 121: 193-202.

Weiss, E. (2008). *Reburying the Past. The Effects of Repatriation and Reburial on Scientific Enquiry*. Nova, New York.

Weiss, E. (2015). Examining Activity Patterns and Biological Confounding Factors: Differences between Fibrocartilagenous and Fibrous Musculoskeletal Stress Markers. *International Journal of Osteoarchaeology* 25: 281–288.

Weiss, E. & Jurmain, R. (2007). Osteoarthritis Revisited: A Contemporary Review of Aetiology. *International Journal of Osteoarchaeology* 17: 437–450.

Weiss, E., Corona, L., & Schultz, B. (2012). Sex Differences in Musculoskeletal Stress Markers: Problems with Activity Pattern Reconstructions. *International Journal of Osteoarchaeology* 22: 70–80.

Weiss, K.M. (1973). *Demographic Models for Anthropology*. Memoirs of the Society for American Archaeology No. 27.

Weiss-Krejci, E. (2016). 'Tomb to Give Away': The Significance of Graves and the Dead in Present-Day Austria, pp. 345–366 in H. Williams & M. Giles (eds) *Archaeologists and the Dead. Mortuary Archaeology in Contemporary Society*. Oxford University Press, Oxford.

Weitzel, M.A. & McKenzie, H.G. (2015). Fire as a Cultural Taphonomic Agent, pp. 203–217 in C.W. Schmidt & S.A. Symes (eds) *The Analysis of Burned Human Remains* (2nd edition) Academic Press, London.

Welker, F. (2018). Palaeoproteomics for Human Evolutionary Studies. *Quarternary Science Reviews* 190: 137–147.

Wellcome Institute. (2013). *Repatriation of Māori/Moriori ancestral human remains*. https://wellcomecollection.org/pages/WyjZcCgAAKgALCuN

Wells, C. (1993). Human Remains, pp. 100–107 in A. Davison, B. Green, & W. Milligan (eds) *Illington: A Study of A Breckland Parish and Its Anglo-Saxon Cemetery*. East Anglian Archaeology Report No. 63.

Wenham, S. (1989). Anatomical Interpretations of Anglo-Saxon Weapon Injuries, pp. 123–139 in S.C. Hawkes (ed) *Weapons and Warfare in Anglo-Saxon England*. Oxford University Committee for Archaeology Monograph 21, Oxford.

Wenham, S.J. & Wakely, J. (1989). Microscopical Features of Blade-Injuries to Bone Surfaces in Six Anglo-Saxon Skeletons from Eccles, Kent, p. 291 in C.A. Roberts, F. Lee, & J. Bintliff (eds) *Burial Archaeology. Current Research, Methods and Developments*. British Archaeological Reports (British Series) 211. British Archaeological Reports, Oxford.

Wescott, D.J. (2006). Effect of Mobility on Femur Midshaft External Shape and Robusticity. *American Journal of Physical Anthropology* 130: 201–213.

Wescott, D.J. & Jantz, R.L. (2005). Assessing Craniofacial Secular Change in American Blacks and Whites Using Geometric Morphometry, pp. 231–245 in D.E. Slice (ed) *Modern Morphometrics in Physical Anthropology*. Kluwer Academic/Plenum Publishers, New York.

Weyrich, L.S., Duchene, S., Soubrier, J., Arriola, L., Llamas, B., Breen, J. et al. (2017). Neanderthal Behaviour, Diet and Disease Inferred from Ancient DNA in Dental Calculus. *Nature* 544: 357–362.

White, C.D., Longstaffe, F.J., & Law, K.R. (2004). Exploring the Effects of Environment, Physiology and Diet on Oxygen Isotope Ratios in Ancient Nubian Bones and Teeth. *Journal of Archaeological Science* 31: 233–250.

White, C.D., Longstaffe, F.J., Pendergast, D.M., & Maxwell, J. (2009). Cultural Embodiment and the Enigmatic Cultural Identity of the Lovers from Lamanai, pp. 170–191 in K.J. Knudsen & C.M. Stojanowski (eds) *The Bioarchaeology of Identity in the Americas*. University Press of Florida, Boca Raton.

White, L. (2019). Conflicts over the Excavation, Retention and Display of Human Remains: An Issue Resolved? pp. 91–102 in S. Campbell, L. White, & S. Thomas (eds) *Competing Values in Archaeological Heritage*. Springer, Cham.

White, M.J. (2006). Things to Do in Doggerland When You're Dead: Surviving the OIS3 at the Northwestern Fringe of Middle Palaeolithic Europe. *World Archaeology* 38: 547–575.

White, T.D. & Folkens, P.A. (2005). *The Human Bone Manual*. Academic Press, London.

Whittle, A., Bayliss, S., & Wysocki, M. (2007). One in a Lifetime: The Date of the Wayland's Smithy Long Barrow. *Cambridge Archaeological Journal* 17(Supplement 1): 103-121.

Whittle, A., Brothwell, D., Cullen, R., Gardner, N., & Kerney, M.P. (1991). Wayland's Smithy, Oxfordshire: Excavations at the Neolithic Tomb in 1962-63 by R.J.C. Atkinson and S. Piggott. *Proceedings of the Prehistoric Society* 57: 61-101.

Wicher, K., Wicher, V., Abbruscato, F., & Baughn, R.E. (2000). *Treponema Pallidum Subsp. Pertenue* Displays Pathologic Properties Different from Those of *T.pallidum Subsp. Pallidum. Infection and Immunity* 68: 3219-3225.

Wieberg, D.A.M. & Wescott, D.J. (2008). Estimating the Timing of Long Bone Fractures: Correlations between Postmortem Interval, Bone Moisture Content, and Blunt Force Trauma Fracture Characteristics. *Journal of Forensic Sciences* 53: 1028-1034.

Willcox, R.R. (1972). The Treponemal Evolution. *Transactions of the St Johns Dermatological Society* 58; 21-37.

Willey, P., Galloway, A., & Snyder, L. (1997). Bone Mineral Density and Survival of Elements and Element Portions in the Bones of the Crow Creek Massacre Victims. *American Journal of Physical Anthropology* 104: 513-528.

Williams, H. (2016). Firing the Imagination: Cremation in the Museum, pp. 293-329 in H. Williams & M. Giles (eds) *Archaeologists and the Dead. Mortuary Archaeology in Contemporary Society*. Oxford University Press, Oxford.

Williams, H., Cerezo-Román, J.I., & Wessman, A. (2017). Introduction: Archaeologies of Cremation, pp. 1-24 in J. Cerezo-Román, A. Wessman, & H. Williams, (eds), *Cremation and the Archaeology of Death*. Oxford University Press, Oxford.

Wilson, A.S., Dixon, R.A., Dodson, H.I., Pollard, A.M., Stern, B., & Tobin, D.J. (2001). Yesterday's Hair - Human Hair in Archaeology. *Biologist* 48: 213-217.

Wilson, A.S. & Tobin, D.J. (2010). Hair After Death, pp. 249-261 in R.M. Trüeb & D.J. Tobin (eds) *Aging Hair*. Springer, Berlin.

Wilson, L.A., MacLeod, N., & Humphrey, L.T. (2008). Morphometric Criteria for Sexing Juvenile Human Skeletons Using the Ilium. *Journal of Forensic Science* 53: 269-278.

Wilson, L.A.B. & Humphrey, L.T. (2017). Voyaging into the Third Dimension: A Perspective on Virtual Methods and Their Application to Studies of Juvenile Sex Estimation and the Ontogeny of Sexual Dimorphism. *Forensic Science International* 278: 32-46.

Wilson, L.A.B., Ives, R., Cardoso, H.F.V., & Humphrey, L.T. (2015). Shape, Size and Maturity Trajectories of the Human Ilium. *American Journal of Physical Anthropology* 156: 19-34.

Witkin, A. & Boston, C. (2006). The Human Bone Assemblage, pp. 44-99 in C. Boston, A. Boyle, & A. Witkin (eds) *'In the Vaults Beneath'- Archaeological Recording at St George's Church, Bloomsbury*. Project Report. Oxford Archaeological Unit, Oxford.

Wittwer-Backofen, U. (2012). Age Estimation Using Tooth Cementum Annulation, pp. 129-143 in L.S. Bell (ed) *Forensic Microscopy for Skeletal Tissues: Methods and Protocols*. Methods in Molecular Biology No. 915. Springer, Berlin.

Wittwer-Backofen, U., Gampe, J., & Vaupel, J.W. (2004). Tooth Cementum Annulation for Age Estimation: Results from a Large Known-Age Validation Study. *American Journal of Physical Anthropology* 123: 119-129.

Woo, S.L.Y., Kuei, S.C., Amiel, D., Gomez, M.A., Hayes, W.C., White, F.C., & Akeson, W.H. (1981). The Effect of Prolonged Physical Training on the Properties of Long Bone: A Study of Wolff's Law. *Journal of Bone and Joint Surgery* 63A: 780-786.

Wood, J.W., Milner, G.R., Harpending, H.C., & Weiss, K.M. (1992). The Osteological Paradox: Problems of Inferring Prehistoric Health from Skeletal Samples. *Current Anthropology* 33: 343-370.

Workshop of European Anthropologists (1980). Recommendations for Age and Sex Diagnoses of Skeletons. *Journal of Human Evolution* 9: 517-549.

Wrathmell, S. (2012). *A History of Wharram Percy and Its Neighbours*. Wharram: A Study of Settlement on the Yorkshire Wolds, XIII. York University Archaeological Publications 15. University of York, York.

Wright, L.E. (2005). Identifying Migrants to Tikal, Guatemala: Defining Local Variability in Strontium Isotope Ratios of Human Tooth Enamel. *Journal of Archaeological Science* 32: 555-566.

Wright, L.E. & Yoder, C.J. (2003). Recent Progress in Bioarchaeology: Approaches to the Osteological Paradox. *Journal of Archaeological Research* 11: 43-70.

Wu, A.H.B. & Bellantoni, N.F. (2003). Stability of Gall Stones after 165 Years of Burial. *Journal of Forensic Sciences* 48: 633-634.

Wysocki, M., Bayliss, A., & Whittle, A. (2007). Serious Mortality: The Date of the Fussell's Lodge Long Barrow. *Cambridge Archaeological Journal* 17(Supplement 1): 65-84.

Xanthopoulou, P., Valakos, E., Youlatos, D., & Nikita, E. (2018). Assessing the Accuracy of Cranial and Pelvic Ageing Methods on Human Skeletal Remains from a Modern Greek Assemblage. *Forensic Science International* 286: 266.e1-266.e8.

Yamamoto, T., Hasegawa, T., Yamamoto, T., Hongo, H., & Amizuka, N. (2016). Histology of Human Cementum: Its Structure, Function and Development. *Japanese Dental Science Review* 52: 63-74.

Yoder, C., Ubelaker, D.H., & Powell, J.F. (2001). Examination of Variation in Sternal Rib End Morphology Relevant to Age Assessment. *Journal of Forensic Sciences* 46: 223-227.

Zerweckh, J.E., Ruml, L.A., Gottschalk, F., & Pak, C.Y.C. (1998). The Effects of Twelve Weeks of Bed Rest on Bone Histology, Biochemical Markers of Bone Turnover, and Calcium Homeostasis in Eleven Normal Subjects. *Journal of Bone and Mineral Research* 13: 1594-1601.

Zhou, L. & Corruccini, R.S. (1998). Enamel Hypoplasias Related to Famine Stress in Living Chinese. *American Journal of Human Biology* 10: 723-733.

Zhu, H., Willcox, M.D.P., Green, R.M., & Knox, K.W. (1997). Effect of Different Diets on Oral Bacteria and Caries Activity in Sprague-Dawley Rats. *Microbios* 91: 105-120.

Ziesemer, K.A., Ramos-Madrigal, J., Mann, A.E., Brandt, B.W., Sankaranarayanan, K., Ozga, A.T. et al. (2019). The Efficacy of Whole Genome Capture on Ancient Dental Calculus and Dentin. *American Journal of Physical Anthropology* 168: 496-509.

Zimmerman, H., Yin, Z., Zou, F., & Everett, E.T. (2019). Interfrontal Bone among Inbred Strains of Mice and QTL Mapping. *Frontiers in Genetics* 10: article 291.

Zimmerman, M.R. & Kelley, M.A. (1982). *Atlas of Human Paleopathology*. Praeger, New York.

Zorba, E., Goutas, N., Spiliopoulou, C., & Moraitis, K. (2018). An Evaluation of Dental Methods by Lamendin and Prince and Ubelaker for Estimation of Adult Age on a Sample of Modern Greeks. *HOMO - Journal of Comparative Human Biology* 69: 17-28.

Zuckerman, M.K. & Armelagos, G.J. (2011). The Origins of Biocultural Dimensions in Bioarchaeology, pp. 15-43 in S.C. Agarwal & B.A. Glencross (eds) *Social Bioarchaeology*. Wiley-Blackwell, Chichester.

Index